The World of ECONOMICS

Second Canadian Edition

A. H. MacDonald

Leonard S. Silk

Phillip Saunders

McGRAW-HILL RYERSON LIMITED

Toronto Halifax Montreal Vancouver

THE WORLD OF ECONOMICS, SECOND CANADIAN EDITION

ISBN 07-082898-9

4 5 6 7 8 9 0 D 8 7 6 5 4 3 2 1

Printed and Bound in Canada

THE AUTHORS

A. H. MacDonald has taught senior high school economics in Nova Scotia and New Brunswick. He has been involved in economics curriculum development and evaluation for the New Brunswick Department of Education, in teacher training with the University of New Brunswick and the Canadian Foundation for Economic Education, and in evaluation for Educational Testing Service. He is currently Maritime Educational Consultant for a major Canadian publisher.

Leonard Silk has had wide experience in university teaching, including the Brookings Institution and Carnegie-Mellon University, and in economic journalism. He is the author of a number of widely acclaimed books, including *The Research Revolution* (McGraw-Hill, 1960) and *The Economists* (Basic Books, 1976). A former chairman of the Editorial Board of *Business Week,* he is currently economic columnist with *The New York Times*.

Phillip Saunders is a university teacher in economics who has written widely for the high school level. He has also made major contributions to the development of economics curricula and methods of teaching through publications of the Joint Council on Economic Education. He is currently on the faculty of Indiana University.

CORRELATED MATERIALS

Workbook and Study Guide to Accompany The World of Economics—07-082899-7
Readings in the World of Economics—0-07-077305-X
The World of Economics Transparency Masters—07-077847-7
Teacher's Manual to Accompany The World of Economics—07-077846-9

Canadian Cataloguing in Publication Data

MacDonald, Alexander Herbert, date
The world of economics

Bibliography: p.
Includes indexes.
ISBN 0-07-082898-9

1. Economics. I. Silk, Leonard S., date.
II. Saunders, Phillip. III. Title.

HB171.5.M142 1979 330 C79-094565-7

PREFACE

In recent years, economics has become an accepted part of the high school curriculum. The evolution of this trend is an important one. The result is that many students who otherwise might not have even an introduction to a crucial set of concepts now have an opportunity to gain insight into the economic structure of their society.

An understanding of economic principles requires an effort, even if those principles are examined at an introductory level. This book and its accompanying aids are designed to make that effort as interesting and rewarding as possible while providing young people with the concepts they will need to understand the major economic problems of our country and of the world.

Economics does not offer any simple or definite set of absolute answers to these problems. Instead, it presents a method of approaching them or a way of thinking about them. This way of thinking, which should help each person come to rational conclusions in a clear and orderly manner, is the essence of economics.

Promotion of this ability to consider economic problems in a clear and rational way is the primary objective of this book. In the pursuit of this objective, the contents have been structured so as to avoid undue concern with descriptive trivia or overly elegant analytical refinements. The concern has been to concentrate on the key basic concepts and their application in a way which will enable the students to come to grips with crucial economic issues.

Economics has a rather large technical vocabulary. The student must come to understand the language of economics, not merely memorize it. Terms have no real meaning in isolation. Only in their proper context do they acquire any true significance. The vocabulary of economics, hence, is treated as an integral part of the text. However, to aid the student in checking or relocating terms, each key word or phrase is placed in **bold-faced type** when it first appears, is listed at the end of that chapter, and is included in a complete Index of Key Concepts at the end of the book with its initial chapter location.

The reader must make serious use of the photographs, cartoons, tables, and diagrams. These items have been used to present important messages and concepts; their presence is not just for the sake of providing visual relief from the text.

Also included in the book are numerous excerpts from the writings of great economists, past and present, and views of other persons on important economic issues. These selections will help the student gain some sense of the historical depth of economics, some flavor of the rich diversity of the literature of economics, and some insight into the deep feelings which economic issues arouse in thoughtful people.

A. H. MacDonald
Dartmouth, Nova Scotia,
April 12, 1979

CONTENTS

UNIT 1 INTRODUCTION AND BASIC CONCEPTS

UNIT 2 THE MARKET

UNIT 3 INSTITUTIONS IN OUR ECONOMIC SYSTEM

UNIT 4 THE ECONOMIC SYSTEM AS A WHOLE

UNIT 5 THE INTERNATIONAL ECONOMY

UNIT 6 CONCLUSION

LIST OF TABLES AND FIGURES

INTRODUCTION AND BASIC CONCEPTS

Economics has much to contribute to an understanding of one's social, political, business, and personal behavior. Economics aspires to be a science—to observe the world objectively and accurately, and to make sense of it through general concepts and analytical models. But economics passes beyond the limits of science because it seeks not only to explain events but to help individuals, groups, or nations decide how best to improve their welfare.

CHAPTER 1

WHY ECONOMICS IS IMPORTANT

■ THE IMPORTANCE OF ECONOMICS TO THE INDIVIDUAL ■ THE IMPORTANCE OF ECONOMICS TO BUSINESS ■ THE IMPORTANCE OF ECONOMICS TO NATIONS ■ THE WEALTH—AND POVERTY—OF NATIONS ■ ECONOMIC DEVELOPMENT AND FREEDOM ■ THE NEED FOR ECONOMIC GROWTH IN CANADA ■ SUMMARY

It is much easier to say what economics is *about* than what economics *is*. In general, economics is about the way people make a living and spend their income. It is about the ups and downs of business. It is about the wealth and poverty of nations. It is certainly about money, but it is about much more than money. Put most broadly, economics is about individual and social behavior and values.

■ THE IMPORTANCE OF ECONOMICS TO THE INDIVIDUAL

To see why economic questions are important, start with yourself. What do you want out of life?

Some people might start to answer that question on a high moral plane, saying that their aim is to help their fellow man or to contribute something significant to human knowledge. Some might say their aim is to be a big success in the world, to have a good apartment in town and a fine house in the country, and to travel a lot. Others might set more modest goals for themselves—to be happy, to marry and raise a family, to live in peace and quiet. And some people might be still more modest and say that all they want is three meals a day and a clean bed at night.

Perhaps none of us would answer the question of what we want from life in exactly the same way; our specific wants are as unique as our fingerprints. Yet, given our aims in life, we all want *enough income to enable us to live as we like.*

The seeker after knowledge needs income for his education, his books, his travel, his sustenance. The seeker after beauty—say, a painter—needs canvases, brushes, tubes of paint, turpentine, a studio, furniture, food, clothing, and so on. The person who says that he seeks only peace and quiet needs enough income to keep not only himself but his landlord quiet. He must stay at peace not only with himself but with the grocer, the butcher, and other bill collectors. Nothing is more disruptive of peace of mind than not to know where your next meal is coming from or where you will get enough money to provide for your family. Alfred Marshall, a leading British economist of the late nineteenth and early twentieth centuries, observed that the poor in the slums of cities "have little opportunity for friendship; they know nothing of the decencies and the quiet, and very little even of the unity of family life; and religion fails to reach them. . . . No doubt their physical, mental, and moral ill-health is partly due to other causes than poverty; but this is the chief cause." It remains true that an adequate income is essential if men are to achieve a sense of personal dignity, psychological security and well-being, and a life that is rich in moral values, rather than one that is mean, cramping, and debasing.

Economic factors affect the lives of all

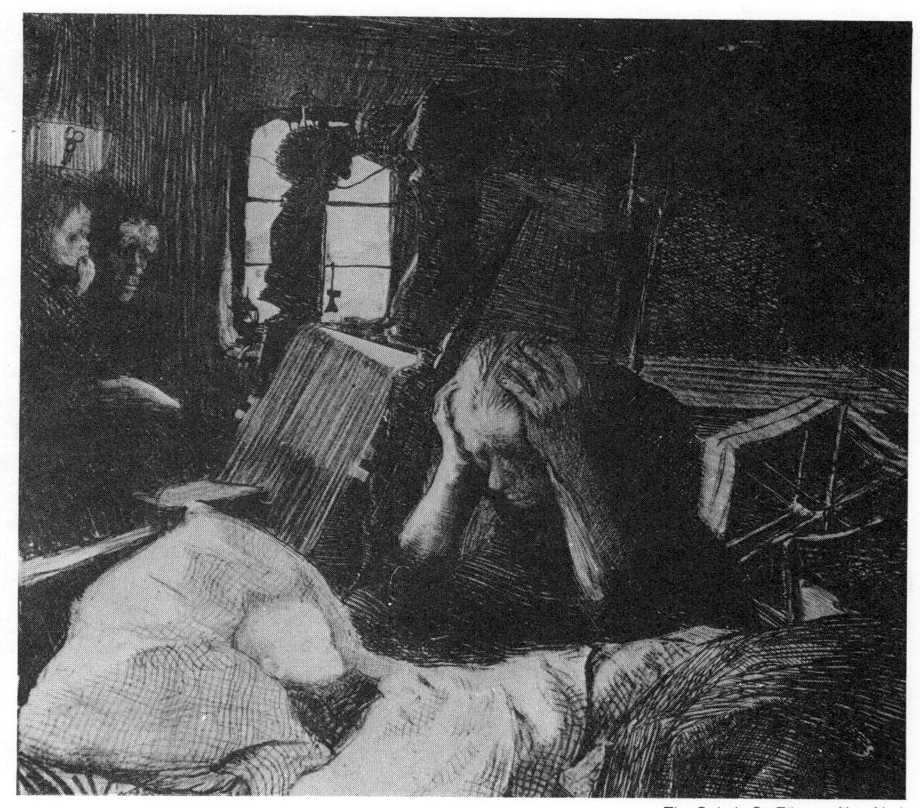

The Galerie St. Etienne, New York

The hope of wiping out poverty has always been a primary reason for efforts to increase economic knowledge. In this picture, a great German artist, Kaethe Kollwitz, depicts the misery of a family dependent upon the meager income it gets from weaving cloth at home, as was still a common practice in industrialized countries at the end of the nineteenth century (this lithograph was made in 1897). The artist Kollwitz graphically shows the meaning of the economist Alfred Marshall's words: "No doubt their physical, mental, and moral ill-health is partly due to other causes than poverty; but this is the chief cause."

men, and not just the poor. They affect our decisions on whether to quit school or go to college, on what careers we choose, on where we live, and other major personal decisions we must make. Economic considerations also influence a multitude of lesser decisions we all must make in our day-by-day lives. They affect what we eat for breakfast, lunch, and dinner; whether we walk or ride to town; whether we fly or take a train to another city; whether we go to a dance or not; whether we buy a car or put our money in the bank, and a host of other decisions that add up to a substantial part of the way we live our lives, exercise our taste and judgment, and achieve our personal objectives.

Of course, economic considerations—in the narrow sense of monetary gains or losses—are not the only factors that influence personal decisions. Our talents, tastes, social attitudes, psychological makeup, values, and aspirations also affect the choices we make, including the economic choices. Some people may choose a lower-paying job rather than a higher-paying one out of a sense of social responsibility (for example, choosing a career as a social worker rather than a stockbroker). Others may choose a

Economics: A Study of Mankind

Alfred Marshall (1842-1924) was one of the greatest economists of all time. Here, Marshall explains why the study of economics is essential to an understanding of the history—and current behavior—of individuals and societies.

Political Economy or Economics is a study of mankind in the ordinary business of life; it examines that part of individual and social action which is most closely connected with the attainment and with the use of the material requisites of well-being.

Thus it is on the one side a study of wealth; and on the other, and more important side, a part of the study of man. For man's character has been moulded by his everyday work, and the material resources which he thereby procures, more than by any other influence unless it be that of his religious ideals; and the two great forming agencies of the world's history have been the religious and the economic.

Here and there the ardor of the military or the artistic spirit has been for a while predominant: but religious and economic influences have nowhere been displaced from the front rank even for a time; and they have nearly always been more important than all others put together. Religious motives are more intense than economic, but their direct action seldom extends over so large a part of life. For the business by which a person earns his livelihood generally fills his thoughts during by far the greater part of those hours in which his mind is at its best; during them his character is being formed by the way in which he uses his faculties in his work, by the thoughts and the feelings which it suggests, and by his relations to his associates in work, his employers or his employees.

From Alfred Marshall, *Principles of Economics,* New York: The Macmillan Co., 1948. Reprinted with permission.

lower-paying job not out of a sense of social responsibility so much as out of anxiety about the pressures or risks of the higher-paying job. In such cases, however, one still could say that the decision to take the lower-paying job was an economic choice. The higher income offered was simply not enough to overcome the individual's sense of social obligations—or fears about the pressures or uncertainties found in the higher-paying job. Conceivably more income—and more stable income—might still have caused a person to give up the career of a social worker. The world is full of would-be musicians, actors, artists, writers, and others who decided that they could make a better living doing something else.

It thus appears that economic factors are remarkably pervasive and potent in affecting personal choices and decisions. There is all sorts of evidence for this conclusion. A department store, with heavy stocks of goods left over from Christmas, can pretty safely count on clearing out its stock if it slashes prices. A college seeking to improve its faculty can probably attract excellent people by offering higher salaries to outside professors than they are presently earning. A landlord with vacant apartments can usually reduce the number of vacancies by lowering the rents, offering to redecorate without charge, or granting some months of rent-free occupancy.

The individual is often affected by economic events that lie beyond his or her personal control. If the nation enters a period of rapidly rising prices, the value of cash and savings accounts at the bank will diminish. If the nation is forced to reduce its imports from other countries because it is not exporting enough goods, the individual may find that it may cost more for domestically produced substitutes, or that one may have to do without some goods. If the nation falls into a

Courtesy of the Steel Company of Canada, Limited

The well-being of workers depends on what wages they earn—and whether they have a job at all. When the national economy is prosperous and growing, wages are rising and jobs are easy to get. If the national economy slumps, wages will not rise much (or may even drop), and unemployment will increase.

serious business decline, the individual may lose a job—and also may lose his or her home, car, the chance to send children to college, even self-respect. If the national economy slumps, business owners or investors may sustain serious financial losses or even lose their assets as a result of the slump.

THE IMPORTANCE OF ECONOMICS TO BUSINESS

Business activity, in large measure, consists of collecting and evaluating economic information and making decisions based on that information. The basic goal of a business is to make a profit. In pursuit of that, owners and/or managers must seek to determine what the market for their products is and will be, whether they should maintain prices, increase or reduce them, increase or decrease advertising expenditures, add to or reduce sales staff.

They must seek to reduce the costs of doing business to meet the pressures of competition. They must decide whether to buy new machinery to increase the productivity of the plant; they must seek to substitute less expensive for more expensive materials; they must try to employ workers who will produce more than they must be paid.

Business people must be alert to new industrial developments that may create new opportunities; they must decide whether to switch to different lines of production or to try to develop new products. They must determine whether there is enough productive capacity to meet the demands for their products, whether they have enough warehouse space for their goods, whether there is a good enough distribution system for getting goods to possible buyers.

Business people must study the financial situation continuously. Do they have sufficient funds to realize the market opportunities they see ahead? Can they borrow additional money from the bank? Will the cost of the money be greater than the opportunity they see for profit? How risky would it be to increase debts? How risky may it be to do too little, while competitors are moving?

Determining the answers to all such questions involves information-gathering, economic and financial analysis, rational decision-making, and a certain intuition about the prospects or dangers of particular actions. The business person lives in a somewhat uncertain world that cannot be perfectly measured or determined, and must have the courage to back intuitions and hunches. But clear economic information and analysis can help in making better business decisions by reducing areas of uncertainty and thereby help business to prosper and grow, rather than stagnate or fail.

THE IMPORTANCE OF ECONOMICS TO NATIONS

As with individuals or businesses, economic factors vitally affect all nations, individually and collectively. Throughout history, economic progress or stability has generally promoted the advance of civilization within nations and frequently helped foster peace among national states. Conversely, lack of economic stability or long-run economic progress has often contributed to social and cultural decay, discontent or revolution within countries, and rivalries or wars between or among states.

While drawing lessons from history and fitting them to other times and places is a risky process, the premises in the above paragraph are, in fact, valid. The twentieth century provides many examples of how economic factors affect nations.

On the positive side, more people have greater material well-being than ever before. Technological changes, together with changes in the proportional distribution of wealth, have brought these benefits. Progress has gone beyond simply the realm of the material. Access to education, to culture and to more leisure time have raised the quality of life for many. Expansion of trade and travel has promoted the international flow of goods and services. The movement of ideas and the extent of personal contacts have also increased, bringing many positive results.

But this century, in which so much more has become available to so many more, has also had perhaps more than its share of misery, hostility and war. Economic factors are at least partly to blame.

International rivalries, such as the one between Great Britain and Germany in the pre-1914 period, were intensified by clashes over sources of raw materials and markets. These conflicts helped to draw much of the world into war in 1914.

Famine and economic misery were root causes of the collapse of the Romanov dynasty in Russia, a collapse which led to the establishment of the world's first communist government under Lenin. Domestic and international economic problems emanating from the First World War and the widespread depression in the decade of the 1920s were factors in the rise of fascism in Italy, Germany and Japan. The quest for economic power, combined with the nationalistic, militaristic, racist and ideological elements of fascism plunged most of the world into war again in the late 1930s.

In the two decades after 1918, some nations opted for solutions to their severe economic problems by following paths different from those of Italy, Germany, Japan and the Soviet Union. These states were mainly political democracies with advanced levels of economic development. They introduced or speeded up social and economic change through government action and an increased government role in the economy. The rise of various degrees of what is, in fact, some form of democratic socialism, has been a continuing example of an evolutionary rather than a revolutionary response to economic and political pressures.

In the post World War II period, a focal point of economic unrest has been the so-called "Third World." The push for political independence from direct or implicit colonial rule was accompanied by what has been called "a revolution of rising expectations." This is a simple desire to share in the rising standards of living which exist in what might be called "developed countries." In

Saskatchewan Archives Photograph

The political and social stability of a nation depends in major part on its economic health. During the Great Depression, Canada was fortunate in some ways. Despite the high levels of unemployment and widespread suffering, Canada did not experience the swings to political extremism and violence which were to sweep many nations. One of the few open outbreaks of unrest took place in Regina in 1935 during a march of the unemployed from Western Canada to Ottawa. This photo shows one scene from the Regina Riot. Obtain a copy of the "Jackdaw" kit on the Great Depression to see a reprint of the Regina Leader-Post published the day after the riots.

some nations such as China or Cuba, the results were revolutions which brought communist governments to power. Other states, such as Tanzania, have followed socialist courses, while trying to stay neutral in the rivalries between communist and non-communist blocks. Still other states, such as Singapore, have taken a basically non-socialist route to development.

Generally economic forces within countries are connected to social and political pressures. What is happening within a country is often further complicated by the interests and involvements of other nations, especially the "Great Powers." As a result, the economic forces at the national and international level discussed in your morning newspaper will often be interwoven with references to interests and goals of many different groups within a country, or connections to the complex fabric of international relationships.

THE WEALTH—AND POVERTY—OF NATIONS

When considering such a trend as the drive of the poor countries for economic and political development, we must examine the oldest and most basic question of economics. What makes a nation wealthy?

Nothing is more striking than the enormous range of economic differences among nations. The GNP per capita data in Table 1-1 provide some idea of the contrasts which exist. Try to find some comparative informa-

Table 1-1. PER CAPITA GROSS NATIONAL PRODUCTS* OF SELECTED COUNTRIES, 1976

Very Low (under $1000)		Low ($1000-2499)	
Bolivia	390	Brazil	1140
Burma	120	Bulgaria	2310
Egypt	280	Iran	1930
Ethiopia	100	Jamaica	1070
Haiti	200	Mexico	1090
India	150	Panama	1310
Nigeria	380	Portugal	1690
Sri Lanka	200	Taiwan	1070
Turkey	990	Yugoslavia	1680
High ($2500-4999)		**Very High (over $5000)**	
Czechoslovakia	3840	Australia	6100
German Democratic Republic	4220	Austria	5330
Israel	3920	Canada	7510
Japan	4910	Denmark	7450
New Zealand	4250	Iceland	6100
Saudi Arabia	4480	Kuwait	15 480
Singapore	2700	Sweden	8670
U.S.S.R.	2760	Switzerland	8880
United Kingdom	4020	United States	7890

* Per Capita Gross National Product is the value of a nation's output of goods and services in a year divided by the total population at that time.

Note: National currencies have been converted to U.S. dollars at official exchange rates. The data are preliminary for 1976 and subject to revision.

Source: International Bank for Reconstruction and Development.

tion about income levels, infant mortality rates, literacy rates, the number of doctors or automobiles per thousand of population. These will provide a vivid indication of the extremes to be found among nations. Examine the photographs on page nine closely. The contrasts here speak even more loudly than all the statistics in the world.

Can you imagine living on a dollar or two a week, as many people do in India, Pakistan, China, Burma, Nigeria, Bolivia, Vietnam, and many other countries? Try to imagine the lifestyle of the average resident of this planet, a resident of the "Third World," a farmer who seeds and harvests the land by hand, suffers sieges by insects and rats that eat the crops, often knows the dry pangs of hunger, and usually grows old and dies at an age when you would still consider yourself a young man or woman. No wonder that such people, who constitute more than half the world's population, are determined to raise their standard of living.

ECONOMIC DEVELOPMENT AND FREEDOM

The methods that the poorer nations use to achieve economic development matter to us as well as to them, for these policies will affect us politically and economically. We would like them to use many of our methods of achieving economic growth. In particular, we are inclined to be unhappy about policies involving the sacrifice of freedom in the pursuit of economic gains. The Communist nations are also interested in seeing their methods adopted. In the middle, the poorer nations are often caught in a vise. Regardless of our views, however, we must remember to avoid trying to push our methods and our values on other nations. This is something which must be carefully avoided in dealings with newly independent nations where nationalistic pride is often very strong.

In addition to being caught in the ideological vise between "Western" and "Com-

George Weston Ltd.

A world of contrasts.

Oxfam

A. H. MacDonald

Developed countries—such as Canada—face plenty of problems too. Coping with increasing needs for urban services is just one of these. Governments at all levels face pressures for provision of or improvements in a wide range of public services and goods, symbolized here by a large bridge in Saint John, New Brunswick.

munist" approaches, many poorer nations are also saddled with both political and economic tyranny of a domestic variety. Thus a crucial problem facing many of these nations is not simply how to increase economic wealth, but rather how to increase it while also achieving more individual freedom. From our democratic perspective, it seems unfortunate that, as one statesman has phrased it, the "promise of freedom with equal material benefits to the oppressed" is often rejected in favor of "the allurement of a material revolution coupled with enslavement to the free."[1]

THE NEED FOR ECONOMIC GROWTH IN CANADA

In Canada, many of our economic problems are unresolved and consequently provide keys to much of our political and social discontent. Such issues as regional disparity have become topics for everyday discussion. All too frequently, however, the degree of progress toward the solution of major economic problems does not match the volume of discussion about the problems themselves.

The Canadian population has been growing by about a third of a million per annum in recent years. Economic growth is doubly necessary: first, to produce enough additional goods and services to maintain output on a per capita basis; and secondly, to enable Canadians to acquire a better standard of living by providing all with access to more and better goods and services despite a growing population.

Our labor force is also growing rapidly, as is the efficiency of our machinery and our productive techniques. We therefore must be able to apply our improved technology suitably, or we may be faced with growing unemployment and the problems it brings with it.

We must keep our own economy stable, primarily for our own good, but also for the benefit of others. As Louis Rasminsky, former Governor of the Bank of Canada, once paraphrased John Donne: "No economy is an island." It is, therefore, equally important to us that economic stability is maintained in other nations. If this is not the case, we shall be affected by what happens elsewhere, especially, of course, by what happens in the United States.

[1] Charles Malik, "Will the Future Redeem the Past?" address at Williamsburg, Virginia, July 11, 1960. Mr. Malik, a Lebanese philosopher, educator, and diplomat, had just completed a term as president of the General Assembly of the United Nations.

SUMMARY

Economic issues play a crucial role in the lives of all men—as private individuals, as citizens of a nation, and as inhabitants of a troubled and rapidly changing world. While economics cannot provide a complete explanation of all individual or social or political behavior, it has much light to shed on the forces that motivate men and nations. The basic aim of the study of economics is to increase understanding of human life and, if possible, to increase human welfare.

QUESTIONS FOR REVIEW AND DISCUSSION

1. Write a brief statement of what economics is about.
2. Give a specific example of the importance of economics to an individual, a business firm, and a nation.
3. Can you think of a situation in which economic considerations are *not* important to an individual, a business firm, or a nation? Be prepared to defend your reasons for selecting or for not selecting a particular situation that may arise in a class discussion of this question.
4. Give two examples of how economic problems and political problems are related in the world outside Canada and inside Canada.
5. How do you think that the study of economics can increase your understanding of human life?

PROBLEMS AND EXERCISES TO SHARPEN YOUR UNDERSTANDING

1. Obtain a copy of a recent newspaper or weekly news magazine. List the articles and stories dealing with economic topics. List the articles and stories dealing with political topics. How many of these articles or stories have you put on both lists? Why?
2. Check the location of a number of countries in Table 1-1 in an atlas. Are there any apparent trends in the location of "poor" or "rich" nations? To what can you attribute these trends?

CHAPTER 2

WHAT IS A SCIENCE?

■ SCIENTIFIC METHOD ■ THE CONCEPT OF A SYSTEM ■ PITFALLS TO AVOID ■ SUMMARY

In starting your study of economics, it is important to note that economics has much in common with all other sciences, including the abstract sciences of logic and mathematics, the natural sciences of physics, chemistry, and biology, and the human or social sciences of psychology, sociology, and anthropology. What all of these sciences have in common is their dependence on observation to assemble data that can be organized and interpreted by means of concepts and mental models.

Both of these last two terms demand careful definition. By the term **concept**[1] we mean a generalized idea of a class of objects or phenomena, based on particular instances of the class. Thus, having observed such animals as elephants, mice, and human beings, biologists derived the concept of *mammalia*, a class of vertebrates, the females of which have milk-secreting glands for feeding their offspring. Or, having observed particular forms of government dominated by a single leader, such as Caesar's Rome, Mussolini's Italy, or Hitler's Germany, political scientists or historians derive the concept of *dictatorship*. Having observed the behavior of particular businessmen, such as Lord Strathcona, Sir James Dunn, Lord Beaverbrook, or Henry Ford, all of whom assumed large financial risks in promoting and developing business, economists derive the concept of *entrepreneurship*.[2] These concepts enable scientists—or anyone else—to understand and interpret new experiences and observations more intelligently.

By a **mental model** (as contrasted to a physical model, such as a model airplane or model ship) we mean a representation of some aspect of the real world that is constructed of symbols—words, diagrams, or mathematical expressions. "The earth is a sphere," is a very simple mental model of our planet. Physical scientists create far more complex mental models of atoms, molecules, sound waves, radio waves, or other natural phenomena. Economists develop mental models of consumers, business firms, markets, the national economy, and even the world economy.

The purpose of mental models (which we shall hereafter refer to simply as models) is to provide a set of assumptions from which a conclusion or set of conclusions can logically be deduced. Models need not be highly complex to be useful; whether simple or complex, their purpose is to provide us with a means of analysing still more complex reality. Both concepts and models help us form *a more systematic organization* of observations and facts. This organization helps us to understand better the world in which we live.

[1] Key concepts throughout this book are printed in bold-face type. They are listed at the end of the chapters and in the Index of Key Concepts, found before the main index at the end of the book.

[2] For some excellent biographical sketches of some prominent businesspeople in Canada's history, see: Peter C. Newman, *Flame of Power*, Toronto: McClelland & Stewart, 1959, and Peter C. Newman, *The Canadian Establishment*, vol. 1, Toronto: McClelland & Stewart, 1975.

The Nature of Models

Professors Kalman J. Cohen and Richard M. Cyert of Carnegie-Mellon University explain here the nature and purpose of models, as used in both the physical and social sciences.

The basic procedure which is used by scientists in their efforts to increase our understanding of the world is the formulation of models. A *model* is a set of assumptions from which a conclusion or a set of conclusions is logically deduced. . . . The first point we discuss is the relation of a model to the real world. One obvious connection of a model with reality is, of course, through its assumptions. These assumptions characterize the type of world to which the model is intended to apply. It is important to realize that the assumptions need not be *exact representations* of reality, but they may instead be *reasonable abstractions* of reality. By reasonable abstractions we mean that only certain aspects of reality are contained in the assumptions, namely, those aspects considered to be relevant. . . .

. . . Even though the assumptions of a model may not be literally exact and complete representations of reality, if they are realistic enough for the purposes of the analysis we may be able to draw conclusions which can be shown to apply to the world. A good example is provided by plane geometry. Certain geometrical objects are assumed which in a strict sense do not exist in the world; for example, there are no physical embodiments of angles exactly 90 degrees and lines possessing zero width. Nevertheless, these postulated geometrical objects correspond sufficiently closely to existing physical objects so that for certain purposes, e.g., surveying, the conclusions obtained about the properties of these abstract geometrical objects are valid for the corresponding real world objects.

Some scientific models with intentionally unrealistic assumptions are developed for special types of analysis, as, for example, the model of a frictionless world in physics. The situations characterized by these models are admittedly hypothetical. Nonetheless, such hypothetical models are important in any science. These models are intended to be intellectual experiments. They are created for the purpose of isolating and determining the nature of certain crucial variables. Sometimes they may also be used as criteria against which the current state of the real world is evaluated. Thus the economist's perfectly competitive model may be used as a standard for judging the performance of real agricultural markets. The one warning that must always be kept in mind, however, is that conclusions which are logically deduced from a set of assumptions which do not correspond to the real world do not necessarily apply to the real world.

■ SCIENTIFIC METHOD

Economics shares with other disciplines, then, a common approach known as **scientific method**. The four basic elements of scientific method, as defined by one of the first modern philosophers of science, Sir Francis Bacon (1561-1626), are *observation*, *measurement*, *explanation*, and *verification*. There are actually many other possible ways of breaking down the complex process by which scientists make discoveries, but Bacon's formulation will probably serve as well as any, and it has the great merit of simplicity. But its four elements require amplification.

SOME EXAMPLES OF MENTAL MODELS

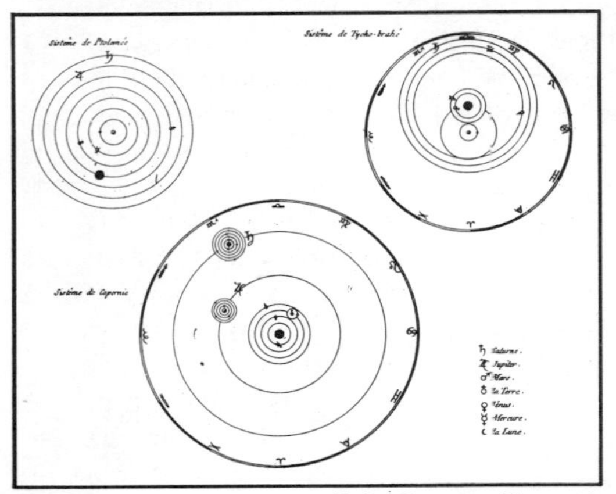

Yerkes Observatory Photograph

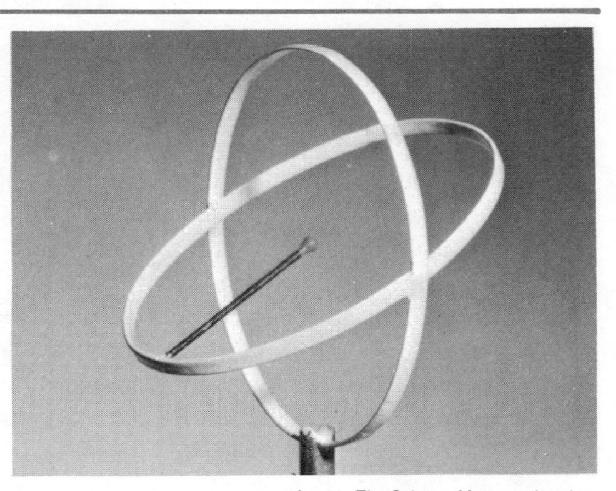

Lent to The Science Museum, London, by Sir Lawrence Bragg, F.R.S.

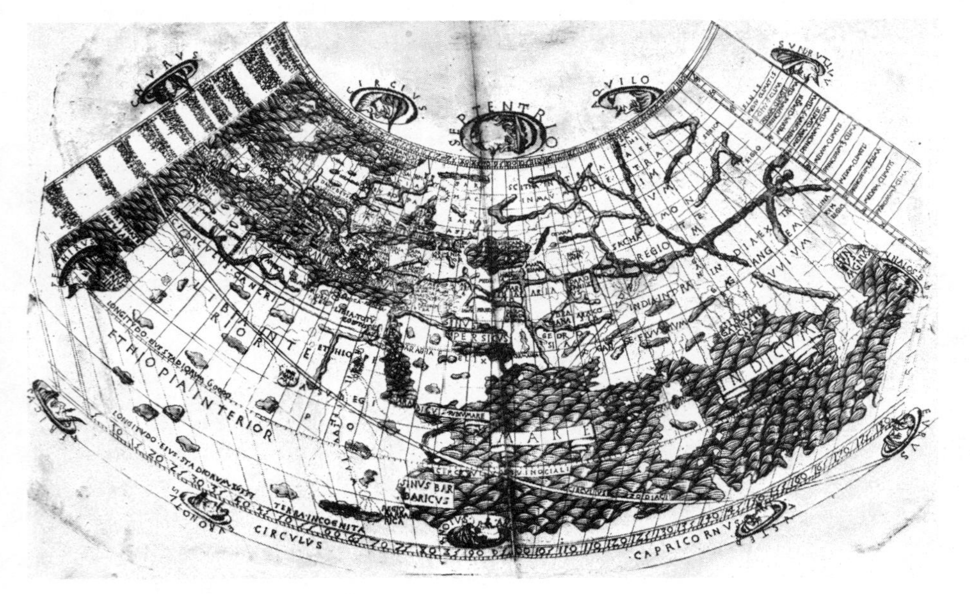

Courtesy The New York Public Library, Rare Book Division

People seek to comprehend reality through the use of models. On these pages we see a wide variety of models that have been used since early times to organize information about complex matters. The bottom illustration on this page is an early model of the world—a map of Ptolemy, the last of the great Egyptian astronomers, who lived from about 100 A.D. to 170 A.D. The illustration above the map at the left shows three conceptions of the solar system—according first to Ptolemy, then to Tycho Brahe (1546-1601), and then to Nicholaus Copernicus (1473-1543).

The illustration at the top right of this page is a model—made of metal—of a helium atom. The illustration at the top of page 15 shows a chemistry teacher constructing a model of molecule out of verbal symbols (C means carbon, H means hydrogen). The illustration at the bottom of page 15 depicts a chemical molecule—this time the DNA molecule—through a drawing.

Einstein's famous formula $E = mc^2$ (energy equals mass times the speed of light squared) is a mathemetical model used by physicists.

Economists, too, employ models. The diagram at the center right of page 15 represents the buyers and sellers in a market and shows how their interaction determines the price of a good and the quantity of it that will be sold.

Ford Foundation (Roy Stevens)

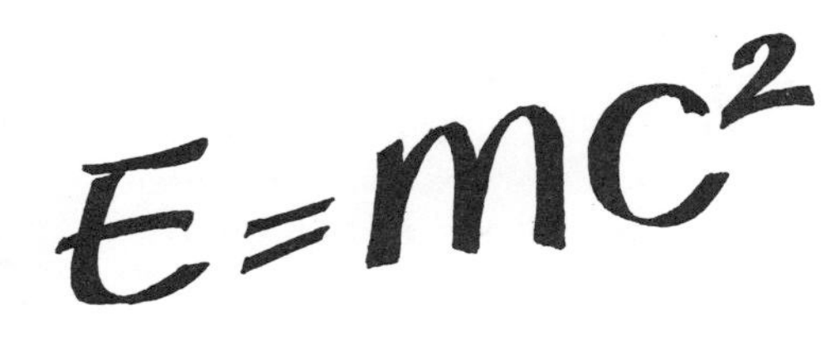

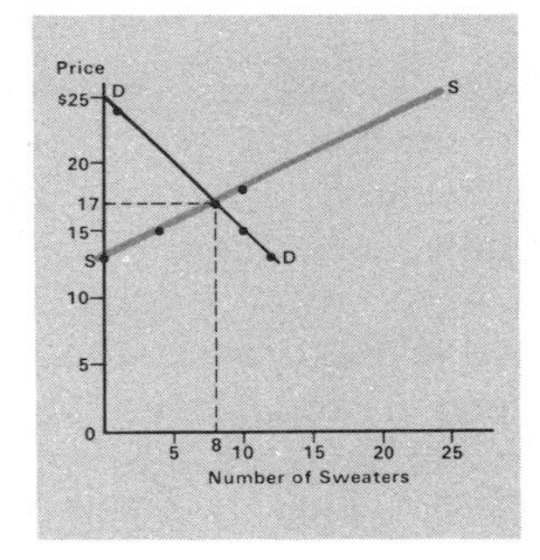

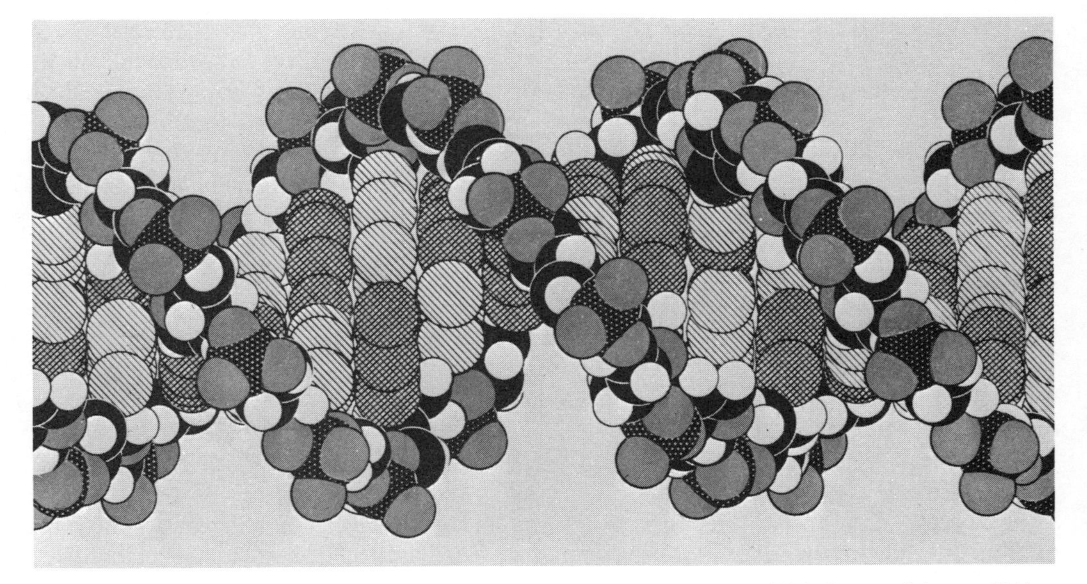

Courtesy of the Upjohn Company. Kalamazoo. Michigan

Observation

Measurement

The process of observation starts with the decision of *what* to observe—that is, with the posing of an interesting question about nature or society. Since earliest times people have been asking such questions as, Why does the sun rise in the morning? Why do leaves turn red and brown in the fall? Why are some people better warriors than others? Why does fire consume some objects and not others? Why are some people richer than others? Why does an apple fall to the ground? Answers to such questions can be found in ancient myths. But even when people stopped inventing tales or myths to explain such events, they did not immediately begin to answer the questions scientifically, in the sense that we would use the term today.

Scientists seek to exercise great care in making the observations on which their questions are founded. Thus, the physicist asks: Exactly how does the apple fall to the ground? At exactly what speed? Does the speed of its fall depend upon the shape of the apple? Does it depend on the wind? What if there were no wind? Does its speed accelerate as the apple descends? If the apple were hundreds of thousands of miles up, would it still fall to the ground? How do I know?

Similarly, an economist might seek to find out not just *why* some people are richer than others, but exactly *how much* wealth or income different people have. Can economists find out by asking them? Will they tell the truth? Can it be told from their dress or houses? If a nation collects income taxes, will that provide the economist with better information? What if it is a primitive society that does not collect taxes or even possess money? How would wealth be accumulated or measured in such a society?

The *how* of any phenomenon will tell the scientist much about the *why* of it. The answer to a problem and a careful or exact understanding of the problem are intertwined.

Therefore scientists—whether physicists, economists, or any other—seek to collect *evidence* about what they observe. Wherever possible, they try to measure things. The anthropologist will measure the size of different people's skulls. The biologist will measure the rate at which a culture of microorganisms grows in the earth. The astronomer or astro-physicist will measure the distances to the stars, the speed at which stars move in space, how they expand or contract, change color, emit radiation. Similarly, the economist will seek to measure the production of goods in a nation, the number of unemployed workers, the velocity with which money changes hands among different people, the volume of a nation's imports and exports, and the rate at which a given nation is increasing its wealth.

All such facts, once they have been ascertained, will be recorded, either on paper, microfilm, magnetic tape, or some other device. These recorded observations we call *data*.

Not all the data resulting from a scientist's observations and measurements can be stated in numbers. It is hard to measure numerically just how much more militant one primitive tribe may be than another, or how much satisfaction different people may derive from food as compared with clothing, or from music as compared with air conditioners. Nevertheless, the scientist in every field tries to present the evidence as precisely and objectively as possible. This involves an effort to express data quantitatively.

Like other scientists, economists try to use mathematics and statistics whenever they can in order to add precision and rigor to their findings. However, the economist's data are likely to be less exact than those of the physicist, for example, because it is often more difficult to measure social behavior, which is made up of many individual actions, than it is to measure physical objects or natural phenomena. However, natural

Every science seeks to make exact measurements of social or natural phenomena. In this illustration, taken from Tycho Brahe's work, *Astronomiae instauratae mechanica,* published in 1598, we see the astronomical instruments that Tycho used to measure movements of the planets and stars. Similarly, economists collect satistical data to measure changes in wages, prices, production, national income, employment, unemployment, and other economic phenomena.

Courtesy The New York Public Library, Rare Book Division

phenomena cannot always be observed and measured with greater certainty than social phenomena.

Explanation

The purpose of scientific observation and measurement is to find a basis for explaining either natural or social phenomena. Hence, it is necessary to organize the data collected in some coherent way so that one can form an idea—or get a hunch or insight—into what accounts for the occurrences in which one is interested. (In scientific research, the hunch may often in fact precede the organization of data or even the observation of phenomena.) Frequently, the scientist may find that one set of data correlates with another. For example, changes in the weather may be found to correlate with cycles of sun spots or the incidence of lung cancer may be found to correlate with cigarette smoking.

The scientist collects and studies facts in order to reach or to verify a **hypothesis** or *generalization* that will explain the relationship among his measured observations. The way the scientist works to reach fruitful generalizations is illustrated by the career of the great physicist Galileo (1564-1642). As a young man of twenty, Galileo is said to have become fascinated while watching the swinging of the great lamp from the ceiling of the cathedral in Pisa. He timed the swings of the lamp by his pulse beat. These observations led Galileo to conceive the laws of the pendulum. He later suggested using the pendulum to time the pulse beats of medical patients, as a means of diagnosing their illnesses.

In his mid-twenties, Galileo began to experiment with falling bodies. His observations led him to an astonishing conclusion which conflicted with the sacred beliefs of his time, dating back to the ancient Greek philosopher Aristotle. He found that all objects are accelerated at the same rate as they fall toward the earth regardless of their weight, when under the influence of gravity alone. This discovery so enraged the Aristotelians that they forced Galileo out of the University of Pisa. (Social scientists, including economists, must also be willing to pursue the facts wherever they may lead, regardless of the effect on the scientist's popularity or the effect on hitherto accepted doctrine.)

Galileo's later observations with a telescope led him to fresh discoveries about the nature of the moon, of the Milky Way, of the four satellites of Jupiter, and of much else. But, as important as the specific findings of Galileo were, even more important was the method he used to achieve his discoveries and laws. For Galileo was the first physicist to use measurement in a systematic way, to conduct time experiments, and to apply mathematics to the explanation of physical phenomena. His greatest contribution of all was to raise **induction** (reasoning from specific facts to general conclusions) above **deduction** (reasoning from the general to the specific) as a means of establishing scientific principles.

The ancient Greek philosophers and scientists, and the churchmen and philosophers who followed them down to Galileo's day, had given *deduction* the primary role. They stated certain allegedly self-evident or intuitively perceived axioms (or divine truths) and sought to derive valid conclusions from them. But no conclusion can be valid if the axiom or premise on which it is founded is invalid. Frequently, what seemed self-evident was not so at all. Every axiom, theory, or concept is based on a particular set of assumptions.

What Galileo did was to focus attention on the way axioms, premises, or basic principles were to be formed. According to Galileo's inductive method, axioms must be modified as needed to be applicable to the real world.

Fig. 2-1. Inductive and Deductive Reasoning

INDUCTION

1. start with facts
2. reason to general conclusions
3. if tested and verified, these conclusions can become basic principles

DEDUCTION

1. start with basic principles
2. reason to specific facts
3. if tested and verified, these facts can be the basis for more general conclusions

The interaction of inductive and deductive reasoning can lead to scientific progress.

This inductive method implied, however, that scientific generalizations could never be absolutely certain. They are limited by the set of assumptions originally selected.

Many scientific generalizations of the past have been upset or modified by new or more precise observations. For instance, Galileo's laws, in their original form, were refined by the work of later scientists. Sir Isaac Newton, building on the observations of Galileo, Tycho Brahe, and Johannes Kepler, as well as on his own observations and measurements, arrived at his three famous laws of motion and his great generalization, the law of universal gravitation. In time, Newton's great work was encompassed by Einstein's theory of relativity; Newton's law of gravitation became just a special case in Einstein's theory that gravitation is a manifestation of the geometry of space and time.

The heavy stress upon the inductive method in science does not mean that deduction is no longer important. On the contrary, a major reason for working so hard to reach valid generalizations is that one may then deduce further facts, discoveries, inventions, and applications from these generalizations. The tools of logic and mathematics are essential to tracing out the implications of well-founded generalizations.

A combination of induction and deduction—and intuition—is necessary to discover scientific truths. Intuition often leads to an exciting hypothesis—that is, a generalization that *might be true*. But no scientist is content to reason from hypotheses that have no correspondence to the real world. Social scientists, such as economists, are no different from natural scientists, such as chemists, in this respect.

Verification

In order to be useful, it is essential that a generalization or hypothesis have some correspondence to the real world. To determine whether a generalization is valid, one must compare predictions based on the theory with experimental data. Thus, laws of genetics can be tested by applying them in the breeding of different strains of cereals or different varieties of animals. And in economics, theories of employment can be tested by seeing whether policies founded on those theories can solve a nation's unemployment problem. When a theory does not work in the real world, it must be discarded, or modified until it does work.

In the social sciences, it is often very difficult to find adequate verification of a theory. For instance, one might find much evidence that when the population of a country is increasing, the income of that country is also increasing. But does this mean that an increase in population causes an increase in income? Or does it mean that an increase in income causes an increase in population? Or does it mean that each causes the other, in a chicken-and-egg process? Or may both phenomena be caused by some outside factor, such as an improvement in technology? Or can we even be sure that there is a positive correlation between population and income? Many generalizations in the social sciences may remain uncertain for centuries—perhaps indefinitely.

Unfortunately for both peace of mind and the prestige of the science, the economist is often at a disadvantage compared with the natural scientist in the firmness with which generalizations and theories can be established. The natural scientist frequently can test theories rigorously in a laboratory. But the laboratory of the economist is, generally speaking, the real world itself. Though trying to abstract from that vast world in order to develop theories, the economist cannot experimentally validate those theories with the same assurance as the natural scientist.

THE CONCEPT OF A SYSTEM

A system, to the scientist, is an organized scheme for studying nature or society. In effect, the scientist, in building a system, creates a special model of the world. This model can be experimented with, as a child can play with an airplane model or an engineer can test a model of a bridge, to discover new implications of theories and concepts.

Every science constructs a system of its own, a representation or abstraction from the inconceivably complex world of reality. But some scientists can be more abstract than others in their system-building—that is, in ruling out factors they do not wish to study.

The reason that the laws or principles of the social sciences tend to be less regular or certain than those of the natural sciences is that the two types of sciences use different systems. The problem of economists is that they cannot usefully limit themselves to a system as precise, orderly, and abstract as the system of the physicist or other natural scientists.

Closed Systems

Albert Einstein observed that "man tries to make for himself, in the fashion that suits him best, a simplified and intelligible picture of the world; he then tries to some extent to substitute this cosmos of his for the world of experience, and thus to overcome it." This, said Einstein, is what the painter, the poet, the speculative philosopher, and the natural scientist—such as the theoretical physicist—try to do, "each in his own fashion." What place does the theoretical physicist's picture of the world occupy among all these possible pictures of reality? "Physics," said Einstein, "demands the highest possible standard of rigorous precision in the description of relations, such as only the use of mathematical language can give. In regard to his subject matter, on the other hand, the physicist has to limit himself very severely: he must content himself with describing the most simple events which can be brought within the domain of our experience; all events of a more complex order are beyond the power of the human intellect to reconstruct with the subtle accuracy and logical perfection which the theoretical physicist demands. Supreme purity, and certainty at the cost of completeness!"[3]

In effect, the physicist deals with events in what is considered, with little or no harm to the aims of the work, to be a **closed system**—that is, a rigidly limited system that is not subject to influences or disturbances coming from outside this particular logical system. Thus, the physicist who is studying the properties of matter need not be concerned with such outside disturbances as national elections, changes in social moods, conflicts between nations, ups and downs in business, or many other factors. The physicist's findings may affect the outside political, social, and economic world, but that world will not affect the physicist's own physical system, ideas about matter, or abstract picture of the universe or the atom.

Open Systems

The economist, however, is concerned with events in an essentially **open system**—one that cannot be closed off in order to enjoy the "purity, clarity and certainty" that the theoretical physicist may enjoy in his realm. The economist's system is, on the contrary, subject to all the disturbances and influences of exactly the sort that the physicist can exclude—national elections, international conflicts, and the technological changes that the physicist helps to cause. Indeed, all sorts of political, social, psychological, biological, technological, and meteorological factors may affect the state of business, the growth of a nation's economy, the stability of the value of money, or other matters that are the economist's primary focus of interest. It does economists no good to complain about these outside disturbances; they are expected to analyse and explain the real political-economic world, not to dwell within a realm of abstractions.

Not every analytical system in the natural sciences—especially the applied sciences—is as closed, simple, and pure as that of the theoretical physicist. When natural scientists must deal with the problems of an open system, they are unlikely to be more certain of their findings or more dependable in their predictions than the economist or other social scientist. For instance, the prediction record of the science of meteorology is far from distinguished. The meteorologist may be even more notorious for errors in forecasting than the economist. The reason is that the meteorological system is actually *open*, like the economic system.

To predict next year's weather accurately, the meteorologist would need extremely detailed knowledge of present conditions (because a small local deviation can cause an ever-expanding influence) and information about the state of the sun (in order to predict the changes in the heat and corpuscular radiation it sends to us). Also needed would be data from the inside of the earth (to predict volcanic eruptions that might spread a dust screen over the atmosphere) and penetration into the human mind and into economic and political events (since a coal strike or a war or an outbreak of nuclear testing would affect the atmosphere, and even a carelessly thrown match might cause deforestation, which in turn would change rainfall and climate). In fact, all of these things cannot be known in advance. The system therefore remains open, and the forecasts are more unreliable than they would be if they were based

[3] Albert Einstein, *Essays in Science*, New York: Philosophical Library, 1954, p. 3.

only on a few factors about which a great deal is known.

The economist is, of course, in the same boat as the weatherman—or possibly a worse one. An English economist, John Maynard Keynes, observed that Max Planck, a famous German physicist who invented the quantum theory, had in his early life thought of studying economics but had abandoned the idea because he found economics too difficult! "Professor Planck," said Keynes, "could easily master the whole corpus of mathematical economics in a few days. He did not mean that: But the amalgam of logic and intuition and the wide knowledge of facts, most of which are not precise, which is required for economic interpretation in its highest form is, quite truly, overwhelmingly difficult for those whose gift mainly consists in the power to imagine and pursue to their furthest points the implications, and prior conditions of comparatively simple facts which are known with a high degree of precision."

Lest the student despair, however, it should be noted that far less brilliant men than Max Planck have managed to make a career as economists; indeed, anyone who is willing to make the effort can learn much about economics that will help to make the real economic world in which we live more intelligible. Indeed, just as Molière's character M. Jourdain learned to his astonishment that he had been talking prose all his life and had never known it, you will doubtless learn that you have been talking economics all your life.

You will discover that economics, like every science, is fundamentally common sense—but common sense organized, refined, and documented to the point where it is anything but common or obvious. Economics can be as potent as other sciences for affecting the development of the real world and, when wisely used, for increasing the welfare of mankind.

PITFALLS TO AVOID

There are always pitfalls awaiting one, especially in a new subject. Therefore, a brief word of warning about some potential dangers is in order.

First of all, be prepared to find out that some of your existing knowledge of economic matters may be ill founded. Everyone knows a little economics; but all too often, ideas which are only partly true or completely false become widely accepted. Don't be too disillusioned when this happens to prove true of you, for it happens to everyone. A possible example may appear with the following question: "What is the connection between gold and the Canadian dollar?" Do you or some of your classmates want to reply: "Our dollar is backed by the gold held by the government."—What is the correct answer to the question? After getting your answers, your teacher will discuss this with you.

As you well know, words cause confusion. Economics as a discipline has its own problems here. Sometimes, different words or terms refer to the same thing. On other occasions, words have meanings in economics which differ somewhat from the everyday meaning. This is not done just to confuse the student, but it is something to watch out for. Two classic examples are the terms "supply" and "demand." In Unit 2, you will find that they do not mean the same thing to the economist as they do to you right now.

Two other problems may arise from faulty logic. The first is often called the **post hoc fallacy** from the Latin *post hoc, ergo propter hoc* which means "after this, therefore because of this." Remember, just because "B" takes place after "A", it does not necessarily follow that "A" was the cause of "B." The second of these fallacies is called the **fallacy of composition**, an invalid statement where something which is true of a part is assumed to be true of the whole. An example is a classic quotation from a former American Secretary of Defense who once said: "What is good for General Motors is good for the country." What he meant was: "What is good for American business is good for America." This, however, is not necessarily true—for any country.

SUMMARY

Economics has much in common with other sciences, especially in its use of scientific method. This method seeks to discover truths about nature or society by a process of *observing* events in the real world, *measuring* them, *developing generalizations or hypotheses* to explain these facts, and finally testing and *verifying* the generalizations or hypotheses. Thus, the basic approach of science is through *induction*, drawing conclusions from empirical observations. But every science also uses *deduction* in order to discover the further implications (or applications) of valid generalizations. A scientist capable of making important discoveries also needs that mysterious quality variously called intuition, imagination, or creativity.

Every science seeks to build a system with which to view the real world; such systems are abstractions from reality. Some sciences, such as theoretical physics, build an abstract system that is *closed*—that is, a system that excludes outside disturbances. Other sciences, such as meteorology and economics, must be content to work with *open* systems, in which outside disturbances cannot be excluded nor wholly understood and in which analysis and prediction are therefore less dependable. Further, the data of the social sciences, such as economics, are likely to be less precise than those of the natural sciences, such as physics.

These problems of imprecise measurement and of open rather than closed systems generally make the work of economists less certain and less systematic and their predictions less dependable than those of natural scientists. But these limitations are inescapable, because the economist is charged with the task of coping with the complexities of society itself, not with the greater abstractions from reality to which the natural scientist may practically limit himself. Yet the economist, while compelled to depend more heavily on guesswork, intuition, and judgment, still strives for the objectivity and logical rigor of the other sciences.

KEY CONCEPTS

concept
mental model
scientific method
hypothesis
induction
deduction
closed system
open system
post hoc fallacy
fallacy of composition

QUESTIONS FOR REVIEW AND DISCUSSION

1. What is it that all sciences have in common?
2. What are each of the basic elements in the scientific method? Explain how these elements are related.
3. Explain the inductive and deductive methods of reasoning. Why are *both* induction and deduction useful in scientific investigations?
4. Why is it that the laws or principles of economics and other social sciences tend to be less regular or less certain than those of the natural sciences?

PROBLEMS AND EXERCISES TO SHARPEN YOUR UNDERSTANDING

1. Models (or theories) can be expressed in different ways. Examine the following data and state in words a model that explains your observations.

Consumer Income	*Consumer Spending*
100	90
200	180
300	270
400	360

2. Can the verbal model you stated above be illustrated on a graph? How?
3. Show that the verbal or graphical model may also be represented by the following equation:

$$\text{Consumption} = 9/10 \text{ of Income}$$
$$C = 9/10\ I$$

4. According to this model, what will be the amount of consumer spending, if consumer income is increased to 500? If it is decreased to 50?
5. What would you call these predictions? How would you verify whether your predictions were correct or not?

CHAPTER 3

ECONOMICS: THE SCIENCE OF SCARCITY AND CHOICE

■ THE CONCEPTS OF SCARCITY AND REAL COST ■ THE CONCEPT OF RESOURCES ■ THE CONCEPT OF GOODS AND SERVICES ■ THE CONCEPT OF WANTS ■ THE CENTRAL PROBLEM OF ECONOMICS: CHOICE ■ SUMMARY

Although economics has much in common with other sciences, it has a perspective that is uniquely its own. **Economics** *is the science that investigates problems arising from the* **scarcity** *of resources and goods that can be used to satisfy human wants.* It studies how men allocate and develop their scarce resources to satisfy their wants and needs in a way that is compatible with the basic values of their societies.

This definition contains a number of concepts—scarcity, resources, goods, wants—that need to be spelled out. This will be the task of this chapter. The concept of values or social goals also requires some elaboration. This will be the task of Chapter 4.

■ THE CONCEPTS OF SCARCITY AND REAL COST

Any resource or good is considered by economists to be scarce whenever people cannot obtain as much of it as they would like to have *without giving up something else.* If a family chooses to eat sirloin steak rather than hamburgers, the difference in cost represents something else which must be sacrificed if the steak is purchased. Even more fundamentally, one could say that the time and energy spent to earn the dollars needed to buy the steak represent another form of the cost of the steak dinner. This is the true meaning of the old saying, "There is no such thing as a free lunch." Somebody must give up something to create or acquire scarce goods.[1]

Whatever is given up in order to acquire goods and services constitutes a **real cost**, a key economic concept. Scarce resources used for one purpose cannot be used for something else. Steel used to make rockets is not available to make cars. The real cost of satisfying one economic want is the loss of all the other satisfaction producing goods and services that might have been produced with the same resources. Every time a scarce resource is allocated to the production of a particular good or service, the real cost is not having that resource available for the production of other goods or services. Goods that are scarce—whether turkeys, electronic computers, spaceships, or rides on a roller coaster—are called *economic goods.* All economic goods have a real cost.

Some goods are free in the sense that one must not sacrifice anything in order to have as much of them as one likes. For instance, we usually think of air or ocean water as free goods. But whether these goods are free or not depends upon actual circumstances.

For purposes of equipping a submarine, air becomes an economic good, since storing air in tanks in a submarine involves expenditure of effort and means giving up of space

[1] Robbery might seem to be an exception. But then it is the victim of the robbery who has given up something.

and resources that could have been used to carry more equipment, torpedoes, and similar items. And if you lived in Saskatchewan and wanted to bring in ocean water for some reason, that water would not be costless to you. This corresponds to common sense. Ocean water is obviously scarce in Saskatchewan; somebody has to give up something to get it there.

It has been asserted by one contemporary economist, Professor John Kenneth Galbraith, that, thanks to the rate of economic progress in some nations, many people have passed from the Age of Scarcity into an Age of Affluence.[2] However, granting that our society is richer than it once was does not mean that all sorts of goods and resources are no longer scarce in the sense that we have defined scarcity. People still must work if they want a car or a house; they still must give up claims on other goods if they wish to acquire a pair of shoes or a motorboat, or any other economic good.

THE CONCEPT OF RESOURCES

By the term **productive resources** economists mean anything that can be used to create economic goods or services. Originally, economists considered that there were just three basic resources or factors of production: land, labor, and capital. Subsequent consideration, however, has refined these original notions and added other factors that can be considered basic economic resources.

The concept of *land*, for example, has been broadened to include not only the fertile earth itself but all **natural resources** such as mineral deposits, oil reserves, waterfalls, and rivers. Natural resources, then, are the gifts of nature that are useful in producing the goods and services that men want.

The concept of *labor* has also been broadened to include all **human resources**—not only physical labor, but also mental effort and the other contributions that human beings can make to the production of economic goods and services. Of particular interest here is a human contribution that is so special that it is often considered a separate resource in itself—the resource of **entrepreneurship** or enterprise. Entrepreneurship refers to the contribution that the businessperson, promoter, manager, risk taker, or inventor makes to the productive process. The entrepreneur organizes and directs the other factors of production, thinks up new things for the business to do, and seeks to develop new products, new productive processes, new materials, and new ideas for selling goods. The entrepreneur also bears the risks for the success or failure of the business. Thus, the quality of a nation's human resources consists of the health, strength, education, and skills of its people, including their ability to organize economic activity and get things done.

Real capital goods refers to all goods produced to aid in the production of other goods and services. Thus, capital as a real factor of production, or as a productive resource, means such things as machines, factories, highways, power dams, generators, tools, steamships, trucks, and warehouses.

The above definition of capital covers only one of the senses in which it is used by economists. *Capital* is also used by businesspeople and economists to refer to money available in a business for buying machinery, equipment, or other productive facilities. Fundamentally, however, no one can plow a field or build a house or knit a sweater out of money. One can only use money to acquire land, labor, or capital goods to do any of those things. Thus, it is useful to distinguish between *real* capital goods and *money* capital, the funds used to buy real capital goods or other productive resources. Throughout the rest of this book, therefore, we shall try to keep these two meanings separate by prefixing the word *capital* with the word *real* or the word *money* to make it clear which type of capital we are talking about.

[2] J. K. Galbraith, *The Affluent Society*, Boston: Houghton Mifflin, 1958.

FIG. 3-1. SCARCE PRODUCTIVE RESOURCES

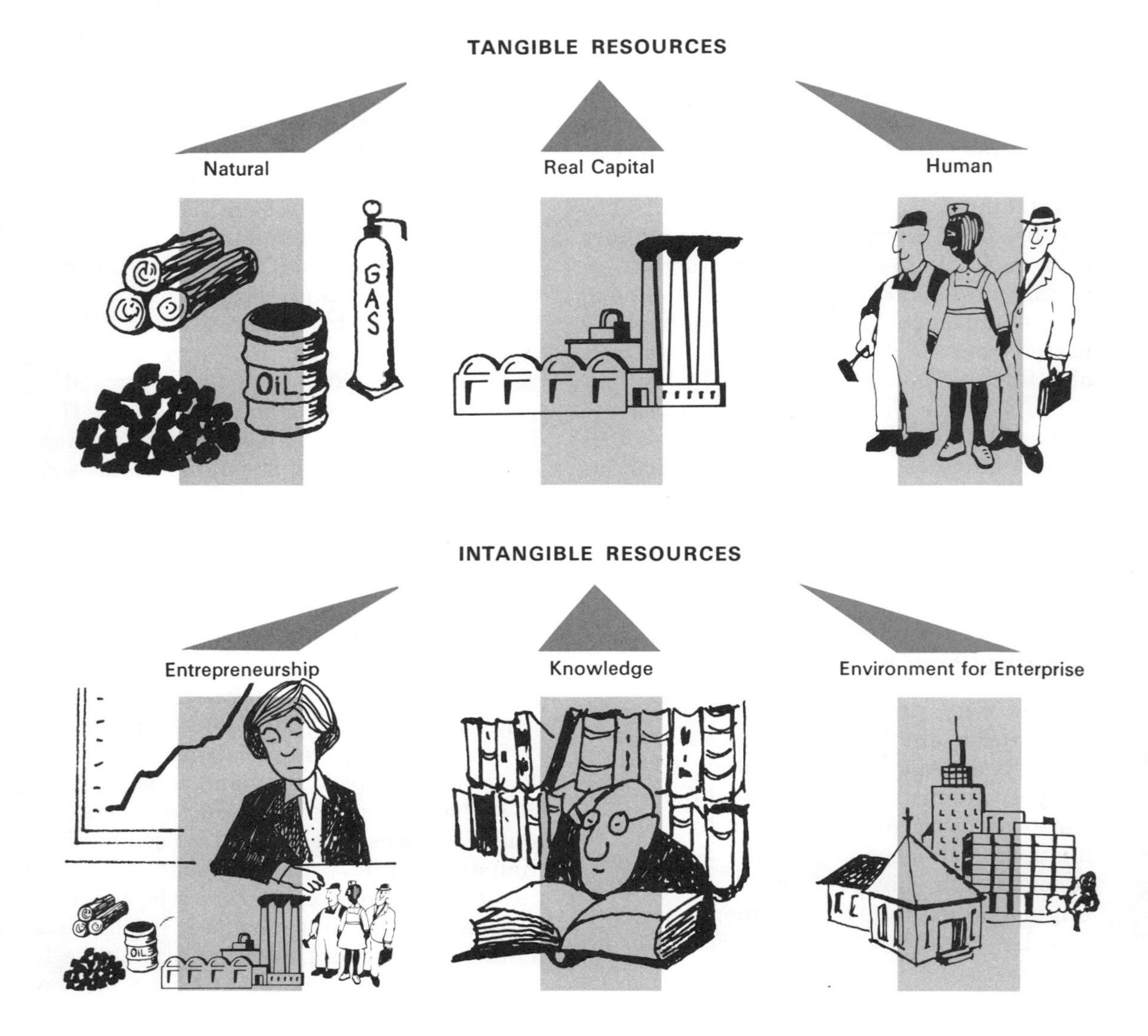

Some of the factors of production, such as natural resources, human resources, and real capital goods, are *tangible resources*. They have a physical existence that can be seen and touched and counted, measured, or weighed—as so many tonnes of coal, so many people in the labor force, or so many kilometres of railroad track. In recent years, however, economists have become aware of *intangible resources* that also contribute to the production of goods and services. Entrepreneurship, for example, is really an intangible factor of production. It is harder to see and measure directly than, say, a tonne of coal, but we know that entrepreneurship is important by the effect that certain risk-taking and organizational activities have on the output (or productivity) of tangible resources. Two societies, for example, might have the same physical amounts of tangible resources, but one society might be able to produce more with these factors of production because it has a greater capacity for entrepreneurship.

In recent years, many economists have emphasized **knowledge** as still another factor of production. Knowledge, including scientific, technological, and other forms of knowledge, can indeed contribute to improving the productive powers of natural resources, human resources, real capital goods, and even entrepreneurship. New knowledge may increase the productivity of land, for instance, through crop rotation or by the discovery of new uses for natural resources.

New technological knowledge may be embodied in capital goods and thereby increase the productivity of real capital. For example, an electronic computer, based on new scientific and engineering knowledge, is vastly more productive or efficient than older computing machines. Similarly, new knowledge may be embodied in labor; workers with higher education and greater skills can produce more efficiently than those with less knowledge. Knowledge and information which is accurate and timely increase the efficiency and managerial productivity of entrepreneurs.

A final, and even more intangible, factor that is recognized as important in producing economic goods and services is a society's total **environment for enterprise.** By environment for enterprise, we mean the basic social and cultural values of the society and its economic and political institutions that can play a vital role in creating an atmosphere or a climate that can aid or hinder the production of economic goods and services.

The kinds of things that a people think are important can significantly affect their economic behavior. For example, a society that reserves its highest tribute and prestige for soldiers and statesmen, while considering others to be engaged only in menial work, might have a lower economic output than one that considers entrepreneurs as the most important people in society. Values concerning the role of women and children in society will affect the economic productivity of the society. Values concerning the proper use of land will affect the economic productivity of natural resources.

Modern economists have broadened the concept of resources to include not only tangibles but also intangible resources such as knowledge and specialized skills—such as those being acquired by university students. The photograph shows the campus of Simon Fraser University, one of the many newer universities in Canada.

While it may seem strange to classify a society's religious and cultural values as productive resources, attempts to improve the economic output of some of the underdeveloped nations mentioned in Chapter 1 have emphasized the importance of intangible resources, as well as the more tangible factors of production. In economics it is necessary to recognize the importance of *all* of these resources, and it is dangerous to try to single out any one resource or factor of production as *the* important one. The vast natural resources of North America, for example, would have been of little value if large amounts of human resources, real capital, knowledge, entrepreneurship, and a favorable environment for enterprise had not also been applied to these natural resources. Look at the economic performance of the North American Indians—did they not have the same natural resources as the subsequent settlers? Yet, why did the real economic output per person grow faster under the settlers than it had under the Indians? Would not all of the above factors have to be mentioned in adequately answering this question?

Thus, in the final analysis it is *all* of the resources described previously (and their combination) that is the real source of a nation's wealth: its tangible resources—natural, human, and real capital—and its intangible resources—entrepreneurship, knowledge, and the environment for enterprise. It is not money that really matters. Money can always be printed by a nation's government; obviously, however, simply producing bales of money in such poor nations as India or Pakistan will not make such countries rich in terms of food, clothing, housing, or other goods essential to the welfare of their populations. If any nation could make its people prosperous and healthy just by printing money, what nation would ever stay poor?[3]

THE CONCEPT OF GOODS AND SERVICES

Throughout this book we shall be talking of *goods* and *services*.

Goods are objects that are capable of satisfying human wants. *Durable* goods, such as automobiles or refrigerators, are simply goods that last for a long time and can be used over and over; *nondurable* goods, such as fruit or paper napkins, spoil or are quickly worn out in usage.

Services are economic actions performed by a person or business that are capable of satisfying human wants. Services are goods that do not take lasting physical form but expire as soon as they are performed—such as a doctor's examination or a housekeeper's dusting. We often use the words *goods* to cover both goods and services.

Just as money is not a resource or factor of production, neither is money a good or service in the sense the economist uses these terms, since it cannot of itself increase your welfare. You can nourish yourself with goods such as milk or bread, but you cannot eat money. You can be helped by a waiter who brings you your food, or by a dentist who cleans your teeth, but money cannot serve you. You can use money only to acquire some good or service that *will* benefit you.

THE CONCEPT OF WANTS

People have a tremendous variety of wants—for the nourishment of their bodies, for protection against cold or heat, for communication with their fellow humans, for knowledge, beauty, excitement, fun, comfort, luxury, pleasant experiences, impressive possessions, respectability, or honor in the eyes of their neighbors. We may think of some goods and services as essentially satisfying physical wants and others as essen-

[3] But this does not imply that an effective monetary system and an adequate supply of money are not important to a well-functioning national economy. The role of money and its importance in economics is discussed in more detail later on in this book. See Chapter 16 and 17, and Unit 4.

FIG. 3-2. THE BASIC ECONOMIC PROBLEM OF SCARCITY

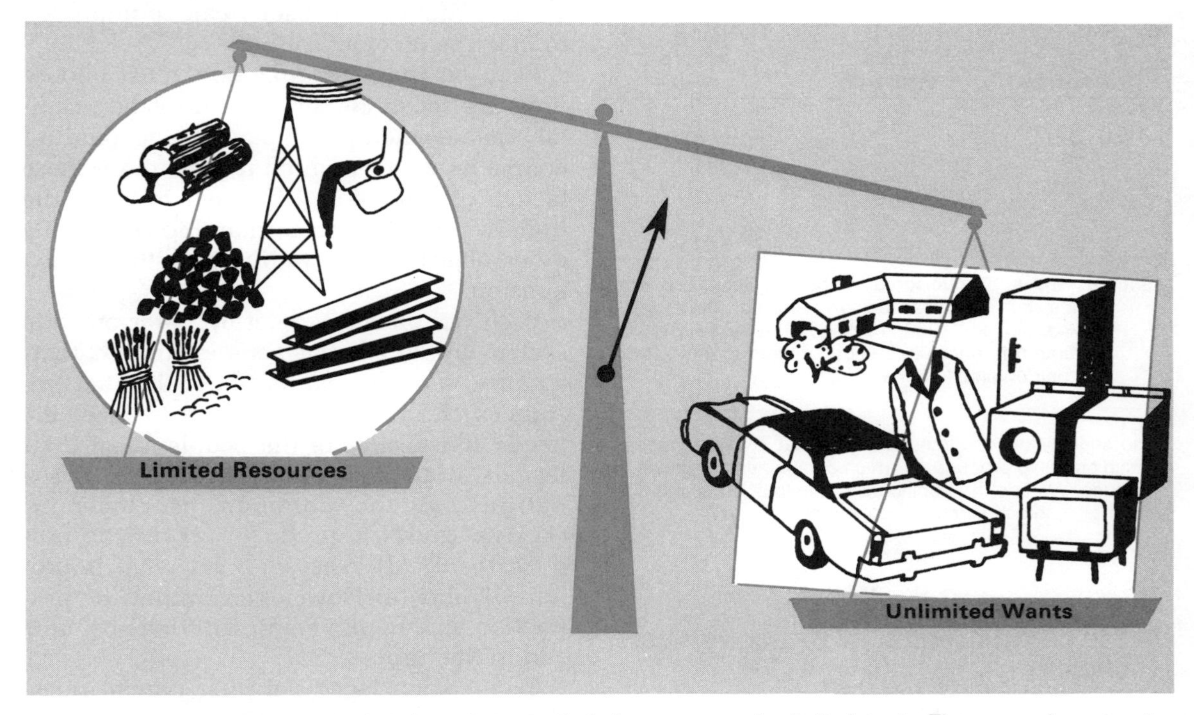

The basic economic problem is the imbalance between limited resources and unlimited wants. The economic answer to this problem involves: (1) getting the *most* out of existing limited resources and seeking to *increase* resources, and (2) choosing to satisfy only those *wants that are the most important.*

tially satisfying psychological wants. In an advanced civilization, many goods satisfy both physical and psychological wants.

The variety of human wants is so great, and the range of aspirations is so wide, that economists customarily say that human wants are unlimited. Of course, the wants of a single individual for any particular good are by no means unlimited; people may easily reach the limits of their appetites for food. But it is unlikely that very many individuals can satisfy *all* of their wants. Even very rich people never seem able to afford all the paintings, jewelry, servants, horses, yachts, country houses, or parties that they might conceivably want.

It is not, however, necessary to agree that human wants are truly unlimited (whatever that may mean) to see that, for the overwhelming majority of individuals, for every nation, and for the world as a whole, human wants at this stage of history greatly exceed the goods and resources with which those wants can be satisfied.

As the index of wealth and poverty used in the first chapter implies, most nations are very poor, and, even in the richest nations, virtually everyone wants more than he or she now has. This condition is likely to remain true for centuries to come. One can be sure that the science of economics has a long life expectancy.

Table 3-1: PRODUCTION POSSIBILITY CHOICES

Possibilities	Guns, thousands	Butter, millions of kg
A	15	0
B	14	1
C	12	2
D	9	3
E	5	4
F	0	5

Source: Paul A. Samuelson and Anthony Scott, *Economics,* first Canadian edition, Toronto: McGraw-Hill Co. of Can., 1966, Table 1, Chapter 2. (The volume references have been altered to metric from their original Imperial structure.)

The scarcity of resources requires that society chooses which goods to produce, or which combination of goods to produce. We use the traditional example of guns and butter (that is, the choice between war and peace).

THE CENTRAL PROBLEM OF ECONOMICS: CHOICE

We can now combine our four central concepts—scarcity, resources, goods and services, and human wants—to formulate the central problem of economics.

Because of the inequality between human wants and the scarcity of resources and goods capable of satisfying those wants, men must make choices on how to make the best possible use of the resources and goods that they have, and on how to develop and improve the resources at their disposal. Hence, economics is sometimes called the "science of choice." Millions and billions of economic choices must be made every day by all the individuals, organizations, and nations of the world.

Each *individual* must choose how best to satisfy wants by allocating limited time and energy to different uses and by distributing income among the different goods and services actually bought. Consideration should also be given to savings which may be needed to meet future needs, and ways in which productive capacity can be improved to increase income.

Each *business organization* must choose how to allocate its limited land, labor, capital, management, and knowledge (and of course its money, which is a claim on these factors of production) in order to make the highest profits it can earn and to achieve its other objectives, including growth and expansion.

Each *nation* must determine—or create a system by which the people through their actions can determine—how limited resources can best be employed to meet the needs and desires of the people, or of their leaders, both now and in the future. Every nation has the common problems of: (1) What goods to produce? (2) How to produce them? (3) Who shall get what is produced? and (4) How much output, or production and employment, will there be, now and in the future?

Each nation faces a further crucial question involving a very serious complication. *How can it best solve the fundamental questions of what to produce, how to produce it, for whom, and how much, in a way that is consistent with its social, political, and moral values?* Different nations may resolve their fundamental economic questions with varying degrees of infringement of individual liberty, central control over the national economy, inequality among individuals in wealth and income, and stability and change in the economic lives of its people. Canada, the United States, the Soviet Union, China, and every other nation must solve the same basic economic questions of what, how, for whom, and how much, but they may answer these questions in ways that run the gamut from great freedom for the individual to almost total dictatorship. Given this fact, how do we know which economic system is best? This question of values and goals will be discussed in the next chapter.

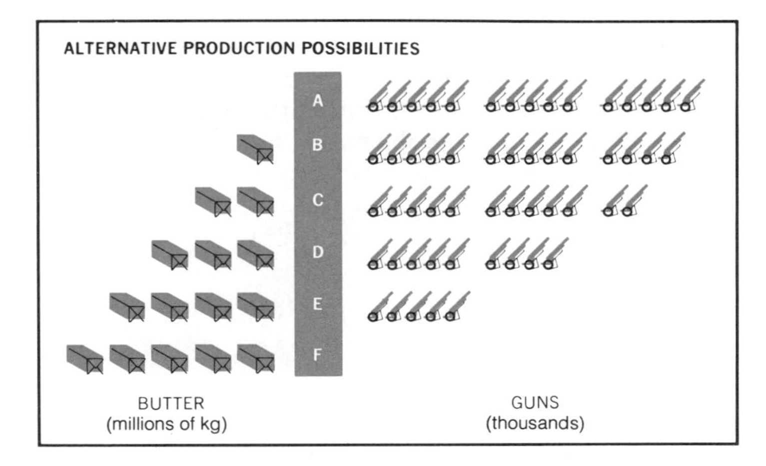

FIG. 3-3. ALTERNATIVE PRODUCTION POSSIBILITIES

Table 3-1 can be shown pictorially. The cost of getting extra guns may be measured in terms of the butter production which must be sacrificed.

Source: Samuelson and Scott, *op. cit.*, Figure 1, Chapter 2, p. 18.

FIG. 3-4. GRAPHING PRODUCTION POSSIBILITIES

Each point marked is a careful plot of each gun-and-butter numerical combination from Table 3-1. (Guess where the point midway between *B* and *C* might approximately fall. Read off its guns-butter numbers, and pencil them into Table 3-2 at about the right place.)

Source: Samuelson and Scott, *op. cit.*, Figure 2, Chapter 2, p. 19.

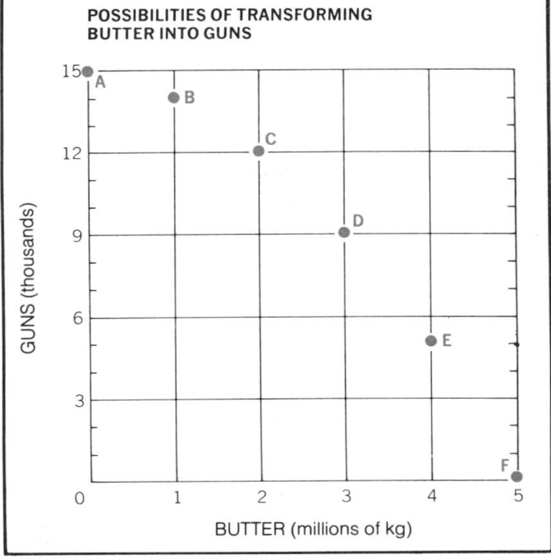

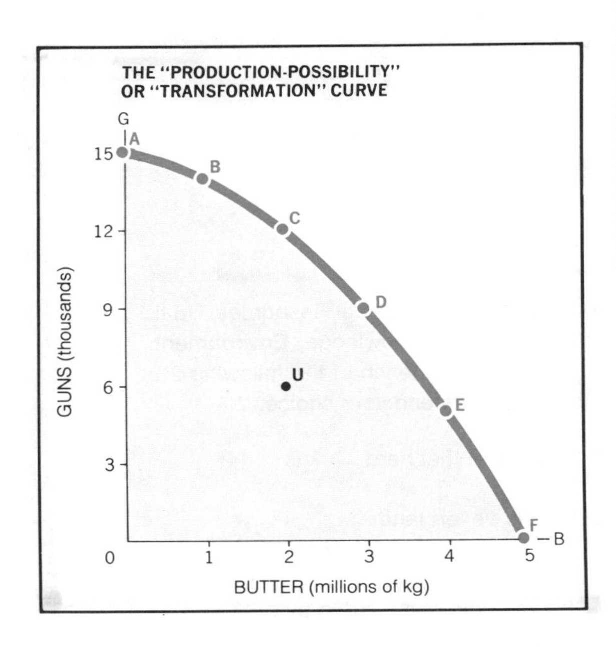

FIG. 3-5. THE PRODUCTION POSSIBILITY CURVE

This shows how society can choose to substitute guns for butter, assuming a given state of technology and a given total of resources. Any point *inside* the curve, such as *U*, indicates that resources are not being fully employed in the best known way. (Source: Table 3-1. A smooth curve has been passed through the points of the previous chart.)

Source: Samuelson and Scott, *op. cit.*, Figure 3, Chapter 2, p. 20.

■ **SUMMARY**

Individuals, businesses, and nations must continuously make choices as to how best to use scarce resources and goods to satisfy their virtually unlimited wants. Because this is the fundamental economic problem, economics is often called the science of choice.

KEY CONCEPTS

economics
productive resources
scarcity
real cost
natural resources
human resources
entrepreneurship
real capital goods
knowledge
environment for enterprise
goods
services
production possibility curve

QUESTIONS FOR REVIEW AND DISCUSSION

1. How do *economic* goods differ from *free* goods?
2. Write your own definition of the terms *economics, scarcity, cost,* and *productive resources.*
3. What are three different kinds of tangible productive resources and three different kinds of intangible productive resources? Give a specific example of each.
4. In what ways are goods and services alike, and in what ways are they different?
5. Do you agree or disagree with the statement, "Human wants are unlimited"? Defend your position with a good argument supported by specific examples.
6. Explain why economics is often called the *science of choice.*

PROBLEMS AND EXERCISES TO SHARPEN YOUR UNDERSTANDING

On a separate sheet of paper, make seven columns labeled: Natural Resources; Real Capital Resources; Human Resources; Entrepreneurship; Knowledge; Environment for Enterprise; and Not a Productive Resource at All. Write each of the following 20 items in one of the seven columns, and be prepared to defend your choice.

1. codfish off the coast of Newfoundland
2. college-trained engineers
3. computers
4. the discovery of atomic energy
5. the Athabaska tar sands
6. Gerald Bouey
7. a belief that hard work is good
8. arid desert land
9. unpicked but edible fruit growing wild in the jungle
10. an apple being eaten by a small child
11. Florida climate

12. jet airplanes
13. a hangar at an airport
14. land made fertile by irrigation
15. a law prohibiting work on Sunday
16. public school systems
17. Montreal Canadiens
18. mimeograph machine
19. the development of synthetic fiber for clothing
20. railroad cars

THE PROBLEM OF VALUES AND SOCIAL GOALS

■ VALUE JUDGMENTS ■ THE PROBLEM OF OBJECTIVITY ■ ECONOMICS AS A WAY OF THINKING ■ WHAT ECONOMISTS DO ■ ECONOMIC CHANGE ■ SUMMARY

Economics has the reputation of being a highly controversial subject. In part, this reputation is deserved, for controversies among the general public, as well as among economists, are common over what to do about a particular problem and how the nation should deal with some economic issue, such as poverty or inflation.

However, it is important to recognize that it is possible to separate the facts about a particular economic problem and an analysis of its causes and probable consequences from a judgment as to what to *do* about that problem. Judgments about the preferred answers to economic problems are heavily influenced by the values or interests of the person making the judgment. Understanding economic issues requires that one clearly recognize *one's own* values and goals, as well as those of other people.

■ VALUE JUDGMENTS

What economic system is "best" depends on which social goals or which *values* you think are most important. **Value judgments** concern judgments or feelings about what *ought to be*, whereas facts concern observations or statements about what *is*. In attempting to get at the facts of how a society answers its basic economic questions, the economist uses the kind of *analysis* described in Chapter 2. While this type of economic analysis is helpful in deciding what *is*, it is not very helpful in deciding what *ought to be*.

What seems good to one person or one society may seem bad to another. The economist, as such, is not particularly competent to judge who is right and who is wrong.

This crucial point was well brought out in a 1961 report by a number of prominent economists and educators in the United States. This report, which has had a major effect on the teaching of economics at the high school level in a number of countries outside the U.S.A., Canada included, made the following observations about value judgments.

> Since different people want economic systems to achieve different goals, they understandably differ on how well their and other economies work. As between communist leaders and most Americans, this point is obvious. But even within American society, economic goals differ widely. Some value individual freedom most highly. Others stress security, or rapid economic growth, or maximum output of goods and services. Some believe incomes should be distributed more equally, others less equally. In a democratic society, everyone has an equal right to his own views—and by the same token a special responsibility to have informed views rather than opinions based on ignorance and prejudice.
>
> Thus, it is understandable that wide differences arise as to how the economic system should be modified to achieve better one or another of these goals. Economic analysis and understanding can aid straight thinking on such questions. But it cannot tell anyone what economic goals he should place high-

Collins in the Montreal Gazette

The cartoonist's comments about inflation show how value judgments and personal interests may affect one's point of view. Rising prices and wages are not concerned about John Doe, though obviously the leak at his end of the boat will affect them as well.

> est—or that the goals held by someone else are "wrong."[1]

As a social science, economics does not have an *ideology* or a particular set of value judgments of its own. Individual economists may hold to any value judgments or political beliefs they wish—just as may physicists, chemists, or, for that matter, any other citizens. As we say, "it's a free country"—and your beliefs and values are your own.

THE PROBLEM OF OBJECTIVITY

Conscientious economists, however, strive to keep their value judgments and political beliefs from biasing their economic analyses. This is not always easy to do because value judgments and political beliefs are frequently intertwined with particular economic issues and economic policy recommendations. Economists sometimes differ sharply among themselves, especially on policy matters, because of their different social and political values.[2] Some economists may be more willing than others to use the powers of government to serve what they regard as the interest of all the people, while others may be more inclined to regard many types of government activity as an infringement of individual rights. Economists may sometimes commit themselves to the interests of a particular group or client. Some economists may serve the interests of business, some those of labor unions, some those of farm organizations, while some maintain that they serve only the *public* interest. This concept of the public interest is not easy to define, since the individuals who make up the public differ a great deal among themselves in wealth, income, and the way they would define their separate interests and values. More briefly, one might say that some economists serve the interests of a particular government or political party.

It is inevitable that economists, like other citizens, should often be involved in controversy—both among themselves and in debates with other citizens. This is as it should be. In a free society we do not expect to find a single philosophy or point of view about important political issues. We regard controversy as not only inevitable but desirable, since it is the democratic belief that the truth will emerge from "the free marketplace of ideas." But it is helpful to know whether the basic controversy concerns differences in value judgments or whether it concerns differences in economic analysis.

Therefore, despite their political differences or interest-group allegiances, economists do generally strive to maintain a sci-

[1] *Economic Education in the Schools Report of the National Task Force on Economic Education,* New York: Committee for Economic Development, 1961, p. 26.

[2] The fundamental policy question is always, "What shall we do about this?"

The Limits of Economics

Sir Eric Roll, who, after a distinguished career as academic economist and British civil servant, became an investment banker, explains in this passage why economists disagree as to whether their subject is or is not a science.

Most professional economists today would say that the primary purpose of economics is analytical, that is, to discover what is. In other words, whatever other aims some of them may have in mind, and whatever hypothetical examples they may devise for expository purposes, economists' concern is to establish the principles upon which the present economic system works. It is sometimes argued that economics is capable of becoming as exact and as "universally valid" as the physical sciences; by implication, the essentially social and historical nature of economics is denied. These views, however, are put forward only on the occasion of methodological discussion and do not seem to affect the scope of the bulk of the work of members of this school of thought: they are still mainly interested in the working of the present-day economy.

It should be said at once that the general public is very rarely aware of this positive and analytical purpose which the professional regards as the paramount, or even as the only legitimate one. The public knows that it can justifiably demand of the economist a statement of how the system works (though its faith in the explanation which is forthcoming is not always great); but it generally wants to know also what is the right thing to *do*. Economists cannot always shirk this question; and when they answer they reveal more far-reaching differences of opinion than any that arise in the analysis upon which they all claim to base their advice. Such disagreement over the diagnosis of an actual economic problem and the prescription of a remedy, more than a desire for scientific neatness, leads economists from time to time to an examination of the limits of their discipline.

From Eric Roll, *A History of Economic Thought,* London: Faber and Faber, Ltd., 1961, pp. 19-20.

entific attitude in their professional analysis. The development and growth of economics as a science makes it easier for economists to be objectively analytical. They strive to develop useful concepts, models, and data about economic problems as a means of recommending how to deal with those problems and as a means of helping other policymakers decide what to do. Thus, economists try to employ, in their analytical work, the scientific method described in Chapter 2, without necessarily imposing their own value judgments on those who must decide what to do about a particular problem.

■ ECONOMICS AS A WAY OF THINKING

In trying to develop an approach that separates their professional analysis from their personal value judgments, most economists use a special *way of thinking* about economic problems. This way of thinking can be called the **problem-solving method**, and it consists of six distinct steps.

1. *Define the problem.* Find out where you are and how you got there. Get the facts, and state the important issues.

2. *Identify the goals* or values that you want a solution to achieve. Find out where you want to go. Then state your objectives clearly, and give them a rough order of priority.

3. *List alternative courses of action.* There is usually more than one way to get from where you are to where you want to go. Try to make sure that you think of most of the main alternatives.

4. *Weigh each alternative.* Think about what is likely to happen if you choose each

course of action. What are the most probable results of each alternative? Compare the likely results of one action against the likely results of another action.

5. *Choose* the alternative that seems to solve your problem best in terms of the goals or objectives you have stated, *and* then *act* on it.

6. *If possible, after you have acted,* you should go back and *check your results.* Ask: Did my solution work out as I expected? What have I learned that will help me in solving other problems in the future?

This method has the advantage of separating the economic analysis needed in defining the problem (step 1) and in evaluating the alternatives (step 4) from the value judgments needed in stating the goals and values in step 2.

The use of this method explains why economists can use the same analysis and still disagree on particular policies—they often have different values in step 2 of the problem-solving process. The use of this method also explains why disagreement among economists on most policy issues is usually narrower than the disagreement of noneconomists on the same issues. The reason for the resulting narrowness of disagreement among most economists is that once differences in values are recognized and a particular goal accepted,[3] economists usually use the same *tools of analysis* in defining the problem and evaluating the alternatives. The models of the economist, based on the analytical techniques described in Chapter 2, give them a systematic way of explaining economic phenomena that noneconomists do not have.

WHAT ECONOMISTS DO

It has sometimes been said that economics really *is* what economists *do*. In fact, the growing ability of economists to deal use-

[3] For further discussions of this, see J. K. Galbraith's "Economics and Goals," reprinted in *Readings in the World of Economics.*

"You'll just have to imagine the rabbit."

Collins in Montreal Gazette

Economists have to advise government leaders about just how much may be "pulled from the hat" and also what the cost will be, for whom, for each performance.

fully with the problems of business, labor, or the nation as a whole through the techniques of their science has led them to play an increasingly active role in practical affairs.

Within Government

Within government, economists work on a broad range of problems, including the fluctuations of the national economy, employment and unemployment, the movement of prices, the flow of tax revenues to the government, and the allocation of those revenues to different public uses. On the basis of their analyses, economists advise key government officials on the best means of dealing with their problems.

In Canada, for example, many economists play prominent roles in all government departments and act as special policy advisors

Careers in Economics:

The Guidance Centre, Faculty of Education, University of Toronto has issued an excellent monograph on the educational requirements for and career opportunities within the field of economics. This would be of interest for your course in economics and, perhaps, your own future. Check with your guidance office. If the monograph is not there, perhaps they can obtain it.

to Ministers. Federal advisors must try to forecast the future development of the national economy, and also predict regional trends and problems since government policies must be oriented toward the future. On the federal level, other economists in institutions such as the Bank of Canada (see Chapter 27) and the Economic Council of Canada (see Chapters 25 and 26) give recommendations to the Cabinet and the public regarding the promotion and preservation of economic growth and stability. Economists have also been key figures in many Royal Commission studies. An example is Professor Melville Watkins, who headed a study on the implications of increasing foreign ownership of Canadian industry, a topic we will deal with later.

In foreign governments also, economists play equally vital roles. In some cases, the position held automatically means that the holder's actions will be of importance to other countries. The head of the Federal Reserve, the central bank of the United States, is one such position.

Economists frequently become heads of governments as well. Examples are Harold Wilson in the U.K. and Alexis Kosygin of the U.S.S.R. Considerable economic training may also be a prime requirement for many positions in government in Canada and elsewhere, despite the fact that the jobs do not involve full-time work in economics.

Economists also play an important part in such international agencies as the United Nations, the International Monetary Fund, the International Bank for Reconstruction and Development, the Organization for Economic Cooperation and Development, and others. Here the economists tend to focus on problems involving monetary problems, trade, and other economic relations among different countries. International economic cooperation is highly important for the prosperity and progress of each individual country.

Within Business and Economic Institutions

Economists are frequently employed by large business organizations, banks, and trade associations to work on such problems as forecasting the development of the national economy and trying to anticipate how such developments may affect the particular business institution for which the economist works. Business economists try to spot price, wage, production, and other trends, in order to help business managers plan more effectively and to reduce their costs of operation. In some business organizations, economists try to determine how the company can best invest its funds or which new projects the company should undertake at home or abroad. Economists working for business sometimes serve a public relations role as well. They may often speak before business or other public groups or help company officials to prepare economic policy statements of their own. Bank economists frequently offer economic information or advice to customers of the bank, as well as to their own top management.

Within other economic institutions, such as labor unions or farm organizations, economists also prepare analyses and recommendations affecting the important decisions and actions of those organizations. A labor economist will, among other tasks, analyse wage, cost, price, and profit trends in a particular industry as a basis for shaping his union's demands upon an employer or presenting a case before a government agency. In a farm organization, the economist will develop analyses and recommendations to guide his organization's position on needed Federal legislation affecting farm prices, subsidies, or crop controls.

Within Education

Within colleges, universities, and research institutes, economists, in addition to their teaching responsibilities, carry on research activities designed to achieve two fundamental objectives: (1) to improve economics as a science, by developing better and more useful concepts, models, and theories, and (2) to make factual studies that will contribute to the solution of major economic problems affecting the world, the nation, business, labor, or other groups. Many academic economists also serve as consultants to government agencies or business organizations, either on a part-time basis or on leave from their academic institutions. For instance, many of the most prominent economists who have served on the Economic Council of Canada or headed Federal Royal Commissions have been professors who have been on leave from their academic duties.

There is no clear line that divides the practical from the academic economists; all economists aim to develop knowledge, models, and tools of analysis that will—whether immediately or eventually—contribute to the solution of real economic problems.

ECONOMIC CHANGE

Although some economists are more concerned with theoretical research and others with immediate practical problems, all are concerned with **economic change**. Economists seek to explain the factors that have been responsible for past changes and which are likely to be responsible for future changes in economic conditions. Economists are interested in many types of changes, such as:

1. *Prices*. What causes the price of some particular good or service to go up or down? Why does the general level of prices increase or decrease? Can one predict the course of prices of individual goods or of all goods collectively?
2. *Production*. What determines whether the production of particular goods—or all goods together—will increase, decrease, or remain the same? What causes national economies to rise and fall?
3. *Consumption*. Why do people change the ways in which they spend their money? What determines whether consumers will increase or decrease the portion of income that they spend or save? What effect do their decisions to spend or save have on the overall economy?
4. *Employment*. Why, at some times, are jobs plentiful and, at other times, hard to find? What causes unemployment to grow or diminish among different groups in a population? How can unemployment be reduced? What effect does unemployment have on the level of prices?
5. *International trade*. Why do the imports and exports of particular nations, or of all nations, increase or decrease? What effect do these increases or decreases in international trade have upon the welfare of people within individual nations?
6. *Economic systems*. Why does the economic system of a particular nation change? Can such changes in the system be controlled to increase the economic efficiency of a nation and to serve other political purposes; that is, can such changes be controlled to increase individual freedom or to reduce the dangers of depression and unemployment?

* * *

In this book, we hope to present to you some knowledge of what economists have learned in each of these areas, and we hope that you will share in the sense of excitement and accomplishment that comes from understanding and analysing such vital problems in a systematic way.

SUMMARY

Economists strive to achieve a scientific attitude toward economic problems—that is, one that keeps their political, moral, or personal values separate from their economic analyses. Obviously, this is often quite difficult to do. Nevertheless, the claim that economics is a science rests on the belief that it is indeed possible objectively to explain economic events, apart from one's own values or goals. To achieve this scientific purpose, economists gather facts and try to develop models that explain the facts.

The special task of the economist is to solve problems, which can range from such questions as how a business can increase its profits to how a nation can increase its rate of growth. The problem-solving method involves a six-step process: (1) clearly defining the problem; (2) identifying the goals or values sought; (3) laying out alternative courses of action; (4) weighing each alternative; (5) choosing the alternative that seems best, and acting on it; and (6) checking to see how it worked out.

Economists use their problem-solving techniques in their roles within government agencies, in business, labor, or other organizations, and as researchers within educational institutions. Their general mission is to explain economic *change*, to predict it, and to influence it in order to serve human and institutional needs and aims.

KEY CONCEPTS

value judgments | problem-solving method | economic change

QUESTIONS FOR REVIEW AND DISCUSSION

1. Explain the terms *value judgments* and *social goals.*
2. What goals and values do you think are the most important for Canada's economy? Do you think that everybody else has the same goals and values that you have? Why or why not?
3. Explain how differences in values and goals may account for the fact that economists often disagree on what is the best solution for a particular problem.
4. How does the problem-solving method help economists prevent biases and personal values from entering into the scientific analyses? Do you think that economists are always successful in this effort? Explain.
5. In what ways to all professional economists tend to be alike? In what ways do they tend to differ?

PROBLEMS AND EXERCISES TO SHARPEN YOUR UNDERSTANDING

1. Following is a list of professional economists. Not all are Canadians. Using the resources in your school or community library, find out whether these economists work primarily for government, business, labor unions, or colleges and universities. Are there any economists who would fit in more than one category? If so, give the various categories for each.

1. Judith Maxwell
2. John Kenneth Galbraith
3. Barbara Ward
4. James E. Coyne
5. Milton Friedman
6. Melville Watkins
7. Dian Cohen
8. Sylvia Ostry
9. Paul Samuelson
10. Yevsei Liberman
11. Arthur Burns
12. T. N. Brewis
13. Gerald Bouey
14. Gunnar Myrdal
15. Jacques Parizeau

2. John Maynard Keynes, probably the most influential economist of this century, once made an observation about men being slaves "to some defunct economist." During your study of economics, you should be constantly reading about outstanding economists. Two excellent books to start with are *The Worldly Philosophers* by Robert Heilbroner, Englewood Cliffs, N.J., Prentice-Hall, 1975 and *The Economists* by Leonard Silk, New York: Avon Books, 1976.
3. Find the names of Nobel prize winners in economics since the prize was established in 1969. Prepare brief sketches of three of the winners. (Keep these names in mind. You may encounter them again.)

AN OVERVIEW OF ECONOMIC SYSTEMS

■ TYPES OF ECONOMIC SYSTEMS ■ A THREE-FOLD CLASSIFICATION OF ECONOMIC SYSTEMS ■ COMBINATIONS OF ECONOMIC SYSTEMS ■ SUMMARY

The term **economic system** refers to the way different economic elements (individual workers and managers, productive organizations such as factories or farms, and government agencies) are linked together to form an organic whole. The term economic system also refers to the way decisions are made as to what these different economic elements will do in determining the answers to those basic economic questions which every nation faces: what to produce, how to produce it, who will receive the fruits of production, and how much the economy will produce over a period of time.

■ TYPES OF ECONOMIC SYSTEMS

It is no easy matter to find the right names for the different types of economic systems that exist in the world today. One problem is that the concept of an economic system is so vast that it overlaps the concepts of political systems, social systems, even religious systems, and it is difficult (perhaps impossible) to separate political, social, religious, or moral elements when defining an economic system.

Another problem is that real-world economic systems are extremely complex and contain elements from different pure systems. In an economy like that of the Soviet Union, the government may make most of the important decisions, but some goods and services are sold in markets, without central government planning. In Canada, where most goods and services are produced by private individuals and businesses and freely sold in markets, the government still plays an important role in determining the production of certain goods (such as military equipment, highways, and schools), in influencing who gets what through the tax system and its expenditure and welfare programs, and in regulating parts of the private sector of the economy.

A third problem is that the real content of economic systems changes from one country to another and within a single country over a period of time. Capitalism in Canada is not precisely the same as that in the United States, France, or Japan. Soviet communism is not precisely the same as Chinese communism or Yugoslav communism. And Spanish fascism changed considerably between Franco's rise in the late 1930s and the end of the regime in the 70s.

Still, we do need general labels for the main classes of economic systems. One set that we might employ would go as follows. (See Figure 5-1.)

1. **Capitalism** refers to an economic system in which most productive resources are privately owned; in which the market is the principal institution for setting values upon goods or services and exchanging them; and in which the society is characterized by a democratic political system and individual freedom. (The institution of the market is discussed in Unit 2 of this text.)

2. **Fascism** refers to a system in which there is a combination of private ownership

FIG. 5-1. LABELING COMBINATIONS OF ECONOMIC AND POLITICAL FACTORS

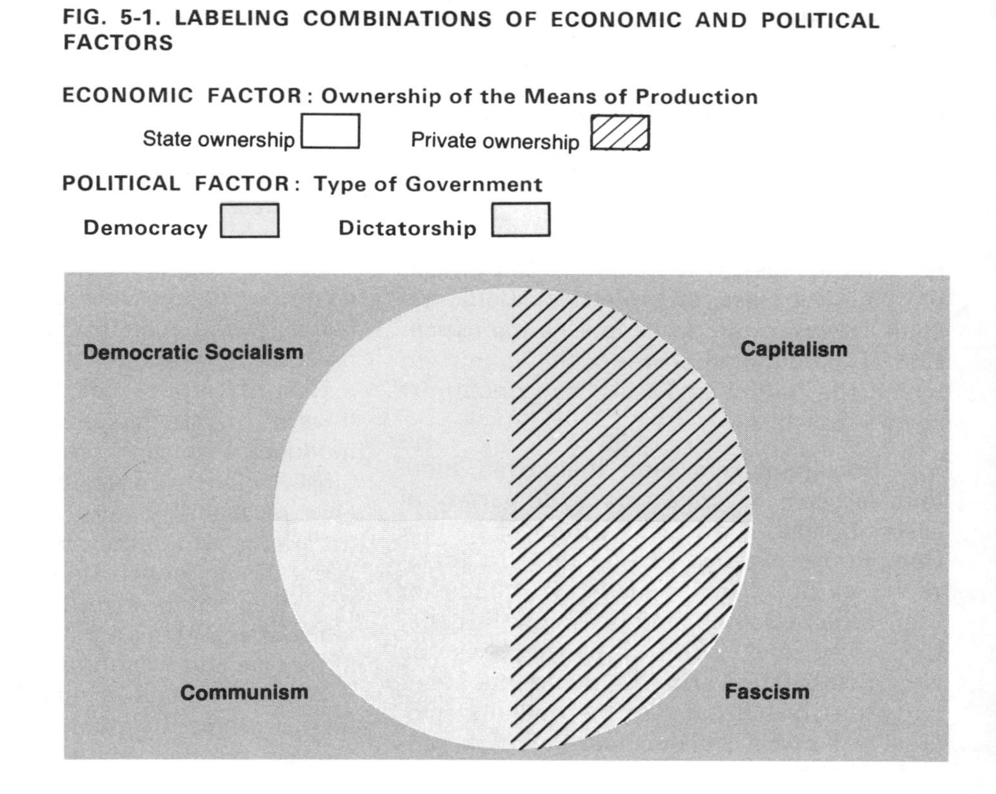

and a dictatorial political system, with major restrictions upon individual political, economic, social and religious freedom. The Nazi regime in Hilter's Germany differed in many respects from Fascist Italy under Mussolini; and both differed from Fascist Spain under Franco. In all Fascist systems, however, the government assumes a great deal of control over the nation's business organizations, labor unions, and other private economic groups—where these are not wiped out or converted into out-and-out state institutions.

Despite differences in terminology or ideology (the official expression of a political creed), Fascist systems have much in common with Communist systems. Both embody a great deal of central planning and control aimed at furthering state rather than individual private objectives. The chief economic differences between fascism and communism are these:

1. Communist economic planning tends to be more detailed and more highly developed than Fascist planning.
2. The right to the ownership of the means of production by private individuals and groups is likely to be partially preserved under fascism but much more restricted under communism.
3. The market plays a larger role under fascism than communism, though, in both, the state makes the big overall economic decisions.

Besides the economic differences, there are interesting political differences in the style, tone, and objectives of fascism and communism. Fascism tends to be a system that is highly *nationalistic;* that is, it seeks to glorify a particular nation or race (as Nazism did Germany and the so-called "Aryan" race), whereas communism—at least according to its official creed—emphasizes *internationalism,* the common interests and brotherhood of workers in all nations. Fascism tends to glorify the values and prejudices of the middle class, while communism praises the working class, or proletariat. Both systems, however, are prone to seek the expansion of the national power of the country in which the particular Fascist or Communist party is based.

3. **Socialism** is a term that, even more than fascism, covers a very wide variety of cases. Indeed, the Soviet Union and other Communist regimes like to refer to themselves as Socialist (the U.S.S.R. stands for the Union of Soviet *Socialist* Republics). On the other hand, political parties, like the New Democratic Party in Canada, the Labor party in Great Britain, or the Social Democrats in Norway, Sweden, and Denmark, proclaim that their ideology is Socialist. Democratic Socialists tend to put relatively less stress upon government ownership and control over the detailed operations of the economy; they do not wipe out private ownership of the means of production; and they are committed to the principles of political freedom and democracy.

Initially, to be sure, socialism was generally taken to mean the control of production and distribution by the society as a whole, rather than by private individuals and businesses, through the working of the market. But modern Socialist parties differ greatly in their interpretation and enactment of this initial principle of public control. Western Socialist parties have made minor modifications of existing capitalist systems and have largely been content to expand national welfare programs. In fact, there are few, if any, market systems in the world today in which the society does not play a fairly large role through welfare programs and through its tax and expenditure programs.

Curiously enough, the discovery that modern market or capitalist governments could, through their fiscal and monetary policies, keep their economies healthy and growing and, thereby, serve the interests of all their citizens, has tended to cause Socialists to put less stress in Western democratic nations upon public ownership of the means of production. They have put greater stress upon governmental policies designed to create a better overall economic and social environment for individuals.

Hostility on the part of Western Socialists toward private business has considerably moderated since World War II. However, most Socialists do retain a measure of suspicion or hostility toward big business corporations, which they believe should be regulated or controlled by government. Socialists also generally stress the importance of achieving a more equal distribution of income and wealth than currently exists.

Despite some blurring of the line between market-oriented capitalism and socialism in modern Western democratic countries, it is still possible to distinguish Socialists from capitalists by the Socialists' relatively greater emphasis upon public control, rather than private control, of the economy; by the Socialists' greater liking for national economic planning to serve the nation's welfare objectives, rather than relying so much upon the market to advance the welfare of individuals; and by the Socialists' stress upon government action to increase equality of income.

In modern capitalist or market systems, however, many individual citizens, and the political parties that seek their support, combine various capitalist (market) and Socialist (command) elements in their programs.

4. **Communism** or Marxism or Marxism-Leninism may be briefly described as radical or extreme socialism. It is characterized by a higher degree of state ownership of the means of production and general state control over most decision-making in the econ-

FIG. 5-2. A THREE-FOLD CLASSIFICATION OF ECONOMIC SYSTEMS

Traditional economies answer the basic economic questions by relying on the familiar customs of the past.

Command economies answer the basic economic questions through central planning.

Market economies answer the basic economic questions through a system of interrelated prices.

omy within a framework of economic plans directed by the state. Politically, communist states are one-party systems where opposition, either by groups or individuals, is either suppressed or regulated.

A THREE-FOLD CLASSIFICATION OF ECONOMIC SYSTEMS

In an effort to avoid confusion, we might follow the classification suggested by Robert Heilbroner, who offers a simple three-fold way of classifying the principal economic systems: economies run by *tradition*, economies run by *command*, and economies run by the *market*.[1] (See Figure 5-2.) None of these three types exists in pure and perfect form in any actual nation today. Nevertheless, it may be useful to see how each of these basic systems goes about the task of answering the basic economic questions of *what, how, for whom,* and *how much.*

Systems Run by Tradition

Nations with **traditional economic systems** permit the customs of the past to make the basic economic decisions for them. A traditional economy answers the question of what to produce very simply. It says: "Produce what has always been produced." Similarly, a traditional economy answers the question of how by saying: "As we have always done." The custom of assigning the jobs of parents to children, for example, assures that things will be done now and in the future much as they have always been done

[1] Robert L. Heilbroner, *The Making of Economic Society*, Englewood Cliffs, N. J.: Prentice-Hall, 1975. This is an excellent introduction to the whole field of economic history and is highly recommended for frequent use.

The Traditional Economy

Social scientists have long been fascinated with the structure of traditional societies. The following brief excerpt provides a concise view of the economic structure of traditional Inuit life. Does Diamond Jenness seem to suggest in any way that there were possible advantages to such an economic pattern?

To the pre-European Eskimos, trade meant only the simplest barter, and in Canada even that occurred but rarely. A man expected to support his wife and children by his own efforts from the sea and the land around him. Food he obtained by hunting and fishing; with his own hands he made all his tools and weapons. Snow, hard-packed by the wind, furnished the building blocks with which he erected his winter dwelling, and the skins of caribou and seals supplied the covering for his summer tent. The same skins or furs, carefully cut by his wife and stitched together with sinew-thread from the back of the caribou, provided clothing for himself and all his family. For food, clothing, and shelter, therefore, he depended on no man; he was completely self-supporting, as no European has been since some of our ancestors 15 000 years ago crouched for warmth and safety in the caves of central France during the closing centuries of the Great Ice Age. Once or twice in his lifetime, perhaps, our Eskimo exchanged his home-made knife for a soapstone cooking-pot, or a strip of white fur from the belly of a caribou for a long wooden pole that could serve as a fish-spear handle; but to a degree that we today can hardly comprehend, he was free and independent, master of his own fate, as far as any living creature can be master of its fate in this our imperfect and ever-changing world.

From Diamond Jenness, *Eskimo Administration: II, Canada,* Arctic Institute of North America, Technical Paper #14, 1964, p. 99. Reprinted by permission of Mrs. Jenness and the Arctic Institute of North America.

in the past. Custom and force of habit also answer the questions of for whom and how much. Economic and social progress from one generation to the next tends to be determined by social or economic class. And productive units (whether potters or cobblers or farmers) tend not to alter their output, in quantity or quality. The economies of many of the countries of the Middle East, Asia, Africa, and Latin America, especially in their large rural areas, are essentially run by tradition.

Systems Run by Command

Command economic systems are those in which a small group of leaders and planners answer the basic economic questions, relying on their authority to have their decisions carried out by all elements in the system. Centralized authority thus does the job of allocating and developing scarce resources. Sometimes the decision-makers seize or inherit their power; sometimes they gain power by election or by being designated by the political party that dominates the state. But no matter how the economic policy makers get their power, a command economy relies for its basic decisions upon a small number of people who can enforce their authority upon all elements in the system.

In answering the question of what to produce, the decision-makers in a command system might decide to use the scarce resources to make what they think the people themselves want; or what they think the people need, no matter what they want; or what

TYPES OF ECONOMIC SYSTEMS

Radio Times Hulton Picture Library

Sovfoto

A. H. MacDonald

There are three basic types of economic systems—those run by tradition, by command, and by the market. The first picture, taken from a 15th century manuscript, *Le Livre de Rusticon,* shows agricultural pursuits being carried out on a French manor—in which everyone's station and role in life was determined by custom and tradition. Notice that the lord of the manor comes strolling by with his aide while the serfs work.

The second picture shows a critical moment in the life of a command economy—that of the Soviet Union. The Premier, Alexei N. Kosygin, is addressing the Supreme Soviet Council of the U.S.S.R., laying out the economic plans and programs for all sectors of the nation, which the top policymakers have made.

The third picture shows a typical scene in a market economy—a street with a number of privately owned stores, ranging from a branch of Eaton's, a nation-wide chain, to the independent furniture store next door.

those who run the society want for themselves, regardless of what the people want or need. Thus, the people at the top will decide whether the system should produce more guns or more butter, more schools or more steel mills, more housing or more atomic bombs.

The decision-makers also decide how to produce things. They lay down rules for the managers of farms or factories. They decide who is allowed to work where, who can or cannot change a job, what machines will or will not be available to assist production, and so on.

The planners in the command economy also determine how much everyone shall be paid—and hence who will get what. They will not only determine what pay everyone receives but also what privileges everyone is entitled to: who shall have a villa in the country, who shall be permitted a trip abroad, who shall be given the right to move into a new apartment house, or who shall have an automobile.

And the decision-makers and planners will determine how much the economy will produce—how many resources will be devoted to satisfying the wants of the people now, and how many resources will be devoted to building up the mills and factories and dams and other capital goods so that more can be produced in future years.

Carrying out decisions in a command economy will reflect the political and social nature of the state. Decisions may reflect the popular will, in which case there will be no problem. Persuasion, propaganda and coersion, may be necessary if the nation is undemocratic in nature.

Systems Run by the Market

Market economic systems rely on a whole network of prices to shape the decisions as to what gets produced, how, for whom, and in what amounts. The functioning of the markets determines what proportion of resources will go to producing consumer or capital goods for future use; it therefore regulates the rate at which the total economy grows. And the functioning of markets also determines how much of all the resources of the society will currently be used—that is, how much employment or unemployment of men and machines there will be at any given time.

Given the crucial role of prices in a market system in answering the basic economic questions, it is essential that we come to see how prices are determined and what they do. All of Unit 2 of this book will be devoted to increasing your understanding of how prices are set in markets and how the market system works to allocate scarce resources.

A market system gives a more limited role to government (or the community as a whole) than traditional or command systems in determining the answers to the basic economic questions. Rather, the answers are determined as a consequence of large numbers of individuals and heads of business acting, not for the community or state, but for themselves. The market system harmonizes these individual actions as though by—in the immortal phrase of Adam Smith—an *invisible hand,* rather than by a central planning authority. The "invisible hand" ensures (if the system is working well) that when farmers want to buy tractors or shovels, tractors or shovels will be made available; that when students or teachers want to journey to Europe on summer vacation, airplanes and ships will be available to move them; that when airlines and ships want gasoline and oil, producers and distributors of gasoline and oil will have it ready for them. Thus, the whole market system will be closely organized and integrated, although no central authority will do the organizing or integrating.

Those who live in a market system often take it for granted, without understanding it or its institutions very well. There are basically four institutions in market economic systems:

THE SPECIALIZATION OF LABOR

Radio Times Hulton Picture Library

Division of labor—resulting in greatly increased efficiency in production—was the basic reason why the tradition-bound manorial system gave way to the market system. In the top picture we see the old-style type of unspecialized labor, with serfs breaking up the ground with mallet-like implements on a 14th century manor. In the lower picture we see the progress that had been made toward greater division of labor. This picture shows a tin worker's shop, with all kinds of tinware being cut, hammered to shape, soldered and finished—for sale from the front of the same room. Today, of course, the division of labor involved in producing pots, pans, paper, or other manufactured goods has increased by several orders of magnitude. And so has the efficiency of production.

Radio Times Hulton Picture Library

1. **Private property**—the legal right of individuals or businesses to own productive resources.

2. **Freedom of contract** (or freedom of enterprise)—the right of resource owners to use these resources as they see fit, and to exchange them with others as they see fit, largely unrestrained by custom, tradition, or central control.

3. **The profit motive**—the desire of individuals or businesses to use their resources in such a way as to earn a return for themselves, and their freedom to make this desire for profit the chief motivation of their economic actions.

4. **Competition**—the striving of one person or business against another, each for his or its own advantage. This competition ensures that if a person is not well served by a particular producer, he can turn to another; or if a business does not like the job done by a particular worker, it can dismiss him and hire another who wants his job.

These four basic institutions of private property, freedom of contract or enterprise, profit motive, and competition underlie the markets in which prices are set. These markets, in turn, determine the answers to the economic questions of what, how, for whom, and how much.

Compared to the economic systems of tradition and command, the basic institutions necessary for a market system are of fairly recent historical origin. Through most of history, men have not lived in societies in which the widespread exchange of resources, goods, and services in the marketplace was common.

COMBINATIONS OF ECONOMIC SYSTEMS

No contemporary society relies exclusively on tradition, command, or the market—although some societies rely more on one basic type of system than the others.

The Canadian economy, for instance, is predominantly a market economy. But we do rely to some extent on a system of command in allocating some of our scarce resources to achieve national goals. We use taxes and government spending to take resources away from the private economy and use them on a wide variety of government programs; we pass laws to require children to stay in school up to a certain age; we pass other laws to deny businessmen the right to build factories in certain residential areas, and so on. There are also elements of prejudice that persist in our society. For example, if you are a Black, it may be difficult for you to buy or rent a home in neighborhoods where white people may discriminate against you. If your family has a famous name and your father went to certain private schools or colleges, it may be easier for you to go to those schools or colleges. Can you think of any other examples where tradition or custom plays a role in our society or economy?

Likewise, contemporary societies that answer most of their economic questions through the central planning and control of a command system, such as that of the Soviet Union, also have elements of tradition and the market in their systems. And some primitive or backward economies relying heavily on tradition often have some elements of the marketplace or of command at the top within their systems.

In the next two units of this book, we shall examine in more detail the way the major elements fit together in a modern market system and how the total output of such a system expands or contracts. In looking at how prices are set in particular markets, we shall in Unit 2 emphasize **microeconomics**, the economics of the parts of a market economy. In Unit 3, we will examine a number of the key institutions within our market system. In Unit 4, we will emphasize **macroeconomics**, a study of measurement of and changes in total economic output. Unit 5 will examine international aspects of economic activity from both Canadian and world perspectives.

SUMMARY

The term *economic system* describes the way different elements are organized and integrated and the way decisions are made as to what those elements will do in solving the basic economic questions that every nation faces: what to produce, how to produce it, for whom, and how much.

Although every nation must deal with the basic problem of managing scarce resources in answering those questions, different nations go about the job in very different ways. The three basic types of systems are those run by *tradition*, by *command*, and by the *market*. In actual cases, however, there are always combinations of these three elements, although some nations are predominantly characterized by one element or another. The Soviet Union, for instance, is primarily a *command* system; its system is also called *communism*, of course. Canada is primarily a *market* system; its system is also called *capitalism*. The four dominant institutions of a market system or capitalism are private property, freedom of contract and enterprise, the profit motive, and competition.

KEY CONCEPTS

economic system	traditional economic systems	the profit motive
capitalism	command economic systems	competition
fascism	market economic systems	microeconomics
socialism	private property	macroeconomics
communism	freedom of contract	

QUESTIONS FOR REVIEW AND DISCUSSION

1. What is the basic problem that all national economies have to face? What basic economic questions must they answer? Why do different nations have different types of economic systems?
2. What are the basic differences between capitalism, fascism, socialism, and communism? Are these differences confined to economics alone?
3. If your main objective is stability, which type of economic system would you prefer: a traditional system, a command system, or a market system? What if your main objective is individual freedom? What if it is rapid economic growth? What if your objective includes all three of these goals? Explain each of your answers.

PROBLEMS AND EXERCISES TO SHARPEN YOUR UNDERSTANDING

1. Below is a list of statements describing various economic actions. Label or classify each statement according to whether you think it is typical of a traditional economy (T), a command economy (C), or a market economy (M).
   a. "On the farms, the working day lasts from before sunrise until dusk or dark. As they have done for centuries, women follow the reapers and binders on foot to gather the gleanings from the fields. . . ."

b. "The problem of finding skilled workers was immense. There were simply not enough trained men available. His competitors were fighting for their share of the labor supply. [He] decided to introduce a five-dollar-a-day minimum wage. The new minimum more than doubled the existing wage. . . ."

c. "The practice of giving certain industries [first call on scarce materials] has brought more rapid overall economic growth than otherwise might have been possible."

d. "The proclamation of the [head of state] declared that no banking operations should be carried on throughout the country until further notice."

e. "The [people being studied] were still living on seal meat and were making no attempt to kill any of the numerous caribou that were continually migrating past. I thought at first that there might be some taboo preventing them from hunting caribou on ice, but this they told me was not so. It was simply that they had never hunted caribou on the ice and had not considered it possible. . . ."

f. "Holding prices in check was difficult. A great burden fell on the Office of Price Administration, created to keep the lid on prices by setting price ceilings on a large list of commodities which were much in demand."

2. Might it be possible for all of these statements to be describing actions in the same national economy? Why or why not?

3. Assume that a delegation from an economically less-developed country is visiting your class and asks you to answer the following three questions:

   a. What are the most essential features of the way your economy answers the "what, how, and for whom" questions at the core of all economies?

   b. What are the most essential features of the way today's Soviet economy answers these same questions?

   c. What conclusions might a less-developed economy draw from a comparison of these features with respect to a list of goals that a country might reasonably be expected to have? (Specify the goals and make comparisons with each goal as well as an overall comparison.)

4. After you have written your answer to each of the preceding questions, compare your answers with those of other members of your class and try to reach an agreement on the best answers to give to the visiting delegation.

UNIT 1 REVIEW

1. Can scarcity ever be eliminated from the world? Why?

2. In what respects is economics a science and in what respects is it not? Is it necessarily a weakness of any field of study not to be a science? Explain your answer.

3. If everyone had a good understanding of economics, would this eliminate economic controversies? Why?

4. If it can be shown that modern market economies can consistently outproduce command economies, would this cause communists to convert to a belief in capitalism? Or, if the reverse were true, would it cause capitalists to convert to communism? Why?

5. What are the main differences among the economic systems? What are their main similarities?

THE MARKET

The key institution of national economies such as that of Canada is *the market.* Through their interactions in a vast number of markets, the private individuals and businesses of the nation determine most of the answers to the basic questions that every economy faces: What goods to produce, how to produce them, who will receive what share of the national product, and how much total output will increase over time. However, in all modern democratic societies, government is assigned an important economic role to supplement the workings of the market.

MARKET PRICES

■ THE INSTITUTION OF THE MARKET ■ THE PRICE SYSTEM ■ RELATIVE PRICES ■ AN EQUILIBRIUM MODEL ■ PARTIAL-EQUILIBRIUM MODELS ■ SUMMARY

As we noted in the last chapter, modern nations differ in the structure and functioning of their economic systems. Some are highly decentralized, with great freedom for elements in the system—individual persons and separate business organizations—to determine their own behavior in response to what other elements in the system do. Other national economic systems are highly centralized, with a great degree of government control over the behavior of the individual elements in the system.

■ THE INSTITUTION OF THE MARKET

Resting on the pillars of private property, freedom of enterprise, the profit motive, and competition, the primary economic institution of the essentially free, decentralized economic systems is *the market.* A **market** is a place where buyer and seller transact business. But it is not necessarily, or even usually, a single physical location. Indeed, the distinguished British economist Alfred Marshall stated that, "A market is an area within which buyers and sellers are in such close communication with each other that price tends to be the same throughout the area." One could in fact, take this approach to the meaning of the term even further and simply say that the market is a method or system permitting buyers and sellers to deal with each other, either directly or through intermediaries. In a market economy every good or service can be regarded as having a market, in which certain quantities of the good are bought and sold. In a market economy private persons and businesses, freely exchanging goods and services chiefly through the medium of money, largely determine by their actions *what goods are produced by the nation, how those goods are produced, who gets them, and how much will be produced in total*—both now and in the future. However, the governments of all market economies in the real world regulate, modify, and supplement the workings of markets in order to achieve particular social objectives, such as the military defense of the nation, the preservation of natural resources, the provision of common facilities such as highways and schools. But the marketplace remains the primary economic institution of a free, decentralized economy.

One of the major discoveries made by early economists, including Adam Smith, the noted eighteenth-century British economist, was the way that markets work in a free enterprise economy to allocate resources efficiently and spur national production and the growth of income. Adam Smith was so impressed by the way free markets worked to solve human problems that he said it was as though the economy were guided by an "invisible hand."

What was true in Adam Smith's day is still essentially true in market economies, despite great growth in the size of government and business organizations. Nor is it any less miraculous today than in Smith's day that,

The Invisible Hand

In the following passage from The Wealth of Nations, *Adam Smith created the most famous metaphor in all of economic literature—the invisible hand—which, Smith held, guided individuals, in pursuit of their self-interest, to promote the good of the whole society.*

. . . The annual revenue of every society is always precisely equal to the exchangeable value of the whole annual produce of its industry, or rather is precisely the same thing with that exchangeable value. As every individual, therefore, endeavours as much as he can both to employ his capital in the support of domestic industry, and so to direct that industry that its produce may be of the greatest value; every individual necessarily labours to render the annual revenue of the society as great as he can. He generally, indeed, neither intends to promote the public interest, nor knows how much he is promoting it. By preferring the support of domestic to that of foreign industry, he intends only his own security; and by directing that industry in such a manner as its produce may be of the greatest value, he intends only his own gain, and he is in this, as in many other cases, led by an invisible hand to promote an end which was no part of his intention. Nor is it always the worse for the society that it was no part of it. By pursuing his own interest he frequently promotes that of society more effectually than when he really intends to promote it. I have never known much good done by those who affected to trade for the public good. It is an affectation, indeed, not very common among merchants, and very few words need be employed in dissuading them from it.

From Adam Smith, *An Inquiry into the Nature and Causes of the Wealth of Nations,* New York: Random House, Inc., 1937, p. 423.

with very little central economic planning or control over the decisions of individual producers or consumers, millions and millions of different goods and services are produced and delivered in the quantities desired, in the qualities and types wanted, at the right places, and at the right time. This is, if anything, more remarkable today than in Smith's day because of the complexity of the modern industrial process with the long lead-times involved in planning production, the highly specialized nature of industrial production, and the masses of people involved in producing even the seemingly most simple objects.

To get a sense of the remarkable complexity of determining in a modern industrial economy what to produce, how to make it, for whom, and how much in total, consider some object of our society, such as this book. Think what was involved in producing it: the building and running of the printing press; the manufacture of the steel that went into the press; the assembly of the iron ore, coke, steel scrap out of old automobiles and so on; the metal alloys that were needed to make the steel; the building of the machine tools needed to make the steel equipment, the printing press, the structures in which all this activity was housed; the mills in which the paper for the book was made; the chemicals that went into the paper-making process; the inks; the textiles for the book's hard cover; the thread for its binding; and so on. Consider the diversity of human labor involved in making and marketing this book: the steel workers, printers, farmers, engineers, chemists, railroad engineers, fork truck operators, book salesmen, publishing executives, truck drivers, secretaries, and even authors—authors who needed typewriters, typewriter ribbons, paper, other books, calculators, pencils, pens, desks, and offices. Think of the transportation system by which this manuscript was carried between the authors in different cities to their editor and finally to the publisher and printer. Think of the post office system and telephone system over which all these people communicated. This is of course only the most superficial sketch of what was involved. Quite exact calculations had to be made of just how many copies of the book, and how much paper, steel, chemicals, and other products had to be produced; how much they should cost; how they should be made; when they should be delivered; and so on. All of this had to be done without any single person or institution controlling the vast, integrated productive process. In fact, there was not even direct personal acquaintance or communication among the vast majority of the people who were involved in working together so that this book could finally be published and put into your hands.

How in fact was this fantastic project organized and carried through so efficiently?

THE PRICE SYSTEM

The answer is that the job of coordination and integration was done through a *system*—a system of market-determined prices. Information produced by the system triggered appropriate responses from the vast array of independent elements in the system; each element—each business firm and individual—decided for itself what it would do. The same system is responsible for producing not just this book but the billions and billions of dollars worth of other items produced by our nation every year.

In a complex economy like ours, we live in a universe of prices. Almost everything imaginable bears a price—not only goods like this book, but the stocks and bonds of corporations, the right to use somebody else's money, the right to use somebody else's land or house or apartment, the right to receive the services of some other human being. It is the price that any of these things commands that will determine whether its owner will or will not be willing to do a particular job or hand over the desired good or let another person use his money, his land, his house, his apartment, or anything else he owns. Prices, in effect, glue the system together and establish a relationship between one thing and all other things.

Every price is a **ratio** between the value of one unit of a particular thing and the value of all other things—or, at any rate, of all other things that bear a price. (There are, after all, some things that do not bear a price—a mother's love or a sunny afternoon.) Thus, prices really state that the ratio between a carton of milk and a bus ride is 2:1, if the carton of milk costs $.60 and the bus ride $.30. Similarly, prices establish a 10:1 ratio between automobiles and color television sets, if the automobile costs $5000 and the color television set $500. Of course, prices in the real world fix such ratios with far greater exactitude than we have done here, and for every single item, and in relation to all other items.

While few things look more ordinary than a mass of price data, the concept of price is, like the wheel or the alphabet, one of the most important creations of the human imagination that has made possible man's social development.

Prices are so much a part of our environment that it may come as a shock to realize that literally nothing in nature bears a price. Every price is a human fiction, a creation that results from the interaction of human beings.

RELATIVE PRICES

It is important to bear in mind that a price is a ratio, because the absolute numerical value of the price of any good (or of all goods together) is meaningless. It is **relative prices**, not **absolute prices**, that matter.

What people really care about is whether one hour of their labor will enable them to purchase, say, a dozen eggs or two dozen tomatoes or some quantity of other goods. Or will a month of the labor permit them to purchase a new car or only a set of tires? It is the

Lynn Millar from Rapho Guillumette

Sovfoto

Even traditional and command economies make some use of markets. In the top picture we see a market in Arusha, a town in Tanzania in East Africa; and in the lower picture we see Russian shoppers buying candy in the Gastronom—the grocery and provision store of the State Department Store.

price of labor in relation to the price of different goods that determines how much one's earnings are really worth in any country.

Although most people instinctively understand the concept of relative prices, they are often misled by changes in absolute prices. Thus, a factory worker may think that he is better off making $250 a week than he was 10 years ago when he made only $150, but, if the prices of everything he buys have risen 75 percent, he is worse off. This misconception on his part is called **money illusion**. As a British economist, the late Sir Dennis Robertson, put it, "People tend to confuse the pieces of money, which are mere certificates of a right to draw goods which may not even exist, with the goods themselves, and to lay up all sorts of trouble and disillusion for themselves."

Although individual people or business organizations feel free to set prices on their goods or services as they choose and to pay or not pay the prices that other people or businesses charge, the fact is that *all prices are affected in some degree by all other prices*.

If, for example, the price of food goes up, this may cause workers to ask for more money from their employers, who may in turn raise their prices, which may cause landlords to put up rents, which may cause workers to ask for still more money, and so on. (This chain of events is by no means inevitable, but is only set forth to show the interrelationship among different prices in a system.) Even if the rise in the price of food does not cause the workers to demand more money, their real wages will still be affected—in a negative direction.

A witty American economist, H. J. Davenport, sought to describe some of these complex price interrelationships in a poem:

> The price of pig
> Is something big;
> Because its corn, you'll understand
> Is high-priced, too;
> Because it grew
> Upon the high-priced farming land.
>
> If you'd know why
> That land is high
> Consider this: its price is big
> Because it pays
> Thereon to raise
> The costly corn, the high-priced pig.

Davenport's poem thus declares that all prices in a market system are interdependent. The price of a pig is what it is partly because the prices of corn and other things are what they are. In turn, the prices of corn and other things are what they are partly because the price of a pig is what it is. Both corn and pig are priced as they are partly because the cost of farmland is what it is. And land prices are what they are partly because of the prices of pig, corn, and everything else.

These statements of **interdependence** can readily be translated into a system of mathematical equations representing all the prices resulting from the interactions of buyers and sellers in all markets in a national economy. The creation of such a mathematical model was actually done for the first time in 1874 by a French economist, Marie-Esprit Leon Walras. Walras's model for explaining the structure and functioning of a private enterprise economic system assumed that all prices were freely set in competitive markets, and that resources would readily shift to lines of production where earnings were higher.

We shall try to show, in extremely condensed form, how Walras's model works, concentrating our attention on two sectors of the economy, agriculture and the steel industry.

AN EQUILIBRIUM MODEL

Let us examine such a market system, seen as a network of relations among many buyers and sellers of many different types of goods and services. We will assume that our system is initially in a state of balance (or, to use the economist's favorite term for this condition, is in **equilibrium**—at rest). In this state of equilibrium, the prices of wheat, steel, and other goods are stable; and the wages of farm labor, steel workers, and other workers are stable; as are the earnings of farm owners, steel companies, and other firms.

Now let us assume that this state of equilibrium is disturbed in some way—for instance, by the development of a cheap and practical automobile; the resultant growth of the automobile industry and related industries, such as rubber, glass, and highway construction, greatly increases the demand for *steel*.

The increase in the demand for steel causes the price of steel to rise. Resources currently engaged in producing steel bring higher incomes. These higher earnings in steel then attract additional resources, such as labor and both real and money capital, away from other industries, say farming. As steel producers increase their output to meet rising demand for steel and put additional resources into production, the cost of making steel eventually begins to rise. As costs and prices go up, the amount of steel that people have the ability to buy is at last restrained. And, as costs of making steel rise and the sales of steel level off, the extra profits initially resulting from the increase in the demand for steel are squeezed. The movement of resources to the steel industry slows down.

At the same time, let us consider what has been happening over in the farm sector of our model economy. The rise in earnings in the steel mills first attracted factors of production away from wheat. Farm labor took off for the steel and other industrial towns. The workers making more money in industrial jobs increased their demand for wheat, and the price of wheat rose. As a result of the migration from the farms to higher paying industrial jobs, there are now fewer farmers left on the land. The income of the average remaining farmer is rising, both because the number of farmers has been reduced and because the price of wheat is higher.

Farmers can now afford to invest in more agricultural machinery. This further increases the demand for steel. Farmers can also afford automobiles and other consumer goods for themselves.

Bankers and others with funds to lend, noting these favorable developments in agriculture, put these funds into more farmland and farm equipment. At the same time, they slow down their rate of lending in the steel industry, whose profits are now squeezed by rising costs, but who are no longer in a position to raise their prices.

So the influx of resources into the steel industry slackens and finally ceases when the incomes of suppliers of steel are no greater than those to be obtained by equally efficient resources employed in agriculture or other industries. Prices throughout the economy are again stable. The economic system is at rest—in equilibrium. We are back in the steady state in which we were before the invention of the cheap automobile and the growth of related industries boosted the demand for steel.

Remember that the above discussion is not intended to be a description of Canadian economic history, but simply a tracing out of the course of events resulting from the way we set up our theoretical *model* of an economic system. However, the course of events described above does have *some* correspondence to reality.

That our model does not correspond closely enough to the real world is shown by the persistence of low incomes on a great many Canadian farms. Even if prosperity in other economic sectors, such as the steel industry, has drawn and still does draw low-income labor off the farm, it may not do this fast enough to eliminate poverty in many farm districts because of other changes that have occurred in the economy—including some changes in agriculture itself.

The main purpose of our discussion is, however, to illustrate the concept of a **general-equilibrium** model of the entire economy. It was first at rest, then disturbed by a new technological force, then went through a series of responses and adjustments that stemmed from the basic structure of the model, until finally the adjustment process was completed and the model had returned to a state of rest—waiting to be disturbed by some other new force.

PARTIAL-EQUILIBRIUM MODELS

Economists may develop equilibrium models not only for the economy as a whole but for particular parts of the economy, such as the market for a single product. They will then focus on that one part of the economy, assuming that everything else remains the same.

When they focus on just one sector of the economy, economists build what is called a **partial-equilibrium** model, since they simply assume that no outside force will disturb relations within the model of a single sector. But they know the rest of the economy may not be in equilibrium.

We shall study in greater detail how such partial-equilibrium models of a single sector are constructed and how they can be used for economic analysis of real-world situations in the other chapters of this unit. An understanding of these single-market models is essential to a comprehension of the workings of our economy as a whole—or of any other economy, however different its form of government or social institutions may be.

■ SUMMARY

In this chapter we have seen that prices play a critical role in holding a market system together and in setting off responses among buyers and sellers of goods and services within the economic system. The real significance of any price is its relation to other prices; this is the concept of *relative price*.

We have seen the way a highly simplified model of a market price system works, moving from a state of equilibrium to a state of imbalance as a result of some disturbance, and then making the necessary adjustments to return to a state of equilibrium. A model that traces this process for the entire national economy is called a general-equilibrium model. One that does it for some particular sector of the economy, such as a single market, is called a partial-equilibrium model, since it assumes that other conditions remain the same in the rest of the economy, while equilibrium is reached in the one market being studied.

KEY CONCEPTS

market	absolute prices	equilibrium
ratio	money illusion	general equilibrium
relative prices	interdependence	partial equilibrium

QUESTIONS FOR REVIEW AND DISCUSSION

1. Why might basically command or even basically traditional economies rely to some extent on the market in allocating their scarce resources?
2. Why has the market system often been described as being guided by an "invisible hand"?
3. What are the motivating or driving forces that give the market system its impetus? What are the restraining or regulating forces that keep it in check?
4. If you were told that the price of orange juice was $.80, would this information be very useful unless you also knew the price of other goods (such as tomato juice, grape juice, milk, eggs, or coffee)? Why is it that *relative* prices, rather than *absolute* prices, are important in economics?
5. What do these terms mean: *equilibrium, general equilibrium,* and *partial equilibrium*?

PROBLEMS AND EXERCISES TO SHARPEN YOUR UNDERSTANDING

Prices in a market system are all interdependent. Relative prices, and changes in relative prices and outputs may have far-reaching effects on both producers and consumers of goods. Test your understanding of these fundamental points by working out possible explanations for the following cause-effect relationships. (These may be real or fictitious events and you may well have more than one hypothesis to offer as a prospective explanation.)

1. A war in the Middle East boosts the cost of electricity in Atlantic Canada.
2. Higher interest rates cut purchases of new cars.
3. Crop failures and cold weather in the tropics combine to boost the cost of breakfast in Canadian restaurants.
4. A prolonged rail strike in the USA causes unemployment in the steel producing centers of Ontario.
5. Joint price increases by major coffee-producing nations cause an increase in the price of tea.
6. Major increases in Japanese steel production boost employment of railway and dock workers in B.C.
7. Sharp increases in the price of paper in Western Europe contribute to an increase in the projected cost of this book.

CHAPTER 7

HOW BUYERS BEHAVE

■ WHAT IS DEMAND? ■ THE PRICE EFFECT ■ BUILDING A MODEL OF CONSUMER DEMAND ■ OTHER DEMAND MODELS ■ SUMMARY

In this chapter we shall take a closer look at one side of the market, the buyer's side. We shall try to get at the underlying factors that explain consumers' behavior. These explanations cannot be expected to fit precisely the case of every human individual: each consumer has his own tastes, habits, and idiosyncrasies. What we shall attempt to do instead is to explain what motivates consumers *as a class*—the class that constitutes the demand for any good or service.

■ WHAT IS DEMAND?

To the economist, the term **demand** has a very specific meaning. In order for demand for some product to exist, two conditions must be satisfied: (1) There must be a desire on the part of some people for the product, and (2) These people must possess the ability to pay for the product. There is an old jingle that goes, "If wishes were horses, all beggars could ride." We may paraphrase this to mean, "If wishes constituted a demand for horses, all beggars could ride." Wishes are not demand. Nor is *money* demand—unless people want to spend their money for some good.

Assuming, however, that consumers have both the desire for some good and some money, their actual ability to buy the product depends on two factors: (1) just how much money they have (or what other goods and services they own and are willing to offer in exchange), and (2) how much the product costs.

If consumers cannot afford a particular product today but their incomes rise tomorrow, they may then be able to translate their desire into effective demand for the product, if its price remains the same. Or, if their incomes remain the same but the price of the good falls, the consumers may then translate their desire into effective demand. (However, it should be noted that demanding a good and getting it are not necessarily the same thing. At a particular price that the consumer is willing to pay, there might or might not be enough of that product to go around among all the would-be customers.)

■ THE PRICE EFFECT

If, then, we assume that the money income of consumers remains constant, the principal factor that will cause consumers to buy more or less of a product will be a change in its price. With few exceptions, a reduction in price makes people both more willing and more able to buy a product. Conversely, an increase in its price makes people both less willing and less able to buy it. There is thus, generally, an *inverse* relationship between price and the amount consumers are willing to buy. There are several reasons for this typical consumer behavior.

Diminishing Marginal Utility

Why is a consumer more willing to increase purchases of a product at a lower price? One important part of the explanation is a phenomenon known to economists as **diminish-**

A. H. MacDonald

How might the principle of diminishing marginal utility affect the prices set by the owners of "The Car Park"? Use an illustration containing specific prices for one hour, two hours, additional hours, and for a day in your answer.

ing marginal utility—the shrinking desirability of an extra unit of a particular good to each consumer as he acquires more units of that good.

If you do not own a particular product, you may want one very much (a television set, a car, a pair of ice-skates). But once you have one of these, your desire for a second one is considerably diminished. And the more you have of any product, generally speaking, the less you want each succeeding unit of it.

Hence, in order to induce the individual consumer to buy more of a product already owned, its price will have to be lowered to correspond to the reduced desire for the product. For example, if a hamburger costs $.50, you probably would buy only one for lunch. If, however, that hamburger costs only $.30, you might buy two. To induce you to eat three hamburgers for lunch, how low would the price have to be? Four? Five? (We might have to pay *you*.)

Another example: if phonograph records cost $9 apiece, you might buy ten in a year. If they cost $2 apiece, you might buy thirty or fifty. You would not necessarily spend the same total amount on phonograph records, regardless of their price. The number you actually buy will depend on the strength of your desire for more records—proportional to the price of records. Thus, the principle of diminishing marginal utility tells us something about the *desire* or *want* component of demand, the other component of which is ability to pay.

The Substitution Effect

Another important reason why people will buy more of a product at a lower price is that they may be able to save money by substituting that lower-priced product for higher-priced goods. Economists call this the **substitution effect** of price changes.

Many products are close substitutes for one another. For example, one may substitute fish for meat, lamb for veal, margarine for butter, bus rides for train rides, airplane rides for bus rides, and so on. If the price of owning and operating a car declines *relative to other prices,* motorists will substitute the use of their cars for public transportation. Conversely, if the prices of gasoline; oil; bridge, tunnel, and highway tolls; parking lot rates; and the *time* it takes to get through traffic (time should be considered valuable by all people) all increase, motorists will substitute public transportation, to some extent, for the use of their own cars.

Virtually all goods have substitutes which may sometimes be goods that do not appear to resemble them but are in fact functionally similar. People can and do substitute central heating for clothing, backyard swimming pools for vacation trips, dishwashing machines and vacuum cleaners for domestic servants.

A few goods, however, may not have very

Loblaws Limited

Here we can see the substitution effect at work in a very specific way. The consumer is looking at two products which are quite similar and in fact are bottled by the same company. Consideration of the price per unit of each item along with the unit prices of possible substitutes from other companies may have a major effect on what—if anything—the man will buy.

acceptable substitutes or may constitute so small a part of consumers' living expenses that they will go on consuming about the same amount of them, whether the price of these items goes up or down. A good example of this is pepper. A great drop in the price of pepper (even to zero) would hardly make you consume more pepper than you presently do. The fact that pepper is set out on restaurant tables without extra charge and that you still use only a bit of it, or none of it, depending on your taste, demonstrates this. On the other hand, it would take a very big increase in the price of pepper (or salt) to cause you to cut it out of your diet.

It must be emphasized that, as we discussed in Chapter 6, for the substitution effect to take place, the reduction in the price of a particular good must be *relative* to the prices of other goods. Economists customarily assume that other prices remain the same when studying the effects of price change on the amount of a particular product people are willing to buy. Again, the important concept is not absolute price, but *relative price.*

The Income Effect

When the price of one good declines while the prices of other goods remain the same, the amount of that good that people are willing to buy may increase for another reason, which economists call the **income effect.** This is the effect of the price cut upon the real income of the consumer; a price cut causes the real income of the consumer to rise, and a price increase causes real income to decline. By *real income* we mean the ability of the consumer to buy actual goods and services—as contrasted with *money income.* Changes in money income may or may not

THE INCOME EFFECT

Exxon

These two photos illustrate "the income effect." In the first picture, taken in relatively "low-income" India, we see an indication of the extent to which urban transport depends on bicycles. In the lower photo, taken in relatively "high-income" Singapore, we see the impact of higher incomes on traffic conditions.

Singapore Ministry of Culture Photo

Public Archives of Nova Scotia

Style Magazine

Changes in social attitudes, customs, technology, trends in design, advertising, and a host of other forces influence the nature of demand for clothing over the long term.

increase the ability of the consumer to buy actual goods and services. If one's salary (the money income) is increased from $10 000 a year to $15 000 a year and the prices of everything bought simultaneously increase by 50 percent, the real income is no greater than it was in the first place. If money income remains the same and prices decline, real income increases. Similarly, if the price of *one* product a consumer buys declines, the real income is increased by the amount of the price reduction. One then has, in effect, more money to spend on that good or on other goods.

Whether the income effect resulting from the price cut of a single good will result in the consumer's buying more of that good or of some other goods will depend on the entire structure of tastes and desires relative to income. For instance, if food prices decline so that a family's real income rises, one shopper might go on buying the same shopping bag full of food as before, but use the extra money that is now left over to buy other goods, such as new glassware or clothing. But another shopper, from a poorer family, might prefer, as a result of the decline in food prices, to use the extra real income to increase the amount of food bought for the family.

Habits and Social Attitudes

We are all creatures of habit, and this has an important effect on our behavior as consumers. When we are used to paying a certain price for a product, we are pleasantly surprised when its price is lower than we are accustomed to paying, and we are annoyed when its price is higher than we remember. Pleasant price surprises—bargains—move us to buy; unpleasant surprises in the form of price hikes deter us from buying.

Other types of habits may dull our sensitivity to price changes. If we are in the habit of going bowling on Saturday nights, a rise in the price of an alley may not cause us to change our habits. Or, if we are in the habit of budgeting a certain amount of money for particular purposes, such as our contribution to a charity or a church, we may be highly insensitive to the effect of price increases affecting that institution. In effect these price increases reduce our real contribution to the charity or church.

Much of our buying is conditioned by the habits and customs of the people among whom we live. Many people buy particular products in order to "keep up with the Joneses." If their neighbors are buying expensive cars or outdoor swimming pools or fur coats, they hasten to follow suit. Indeed, some will rush to get *ahead* of the Joneses—"Be the first on your block to own a new. . . ."

Striving for social status may sometimes produce contradictory price effects. Thus, a restaurant that raises its prices may sometimes attract more customers—people who want to be seen in the most exclusive place rather than to dine in a place known to be cheap. Similarly, a perfume may attract more buyers at a higher than a lower price because those who want to give it away as a present want to make a big impression on the recipient of the gift. The fancy restaurant and the expensive perfume are both instances of what an American economist, Thorstein Veblen, called *conspicuous consumption* goods—goods intended to permit the consumer to show off. These constitute, however, exceptions to the generally inverse relationship between price and quantity demanded (and these exceptions are likely to be much more true for a few individuals than for all consumers).

BUILDING A MODEL OF CONSUMER DEMAND

We have now reached the point where we can try to build a simple but practical model of demand, one that can be used by businesspeople, government officials, or high school students. In Chapter 2 we have already defined a model as a symbolic representation of reality. We have said that a model in economics (or in other sciences) may provide a set of assumptions from which a conclusion or set of conclusions can logically be deducted.[1] Those conclusions will have relevance to the real world and permit us to *explain, predict, and control* the real world to some extent—*provided* that the assumptions in the model bear a reasonable correspondence to reality. The assumptions need not correspond exactly to reality; indeed, since every model is an abstraction from reality, by definition, no model will faithfully represent all aspects of any real situation. The important question is whether the *model* reasonably represents the key factors in any problem.

There are six steps in developing a useful model. These are steps that one can use over and over in life to deal with any kind of complex problem—whether in business, science, or any field. The six steps are these:

1. Observe a situation in the real world and define the problem.
2. Formulate a preliminary model—a set of assumptions and the probable conclusions that would appear to follow from them.
3. Collect and lay out actual data that will provide the evidence to support (or refute) your model.
4. Determine how the data are interrelated.
5. Test the model against real-world experience. That is, see whether the model can be used to explain, predict, or control real events.
6. Accept or reject the model. If accepted, it will probably be useful again and again for dealing with similar problems.

All of this sounds rather formidable, but let us show how essentially simple it really is, as applied to the building of a simple but extremely important model of *consumer demand*.

[1] For an excellent account of the concepts of model-building in economics and other sciences, see K. J. Cohen and R. M. Cyert, *Theory of the Firm*, Englewood Cliffs, N.J.: Prentice-Hall, 1965, pp. 17-28.

The Sovereign Consumer

Thomas Balogh, an Oxford don and economic adviser to former British Prime Minister Harold Wilson, here ironically describes the typical consumer—as portrayed in conventional economic literature.

All the best economic textbooks and speeches by the heads of international banks and agencies begin with an appealing reference to that shadowy if convenient concept of the average, yet sovereign, consumer. There he stands, steadfast among millions of temptations, surrounded by a host of goods and services from among which to choose. He is alert, and quite determined. He does not look round to see what the Joneses do; his tastes are all his own. The only pointer he looks for is prices. He reacts instantly and intensely even to their smallest alteration, and he is an expert buyer with a quivering knowledge of the last advantage to be squeezed from every deal. It is his buying which rules the economic system. Through the elastic sway of his favours, new firms spring into being and old ones are instantly eliminated. In this way, what he wants is produced when he wants it and as he wants it. A perfect balance reigns.

From Thomas Balogh, *The Economics of Poverty,* New York: Macmillan Company, 1967, p. 47.

1. Defining the Problem

The six senior class members of Pleasantville High's Athletic Honor Society have been approached by two fellow students who suggest that members might be interested in having society rings. These two students make jewelry as a hobby and indicate that rings with an insignia like the school's could be made for a price somewhere in the range of $15 each. From the discussion that follows, it quickly becomes clear that *the problem* is to determine *how many* rings the members would buy under different price assumptions. The members' situations differ in terms of how much each can *afford* to spend and how much each would *want* to spend on a ring. Here is the picture of each student.

George Adams, 17. Father's occupation: manager of a Pleasantville bank. Personal characteristics: Outgoing, popular (has a girl friend named Sue at Pleasantville High, and another named Betsy in Harborside, where his family spends its summers). If the rings cost $15 apiece or less, Adams would buy three—one for himself, one for Sue, and one for Betsy. If they cost $18, Adams would buy two—one for himself, one for Sue. If they cost $21, Adams would buy one for himself. If they cost more than $21, he would not buy any. (George is Society President.)

Henry Kandinsky, 16. Father's occupation: tailor. Personal characteristics: bookish, shy (nickname: "Lonesome"). If rings cost $7 or less, Kandinsky would buy one. That is his limit.

Sharon Lewis, 17. Mother's occupation: life insurance agent. Personal characteristics: star basketball player, somewhat conceited. If rings cost $7 or less, she would buy two—one for herself, one for her boyfriend. If they cost $11 to $21, she would buy one for herself. That is her limit.

John Mullins, 17. Father's occupation: garage mechanic. Personal characteristics: conscientious, devoted to family—has four brothers, two sisters. Works after school at a supermarket. If they cost $11 or less, Mullins would buy one. If they cost more than $11, he will not buy one.

Peggy Russo, 17. Father's occupation: carpenter. Personal characteristics: fond of music, buys a lot of records. If rings cost up to $15, she would buy one. She would not go higher.

Janet Williams, 16. Mother's occupation: newspaper editor. Personal characteristics: lively, talkative, enjoys dancing (especially with one special friend). If rings cost up to $11, she would buy two—one for that friend and one for herself. If they cost $15 or $18 she would buy just one for herself.

2. Formulating a Preliminary Model

As a preliminary verbal model, we might assert that *the number of rings to be ordered by each student will depend upon the cost of the ring*—or, in mathematical language, *the quantity demanded is a function of price.* This model is based on our knowledge and intuition about the problem as it presents itself to each student.

3. Collecting and Laying Out the Empirical Data

From all of the information we have set forth in (1) above about each student, we *select* the data about how many rings would be bought at each price.

The other information about parents' occupations and students' personal characteristics provides some interesting background material about *income* situations and about the *utility* of rings compared to other preferences. This information, however, is really comprehended by the data about willingness to buy one or more rings at different prices.

The relevant data about our problem, the demand for rings by each at different prices, may be laid out in a table (see Table 7-1). This table is a **demand schedule** (similar to a train schedule).

4. Determining How the Data Are Interrelated

From the above demand schedule, we may set forth the relevant data that show *the quantity demanded as a function of price*, as specified in our preliminary model. The total demand for rings at every price may now be set forth as a series of *ordered pairs*:

Price (in dollars):	7	11	15	18	21	24
Quantity demanded:	10	8	6	4	2	0

These ordered pairs may in turn be set forth on a graph (Figure 7-1), with *price* measured along the vertical Y-axis, and *quantity* measured along the horizontal X-axis. Each *point* on the graph corresponds to an *or-*

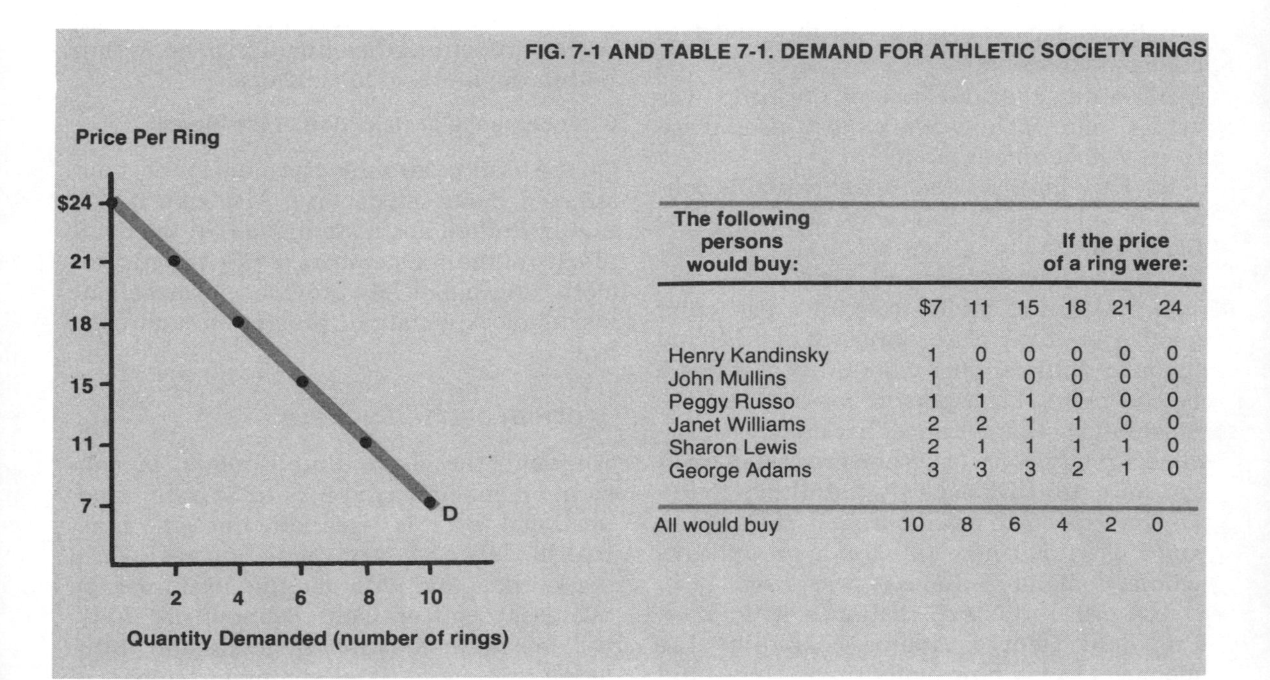

FIG. 7-1 AND TABLE 7-1. DEMAND FOR ATHLETIC SOCIETY RINGS

The following persons would buy:	If the price of a ring were:					
	$7	11	15	18	21	24
Henry Kandinsky	1	0	0	0	0	0
John Mullins	1	1	0	0	0	0
Peggy Russo	1	1	1	0	0	0
Janet Williams	2	2	1	1	0	0
Sharon Lewis	2	1	1	1	1	0
George Adams	3	3	3	2	1	0
All would buy	10	8	6	4	2	0

dered pair of numbers. Thus, the lowest point on the diagram marks the intersection of the coordinates from a price of 7 and a quantity of 10 and the highest point marks the intersection of the coordinates when price is 24 and quantity demanded is 0.

The straight line that may be drawn to connect the points can also be called a **demand schedule**, since it shows how many rings are scheduled to be bought at each price. The diagram in Figure 7-1 is a *geometrical* model of demand.

It should be noted that no one has ever *seen* a demand schedule in the real world; it is a wholly imaginary representation of what buyers in a market would do under certain assumptions. It symbolizes reality; it does not portray it.

5. Testing the Model Against Real-world Experience

We now have a geometric, as well as a verbal and tabular, version of our model. We must now test our model in the real world to see whether it is any good. There are three possible tests of any model: (a) How well does it explain real events? (b) How well does it predict real events? (c) How well does it permit a policymaker who possesses the model to control real events?

Assuming that our case of the rings was actual, here is how we would meet these three tests with our model.

(a) *Explanation*. The model explains consumer behavior in this way. *Assumptions:* Each person in a market has a certain amount of money to spend. Each person has some pattern of preferences for a particular good. The utility of an extra unit of this good tends to diminish, the more units of it that a person owns. Each person wants to get the most satisfaction for his or her money as possible. *Conclusions:* (1) When the cost of owning an extra ring exceeds the utility that a person expects to receive from it, that person stops buying rings. (2) For a group as a whole, demand declines as price rises.

The test of this explanation is as follows. President George Adams asks his club members to say how many rings they would order if the price were $21. Their answer is *two*. He asks how many rings they would buy if the price were $7. Their answer is *ten*. The explanation appears valid.

(b) *Prediction*. George checks with a local jewelry maker, and finds that a reasonable price on the type of ring would be $15. The model predicts that, at that price, there would be orders for six rings. When George asks his members for orders, lo and behold, six rings are actually ordered! The model has proved to be good for predicting demand.

(c) *Control*. George notices that at the price of $15, two members, Kandinsky and Mullins, are not buying any rings. If he wants to *control* (or influence) the situation so that, say, *every* member will get a ring, he must find some way to reduce the price to $7. Perhaps he can do this by getting the school authorities to subsidize the cost of buying the rings.

Or perhaps President Adams, wanting to spare the feelings of the two who won't or can't buy, decides to control the situation by eliminating *everyone* from the market for rings. He might then report the price of a ring as $24, to which all members, including himself, would say no. Either way, the model would, in fact, permit President Adams to control the situation as he wishes within the limits of his powers.

6. Acceptance or Rejection of the Model

On the basis of all three tests, the model constructed looks satisfactory. Although it is a highly limited abstraction from all the complexity of the six members of the Athletic Society, the model has provided an excellent means of explanation, prediction, and control.

OTHER DEMAND MODELS

Although the above simple model of consumer demand may appear to be only an educational toy, it is essentially the same as actual models of demand based on real-world market data and with genuine usefulness to business or government. Economists, studying data on the quantity of goods sold at different prices and times among consumers of

FIG. 7-2. DEMAND FOR SIRLOIN STEAK

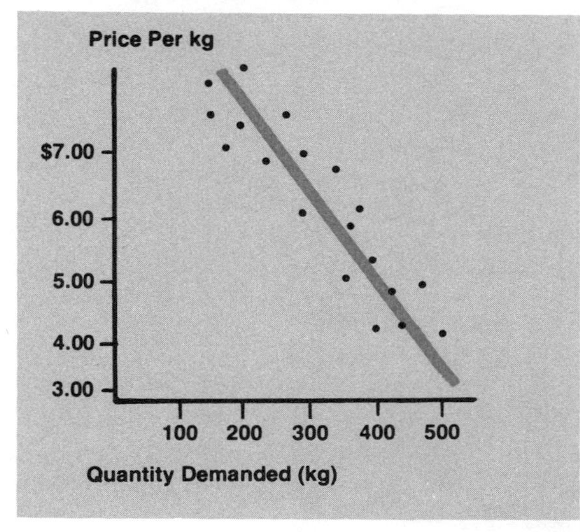

FIG. 7-3. DEMAND FOR TENNIS BALLS

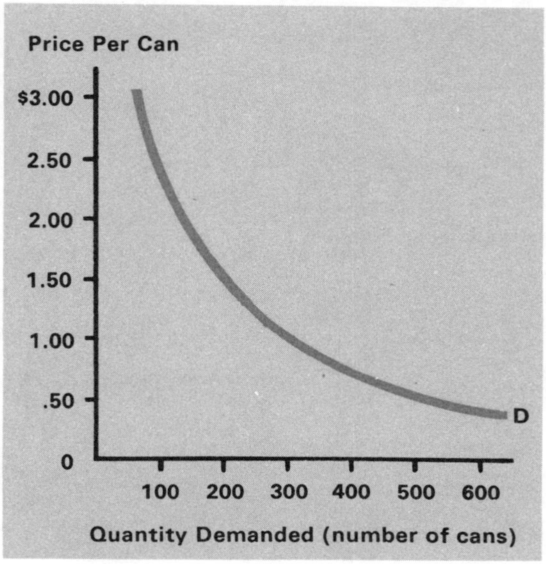

Price Per Can
$3.00
2.50
2.00
1.50
1.00
.50
0
D
100
200
300
400
500
600
Quantity Demanded (number of cans)

varying incomes, have worked out estimates of demand functions of many different products. The real world may never provide data with so perfect a linear relationship as that contained in our fictional case study above. Yet it is often possible to *approximate* a linear relationship between quantity demanded and price, even though the actual data recorded in market transactions do not fall precisely on a straight-line demand schedule. Typically, plots will scatter along and around a straight line, as in Figure 7-2.

Often economists find that the relationship between demand and price for a particular product is best represented by a curve rather than a straight line. This is because quantity demanded for the product may at first not increase very much as price begins to decline from a high level, but then quantity demanded may increase more rapidly as price continues to decline, as shown in Figure 7-3. Economists often speak of a demand graph as a **demand curve,** even when it is a straight line.

As a result of the general appearance of the normal curve and the inverse relationship which is normally found between price and quantity demanded, the phrase **downward-sloping demand** is sometimes used to describe the pattern.

Economists sometimes find it important to include in their model of demand more variables than just *price* and *quantity demanded.* For instance, economists might wish to make the quantity demanded of some product, such as pork, a function not only of the price of pork but also of the *income* of consumers, of the *prices* of other substitute goods, such as steak or lamb, or of food prices or consumer prices generally. Economists may also make quantity demanded a function of *time* (which will reflect growth in population or national income). They may add still other variables on which to make the quantity demanded of other goods dependent.

All of these more complex models of demand are, however, refinements or improvements upon the basic model of demand presented in this chapter in our example of the rings. Like it, all demand models give the economist and the retailer who uses it a means of *explaining* the functional relationship between the sales of a product and its price (or other variables); of *predicting* how large the sales of a product will be; and of *controlling* to some extent the number of

A. H. MacDonald

What demand model is likely being used by the retailer in this bookstore display?

units of the product that will be sold.

Models of demand are of great practical value to businesspeople. For instance, the growth of the Woolworth Five & Ten Cent Store empire was founded on a model—in the head of the founder—that implied that there would be enormous increases in the quantity demanded for a wide range of products if these prices could be reduced. Also the rise of the chain store and later the supermarket and the discount house in North America was founded on such demand models. So was the growth in sales of Henry Ford's Model T automobile, ball-point pens, radio and TV sets, and other products that experienced huge increases in sales with lower prices.

In the chapter that follows we shall consider more carefully some of the factors that cause the sales of products to change from one day to the next or over a longer period of time.

SUMMARY

To the economist, demand means both the ability and the willingness to buy goods. A consumer's ability to buy some particular good depends upon income or wealth in relation to the price of the good; willingness to buy depends upon a judgment of the utility or desirability of the good in relation to its price. The utility of an extra unit of the good to a person generally declines as the number owned increases.

People are likely to increase their purchases of any good when its price declines for these reasons: (1) At a lower price, the good may be judged to have enough utility to make additional units of it worth buying. (2) At a lower price, the buyer may substitute it for other comparable goods. (3) At a lower price, the customer will have more real income with which to buy the good. Occasionally, people may prefer higher priced goods to lower priced goods for reasons of display or snobbery. People's spending is affected by their social attitudes and habits.

A simple but useful model of demand was developed. This model was expressed in three forms: (1) *verbally*, by the statement that "the quantity demanded of any good depends upon its price"; (2) in a *table* where different prices were listed and the quantity demanded at each price was tabulated and shown; and (3) *geometrically*, as a downward-sloping straight line—a demand schedule—on a graph, with price measured along the vertical or Y-axis and quantity demanded measured along the horizontal or X-axis. This model was found to be useful for purposes of explaining, predicting, and controlling sales of a product.

Although this model developed for demand is simple, its structure is basically similar to more complicated models that can be used for analysing the demand for all sorts of products in the real world.

More generally, this chapter sought to show an approach by which many complicated real-world situations can and should be analysed. This approach involves (1) carefully *defining* the problem; (2) formulating a preliminary model—a set of assumptions from which a conclusion or set of conclusions can be deduced; (3) collecting data about the problem; (4) finding out how the data fit together; (5) testing the model in the real world; and (6) finally deciding whether or not to accept the model for use and reuse.

Even though one cannot always proceed in a very scientific way to analyse actual situations, one of the most important values of studying economics is to learn this approach to problem defining and problem solving.

KEY CONCEPTS

demand
diminishing marginal utility
substitution effect
income effect
demand schedule
demand curve
downward-sloping demand

QUESTIONS FOR REVIEW AND DISCUSSION

1. What two conditions must exist before we can say that there is a demand for a product? If you are hired to estimate the number of people with a demand for a packaged product (say brand X), which of the following people would you include in your estimate? Why?
   a. Person 1 has no money and says: "I think brand X is the greatest. I would like to have three or four packages of brand X."
   b. Person 2 has $8000 and says: "Brand X stinks."
   c. Person 3 has $1000 and says: "Brand X is by far the best of the packaged products on the market. It can't be beat at any price."
   d. Person 4 has $2000 and says: "Brand X is o.k., but I wouldn't pay more than $.50 a package for it."
2. If brand X is now priced at $2.00 a package, and there are no changes in people's incomes or the prices of other goods, why might the sales of the product increase if the price was lowered to $1.50? Give three reasons. Give two reasons why the sale of brand X might *not* increase if its price fell to $1.50. Which of these sets of reasons do you think is most likely, i.e. do you think the sales of brand X will increase or not? Why?
3. If the price of bowling a line of ten pins is increased from $.75 to $1.25 a line, and there are no changes in people's incomes or the prices of other goods, what reasons explain why the number of lines bowled might decrease? What reasons explain why the number of lines bowled might remain the same? What reasons explain why the number of lines bowled might increase? Which of these reasons do you think are the strongest? Would you predict that the number of lines actually bowled after the price increase would decrease, stay the same, or increase? Why?
4. What type of model have you been using in answering the preceding questions? What were the key elements in your model? How did you relate these elements?

PROBLEMS AND EXERCISES TO SHARPEN YOUR UNDERSTANDING

Below is a table showing a list of prices for a litre of ice cream and a list of the number of litres of ice cream that consumers would be willing to buy at the different prices in a typical city on a typical summer day.

Demand for Ice Cream in a Typical City on a Typical Summer Day

Price per Litre	Number of Litres Consumers Would Be Willing To Buy
$2.00	5000
1.80	10 000
1.60	15 000
1.40	20 000
1.20	22 500
1.00	25 000

1. On a sheet of graph paper, sketch a vertical axis (up and down) and label it

"price." Make a horizontal axis (across the page) and label it "quantity demanded." Plot the data from the above table, letting each unit on the vertical axis represent price intervals of $.20, and letting each unit on the horizontal axis represent 5000 litres.

2. Describe in words what the graph shows you.
3. Make a new table and a new graph indicating your estimate of the demand for ice cream in a typical city on a typical *winter* day, and explain why your new table and graph are or are not different from the previous one.

Note: Be sure to keep the work on the above problems. This ice cream situation will reappear several times in subsequent chapters. (We hope we won't spoil anyone's taste for ice cream!)

WHY SALES OF A PRODUCT RISE OR FALL

■ PRICE-ELASTICITY ■ WHAT CAUSES ELASTIC OR INELASTIC DEMAND? ■ INCOME-ELASTICITY OF DEMAND ■ CHANGES IN THE DEMAND SCHEDULE ■ REASONS FOR SHIFTS IN A DEMAND SCHEDULE ■ FORECASTING CHANGES IN DEMAND ■ SUMMARY

Economics, we have said, is a study of change. We shall now examine the factors that make the quantity demanded for some products respond sensitively or insensitively to changes in price and to changes in the incomes of consumers. We shall also look into the causes of upward or downward shifts in the demand schedule for individual products over a period of time. Understanding the causes of changes in demand is essential to predicting sales, a matter of the greatest concern to businesses.

■ PRICE-ELASTICITY

As we know from Chapter 7, the quantity demanded is a function of price; hence, a change in price generally produces an inverse change in the quantity demanded. But this relationship between price and quantity needs to be examined more exactly if it is to be of practical usefulness, for the *degree* to which a given price change may cause a change in the quantity demanded varies widely.

Sometimes a small price decrease results in a big increase in the quantity demanded. Sometimes the reverse happens; a big price decrease results in only a small increase in the quantity demanded. And sometimes a given price decrease results in a proportionately *equal* increase in the quantity demanded.

The degree to which the quantity de-

FIG. 8-1. ELASTIC DEMAND

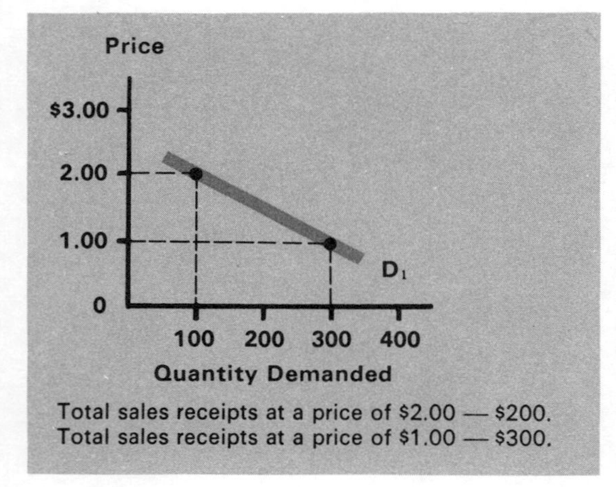

FIG. 8-2. INELASTIC DEMAND

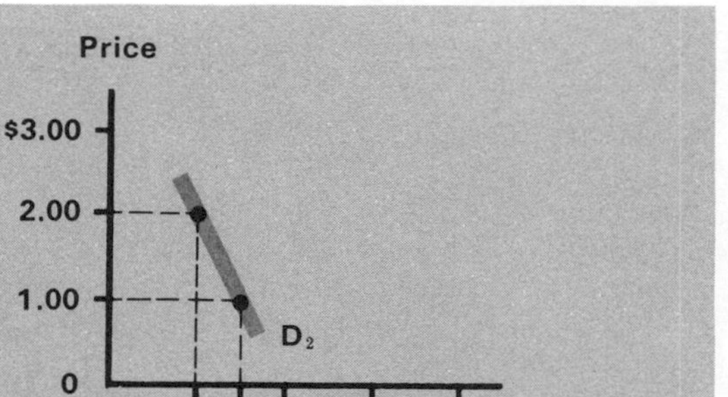

FIG. 8-4. ELASTICITY OF DEMAND FOR ATHLETIC SOCIETY RINGS AT DIFFERENT PRICE-QUANTITY INTERVALS

Price Per Ring

$24, 21, 18, 15, 11, 7

E Elastic, price cuts raise receipts, price increases lower receipts

E Elastic, price cuts raise receipts, price increases lower receipts

E Elastic, price cuts raise receipts, price increases lower receipts

I Inelastic, price cuts lower receipts, price increases raise receipts

I Inelastic, price cuts lower receipts, price increases raise receipts

D

2 4 6 8 10 12

Quantity Demanded (number of rings)

TABLE 8-1. SALES OF RINGS

Price	Quantity	Dollar Receipts
$24	0	$ 0
21	2	42
18	4	72
15	6	90
11	8	88
7	10	70

manded of any good changes in response to a price change measures the **price-elasticity of demand** for a product. Goods for which the quantity demanded is highly responsive to price change are said to have *high* price-elasticity. Goods for which the quantity demanded changes only slightly in response to price change have *low* price-elasticity. And goods for which the quantity demanded changes proportionately with price change have *unitary* price-elasticity. Diagrams showing demand schedules that are *elastic*, *inelastic*, and *unitary* are presented in Figures 8-1, 8-2, and 8-3.

FIG. 8-3. UNITARY ELASTICITY OF DEMAND

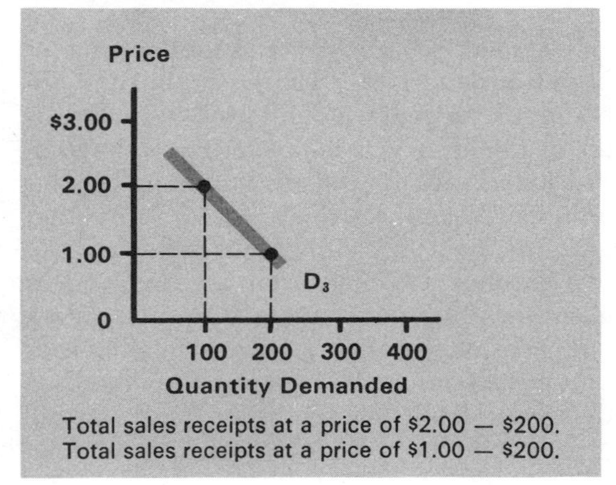

If demand for a product is **elastic,** a given price decrease will cause the *total dollar amount* of sales receipts to increase.

If demand is **inelastic,** a price cut will cause total dollar sales receipts to decrease.

And if demand has **unitary price-elasticity,** a price reduction will cause no change in total dollar sales receipts.

Table 8-1 (above) drawn from our Athletic Society rings example will illustrate these relationships.

We see that between prices of $24 and $15, demand is elastic. Price reductions will cause total sales receipts to increase. But price reductions from $15 to $11 or $11 to $7 will cause total sales receipts to fall. This is shown graphically in Figure 8-4 where we have labeled each interval on the demand curve *E* for elastic and *I* for inelastic.

The converse of the above relationship is also important to note. When demand for a product is elastic, price increases will cause total sales receipts to decline. When demand is inelastic, price increases will cause total sales receipts to rise. It therefore follows that a producer or any other seller of a product who perceives that the demand for the product is inelastic will tend to hold the price of the product up—or try to raise it higher—in order to increase total sales receipts. This is why farmers, acting together as a bloc as they frequently do in many countries, try to keep farm prices up or induce governments to help them raise farm prices still higher. For farmers perceive that the demand for their products is *inelastic* and that increases in farm prices will cause their total receipts from sales to increase, while decreases in farm prices will cause total receipts to decline.

And this same perception of inelasticity of demand explains why Brazilian coffee growers have sometimes been known to burn thousands of coffee trees because the resulting rise in the price of coffee and consequently of their total receipts more than compensates them for the loss of their coffee trees. This is also why French wine growers have been known to spill thousands of gallons of wine onto the earth—as a means of getting wine prices and total sales receipts up, since they perceive that the demand for wine is *inelastic*. And it is why milk producers have sometimes banded together to spill part of their milk on the ground rather than bring it to the market.

Conversely, this is the reason that different sellers, perceiving that the demand for their product is *elastic*, cut their prices as a means of increasing their total sales receipts. Henry Ford cut the price of his cars not as an act of charity but as a means of increasing total dollar volume of sales. He sensed that the demand for a simple and efficient automobile was highly elastic. But the makers of Rolls-Royce cars perceived that demand for their

A. H. MacDonald

more elegant product was relatively inelastic, and they maintained a high-price policy. Both Ford and Rolls-Royce were right, each in its own way and at a particular time in history.

In some cases, the demand for the product of one producer may be elastic, but the demand for the product of all producers or sellers in a field may be inelastic. Thus, the high price-elasticity of demand for any particular brand of gasoline explains why individual gasoline distributors often cut prices against one another and may even get involved in gasoline price wars. Price wars also break out occasionally among sellers of such products as cement, milk, or drugstore merchandise—all fields where the demand for the

A. H. MacDonald

In the picture here, and on page 78, we see the potential impact of price-elasticity in two situations. How many examples can you give of personal experiences within the last month when price-elasticity had an impact on a purchase you made or were seriously considering?

goods of *any particular producer* is elastic.

WHAT CAUSES ELASTIC OR INELASTIC DEMAND?

Basically, there are three factors that cause the demand for a product to be elastic or inelastic. The first of these is the most important. They are: (1) whether acceptable substitutes for the product are available; (2) whether the item is important in a consumer's total budget; and (3) whether the product is regarded as a luxury or a necessity.

The elasticity of demand for a product *increases* (1) when it is easy to find a substitute for it; (2) when it constitutes a big expense in a family's budget; and (3) when it is considered to be a luxury or, at any rate, something one can do without.

So it is easy to see why any single gasoline distributor faces elastic demand. First of all, car owners can readily substitute another brand of gasoline and, secondly, gasoline is a pretty big expense to a person who drives a great deal. However, while the demand for any single brand of gasoline is elastic, the demand for all gasoline is inelastic because if a person owns and intends to drive a car, then gasoline is a necessity for which no acceptable substitutes are available.

The demand for a product such as color television is likely to be quite elastic, because it has many substitutes (black-and-white television sets, motion pictures, radio, phonographs, and indeed all other forms of entertainment). Furthermore, a color television set makes a pretty good dent in the typical family's budget. When color television set makers were able to reduce their prices—closer to black-and-white television set prices—they enjoyed a much greater than proportional increase in their dollar sales receipts. Since, however, color television is regarded as a superior product to black-and-white television, it is not necessary for color set makers to get prices down as low as black-and-white television sets.

The demand for household refrigerators is also elastic. The problem of determining the price elasticity for refrigerators is greatly complicated by changes in the quality and design of refrigerators over a period of time. Yet it is apparent that, since consumers can either decide to buy a new refrigerator or to keep the old one—and, if necessary, to keep the old one going through repairs—there is considerable elasticity on the part of consumers in response to changes in refrigerator prices.

The elasticity of demand for different goods or services may be quite *irregular* at different price ranges, as was true in the case of our rings. For example, in the case of demand for airline transportation, demand might be quite *inelastic* at the upper-price ranges (since some people must frequently get to their out-of-town appointments on time and not waste working hours). However, the demand for airline transportation might be elastic at lower prices, since those who must travel may not choose to take their spouse or other members of their family along and because other people, with less money to spend and less urgency about time, can substitute travel by train, bus, or their own car for air transportation. Airlines, in fact, often work out differential fares in order to maximize their total dollar receipts. The airlines may seek to do this by raising the rates for first-class tickets on flights that are convenient for business travelers (whose demand for space is inelastic) while giving cut-rate fares to students, or to children accompanying an adult, or offering reduced tourist fares for noncommercial travelers (whose demand for air transportation is elastic). Various types of group or advance bookings are another means used to increase total airline receipts under conditions of elastic demand.

INCOME-ELASTICITY OF DEMAND

Economists identify not only the *price-elasticity* of demand for particular goods but also income-elasticity. **Income-elasticity of demand** is the change in demand for particular goods that results from changes in the income of consumers. Where the price-elasticity of most goods is negative (the higher the price, the less a consumer wants of it), income-elasticity is ordinarily positive (the more income the consumer has, the more he will buy of most goods). For instance, if a family's income rises, it will tend to consume more steak, more bacon, more oranges, more electricity, more theater tickets, more butter.

However, the income-elasticity of some goods is negative. For instance, if a family's income rises, it may consume less margarine (it may substitute butter for margarine), less spaghetti (it may substitute meat for spaghetti and other cereal products), and less bus or subway transportation (substituting transportation by private automobiles).

Indeed, one can clearly see the effect of rising income upon the demand for particular goods for entire nations. As nations move up the income ladder, they first substitute bicycles for walking, and then substitute automobiles for bicycles.[1] Similarly, as income rises, nations consume more animal products, more housing, more electrical appliances.

[1] Such a trend in the USA prompted humorist Will Rogers to observe during the Depression that his was the first country where the average family could go "over the hill to the poorhouse—in an automobile!"

FIG. 8-5 AND TABLE 8-2. INCREASE IN DEMAND SCHEDULE FOR ATHLETIC SOCIETY RINGS

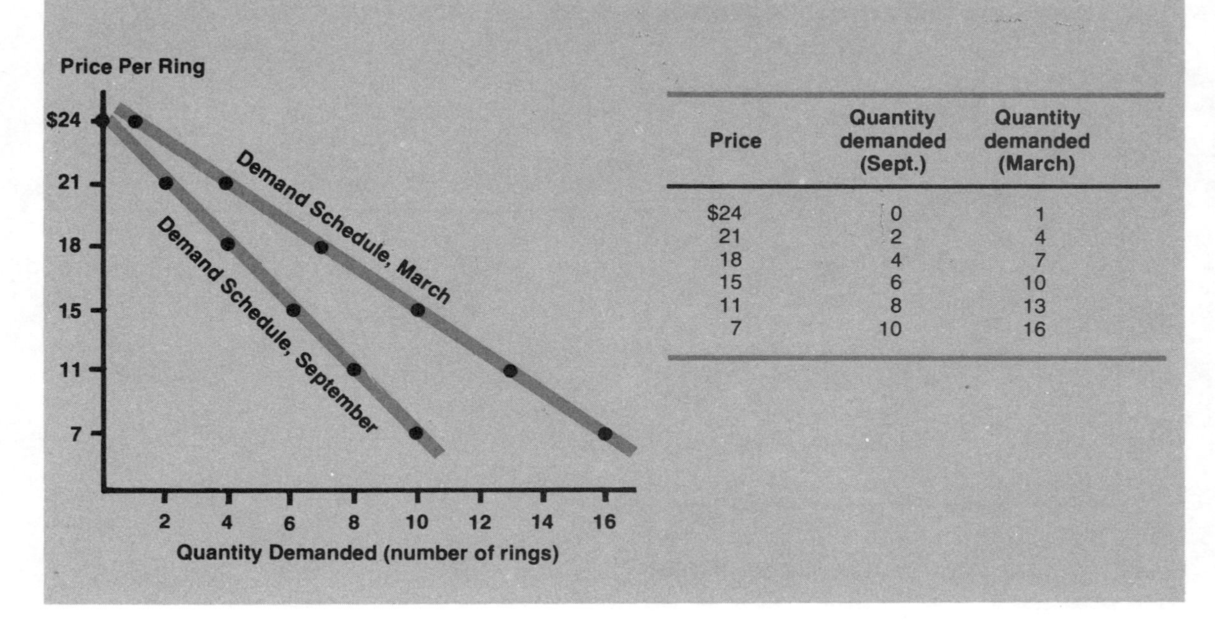

Price	Quantity demanded (Sept.)	Quantity demanded (March)
$24	0	1
21	2	4
18	4	7
15	6	10
11	8	13
7	10	16

A German statistician, Ernst Engel (1821-1896), was one of the first to note the common patterns of income-elasticity for different types of goods; he formulated what is known as *Engel's Law:*

As income rises,

1. The amount spent on food increases, but the share of total income spent on food decreases;
2. The percent of income spent on housing increases up to a point, and then stays at a roughly constant proportion of income;
3. The percent of income spent on clothing, transportation, medical care, education, and recreation rises.

In a general way, Engel's Law still appears valid—though it certainly does not hold for every individual family.

CHANGES IN THE DEMAND SCHEDULE

When economists refer to a change in demand, they usually mean a change in the entire *demand schedule* for a product. Thus, to the economist, an increase in demand means that *more units of a product will be demanded than before at any given price.* And a decrease in demand means that fewer units of a product will be demanded than before *at any given price.*

A change in demand, represented by a shift in the demand schedule, can easily be illustrated if we go back to our demand schedule for rings from Chapter 7. We shall describe two changes in demand for rings—first an increase, then a decrease.

Increase in Demand

Suppose that the original demand schedule for rings was computed on September 29, but that on March 1 (after the hockey and volleyball seasons), six new members of the society were elected. Then the demand for rings might change, as shown in Table 8-2.

This increase in demand can be represented, using our geometric model, by an upward and rightward shift of the entire demand schedule on the graph, as shown in Figure 8-5.

FIG. 8-6 AND TABLE 8-3. DECREASE IN DEMAND SCHEDULE FOR ATHLETIC SOCIETY RINGS

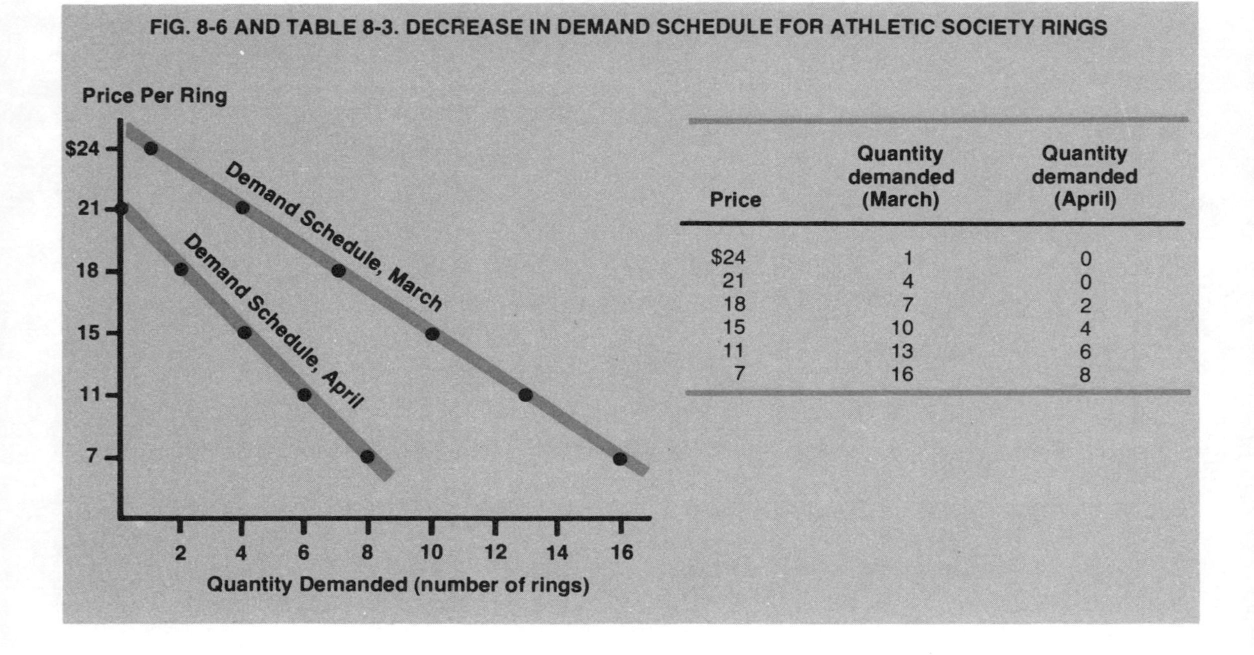

Price	Quantity demanded (March)	Quantity demanded (April)
$24	1	0
21	4	0
18	7	2
15	10	4
11	13	6
7	16	8

Decrease in Demand

Now suppose that in April, the biggest employer in Pleasantville, the Shakey Chair Company, closes its plant. The parents of two new members have lost their jobs—and so have two other parents who did not work for Shakey but whose jobs depended on spending by people who *did* work for the big furniture company. Indeed, the incomes of other families who work for themselves had also been reduced, and they were worried about the future. The effect of all this was to decrease the demand for rings by the students in the group, as shown in Table 8-3.

When graphed, this demand schedule shifts downward and to the left, representing a decrease in demand, as illustrated in Figure 8-6.

REASONS FOR SHIFTS IN A DEMAND SCHEDULE

Many different factors can cause shifts in a demand schedule. Some of the most important of these causes are the following.

1. Changes in Income

As in the above example, decreases in income tend to reduce demand; increases in income tend to increase demand.

At this point, we shall not consider the question of how the total income of a nation rises. However, individual persons may experience a rise in their incomes for a host of reasons. Improved business in the place where they live or in the company for which they work are primary causes. Incomes of a whole community may rise as a result of the opening of a new plant, the building of a new railroad or airport, the growing attractiveness of the products or facilities of the region, or a growth in incomes resulting from a boom in the national economy.

Conversely, the loss of markets for the product of a company, the exhaustion of the mineral resources of a region, a business depression and growth of unemployment, or any other development that causes incomes to fall will reduce demand for most individual products.

For the purpose of discovering what the

effects of changing income will be on the *price* of a product and on the quantity of the product that will actually be purchased, we depict this change by drawing a new demand schedule, as shown above in Figures 8-5 and 8-6.

2. Changes in Taste

If people acquire a taste for some good, its demand increases; if people lose their taste for it, demand shrinks. European travel may, for example, lead Canadians to acquire a taste for French wine and perfume and boost their demands for French imports. When people move from rural to urban areas, they may acquire many new tastes in food, clothing, and entertainment. A major function of advertising is to change the taste of people for particular goods.

3. Changes in Relative Prices

Although the price of a particular good may remain the same in actual dollars and cents, the demand for it may change as a result of changes *in the price of other goods that are substitutes for it*. For instance, if the price of sailboats remains the same but the price of speedboats comes down, people will *decrease their demand for sailboats*—because of the *increase in the relative price of sailboats*. Or if the price of plastic pocketbooks remains the same but *the price of leather pocketbooks rises*, the *demand for plastic pocketbooks will increase because of the reduction in their relative price*.

4. Joint or Derived Demand

The demand for some goods is linked to the demand for other goods or services. For instance, if the demand for big lawns and gardens increases, the demand for power mowers will increase; and if the demand for power mowers increases, so will the demand for motor oil. If people demand more steel, they demand more of the services of steelworkers. Conversely, if the demand for seats in movie houses declines, the demand for popcorn and ushers will decline.

5. Population Change

If the population of a locality, region, or nation increases, the demand for certain goods and services, such as schools, housing, food, clothing, and hospitals, will increase. But if the growth of real income does not keep pace with this growth of population, it is likely that the growth in demand for certain items resulting from more children and old people will reduce the demand for other items which working people who must *support* more children or old people can no longer afford. Thus, if there are relatively more young and old people and fewer middle-aged people, this may increase the demand for some goods such as high-chairs, baby carriages, and phonograph records (for the infants and teenagers) and for retirement homes, rest homes and hospitals, hearing aids, and medical services (for the aged). But it may reduce the demand for household furnishings, household help, and holiday travel (for the middle-aged).

6. Seasonal Changes

The change in the seasons produces changes in the demand for different goods. Obviously people increase their demands for fur coats, skates and snowshovels in the winter, and for water skis, bathing caps, and sun tan lotion in the summer. This is why you can save money if you buy out of season. Demand for department store merchandise booms before Christmas, Easter, and in the autumn when children go back to school. It slumps in the summer and after Christmas. Many businesses have special seasonal patterns of their own.

7. Changes in People's Expectations about Prices and Business Conditions

If people *expect* prices of goods to go higher, they may rush to buy immediately. If they expect prices to fall, they may delay their purchases in order to save money. If people expect business conditions to stay good or to improve, they are likely to increase their purchases of many types of goods that they

General Motors

These two photographs illustrate the concept of alternate production possibilities which was introduced in Chapter 3. The situations use somewhat similar materials, production techniques and skills. As a result, they convey the idea of one possible result of a change in demand which was caused by a change in military or political considerations or priorities.

A. H. MacDonald with the cooperation of Volvo (Canada) Limited

might otherwise postpone, such as new cars, appliances, housing or house furnishings. If they expect business conditions to worsen, they may cut such expenditures. The buying behavior of most people who work for a living is markedly affected by the *outlook* for their jobs and incomes, as these may be affected by business conditions.

8. Political Changes

Changes in political attitudes, in the government in office, or in the political pressures upon a nation, can have significant effects upon the demand for different goods and services. If a nation decides to pursue a tougher international military policy, this

How many concepts contained in Chapters 7 and 8 can you find represented in the photograph and the following information about the situation?

The boys shown wanted to have a television set of their own, separate from the existing "family set." They had reason to believe that the family budget could permit the purchase without undue financial strain. They also had become familiar with prices and, in this photograph they are shown examining a satisfactory set with a considerable reduction from its normal price. This set, however, was not purchased. The money which could have been spent on the set was used, along with more money, in the purchase of a new stereo by the boys' parents.

A. H. MacDonald

may increase the demand for such goods as airplanes, rockets, tanks, radar, and other electronic equipment. If a national administration decides to try to raise the level of living and literacy of the poor, this will increase the demand for schools, books, teachers, teaching machines, and so on. If governments reduce taxes, this will increase demand for goods in the private sector, such as automobiles and homes. If governments boost their spending, this will increase the demand for goods in the public sector, such as schools, highways, military goods, etc.

Each of the eight types of factors described above will cause shifts in the demand schedules of different goods and services—"of shoes and ships and sealing wax, of cabbages and kings," and countless other goods not yet invented when the famous conversation in "The Walrus and the Carpenter" was written by Lewis Carroll over a century ago.

FORECASTING CHANGES IN DEMAND

One of the most important jobs of the economist is forecasting the effects of various changes upon the demand for goods of different types. Generally speaking, the main question the business executive wants the economist to answer is, "What will these changes in the world around us do to the demand schedule and hence to the sales of the products we make?" Whether the business executive actually has an economist of whom to ask this question or not, the answer must be sought on the basis of all the information available.

However, sales forecasting requires time and work and, for the best results, real economic skills. Many businesses have grown so big and complex that their managers find themselves faced with tasks where decisions based on guesses or wishful thinking may result in large and costly mistakes. But objective analysis of the factors influencing consumer demand, through the use of models similar to those employed in this chapter and the assembly of relevant data, may do much to reduce the risks facing business owners. It may also help to put business decision-making on a firmer foundation. We shall discuss forecasting in detail in Chapter 25.

SUMMARY

In this chapter we have examined the factors that cause the sales of particular products to increase or decrease. Three fundamental concepts were discussed: (1) the price-elasticity of demand—the responsiveness of the quantity demanded of a product, when its price changes; (2) the income-elasticity of demand—the responsiveness of the demand for a product to changes in the income of consumers; and (3) changes in the demand schedule for a product which are caused by all such factors as changes in income, taste, relative prices, demand for related products, change in population size and age composition, seasonal change, consumers' expectations as to prices and business conditions, and political changes. One of the most important tasks of the economist is to forecast the effect of all such changes upon the demand for particular products. This is a question vital to everyone who works for a living or depends on those who do.

KEY CONCEPTS

price-elasticity of demand	elastic demand	unitary price-elasticity
	inelastic demand	income-elasticity of demand

QUESTIONS FOR REVIEW AND DISCUSSION

1. Give a verbal definition of *price-elasticity of demand*.
2. State in words the simple total receipts test of the price-elasticity of demand. How do changes in total receipts indicate whether the demand for a product is elastic, inelastic, or unit elastic over a given price-quantity interval?
3. Why is the demand for a particular *brand* of gasoline more elastic than the demand for all gasoline in general?
4. How does the concept of a change in demand differ from the concept of the price-elasticity of demand?
5. What accounts for the positive income-elasticity of some goods and the negative income-elasticity of others?
6. What is Engel's Law?
7. If you are a market analyst for a business firm, and you are told that sales have increased, what question would you ask to determine if there has been a change in demand or merely a move along a given demand schedule?
8. What are some factors that could lead to an increase in the demand for a product? What are some factors that could lead to a decrease in demand?

PROBLEMS AND EXERCISES TO SHARPEN YOUR UNDERSTANDING

1. Take the data given at the end of the last chapter on the demand for ice cream in a typical city on a typical summer day. Determine whether the demand curve is elastic, inelastic, or unit elastic for price changes over each interval shown (i.e., \$2.00 to \$1.80, \$1.80 to \$1.60, \$1.60 to \$1.40, etc.). Explain the procedure you used in giving your answer for each interval.
2. From the data at the end of the last chapter and the format given below, indicate an increase in demand and a decrease in demand. In each case indicate the factors that would lead to the changes in demand that you have shown.

Quantity Demanded With a Decrease in Demand	Price Per Litre	Quantity Demanded With an Increase in Demand
	\$2.00	
	1.80	
	1.60	
	1.40	
	1.20	
	1.00	

3. Using the same graphing scales you used at the end of the last chapter, plot on one set of axes the original demand for ice cream and the increase and the decrease in the demand for ice cream you have developed for problem 2. Label each of your three demand curves.
4. As an indication of market study in the real world, watch for current references to business expectations about the market made up of high school and college students. One academic study, unfortunately out of date, which would indicate the approach to the analysis of a particular segment of the population, is *The Teenage Market in Canada* by S. Govin, B. Portis and B. Campbell. Based on a detailed analysis of high school students in London, Ontario and Chicoutimi, Quebec, it was published in 1967 by the School of Business Administration, University of Western Ontario, London.

HOW PRICES ARE SET

■ WHAT IS A MARKET? ■ THE CASE OF THE OLD MASTER ■ BARGAINING ■ COLLUSION ■ RATIONING ■ NONPRICE RATIONING ■ EFFECT OF CHANGES IN DEMAND ON PRICE ■ OTHER CASES OF FIXED SUPPLY ■ SUMMARY

In this chapter we shall begin a more careful study of the way prices are set in markets. Up to this point we have treated the demand for a product—meaning its demand schedule—as the quantities that buyers would demand of a good at a *hypothetical* list of prices. We have regarded *quantity demanded as a function of price.*

Now, however, we wish to find out what *actual* price will be set at any given point in time. Using simple cases of fixed supplies we shall see that price plays a crucial role in *rationing* the available quantity of goods—that is, in determining who gets what and who gets nothing—in a market.

■ WHAT IS A MARKET?

We may define a **market** as a relationship between prospective buyers and prospective sellers of some goods or services. Some markets exist at a particular meeting place, such as the grain pit in Winnipeg, the Montreal Stock Exchange, the garment district in New York, the London Gold Market, or the Flea Market in Paris. Other markets are widely spread geographically, such as the markets for school teachers or college professors, textbooks, stamps, rare coins, typewriters, steel, coal, oil, or wheat. Markets differ enormously in the way they work. In some, buyers and sellers see each other in person, exchange information, bargain about terms, and settle deals directly. In others, buyers and sellers have very little or no face-to-face communication with one another and do not bargain, but simply react to one another's moves or to the prices which are the consequences of the behavior of all buyers and sellers in the market, no one of whom has any control over the prices established.

All of this is rather abstract. We shall get further in understanding the way markets work if we get down to cases.

■ THE CASE OF THE OLD MASTER

Let us start with the case of a fictitious painting which we will pretend was found in an attic in 1924—namely, a hitherto unknown work of Rembrandt's titled "Lady with a Dog." An art dealer named Mr. M puts the painting up for sale at auction (that is, he invites open bidding for the picture among all interested customers). How much is the Rembrandt worth? That will depend primarily upon the desire and wealth of the people who come to buy it.

In fact, five customers come, each of whom either has considerable money or represents an art museum with plenty of money. The five bidders, however, have not only different amounts of money available, but different judgments of the value of the picture. The highest price each is prepared to pay is as follows.

A will go as high as $50 000
B will go as high as $60 000
C will go as high as $70 000
D will go as high as $90 000
E will go as high as $110 000

These top prices constitute a demand schedule (Figure 9-1). But how much will the picture actually be sold for? Obviously, this is up to M, the *seller*, as well as to the prospective *buyers*. We must therefore take a look at the seller of the painting and consider his position. M does not know what the buyers will bid, but he is desperate for money. He might have decided that he is willing to sell it *at the best price he can get*, whatever that might turn out to be. In that case we can draw a graph of his *supply* schedule (SS), which is a vertical line, as in Figure 9-1.[1] The supply schedule in this case is a vertical line because M has only one Rembrandt and would be willing to sell his picture for any amount—for a price of $1 000 000 if it would bring that much, or for $1000, or theoretically for $.01 if it would only bring that amount. Thus, the supply schedule at Quantity 1 (for 1 painting) goes straight up with higher prices.

This will of course strike you as unrealistic. If Mr. M really thought the bidders would not pay more than some minimum price he had in mind, he would keep it himself. In this sense, we may regard Mr. M. *himself* as one of the bidders for the picture. Let us suppose that he would refuse to sell it for less than $30 000 (this is called his *reservation* price). So we have added M to the demand schedule for the Rembrandt painting (Figure 9-1).

Now the buyers are assembled in Mr. M's gallery. The bidding is opened by A at $25 000 and quickly climbs to $65 000, at which price only C, D, and E are left. E bids $75 000, and C drops out, leaving only D and E. The bidding goes on until D bids $90 000 (as high as he is willing to go). It is now up to E.

FIG. 9-1. MARKET FOR REMBRANDT PAINTING, 1924

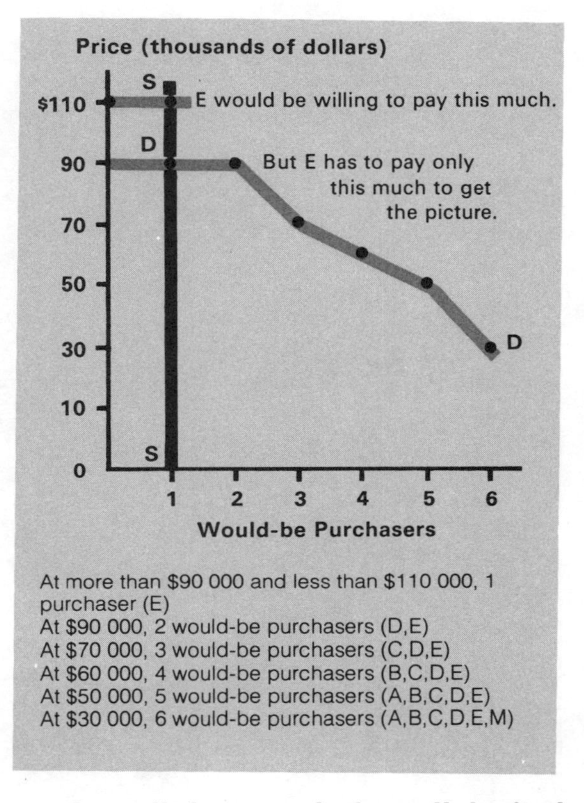

What will she say and what will the final price be?

E would be *willing* to go as high as $110 000, if it were necessary; but in fact, she does not yet know how high she must go, since D has simply made a bid of $90 000. But E does not want to pay any more than she has to, so (perhaps sensing that D has come close to the end of his limit) E says $91 000. D fails to top this bid, and E takes the painting at that price.

All of this is represented diagrammatically in Figure 9-1. As the diagram shows, the price of the Rembrandt has been determined at approximately the point where the demand schedule, DD, intersected the fixed supply schedule, SS. That is where E's last bid knocked out D, and only one buyer was left for the one painting—in other words, where demand (1) equalled supply (1) at a price a bit above $90 000.

[1] The supply schedule is the counterpart of the demand schedule. The supply schedule shows the quantity of a good that would be offered at various prices. As price rises, suppliers ordinarily tend to offer more of the good but, in this case, with only one painting available, the quantity supplied does not vary with the price—the supply schedule is a vertical line at a quantity of 1 unit.

Courtesy of the McMichael Canadian Collection, Kleinburg, Ontario

The working of a fixed-supply market in the real world is best illustrated by such unique things as paintings. This Tom Thomson oil, "Woodland Waterfall," was bought for $285 000 by the W. Garfield Weston Foundation in 1976. The Foundation donated the painting to the McMichael Collection in Kleinburg, Ontario. The price paid set a new record for Canadian paintings. For your aesthetic benefit, the black and white photograph is most inadequate. Try and locate a full color reproduction of the painting in a book on Canadian art.

Strictly speaking, we cannot say that *demand* determined the price of the painting though it was the dynamic element; *supply* also determined the price. If there were no painting, there would be no price. For, as the economist, Alfred Marshall, used to put it, demand and supply are like a pair of scissors, and though only one of the blades moves on some occasions (and the moving blade may be either supply or demand) it is is both blades that do the cutting.

BARGAINING

Was it absolutely inevitable that the price of the Rembrandt would be set at a little above $90 000? Possibly you might have thought the price would go up closer to $110 000. In fact, it could not be absolutely determined in this case that the price of the old master would be any certain amount between $90 000.01 and $110 000. E did not know for sure what bid would knock D out of the market, and even after D was out, there was still a potential bargaining situation between E and the seller, M. Of course, if M were behaving ethically he would be compelled to sell to E as soon as E had eliminated A, B, C, and D. But suppose that M sensed that E was willing to go still higher, and that M had an agent named N working for him, who was planted among the customers. Then M might signal to N to make another bid after E said, "$91 000." Suppose that M's agent N said, "$95 000," and E came back and said "$100 000." This might go on until N had forced E to go up to her $110 000 limit.

However, since M and N do not know in advance what E's real limit is, they are taking a big risk. It is possible that E might drop out of the bidding sooner than M and N expect, and they will be left without a buyer at all. Therefore, even an unethical M is going to be wary of pushing E much above $91 000—unless M has some dependable information on E's true limit. (It would have meant a lot to M if he had had a secret agent who could have found that out in advance.)

In fact, many bargaining situations are like that, in which a buyer and a seller seek to detect each other's true positions, to feel one another out, to outguess or outbluff one another, as in a game of poker. In primitive or old-fashioned markets (as in Oriental bazaars) each buyer and each seller engages in this kind of bargaining over every exchange. The seller tries to make the buyer think that such valuable property would not be parted with except at a much higher price, and the buyer acts as though the property has little value and is not really wanted or needed.

COLLUSION

Suppose that it was not the art dealer M who tried to trick E into paying a higher price than she had to, but rather that E decided to pay a much lower price than she was willing to pay by making a side deal with D.

E, knowing D from many past art sales, might have gone to D before M's Rembrandt came up for sale and said, "Look, D, I know that you want that picture, but I also know that I am in a position to outbid you for it. Why can't we work together? You cooperate with me on this Rembrandt and I'll do you a favor next time."

"What do you want me to do?" asks D.

"When A, B, and C drop out of the bidding, you drop out, too," says E.

"What's in it for me?" asks D.

"I've already told you I'll work with you next time, but if you want something immediate out of this deal, I'll give you $1000," says E.

"I don't know," says D.

"Look," says E, "I've already told you that you're not going to get that picture anyway. I can outbid you. So you have the choice of taking $1000 or getting nothing."

D agrees.

Now when the bidding reaches $70 000 (C's last bid), D says $"71 000." E says $"72 000." C drops out. And D drops out, too. So E gets a picture for which she was prepared to go as high as $110 000 for only $72 000. Had D stayed in, E would have had to pay more than $90 000. As it is, E's total outlay is $73 000, including the $1000 she pays to D. E has saved herself at least $17 001. (In fact, E could have afforded to bribe D much more than $1000—up to $18 000[2]—and still saved money. But neither D nor E knew the true situation in advance or how high, A, B, and C would go.)

Thus, in this case of collusion, we can see that the price of the picture was not set simply by the intersection of the demand and supply schedules but by the *behavior of human beings*. Although economists like to

[2] Based on the difference between E's purchase price of $72 000 and $90 001, the amount she might have had to pay had D bid to his true limit. A bribe of $18 000 would have saved E a total of $1.00 in this hypothetical consideration of possible events.

FIG. 9-2. MARKET FOR REMBRANDT PAINTING AFTER E'S COLLUSION WITH D

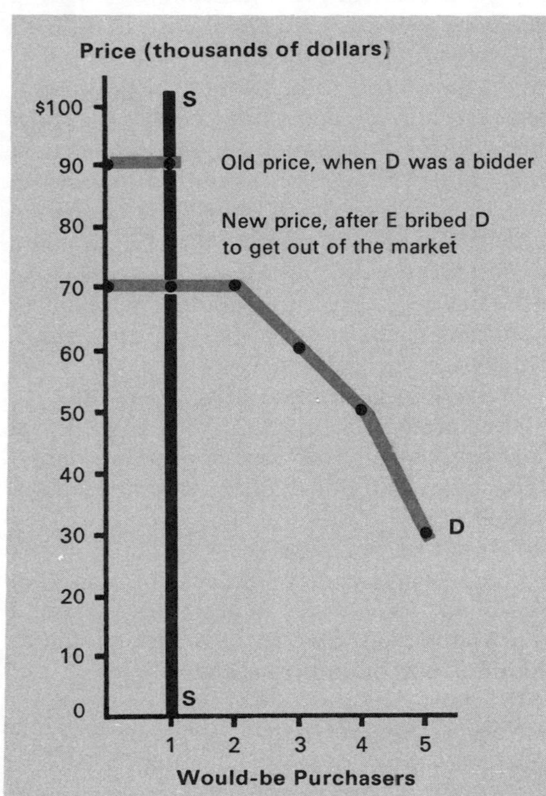

use geometrical or algebraic models to show how demand, supply, and price are interrelated, it is essential always to remember that what we are really studying is *human beings*, who may behave in ways quite different from what particular models suggest.

However, this only means that, if we want to use models for purposes of explaining or predicting human behavior, we must make sure the models fit people's behavior and not waste time pretending that the people's behavior must fit the models. So if some models do not work right, we must make new and better models. Actually, the result of D's collusion with E can easily be represented by a small change in our model—that is, by a downward shift in the demand schedule. After D's collusion with E, demand equalled price at slightly above $70 000, C's last bid, rather than at a bit above $90 000 as implied by the first model. This is shown in Figure 9-2.

RATIONING

The market mechanism not only sets a price but determines who gets what. To show how this **rationing** effect works, let us go back to our description of the bidding for the Rembrandt painting before the collusion between D and E.

In M's gallery, there was one painting to be disposed of and five people (six including the seller, M) who wanted it at some price. After the price was set at $91 000, everybody in the market was *satisfied*—or at least as satisfied as possible under the circumstances—for the following reasons.

M was satisfied because, although he would have been willing to sell his picture for any price higher than $30 000, his reservation price, he was delighted to get $91 000 for it. (We may tell you that M got the painting in the first place for only $10 000 from some careless person who did not check into its true value.)

E was satisfied both because she *got* the picture and because she got it for only $91 000, whereas she would have been willing to pay as much as $110 000. It was, in other words, worth more to her than she had to pay for it.

A, B, C, and D were satisfied because they *did not* spend more than the picture was worth to them. They were quite content to let E take the picture at that price.

NONPRICE RATIONING

What if price had not rationed demand in that way? How would the picture have been disposed of, to whom, and with what effect on the other would-be buyers?

Suppose that, for some reason, M had wanted to dispose of the painting for *less* than the maximum price he could get for his Rembrandt in the market. For instance, M might regard himself as a public benefactor and a patron of the arts who is not greedy. The Rembrandt had cost him only $10,000, so he decides that he is getting more than enough if he sells it for $20 000 and at the same time makes a valuable painting available to the public.

Who then will get the painting? Remember that all five would-be buyers are willing to go as high as $50 000. Thus, when M announces that his Rembrandt is offered for only $30 000, A, B, C, D, and E all say they want to buy it. Now M must make a decision as to which one of the five he shall give it to. (This has become *his* decision, and not simply a market decision.) Shall M give it to A, who was his father's business partner? Shall he give it to B, who is the same religion as M? Shall he give it to C, who represents the Museum of Art? Shall he give it to D, who is an old friend? Or shall he give it to E, who has been a good customer of his for years and who has an absolute passion for Rembrandt?

Obviously, M has a problem on his hands, which he can solve only by basing a decision upon his own personal values and objectives. To whom do you think M should give the painting for only $50 000? Is it more ethical or less ethical for M to sell the painting on the basis of sentimental, humanitarian, religious, or some other grounds than to let the picture go to the highest bidder?

Obviously, such a problem takes us beyond the boundaries of economics itself, into more philosophical territory. Some people would approve, for example, a decision by M to sell the picture to his co-religionist B, but others would say this is practicing religious discrimination against A, C, D, and E. Some might feel that friendship should be served in the case of D, but others would question M's motives. Some people would feel that C, the representative of the Museum of Art, should get the picture on the grounds that most people would see it there, but others would argue that, with all the great works of art that the Museum already has, this Rembrandt would do far more good and would find a more appreciative audience elsewhere. And some people would say that it would be far more ethical for M to reinstitute bidding for the painting and let the highest bidder, the one who values it most, take it, but others would protest that the best things of life should not necessarily go to those who are richest.

Whatever your own view, however, of who should get the Rembrandt, notice the main point, from the standpoint of economics: The interaction of buyers and sellers in a market, in determining the price of the good, also determines who will get the good. But this, as we have seen, is only one way of rationing goods. If we do not let the marketing price ration demand, then we must choose some *other* rationing system. Notice that any non-price system is likely to leave other would-be buyers, who can afford to buy the good but do not get it, dissatisfied. For instance, if M decides to sell the Rembrandt painting to B, all the others will feel that M discriminated against them.

EFFECT OF CHANGES IN DEMAND ON PRICE

In our study of price-elasticity of demand in Chapter 8, we noticed that changes in price caused the quantity of any good demanded to change—in the usual case, quantity demanded varied inversely with the change in price.

Now we have seen that changes in demand cause price to change—in the usual case, price will vary directly with demand. That is, increases in demand cause prices to rise, and decreases in demand cause prices to fall. This statement assumes that *supply remains the same* (is fixed).

We may now state the fundamental relations between demand, **fixed supply,** and price, as follows:

1. When, at a given price, the quantity

FIG. 9-3. CHANGE IN DEMAND FOR AND PRICE OF A PAINTING

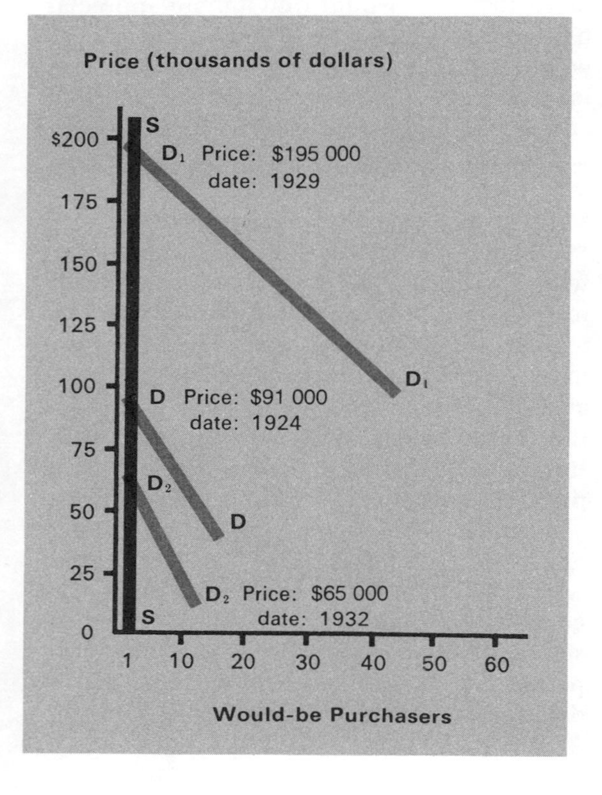

demanded exceeds the quantity supplied, price will be bid up.

2. When, at a given price, the quantity demanded is less than the quantity supplied, price will be reduced.

3. When the quantity demanded is brought into equality with the quantity supplied at the same price, the price will be at equilibrium—at rest. (See our discussion of equilibrium models in Chapter 6.)

Let us now use our case of the Rembrandt to illustrate these three situations. Suppose that the first auction of the painting, at which E purchased the "Lady with a Dog" for $91 000, occurred on January 14, 1924. Then suppose that, five years later, on January 23, 1929, E decides to sell her picture. How much will she get for it? There has been a rising boom in the stock market and prosperity in the nation as a whole. Art collectors are now much more wealthy than they were in 1924. There are also in 1929 more people interested in acquiring old masters. The museums are richer than they were, thanks to lavish gifts of private donors. In 1929, when E puts her Rembrandt, for which she paid $91 000, up for sale, it brings $195 000. How this happened is shown in Figure 9-3. The original demand schedule for the Rembrandt was at DD in 1924; then by 1929, the demand schedule had shifted upward to D_1D_1 and the price of the Rembrandt "Lady with a Dog" was bid up until it reached $195 000, where it was purchased by a wealthy investor named Mr. F. At that level, price was again in equilibrium since demand equalled supply.

Now three more years go by, and a lot has happened to the art market. The stock market has crashed in November, 1929, and many wealthy people have had their fortunes wiped out. (In 1932, art museums are receiving much smaller contributions from donors and are not able to bid as much as in 1929 for paintings.) Many people no longer can afford valuable works of art, and some who own rare paintings no longer want to keep them. Mr. F, the wealthy investor, has sustained huge financial losses in the stock market and decides that he must sell the Rembrandt painting for which he paid $195 000 in 1929. When Mr. F puts his picture up for sale on January 17, 1932, the demand schedule for Rembrandt's "Lady with a Dog" has dropped from D_1D_1 (where it was in 1929) to D_2D_2—below where it was back in 1924 when M sold it to E for $91 000. On January 17, 1932, F sells the picture to G for $65 000, the new equilibrium price.

Thus it is evident that changes in demand have been the critical factor in determining the market value of this old master. The actual paint and canvas of which the painting is physically composed is virtually worthless. If it should happen that the picture turned out to be a forgery, its price would fall from $65 000 in 1932 to some very low figure, perhaps less than $1000 (even a clever forgery is worth something), because buyers care about the authenticity of a picture and not just about its appearance.

If, on the other hand, the picture is not a forgery, business prosperity returns, art collectors recoup their fortunes, and tastes for Rembrandts grow as a result of the judgment of art critics—and the "Lady with a Dog" is judged to be one of the artist's very greatest works—then the demand will swing up again. By the year 1985, the Rembrandt painting, once purchased by M from the foolish seller in 1924 for $10 000—and originally painted by the master at a cost of a few guilder for paint, canvas, studio space, and model time plus the cost of his labor—might sell for $1 000 000 or even more.

OTHER CASES OF FIXED SUPPLY

You may suppose that the case of the old master used in this chapter is a rather special one, which of course it is. Yet it describes the fundamental relations among demand, supply, and price that can be found in any market. The only really special characteristic of our old master example is that it assumed that the supply was fixed (there was just one original painting named "Lady with a Dog" by Rembrandt, and its number could not be increased in response to any higher price, no matter how high the price went—excluding the possibility of forgery or of photographic reproduction).

But even that fixed-supply assumption is not particularly special. There are many examples of goods whose supply is essentially fixed, either in the short run or in the long run. For example, there was only one Elvis Presley. When he started his career, there was little demand for his services and he earned little. Later, when he became a famous personality, demand for his services increased enormously, and he was able to command very high prices for stage, TV or film appearances.

The supply of land along beaches in Nova Scotia is essentially fixed. If demand for that limited land climbs, its price will climb; if demand falls, its price will fall. People who own beach property will be richer or poorer depending on what happens to demand. Population growth will increase the demand for beach property; so will rising incomes, more vacation time and longer holidays among working people, and better highways and speedier transportation to beach areas. What may cause the demand for the fixed supply of beach land to fall?

Other examples of essentially fixed supply include (in the short run) the number of tables at the best restaurant in town, the number of habitable apartments in a city, the number of brain surgeons or pediatricians or licensed barbers in the nation, the number of used station wagons in the hands of a particular automobile dealer, the number of seats available for a Vancouver theater showing a hit musical, the number of hospital beds available in a community, the number of places for students at each Canadian university, the number of seats available on commercial aircraft flights between Montreal and Winnipeg, and the number of telephone communication channels between Regina and Fredericton.

There are plenty of examples of long-run fixed supply as well. These include the land at the southeast corner of Yonge and Bloor Streets in Toronto, the number of seats available for a hockey game in Edmonton, paintings by Ken Danby, the iron ore deposits in Labrador, the diamonds in South Africa, and the original pressings of the first album by the Beatles. All these are cases of long-run fixed supply, although exactly what one means by long-run may vary from case to case.

SUMMARY

In this chapter we have seen that, while the quantity demanded depends upon price, the actual price that is set in a market, where supply is fixed, depends upon changes in demand. In these circumstances, the following principles hold: (1) If, at a given price, the quantity demanded exceeds the quantity supplied, price will rise. (2) If, at a given price, the quantity demanded is less than the quantity supplied, price will fall. (3) When the quantity demanded equals the quantity supplied at the same price, price will be at rest.

The above three principles are statements of tendency and not rigid laws. Human actions may make actual prices in markets different from those implied by models based on false assumptions. But then one must design a new model to represent actual human behavior more faithfully, rather than junk the idea of using a model.

Market price rations the demand for any good. If price is not permitted to ration demand, some other rationing system—based on other than market values—must be used.

KEY CONCEPTS

market | rationing | fixed supply

QUESTIONS FOR REVIEW AND DISCUSSION

1. What is a *reservation price?* Give two examples of how reservation prices might be determined in particular markets.
2. If the supply is fixed, does it make sense to say that *both* demand and supply determine price, or can one simply say that in this case, since the supply is fixed, that demand alone determines price?
3. What is meant by *collusion?* How can collusion among buyers affect the price in markets with fixed supplies? Do you think collusion would work in the same way in markets where supplies were not fixed but varied with price changes?
4. Can you explain how prices act as rationing devices? What are some nonprice rationing devices that might be used instead of allowing market prices to determine who gets what? Would you prefer a price or a nonprice rationing system for Rembrandt paintings? Color TV sets? Milk? Polio vaccine? Why, in each case? Does your answer differ with each case and, if so, why?
5. If you pay $5000 for a plot of ground today, what will determine whether or not you will be able to sell the same plot of ground for more or less than $5000 at some date in the future?

PROBLEMS AND EXERCISES TO SHARPEN YOUR UNDERSTANDING

1. Using the data given to you at the end of Chapter 7 on the demand for ice cream in a typical city on a typical summer day, what would be the market price of ice cream if the supply of ice cream for that day was fixed at 10 000 litres?
2. How would this fixed supply be shown on a graph?
3. What would happen to the price of ice cream in (1) above if the demand for ice cream increased? If it decreased? How would these changes in demand for ice cream be shown on a graph?
4. If each litre of ice cream was demanded by a different person, how many people would be rationed out of the market at the price determined in (1) above? Is this price rationing system fair? What other system might be used to ration out the 10 000 litres of ice cream? Who would gain and who would lose if a nonprice rationing system were used?
5. Assume you inherit from a distant relative a collection of fifty oil paintings by Tom Thomson. Let us also assume these had been bought from the artist himself between 1900 and 1910 and that the very existence of the paintings had not been suspected by art critics, museums, etc. If you wanted to sell the paintings, what do you think would be the effect on the prices you would receive of each of the following:
   (a) offering all the paintings at the same time (i) as a group or (ii) individually?
   (b) offering them for sale singly over a ten-year period?
   (c) offering them for sale only to museums or public galleries?

CHAPTER 10

THE STOCK MARKET

■ WHAT IS THE STOCK MARKET? ■ HOW ARE THE VALUES OF SHARES OF STOCK DETERMINED? ■ STOCK INDEXES ■ MOVEMENTS IN THE STOCK MARKET AS A WHOLE ■ SUMMARY

On the surface it would appear that no two markets could differ more completely than the auction in an art gallery of a single painting that we studied in the last chapter, and the stock market, in which millions of individuals and business and financial institutions hold and exchange hundreds of millions of shares of stock.

Yet the same basic model that we used to explain the relationships among demand, supply, and price of a unique Rembrandt painting can be applied to the almost unbelievably complex stock market as a means of explaining the upswings and downswings in the average of all stock prices, or the rises and falls of the value of the stock of any single company or corporation. A share of **stock** may be defined as a certificate of ownership in a corporation. Legally, it represents a contract stating the terms under which the corporation accepts money from its owners, the stockholders. If the corporation is profitable, it usually pays part of its profits to the stockholders in the form of dividends of so much money per share of stock. In addition to buying stock in hopes of dividend income, many people buy stock in hopes that the value of each share of ownership, that is the stock itself, will increase in price.

■ WHAT IS THE STOCK MARKET?

Actually, there is no single **stock market** but rather many stock markets (or exchanges or bourses) in major cities of Canada, the United States, Britain, France, the Netherlands, Japan and many other countries throughout the world. All of these different stock markets do have some interconnections. In Canada there are a number of stock exchanges, of which two, the Toronto Stock Exchange and the Montreal Stock Exchange, account for most of the stock trading in this country.

There are two basic types of shares or stock issued by companies. **Common stock** represents the rights of the ordinary owner of a company. The proportion of a company that any individual shareholder owns is determined by the *number* of shares he holds. (If you own one share of Massey-Ferguson, for example, you own about 1/18 000 000th of the company. The value of your share depends on what it will currently bring in the stock market; in early 1979 Massey-Ferguson was selling for about $13 a share.)

Preferred stock is so called because those who own it have a right to receive dividends that the company pays out, or to get a share of the assets of the company should it be liquidated, before the common stockholders get anything. Common stock carries the right to vote on company matters; preferred stock usually does not.

Stock in corporations has the legal right of limited liability. If you buy one share of a

Canadian Pacific Limited

Here is what a stock certificate looks like. This one, obviously blank, would be issued to a buyer of less than one hundred shares. The seller, of course, ceases to be a shareholder and, if his certificate had been made out in his own name, it would be destroyed. The $5.00 par value indicates the original issue price or company valuation—not necessarily the market value after the shares have been issued, that is, after they are acquired by their first buyer. Remember that, with a few minor exceptions, purchases of shares through the exchanges are purchases of "second-hand" shares. Companies selling new or additional shares to raise more capital ordinarily have an investment dealer or underwriter act directly on their behalf to find buyers for new issues.

company for, say $100, all you can lose is the $100 you paid—you are not assuming the obligations of the corporation as a whole if it should fail and wind up owing millions of dollars, of which your theoretical share might be far greater than your original investment.

Originally, this feature of limited liability enabled corporations to raise the hundreds of millions of dollars from individual and business savers and investors that the corporations needed to establish huge industrial and financial organizations in a modern economy. The buyers were attracted because they could limit their potential loss to the price they paid for stock. The corporations benefitted by attracting investors who would not have been willing to risk their money if they had to become responsible for all the company's obligations—if, that is, their liability was unlimited.[1]

The companies listed on the stock exchanges represent the biggest firms in every important industry—aircraft, automotive,

[1] For a further discussion of limited and unlimited liability, see pages 162-165, Chapter 15.

Montreal Stock Exchange

The photo shows the trading floor of the Montreal Stock Exchange. On the floor are the traders who represent the brokers and other exchange members. On the back wall are massive quotation boards providing up-to-date information on all listed shares. This covers bid and offering prices, would-be buyers or sellers, number of shares sold during the day, and price ranges. The boards are linked to the floor by the trading "desks" in mid-floor, where transactions are recorded for the information system. Here, data processing equipment feeds the information onto the boards, into the exchanges' records, and out of the exchange across the nation to all who receive the constant electronic flow of data from the markets.

chemical, electrical, foods and commodities, machinery, oil and natural gas, retail trade, steel, utilities, and others. When you buy a share of stock, you own a piece of Canadian industry.

On any business day, widely scattered individuals who own stock will decide whether they want to buy more or get rid of all or part of the stock they are already holding. And some people who do not own any stock will be making up their minds about whether to buy into the market.

Those who decide that they do want to trade on a particular day will place orders to buy or sell securities listed with the stock exchange. They will usually do this by telephoning their buy or sell orders to a stockbroker. Often broker and customer will exchange some words about the state of the market and what might be a good stock to buy or get rid of.

The broker, once given instructions, will

wire or telephone these buy or sell orders to brokers' representatives on the floor of the stock exchange. There are many specific individuals at the exchanges representing brokerage firms all over the country; only these members are permitted to trade securities on the floor of the exchange. Therefore, any person wanting to buy or sell securities listed with the exchange must trade through a broker who is represented on the exchange.

The brokers' representatives on the floor of the exchange move swiftly to make deals that will bring together orders to buy and sell at the same price at the same time. They will hustle over to the trading post of the stock they want to buy or sell; each of the securities listed on the exchange has its own trading area at one point, or around one of the counters on the floor.

When a trade has been made on the floor of the exchange—say to exchange 100 shares of Massey-Ferguson at a price of $13.25 per share—word of this deal goes back to the brokers, who in turn notify their customers. Simultaneously, employees of the Stock Exchange send out word of this transaction on the stock ticker to machines in brokerages and other business and news offices all over the country. Newspapers in the major cities rush these stock quotations into print. And investors, reading the news in the papers or watching the stock tickers, decide whether or not to make further trades. They also keep a close eye on other news developments that may affect the value of individual stocks or the stock market in general, such as favorable reports on a company's profits or sales or unfavorable reports on the trend of the national economy.

HOW ARE THE VALUES OF SHARES OF STOCK DETERMINED?

Stock traders like to say that there is no such thing as the stock market, but rather a *market of stocks*. By this they mean that the stock of each corporation has a market value of its own. Any single stock may move with the general average of prices, or hang at about the same level while the market averages rise or decline, or move counter to the trend of the market as a whole.

The market value of any stock is determined basically, like the value of a Rembrandt painting, by what investors really *think* it is worth, as shown by their willingness or unwillingness to own it. Each investor who currently owns a share of stock in a company, continuously asks (unless he or she is sick or careless): "Do I want to continue holding this stock at its present price?" And each investor with money to invest (or other stocks or assets which could be liquidated to get money) continuously asks: "At its present price, should I be buying the stock of company X?"

What affects the judgment of investors as to whether a particular stock is worth holding? There are many factors, of which the following are the most important.

1. The Price-earnings Ratio

The **price-earnings ratio** (p-e ratio) is the earnings per share of a company[2] divided into the current market price of its stock. If a company, which we shall call GBM, is earning $1.00 per share in the current year, and its stock is now selling for $10.00 per share, its price-earnings ratio is 10.0:1. (When these are reported in the press, the 1 on the right hand side is ignored and the ratio colon is dropped also.)

$$\frac{\text{Price per share}}{\text{Earnings per share}} = \frac{\$10.00}{\$\ 1.00} = 10.0$$

Investors use this price-earnings ratio to

[2] If a company's current rate of annual earnings or profit is $16 million and it has 16 million shares outstanding, its earnings per share equals $1.00.

Reading Stock Exchange Data

Almost all papers carry exchange data, some in more detail than others. If GBM, referred to below, were to be found, it might appear as follows:

GBM 1400 10¼ 9¾ 10 + ½

This would mean exactly what the headings at the top indicate: Volume—1400 shares traded; High—$10.25, the highest price of the day; Low—$9.75, the lowest price of the day; Close—$10.00, the final or latest price of the day; Change of + ½, an increase of ½ or 50 cents from the close of the previous day to the closing price for the day being reported.

In addition to these, some papers will give E.P.S., earnings per share; P.E. ratio, price earnings ratio; Dividends paid; and Yield, which is the amount of dividends per share divided by the present cost. In other words, the percent return on your investment at present dividend and price levels.

compare the value of one company's stock with the stocks of similiar companies in the same industry. If GBM has a price-earnings ratio of 10, and its three major competitors, which are basically similar, have price-earnings ratios of 12,14 and 17, then GBM would normally look like a good buy.

But it is the *future* of the stock that matters most, not its past. So, if investors thought that GBM's earnings were likely to fall from $1.00 per share to only $.40 per share in the year ahead, GBM would *not* look like a good buy, because its *projected* price-earnings ratio would (at its current price of $10.00) be 25—or much higher than similar companies in its field.

Similarly, if the investor expected the earnings of another company (say, the All-out Corp., GBM's competitor that now has a price-earnings ratio of 14) to climb markedly because of a terrific new product with which All-out may capture most of the market, then All-out might look like a much better buy now than GBM, despite their respective current price-earnings ratios.

Investors may benefit from an increase in the earnings of a corporation in two ways: (1) through *capital gains* or (2) through an increase in *dividends*. A **capital gain** may be realized when the investor can sell the stock at a higher price than was originally paid for it because the price of the stock has increased in the market. A *dividend*[3] represents that part of earnings which the corporation distributes to stockholders; thus a corporation might earn $4.00 per share of its outstanding stock, and actually pay out as a dividend $2.00 per share to each stockholder (retaining the $2.00 balance for various corporate purposes, such as to pay for an increase in plant and equipment).

Anything that is likely to affect the future earnings of a company is likely to affect both dividends and the value of its stock. Several of these critical factors affecting future earnings are discussed below.

2. Business Trends in the Industry of Which the Company Is a Part

If, for example, the company is in the field of space exploration, and government contracts are going up, this may boost the sales, earnings, and stock value of the company. Or if industry sales are likely to decline in, say, the housing field, prospective earnings of a company selling building materials will

[3] References to dividends are often made by referring to the "yield" on a stock. This is the ratio of the current dividend rate per year to the present market value. For example, if GBM were paying dividends of $.85 per year, when its market value was $10.00, the yield to an owner of GBM shares would be 8.5%.

look bad to investors, and its stock price will fall.

3. Business Trends in the National Economy

If the national economy is likely to climb, the great majority of industries will be favorably affected; and stock prices of companies generally will reflect these anticipations of higher sales and earnings. Just the reverse will happen when a business recession is generally expected. But some companies will always buck a national decline, and others will lag or drop despite overall good business.

4. Company Management

Investors seek to appraise the particular situation of a company and its management from reports published in the business press; from studies by financial services and research organizations, including those of stock brokerages; and from whatever other sources of information are available—including rumors or observations of personal friends who know something about the company or work for it. If a company's presidency has been assumed by a brilliant new executive who is likely to shake things up, get rid of some managerial dead wood, strengthen some divisions of the company that have been earn-

Norris in Vancouver Sun

"What's Canada coming to ??. legalizing lotteries and gambling games."

Norris' cartoon illustrates, in rather wry form, the risks inherent in stock-buying. The name of the firm contains a number of puns based on the jargon of the stock market. Try to trace the sources of the names given to the firm.

FIG. 10-1. PRICE TRENDS: TORONTO AND NEW YORK STOCK EXCHANGES

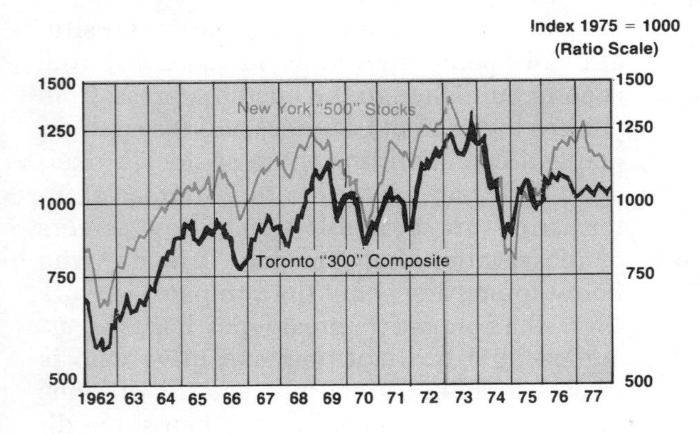

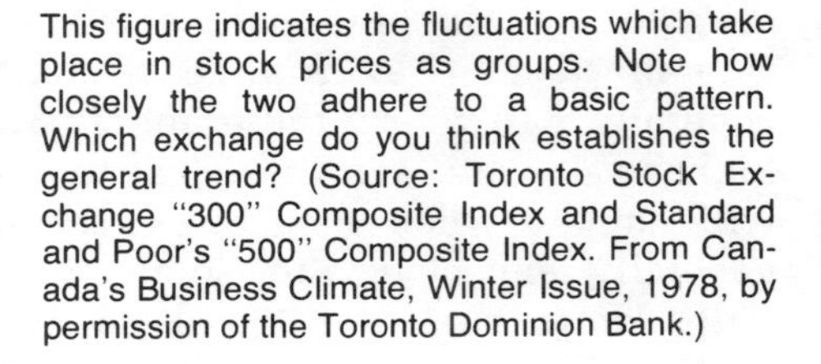
This figure indicates the fluctuations which take place in stock prices as groups. Note how closely the two adhere to a basic pattern. Which exchange do you think establishes the general trend? (Source: Toronto Stock Exchange "300" Composite Index and Standard and Poor's "500" Composite Index. From Canada's Business Climate, Winter Issue, 1978, by permission of the Toronto Dominion Bank.)

ing no money, and do a generally more effective sales job, the news that this president is in charge will affect the company's stock values favorably. If a company has acquired an outstanding group of research scientists and engineers, this news is likely to increase demand for the company's stock. But if key executives of a company are reportedly in conflict and some are resigning in disgruntlement, this will affect the value of a company's stock adversely.

STOCK INDEXES

Although each company's stock is affected by some factors peculiar to itself, there are nevertheless tidal waves that affect the stock market as a whole. Some companies may swim faster than the wave; others may swim against it. But all know that the great waves are strong forces affecting the values of all securities.

Measuring the overall waves in market activity requires that we have some sort of index number that will show ups and downs of selected stocks. Conceptually, it is simple to define an **index number**. If we let 100 stand for some number in the base year (such as sales of $5000 in the year 1970) then the index number for the year 1985 will rise to 150 if sales in 1985 rise to $7500. And if, in 1985, sales fall to $4000, the index number will fall to 80 (1970 = 100). The following formula sets forth the proportion for computing index numbers:

$$\frac{\text{Quantity in given year}}{\text{Quantity in base year}} = \frac{X}{100}$$

or

$$\text{Index for any year} = \frac{\text{Quantity in given year}}{\text{Quantity in base year}} \times 100$$

Actually, computing an index for an entire stock market is, however, a very complex statistical problem, for there are hundreds of companies listed on the stock exchange; each with varying amounts of stock outstanding, and all selling at different prices.

For our purposes it is unnecessary to discuss the details of how stock indexes are compiled and weighted to produce a more or less accurate index of movements in the market as a whole. There are many indexes, all of which use somewhat different procedures in their construction but which nearly always show similar movements. All of these indexes are constructed by taking a base year or period of years, finding the weighted average of the value of certain selected stocks in that base period, and calculating averages for subsequent dates. Each stock price index makes adjustments for changes in the number of shares of stock outstanding of the companies included in the index. If this adjustment were not made when additional shares were issued, then the stock price index would tend to misrepresent the changes in value of the stocks listed. Owning shares of a company is essentially like owning "shares" of a painting, to use our old example. If in 1960 a painting is worth $1000 and J owns 100 percent of it, the one "share" is obviously worth $1000. If in 1970, J sells half-interest in the picture to K, then (if the picture is still worth $1000) each of the two "shares" held is worth only $500. But if we want to see what happened to the value of the painting, we should adjust for the number of "shares" issued. In fact, of course, the value of the painting had not changed from 1960 to 1970. If in 1980, the "shares" of J and K in the painting are *each* worth $1000, the value of the picture has actually doubled from the years 1970 to 1980, since the painting is now worth $2000.

The stock market averages make similar adjustments to take account of changes in the number of shares of stock outstanding, in order to ensure that the index will reflect only price movements.

In effect, then, a stock exchange index shows us price movements of a *fixed supply* of the rights of ownership in its companies. Whenever the demand for ownership of these companies moved up, the index moved up. When demand for shares of these companies fell, the index fell.

FIG. 10-2. HOW CHANGES IN DEMAND AFFECT THE STOCK MARKET

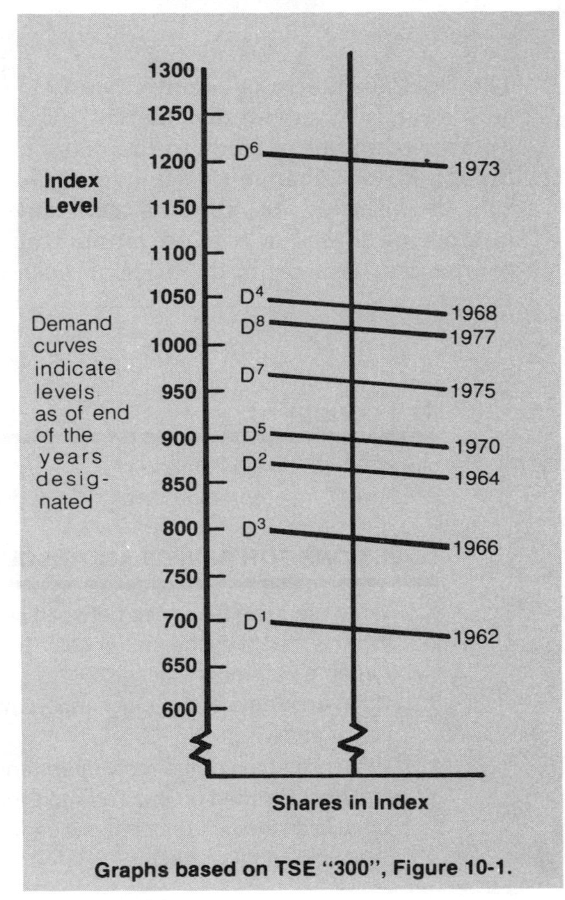

This figure illustrates the changes in demand for shares of stock over a fifteen year period as they have been reflected by the level of the TSE "300" at the end of each chosen year. Where would the present level of the TSE "300" fit into this figure?

MOVEMENTS IN THE STOCK MARKET AS A WHOLE

If the trends illustrated in Figure 10-1 were to be projected back to the earlier part of the century, we would find the same basic pattern, a long-term upward movement with shorter-term fluctuations both up and down. The long-term pattern is produced in part by growing levels of profitability associated with real growth in the economy, partly by inflationary trends which boost stock prices in the long run, and partly by increasing demand for shares.

Over the shorter time periods, due to factors such as those mentioned in the previous section plus many other economic pressures, the demand for shares may alter considerably. The result is the up and down movements in prices for individual companies and for market trends as a whole. These shifts in demand can be illustrated, as in Figure 10-2, by normal demand curve techniques. The demand shifts reflect the willingness or unwillingness of investors to buy or hold shares at existing price levels.

SUMMARY

The stock exchange is essentially an example of a fixed-supply market. The number of shares of stock in the market, though it does change slowly over time, can be adjusted to show a constant number of shares in a fixed number of companies. Changes in the price of those stocks depend, then, upon upswings and downswings in the demand of investors for those stocks.

Investor demand for stocks depends upon a number of factors, especially the price-earnings ratio, the trend of particular industries and of the national economy, and expectations about specific companies and appraisals of the quality of their management.

KEY CONCEPTS

stock	stock market	preferred stock	capital gain
dividends	common stock	price-earnings ratio	index number

QUESTIONS FOR REVIEW AND DISCUSSION

1. What are the differences between common stock and preferred stock?
2. What is meant by the statement, "There is no such thing as the stock market, but rather 'a market of stocks' "?
3. What are some of the most important factors affecting the market price of a particular stock?
4. What are some of the most important factors affecting the average price of all of the stocks traded on the Toronto Stock Exchange?
5. What is an index number? How can an index number be used to keep a record of changing stock prices?

PROBLEMS AND EXERCISES TO SHARPEN YOUR UNDERSTANDING

1. Choose a public Canadian corporation to (a) get as much information about its activities over the past two years as is possible, and (b) observe during the rest of the school year.
2. Trace the value of the company's stock during this period and try to find explanations for changes in value.
3. Analyse your company's shares against general market trends. Have the shares performed better or worse than market averages? Can you offer any explanation for the relative performance?
4. Research the "Great Crash" of 1929 from both Canadian and American perspectives. Why did the stock market "crash" take place? Did the "crash" cause the "Great Depression"? An excellent basic book on the "crash" is *The Great Crash* by John Kenneth Galbraith, Boston: Houghton Mifflin, 1961. For a Canadian perspective, read chapter 12 in *Decisive Decades* by A. B. Hodgetts and J. D. Burns, Thomas Nelson and Sons (Canada) Limited, 1973.

CHAPTER 11

SURPLUSES AND SHORTAGES

■ DOWNTOWN PARKING PROBLEMS ■ DINNERS AT A FINE RESTAURANT ■ SOCIAL VALUES AND RATIONING PROBLEMS ■ SUMMARY

In the preceding chapters we have observed how prices *tend* to rise or decline in response to shifts in demand until a new equilibrium between demand and supply is established.

However, in the real world, market prices do not necessarily adjust to that point where they bring about a nice balance between demand and supply. When prices fail to rise enough to bring about equality between demand and supply, *shortages* result; and when prices fail to fall enough to bring about equality between demand and supply, *surpluses* result. Imbalances between supply and demand at current prices confront policy makers in business, government, or nonprofit institutions with some of their most difficult problems. In this chapter we shall examine a few such problems—all of which may affect you quite personally.

■ DOWNTOWN PARKING PROBLEMS

Let us now consider a quite different type of shortage-surplus problem: the rationing of downtown parking space, which is an acute problem in virtually all cities. Downtown merchants want their customers to be able to drive to their stores and park conveniently—or they will lose sales. The customers, on their side, want to avoid wasting time looking for some place to park (or spending a lot of money putting their cars into off-street garages or parking lots); otherwise they will shop in the suburbs.

The mayor and other city officials want downtown businesses to prosper, so that they can collect enough taxes from them to help pay for all the city's facilities, police, schools, welfare costs, and similar items. So they would like to make more parking space available on the streets for shoppers. But the people who *live* downtown and own cars would like to be free to leave their cars on the street.

There is only so much parking space along the streets in the downtown area. How can parking space best be rationed, especially since some of the time the streets are heavily crowded with traffic and at other times the streets are virtually deserted?

Take the mythical case of Crane City. On weekdays, the downtown area of Crane City is choked with private cars, delivery trucks, taxis, and buses during the business hours from 09:00 to 18:00.

The downtown area of Crane City is still fairly busy during the evening hours from 18:00 to 24:00, when many people go out to restaurants, movies, theaters, concerts, sporting events, and other social or entertainment activities in town.

From 24:00 to 09:00, the streets downtown in Crane City are deserted. The mayor of Crane City, Peter Rossi, wants to install parking meters to reduce downtown congestion during the day and evening hours. But, before installing a system of parking meters and before deciding how much to charge for an hour of parking, Mayor Rossi asks the Crane City Planning Commission to do a survey of the supply and demand for downtown parking spaces.

In the congested center of the town, the

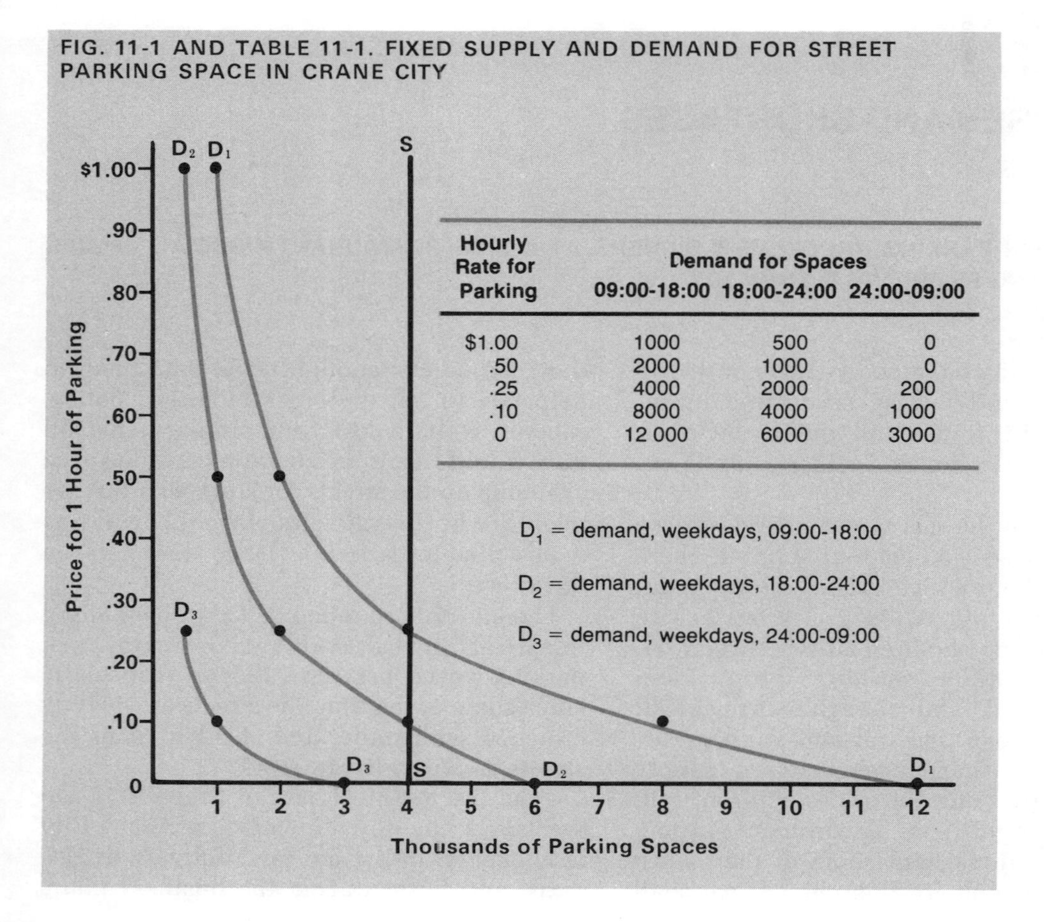

FIG. 11-1 AND TABLE 11-1. FIXED SUPPLY AND DEMAND FOR STREET PARKING SPACE IN CRANE CITY

Hourly Rate for Parking	Demand for Spaces 09:00-18:00	18:00-24:00	24:00-09:00
$1.00	1000	500	0
.50	2000	1000	0
.25	4000	2000	200
.10	8000	4000	1000
0	12 000	6000	3000

Commission finds, there are 4000 parking spaces. And the Commission's survey finds that the demand for parking space is as shown in Figure 11-1—depending on the time of the day and the amount to be charged.

Should Crane City install parking meters and if so, how much should it charge for an hour of parking time? These are the two key questions that the Mayor puts to his Commission.

The Commission recommends installing meters. If this is not done, then (the data indicate) the city will normally have 12 000 *cars* fighting for 4000 downtown parking spaces from 09:00 to 18:00 during business days. Those people who most want to park, in order to do their shopping, may be unable to because most of the street spaces will be occupied by people who live downtown (and can easily find spaces first), or by the downtown merchants themselves. Many shoppers will take their time about moving their cars, if they do not have to pay for space. But other would-be shoppers will be forced either to buy much more expensive off-street parking or to shop elsewhere. The Mayor accepts the Commission's recommendation to install meters.

But how much should the hourly charge be?

Should Crane City charge $.25 for one hour of parking? That would make the 4000 automobile drivers who are willing to spend

$.25 an hour to park equal the 4000 parking spaces available from 09:00 to 18:00.

But from 18:00 to 24:00, there would be only 2000 spaces occupied at a price of $.25. And from 24:00 until 09:00, there would be virtually no spaces occupied at $.25 an hour.

In the evening, from 18:00 to 24:00, the restaurant owners and other downtown businesspeople would resent the city's making it unnecessarily expensive for their customers to park. The customers would resent it even more, since they would have to rush out of theaters to feed parking meters.

From 24:00 to 09:00, there would be even more resentment from downtown residents about the high parking charges and the impossible inconvenience of having to keep feeding the parking meters through the night when the streets are deserted.

Clearly, says the Planning Commission, if Crane City charges $.25 from 09:00 to 18:00, it can bring about a balance between an hourly demand of 4000 and a supply of 4000 parking spaces.

But from 18:00 to 24:00, recommends the Commission, the city ought to reduce the hourly meter charge to $.10; this will balance supply and demand at 4000. From 24:00 to 09:00, says the Commission's report, its object is to raise some extra money from the parking meters. At $.10 an hour, it can take in $100 an hour from the 1000 parking spaces that would be occupied. But against this, the city would have to pay for the additional costs of hiring nighttime collectors or extra policemen to patrol the streets and give tickets for overtime parkers. More seriously, the town's officials would have to cope with the complaints of downtown residents and taxpayers who would bitterly object to having to pay for parking when there was absolutely no problem in finding enough space to park.

Thus, the Crane City Planning Commission recommended to Mayor Rossi that the city charge $.25 an hour from 09:00 to 18:00 for curb parking, $.10 an hour from 18:00 to 24:00, and free parking from 24:00 to 09:00.

Alberta Government Photo

As this Edmonton street scene indicates, space on city streets for cars and trucks is not a free good. How can the shortage of space be rationed? Obviously, parking meters provide one means of rationing space available along the curbs. But what might be done to ration the rest of the space on city streets? Would more costly license fees do this? Higher toll charges on bridges or expressways? Any other ideas?

However, the mayor and the other city commissioners rejected this advice. They installed the parking meters at a charge of $.10 an hour from 09:00 to 18:00, because they were impressed by the complaints of those who objected to paying $.25 an hour when other nearby communities charged less for street parking. Even downtown store owners were afraid of the $.25 hourly meter fee, for they suspected that it would keep too many cars out of the downtown area and actually hurt their business.

So it is still difficult to park downtown in Crane City on working days, though one-third less difficult on the average than it was before the $.10 meters were installed. In the evenings, parking is still a moderate prob-

FIG. 11-2. GETTING A TABLE AT "LE GOURMET" (CAPACITY: 100 PEOPLE)

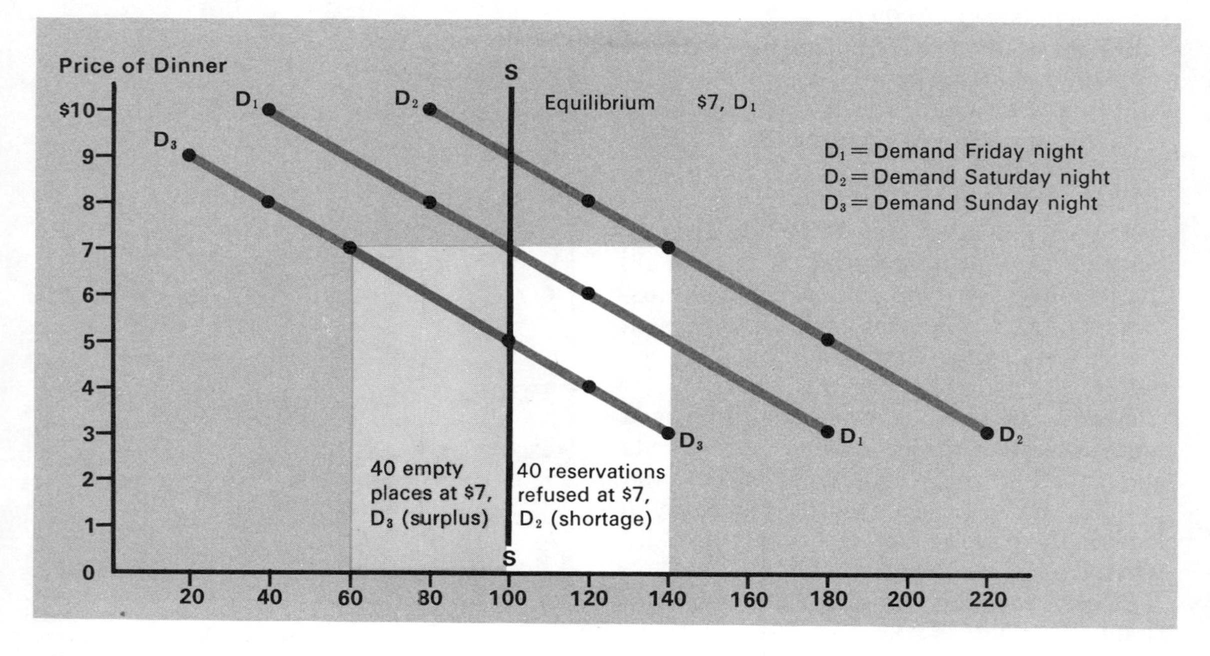

lem, but from night till morning, it is no problem at all. The city collects $400 an hour from parking meters (4000 meters × $.10), or $3600 a day from 09:00 to 18:00 on business days.

Everyone is pretty happy, except those frustrated drivers (4000 each hour) who still cannot find a place to park downtown from 09:00 to 18:00, and who either have to put their cars onto parking lots or garages for as much as $1 per hour, or park outside the central area, or leave their cars home and ride the buses, or shop elsewhere. The downtown merchants are still worried about the loss of customers to the suburbs because of the shortage of downtown parking space, though the situation seems moderately improved since the $.10 meters were installed. Did the city make a mistake in not choosing $.25 parking meters?

DINNERS AT A FINE RESTAURANT

Some business managers find themselves in a situation where, with a fixed supply of goods or services to sell and a rather rigid price structure, their market keeps swinging from balance to surplus to shortage and back again. These swings around a balance point confront managers with a difficult problem, if they are to avoid hurting their customers by not being able to take care of them or hurting themselves by not having enough customers to take care of.

Take the case of a fine fictional Montreal restaurant called Le Gourmet—Gaston Elouard, proprietor. M. Elouard can take care of 100 diners a night, and no more. He puts out a splendid dinner for which he charges a *prix fixe*—a fixed price—of $7.00. Each such dinner costs him $3.00.

Table 11-2: THE BUSINESS PICTURE AT "LE GOURMET" (CAPACITY: 100 PEOPLE)

Price of Dinner	Cost of Dinner	Profit per Dinner	Demand, Friday Night	Total Profit, Friday Night	Demand, Saturday Night	Total Profit, Saturday Night	Demand, Sunday Night	Total Profit, Sunday Night
$10.00	$3	$7.00	40	$280	80	$560	0	0
9.00	3	6.00	60	360	100	600	20	120
8.50	3	5.50	70	385	110	605	30	165
8.00	3	5.00	80	400	120	600	40	200
7.50	3	4.50	90	405	130	585	50	225
7.00	3	4.00	100	400	140	560	60	240
6.50	3	3.50	110	385	150	525	70	245
6.00	3	3.00	120	360	160	480	80	240
5.00	3	2.00	140	280	180	360	100	200
4.00	3	1.00	160	160	200	200	120	120
3.00	3	0.00	180	0	220	0	140	0

On three successive nights one week, M. Elouard's business swung from good to *too* good to bad. On Friday night, 100 people came to Le Gourmet, and M. Elouard seated all of them. On Saturday night, 140 people sought tables at Le Gourmet, but M. Elouard had to turn 40 customers away. They were bitterly unhappy. But on Sunday night, Le Gourmet had only 60 customers and 40 empty places. (see Figure 11-2.)

As a result, M. Elouard served his $7 dinner to 260 people during the three nights, Friday, Saturday, and Sunday, and made a profit of $1040 (because he made $4 on each dinner—the difference between a $7 price and a $3 cost). However, M. Elouard suspected that he could have made more money (1) if he could have charged a higher price and thus disposed of the less affluent guests on *Saturday* night, while seating some of the richer people he had been forced to turn away, and (2) if he had charged a *lower* price on *Sunday* night, and filled some of those empty 40 places with people who might have come to eat his special dinner at a bargain price.

The complete demand, price, and profit situation facing M. Elouard on the three nights was as shown in Table 11-2.

Bearing in mind that the maximum number of diners M. Elouard can take care of any night at Le Gourmet is 100, how could he have made the most profit? Would he have been better off to charge $8 than $7? How about $9? And what if he had announced a new policy, establishing a price for his special dinner of $7.50 on Friday nights, $9.00 on Saturday nights, and $6.50 on Sunday nights? Would that have given him the largest total profit? Would such a flexible pricing policy be feasible, if desirable?

What prices should M. Elouard charge to fill his restaurant on each of the three nights? Would it make sense for him to do that in terms of his *total* profit? What if he charged a low enough price to fill the restaurant (regardless of profit) each night—say, $5.00—would he be doing a favor to his customers? What about the 40 people he would have to turn away on Friday night and the 80 people he would turn away on Saturday night? Would he make more friends among those who got a bargain or lose more among those who could never count on getting a table? Would he not then be tempted to favor his friends or people he liked and discriminate against people he did not know or did not like? Is this a good thing or a bad thing from the standpoint of society? What if M. Elouard is a biased man, who practises racial discrimination? What if he is a snob? On the other hand, what if he is a champion of modest and simple folk, and does not like people who look too wealthy or proud?

In brief, is it better to let the price system

discriminate or is it better, from a social standpoint, to have M. Elouard underprice his meals and discriminate among his customers on personal grounds?

If meals are underpriced at Le Gourmet relative to the demand for those meals, will customers anxious to get a table not begin to make excessively large tips to win the patron's favor or, if there is a headwaiter, to slip him extra sums of money in order to be seated when others are waiting?

SOCIAL VALUES AND RATIONING PROBLEMS

Economics, as we have noted earlier, is basically about scarcity. The scarcity of goods confronts us with a host of rationing problems that force us to think very hard about our social values. When should we let market prices and the incomes of customers ration available goods and when should we use other criteria and rationing techniques in the case of each of the following things?

Library books (old books, scholarly books, newly acquired popular novels or nonfiction); school supplies; tickets for commencement exercises at high school graduation; tickets for symphony orchestra concerts; tickets for Shakespeare plays; the supply of housing near a military base in wartime; the supply of butter and meat in wartime; space on commercial airlines in wartime; education in the primary grades, secondary grades, college, graduate school, or adult education; drugs and pharmaceuticals; innoculations with anti-polio vaccine; lunches for school children; admission to art museums; access to tennis courts and golf links; use of the national parks, like Jasper or Fundy; services of psychoanalysts and psychiatrists; services of lawyers for people charged with criminal offenses; admission to school football games; care for old people in nursing homes; food and clothing for flood victims; food and clothing for families with incomes below $5000 a year; books in braille for the blind; books for people in less-developed countries; fire extinguishers in homes; use of superhighways; use of tunnels and bridges; membership in churches or synagogues; membership in country clubs; beachfront property along the Atlantic coast; and lakefront property in the mountains.

The primary justification for the use of market price as a rationing device is this: In a free society, people who most want a good and are willing to back their desire with cash should have it. People should pay for what they get and not expect others to pay for them. And sellers of goods or services are entitled to get the value for their property that is established in a free market.

But the primary justification for the use of other devices than market price for rationing limited goods is this: There are cases where undue harm would be done to individuals or to society if market price were permitted to do the rationing. And there are social goals (such as health, education, or equality of opportunity) that may sometimes best be served by distributing goods or services on a wholly or partially subsidized non-market basis. This may, however, produce a shortage of supply relative to demand and necessitate nonprice rationing (as, for instance, by putting popular library books on short loans, restricting seats at a graduation to parents of graduates only, limiting the time permitted any one player on a public tennis court, or limiting the food and drink that any single flood victim may have).

In each of the cases listed above, which principle—market price or nonprice rationing—should apply? Are there some cases in which *both* principles should be applied? If so, how can they be reconciled or combined? Do private sellers of goods ever use nonprice rationing devices ("one to a customer"; "take a number and wait your turn"; "I've been saving this for *you*, Mrs. Gilhooley"; "I'm sorry, but I don't think you would like this neighborhood"; "Sorry, these tables are reserved"; "Sorry, no vacancies"; and so on)? If nonprice rationing is to be done, is it better done by society or by individuals? Is it better done according to legal principles or according to individual judgments of each situation or of each would-be customer?

SUMMARY

In this chapter we have studied the way surpluses or shortages of goods and services result from the failure or inability of market price to rise or decline enough to bring about a balance between demand and supply. When demand exceeds supply at a given price, and price does *not* rise sufficiently, shortages result. When demand is less than supply at a given price, and price does not fall sufficiently, surpluses result.

Particular institutions do not always wish to rely on market price to ration demand—that is, to bring about equality between demand and supply. For instance, colleges and universities often prefer to have more applications than they are willing to accept, in order to choose the best students, according to their own criteria. And although business executives might wish to establish a price that would bring demand into closer balance with supply, they may be unable sometimes to do so, because of factors peculiar to their situation (such as the market for tables at a popular restaurant).

Difficult problems of social values and principles are involved in deciding which goods and services should be made available to the public on a subsidized basis, with nonprice rationing to handle the excess demand, and which should be kept within the regular market economy, with price doing the rationing by bringing demand and supply into equilibrium.

QUESTIONS FOR REVIEW AND DISCUSSION

1. Should a city try to set the price on its parking meters at a level that would always equate supply and demand? What might be some of the difficulties in adopting such a policy? What might be some of the advantages?
2. Why is some normal surplus of seats usually available at current prices at most sports stadiums? Is lowering the price to get rid of these surpluses always a good idea? Why or why not?
3. How would a flexible pricing policy (different prices at different times, or different prices to different groups—half price for children under 18, and so on) help solve the surplus problem at sports stadiums? At movie theaters? At restaurants? What are some of the problems involved with a flexible pricing policy?

PROBLEMS AND EXERCISES TO SHARPEN YOUR UNDERSTANDING

Select one of the cases listed above, and draw a supply and demand diagram illustrating the number of people who would buy the good or service at a market equilibrium price, compared to the number who would buy it at a price set above the market equilibrium, and compared to the number of people who would want to buy it at a price below the market equilibrium price. Label the axes and all other parts of your diagram clearly, and be able to explain in words what your diagram shows.

CHAPTER 12

VARIATIONS IN SUPPLY AND DEMAND

■ THE PROFIT MOTIVE ■ PRICE-TAKERS AND PRICE-SEARCHERS ■ POLICY PROBLEMS OF PRICE-TAKERS ■ OPPORTUNITY COST ■ CONSTRUCTING A SUPPLY SCHEDULE ■ SUPPLY AND DEMAND: THE MARKET MODEL COMPLETED ■ OTHER CASES OF VARIABLE SUPPLY AND DEMAND ■ ELASTICITY OF SUPPLY ■ SUMMARY

Up to now we have been studying market situations in which the supply of goods is fixed, while demand fluctuates up or down. We have seen that in the real world there are plenty of situations where the quantity supplied of some goods does not vary appreciably, regardless of how much demand and price may change. Among such fixed-supply cases we have considered those of the markets for a work of art, shares of stock of one corporation or of all the companies listed on the Toronto Stock Exchange, and others.

Now we must turn to an even more common class of market cases—those where the quantity of goods or services that people are willing to sell, as well as the quantity that people are willing to buy, is *variable*. Often the quantity supplied changes as the price of a good or a service changes and a *supply schedule* tells us how much of a particular good or service will be supplied under certain carefully defined conditions.

Generally speaking, the higher the price, the more units of a good will be offered by suppliers. Thus the supply schedule normally slopes upward. We must now study how suppliers interact with their customers.

■ THE PROFIT MOTIVE[1]

To begin, we must make explicit an assumption about the behavior of producers or suppliers of goods. We shall assume that the aim of producers is *to make as much profit as possible within the constraints of the laws and customs and pressures of their environment.*

There is actually a good deal of debate among economists as to whether the assumption that business seeks to maximize profits closely corresponds to the actual behavior of manufacturers, farmers, or other producers. Certainly not all individuals are equally motivated by the aim of making money. Some people put professional or artistic accomplishments above profit. Some aim mainly at winning fame, or power, or a reputation for social responsibility or patriotism. Some regard their business careers as stepping stones to political office. And some may primarily seek a quiet life rather than maximum profits.

Some people may be motivated chiefly by their social or psychological biases. Hatred, personal insecurity, or racial and religious prejudice may move some individuals to act against their own business interests. Indeed, the eighteenth century author, Samuel Johnson, once remarked that he thought a person was never so innocently engaged as when making money. But not all people are "innocent"; some may refuse to hire Blacks, Jews, Catholics, or others not because of, but at the *expense* of, profit. Others may refuse to sell real estate at a better price to minority groups against whom they are prejudiced rather than to those of their own race, reli-

[1] In conjunction with this, it might be appropriate to examine the Toronto-Dominion Bank reading on "The Role of Profits" reprinted at the end of Chapter 15.

gion, or national background. Bigotry may frequently come at a loss rather than a profit. In addition, it should also be pointed out that not only is such behavior morally wrong, in general it is also contrary to the law.

Whether people's motives are regarded as worthy or unworthy, however, it is clearly an oversimplification to say that people are motivated solely by the aim of making as much profit as possible. Although some may come close to behaving as though making as much money as possible were their sole aim in life, people are more complex in their aims. This applies to those in business as well as to any other group of people. For instance, some businesspeople may care about producing the best quality of products as an end in itself, even though maintaining or improving quality may involve making less than the largest possible immediate profit. However, business executives commonly contend that making a better product will, in the long run, increase their profits.

Long-run considerations rather than immediate profits also affect business decisions in many other respects, such as the types of services or courtesies businesses provide to customers, their willingness to replace a product if the customer finds it defective, their decisions not to take advantage of an opportunity to raise prices in the short-run if they think customers would resent it, and concerns about the welfare or morale of their employees. Obviously, however, businesspeople differ considerably among themselves in all these respects. On prices and profits, for example, some are what an economist, John R. Hicks, calls "stickers" while others are "snatchers". "Stickers" try to stick to their existing prices, as they worry about the long-run relationship with their customers, while "snatchers" try to snatch the greatest possible price and profit immediately. What would be the expected behavior of each type in a situation like a prolonged heat wave? In such an emergency, in what fields would the division between the two groups quickly become apparent?

Even if producers cared only about making as much profit as possible as fast as possible, nowadays they would encounter all kinds of limitations that would prevent their behaving the way some ruthless employers behaved in the late eighteenth and early nineteenth centuries. Statute laws now prevent employers from exploiting child labor or from working their employees too many hours a day. Other laws require employers to install safety devices on their machinery and in their factories; to safeguard the health of their workers against silicosis, radiation poisoning, or dangers of mine disasters; to pay minimum wages; to bargain collectively with their workers over wages and working conditions; to describe accurately their merchandise to consumers; and not to fix prices in collusion with other companies.

Employers face many other types of constraints on their ability to make maximum profits. They often face pressures from their workers to slow down the pace of production, to lighten work loads, or to hold off from introducing new labor-saving machinery. Workers may demand not only higher pay than the employer wants to give but may put on pressure for longer relief breaks from the production line or time off for holidays, shorter working hours, or seniority preferences for dismissal from jobs or for rehiring.

Yet, even though aware of all the different types of constraints imposed upon business by laws, pressures of employees and customers, together with the civic concerns or personal morality of businesspeople themselves, the great majority of businesspeople still regard maximizing profit as their cardinal aim. Indeed, they generally insist upon this point and complain because the public does not understand the importance of profits. They call our economy a *profit* system, or, more exactly, a *profit-and-loss* system.

While it is doubtless an oversimplification, we will probably find that we can come *reasonably* close to explaining most business behavior if we assume that businesses ordinarily *aim to maximize profits (or minimize losses) within existing constraints.* This will hold for the vast majority of cases.

FIG. 12-1. HOW DEMAND FOR WHEAT LOOKS TO THE INDIVIDUAL FARMER (A PRICE-TAKER)

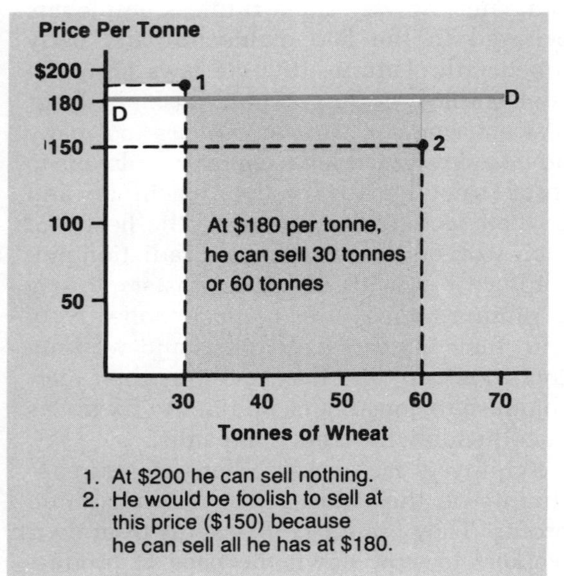

If you doubt this, ask yourself some simple questions. Would the head of a large corporation prefer to have the company earn $35 million rather than $30 million? Would that President prefer a salary of $100 000 rather than one of $75 000? Would a hardware store owner prefer to clear $17 000 from the business in a year rather than $16 000? Would the owner prefer to sell that business for $100 000 rather than $90 000? Would *you* rather sell your used typewriter for $20 or $19? If you think the answer to all those questions is "yes, under normal circumstances," then the assumption that suppliers seek to maximize profits should impress you as reasonable.

The chief question that usually concerns business is not *whether* to maximize profits but *how* to maximize profits. The answer to that question varies from producer to producer depending on (1) the prices that can be charged, (2) the costs of doing business, and (3) the volume of business that can be done.

PRICE-TAKERS AND PRICE-SEARCHERS

Managers and owners of businesses differ in their ability to set a price and hold to it. Some are *price-takers,* others are *price-searchers.*

Price-takers

Price-takers are producers who must accept as given the price that exists in the market for their products. They alone are unable to increase that price without losing all sales, and it would be foolish of them to cut that price because they can sell all they have at the market price. This is the situation that faces, say, a farmer who can sell *all* of the wheat he produces at the going market price. He will not sell one tonne if he tries to hold out for a higher price.[2] And it would be silly of him, since he can sell everything he has produced at the existing price, to offer his supply of wheat at a price below the market level.

The situation that faces our farmer as a price-taker may then be depicted as a perfectly elastic demand curve for his product (Figure 12-1). If, at a going price of $180 per tonne, the farmer offers 30 tonnes for sale, he will sell all of it; if he offers 60 tonnes at $180, he will sell it all, too. But if he tries to sell his wheat at $200 a tonne, arguing that it cost him that much to produce it, he will sell none of it. Few care how much it cost the farmer to produce it (except the farmer himself).

The same sort of situation affects many individual producers. Inshore fishermen, woodlot operators and others in primary industries are especially affected by this situa-

[2] If he were operating in a completely free market without any government income stabilization plans, he might wish to hold his wheat off the market, gambling that the market price might later go higher. However, since he alone could not affect the future price any more than he can affect the present price, it is quite likely that the future price might be lower rather than higher than the present price, despite the fact that he had held his wheat off the market.

tion—while often facing costs set in markets where there is much less price competition.

The characteristics of the type of market in which the individual producer is a price-taker are these:

1. The product is relatively homogeneous—so it is extremely easy and natural for customers to substitute the output of one producer for that of another.

2. There are lots of producers—enough so that if any one producer tries to raise the price above the market level or hold goods off the market, this will have no appreciable effect on the overall market, and that producer alone will be affected by the loss of sales, revenue, and profits.

Price-searchers

The situation facing the **price-searcher** differs from that of the price-taker in both of those fundamental respects. The characteristics of a market in which the individual producer is a price-searcher are these:

1. The product of the price-searcher is recognizable and exclusive in some way, so that some people will continue to want to buy the product, even if it costs more than competing ones (although some sales may be lost).

2. Although there may be several other producers of the product or close substitutes for it, the price-searcher deals in a market that *is* affected by his or her own decisions on *what price to charge* or *how many units to produce and offer for sale.*

The price-searcher may be able to affect the market price, either because it is a very small market, which is cut off from outside competition and in which the producer is a relatively "*big fish*" or the producer may be so big that that firm's decisions on prices set the level for the whole industry. Or the price-searcher may be the producer of a good for which there are few or no acceptable substitutes.

Here are some examples of these different types of price-searchers.

1. The "big fish in little ponds": a local builder who can determine prices without too much concern about outside competition, the company with a concession to operate an airport restaurant, the one playhouse doing live productions in a small city where many people want to see live theater, the grocer in a relatively isolated town.

2. The "big fish in big ponds": the Steel Company of Canada, Alcan Aluminum, International Nickel, General Motors, MacMillan-Bloedel, and other large producers of products which, though they may face competition in the market, can still affect by their own individual actions the market price of a product.

3. Sellers of unique goods; producers of goods on which they hold special patents, such as particular copy machines, drugs or pharmaceuticals, machine tools, or systems of shorthand; makers of fine violins or cellos, of specially ground and blended coffee, ceramics, high-style fashion clothes, handmade jewelry; and all other kinds of goods or services that are identifiable as the product of a particular producer and are desirable for that reason.

Some price-searchers may of course fit into more than one of the above three categories. The International Business Machines Corporation, for instance, is both a big fish in a big pond and a producer of its own brand of electronic computers, typewriters, dictation machines, and cash registers. Similarly, a local lawyer may not only be a big fish in a small pond but may be a recognized expert on tax law or a specialist on patents and copyrights.

All price-searchers face a market situation in which, if they charge higher prices, they may lose some of their customers but will keep others. And price-searchers can usually expand their businesses by reducing their prices, if they so choose. The situation of the

FIG. 12-2. HOW DEMAND LOOKS TO AN INDIVIDUAL FASHION HOUSE (A PRICE-SEARCHER)

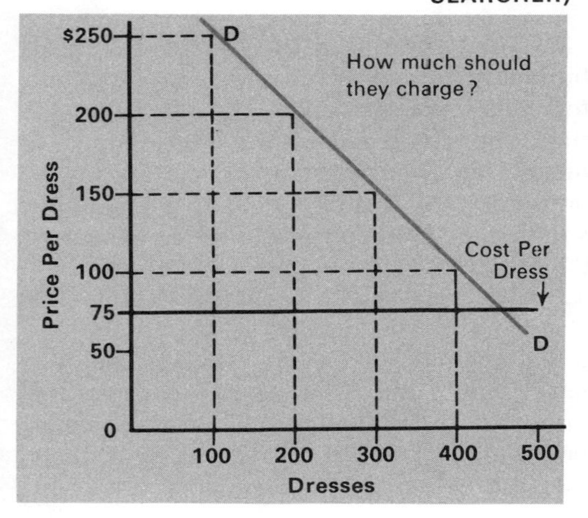

individual price-searcher is represented, therefore, as in Figure 12-2, by a downward sloping demand curve. The price-searcher will try to set a price for a product that will give the greatest total return above total costs. The price-searcher wants to make a good profit on *each item* produced, but also wants to have a large enough *volume* of sales to give the *largest total profit*.

If, for instance, as shown in Figure 12-2, a high-fashion dress house sells its garments (which cost it $75 apiece) for $250 each, it may make a huge $175 profit per dress, but it may sell only 100 dresses. Thus its profits would total $17 500. If it sold its dresses for $150 apiece, it would sell 300 dresses, at a cost of $75 per dress; and its profits would total $22 500, or $5000 more. But it would not want to cut prices too low or its total profits would drop. If it reduced the price per dress to $100, its volume would rise to 400 dresses but, at a cost of $75 per dress, it would earn total profits of only $10 000. Actually if our fashionable dress house proprietor wants to *maximize* profit, how much should be charged per dress and how many should be sold?

What the price-searcher aims at, then, is the *right combination* of price, volume, and cost. Beyond some point, costs will rise faster than sales revenues, and that is the point to stop reducing prices in order to increase volume.

■ POLICY PROBLEMS OF PRICE-TAKERS

The basic policy decision of price-takers, who by definition cannot set the market price of a product but must accept it as given, is what to produce and how much to produce in order to maximize profits.

To illustrate the basic principles involved, let us consider a simple hypothetical example involving two high school students, Lisa and Jack Bennett, who wish to supplement their incomes. They are both interested in various aspects of gemcraft and recognize that their school, Pleasantville High, contains a potential market for a commercial venture growing out of their hobby. (The demand side of this market is the model referred to in Chapters 7 and 8.)

Lisa and Jack know there are other prospects for part-time jobs. In order to achieve their objective efficiently, they must compare the relative returns, based on the amount of time needed plus the cost of raw materials used in making rings, with the potential return per hour from other jobs.

In addition to measuring the mathematical relationships of time and materials to dollar returns, another factor must also be considered. They realize that their school work is of long-run importance and time spent on anything else cannot be spent on school work. In addition, time spent at work on an economics course or serving hamburgers at a part-time job in a restaurant cannot be spent with friends, at a movie, participating in sports or other social or leisure activities.

■ OPPORTUNITY COST

This consideration, as obvious as it sounds, is one of the most important concepts in economics. It is the concept of **opportunity** or **alternative cost**—that is, the cost of doing one thing instead of something else, or the cost of using resources in one way and thus eliminating the possibility of using them in another way. (This idea was originally introduced to you in Chapter 3, where the term "real cost" was used.) This is a cost a business faces when deciding if a plant and other resources will be used to make washing machines or anything else. This is a cost a farmer faces when deciding whether to use land to grow wheat or corn. It is the cost a nation faces in making choices such as that between butter and guns. (Figure 3-3). Any choice about allocation of resources in a given way instantly rejects all other opportunities for their use. In the case of Lisa and Jack, time is an important resource and any use they put it to eliminates its use in another way.

Because of the importance of free and flexible time to them, Lisa and Jack each feels that, other things being equal, the idea of taking a regular part-time job outside the home is not too attractive. Neither wishes to make the commitment of a regular number of hours per week at designated times. The opportunity cost of such a commitment is too high for them. In such a case, the possibility of income being produced from a hobby where time allocation can be flexible is a rather attractive situation.

CONSTRUCTING A SUPPLY SCHEDULE

In the case of Lisa and Jack, let us assume for the sake of simplicity that the practical option for a job outside the home is at a local take-out restaurant where either would earn $1.50 per hour. This gives them (and us) a figure to use in placing a dollar value on an hour of their labor. Let us make several other assumptions as well. The material needed to fashion rings to meet the school Athletic Society's specifications would cost $4.00 for each ring. The time either would need to make a ring would be an hour and a half. Finally, let us assume they presently have all the equipment needed for such a venture. No investment is needed other than for material. Looking at the above data and considering their labor to be worth a minimum of $1.50 per hour, the production cost per ring would therefore be $6.25.

In terms of time, assuming for the moment that any quantity of rings made could be sold, Lisa and Jack are willing to spend up to three hours each per week on this venture. This would produce a total of six hours labor per week, or twenty-four hours in a month. At a production time of 1.5 hours per ring, this would permit a maximum output of sixteen rings in a month.

If the price they can get per ring is relatively low, there is relatively little incentive to devote maximum time to making rings. If, on the other hand, the price they can get per ring is relatively high, so will be their income and profit both per ring and in total. Such would obviously increase their incentive to spend more time on the venture.

Prior to any more detailed investigation of their potential market, Lisa and Jack determine that, as a generalization, their response to various prices would be one of alternating output between four rings per month (if the price were relatively low, i.e., about $7.00, which is only slightly above their minimum cost) and sixteen rings per month (if the price were anything above $20.00, which they feel is about the highest price they can expect to get.) This response is summarized in Table 12-1 and then graphed in Figure 12-3.

What Lisa and Jack have prepared is a **supply schedule,** a model which reflects responsiveness of producers to changes in price for the product or service they produce.

Notice that within this supply schedule, quantity is positively correlated with price while in our typical demand schedule, quantity is negatively correlated with price. In other words, an increase in price tends to cause the quantity demanded to drop but tends to cause the quantity supplied to increase. Basic information about **supply** can be illustrated by a **supply curve,** which normally slopes upward from left to right. The nature of supply, when it is graphed, is

FIG. 12-3 AND TABLE 12-1. MONTHLY SUPPLY OF RINGS

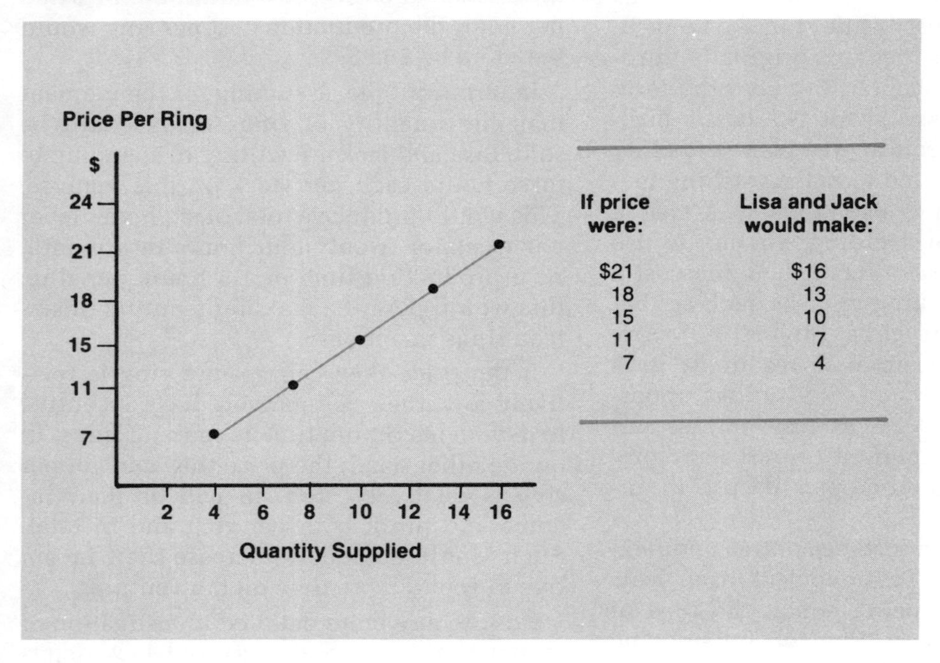

If price were:	Lisa and Jack would make:
$21	$16
18	13
15	10
11	7
7	4

sometimes described as **upward-sloping supply.** This is a pattern opposite to that found in downward-sloping demand, referred to in Chapter 7. The basic pattern of Figure 12-3 is a direct contrast to the normal pattern of demand curves you have seen in previous chapters.

SUPPLY AND DEMAND: THE MARKET MODEL COMPLETED

Let us now assume that our market model becomes reality. Lisa and Jack try to make an agreement to produce the rings for the Athletic Society. Members of the society are in general agreement and a meeting is held on March 1 to resolve the terms of the agreement.

Information about the supply side of the market is found in Table 12-1 and Figure 12-3. Information about the demand side can be brought forward from Chapter 8, from either Table 8-2 or Table 8-3.

The data are combined for you in Table 12-2, and Figure 12-4 illustrates it in graphic form.

Looking at either (and making one final assumption—that members would like to have the rings within a period of about a month), we can conclude that the two sides in our market are likely to reach an agreement for the supply of about 10 rings at a price of about $15.00 per ring.

The model tells us that the market price and quantity, where demand and supply are equal, will determine the likely terms of transactions. To test your understanding of the concepts, determine the effects of each of the following on our market situation:

(1) What if some outside authority, such as the Student Council, tried to step in and impose a price of $10.95? a price of $19.95?
(2) What if Jack and Lisa found that at the end of the month, they had only produced five rings?
(3) What if Lisa and Jack actually produced sixteen rings and offered all at the agreed price of $15.00?

Consider each of the three above changes in our market situation with the following questions in mind: With such imposed changes in price and/or quantity produced, how would quantity offered compare with

FIG. 12-4 AND TABLE 12-2. SUPPLY OF AND DEMAND FOR RINGS

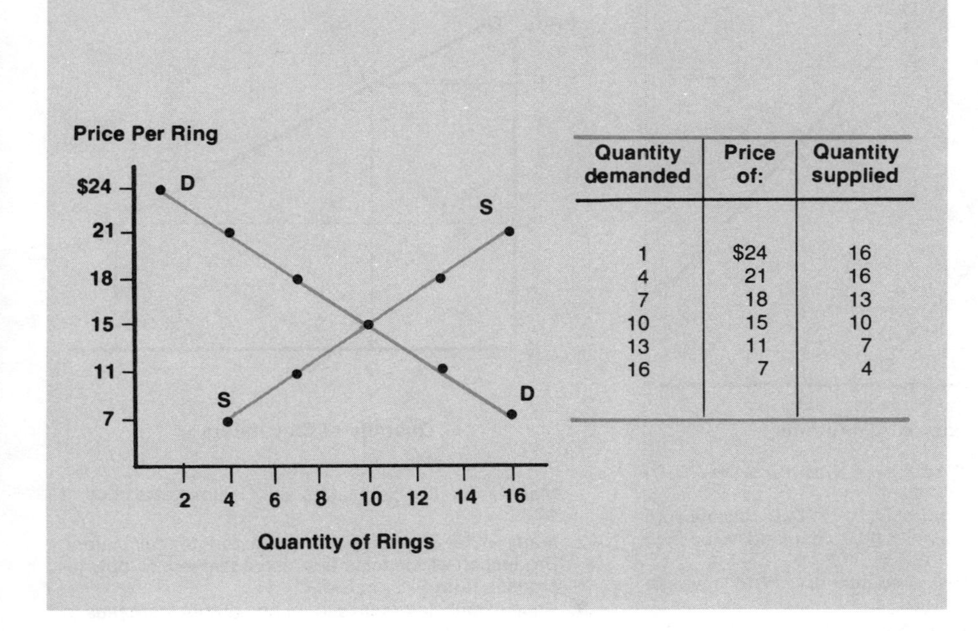

Quantity demanded	Price of:	Quantity supplied
1	$24	16
4	21	16
7	18	13
10	15	10
13	11	7
16	7	4

quantity demanded? What would the effect tend to be on the number actually sold or the price at which sales actually take place? Would there tend to be a surplus or a shortage? What effect would such a surplus or shortage tend to have on actual selling price? An analysis of these three situations would indicate that if any of these conditions were to become reality, some form of imbalance would occur. If any of the three problems were to occur, but the market were left with some flexibility, the problems would tend to be resolved through such adjustments as lower prices (if Lisa and Jack overproduced), or a "black market" at prices approaching $15.00 (if the Council tried to impose a price of $10.95). If the market were not permitted flexibility to deal with such changes, either a surplus or shortage would then continue.

Consideration of these problems is the essence of understanding the theory of supply and demand. In any real market, change in either supply or demand is likely at any time. Many external forces constantly influence any specific market. At the same time, however, this model illustrates how the upward and downward pressures on both price and quantity from both sides of the market tend to move the two sides toward a point of agreement. It is desirable, however, for you to think of the "point" not as an extremely precise or specific one, as Figure 12-4 indicates, but rather as one representing a range of price-quantity combinations within a reasonably narrow circle around the "point."

OTHER CASES OF VARIABLE SUPPLY AND DEMAND

Our market for rings has of course been a hypothetical case, designed to show as simply as possible the interactions of variable supply, variable demand, and market price. But we can find any number of real-world examples to which the simple market model that we have developed closely corresponds. Here are a few such cases.

1. At the existing price of soybeans, demand exceeds supply, because new uses have been found for soybeans by chemical and plastic companies. The price of soybeans rises. Farmers shift some of their acreage, presently planted in other crops,

FIG. 12-5. THE CASE OF SOYBEANS

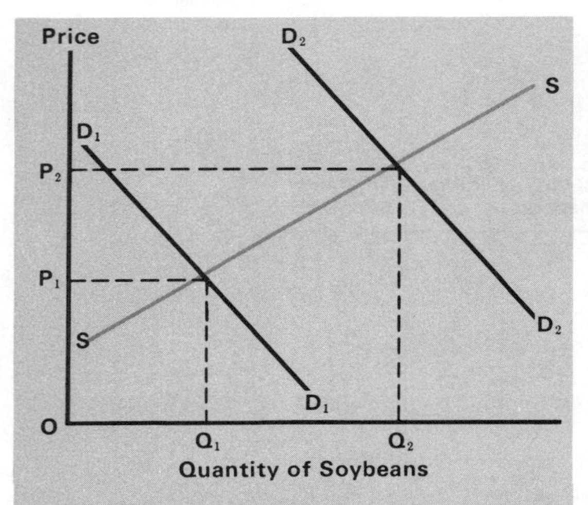

1. Originally, price of soybeans was P_1, where D_1D_1 intersected SS.
2. Demand increased from D_1D_1 to D_2D_2 because of new uses for soybeans. New demand exceeded supply at old price of P_1.
3. As price rose, suppliers switched land to soybean production.
4. New equilibrium price set at P_2 where D_2D_2 intersects SS. Output increases to Q_2.

FIG. 12-7. THE CASE OF CALCULATORS

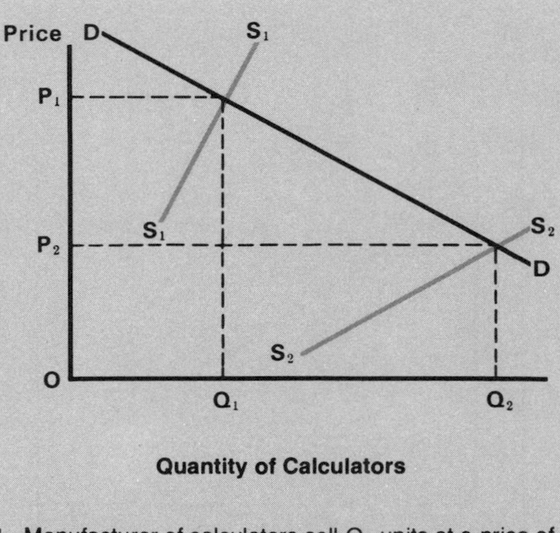

1. Manufacturer of calculators sell Q_1 units at a price of P_1.
2. Many other suppliers are attracted to calculators. Production efficiencies are also achieved. Supply increases from S_1S_1 to S_2S_2.
3. Price of calculators falls to P_2 and output increases to Q_2, where S_2S_2 intersects DD.

FIG. 12-6. THE CASE OF BLACK AND WHITE TV SETS

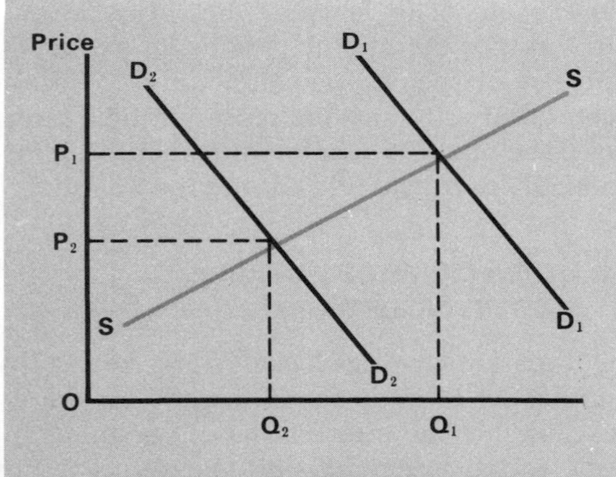

1. Price of sets is originally set at P_1, where D_1D_1 intersects SS.
2. Demand for sets is reduced to D_2D_2, as a result of advent of color television sets.
3. Price of sets falls and output is reduced until new price of P_2 and new production level of Q_2 are established, where D_2D_2 intersects SS.

into soybean production, and the quantity supplied increases. Then the price stabilizes. (See Figure 12-5.)

2. Color television sets come on the market at price ranges most consumers can afford. Public demand for black and white sets declines. Manufacturers shift resources from making black and white sets to making color sets. Price levels and quantities sold of black and white sets both decline (see Figure 12-6).

3. A manufacturer develops the pocket calculator and markets it at $100.00. Demand for the product is strong and sales grow rapidly. Other manufacturers, attracted by high price and profits, shift their resources to turning out calculators. At the same time, more efficient means of production are developed. The supply increases. (The supply schedule shifts from S_1 to S_2 in Figure 12-7.) The competition among the producers drives prices down closer to production costs. The price of a calculator falls

FIG. 12-8. THE CASE OF BOX OFFICE PRICES TO SEE "GALAXY WARS"

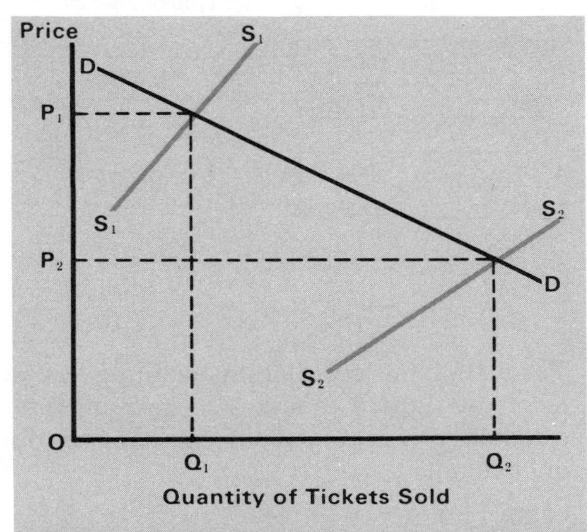

1. Distributors of the film wish to charge high admission prices, so the supply schedule is at S_1S_1. At a market price of P_1, box office ticket sales amount to only Q_1.
2. Distributors decide to change pricing policy and offer more screenings at lower prices; so supply schedule shifts to S_2S_2.
3. Price is set at P_2 and box office attendance increases greatly to Q_2.

FIG. 12-9. THE CASE OF MUSICIANS

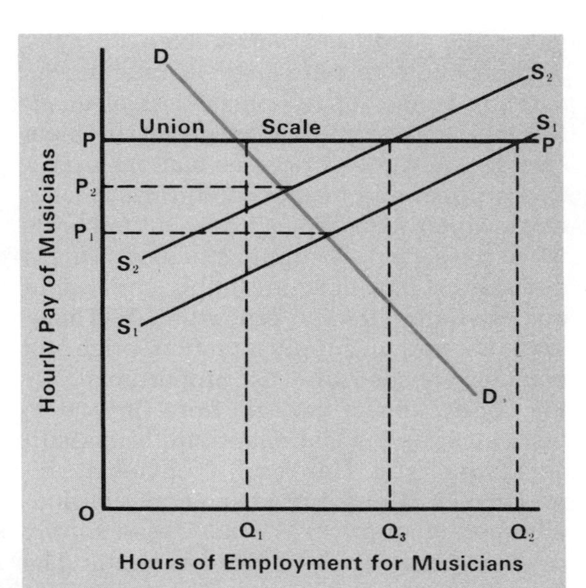

1. The original market for musicians is represented by the demand curve DD and the supply curve S_1S_1. However, the musicians' union fixes the hourly pay scale at a rate of P, which is much higher than the equilibrium market price of P_1.
2. At a price P, the demand for musicians is only Q_1. But at the price P, the supply of musicians (the number of hours that musicians want to work) is Q_2. Therefore, there is an oversupply of musicians equal to Q_2 minus Q_1.
3. Many discouraged musicians, unable to get employment, switch to other lines of work and give up their musical careers. So the supply curve shifts from S_1S_1 to S_2S_2. However, union scale remains the same, at P, and there is still an oversupply of musicians, though a smaller one. At the new supply schedule S_2S_2, the oversupply is now equal to Q_3 minus Q_1.
4. The oversupply of musicians continues to hold back rises in the pay of musicians.

sharply. Masses of calculators are produced at prices ranging from $6.99 up.

4. A film producer brings out a super-colossal science-fiction film. It is initially shown only at a high price in selected motion picture theaters. After a while attendance at the high price begins to fall off. The film distributor cuts the film's cost to make it available for the market at neighborhood theaters. Attendance at showings is high and the film does excellent business at the lower prices. (See Figure 12-8).

5. The supply of musicians exceeds the demand for live music at the existing pay scale for musicians. The musicians' union struggles to hold up the pay scale, and even to increase it. But the oversupply of musicians persists. Fewer youngsters decide to make music their vocation, and more treat it as an avocation. Some professional musicians switch to other lines of work, and the supply of musicians decreases, but not enough to raise the price to the union scale. Despite the efforts of the musicians' union, the pay of the average musician declines relative to the pay of professionals in other fields. (See Figure 12-9).

ELASTICITY OF SUPPLY

In chapter 8, we examined the relationship between prices and quantities in demand situation. Different types of price-elasticity measured the degree of response of quantity to changes in price. This relationship exists in non-fixed supply situations and may be an equally significant market force.

The same terms are used to refer to the varying degrees of responsiveness of quantity supplied to price changes. A problem emerges, however, since the relationship between prices and total expenditures or revenues, which was used as a rule in Chapter 8, is not the same in a supply situation. This is due to the fact that, in supply, price and quantity are directly proportional. Therefore, in a normal supply situation, price and revenue are also directly proportional. By the application of the rule from Chapter 8, then, all supply situations would be classifiable as inelastic. This result is obviously unreasonable. If quantity changes proportionally more than price, as it may, then supply in that case should be defined as elastic. The "revenue rule," therefore, must be classed as invalid and an alternative must be found. Better still, why not a rule that measures price-elasticity for either supply or demand, regardless of circumstances? This rule, based on the **elasticity coefficient** is the solution to the problem. Remember—it is the only valid way to measure **elasticity of supply**, and it may also be used for demand situations if desired.

Examining the response of quantity to each price change in Table 12-3, one can see that the degree of change in quantity increases as price rises. Let us remember precisely what elasticity is—the measure of response of quantity to changes in price. How does one measure it—if one wishes to be precise? Use a bit of common sense and it will be apparent that what is needed is to compare the average percentage change in quantity with the average percentage change in price. Why the average change? Because elasticity measures changes between price and quantity levels, valid for changes in either direction. Our formula, then, is:

$$\frac{\text{Average \% change in Q}}{\text{Average \% change in P}} = \text{Elasticity Coefficient}$$

Table 12-3. TYPES OF ELASTICITY OF SUPPLY

Price	Quantity Offered	Type of Elasticity between prices
1.00	1000	
		Inelastic
2.00	1200	
3.00	1800	
4.00	4000	
5.00	9000	

Dealing with the first price interval from Table 12-3, our calculations would go as follows (we ignore ± signs, for we are interested only in degree of change, not direction of change):

$$\frac{\dfrac{\frac{200}{1000}+\frac{200}{1200}}{2}}{\dfrac{\frac{1.00}{1.00}+\frac{1.00}{2.00}}{2}} = \frac{\dfrac{20\% + 16.67\%}{2}}{\dfrac{100\% + 50\%}{2}} = \frac{18.34\%}{75\%}$$

When this is taken one more step, the result is .244, the elasticity coefficient. What does all this tell us? Obviously, when we look at the two average figures, 18.34% and 75%, we see that quantity changes proportionally less than price; or, to put it another way, quantity is unresponsive to the price change; therefore, between the prices of $1.00 and $2.00, supply is inelastic.

The coefficient, the final fraction in decimal form, provides a way to express the rule in concise terms. If, as was the case in our illustration, the coefficient is less than 1.0 (but greater than zero), supply (or demand) is inelastic. If the coefficient is exactly 1.0, supply (or demand) is of unit-elasticity. If the result is greater than 1.0, then supply (or demand) is elastic. Unlike the "revenue rule," this technique is valid without limitation.

Work out the types of elasticity in the intervals between prices of $2.00 and $5.00 to be sure you are familiar with the technique.

SUMMARY

Although the world offers many examples of fixed supply, as we saw in earlier chapters, the quantity supplied is ordinarily *variable*, just as is the quantity demanded. But the quantity supplied tends to *increase* as price *increases*, while the quantity demanded tends to *decrease* as price *increases*.

Suppliers can be divided into two broad classes, price-takers and price-searchers. Price-takers operate in markets where no single producer can determine the market price; in fact each price-taker faces a perfectly elastic demand for his or her products.

Price-searchers, who may be either "big fish in little ponds," "big fish in big ponds," or producers of unique goods, can set prices above those of their competitors, without necessarily losing all their customers. *Price-searchers aim at that combination of prices, costs, and volume of business that will enable them to maximize their profits.*

Price-takers cannot find any buyers for their goods at prices above the market level and need not offer lower than market prices to sell all they can produce. Their policy decisions boil down basically then to these: *what goods to produce, how much of them to produce, and how to produce them most efficiently.*

Both price-searchers and price-takers must make a careful calculation of their *market opportunities* and of their *opportunity costs.*

In this chapter we have presented a simple model of any market in which both the quantity supplied and the quantity demanded are variable. This model, represented by crossing supply and demand schedules on a graph, means that if the quantity supplied varies positively with price, and if the quantity demanded varies negatively with price, then price and quantity exchanged will be determined at the point where the curves intersect. This is where quantity supplied equals the quantity demanded *at the same (equilibrium) price*.

The model thus provides a succinct statement of the so-called laws of supply and demand.[3] For all cases when both supply and demand are variable:

If, at a given price . . .

1. demand exceeds supply, then price will rise and the quantity exchanged will increase;
2. demand is less than supply, then price will fall and the quantity exchanged will decrease;
3. supply exceeds demand, then price will fall and the quantity exchanged will increase;
4. supply is less than demand, then price will rise and the quantity exchanged will decrease; and
5. demand equals supply, then market price and quantity exchanged will be at equilibrium.

All of these relationships are represented graphically in Figures 12-10 and 12-11. See page 126.

[3] See also the statement of the laws of demand in Chapter 9, which assumed fixed supply.

KEY CONCEPTS

price-taker
price-searcher
opportunity cost
alternative cost
supply
supply curve
supply schedule
upward-sloping supply
elasticity of supply
elasticity coefficients

FIG. 12-10. CHANGES IN DEMAND, SUPPLY SCHEDULE CONSTANT

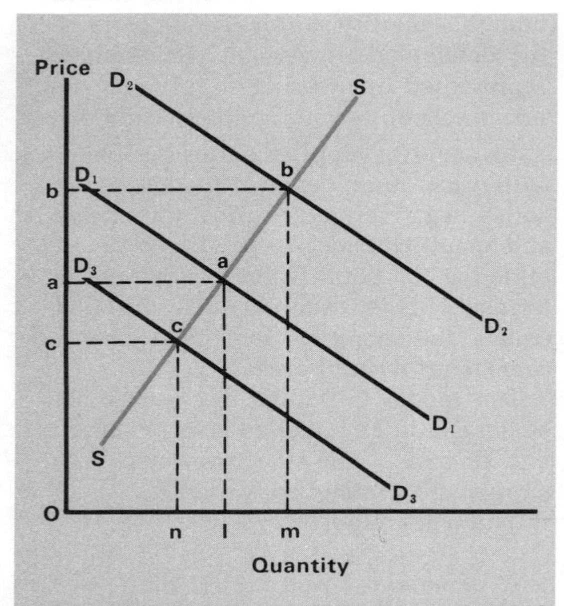

1. Initial market price set at a, where D_1D_1 intersects SS. Quantity exchanged equals l.
2. Demand increases to D_2D_2. Price increases to b. Quantity exchanged increases from l to m.
3. Demand decreases to D_3D_3. Price decreases to c. Quantity exchanged decreases to n.

FIG. 12-11. CHANGES IN SUPPLY, DEMAND SCHEDULE CONSTANT

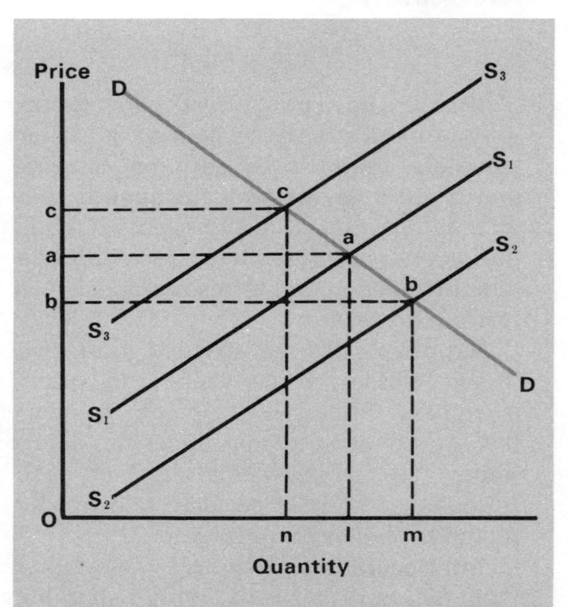

1. Initial market price set at a, where S_1S_1 intersects DD. Quantity exchanged equals l.
2. Supply increases to S_2S_2. Price decreases to b. Quantity exchanged increases to m.
3. Supply decreases to S_3S_3. Price increases to c. Quantity exchanged decreases to n.

QUESTIONS FOR REVIEW AND DISCUSSION

1. Do you think that the assumption that suppliers seek to maximize profits is a reasonable one? Why or why not? What is the advantage of making this assumption in economic analysis? Does any other single assumption you can think of have as many advantages? What is the disadvantage of making this assumption in economic analysis? Can you think of any other single assumption about sellers that has fewer disadvantages?
2. What are the basic differences between *price-takers* and *price-searchers*? How do these differences show on a graphical picture of the demand curve facing each type of seller?
3. Explain in your own words the concept of opportunity cost. Give two specific examples of the opportunity cost of using one hour of your time this evening to watch television.
4. What are the two main factors that account for the positive (upward) slope of typical supply schedules? Explain why each of these factors might cause the quantity supplied to increase as the price of a particular good increases.
5. Explain in your own words how the forces of supply and demand interact to determine equilibrium price and quantity. If price is temporarily above equilibrium, what forces are set in motion to move the price down toward the equilibrium

price? If price is temporarily below equilibrium, what forces are set in motion to move the price up toward the equilibrium price? Do these forces always work in all markets?

6. Explain why the "revenue rule" used for measuring elasticity of demand is not useful for supply.

PROBLEMS AND EXERCISES TO SHARPEN YOUR UNDERSTANDING

Below is a table showing a list of prices for a litre of ice cream and a list of the number of litres that producers (given time to adjust their output schedules) would be willing to sell at the different prices shown.

Supply of Ice Cream in a Typical City on a Typical Summer Day

Price per Litre	Number of Litres Producers Would be Willing to Sell
$2.00	30 000
1.80	25 000
1.60	20 000
1.40	15 000
1.20	10 000
1.00	5 000

1. On a sheet of graph paper, using the scales you used at the end of Chapter 7, sketch a vertical axis and label it price. Make a horizontal axis and label it quantity. Plot the data from the above table, letting each unit on the vertical axis represent a price of $.20 per litre and letting each unit on the horizontal axis represent 5000 litres.
2. Describe in words what the graph shows you. How does the shape of this supply curve differ from the shape of the demand curve you drew for the exercise at the end of Chapter 7? Can you explain this difference?
3. On the same piece of graph paper you have just used, plot the demand data from the table in the exercise at the end of Chapter 7. What is the equilibrium price of ice cream in a typical city on a typical summer day? How many litres of ice cream would be bought and sold at this price?
4. On your supply and demand graph, add a new supply and a new demand, each somewhat closer to a horizontal position in relation to your "Q" axis. What can you conclude about the relative elasticity of the two supplies or demands?
5. Finally, sketch two more curves, one supply and the other demand, only make them more vertical than the first lines. What conclusions can you draw about graphic illustration of elasticity as long as the graphs being compared are drawn to the same scale?
6. Show how conclusions reached in exercise 5 may be invalid if two graphs drawn to different scales are being compared.

CHAPTER 13

COMPETITION AND THE MARKET MECHANISM

■ AN OVERVIEW OF A MARKET ECONOMY ■ THE CONCEPT OF PERFECT COMPETITION ■ LONG-RUN COMPETITIVE EQUILIBRIUM ■ THE FLOW OF GOODS AND MONEY ■ DIFFICULTIES OF MAINTAINING PERFECT COMPETITION ■ SUMMARY ■ APPENDIX: THE ECONOMIC ORGANIZATION OF A PRISONER OF WAR CAMP (PART 1)

In the preceding chapters we have been studying how the price of a particular good or service would be determined, given certain assumptions about how buyers and sellers would behave in competitive markets. In this chapter we shall consider what economists mean by **perfect competition.** And we shall examine how a market economy's scarce resources would be allocated if *every* market in the economy were a perfectly competitive one. Finally, we shall discuss the problems of maintaining competition in real-world markets, and we shall ask this question: If we could have a perfectly competitive market system, would we *really* want it?

■ AN OVERVIEW OF A MARKET ECONOMY

Let us begin with a summary of how a perfectly competitive market economy would be organized. Figure 13-1 provides a simplified overview of such an economy. This system would be based on the four underlying capitalist institutions of private property, freedom of enterprise, the profit motive, and competition. Let us remind ourselves of just what these institutions mean. *Private property* means that the economy's scarce resources or factors of production are owned by individuals and private businesses. *Freedom of enterprise* means that these resource owners are free to use their resources as they see fit, unrestrained by tradition or command. The *profit motive* (or self-interest) means that these resource owners will seek to sell their resources where the money rewards are the greatest, and that business firms buying these services will attempt to make finished goods and services to sell for as large a gain (or profit) as possible. *Competition* means that resource owners seeking to sell their productive services and firms seeking to buy these services (as well as firms seeking to sell finished goods and services, and resource owners seeking to buy these goods and services) are acting independently of each other. Each must compete with many other like-minded individuals or firms.

All of these basic institutions, or underlying pillars, are necessary if a pure market economy is to function effectively. If we have private property and freedom of enterprise, however, the desire for gain will drive a market economy forward, and competition will serve as the regulator that keeps the profit motive from getting out of hand.

Interaction of Resource and Product Markets

Thus, above the four basic pillars in Figure 13-1, we show the basic organization of a market economy consisting of the interaction of resource owners and business firms facing each other on two broad fronts—a set of markets for productive services and a set of markets for finished goods and services.

In the markets for productive services, the colored lines S_1 and D_1 indicate that the supply and demand for resource 1 (say, electricians of a certain skill) interact to set a price (P_1) for electricians of this skill. Likewise the lines for resource 2 (say, building lots) indicate that supply and demand for land interact to set a price for this resource (P_2), and the lines for resource 3 (say, a capital good such as a piece of machinery) indicate that a price (P_3) is established for this resource by the interaction of S_3 and D_3.

In the markets for finished goods and services, the same sort of conditions are indicated by the grey S and D lines on the top part of Figure 13-1. If S_1 and D_1 represent the supply and demand for houses, the price P_1 would represent the equilibrium price in the housing market. You can let S_2, D_2 and S_3, D_3 stand for the supply and demand for any finished goods or services you want (maybe wheat and speed boats), and the prices P_2 and P_3 would represent the prices established by the forces of supply and demand in these markets.

Of course, in a market economy there are many more markets than the six represented in Figure 13-1, but this simplified overview of a pure market economy illustrates how productive resources, goods, and services are organized and tied together. It shows how market prices play the key role in allo-

FIG. 13-1. A PERFECTLY COMPETITIVE MARKET ECONOMY

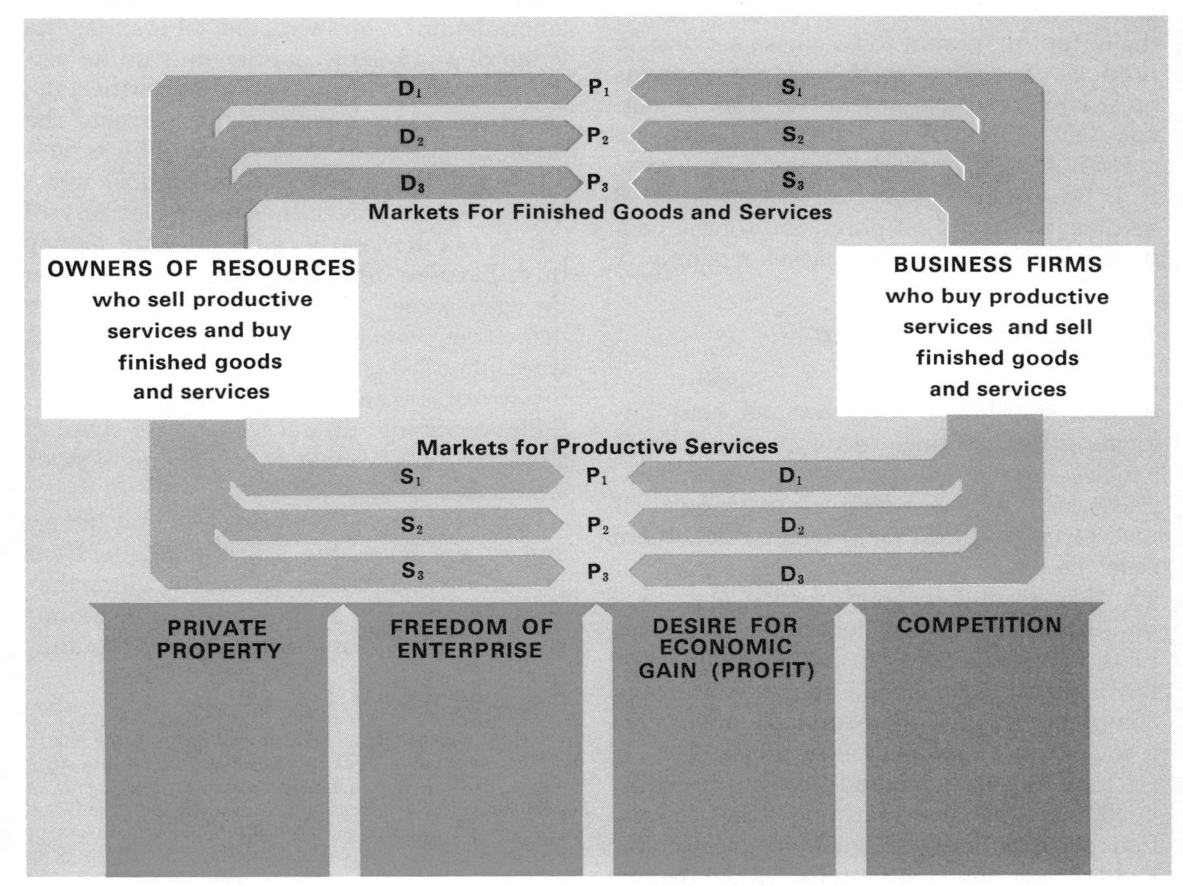

cating scarce resources in such an economy, and it shows how prices in one market are related to prices in other markets.

Interdependence of Prices and Incomes

We can see that product market prices depend on the interaction of what people are willing to pay for various quantities of goods and services and what firms are willing to sell these goods and services for. But what people are willing to pay for finished goods and services depends on what prices (incomes) they receive in the market for their productive services. And these prices are influenced not only by what people are willing to sell their services for, but also by what firms are willing to pay for these services.

Yet, what firms are willing to pay for productive services depends upon the price of the output they want to use these services to produce. The price of this output depends on what people will pay in the product market. This depends upon the prices they receive in the factor market, and so on it goes. H. J. Davenport's poem back in Chapter 6 emphasized a crucial point, the interdependence of prices in a pure market economy.

THE CONCEPT OF PERFECT COMPETITION

In analysing how market systems would allocate scarce resources, economists often use a model based on the concept of perfect competition. Several conditions must prevail if perfect competition is to exist. First, there must be *many buyers* and *many sellers* of *identical* resources, goods, or services. Second, the buyers and sellers must have complete *knowledge or information* about market conditions. Third, they must have complete *mobility* or freedom to move their resources from one market to another.

These are very demanding conditions indeed, but remember that models are simplified constructions designed to give us insight into complex situations. To be useful, a model does not have to describe reality completely. Therefore, as a working model, economists say that there are many buyers or many sellers when each buyer and each seller is so small in the total market that, acting independently, no one can appreciably affect the market price. This condition is obviously more true for some real-world markets (say, the market for wheat or shoes or the market for a particular stock on the Toronto Stock Exchange) than it is for other markets (say steel or helicopters). In a perfectly competitive market economy, however, *all* markets would have to have so many buyers and so many sellers that the actions of any single one could not appreciably affect the market price.

Likewise, it is difficult to find actual markets where all the resources or goods or services are *identical*. The value of an hour of labor depends on who the laborer is; the value of a tonne of coal depends on its carbon content or the amount of impurities; the value of a car depends on the year and the model, and so on. Nevertheless, the economist says that products are identical when buyers do not care from whom they buy. If buyers want wheat and do not care if they buy Farmer Smith's wheat or Farmer Brown's wheat, then we can talk about the market for wheat as though this product were identical, regardless of who produces the wheat. Likewise, if you want a share of C.P.R. stock and do not care whose share of stock you buy, we may say all shares of stock are identical.[1]

Complete knowledge requires that buyers and sellers know the prices and quantities prevailing in all of the markets in which they might participate in the quest for economic gain. And *perfect mobility* requires that they

[1] This may seem self-evident. However, note that a particular buyer of stock might *indeed* care whose stock was bought—if, for instance, the buyer were trying to gain control of a corporation from its present dominant group of owners, in which case their stock might be worth more to the buyer than the company's stock in general.

be able to participate in any market they choose—if not in the short run, at least in the long run, after they have had sufficient time to end their present commitments and free their resources for the most profitable use. As in the case of many buyers, many sellers, and identical products, the amount of knowledge and the amount of mobility existing in actual markets vary. But, by assuming that all of these conditions of perfect competition exist, the economist can make some rigorous predictions about how resources would be allocated and rewarded in a perfectly competitive economy.

LONG-RUN COMPETITIVE EQUILIBRIUM

In the long run, after all resource owners and firms have had sufficient time to adjust to their most profitable opportunities, all the prices in a market system are interrelated. With many buyers, many sellers, identical products, complete information, and perfect mobility, forces are set up to move prices in such a way that:

1. *All the productive resources in the economy will be employed where their contribution to fulfilling consumer demand is the greatest.* Why? Because if this were not so, it would pay some resources to move. And they would continue to move until there were no further gains to be obtained from moving, as opposed to remaining in their present occupation.

2. *The cost of production will be driven down to the lowest point possible, consistent with existing consumer taste and technology.* Why? Because if it were possible to produce any product more cheaply than it was currently being produced, entrepreneurs in search of greater profits would adopt the cheaper methods and drive high-cost producers out of business.

3. *All resources and goods of the same quality or ability to satisfy consumer demand will receive the same return.* Why? Because if resource owners of the same skill or firms of the same productive efficiency receive different prices for their services or for their goods, it pays the lowest paid resources or firms to move toward the higher prices. As they move into the markets with the higher prices, they tend to increase quantity and lower prices in these markets; and, as they leave the markets with the lower prices, the reduced quantity tends to raise the prices in these markets. Only when prices for identical goods and services are equal would the incentive to move cease and the economy come to rest (that is, be in equilibrium).

4. *Differences in relative prices will reflect differences in productive ability to satisfy consumer demand.* Why? Consider the case of a group of workers each of whom can produce 10 units of output in an hour, and a group of machines that can produce 20 units of the same output in an hour. If the price of one hour of worker time were the same as one hour of machine time, firms seeking to keep costs to a minimum would obviously prefer to hire the machines rather than the workers. But would their prices be the same? No. Even if the workers and the machines started with the same price, the higher output for each dollar of cost in the case of machinery would increase the demand for machines and reduce the demand for workers. The price of an hour of machine time would increase, and the price of an hour of worker time would fall. When would the prices stop changing? Only when the relative prices between one hour of machine time and one hour of worker time reached a ratio of two to one would the changes stop and come to rest at a set of equilibrium prices for these two resources. What relative prices would be established in long-run equilibrium between two goods, say wheat and corn, if wheat provided 30 units of consumer satisfaction per tonne and corn provided 10 units of consumer satisfaction per tonne? Three to one, of course.

5. *All of these adjustments will be made impersonally and automatically.* A perfectly competitive market system's rewards and

FIG. 13-2. THE CIRCULAR FLOW OF MONEY, GOODS, AND SERVICES

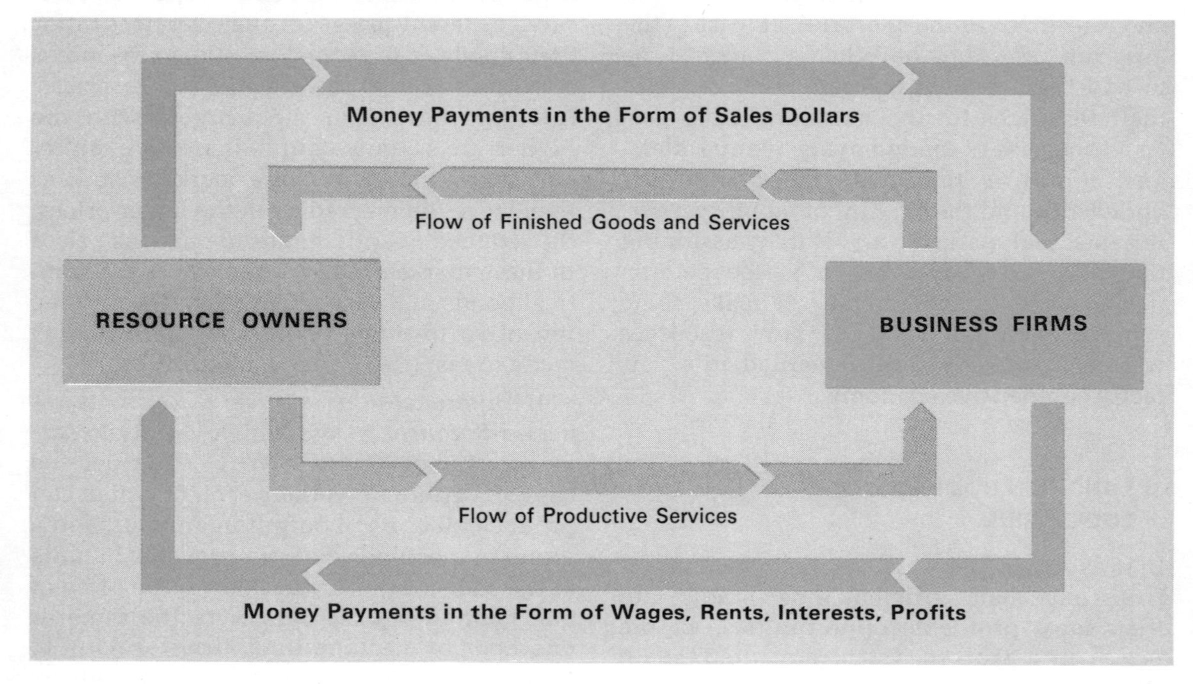

penalties are strictly monetary. They take the form of gains and losses in money terms. But no single person or group determines what these gains or losses will be. Rewards and penalties are the outcome of the combined actions of many participants, producers, consumers, buyers, and sellers in many different markets. Rewards or penalties are passed out with regard to only one test, how much do *you* contribute to what consumers want to buy? You might be a clean-living, warm-hearted producer of hula hoops but if consumers want to buy skate boards, you will be punished with money losses and skate board producers will be rewarded with money gains, even if they happen to be mean people who yell at children and tie cans to dogs' tails.

Decisions from a judge or a jury can be questioned or appealed, but a perfectly competitive market mechanism only reflects consumer taste and technology; it does not judge them, nor does it provide any mechanism for appeal.

We have now completed our analysis of how a perfectly competitive market economy would operate in answering the basic economic questions of what, how, for whom, and how much. Resource owners in a market economy sell the productive services of their resources to firms who pay them money in the form of wages, rents, interest, and profits in return. Firms then use these productive services to make finished goods and services which they sell to resource owners in return for money in the form of sales dollars.

THE FLOW OF GOODS AND MONEY

Figure 13-1 was an attempt to give an overview of this process in order to illustrate how prices in different markets are determined by the forces of supply and demand, and to illustrate how prices in different markets are related to each other. Once these prices have been established and come to rest in equilibrium, however, we can use Figure 13-2 as a more general summary figure to illustrate how the transactions at the various market prices give rise to a flow of goods and services one way and a flow of money payments in the other direction. Money flows from resource owners to firms for finished goods and services, and money flows from firms to resource owners in return for the productive services purchased from resource owners.

Thus, in a purely competitive market economy:

What is produced depends on the prices firms receive in the markets for goods and services. If consumers are willing to pay a price that covers the cost of production (including a normal rate of profit to entrepreneurs) and if the manufacturer receives a profit equal to what could be received in other lines of production, a good or service will be produced in a market economy. If these conditions are not met, it will not be produced.

How goods are produced depends on the prices firms have to pay in the market for productive services. Firms will always seek the cheapest or least cost combinations of resources; if they do not, competition will drive them out of business.

For whom goods are produced also depends on the prices that resource owners receive in the markets for productive services. Those with relatively scarce resources that are in great demand (such as great hockey players or owners of land on a busy downtown street corner) will receive higher incomes and have a greater influence in the market for finished goods and services than those whose resources are relatively more abundant and have lower market prices.

How much, in total, is produced in a market economy depends upon what part of the money incomes received by resource owners is *spent* on consumer goods and services and what part is *saved*. It also depends upon the desire of business firms to borrow these savings for *investment* expenditures on new capital goods.[2] This process of savings and investment will be discussed in more detail in Units 3 and 4 of this book.

While you may have to postpone your complete understanding of a market system's answer to the question of *how much* until later, you should now be able to describe in your own words how a system of relative prices answers the basic questions of *what, how,* and *for whom* in a perfectly competitive market economy.

DIFFICULTIES OF MAINTAINING PERFECT COMPETITION

Economists from Adam Smith on have been impressed with the beauty and the unplanned efficiency of a smoothly working model of a perfectly competitive market-price system. But we must remember that we have been using a model. It is not a good description of reality. Nor is it necessarily an ideal toward which all real-world economies should strive, although the list of results that would be obtained in long-run, perfectly competitive equilibrium (discussed earlier) impresses many people as containing very desirable things to achieve.

Remembering that we should keep value judgments separate from analysis, let us now consider the question, "Is it possible to have an entire economy organized on a perfectly competitive basis?" At the end of this chapter we shall also ask, "Would we want to live in such an economy?"

The Problem of Maintaining Many Small Producers

In many real-world markets, technology is such that it may cost more to produce certain goods and services with many small produc-

[2] Business firms themselves may save part of their sales receipts for investment purposes by not paying out all of their income. Operating costs must of course be paid for. If a firm does save and re-invest, where do you think the funds come from? Note we refer to money saved, not new money raised from some external source.

Imperial Oil Limited Photo

Very large corporations have emerged in many fields such as oil exploration and refining because of the large amounts of capital investment required. The photo shows part of Imperial Oil's Strathcona Refinery in Edmonton. In 1977, Imperial Oil had assets over $3 billion, total sales revenues of $5 billion, and after-tax profits of $289 million. The Strathcona Refinery, which has a replacement value of over $500 million, is the company's largest, with a capacity of about 150 000 barrels per day, about one-third of Imperial's total refinery capacity.

ers than it would with a few larger ones. Take automobiles for example. You and thousands of other people probably could make cars in your own garages. But four or five large corporations, with special tools, special knowledge, and special organizational abilities, are likely to be able to make cars much cheaper. Here is the problem: Perfect competition might force many small producers down to their least cost point, but their least cost point would be much higher than the least cost point for a few larger producers. Yet, with a few large producers, there may not be enough competition to force them down to their least cost point; they might have enough market power to raise prices, restrict output, and make higher profits than perfect competition would allow. Instead of passing all of their cheaper cost advantages on to the consumer, the lack of perfect competition may permit them to keep some of their extra profits for their own use.

We might like to have the cheaper cost of a few large producers and the competitive pressure of many small producers. But if we cannot have both, which do we take, the higher cost of many small producers with no chance for monopoly profit, or the lower cost of a few producers who might be strong enough to make some monopoly profit?

To further complicate things, there may be

even more extreme cases where it makes sense to have only one producer of a good or a service. How many competing sets of railroad tracks should be laid between two points? How many competing telephone companies, water companies, gas companies, or electric companies should a single town have? A thoughtful answer to these questions might be only one. If so, these **natural monopolies** can pose serious problems for any economy that wants to rely solely on competition in the market place to regulate the allocation of its scarce resources.

The Problem of Maintaining Independent Action

Even when there are many buyers and many sellers, a market economy is confronted with the problem of preventing them from getting together and colluding to fix the prices at which they are willing to buy or sell. If many buyers and many sellers act independently and compete with each other, the market system works well. But, if they combine and refuse to compete independently, it may work clumsily and inefficiently.

The Problem of Dullness and Uniformity

The perfectly competitive model assumes that in each market many sellers produce identical products, and that many buyers are indifferent as to which one of the identical products they buy. Yet this sameness makes for dullness. Buyers often like variety and different styles. People often do not want just shirts, they want white button-down collars, or blue striped snap-tabs, or pastel shirts with French cuffs, plus many other styles as well.

In catering to this desire for something different, sellers are often able to cut down the amount of competition to which they are exposed. There may be many producers of gasoline for example, but there is only one producer of Texaco, Shell, Irving, Gulf, or Esso.[3] To the extent that producers can get people to believe that their products are different, they can cut down on the amount of competition faced since only they produce these products.

This desire for product differentiation often gives rise to advertising, style changes, "free" delivery, and other forms of nonprice competition that really do not change the basic nature of the good or service, but do increase the cost of producing and selling it. Therefore, some critics argue that the scarce resources used in these areas are wasted and could better be used doing other things. Critics also argue that buyers have to pay higher prices as a result of these extras, even if they do not want or use them. On the other hand, these practices do add variety and avoid dullness in a market economy.

We shall not try to resolve here the complex argument over the advantages and disadvantages of advertising and sales promotion of many different types of goods and services. It is a subject that you will doubtless wish to ponder yourself. Suffice it to say here that if we were to have a perfectly competitive economy, there would have to be identical products. And this would mean giving up much of the variety and product differentiation that exists in our economy today.

The Problem of Imperfect Knowledge

A perfectly competitive market system relies on the signals of prices and profits to allocate resources, goods, and services from one sector of the economy to another. But these price and profit signals must be seen or heard if they are to influence producers' or consumers' actions. How does a farmer know about alternative employment opportunities? How does a secretary in a high school know what salaries secretaries in industry are making? How does a producer of widgets know or find out about the profit opportunities in the gadget market? How does a consumer know if the contents of two boxes of breakfast cereal have the same or different net weights? How does one maga-

[3] At least in theory this is the case. What, however, if oil company A buys from company B to supply its chain of A service stations in a particular area?

zine publisher know what profits particular competitive magazines are making?

All of the information assumed by the perfectly competitive model is not readily available in many real-world markets. And obtaining such information involves costs. Is the cost of gathering and making available complete information worth the benefits that would result from moving actual markets closer to the kind of markets assumed in the perfectly competitive model? If so, how should such an information system be developed?

Problems of Immobility

Even if information is freely available, some resources in real-world markets may be immobile. A person with a large family and no savings may not be able to get to the job openings elsewhere or may simply prefer not to move elsewhere because the family has always lived there. Or if the market price of engineers with Ph.D.'s goes way up, it still will take a long time for the market to bring forth a substantial increase in the number of such Ph.D.'s.

The fact that the market may solve such problems in the long run has not deterred many thoughtful persons from asking, "Can we think of any nonmarket devices that would increase mobility and speed things up?" Swifter adjustments would make the economy more productive and increase individual incomes.

The Problem of the Unrestrained Consumer

Ignoring the real-world possibility that producer advertising may influence consumer demand, the perfectly competitive model assumes that the consumer rules. The whole competitive system is geared to the consumer's tastes and desires, so long as these are backed up with dollar votes in the market place.

An unrestrained, perfectly competitive market system will use its limited resources to produce gold-plated bird cages and allow babies to go without milk if that is the way the dollar votes are cast in the market place. The greatest concert violinist in the world will starve and singers whose names will be forgotten in a year will prosper if consumers do not want to attend classical concerts but do want to buy millions of copies of pop records. Even narcotics and many other undesirable goods and services will be produced if they prove to be the most profitable ways of using scarce productive resources.

In cases such as these, many people feel that some restraints *should* be placed on the market mechanism. It is a question of compassion and value judgments, not analysis, that says we should not allow people to starve, even if they cannot contribute to the production of anything that people want to buy in the marketplace. Similarly, many people's social values lead them to say that we should *prohibit* the production of certain goods and services, even if people are willing to pay for them at profitable prices. Some feel that we should *encourage and subsidize* other types of production, such as classical music or public education.

The Problem of Unrestrained Competition

Another problem that arises when we try to apply the purely competitive model to actual markets is the problem of excessive competition. Firms and resource owners are encouraged to compete freely and as hard as they can in pursuit of their own self-interest. But what if they do not compete fairly? What if they lie? What if they cheat? What if they sell spoiled meat or sawdust-filled hamburgers?

Freedom of contract has no meaning if contracts are not enforced. Some might argue, however, that in the long run the market can punish such practices. The liars and the cheaters will find it increasingly difficult to do business. As their tactics are found out and information gets around, nobody will deal with them and they will be punished in the currency of the marketplace by money losses. For instance, people who sell spoiled meat or "doctored" hamburgers will be driven out of business.

While such punishment may eventually take care of the cheaters and spoiled meat dealers, however, it does not do much for those who suffered from these harmful practices in the first place. If you become violently ill because of meat poisoning, it is little consolation to know that your suffering will contribute to the economic demise of an unscrupulous competitor. Nor will you be particularly cheerful to learn that a particular drug that ruined your health is starting to lose customers.

However, this is an area of intense controversy on specific issues as to what the government should or should not do to protect consumers by regulating business in particular areas. Should the government promote automobile safety, ensure truth in packaging and advertising claims, or ensure pure food and drugs? Does holding a new drug off the market—a drug which could have saved many lives—hurt the public more or less than permitting it to be marketed before it can be certified as absolutely safe?

Even the staunchest advocates of a pure market system admit, however, that there should probably be some ground rules to keep competition within acceptable limits—ground rules that might not be established by a purely competitive market system acting on its own.

The Problem of Third Party Costs

In a perfectly competitive market economy, the cost of production (including a normal profit) is paid by people who buy the product in the market. But the production of some goods can involve real costs not recorded or covered by market transactions—that is, costs not paid for by the person who buys and gets the goods. These costs are called **third party costs.**

If, for example, the production of good X involves a discharge of smoke into the air and sewage or other wastes into rivers and streams, the air and water resources of the country are being spoiled. But the cost of spoiling these resources is usually not paid for by the firms that produce good X, or by the particular consumers who buy this good. The real costs of air and water pollution are usually paid by third parties or by society itself in the form of the extra discomfort endured and property values ruined because of foul air and putrid water, or in the form of the expense involved in cleaning the air and water. In either case, a perfectly competitive market often has no way of directly charging these third party costs to the people who produce and consume good X.

The Problem of Third Party Benefits

Just as the price recorded in a perfectly competitive marketplace might not reflect all of the costs to society, so might it be that the market price will not reflect all of the **third party benefits** to society arising from a private market transaction. If Mr. and Mrs. Y hire a painter to improve the appearance of their home, this might also have the effect of increasing the property value of the surrounding houses in the neighborhood. Yet, in a purely competitive market system, they have no way of collecting any of the tangible benefits their activities bestow on the third parties living in the neighborhood.

In the case of third party costs, the problem for society is that too many of the underpriced goods might be produced. In the case of third party benefits, however, the problem is that not enough of the over-priced goods or services will be produced. Indeed, there may be some goods (such as a public park) that clearly benefit the community as a whole. Yet these goods might not be produced at all in a perfectly competitive market economy, since it would not be profitable for one individual to pay the entire cost, and since there would be no way of charging other people who would benefit from this expenditure. As a result, expenditures on goods and services which provide in whole or in major part third-party benefits are most

THIRD PARTY COSTS AND BENEFITS

A. H. MacDonald

Third party benefits are those like the positive impact on an entire neighbourhood which comes from a project such as the restoration of these pre-Confederation townhouses in Charlottetown, P.E.I. Third-party costs are those carried by a community. The air pollution from the stacks of the steel plant in Sydney, N.S., is such a cost.

A. H. MacDonald

likely to be carried out by some level of government. If they are incurred by individuals or the private sector, it is likely to be for charitable or humanitarian reasons—though "public relations" benefits may be obtained from the expenditure.

The Problem of Research and Development

The problem of research and development (sometimes shortened to R & D) is related to two of the problems mentioned above: size of firm and third party benefits. If there are many small, no-extra-profit producers, the competitive firms in an industry might not have enough money to pay for R & D on new and better goods or production methods. Even if funds or resources were available, would the problem of third party benefits kill incentives to spend on R & D? What if the head of a business says, "Most of the results of my company's research will soon benefit all the other producers in my industry and society in general. Since I have no sure way of charging them enough to make certain that my research is profitable, why should I bother?" This might slow down economic progress.

On the other hand, the capacity for R & D, which comes as a result of size, does not guarantee that the R & D will be carried out, or, if carried out, that the benefits will be placed at the disposal of the consumer. What would a manufacturer of light bulbs do if it were found that an additional $.05 production cost would yield a light bulb which would last for five years? Consider it from the manufacturer's point of view, not your own.

Market Power in The New Industrial State

The New Industrial State by John Kenneth Galbraith provides a view of contemporary capitalism which is frequently critical. The book, its author, and his other works are well worth further detailed examination.

Markets can also be controlled. This consists in reducing or eliminating the independence of action of those to whom the planning unit sells or from whom it buys. Their behavior being subject to control, uncertainty as to that behavior is reduced. At the same time the outward form of the market, including the process of buying and selling, remains formally intact.

This control of markets is the counterpart of large size and large size in relation to the particular market. A Wisconsin dairy farm cannot influence the price that it pays for fertilizer or machinery. Being small, its decision to purchase or not to purchase is of no appreciable significance to the supplier. The same is true of its sales. Having no control over its suppliers or its customers, it pays and receives the going prices.

Not so with General Motors. Its decision to buy or not to buy will usually be very important to its suppliers; it may be a matter of survival. This induces a highly cooperative posture. So with any large firm. Should it be necessary to press matters, General Motors, unlike the dairyman, has always the possibility of supplying a material or component to itself. The option of eliminating a market is an important source of power for controlling it.

Similarly, size allows General Motors as a seller to set prices for automobiles, diesels, trucks, refrigerators and the rest of its offering and be secure in the knowledge that no individual buyer, by withdrawing its custom, can force a change. The fact that GM is one of a few sellers adds to its control. Each seller shares the common interest in secure and certain prices; it is to the advantage of none to disrupt this mutual security system. Competitors of General Motors are especially unlikely to initiate price reductions that might provoke further and retributive price-cutting. No formal communication is necessary to prevent such actions; this is considered naïve and arouses the professional wrath of company counsel. Everyone knows that the survivor of such a contest would be not the aggressor but General Motors. Thus do size and small numbers of competitors lead to market regulation.

Control of prices is only a part of market control; if uncertainty is to be eliminated there must also be control of the amount sold. But size also makes this possible. It allows advertising, a well-nurtured sales organization and careful management of product design which can help to insure the needed customer response. And since General Motors produces some half of all the automobiles, its designs do not reflect the current mode, but are the current mode. The proper shape of an automobile, for most people, will be what the automobile majors decree the current shape to be. The control of demand, as we shall see later, is not perfect. But what is imperfect is not unimportant for reducing market uncertainty.

Finally, in an economy where units are large, firms can eliminate market uncertainty for each other. This they do by entering into contracts specifying prices and amounts to be provided or bought for substantial periods of time. A long-term contract by a Wisconsin dairy farmer to buy fertilizer or sell milk accords no great certainty to the fertilizer dealer or the dairy receiving the milk. It is subject to the capacity of the farmer to fulfill it: death, accident, drought, high feed costs and contagious abortion can all supervene. But a contract with the United States Steel Corporation to supply sheet steel or to take electric power is extremely reliable. In a world of large firms, it follows, there can be a matrix of contracts by which each firm eliminates market uncertainty for other firms, and, in turn, gives to them some of its own.

From: J. K. Galbraith: *The New Industrial State,* Boston: Houghton Mifflin Company, 1967, pgs. 28-31. Reprinted by permission of the publisher. (The footnotes have been deleted in this reprinting. See pg. 29 in the original work.)

Competition and Size

The reading from *The New Industrial State* clearly points out the potential dangers in any situation where a few large firms dominate a market, a situation commonly referred to as **Oligopoly**. Types of competition may continue to exist, but it will not necessarily be competition as it is understood in a truly free market situation. The primary danger is the minimization of the effects of supply and demand through efforts by firms to avoid price competition. This potential effect on market prices is, to the consumer, a most undesirable result. This view of the structure of many markets within our capitalistic system should, however, be considered in relation to another proposition of Galbraith's, the concept of **countervailing economic power.**[4]

This thesis, in most elementary form, is that strong selling power produces strong buying power, that the concentration of power in the hands of producers may be matched by a growing concentration of power in the hands of smaller numbers of retail chains, by more powerful unions representing employees, and by the emergence of

[4] See J. K. Galbraith, *American Capitalism,* Boston: Houghton Mifflin, 1952. For a concise overview of the Galbraithian approach to the operation of markets, see "The Galbraithian Revolution" in the book of readings correlated with this text, *Readings in the World of Economics,* Toronto: McGraw-Hill Ryerson, 1973. The implications of this view of the market will be encountered again in Chapter 30, which deals with wage and price controls.

a stronger and more active governmental role in the economy. In short, the result may be the evolution of an economic balance of power, in some ways comparable to this tendency in international relations.

One question remains: What of those buyers or sellers who are not in a position to acquire greater strength or gain governmental support or protection? They are likely to suffer. It would be naïve to express it any other way. As a result of all this, it must be recognized that the market system, like its alternatives, is not a perfect mechanism. Two basic questions then arise. First, how much regulation by government is appropriate and what form should it take? Secondly, once the first is answered, who should regulate the regulators? Neither is easily answered. Answers that are offered must be carefully examined, for this is an issue where subjective values and vested interest may determine the position taken.

Is Fear of Corporate Growth Declining?

This column by John Meyer, a Canadian business executive and commentator, appeared in May, 1977. Reference to the Royal Commission on Corporate Concentration will be found in Chapter 19, Appendix. Chapter 15 contains outlines of the range of activities of Argus Corporation and Power Corporation.

The government has now confirmed that it will not appoint a successor to Robert Bryce. Mr. Bryce resigned his chairmanship of the Royal Commission on Corporate Concentration early in the month for reasons of health. The appointment of a new chairman, the government says, would delay the publication of the report which is expected in September.

No doubt it would. Might there not be other reasons, possibly more compelling, for allowing the two remaining commissioners and commission staff to complete the report on their own? There is speculation in Ottawa, for example, that the government wants to play down the commission because its findings—what is known of them—aren't what was expected. It is doubtful that speculation is entirely idle.

The way the commission conducted its hearings—the direction of its enquiries and the responses they elicited—was anything but encouraging to those who looked upon it as a trust-busting operation. And there is some reason to believe that many in the Department of Consumer and Corporate Affairs looked upon the commission as just that.

Their simplistic equation of corporate size with corporate power, however, did not stand up under examination. What was presented instead were rationales for growth rooted in the operation of a competitive market, along with the limitations it imposed on growth. What also became evident, as the hearings progressed, was the impossibility of determining corporate accountability in areas other than where the public interest was expressly defined.

The commission was launched out of fear of corporate size generated by the bid by the Power Corp. for control of Argus Corp. It was also launched at a time when demands for corporate accountability were riding the crest of consumerism. Since the commissioners retired to write their report, little has been heard of either. The announcement of Power's subsequent increase in its holdings of Argus rated little more than a couple of paragraphs on most financial pages.

What happened in the meantime? Among other developments, the shifts in the focus of public concern from the conduct of business to the conduct of labor and government. Accompanying it has been a clearer public perception of the role of the corporation in contributing to the individual's economic well-being. It is a shift in focus to which the government has since responded through, as one example, the publication last fall of its working paper, *The Way Ahead*, and, as another example, in the emphasis placed on investment in the last budget.

The commission was appointed when, in retrospect, the pendulum of anti-business sentiment had swung to the extreme of its arc. Now that it is swinging back, the commission's findings, whatever they might be, are becoming progressively less relevant.

Having now achieved a structure for consultation with business, the government is not going to welcome a report which, at one extreme, might castigate corporate growth, any more than it might welcome a report which, at the other extreme, gives corporate growth a clean bill. It has troubles enough, as it is, with the new Competition and the new Telecommunications Acts.

Both vest in federally-appointed administrators broad powers of discretion, which is precisely what is objectionable about them. Consumer and Corporate Affairs Minister Abbott does nothing for the government's case when he asserts, as other ministers before him, that only those engaged in the "abusive exercise of market power" have anything to fear from the Competition Act. Quite the contrary—all Canadians have much to fear from powers it vests in bureaucrats.

But it is the support of business that government has been courting most immediately and it has to find ways of making its new legislation more acceptable if that courtship is to succeed. It's not just concern over corporate concentration that has become redundant: it is also the notion that Ottawa knows best how to manage the economy for the best results.

Competition: What Do We Really Want?

Now that we have asked the question, "Is it possible to organize an entire economy on a perfectly competitive basis?" let us turn to the question, "If it were possible, would we want to do so?"

The answer to the first question is that it might be possible, but it would be extremely difficult and would involve many problems. Indeed, it would involve so many problems and sacrifices of public interests that most people would probably answer no to the second question. Yet the results of a competitive economy have many attractions, and its emphasis on freedom, flexibility, and automatic controls are values most Canadians think are very important. Therefore, the challenge is, if we cannot have perfect competition, can we at least have workable competition? Can we work out a system that maintains as many strengths of the market mechanism as possible but reduces some of the problems inherent in a perfectly competitive market economy?

To answer this challenge, the Canadian economy turns to the institution of government. Along with individuals and business firms, government is one of the basic elements in our economic system. In a later chapter we shall see how the Canadian people have used government to modify what is still basically a private enterprise, free market system.

SUMMARY

In a competitive market economy, prices play the basic role of linking buyers and sellers of all types of resources, goods, and services together, and of allocating all resources to their preferred uses. Through the price mechanism, all markets are interrelated, setting in motion a flow of productive services from individuals to business firms, and a flow of goods and services from these business firms to individual consumers. Against these flows of real goods and services, there is a counterflow of money through which business pays for the services of individuals, and individuals pay for the goods produced by business.

Our economy is, however, not perfectly competitive. Perfect competition would require that in all markets there be so many buyers and sellers that no single one could make a difference; that all products in each market be identical; that buyers and sellers have perfect market information at all times; and that all resources have complete mobility in adjusting to their best uses.

In the real world, many problems inhibit total reliance on market competition as a regulatory force, even in economies that are essentially free private enterprise economies. These problems develop out of technological change and the huge increases in size of firms to which it leads; the desires of consumers for variety; the need of consumers for protection with respect to certain hazards of unlimited competition; the difficulties of charging third party costs to the buyers or sellers of particular goods or of collecting third party benefits; the need to promote social and economic progress by ensuring that businesses spend enough on research and development; and the importance of providing certain public goods, including national defence, public transportation, and public education. Even if a perfectly competitive system were possible, the vast majority of Canadians might not want it. We tend to prefer to supplement and modify our basically competitive system through the institution of government, covered in chapter 19.

KEY CONCEPTS

perfect competition
natural monopolies
third party costs
third party benefits
oliogopoly
countervailing economic power

QUESTIONS FOR REVIEW AND DISCUSSION

1. What are the four basic institutions or pillars on which a market system rests? How would the operation of a market system be hampered if any one of these four institutions were not present?
2. List the conditions that are necessary if a market is to be a perfectly competitive

market. Do many real-world markets meet all of these tests? Does this mean that an analytical model based on perfect competition is not useful?

3. State in your own words how the basic economic questions of what? how? and for whom? would be answered in a perfectly competitive market system. What characteristics of the long-run equilibrium in such a system do you find desirable? What characteristics of such an equilibrium do you find undesirable? Why?
4. What is meant by the terms third party costs and third party benefits? Give one or two examples of each. Why do these third party effects cause problems for a perfectly competitive market system?
5. In addition to third party effects, what are some of the problems associated with maintaining a perfectly competitive economy? Do you think we should try to make Canada have a perfectly competitive economy? Why or why not? What are the costs of doing this? What are the costs of not doing this?

PROBLEMS AND EXERCISES TO SHARPEN YOUR UNDERSTANDING

1. On a separate sheet of paper, write the numbers 1 to 8 and answer the following questions. Be prepared to explain your answers.

   If we start in equilibrium and people decide they want more skate boards and fewer hula hoops, the price of skate boards will (1) (*rise, fall*) and the price of hula hoops will (2) (*rise, fall*). The output of skate boards will (3) (*rise, fall*), and the output of hula hoops will (4) (*rise, fall*).

   If much labor and little capital machinery is needed to make hula hoops, and much capital machinery and little labor is needed to make skate boards, what will happen to the price of labor (5) (*rise, fall*)? What will happen to the price of machines (6) (*rise, fall*)?

   After these prices change, owners of machines will be able to buy (7) (*more, less*) of all goods, and owners of labor will be able to buy (8) (*more, less*) of all goods.

2. Did market prices in the above exercise decide what, how, and for whom? Give another example of how this process works.
3. As a research project, do a study of a Canadian business noteworthy for some special reason, such as the development of new products or technology, or major breakthroughs into foreign markets. (For reading, watch the financial papers and such books as Alexander Ross, *The Risk-Takers,* Toronto: Maclean-Hunter, 1975.)
4. The reading by John Meyer in this chapter refers to changes in public opinion or attitude toward business. What factors or conditions do you think could induce such shifts in attitude in either direction? Can you offer any evidence of recent swings in public opinion or media treatment of business? This same basic question could and, in fact, should be directed also to the roles of both organized labor and government within the economy at appropriate times, as you move through the book.

THE ECONOMIC ORGANIZATION OF A PRISONER OF WAR CAMP (Part 1)

This appendix contains the first part of a classic study of the development of a market system within a P.O.W. camp during World War II. Written by R. A. Radford, the study appeared in November, 1945, shortly after the end of the war. This segment of the study deals with the initial phases in the development of a market system in a situation which is much closer to a closed system than almost any other that could be found. Look within the reading for illustrations of the concepts of supply and demand, the way they influenced "prices," and the factors which inhibited the operation of markets within the camp. The second half of this study will be found as an appendix to chapter 17.

After allowance has been made for abnormal circumstances, the social institutions, ideas and habits of groups in the outside world are to be found reflected in a Prisoner of War Camp. One aspect of social organization is to be found in economic activity, and this, along with other manifestations of a group existence, is to be found in any P.O.W. camp. True, a prisoner is not dependent on his exertions for the provision of the necessaries, or even the luxuries of life, but through his economic activity, the exchange of goods and services, his standard of material comfort is considerably enhanced. And this is a serious matter to the prisoner: he is not "playing at shops," even though the small scale of the transactions and the simple expression of comfort and wants in terms of cigarettes and jam, razor blades and writing paper, make the urgency of those needs difficult to appreciate, even by an ex-prisoner of some three months' standing.

Nevertheless, it cannot be too strongly emphasized that economic activities do not bulk so large in prison society as they do in the larger world. There can be little production; *the emphasis lies in exchange and the media of exchange.*

But it would be wrong to underestimate the importance of economic activity. Everyone receives a roughly equal share of essentials; it is by trade that individual preferences are given expression and comfort increased. All at some time, and most people regularly, make exchanges of one sort or another.

Between individuals there was active trading in all consumer goods and in some services. Most trading was for food against cigarettes or other foodstuffs, but cigarettes rose from the status of a normal commodity to that of currency. RMk.s [German currency] existed but had no circulation save for gambling debts, as few articles could be purchased with them from the canteen.

Our supplies consisted of rations provided by the detaining power and (principally) the contents of Red Cross food parcels—tinned milk, jam, butter, biscuits, bully [beef], chocolate, sugar, etc., and cigarettes. So far the supplies to each person were equal and regular. Private parcels of clothing, toilet requisites and cigarettes were also received, and here equality ceased owing to the different numbers despatched and the vagaries of the post. All these articles were the subject of trade and exchange.

THE DEVELOPMENT AND ORGANIZATION OF THE MARKET

Very soon after capture people realised that it was both undesirable and unnecessary, in view of the limited size and the equality of supplies, to give away or to accept gifts of cigarettes or food. "Goodwill" developed into trading as a more equitable means of maximizing individual satisfaction.

We reached a transit camp in Italy about a fortnight after capture and received ¼ of a Red Cross food parcel each a week later. At once exchanges, already established, multiplied in volume. Starting with simple direct barter, such as a non-smoker giving a smoker friend his cigarette issue in exchange for a chocolate ration, more complex exchanges soon became an accepted custom. Stories circulated of a padre who started off round the camp with a tin of cheese and five cigarettes and returned to his bed with a complete parcel in addition to his original cheese and cigarettes; *the market was not yet perfect.* Within a week or two, as the volume of trade grew, rough scales of exchange values came into existence. Sikhs, who had at first exchanged tinned beef for practically any other foodstuff, began to insist on jam and margarine. It was realised that a tin of jam was worth ½ lb. of margarine plus something else; that a cigarette issue was worth several chocolate issues, and a tin of diced carrots was worth practically nothing.

In this camp we did not visit other bungalows very much and prices varied from place to place; hence the germ of truth in the story of the itinerant priest. By the end of a month, when we reached our permanent camp, there was a lively trade in all commodities and their relative values were well known, and expressed not in terms of one another—one didn't quote bully [beef] in terms of sugar—but in terms of cigarettes. The cigarette became the standard of value. In the permanent camp people started by wandering through the bungalows calling their offers—"cheese for seven" (cigarettes)—and the hours after parcel issue were bedlam. The inconveniences of this system soon led to its replacement by an Exchange and Mart board in every bungalow, where under the headings "name," "room number," "wanted" and "offered," sales and wants were advertised. When a deal went through, it was crossed off the board. The public and semi-permanent records of transactions led to cigarette prices being well known and thus tending to equality throughout the camp, although there were always opportunities for an astute trader to make a profit from arbitrage. With this development everyone, including non-smokers, was willing to sell for cigarettes, using them to buy at another time and place. Cigarettes became the normal currency, though, of course, barter was never extinguished.

The unity of the market and the prevalence of a single price varied directly with the general level of organization and comfort in the camp. A transit camp was always chaotic and uncomfortable: people were overcrowded, no one knew where anyone else was living, and few took the trouble to find out. Organization was too slender to include an Exchange and Mart board, and private advertisements were the most that appeared. Consequently a transit camp was not one market but many. The price of a tin of salmon is known to have varied by two cigarettes in 20 between one end of a hut and the other. Despite a high level of organization in Italy, the market was morcellated [fragmented] in this manner at the first transit camp we reached after our removal to Germany in the autumn of 1943. In this camp—Stalag VIIA at Moosburg in Bavaria—there were up to 50 000 prisoners of all nationalities. French, Russians, Italians and Jugo-Slavs were free to move about within the camp: British and Americans were confined to their compounds, although a few cigarettes given to a sentry would always procure permission for one or two men to visit other compounds. The people who first visited the highly organized French trading centre, with its stalls and known prices, found coffee extract—relatively cheap among the tea-drinking English—commanding a fancy price in biscuits or cigarettes, and some enterprising people made small fortunes that way. (Incidentally we found out later that much of the coffee went "over the wire" and sold for phenomenal prices at black market cafes in Munich: some of the French prisoners were said to have made substantial sums in RMk.s. This was one of the few occasions on which our normally closed economy came into contact with other economic worlds.)

Eventually public opinion grew hostile to these monopoly profits—not everyone could make contact with the French—and trading with them was put on a regulated basis. Each group of beds was given a quota of articles to offer and the transaction was carried out by accredited representatives from the British compound, with monopoly rights. The same method was used for trading with sentries elsewhere, as in this trade secrecy and reasonable prices had a peculiar importance, but as is ever the case with regulated companies, the interloper proved too strong.

The permanent camps in Germany saw the highest level of commercial organization. In addition to the Exchange and Mart notice boards, a shop was organized as a public utility, controlled by representatives of the Senior British Officer, on a no profit basis. People left their surplus clothing, toilet requisites and food there until they were sold at a fixed price in cigarettes. Only sales in cigarettes were accepted—there was no barter—and there was no haggling. For food at least there were standard prices: clothing is less homogeneous and the price was decided around a norm by the seller and the shop manager in agreement; shirts would average say 80, ranging from 60 to 120 according to quality and age. Of food, the shop carried small stocks for convenience; the capital was provided by a loan from the bulk store of Red Cross cigarettes and repaid by a small commission taken on the first transactions. Thus the cigarette attained its fullest currency status, and the market was almost completely unified.

It is thus to be seen that a market came into existence without labor or production. Despite a roughly equal distribution of resources, a market came into spontaneous operation, and prices were fixed by the operation of supply and demand. It is difficult to reconcile this fact with the labor theory of value.

Actually there was an embryo labor market. Even when cigarettes were not scarce, there was usually some unlucky person willing to perform services for them. Laundrymen advertised at two cigarettes a garment. Battledress was scrubbed and pressed and a pair of trousers lent for the interim period for twelve. A good pastel portrait cost thirty or a tin of "Kam." Odd tailoring and other jobs similarly had their prices.

There were also entrepreneurial services. There was a coffee stall owner who sold tea, coffee or cocoa at two cigarettes a cup, buying his raw materials at market prices and hiring labor to gather fuel and to stoke; he actually enjoyed the services of a chartered accountant at one stage. After a period of great prosperity he overreached himself and failed disastrously for several hundred cigarettes. Such large-scale private enterprise was rare but several middlemen or professional traders existed. The padre in Italy, or the men at Moosburg who opened trading relations with the French, are examples: the more subdivided the market, the less perfect the advertisement of prices, and the less stable the prices, the greater was the scope for these operators. One man capitalized his knowledge of Urdu by buying meat from the Sikhs and selling butter and jam in return: as his operations became better known, more and more people entered this trade, prices in the Indian Wing approximated more nearly to those elsewhere, though to the end a "contact" among the Indians was valuable, as linguistic difficulties prevented the trade from being quite free. Some were specialists in the Indian trade, the food, clothing or even the watch trade. Middlemen traded on their own account or on commission. Price-fixing agreements were suspected and the traders certainly cooperated. Nor did they welcome newcomers. Unfortunately, the writer knows little of the workings of these people: public opinion was hostile and the professionals were usually of a retiring disposition.

One trader in food and cigarettes, operating in a period of dearth, enjoyed a high reputation. His capital, carefully saved, was originally about 50 cigarettes, with which he bought rations on issue days and held them until the price rose just before the next issue. He also picked up a little by *arbitrage;* several times a day he visited every Exchange or Mart notice board and took advantage of every discrepancy between prices and goods offered and wanted. His knowledge of prices, markets and names of those who had received cigarette parcels was phenomenal. By these means he kept himself smoking steadily—his profits—while his capital remained intact.

Sugar was issued on Saturday. About Tuesday two of us used to visit Sam and make a deal; as old customers he would advance as much of the price as he could spare then, and entered the transaction in a book. On Saturday morning he left cocoa tins on our beds for the ration, and picked them up on Saturday afternoon. We were hoping for a calendar at Christmas, but Sam failed too. He was left holding a big black treacle issue when the price fell, and in this weakened state was unable to withstand an unexpected arrival of parcels and the consequent price fluctuations. He paid in full, but from his capital. The next Tuesday, when I paid my usual visit he was out of business.

Credit entered into many, perhaps into most transactions, on one form or another. Sam paid in advance as a rule for his purchases of future deliveries of sugar, but many buyers asked for credit, whether the commodity was sold spot or future. Naturally prices varied according to the terms of sales. A treacle ration might be advertised for four cigarettes now or five next week. And in the future market "bread now" was a vastly different thing from "bread Thursday". Bread was issued on Thursday and Monday, four and three days' rations respectively, and by Wednesday and Sunday night it had risen at least one cigarette per ration, from seven to eight, by supper time. One man always saved a ration to sell then at the peak price: his offer of "bread now" stood out on the board among a number of "bread Monday's" fetching one or two less, or not selling at all—and he always smoked on Sunday night.

R. A. Radford, "The Economic Organization of a P.O.W. Camp", *Economica,* vol. XII, No. 48, November, 1945, pp. 189-194. Reprinted by permission of the London School of Economics and Political Science.

CHAPTER 14

POVERTY AND WEALTH

■ THE FUNCTIONAL DISTRIBUTION OF INCOME ■ PERSONAL INCOME DISTRIBUTION ■ WHO ARE THE VERY RICH? ■ THE PROBLEM OF POVERTY ■ WHO ARE THE POOR? ■ SUMMARY

In a market economy, one's income largely depends on the value of what one has to sell in the marketplace. People who own scarce resources or talents that are in great demand receive higher incomes than those without such resources or talents. Such people include movie stars, hockey stars, surgeons, dentists, lawyers, business executives, owners of land and buildings in busy downtown areas, and owners of machinery, oil wells, or patents on important inventions. The poor of our society are those on whose services the market puts a low value. Such people are primarily those who are without skills, bargaining power or public attention. Of course, it is possible for a highly skilled or well-educated person to receive a very low or even zero income, if there is little or no market demand for what is offered. This can be true for certain musicians, actors, authors, poets, painters, and others. Some of these, in order to make a living, will have to develop another skill or ability, or turn their major talent to a more readily marketable use.

■ THE FUNCTIONAL DISTRIBUTION OF INCOME

The process of production in a market economy requires that payments be made to the factors of production. Thus, wages and salaries are the payments for the services of labor; rent is the payment for the use of someone's land or other property; interest is the payment for the use of borrowed money; and profit is the return to business enterprise, when there is an excess of the value of sales over the costs of the goods and services sold. When total income is divided into wages and salaries, rent, interest, and profit, we have a so-called **functional distribution of income,** since it shows the breakdown of income in terms of the functions performed by those who contribute in some way to the productive process.

Following this approach, Table 14-1 shows the income paid to the owners of different factors of production in 1977. Some people may also receive income in the form of transfer payments, such as gifts, unemployment insurance, family allowances, etc. But, since transfer payments do not involve the exchange of any currently produced economic goods or services, we shall temporarily exclude them from our consideration of the functional distribution of income.

If we were to see how the different shares of national income have changed since World War II, we would note a rise in wages and salaries, a slight decline in corporate profits, and a larger decline in the share to unincorporated business.

Many people are surprised at the degree of stability shown by the percentage distribution of our functional income shares, but some cyclical patterns also show up. During depressions, wages and salaries tend to increase as a percentage of the total, while the percentage share of profits tends to fall. During early periods of prosperity, the share of rent and interest tends to fall, while the profit share rises.

A functional income distribution, of

TABLE 14-1. FUNCTIONAL DISTRIBUTION OF NATIONAL INCOME IN CANADA, 1977

Type of Income	Amount of Income in Billions of $	Percent of Total Gross National Product
Wages and Salaries	$ 119.969	57.8
Unincorporated Business Income and Rents	12.065	5.8
Corporate Profits Before Taxes	20.577	9.9
Interest and Investment Income	12.360	5.9
Less Adjustment Items	− .154	−0.1
Total National Income	164.817	79.3

Note: Data are for the preliminary rate of GNP flows at annual rates, as measured for 1977. They are subject to revision.
Source: Statistics Canada, *National Income and Expenditure Accounts, Fourth Quarter,* 1977, cat. 13-001.

course, does not tell us how many people are in each income category. And it does not tell us how many people receive incomes from more than one source. To get information on the **personal distribution of income,** we must use a different set of figures.

PERSONAL INCOME DISTRIBUTION

Table 14-2 shows a personal distribution of income in Canada in 1976. That is, it shows how many households received different levels of income in that year.

Another way of looking at the personal distribution of income in 1975 is presented in Table 14-3. These data break the population into fifths, and show what percentage of the total income received by all households goes to each 20 percent, ranked from the lowest fifth to the highest fifth. The figures indicate that the lowest fifth of the population received 4.0 percent of the income and the top fifth of the population received 42.6 percent of the total income earned in 1975.

Each of the categories in Table 14-3 and Figure 14-2, of course, contains a range of incomes, but the range is the highest among the top fifth of the families where there is no upper limit.

During the depression of the 1930s and World War II, there was an appreciable reduction in the share of income received by the top income group in Canada. However the decline in the share of income received by the top fifth of the population has not gone to the lowest fifth of the population. The biggest increases in income shares between 1935-36 and now have come in the middle-income groups. The middle three-fifths received 42 percent of total income in 1935-36 and 53 percent in 1975.

The rise of this "great middle class" has had important implications for the economy and businesses which now find the largest parts of their markets among families who are reasonably well off but not rich—not rich by our standards, that is, but incredibly rich by the standards of the billions of people in the less-developed countries of the world. Despite the fact that most Canadians are in the great middle class, however, the largest amount of interest and attention in recent years has been focused on the extremes in the scale of income distribution, the very rich and the very poor. Observe the patterns in Table 14-3 for the lowest and highest fifths between 1965 and 1975. Is this a trend you would have expected?

WHO ARE THE VERY RICH?[1]

At the upper end of the income scale, there need be little concern that great fortunes are a thing of the past. Despite the decline in the relative share of income going to the upper fifth of families, the notion that taxes have wiped out those members of the millionaire class who survived the Great Depression is completely false.

Stocks are a favorite form of investment for

[1] See Peter Newman, *The Canadian Establishment,* vol. 1, Toronto: McClelland and Stewart, 1975.

FIG. 14-1 AND TABLE 14-2. PERCENTAGE DISTRIBUTION OF FAMILIES AND UNATTACHED INDIVIDUALS BY INCOME GROUPS, 1976

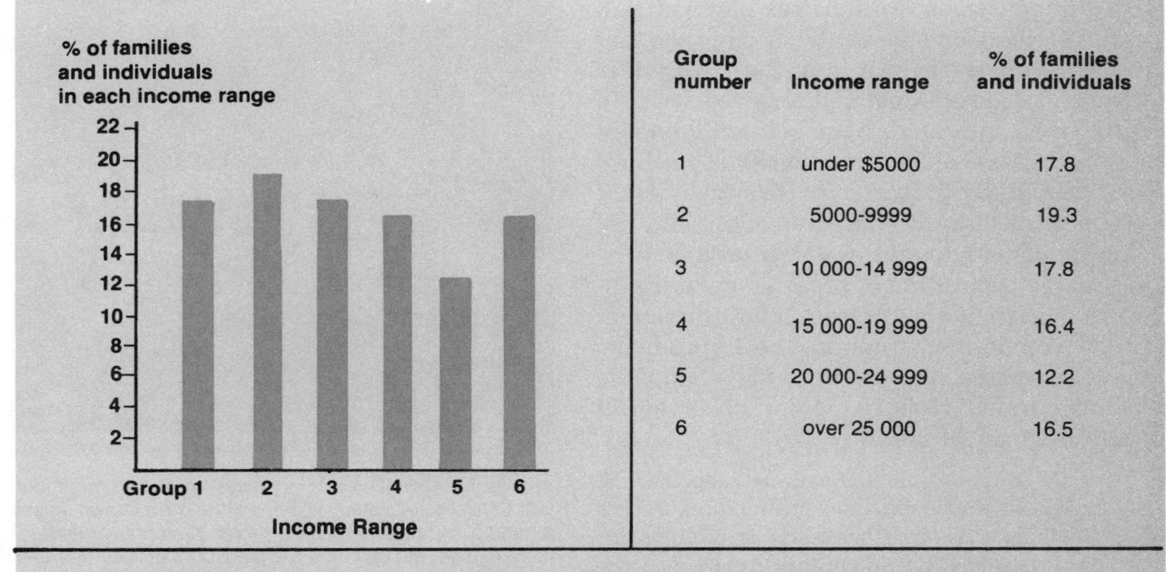

Group number	Income range	% of families and individuals
1	under $5000	17.8
2	5000-9999	19.3
3	10 000-14 999	17.8
4	15 000-19 999	16.4
5	20 000-24 999	12.2
6	over 25 000	16.5

Source: Statistics Canada, *Income Distribution By Size in Canada, Preliminary Estimates, 1976*, cat. 13-206.

FIG. 14-2 AND TABLE 14-3. PERCENTAGE DISTRIBUTION OF TOTAL INCOME OF FAMILIES AND UNATTACHED INDIVIDUALS BY QUINTILES, 1965-1975

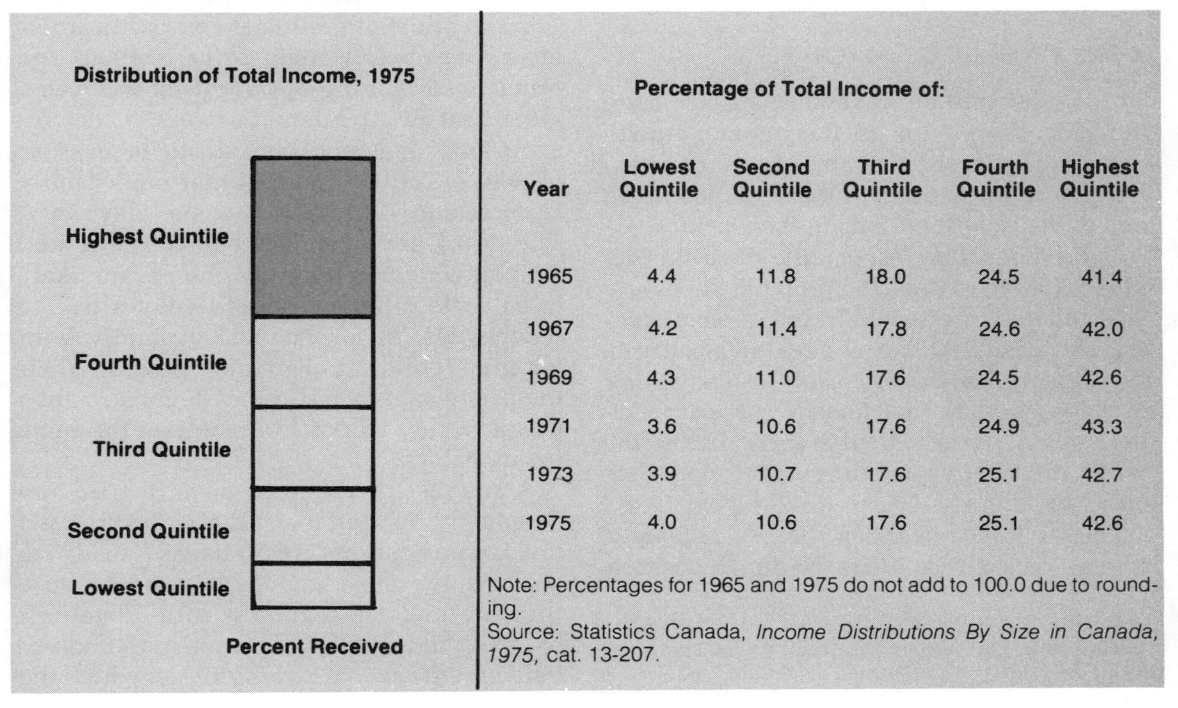

Percentage of Total Income of:

Year	Lowest Quintile	Second Quintile	Third Quintile	Fourth Quintile	Highest Quintile
1965	4.4	11.8	18.0	24.5	41.4
1967	4.2	11.4	17.8	24.6	42.0
1969	4.3	11.0	17.6	24.5	42.6
1971	3.6	10.6	17.6	24.9	43.3
1973	3.9	10.7	17.6	25.1	42.7
1975	4.0	10.6	17.6	25.1	42.6

Note: Percentages for 1965 and 1975 do not add to 100.0 due to rounding.
Source: Statistics Canada, *Income Distributions By Size in Canada, 1975*, cat. 13-207.

millionaires. Real estate and bonds are also favorite investments.

Although some millionaires may get rich quickly, the available evidence suggests that most of them travel a long hard road that takes a lifetime. Most millionaires seem to make their fortune through self-employment in a business. Since the number of millionaires is rapidly growing, it also suggests that the new millions are largely earned and not simply passed down through inheritance.

A large proportion of today's new millionaires gain their wealth from scientific inventions, home construction, new products, new processes, and other socially valuable contributions. Herman Miller observed of the American situation:

> Of course, such innovations keep the rest of us in debt while the millionaires add to their fortunes, but that seems to be the price of prosperity in mid-century America. A dynamic economy requires new ideas and new entrepreneurs who are willing to take chances. We are blessed with an abundance of these men, and it should not be surprising or dismaying that some of them hit the jackpot.[2]

Ontario Ministry of Culture and Recreation

As overall national wealth increases, more and more individuals are able to enjoy luxuries of life once known only to a handful of noblemen and tycoons. Now many others of more modest means know the pleasures of leisure, travel, and high consumption.

THE PROBLEM OF POVERTY

At the other end of the income spectrum are the poor. Despite the great economic growth of Canada, poverty remains a serious problem for a substantial number of people in one of the richest nations in the world.

For a long time, especially since the depression of the 1930s, the problem of poverty was generally neglected in the midst of general prosperity. This may have been because, as Michael Harrington said in *The Other America*, a book that focused American attention on poverty in the early 1960s, the poor are "politically impotent" and "socially invisible."

This is less true today, however, than it was as recently as 1960. National concern has risen over the problem and the demands of the poor for better jobs, more income, and better places to live.

In the midst of the social and political ferment over poverty since the early 1960s, the problem of defining **poverty** itself received a great deal of attention. The reason that income alone may not be an adequate measure of who is actually poor is that other family circumstances besides income may vary. The living and spending habits of a retired couple, who own their own home, are likely to be quite different from those of a pair of newlyweds, or an established family with growing children. Farmers growing their own food may need less cash income than urban factory workers to maintain the same eating habits.

A number of different poverty lines are commonly referred to. Of these, the "revised low income cut-offs" of Statistics Canada are perhaps the most frequently used because they are updated regularly with alterations based on the number of people in the household and the size of community in which the

[2] Herman P. Miller, "Millionaires Are a Dime A Dozen," New York Times *Magazine*. © by The New York Times Company. Reprinted by permission.

The Vicious Circle of Poverty[3]

A young writer, Michael Harrington, did much to make the persistent problem of poverty a political issue in the United States during the booming 1960's. In his book, The Other America, *from which the excerpt below is taken, Harrington showed how the poor are caught in a vicious circle—and live in a "culture of poverty."*

In a sense, one might define the contemporary poor in the United States as those who, for reasons beyond their control, cannot help themselves. All the most decisive factors making for opportunity and advance are against them. They are born going downward, and most of them stay down. They are victims whose lives are endlessly blown round and round the other America.

Here is one of the most familiar forms of the vicious circle of poverty. The poor get sick more than anyone else in the society. That is because they live in slums, jammed together under unhygienic conditions; they have inadequate diets, and cannot get decent medical care. When they become sick, they are sick longer than any other group in the society. Because they are sick more often and longer than anyone else, they lose wages and work, and find it difficult to hold a steady job. And because of this, they cannot pay for good housing, for a nutritious diet, for doctors. At any given point in the circle, particularly when there is a major illness, their prospect is to move to an even lower level and to begin the cycle, round and round, toward even more suffering.

This is only one example of the vicious circle. Each group in the other America has its own particular version of the experience . . . .

The individual cannot usually break out of this vicious circle. Neither can the group, for it lacks the social energy and political strength to turn its misery into a cause. Only the larger society, with its help and resources, can really make it possible for these people to help themselves. Yet those who could make the difference too often refuse to act because of their ignorant, smug moralisms. They view the effects of poverty—above all, the warping of the will and spirit that is a consequence of being poor—as choices. Understanding the vicious circle is an important step in breaking down this prejudice.

From Michael Harrington, *The Other America,* Baltimore, Maryland: Penguin Books, Inc., 1963, pp. 23-24.

The Other Canada[3]

This selection, from a book called The Poverty Wall *by Ian Adams, presents in more personal form a number of the points raised in Harrington's commentary.* The Poverty Wall *is a harsh book, but if examined may well convince the reader its harshness is more than justified.*

You can see them standing grey and mute in the early morning bus lines, holding in one hand a lunch pail or a small brown paper bag of sandwiches. They live in the older, jerry-built suburbs put up immediately after the war, those not-yet-slums but decaying pockets you can find in Halifax, St. Boniface, and Kitsalano. They inhabit the buffer zone between the industrial wasteland and the greener suburbs, where there are picture-window bungalows on streets that are always called Pleasantvale or something like that. The kids are in school, or with grandmother, or with a neighbor down the block. The wives are those harried, unkempt

[3] Despite the fact that the readings are a bit dated, both books are recommended for reference. The conditions described have changed little, though data are now out of date.

women pressing shirts in the corner window of the local drycleaner, serving grilled cheese sandwiches in greasy burger joints, or, if they're lucky, fumbling away time and papers in the lowest echelons of municipal government. The men work at the myriad jobs in the manufacturing, construction, and service industries that are the special domain of the semi- and unskilled worker. They have, on average, a Grade Nine education, and, even if they're not yet middle-aged, they know that all the options of upward mobility are already closed to them. There are usually three or four children to support, which is too many, because the parents earn something between $4500 and $7500 a year. At the bottom end of the wage scale, they know about welfare and living on the pogey during winter unemployment. At the upper end, they moonlight every hour they can, because more than a quarter of their income is gobbled up by exorbitant rents or payments on a wooden frame house that in all probability won't last as many years as the mortgage. There is a four-year-old car to keep running and never enough money to swing a decent trade-in. On average, they are $2500 in debt to the finance company or the bank, and both money-lending institutions charge the highest rates possible, because, you see, they're a "poor risk," although God knows they need the money more than anyone else. For the majority of them, work is drudgery, leisure time is the tube. And their lifestyle is that of one-third of all families—some 7 million Canadians. They are the working poor, the lower middle class, or, to use the inhuman jargon of sociologists, "the lower socio-economic levels without status." Caught in that no-man's land between the slums of the inner city and the slick suburbs, their needs are ignored because they are not poor enough to provide ammunition for the politicians who toss around the political football that is poverty. They are also ignored for the opposite reason; they don't have the money or community machinery that can be used by a politician who is seeking election. They are an ignored and embittered class, which, at this point in our history, neither the government nor industry could do without.

From: *The Poverty Wall* by Ian Adams, 1970, pp. 141-142. Reprinted by permission of The Canadian Publishers, McClelland and Stewart Limited, Toronto.

household is located. The proportion of the population with incomes below this poverty line, or that of the Canadian Council on Social Development, the Senate Committee on Poverty, or other sources varies somewhat, but the rough range has been running from 20-35%, depending on the "line" being used. You should refer to recent data to get specific and current information.[4]

A further problem is access to up-to-date information.[5] The patterns referred to in the following section are based on the best available data from various sources, though they do not always agree completely. The general patterns, however, are quite clear and, unfortunately, quite valid.

WHO ARE THE POOR?

Most of the individuals, families, and groups

[4] Look for the two series from Statistics Canada used as references for Tables 14-2 and 14-3. A prime private source is the Canadian Council on Social Development, which publishes much up-to-date research.

[5] It will have been observed that the data in Tables 14-1, 14-2 and 14-3 are for three different years, even though each had the most "up-to-date " information at the time of writing. Such are the problems of economists, and students of economics.

Fig. 14-3. Percentage Distribution of Low Income Families, 1975

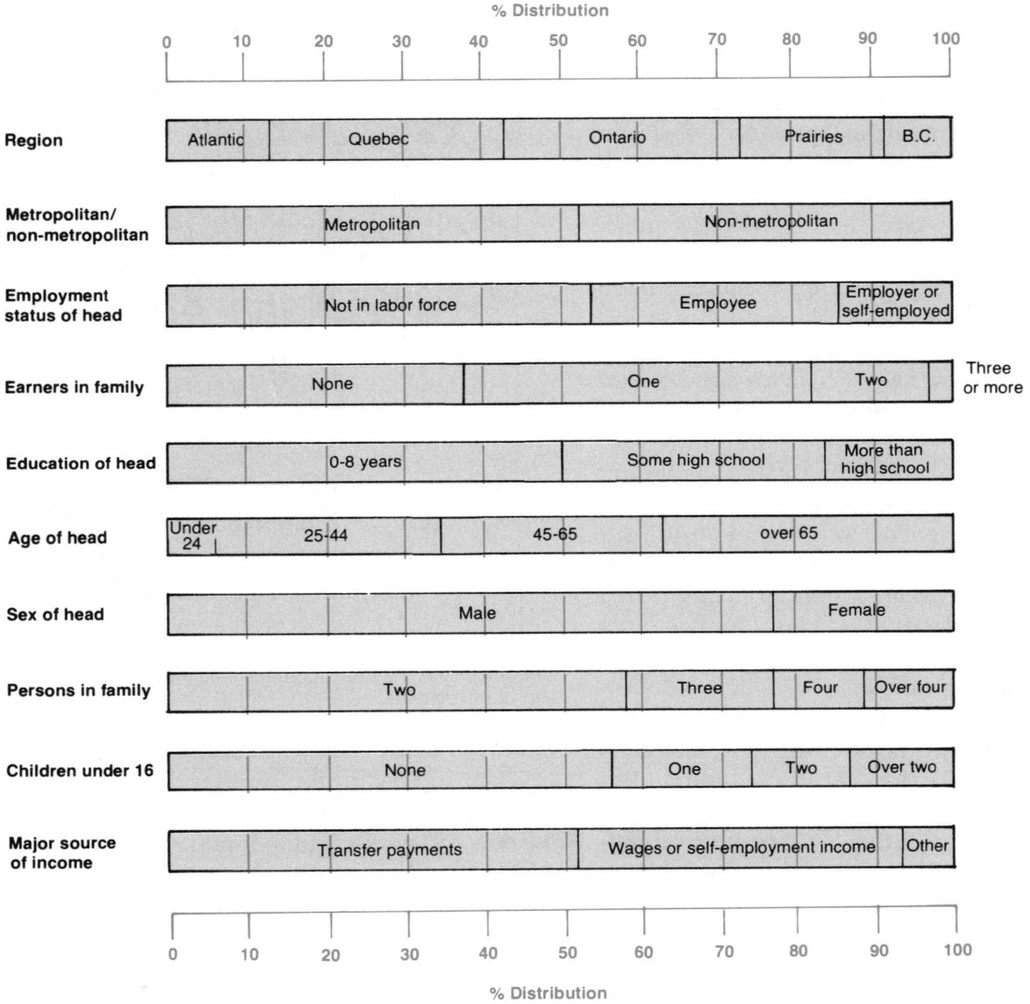

% Distribution
0 10 20 30 40 50 60 70 80 90 100

Region: Atlantic | Quebec | Ontario | Prairies | B.C.
Metropolitan/non-metropolitan: Metropolitan | Non-metropolitan
Employment status of head: Not in labor force | Employee | Employer or self-employed
Earners in family: None | One | Two | Three or more
Education of head: 0-8 years | Some high school | More than high school
Age of head: Under 24 | 25-44 | 45-65 | over 65
Sex of head: Male | Female
Persons in family: Two | Three | Four | Over four
Children under 16: None | One | Two | Over two
Major source of income: Transfer payments | Wages or self-employment income | Other

0 10 20 30 40 50 60 70 80 90 100
% Distribution

Note: This is based on data pertaining to families in the lowest income quintile of families. It does not include unattached individuals and is not directly comparable with data in Tables 14-2 or 14-3.

Source (of data): Statistics Canada, *Income Distributions By Size in Canada, 1975*, cat. 13-207.

The text refers to a number of situations where the proportion of families who are poor is extremely high. Figure 14-3, however, looks at the distribution of the total of all poor families across Canada, and here we find a number of contrasts with the patterns of proportional incidence. Observe that:
(1) 45% of family heads were in the labor force some time during 1975;
(2) 55% of the families have one or more persons who earned wages or salaries some time during 1975;
(3) only 12% were in the Atlantic provinces;
(4) 52% were in large metropolitan centers;
(5) only 23% were headed by females;
(6) 57% have no children under 16;
(7) 48% of heads have at least some high school education.
These facts in the absolute distribution contrast with the proportional trends referred to in the text. Be careful to avoid confusion whenever you are dealing with statistics which might seem to equate proportional and absolute distributions.

ranked within the various categories of poverty mentioned above seem to have certain characteristics that make it difficult for them to move along in the mainstream of our basically market-directed economy. Different studies have shown that, compared to the general population, poverty affects a higher *proportion* of families: (1) who are headed by persons with eight years of education or less; (2) who are headed by non-earners, who because of sickness, a physical or mental handicap, or other disability have no regular, full-time work experience; (3) who are rural farm families; (4) who live in the Atlantic Provinces; (5) who are headed by females; (6) who are headed by persons 65 and over.

If a family is so unfortunate as to have not merely one, but two or more of these characteristics, its chances of falling into the poverty category are increased substantially. Indeed, many of today's poor are caught in a vicious circle of poverty. Many had parents who were also poor, and their children have little to look forward to.

Collins in Montreal Gazette

Doesn't seem to be working at either end

Collins' cartoon aptly summarizes the problems associated with the transfer approach—as viewed from either end of the pipeline.

Since many of the poor are caught up in a cycle of ill health, poor education, and lack of the skills needed to earn an adequate living, some people argue that the best solution to the poverty problem is a **structural approach** that tries to break down the barriers that keep families locked into the culture of poverty and tries to retrain and develop in them the capacity to earn a better living. Others advocate a **transfer approach.** They argue that the basic problem of the poor is simply that they do not have enough money, and they favor various transfer payments to bring poor families up over the poverty line.

Many of the existing transfer programs do not directly benefit many of the families falling below the poverty line, and others are not large enough to raise the recipients out of poverty.

It is estimated that it would take close to $5 billion in transfer or other payments to raise all of the families below the poverty line up to the minimum standards of non-poverty families. This sounds like a lot of money, but compared to total income in Canada it is only slightly above 2 percent. The strongest advocates of the transfer approach argue that it avoids the creation of any new administrative bureaucracy, and leaves the poor free to use their money in ways that seem most effective to them in alleviating their poverty. Opponents of the transfer idea are worried about its effects on people's incentive to work. They argue that, if the poor could be trained to earn the $5 billion or so they need to get out of poverty, the whole society would benefit from the productive output they sell in earning their increased income. They also argue that this would increase the self-respect and morale of those who lift themselves out of poverty.

SUMMARY

In a market economy, such as ours, income is divided up among the people essentially through the interaction of the supply and demand for factors of production. Wages and salaries, rent, interest, and profits are, respectively, the payments to labor, land, capital, and business enterprise for their contributions to the productive process. A functional analysis of income shows that the distribution among these shares has been rather steady over time, although during business upswings and downswings there are variations, with wages rising as a percentage of total income in depressions, and profits rising during prosperity. The personal distribution of income has changed over time, with a reduction over the long term in the proportion of families at the bottom and at the top of the income ladder, and a growing middle class. However, attention in recent years has focused on the very rich and the very poor.

The rich—who have in fairly recent years remained a fairly steady proportion of the total population and are growing in absolute numbers—get a large share of their income from ownership of stocks and other property and from the operation of their own businesses and professions. A growing proportion of the very rich appears to be those who have discovered or introduced innovations that contribute to national economic progress.

The poor are, in general, those who are excluded from the mainstream of national economic development for one reason or another—because they live in poor rural areas, are either unemployed or in low-paying jobs due to lack of skills or adequate education, or are aged or infirm. Efforts to reduce and, if possible, to wipe out poverty have moved to the center of political attention in recent years. *Structural* programs to achieve that end tend to concentrate on increasing the skills and general mobility and employability of the poor. *Transfer* programs concentrate on raising the income of the poor through various welfare payments. But fundamental to any long-run effort to eliminate poverty must be the continuous economic expansion of the nation, which will create more jobs and better-paying jobs. This must be accompanied by the breaking of barriers that have put some people at a disadvantage in the competition for jobs, education, housing, and the other conditions needed for a healthy family life and economic progress.

KEY CONCEPTS

functional distribution of income
personal distribution of income
poverty
structural approach
transfer approach

QUESTIONS FOR REVIEW AND DISCUSSION

1. How does a functional distribution of income differ from a personal distribution of income?
2. Is there a difference between equity and equality in income distribution? Explain your answer.
3. Should the government do something about the poverty problem? If so, how should we define poverty in order to decide who needs help?
4. What is the structural approach to alleviating poverty? How does it compare to the transfer approach?
5. How does an expanding economy help to alleviate poverty? Can continuing economic expansion eventually eliminate poverty completely? Why?

PROBLEMS AND EXERCISES TO SHARPEN YOUR UNDERSTANDING

1. Make up a list of the things you think are essential for a minimum standard of living today.

   How much would it cost a family of four people to buy the things on your list for one year?

   Would the list you have made above have been the same in 1935? Do you think it might be the same if you were to make a minimum standard of living list in 1995? Why or why not?
2. Some assert that some unreasonably low wage rates are a basic cause of poverty among the "working poor." Investigate the range of wages among industries and between provinces. Assuming average work weeks, i.e. in the range of forty hours, how do incomes at these wages compare with poverty line income levels? If minimum wages were to be raised by significant percentages, would this solve the problem? (Be careful to consider effects on employers and employment, as well as on employees.)
3. It appears likely that, some time in the near future, we may have a federally administered Guaranteed Annual Income program. Investigate the arguments for and against such a plan. See what you can find out about experimental programs.
4. "The problems of the welfare recipient" and "welfare bums" are two frequently-heard phrases which tend to establish the two poles of opinion about our welfare system. Investigate the welfare system as it functions within your province and/or municipality.
5. What are the criteria used at present in establishing the various "poverty lines" used by Statistics Canada or the Canadian Council on Social Development? How much variation exists among different lines presently in use?

UNIT 2 REVIEW

1. What is the difference between the quantity of oranges demanded at a price of $1.10 per dozen and the demand for oranges? What is the difference between the quantity of steel scrap supplied at $31 per tonne and the supply of scrap steel?

2. When is a market in equilibrium? What factors will cause it to get out of equilibrium? And what factors will then cause it to return to equilibrium? What factors may cause persistent shortages or surpluses of goods?

3. Do you think there is anything unfair about permitting market prices to ration the available supply of diamonds? Clothing? Housing? College admissions? Aspirin? Penicillin? Milk? Bread? Services of physicians? Space on tennis courts? Seats in concert halls? If everyone received the same income, would you see any need for government action to ensure "fair" distribution of any of the above goods? Would you regard equal distribution of income as fair or unfair?

4. Why is the distribution of income unequal in Canada? What are the basic causes of poverty? How can these best be alleviated? If our national income were twice as high, would you expect poverty still to exist?

5. Is competition essential to the efficient functioning of a market economy? What is the case for—and against—using government to regulate or supplement the working of markets in a democratic society?

INSTITUTIONS IN OUR ECONOMIC SYSTEM

To understand more fully the operation of a market economy such as our own, we must go beyond the mechanism of the market itself. Within this unit, we shall examine a number of the institutions and forces which operate within our market system.

CHAPTER 15

THE ROLE OF BUSINESS IN THE CANADIAN ECONOMY

■ PROPRIETORSHIP ■ PARTNERSHIP ■ COOPERATIVES ■ THE CORPORATION ■ THE ORIGIN OF CORPORATIONS ■ THE ROLE OF SMALL BUSINESSES ■ THE ROLE OF BIG BUSINESS ■ THE ROLE OF PROFITS ■ SUMMARY ■ APPENDIX: AN INTRODUCTION TO CORPORATE FINANCIAL STATEMENTS

In a market economy, individual business firms make the decisions on how to satisfy the demands of the public for goods and services. Businesses, aiming for profit, decide what they shall produce, how much they shall produce, and how they shall produce it. They decide what numbers and types of workers to employ, what machinery to use, where to locate their factories, or mills, or stores. And they decide how much to offer to pay different factors of production and how much to charge for their goods and services.

To be sure, businesses cannot make these decisions like tyrants; in a free economy, each decision must meet some market test. If a producer decides to make a particular product, but finds that the public does not want it and will not buy it, the product must be changed or the firm will go out of business. If it is decided to charge a certain price for a product, but business competitors are charging a lower price and taking sales away, then the price will have to be cut. If it is decided to offer a particular wage to workers, but they will not accept employment at that wage, then the firm will either have to raise the rates of pay or do without labor. The firm often finds that in setting its pay scale, it must negotiate with a labor union representing its workers and other workers in the same industry.

Government also inhibits the freedom of the firm to make certain business decisions. Minimum wage laws may specify that it cannot offer less than a certain wage; child labor laws may specify that it cannot employ youngsters below a certain age; industrial safety laws may specify the conditions that it must maintain in its factories or mines and the type of machinery it may use. A great many other regulations may affect the way it advertises, packages, and sells its products; its right to discriminate among different buyers with respect to prices charged; how it disposes of industrial wastes; where it locates a factory; whether or not it may refuse to bargain with a labor union; whether or not it may refuse to hire specific workers; what methods it may or may not use to drive a competitor out of business; and so on.

Despite all of these limitations on the activities of business, however, it remains true in any market economy, including our own, that the individual business firm remains the center of the economic process and that the individual firm makes daily the basic decisions on what to produce, how much to produce, how to produce it, and how to sell it. We shall now turn to the basic forms of business enterprise in Canada.[1]

[1] Within this chapter, we refer only to privately owned business enterprises. Publicly (i.e. government) owned businesses will be discussed in Chapter 19.

PROPRIETORSHIP

The individual **proprietorship** is the simplest form of business organization. The owner of the business makes all the decisions and gains all the profits—or sustains all the losses to the full extent of his or her ownership of property. Let us suppose, by way of illustration, that a person has total assets (property owned) worth $100 000—including $12 000 in cash, a house worth $55 000, corporate stocks worth $13 000, and land worth $20 000. Assume that $9000 of the cash is invested in starting a shoe store. If the business prospers and pays a return of $7000 a year on the investment, then all that profit (after taxes) belongs to the owner.

But suppose that the business fails. When the business is shut down and all its assets, including the owner's $9000 are gone, there remain debts of $20 000—for unsold merchandise, fixtures and office equipment for the store, money borrowed at the bank to pay for advertising, sales help, and other expenses. The owner will be obligated to cover *all* of these debts, not just the original $9000 invested in the shoe store. Therefore, in order to pay off the creditors, the owner must raise the additional $20 000 in one way or another. The owner could sell the merchandise, fixtures, and office equipment of the store at a loss and sell some other assets to raise cash—for instance, the house, stocks, or land. Indeed, if the total of the debts amounted to $100 000, the owner would have to sell everything to meet the debts.

If the proprietor did not have enough money, the logical result would be to go to court to be declared bankrupt; this would keep the owner from going to jail for defaulting on the debts, but it would not prevent the loss of the assets available, which would go to meet part of the debts. Thus, the individual proprietor has **unlimited liability** for all debts contracted in operating the business.

The logic of unlimited liability for the individual proprietorship is this: An individual might be able to amass a sizable personal fortune by engaging in businesses with heavy risks and avoiding paying off the debts in those businesses that failed. This would be unfair to the creditors, who would have no way of collecting the money due them, even though the individual proprietor who had failed in a particular line might have large personal assets separate from the business—indeed, larger assets than any of the creditors.

Most small businesses—grocery stores, barber shops, bakeries, cleaning establishments, restaurants, auto repair shops, or farms—are individual proprietorships. So are the businesses of some professionals as doctors, lawyers, accountants, architects, authors, individual economists, psychologists, or geologists who do private consulting work (sometimes in addition to other jobs they hold, such as being a university professor). There are about half a million individual proprietorships in Canada, of which about one-third are in farming.

PARTNERSHIP

The **partnership** is a business organization consisting of two or more persons, each of whom is liable for the debts of the partnership to the extent of his personal property. The partnership is thus very similar to the individual proprietorship since it, too, involves unlimited liability for each partner. A partnership ends with the death or withdrawal of any partner, though it may be reorganized to continue as an existing business enterprise.

The essential reason for establishing a partnership is to pool the resources and talents of two or more people where it is desired to expand the size of the business beyond what one of the individuals could handle alone. Several lawyers, for instance, may decide to set up a partnership, so that their law firm can handle a greater number and variety of cases and, thereby, establish a more lucrative and solid business than any of them could manage alone.

Similarly, two people in the retail business (say, a clothing or sporting goods store) might find it advantageous to combine their capital in order to found a store with a better location and a larger stock of goods. This would make it possible for one of them to be away a good part of the time in order to do the firm's buying, while the other would concentrate on running the store. In fact, many of the nation's partnerships are in retailing; the rest cover a wide variety of fields.

Partnerships are rather unstable organizations, not only because they can be dissolved bv the death of a single partner, but because personal conflicts among the partners may easily lead to a dissolution of the firm. Their success involves a high degree of compatibility and trust between the partners, since each one has unlimited liability for all the debts of the partnership. This would make it very difficult to attract small investments from outside persons, who would then become absentee or silent partners. If the business failed, all their personal assets would still be liable to cover the debts of the business, though they had not had an active part in managing the partnership. This unlimited liability of all partners makes this form of business organization unsatisfactory for most large enterprises, where it would be necessary to mobilize the funds of a great many individual investors.

The danger inherent in unlimited liability can be avoided by the establishment of a special type of partnership. Canadian legislation governing partnerships varies from province to province, but in all provinces there is provision for the existence of limited partnerships. The normal pattern for this type of firm is the provision of unlimited liability for at least one partner, and at the same time of limited liability for one or more partners, who frequently must be silent partners, i.e., contributors of capital, but not active participants in the day-to-day activities of the firm. It would be normal to expect that the security of limited liability might carry its costs in the form of reduced levels of voting power or profits, while the greater hazard of unlimited liability could be compensated for in increased shares in areas such as these. Such costs or compensations, however, would be determined by those involved in each individual firm.

The Cooperative

This selection from Samuelson and Scott, a widely used introductory university text, outlines the primary characteristics of the co-op movement. Find out if there is a co-op or credit union in your area. If so, try to get details on its structure and operations.

In certain businesses, cooperative societies are an important alternative to the corporation. They have played a big role in the development of Western Canadian economy (and its politics), where they are relatively more important than co-ops in the United States, though less so than in Europe. St. Francis Xavier University in Nova Scotia is well known for its success in teaching the elements of organizing this kind of business to Maritimers, and recently to visitors from all over the world. . . .

In a *marketing* co-op, a group of farmers, fishermen, or other raw-material producers have formed a society to act as a collector, processor, and distributor of their goods. In place of a corporation's shareholders, each co-op member (who is also a user of the co-op) contributes some capital and is entitled to just one vote.* Thus, the democratic nature of cooperation is stressed. Each year between seasons, the "profit" after all costs (including a price paid to each member for the produce he has deliv-

* Usually, following the famous Rochdale (England) principles laid down by pioneer cooperatives in 1844, members receive a fixed rate of interest on their capital share.

ered) is distributed in proportion to patronage: a farmer who has delivered 4 per cent of the wheat to a pool will get, in addition to his price, 4 per cent of whatever amount the directors choose to distribute to the members. Such co-ops sell about one billion dollars worth of produce every year in Canada.

Often these same people, and city dwellers in Europe too, will form *consumers'* cooperatives, organizing wholesale buying units and running their own retail stores, service stations, medical clinics, and funeral centers. The same Rochdale principles apply. Usually the co-ops do not engage in keen price competition with other retailers, but instead sell at stable prices to their membership and distribute the equivalent of "bargains" in the patronage dividend every year. Consumer co-ops are one of the most important outlets for grocery products in the United Kingdom, though they are having a difficult time competing with the newer chain supermarkets. It appears that the very local and democratic structure of co-ops makes it hard for them to hire and to work with aggressive managers and staff without becoming a commercial business, which of course they wish to avoid.

Cooperatives usually hold evangelical attitudes toward this type of business organization, and work hard to bring about its growth. But in Canada their success has in recent decades been greatest in a third type of business, having rather different historical roots: the credit union. This is a type of savings bank, organized internally on similar lines to producers' co-ops; members often have a common bond, such as belonging to the same parish or co-op, or working in the same factory. Their members deposit savings, and the problem of lending these savings safely (mostly to other members) is simplified by the common bond and the directors' personal knowledge of all their members.

From Paul A. Samuelson and Anthony Scott, *Economics*, second Canadian edition, Toronto: McGraw-Hill Co. of Can., 1968, pp. 105-106.

THE CORPORATION

The **corporation** is, by contrast, ideally designed to provide a means of mobilizing huge financial assets needed for large-scale modern business enterprise, since it is chartered under the law and recognized as a legal body apart from its individual owners, each of whom enjoys **limited liability.** This means that each owner (stockholder) cannot be assessed for debts beyond the amount of the investment in the corporation. Suppose that you buy one share of the stock of a corporation for $50; if the corporation fails, the *most* that you can lose is that $50.

This financial feature of limited liability is the key to explaining why the corporation has become the dominant form of business organization. Not only does it permit the corporation to draw money from a great many individual investors as *owners* but also, since its assets are huge, it permits the corporation to *borrow* great sums of money from banks or other financial institutions or individuals. The corporation issues two basic forms of **securities** signifying either ownership in the corporation or debts of the corporation: (1) **common stocks,** which represent ownership, and (2) **bonds,** which represent debt. The stockholders are the owners of the company, and they elect its board of directors, who provide overall direction and control. The bondholders are creditors of the corporation. They lend money to the corporation at a fixed rate of interest in exchange for their loan to the cor-

The Annual Meeting: Whose Voice Really Counts?

In this selection from The New Industrial State, *Galbraith makes some caustic observations about one result of the tendency for ownership and control to be divorced from each other in the large corporation.*

With even greater unction, although with less plausibility, corporate ceremony seeks also to give the stockholders an impression of power. When stockholders are (or were) in control of a company, stockholders' meetings are an occasion of scant ceremony. The majority is voted in and the minority is voted out, with such concessions as may seem strategic, and all understand the process involved. As stockholders cease to have influence, however, efforts are made to disguise this nullity. Their convenience is considered in selecting the place of meeting. They are presented with handsomely printed reports, the preparation of which is now a specialized business. Products and even plants are inspected. During the proceedings, as in the report, there are repetitive references to *your* company. Officers listen, with every evidence of attention, to highly irrelevant suggestions of wholly uninformed participants and assure them that these will be considered with the greatest care. Votes of thanks from women stockholders in print dresses owning ten shares "for the excellent skill with which you run *our* company" are received by the management with well-simulated gratitude. All present show stern disapproval of critics. No important stockholders are present. No decisions are taken. The annual meeting of the large American corporation is, perhaps, our most elaborate exercise in popular illusion.

From J. K. Galbraith, *The New Industrial State,* Boston: Houghton Mifflin Company, 1967, p. 84. Reprinted by permission of the publisher.

poration, but they do not own the corporation.[2]

If you own a share of stock in a corporation you may receive **dividends** that the corporation pays to its stockholders out of its profits. As profits of a corporation rise, your dividend payments are likely to rise as well; but if the corporation makes no profits, you will receive no dividends. In some cases, corporations may pay no dividends for a long time, but plow back their profits into expanding the business.

By contrast, the bondholder cannot expect that higher profits earned by the corporation will yield a higher interest return; bondholders receive the **interest** fixed on the bond at the time it was issued. If the corporation fails, the bondholder can assert a claim to receive money back ahead of the stockholder, who is an owner. Since bondholders are not owners of the corporation, they cannot vote for the board of directors or on matters affecting the policies of the company.

Corporations often issue a third type of security called **preferred stock,** which stands midway between stocks and bonds. Preferred stock usually has a set rate of dividends, such as $5 per share, which must be paid before any other dividends are paid out to the so-called *common* stockholders. Pre-

[2] You may wish to learn more about corporate securities. In the case of "bonds", there are many types, including some which are in fact not true bonds but debentures. This could make a good topic for research.

From a painting from Franklin Arbuckle, R.C.A. for the Hudson's Bay Company

Corporations—such as the Hudson's Bay Company—played an important part in developing the New World. This painting shows Samuel Hearne building Cumberland House for the Hudson's Bay Company in present-day Saskatchewan in 1774.

ferred stock does not ordinarily carry a vote in the affairs of the corporation. In case the business fails and its assets are liquidated, preferred stock stands *ahead of common stock* in line for payment of claims, but *behind bonds.*

The huge sums of money that corporations can raise through stocks and bonds make possible one of the corporation's prime advantages: the ability to hire outstanding professional managers, who handle the vast job of organizing large numbers of men and capital equipment to produce goods and services efficiently. These professional managers have a great degree of latitude in making the day-to-day decisions of how best to operate the business. They are, however, subject to the overall control of their boards of directors, who are supposed to represent stockholders' interests. In fact, since great corporations may have hundreds of thousands of individual stockholders, there is commonly wide separation between ownership and management of the modern corporation. Finally, the corporate form offers legal status to the institution which, barring failure, remains in effect without any time limit.

THE ORIGIN OF CORPORATIONS

The concept of the corporation is by no means a modern invention. The basic concept of the corporation as *a body of people banded together to act as one* dates back to ancient Rome; from Roman law, this concept passed into English law, and so on to our own law. Corporations played a role in the very early development of our country and continent. For instance, the Hudson's Bay

Company (now a very important Canadian corporation) was chartered in England in 1670 under the name of The Governor and Company of Gentlemen Adventurers to Trade in the Region of Hudson's Bay.

Such corporations were very attractive to early business investors. First of all, they offered limited liability. But, in addition to that, since the corporation was originally regarded as the child of the government that had created it (and was, therefore, subject to special regulation by government in exchange for the privilege of limited liability), owners expected that government would behave in a kindly way toward its own child. The state might invest funds of its own in the corporation—money that had been raised by taxing the people collectively. The state might also grant monopoly privileges to the corporation on the ground that it was doing the state's business and deserved special protections. Such potential advantages made governments the target of pressures (and sometimes of bribes) from those seeking to have states set up corporations from which they could personally benefit.

To correct the inequities of political patronage and unfair monopoly, new corporation laws which granted *any* group the privilege of incorporating by filing the necessary papers, showing only that they were willing to conform to the laws, began to appear by the nineteenth century. The door was thus opened to permit the corporation to be used commonly in all sorts of businesses.

The corporate form of doing business was particularly well suited to the economy of a growing country. It permitted businesses to tap financial resources all over a country—and investors in foreign countries as well. Foreign investment played a big part in the development of many major Canadian businesses. Further, corporations increased the mobility and flexibility of capital. Anyone who owned stock in a corporation would normally find it easy to sell (though not necessarily at an attractive price!) and use the capital in another business—or in some other way.

THE ROLE OF SMALL BUSINESSES

While great corporations unquestionably play a dominant role in the Canadian economy today, one must remember that they have by no means wiped out small business. Although large corporations have grown even more important in manufacturing, small businesses still often find a place for themselves as an adjunct to the activities of large manufacturers or, independently, in other fields. For example, many small businesses provide the retail outlets for large manufacturers. Through franchise arrangements, small businesses account for very large sales volumes by dealers in automobiles and petroleum products, and the many other firms offering a wide variety of services and products: roadside food stores, sales of hearing aids, carpet cleaning, coin-operated laundries, radios and television sets, and others.

Even in manufacturing, there are many niches for small businesses (those, say, with fewer than 250 employees). Many can produce goods for local business users rather than for the national market. Many other small manufacturers find a place making parts for large manufacturers in fields ranging from aircraft to zippers. Small makers of materials required for construction, such as concrete products, millwork, asphalt, and other materials, continue to grow.

In retailing, the corner grocer is fading away as the big supermarkets expand, but specialty stores are increasing in number in suburban shopping centers. And in services, the scale of operation stays relatively small for such businesses as beauty parlors and barber shops, self-service laundries, funeral parlors, service stations, and all the other kinds of businesses you find listed in the yellow pages of your telephone book. There are also ample opportunities for the growth of services to industry—such as public relations, management consulting, computer operations, office services, economic forecasting and advising, accounting, and legal advice.

Creative Destruction

Joseph A. Schumpeter, who was professor of economics at Harvard University until his death in 1950, was perhaps the most brilliant philosopher of capitalism and one of the most sensitive observers of economic change in this century. In the following passage, Schumpeter describes how businesspeople continually destroy old economic orders and create new ones by their enterprise.

The essential point to grasp is that in dealing with capitalism we are dealing with an evolutionary process. It may seem strange that anyone can fail to see so obvious a fact . . . . This evolutionary character of the capitalist process is not merely due to the fact that economic life goes on in a social and natural environment which changes and by its change alters the data of economic action; this fact is important and these changes (wars, revolutions, and so on) often condition industrial change, but they are not its prime movers. Nor is this evolutionary character due to a quasi-automatic increase in population and capital or to the vagaries of monetary systems of which exactly the same thing holds true. The fundamental impulse that sets and keeps the capitalist engine in motion comes from the new consumers' goods, the new methods of production or transportation, the new markets, the new forms of industrial organization that capitalist enterprise creates.

. . . The history of the productive apparatus of a typical farm, from the beginnings of the rationalization of crop rotation, plowing and fattening to the mechanized thing of today—linking up with elevators and railroads—is a history of revolutions. So is the history of the productive apparatus of the iron and steel industry from the charcoal furnace to our own type of furnace, or the history of the apparatus of power production from the overshot water wheel to the modern power plant, or the history of transportation from the mailcoach to the airplane. The opening of new markets, foreign or domestic, and the organizational development from the craft shop and factory to such concerns as U.S. Steel illustrate the same process of industrial mutation—if I may use that biological term—that incessantly revolutionizes the economic structure *from within,* incessantly destroying the old one, incessantly creating a new one. This process of Creative Destruction is the essential fact about capitalism. It is what capitalism consists in and what every capitalist concern has got to live in.

From J. A. Schumpeter, *Capitalism, Socialism, and Democracy,* 3rd Edition, New York: Harper & Row, 1950, pp. 82-83.

The vast majority of home builders are still small business organizations. Here, too, the growth of big industries which manufacture tile, plumbing equipment, plywood, roofing materials, or even prefabricated components, does not obliterate small business. As prefabricated components gradually come into wider use during the years ahead, the growth in the overall demand for housing, as population expands, should more than offset the losses made to large-scale manufacturers of houses. It should serve to keep the small builder a major force in the housing construction industry.

THE ROLE OF BIG BUSINESS

However, despite the survival of a very large number of small businesses, there is no doubt about the growing dominance of the very large corporations in manufacturing, mining, transportation, finance, and many other fields. The reasons for and impact of this trend is in fact one of the main themes in Galbraith's *New Industrial State,* from which you have already encountered two excerpts.

A fairly detailed factual account could be given here to illustrate this trend. Precise figures, however, become outdated rapidly. In-

Photo courtesy of Churchill Falls (Labrador) Corporation Ltd.

Carving Out a Mountain: The corporation is paramount among privately owned forms of business organization in its ability to raise large amounts of capital. Privately owned ventures requiring massive amounts of capital usually utilize the corporate form of organization. This photo was taken during construction of the underground powerhouse at Churchill Falls, the largest single-site power facility now operating in North America, with capacity of over 5000 megawatts. The original privately owned firm was taken over by Newfoundland and Labrador Hydro, a provincially owned utility in Newfoundland and Labrador, in 1974.

First place in terms of size may go to the LG2 site at Hydro Quebec's James Bay development. It is scheduled to come into production in the early 1980s with a capacity slightly above the Churchill Falls site.

stead, it is suggested that research be done to find some up-to-date statistics. Good sources for Canadian data are *The Financial Post* and the *Financial Times of Canada,* two weekly papers, and for the U.S.A., *Fortune,* a monthly magazine.

What precise measures should one look for? Select an industry, such as the steel industry, and obtain as much data as possible on the industry and its major participants. In the case of the Canadian steel industry, the "big three" are Stelco, Dofasco, and Algoma. Examine the total sales, total output, total profits, and total assets of the three (or the two largest firms) in relation to the totals for all firms in the field. Other items which might be considered would be employment, taxes paid, new capital invested, research expenditures, and the like. This type of approach in an industry or over a number of industry groups will indicate in a clearer and more beneficial way the importance of giant corporations in many segments of our economy.

The growth of these corporate giants shows how important the *advantages of scale*—that is, of size—are in exploiting modern technology to supply the demands of mass markets, in developing new products and new technology, and in huge investment programs aimed at expanding sales and profits.

However, these advantages—so important in large-scale manufacturing, mining, trans-

FIG. 15-1. ARGUS CORPORATION: MAJOR INTER-CORPORATE CONNECTIONS

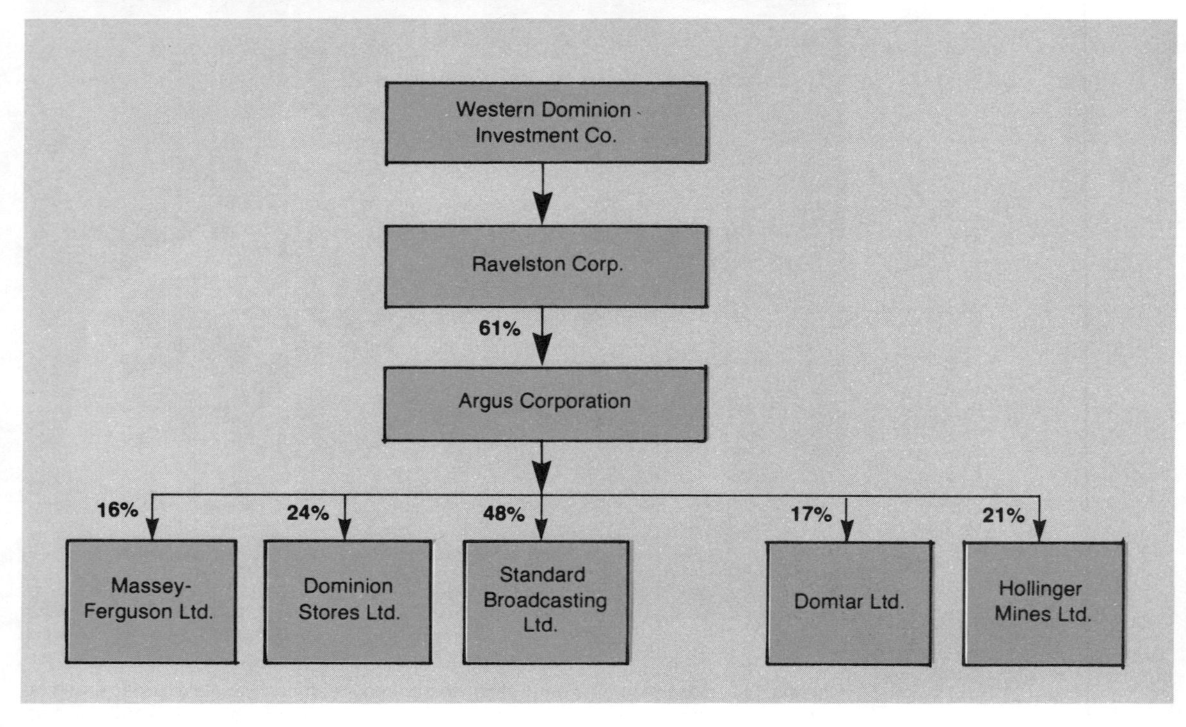

portation, public utilities, and other industrial fields—are not enough to wipe out huge numbers of small businesses in manufacturing, retail trade, housing construction, business services, and other fields where the flexibility and intelligence of businesspeople can be brought into play to deal with local, regional, or even national demands. The Canadian business landscape is still a vast plain of many small and medium-sized businesses, over which loom some mountainously tall corporate giants.

Within the ranks of "big business," many large corporations are in reality corporate "families" or, if you prefer, corporate "empires." Instead of just one corporation, there may be a great many, linked together by one organization that owns a dominating or controlling block of voting shares in each company. In addition, many corporate structures exist for a wide range of reasons. Some distinct corporations may be established for particular types of activity, or to function within a certain legal jurisdiction. Some corporate empires may be made up of many companies operating in different nations (the so-called multinational firms, which will be discussed in the appendix to Chapter 32).

Corporations are not always operating companies directly involved in producing goods or providing services. Some may be managerial or investment companies that invest in and perhaps acquire a major role in the management of other firms. Two prominent Canadian firms of this type, sometimes referred to as holding companies, are Argus Corporation and Power Corporation, referred to in the reading, "Is Fear of Corporate Growth Declining?" found in Chapter 13. In

FIG. 15-2. POWER CORPORATION: MAJOR INTER-CORPORATE CONNECTIONS

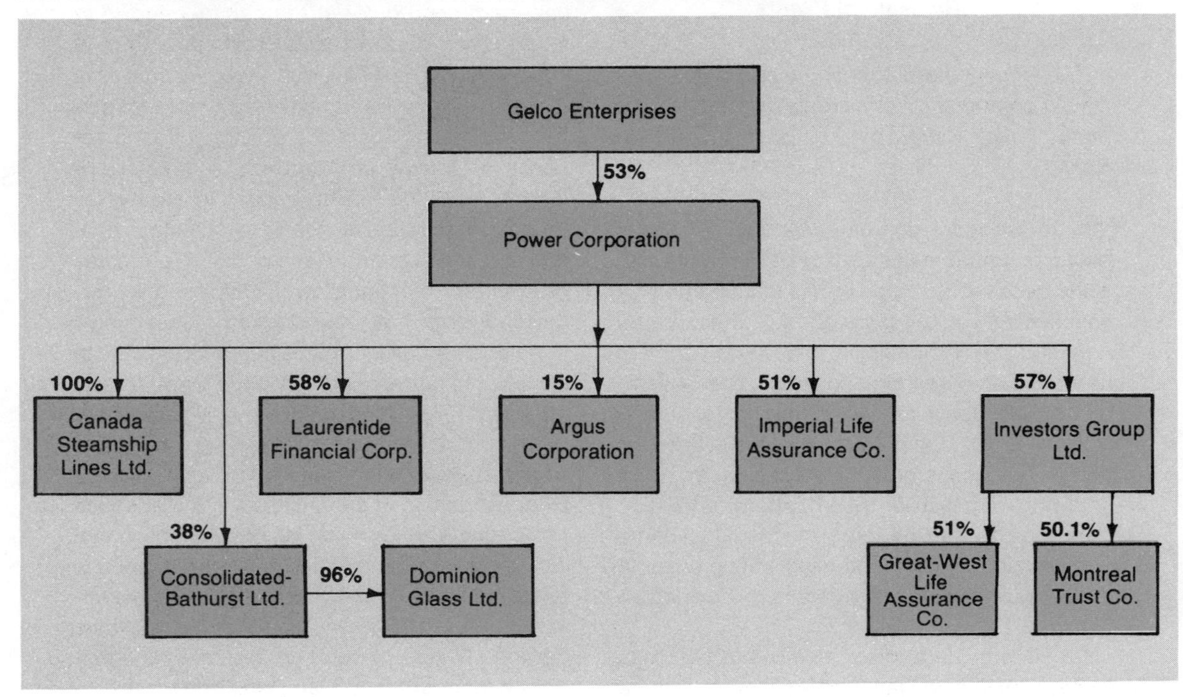

Figures 15-1 and 15-2, outlines are given of the major interests of these two firms.

Within the two figures above, the percentages given indicate the percentages of voting control held by each group over the one below it.[3] In the majority of the cases for Power Corporation's subsidiaries, absolute control (i.e. over 50% of voting shares) is held. In many instances, however, ownership of a smaller block of shares may be quite adequate to provide control, and Argus' investments reflect a policy of control through a "dominating block" of shares.

Note Power's 15% interest in Argus. It was a public bid by Power Corporation for shares in Argus which prompted the establishment of the Royal Commission on Corporate Concentration in 1975, despite an immediate rejection by the group that controlled Argus at that time of any offer from Power Corporation.[4]

You should also be aware that these charts are just preliminary outlines. As an indication of how they extend, refer in Chapter 32, Appendix, to Figure 32A-1 which outlines some (but only some) of the international holdings of Massey-Ferguson, one of the Argus subsidiaries.

[3] As publicly reported in mid 1978.

[4] See Peter Newman's *The Canadian Establishment*, vol. 1. Toronto: McClelland and Stewart, 1975, for an account of this, and also of the key individuals who dominated both firms at that time. The death of J. A. McDougald in early 1978 led to major changes at Argus Corporation which were still evolving in mid 1978. As an initial indication of these, see a profile of the new President of Argus, Conrad Black, in *Maclean's*, June 26, 1978. For detailed backgrounds on the development of these two major firms, see Background Reports #1 (Argus) and #10 (Power) of the Royal Commission on Corporate Concentration.

The Role of Profits

The following analysis of the role of profits is from a commentary on various aspects of economic policy issued by the Toronto-Dominion Bank.

Vital to the resolution of a restructuring of the economy and a revitalizing of economic growth is the necessity to place profits in their true perspective and allow them to play their proper role, and this responsibility falls on government as well as on corporate shoulders. The Government of Canada is to be commended for stressing the need to "increase both the reliance on and effectiveness of the market system." This implicit recognition of the important motivation provided by the market mechanism offers some hope that more attention will be given to the serious problem of profits in the Canadian economy.

Profits provide a major stimulus to business investment in new plant and equipment and are the best measure of success or failure; of efficiency or delinquency; of growth or stagnation. This return for business enterprise has been misconstrued as depriving other factors of production—namely labor—of an assumed greater return. The growth of corporation profits at different times has been used by organized labor as a means of justifying ever-growing increases in wage rates. Governments in turn appear to have perceived profits largely as an irritant to the labor/management scene, thus interpreting corporate profitability negatively and relegating to a minor role the very important positive aspects of profits. *Greater reliance upon the operation of the market system necessarily recognizes the strong motivation provided by corporation profits. Profits represent a return to capital and to initiative. They not only generate dividends but also provide the retained earnings which provide funds for present research and development and are an important contributor to the capital needed in future investment.* To view profits as a form of income in competition with labor income is a disservice to the basic stimulating role that corporation profits play in the economy. In the absence of healthy profit growth, it is not likely that there will be healthy growth in the overall economy. Profitability tends to stimulate economic expansion and in so doing promotes greater employment growth. Unfortunately, organized labor has often looked at seemingly large percentage increases in profits in order to lay claim to correspondingly large labor income increases. This suggests a view of profits as a drain upon labor income, depriving labor of its "rightful" share of income. There appears to be little recognition of the fact that, in the absence of adequate corporation profits, labor income can be adversely affected because economic expansion is thwarted. There also does not appear to be any suggestion by labor that if profits decline, wages should be reduced, thereby having labor share in both gains and losses.

In looking more closely at profits, it must be recognized that their measurement can sometimes be very deceptive. During inflationary times the illusion of massive profit increases is created by the deficiencies of present accounting practices, which fail to take adequate account of inflationary pressures. Depreciation, based upon historical costs rather than current replacement costs, creates distortions that in turn generate the illusion of enormous profitability, an illusion that can only be perceived if all relevant facts are known.

This consideration aside, it is a fact that pronounced profit increases have received widespread attention but declining or weak profits have not. Indeed, profits are traditionally more volatile, falling as well as rising—in marked contrast to the characteristically steady growth of labor income's share of total gross national product (GNP). In the post World War II period, labor's share has in fact risen steadily from approximately 49 per cent of GNP to some 55 per cent in recent years. But corporation profits have generally maintained an 11 to 13 per cent share for several decades. When longer term trends are thus considered, it is apparent that the relative position of corporation profits has deteriorated when compared to the relative position of labor income.

From a social point of view, corporation profits are not the exclusive preserve of the wealthy; increasingly this return is being distributed throughout the entire population, a trend which has accelerated dramatically with the growth of the relative role of pension funds in the economy. The continued health of many pension funds relies on the continued growth of corporation profits in Canada. Such continued growth will, in many instances, provide the future incomes and pensions for many retired workers.

It must become the role of governments to defend the level of profits in the same way they would defend the level of national income. Profits should not be looked upon as a key to a problem in the economy or as an indicator of a new source of taxation. Rather, strong profits should be looked upon as the result of a successful economy, developing strong and viable business enterprises serving Canadian consumers and providing the potential economic growth for future labor force entrants.

Reprinted by permission of the Toronto-Dominion Bank from "Reaction and Reform: Canada's Social and Economic Programmes," in *Business and Economics*, vol. 6, No. 1, January, 1977.

THE ROLE OF PROFITS

At the heart of any business venture is the basic objective of profit. The nature of the profit motive has been discussed previously in Chapter 12. Each business, including any of the types of firms examined in this chapter, must be guided by its own quest for profit within the constraints of the law and the marketplace. And we should note that this quest for profits can serve as a driving force for the whole economy. As outlined in Figure 13-2, business firms in search of profit have a vital role to play in the circular flow. They use resources and pass along money payments to other sectors of the economy in return for the materials, land, labor and capital needed in production.

In recognizing the importance of this role of profit as a catalyst within the economy, we must also recognize the naïvety of the assertion that all profit is basically evil. Likewise, the assertion that any profit, regardless of its level or method of acquisition, is basically good is equally naïve. As with so many other economic issues, opinions on what are "fair," "appropriate" or "reasonable" levels or margins of profit are often based on value judgments or vested interests. Definitive answers or absolute truths about this issue are in short supply.

SUMMARY

The basic forms of business organization in Canada are the individual proprietorship, the partnership, the co-op, and the corporation. Although, in terms of number, the individual proprietorship is the most common, covering small businesses, the corporation has become the dominant form of organization for major industries, such as manufacturing, mining, transportation, and finance. The great advantage enjoyed by the corporation in mobilizing the vast sums of capital required for modern business and industry is the right of limited liability.

Despite the continued growth of huge corporations, neither competition nor small business has disappeared from the scene. Small business still shows great vitality in retail trade, services, small manufacturing, housing construction, and other fields. Yet the great corporations continue to expand in size of assets, sales, and number of employees.

The corporations' great size inevitably thrusts them into the public limelight and raises questions about the appropriate social role to be played by these powerful economic organizations. One of the important issues of our times is how to resolve conflicts, when they emerge, between the interests of the society and the private, financial interests of the great corporations.

Profit, as a return for effort and on capital, plays a basic role as a catalyst for business actions and reactions which, in turn, have far-reaching effects on all other sectors of the economy.

KEY CONCEPTS

proprietorship	securities	preferred stock
unlimited liability	common stocks	interest
partnership	bonds	limited liability
corporation	dividends	

QUESTIONS FOR REVIEW AND DISCUSSION

1. Compare and contrast the advantages and disadvantages of individual proprietorships, partnerships, and corporations with respect to the following points of business organization:
   - control of owner over business operations
   - access to funds
   - liability for business losses
   - stability and length of life
2. Which form of business organization in Canada is the most numerous? Which is most important with respect to the volume of employment and sales? What trends do you expect for the future? Why?
3. What are the basic differences between the common stocks, the preferred stocks, and the bonds issued by a corporation?
4. Do you think that large corporations have a social responsibility to the community over and above their duty to earn money for their owners (the stockholders)? Do you think that large corporations should use stockholders' money for these outside purposes? Explain.

PROBLEMS AND EXERCISES TO SHARPEN YOUR UNDERSTANDING

1. Take a sheet of paper and make three separate column headings for bonds, preferred stock, and common stock. Then for each item listed below put its corresponding letter in each column for which the item is an appropriate description (some items may fit more than one column, some items may not fit any column).
   a. Represents a share of ownership in a corporation
   b. Represents a loan to a corporation
   c. May be sold by the owner to anyone
   d. Has the limited liability feature
   e. Income therefrom is called a dividend
   f. Income therefrom is called interest
   g. Offers absolute assurance of a steady income to the purchaser
   h. Income must be paid in all circumstances short of bankruptcy
   i. Income must be paid before any dividend can be paid on common stock
   j. Income must be paid only when the corporation's board of directors authorizes such payments
   k. Represents a fixed charge for a corporation
   l. Does not represent a fixed charge for a corporation
   m. Its value to the owner is likely to change as the profits of a corporation rise or fall
2. Write a brief essay comparing and contrasting bonds, preferred stock and common stock from (a) the viewpoint of the business firm issuing them and (b) from the viewpoint of the individual person buying them.
3. Why have some corporations grown so large? Why have so many small businesses managed to survive?
4. Research the corporate empires of some of Canada's business giants. Try to contrast differences among holding companies like Argus Corporation or Power Corporation, vertically-integrated companies like Imperial Oil, (which range from raw material exploration through to retailing products), and horizontally-integrated firms (which specialize in one type of activity) like George Weston Ltd.
5. Examine the profits of two similar firms by comparing their profits:
   (a) in relation to total sales
   (b) in relation to shareholders' equity
   (c) in relation to total assets
   (This problem should be done after you have examined the Appendix to this chapter.)

APPENDIX:

AN INTRODUCTION TO CORPORATE FINANCIAL STATEMENTS

If one wished to obtain information about the financial structure, debts, profits, or the like about a corporation, where would one look? One possibility, of course, would be secondary sources such as the financial press or reports from investment dealers. Ultimately, however, the basic source for everyone is financial data provided by the corporation itself. The most important part of this continuous flow of information is the annual report of the corporation, containing the financial statements for the previous year. This section will provide a brief introduction to corporate financial statements. It will do little more than touch on a few concepts of corporate accounting, but it will make it possible for the reader to apply these concepts and be able to look at statements from any corporation with a basic understanding of what the statements present to him. Statements for Dominion Stores for 1977-78 are used as reference points to illustrate these basic concepts.

The three statements reproduced are the three most crucial for the individual interested in the structure and profitability of a firm. There are other statements which will be found in many corporate reports, but these will not be dealt with here for the sake of brevity. Before an examination of each statement in turn, one point might be noted. Each of the statements is referred to as a "consolidated" statement. This means that they have data not just for Dominion Stores Limited, but also for companies owned by and associated with the parent corporation.

The Statement of Earnings, sometimes called the Income Statement or the Profit and Loss Statement, deals with total income, expenditures, taxes, and profits for the company's financial year—which for Dominion Stores ends in March. The basic pattern is to indicate total income, sometimes distinguishing between sales revenues and other income, less all expenditures and deductions which can be made for tax purposes. The table of deductions may sometimes not provide details on a number of items, such as labor costs and raw materials costs, but just include these and other items within one "cost of goods sold" figure. Total revenue or income, less the total of expenses or deductions for tax purposes, yields pre-tax earnings, or what is sometimes referred to as "gross profit". This is the basic amount which is subject to corporate income tax.[1] The gross profit less taxes on income leaves the "net profit" or net earnings for the year.[2]

The major items in this statement thus are revenues, expenditures and the resulting profits or losses for the year indicated, and the one year previous, which is almost always shown for comparison. One can tell nothing about the company's total size, its debts, its previous earning power, payment of dividends, etc. For details on these

[1] The structure of corporate income taxes and eligible deductions is extremely complex. If you wish to check on current rates, etc., consult the Department of National Revenue for introductory information, or check a general source such as a current *Canada Year Book*.

[2] "Minority interest" refers to shares of profits paid to minority shareholders in some subsidiaries which are not 100 percent owned by Dominion Stores.

Consolidated Statements of Earnings and Reinvested Earnings

Consolidated Statement of Earnings

	For the years ended March 18, 1978 (52 weeks)	March 19, 1977 (52 weeks)
	(in thousands of dollars)	
Sales	**$2 215 836**	$2 026 488
Cost of goods sold and expenses except those shown below	**1 853 979**	1 707 647
Employees' salaries and benefits	**286 782**	256 161
Depreciation	**17 511**	15 568
Municipal taxes	**14 609**	12 636
Interest on long-term debt	**7629**	4453
Other interest	**325**	519
Investment income	**(2396)**	(934)
	2 178 439	1 996 050
Earnings before taxes on income	**37 397**	30 438
Taxes on income *(note 6)*	**16 318**	14 113
Earnings before minority interest	**21 079**	16 325
Minority interest	**243**	127
Net Earnings for the year	**$ 20 836**	$ 16 198
Earnings per share	**$ 2.44**	$ 1.90

Consolidated Statement of Reinvested Earnings

	For the years ended March, 18 1978 (52 weeks)	March 19, 1977 (52 weeks)
	(in thousands of dollars)	
Reinvested Earnings—*beginning of year*	**$109 485**	$101 037
Net earnings for the year	**20 836**	16 198
Dividends	**(8181)**	(7750)
Reinvested Earnings—*end of year*	**$122 140**	$109 485

Consolidated Balance Sheet as at March 18, 1978

Assets

	March 18, 1978	March 19, 1977
	(in thousands of dollars)	
Current Assets		
Cash	**$ 3915**	$ 10 295
Short-term investments	**23 905**	—
Accounts receivable	**10 256**	8174
Mortgages receivable	**723**	709
Merchandise (note 1)	**151 354**	121 449
Prepaid expenses	**1818**	1418
Deferred income taxes	**529**	274
	192 500	142 319
Mortgages and other Investments—*at cost*	**284**	434
Investment in effectively controlled company *(note 1)*	**3709**	3312
Fixed Assets *(note 1)*		
Store, warehouse and office equipment	**193 929**	175 899
Buildings and leasehold improvements	**67 312**	60 545
	261 241	236 444
Less: Accumulated depreciation	**123 723**	113 767
	137 518	122 677
Land	**14 319**	13 616
	151 837	136 293
Unamortized Debenture Discount *(note 1)*	**1087**	
	$349 417	$282 358

Liabilities

	March 18, 1978	March 19, 1977
	(in thousands of dollars)	
Current Liabilities		
Accounts payable and accrued expenses	**$ 84 004**	$ 90 780
Income and sundry taxes	**12 804**	2065
Current portion of long-term debt *(note 3)*	**1221**	1351
	98 029	94 196
Deferred Income Taxes	**12 760**	11 370
Long-Term Debt *(note 3)*	**93 557**	44 750
Minority Interest	**1417**	1174
	205 763	151 490

Shareholders' Equity

Capital Stock *(note 4)*		
Authorized—		
20 000 000 common shares without nominal or par value		
Issued and fully paid—		
8 525 831 shares (1977—8 516 596 shares)	**21 514**	21 383
Reinvested Earnings	**122 140**	109 485
	143 654	130 868
	$349 417	282 358

Signed on behalf of the board
A. BRUCE MATTHEWS, T. G. BOLTON,
Directors

Notes to Consolidated Financial Statements

1. Accounting Policies

(a) Principles of consolidation—

The accompanying financial statements consolidate the accounts of Dominion Stores Limited and all its subsidiaries.

(b) Investment in an effectively controlled company.

The equity method of accounting has been used to account for the investment in the effectively controlled company.

(c) Merchandise

Merchandise is located at both stores and warehouses. These inventories have been valued at the lower of cost and market. The term "market" as it applies to store inventories means "net realizable value" and to warehouse inventories "replacement cost."

(d) Fixed Assets

The cost of fixed assets (including significant renewals and betterments) is capitalized at cost. Provisions for depreciation are determined on a straight-line basis over the estimated useful lives of the assets as follows:

Store, warehouse and office equipment	—3 to 10 years
Buildings	—40 years
Leasehold improvements	—term of lease

(e) Amortization of debenture discount

The debenture discount is amortized over the term of the issue.

2. Remuneration of Directors and Senior Officers

In the fiscal year ended in 1978 the company had 12 directors (1977-twelve) and 13 senior officers (1977-thirteen) 4 of whom were also directors. The aggregate remuneration of directors as such was $70 500 (1977-$66 000) and of senior officers as such was $1 493 000 (1977-$1 461 000)

3. Long-Term Debt

	March 18, 1978 $	March 19, 1977 $
Redeemable sinking fund debentures		
9¾% Series "D" maturing December 1, 1990	18 846 000	20 000 000
9¾% Series "F" maturing July 15, 1997	50 000 000	—
9½% Series "E" debentures maturing March 1, 1980	25 000 000	25 000 000
Non-interest bearing note and mortgages payable bearing interest at rates from 6¾% to 11%	931 811	1 101 489
	94 777 811	46 101 489
Deduct: Current portion included in current liabilities	1 220 897	1 351 416
	93 556 914	44 750 073

The principal amounts payable in the next five fiscal years are:

Fiscal years ending March	
1979	$ 1 220 897
1980	26 228 400
1981	1 172 400
1982	1 202 661
1983	1 174 000

4. Stock Option Plan

Pursuant to an employees' stock option plan adopted by the company on August 26, 1969, 112 198 unissued common shares of the company are reserved as at March 18, 1978. During the year 9235 shares were issued for cash of $130 525 upon exercise of stock options granted. Of the options granted to date, the following remain to be exercised (including options on 68 599 shares to senior officers, 3 of whom are also directors).

Number of shares	Option price	Expiry date
74 800	14.13	November 18, 1978
27 999	17.50	April 22, 1980

The exercise of these options would have no material effect on the reported earnings per share.

5. Long-Term Leases

The total minimum rental liability under leases (excluding insurance, property taxes and certain other occupancy charges) to the date of expiry or option, whichever occurs first, for each of the periods shown below, is as follows:

	March 18, 1978	March 19, 1977
	$	$
Within 5 years	110 754 000	97 869 000
Within the next 5 years	90 913 000	83 586 000
Within the following 10 years	114 367 000	104 942 000
Within the remainder of the term	20 078 000	19 009 000
	336 112 000	305 406 000
Minimum annual rentals payable under such leases are	25 943 000	23 578 000

Certain leases contain an option to cancel. Should the company exercise these options, it could be required to purchase the related properties.

6. Income Taxes

Taxes on income have been reduced by approximately $1 748 000 resulting from the 3% inventory allowance provided by recent changes in tax legislation.

7. Pension Plan

As of January 1, 1978, the estimated past service unfunded pension liability amounted to approximately $23 068 000 of which approximately $5 900 000 has vested with employees of the company. This liability is being funded over 12 years by means of annual payments of approximately $2 567 000. These payments are being charged against operations in the year in which they are made.

8. Anti-Inflation Act

The company is subject to restraint of profit margins, prices, dividends and compensation under the terms of the Anti-Inflation Act and Regulations which became effective October 14, 1975.

Auditor's Report to the Shareholders

Coopers & Lybrand
Chartered Accountants

145 King Street West
Toronto, Ontario

We have examined the consolidated balance sheet of Dominion Stores Limited as at March 18, 1978 and the consolidated statements of earnings, reinvested earnings and changes in financial position for the fiscal year then ended. Our examination was made in accordance with generally accepted auditing standards, and accordingly included such tests and other procedures as we considered necessary in the circumstances.

In our opinion, these consolidated financial statements present fairly the financial position of the company as at March 18, 1978 and the results of its operations and the changes in its financial position for the fiscal year then ended in accordance with generally accepted accounting principles applied on a basis consistent with that of the preceding year.

(Coopers & Lybrand)
CHARTERED ACCOUNTANTS

April 12, 1978

points, one must look in the proper places—but those are not in the Statement of Earnings.

The second statement, that dealing with Reinvested or Retained Earnings, follows the Earnings Statement in logical sequence. It indicates (a) how much of the year's net profit has been paid out in dividends and (b) how much profit has been retained throughout the life span of the company. It should be obvious that the total at the end of one year is that for the beginning of the next year. To this is added total profit for the year, less dividends paid out during the year, yielding the balance at the year's end. One important point to note is the fact that while the statement gives the total profit which has not been paid out in dividends, it does not tell how this profit has been used by the firm. Some idea of this, however, might be obtained from the final statement, the Balance Sheet.

The basic purpose of the Balance Sheet is to show, as of the end of each financial year, what the firm is worth, what its debts are, and what the difference between the two is. The latter, sometimes called the "book value," is what the firm is worth to its owners, the shareholders. Hence the term Shareholders' Equity for the section which is equal to Assets minus Liabilities. (Before proceeding, consider what would be the value of a share in a company where Assets and Liabilities were equal. Be prepared to justify your conclusion.)[3]

Within the asset side, there are several general categories which are frequently used in corporate reporting. Current assets are those which are in cash, which will be received shortly (usually within one year) in cash, or which will be turned into cash by the normal course of business. Prudent treatment of any asset requires that it should not be overstated, hence allowances are usually made for the possibility that some accounts receivable will not be paid. Investments are usually recorded at cost or present market value, whichever is lower.

Fixed assets are those in the form of land, buildings, equipment, etc.; i.e. assets which can not be readily sold and for which there might be few buyers willing to pay close to what the assets were actually worth. Total original cost of fixed assets may not be present value. Depreciation can and does take place. The accumulated depreciation total equals the sum of the amounts by which the assets decreased in value each year. (It may be noted that these figures do not necessarily correspond to what has been claimed for tax purposes within the statement of earnings.) "Book value" here is cost less depreciation. But what about appreciation of assets such as urban land? Here again, the basic approach that "it is better to understate than overstate your assets" comes into play.

Other assets outside of these three basic categories may include a wide range of items, but usually represent a low percentage of total asset value. Even in instances where they are obviously very important (e.g., patents for companies such as I.B.M. and Xerox) they are usually entered at nominal value since it is impossible to place an accurate value on this type of asset.

Liabilities are usually broken down into two basic categories, "Current" (i.e. payable within approximately one year) and "Long Term." Deferred Income Taxes are those payable, or which may be assessed against the corporation in the future. It might be noted that "Long Term" debt may run very far into the future. Within the details of the outstanding long-term bonds and debentures (which are listed in a footnote in the report) are found issues which mature between 1980 and 1997. If there are any doubts about the possible amount of any liabilities, the reverse of the accounting adage about assets is usually practiced, i.e. "better to overstate than understate liabilities."

[3] Do not be surprised, when examining balance sheets from corporations, if you encounter a one-page format, which is laid out in the sequence: Assets minus Liabilities equal Shareholders' Equity, in contrast to the two-page format where Assets equal Liabilities plus Shareholders' Equity.

Consequently, "Assets" minus "Liabilities" should equal a Shareholders' Equity, which is a minimum rather than a maximum figure. The reasons for this being the more desirable alternative should be self-evident by this point.

Finally, we come to the Shareholders' Equity, the balancing item. Here, we find details about the number of shares authorized and actually issued,[4] the amount the company has received for these and the total of retained earnings (brought forward from the retained earnings statement) plus any special funds which belong to the shareholders.

The total of Shareholders' Equity and Liabilities must equal that of Assets. The reason is that the two sides are one and the same thing, broken down in different ways. An increase of $10 million in Assets would have to be balanced by an increase of $10 million in either Liabilities or Shareholders' Equity. If the $10 million had been borrowed, it would be added to the former; if it had been raised by selling additional shares or through retained earnings, then the increase would fall into the Shareholders' Equity.

To illustrate this point with a grossly simplified example, prepare a Balance Sheet for a company whose Liabilities exceeded its Assets. The problem is easily solved.

BANKRUPT CORP. LTD.			
Assets	10	Liabilities	12
		Shareholders' Equity	−2
	10		10

The −2 figure is, of course, a mathematical "trick," since the existence of limited liability for the shareholders eliminates their obligation. However, the Balance Sheet balances—as it must every time.

To conclude this appendix, one recommendation is given. Obtain copies of reports from a number of companies to acquaint yourself with a few of the variations in structure and to test your understanding of the basic elements found in the statements.[5] Also, a reminder is in order. This section has only touched on a few highlights of one aspect of a wide field. If you are interested, much may be pursued in this area on your own. Your teacher can recommend sources of additional information on the subject.

[4] Note the increase in the number of shares during 1977-78.

[5] Corporate Reports can often be obtained from brokers and investment dealers and almost always from the companies themselves if they are publicly held. Addresses can be obtained from sources such as the Financial Post's Surveys of Industrials, Mines, and Oils, found in most libraries or investment dealers' offices.

CHAPTER 16

MONEY AND PRICES

■ THREE MAJOR FUNCTIONS OF MONEY ■ FORMS OF MONEY ■ MONEY IN CANADA TODAY ■ CONSTRUCTING A PRICE INDEX ■ INTERPRETING PRICE-INDEX NUMBERS ■ PRICES AND THE VALUE OF MONEY ■ SUMMARY

Ask most people what they think economics is all about, and they will probably say money. Yet here we are up to Chapter 16 in this economics book, and we have really had little to say about money. Up to now, we have been emphasizing the real or physical aspects of the world of economics.

Certainly it is real goods and services that determine the standard of living of a person and the economic strength of a nation; you cannot eat money. And certainly it is the scarcity of real resources that prevents individuals and nations from living as well as they would like. Our study of economics thus far has focused on the questions of how best to use scarce real resources. In microeconomics we emphasized the allocation of scarce resources or goods between one use and another, so that resources would not be permitted to stand idle.

But what does money have to do with all of this? Money is important because of the ways it helps to promote the flow of real resources, goods, and services between one use and another and to facilitate the total use of real resources. Indeed, money plays such a *visible* role in the economic process that many people fall into the trap of focusing only on money itself. Obsessed with dollar signs, they may fail to see the basic flows of goods and services that go on beneath the veil of money transactions in our economy.

In this chapter we shall begin an attempt to lift this veil and see how money works in promoting the real production and distribution of goods and services in our economy. Also, we shall consider the total size of the nation's money supply and see how it is related to the level of economic activity and prices.

■ THREE MAJOR FUNCTIONS OF MONEY

In our economy, money serves as a unit of account, as a medium of exchange, and as a store of value.

Unit of Account

In adding up the total of our economic output, we could see how money can be used as a unit of account, or measure of value. You cannot add apples and oranges. But, if you use the money prices of apples and oranges, you can add the value of apples and oranges. Money thus serves as a means of measuring economic activity, just as metres are basic units of length or kilograms are basic units of mass.

This measuring function greatly facilitates exchanges of goods by enabling every buyer or seller to decide whether or not a deal is advantageous. Money permits exact ratios to be worked out among all goods and services.

In its role as a unit of account, money also permits businesses to establish accounting systems that enable them to determine precisely their costs of doing business and the prices they should charge to realize profits.

This, too, helps to promote the efficient allocation and use of real resources, both for individual businesses and for the economy as a whole.

Medium of Exchange

If an economy is to benefit from the increased production that comes from specialization and the division of labor, it must have a well-developed exchange mechanism. For people cannot each concentrate on doing the things they do best if they cannot exchange the fruits of their production (whether these are strawberries, thumbtacks, tractors, or poems) for the goods and services produced by others, which they need and want. How does the specialist trade his or her goods for the goods of other specialists?

The simplest form of exchange is **barter,** or the direct trading of goods between people. If we had to rely on barter, there would probably be very little specialization in our world. Take the case of a shoemaker who wants his daughter to learn arithmetic from a specially trained teacher. He will have to find such a teacher who also wants a pair of shoes. But what if the arithmetic teacher already has a pair of shoes? What if he really wants a haircut, but the barber has no children and already understands all the arithmetic he needs to know?

Barter requires a *double coincidence of wants*. Carpenters with furniture to trade for shirts must find tailors with shirts who want furniture. But, alas, even when the goods sought are the same, the quantities wanted may differ. If 1 chair is worth 10 shirts, and the carpenter wants only 2 shirts, it is unlikely that he will be able to cut the chair into 5 pieces and trade 1 of the pieces to the tailor for 2 shirts. Who would want one-fifth of a chair?

If money is introduced into this situation, however, both carpenter and tailor can trade for money and then use the money to trade for the other things they want. Money does not require a double coincidence of wants. The shoemaker does not have to look for an arithmetic teacher who needs a pair of shoes, nor the carpenter for a particular tailor. If people are willing to accept money in exchange for goods and services, they can use money as a **medium of exchange** that permits specialization and division of labor throughout a highly complex economy. (Recall Figure 13-2 in Chapter 13, which shows a flow of money in one direction balanced by a flow of goods and services in the other direction; this is a broad picture of money serving as a medium of exchange.)

Store of Value

Closely related to its function as a medium of exchange is the role money plays as a **store of value**. Money lets you exchange something you want to get rid of now for something else you may want to acquire later—perhaps tomorrow, perhaps 20 years from now. If you sell your house for $50 000 you do not want to rush out immediately and buy $50 000 worth of food, clothing, and other goods or services—and you may or may not want to buy another house right away. Likewise, a lumber dealer who sells $50 000 worth of lumber may or may not want to spend his returns at once. Money lets you wait, and lets you provide for your future needs.

Money is not, unfortunately, a perfect store of value. If prices rise, money will, as we have already seen, lose some of its value; if prices fall, money will gain extra value. In times when people distrust money as a store of value, they will try to convert money into things that they think will be better stores of value—land, precious metals (such as gold), rare paintings, or stocks. Conversely, when prices are falling and the value of money as a store of value is rising, people may try to hold onto money and sell goods or assets whose values are dropping.

FORMS OF MONEY

An astonishing variety of things has been used as money throughout history. Money was not invented by some unknown genius;

VARIETIES OF MONEY

BABYLONIAN CLAY DUE BILL

CHINESE TAO

STONE MONEY OF YAP

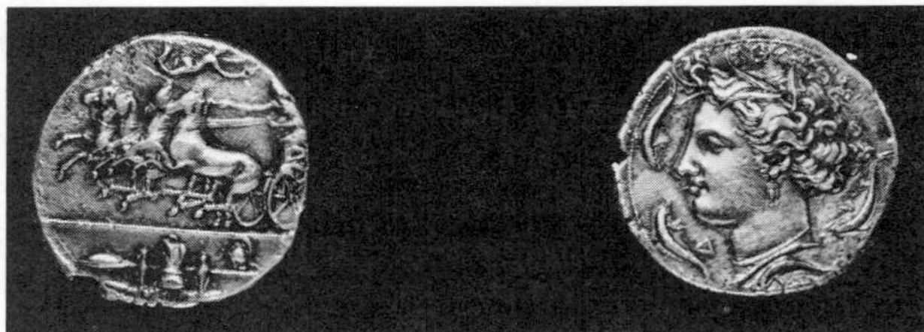

DECADRACHM OF SYRACUSE

Many different kinds of objects can be used to provide the three basic functions of money—as a unit of account, a medium of exchange, and a store of value. On these two pages, we see varieties of money that have been used from ancient Babylonia to Germany in 1923. Obviously, some types of money were much more convenient than others; the stone money of Yap, for instance, could never serve in a complex economy. The elephant tail bristles of Portuguese West Africa and the canine teeth of the Solomon Islands could not permit much increase in the money supply. On the other hand, simple coins—which have scarcely changed from ancient Greece to modern times—were marvelously convenient and (by changing the value upon them) infinitely expandible—as the German one-billion mark coin indicates. The world was rather slow in recognizing that units of money did not have to have any inherent value (as do the silver pieces of eight or bronze bells of Rhodesia) in order to satisfy all the functions of money.

All Photos Courtesy The Chase Manhattan Bank Money Museum

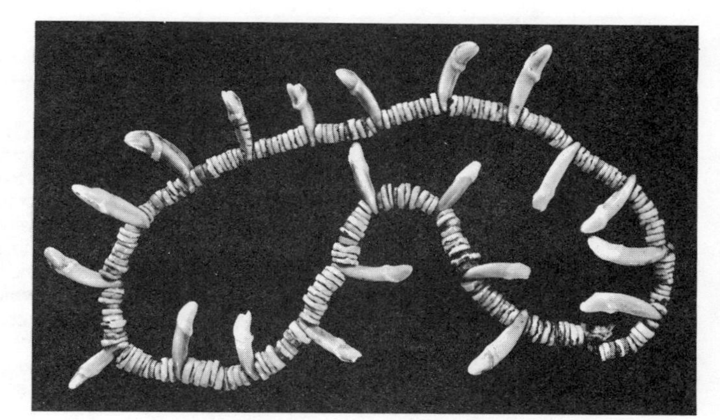

SOLOMON ISLANDS CANINE TEETH

ELEPHANT TAIL BRISTLES

BRONZE BELL OF RHODESIA 19TH CENTURY

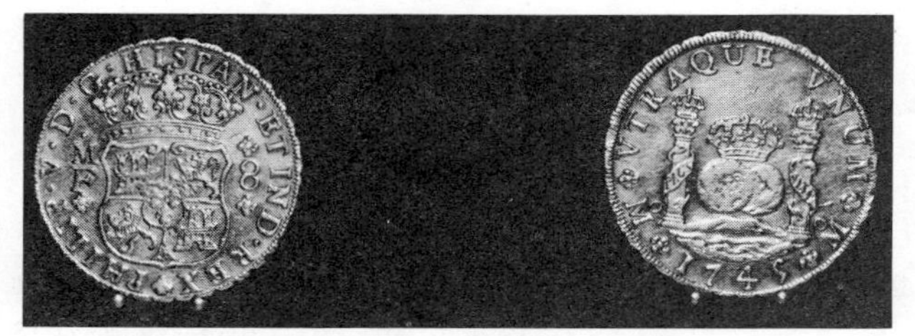

PIECE OF EIGHT 18TH CENTURY

GERMAN ONE BILLION MARK—1923

EARLY CANADIAN PAPER MONEY

Bank of Canada

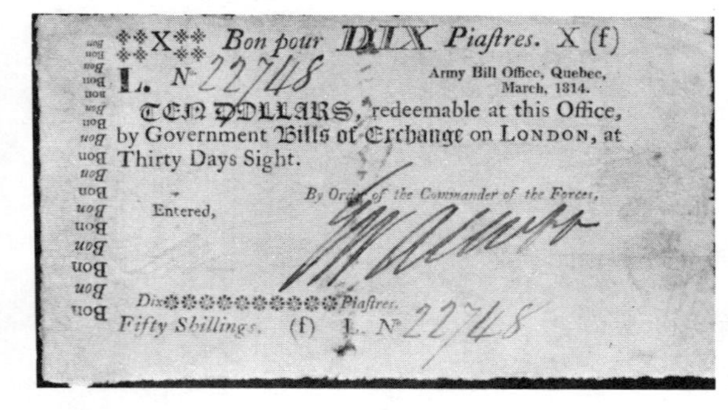

The card money shown in the first photograph has a dramatic history. In the early days of New France it was the practice to send out a supply of coins on the first ship in the spring to be used in paying the troops and to purchase furs and other raw products. When the supply ship returned to France in the fall it took with it most of the coins to pay taxes and purchase manufactured goods for the colony. This resulted in a scarcity of coins every winter and caused considerable inconvenience. Finally, in 1685, the Intendant, Jacques de Meulles, decided to introduce an emergency issue of paper money. As there were no printing presses and no supply of suitable paper available, the notes were handwritten on the backs of playing cards. At the end of the year the notes were redeemed in full. In subsequent years further issues were made. The first five issues were made on playing cards. Their retention after the redemption date was punishable by death and no specimens of this playing card currency have survived. Later issues were made on plain white cardboard and a few of these can be found today in museum collections. The one illustrated here is on plain white cardboard and was issued in 1735.

The War of 1812-14 was financed by the issue of Army Bills, one of which is shown in the second photo, from the headquarters of the British Army at Quebec. At the end of the war these Bills were redeemed in full. This restored trust in paper money and paved the way for the first Canadian banks which appeared on the scene a few years later.

rather, it evolved out of barter. Anything that was generally wanted and was in convenient form could be used as a medium of exchange. The point is that almost anything can serve as money as long as people are willing to accept it in exchange for goods and services. But it is important to note that money does **not** have to have any intrinsic value of its own—you cannot do much with an elephant tail bristle or with wampum beside use it as money. It is people's willingness to accept it that gives money its value in exchange.

Small pieces of paper, engraved with faces of Monarchs or Prime Ministers or stamped with the number of your bank account obviously have little inherent value—but if you can exchange this paper for yachts, steel mills, or bread, the bits of paper are as valuable as the things for which you can exchange them.

MONEY IN CANADA TODAY

What do people accept in exchange for goods and services today? An answer to this question would be that they usually accept *metal coins, paper bills, or checks*. A person who works for $200 a week will take 400 fifty-cent coins, or 800 twenty-five-cent coins, or 200 one-dollar bills, or ten twenty-dollar bills, or 1 check for $200 from the employer for the week's work. You can pay for a new coat with coins, paper bills, or with a check if you have a good checking account in a local bank.

In terms of the different kinds of money accepted today, metal coins and paper bills are not as important as they once were. We have come to rely more and more on checks to pay for the exchange of goods and services in our economy. Table 16-1 shows the total money supply. Note that in this table coins

Table 16-1. CANADA'S MONEY SUPPLY, JANUARY, 1978

	millions of dollars	money supply label[1]
Currency outside banks	7 802	
Demand deposits[2]	12 875	
sub-total	20 677	M 1
Other checkable deposits[3]	7 707	
sub-total	28 384	M 1 B
Personal non-checkable deposits[4] plus non-personal notice deposits[5]	39 673	
sub-total	68 057	M 2
Non-personal fixed term deposits[6] plus foreign currency deposits of Canadians	29 159	
total[7]	97 216	M 3

Notes: [1] These labels are frequently used to indicate which specific measure is referred to. M1 is likely to be the most frequently encountered. It should be noted that the Bank of Canada's structure used here is sometimes altered by economists, or other sources.
[2] Basically, deposits in checking accounts, either personal or other.
[3] Deposits in other accounts with limited checking rights.
[4] Basically, savings accounts plus some deposits which have a set future time for withdrawal.
[5] Non-personal non-checkable deposits which do not have a set future time for withdrawal.
[6] Non-personal non-checkable deposits which have a set future time for withdrawal.
[7] Deposits are those of individuals, businesses or organizations, resident in Canada, which are in chartered banks. All deposits of governments in banks or any deposits in other financial institutions are excluded.

Source: Bank of Canada, *Bank of Canada Review*, February, 1978.

and bills are lumped together and called **currency**. For purposes of figuring the money supply, we do not count currency held outside the country or in bank vaults.

It is very important to understand that checks are to be regarded as money in every sense, precisely because they meet the test of being widely accepted in exchange for goods and services and in payment of accounts. Table 16-1 shows the various totals which are tabulated when we measure the level of the money supply. Some economists also look at other types of assets as "near money." The amount of near money held by the public may influence their feelings of security and their spending habits very much like money itself. An example of this would be deposits in a credit union or trust company or personal holdings of Canada Savings Bonds. We do not formally count near money as part of the total money supply, although it may have an important bearing on the total amount of economic activity.

Credit cards and charge accounts represent another complication, since people sometimes do not pay money immediately for their purchases but instead "charge it." Charging it, however, only delays the ultimate money payment. Eventually, the debts incurred by charging have to be paid in money (usually with interest or service charges, making it more expensive than if the original purchase had been paid for by cash or check).

CONSTRUCTING A PRICE INDEX

In Unit 2, we were concerned with price determination at one point in time in markets for specific products. Now, however, we must examine the changes in the average level of prices for the economy as a whole over a period of time. A **price index** is the tool used to compare average levels of prices over periods of time. This is a table which measures price levels against those of a year which is chosen as the base year and given an index level of 100. An index number of 200 then means that prices were twice as high as in the base year. An index number of 50 would mean that prices are only half as high as in the base year.

In constructing a price index, the first step is to select the market basket of goods and services you want to price. In constructing the *Consumer Price Index*, for example, Statistics Canada uses a market basket that represents the typical purchases of food, clothing, transportation, recreation, medical care, and so on of Canadians.

Table 16-2: SAMPLE MARKET BASKET OF CONSUMER GOODS

Market Basket		Base Year		Current Year	
Item	No. of Units	Price Per Unit ($)	Total Cost ($)	Price Per Unit ($)	Total Cost ($)
Milk	5 litres	.60 a litre	3.00	.80 a litre	4.00
Shoes	1 pair	14.00 a pair	14.00	16.50 a pair	16.50
Movie ticket	1 ticket	1.50 a ticket	1.50	2.25 a ticket	2.25
Bus tickets	1 ticket	.50 a ticket	.50	.50 a ticket	.50
Tooth paste	1 tube	1.00 a tube	1.00	1.75 a tube	1.75
Total Cost			$20.00		$25.00

In constructing a *Wholesale Price Index*, a market basket of basic raw materials and intermediate products used in various types of manufacturing and production is used.

Once the market basket has been selected, prices must be obtained for the various items, and the current prices must be compared to the prices that prevailed for the same goods in the base year. Take the following sample market basket of consumer goods, and the prices that prevailed in the two years shown in Table 16-2.

The market basket that cost $20 in the base year costs $25 in the current year. Thus, we can say that prices have gone up 25 percent between the years shown. Or, using an index number, with the base year = 100, the index number for the current year in this example would be equal to 125.[1]

In computing a price index, there is no hard and fast rule about which year should

[1] To express current year prices as an index number of the base year prices, divide the total cost of the market basket in the current year by the total cost of the same market basket in the base year, and multiply the result by 100.

$$\frac{\text{current year cost}}{\text{base year cost}} = \frac{\$25.00}{\$20.00} = 1.25 \times 100 = 125.00$$

What would the index number be if the cost of the market basket in current prices were $30.00? $18.00? $35.00?

Check up-to-date details on the CPI to see how different categories of goods and services are weighted within the overall index. Any public library will likely have Statistics Canada, *The Consumer Price Index*, cat. 62-001.

Table 16-3. THREE STATISTICS CANADA INDEXES (1971 = 100)

Year	Consumer Price Index	Petroleum Refineries Products	Residential Building Materials
1961	75.0		69.3
1962	75.9		69.7
1963	77.2		72.1
1964	78.6		75.8
1965	80.5		80.2
1966	83.5	83.5	83.9
1967	86.5	84.2	86.8
1968	90.0	86.0	91.5
1969	94.1	87.7	96.4
1970	97.2	90.4	95.3
1971	100.0	100.0	100.0
1972	104.8	102.7	109.8
1973	112.7	117.5	124.0
1974	125.0	160.1	135.2
1975	138.5	184.5	139.7
1976	148.9	211.5	153.6
1977	160.8	239.0(p)	164.2

Note: (p) indicates a preliminary figure.
Source: Statistics Canada, *The Consumer Price Index*, cat. 62-001; *Prices and Price Indexes*, cat. 62-002; *Consumer Prices and Price Indexes*, cat. 62-010; *Industry Price Indexes*, cat. 62-011; *The Canadian Statistical Review*, cat. 11-003.

be selected as the base year. Indeed, more than one year can be used. However, most of the indexes presently maintained by Statistics Canada use 1971 as a base year.

INTERPRETING PRICE-INDEX NUMBERS

In the example we used above, the index number of 125 indicates that, *on the average*, the prices of the goods in our market basket went up by 25 percent between the two years shown. But, does that mean that the price of every single good in the market basket went up by 25 percent? The answer is *no*.

As you can see by going back to the example, the price of milk went up by 33-1/3 percent a litre, the price of shoes went up by 18 percent; the price of movies increased 50%; bus rides were constant at $.50 each; and the price of toothpaste went up by 75 percent. The overall index number of 125 represents the *weighted average* of all of these different price movements, *given the different amounts of each good shown*.

If you do not ride the bus or if you wear out many pairs of shoes quickly, the average, overall index number is not a good measure of your cost of living. The CPI measures your cost of living only if you buy the *same goods* in the *same quantities in the same parts of Canada* that are in the market basket used by those represented in the index. This is more likely to be the case for married urban wage earners than for any other group in our society, but even within this group there are differences in consumption habits that make the CPI an imperfect measure of any individual's cost of living. By shifting your consumption patterns as the prices of some goods rise more than others you may—at least partially—offset the overall rise in the price index.

PRICES AND THE VALUE OF MONEY

If the price index does rise from year to year, this means it will take more and more money to buy the same amount of goods and services. Thus, rising prices reduce the real value of a fixed amount of money; a dollar will not buy what it used to buy—if prices double, a dollar is worth only 50 cents. Similarly, if prices fall, the real value of a dollar will increase.

UPI

The most famous—or, rather, infamous inflation of recent history was the runaway German inflation after World War I. Money was actually better to burn that to spend. This Berlin housewife said it was cheaper to start her breakfast fire with several million marks than to use the money to buy wood, given the soaring price of wood and the deteriorating value of marks.

The phenomenon of generally rising prices (or falling value of money) is called **inflation**. To the public, inflation is a horrid word that conjures up visions of German housewives and clerks trundling wheelbarrows full of marks to the grocery store. Indeed, the German inflation after World War I was a never-to-be-forgotten monstrosity. Consumer prices rose 1.2 trillion times, and life-insurance policies, mortgages, bonds, and other long-term contracts became worthless. In our terms the CPI number would have been 1 200 000 000 000! But to the economist, inflation is a familiar phenomenon that is not necessarily rapid and ruin-

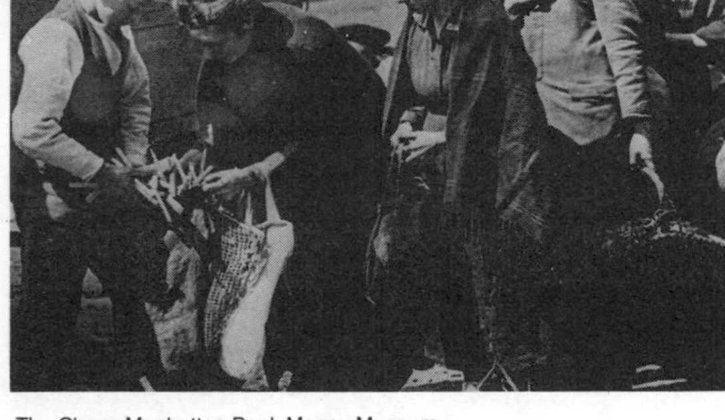

The Chase Manhattan Bank Money Museum

When an existing monetary system breaks down, people revert to barter. Here Germans are exchanging potato peelings for wood. The 1923 catastrophe and the disruption of both the economy and the social order have made the Germans hypersensitive to inflation.

ous. The price indexes of consumer or capital goods may rise a little or a lot. It is all inflation, and it is a common occurrence when unemployment is very low and when business is expanding.

By reducing the purchasing power of money, inflation hurts those whose incomes do not rise as fast as prices increase. Inflation hurts people who lend money, and helps those who borrow money. If you borrow $10, and if prices double before you repay the loan, the $10 you pay back will buy only half as much as it did when you borrowed it. Thus, you gain, and the lender loses. Once people think that prices are going to keep going up, however, too many people may want to borrow for purposes that are not economically sound, and they may overexpand and cause an eventual economic collapse. Or people may simply refuse to lend money and cause the rate of economic activity to collapse for that reason.

In the long run, therefore, inflation places a serious burden on our economy, and we should seek price stability as a national economic goal. The efforts of Government in attempting to restore a greater degree of price stability will be one of our main areas of concern in Unit 4.

The Inflationary Process

This brief overview of causes and effects of inflation is taken from a document called The Way Ahead, *a federal government working paper issued in October, 1976. This was one year after the implementation of wage and price controls. The paper was designed to serve as a basis for discussions among governments, business and labor about the course of economic policy after the period of controls ended.*

A search for future directions must begin with an understanding of current economic conditions and, in particular, the inflationary process. Simplistic explanations of inflation are bound to be incomplete and misleading. Inflation is a complex economic, social and political phenomenon, both in its origins and in its effects. One of the characteristics of a period of continuing, rapid inflation is that expectations that prices will continue to escalate become deeply entrenched. Groups with market power demand higher wages and prices in order to offset not only past inflation but anticipated future price increases. Those individuals and groups who cannot "keep up" in this process—those with fixed incomes, those who cannot work or cannot find work, and many who simply lack market power—suffer a loss of real purchasing power. This leads to increased demands on governments to redress the inequities bred by inflation. Increased government spending can lead to higher prices if the government simply prints the money or if additional taxes levied to finance these expenditures are passed on to others through higher wages and prices. Excessively high wage settlements and pricing decisions impose higher levels of cost, leading directly to higher prices. Expectations escalate and inflation continues to feed upon itself.

The debilitating effects of inflation extend beyond economic considerations to threaten the very nature of our institutions and traditions. The problems that unrestricted inflation creates were spelled out in the Budget Speech of June 23, 1975:

> . . . inflation ultimately inflicts grievous damage to the fabric of society. It lowers the living standards of those on fixed incomes, including pensioners. It leaves people without reliable, understandable guideposts by which to arrange their economic affairs. It injects grave uncertainty into decisions on family budgets, housing, savings and provision for old age. It provokes deep frustration, social tension and mistrust of private and public institutions. Collective bargaining is embittered. Industrial relations are damaged. We in Canada are already beginning to live some of these experiences.

There is a real sense in which the stability and endurance of our economic system and the social and cultural traditions on which it is based will be measured by our ability to respond to the challenge of inflation.

Inflation is not just a recent phenomenon. Escalating prices, and concern about their impacts on the economy and society have been with us for at least the past thirty years. For a large part of this period inflation was fairly moderate, though slowly increasing. It was widely, if reluctantly, accepted as a necessary and fairly tolerable cost of maintaining adequate levels of employment. Only in the late 1960s and early 1970s, when inflation began to accelerate rapidly in Canada and in other countries, were its dangers clearly perceived.

There have been many reasons advanced as to why industrialized countries appear to be increasingly vulnerable to inflation. At one extreme, inflation is seen as a purely monetary phenomenon that can be eliminated by controlling the supply of money. Others argue that governments' monetary and fiscal policies must be viewed together, and assert that excessive government spending in pursuit of social goals together with a government commitment to full employment create inevitable inflationary pressures. There are those, as well, who would argue that even if governments do not incur deficits, increasing levels of taxation required to fund growing expenditures lead to the erosion of incentives, a shift of income from investors to consumers, and a consequent reduction in available output that is accompanied by rising prices.

There is a further view that asserts that inflationary forces are deeply embedded in the very structure of our society. A rapid shift of employment to the service industries and declining rates of productivity growth, as well as broad differences in income and wealth and the ability of powerful groups to protect too narrow interests, are factors which are said to lead inevitably to continuously rising prices. In this view, the market system as we know it does not always allocate resources efficiently and cannot provide a socially acceptable distribution of the fruits of growth.

In addition, there are those who point to the worldwide inflationary experience, in part a result of the rapid expansion of international liquidity, and to the sudden and severe increases in food and energy prices. They argue that Canada, as a trading nation, is extremely vulnerable to imported inflation.

There is a real sense in which the growth experience of the past thirty years has, itself, been seen as a basic factor in the inflationary process. Since World War II, cyclical slowdowns that occurred were short and quickly reversed by expansionary government policies. One of the legacies of this period, fundamental to an understanding of inflation, is a deeply rooted expectation that real growth will continue at past rates and an increasing willingness on the part of both individuals and governments to borrow against anticipated future income to support higher current living standards.

Uluschak in the Edmonton Journal

Uluschak's cartoon provides an amusing though pessimistic note on which to close our initial consideration of the topic of inflation. To provide a note of realism, check with your school librarian or some other source in your school to determine the present list (i.e. school) price of *The World of Economics.* Compare this with the original list price of $6.75 for the first printing of the first edition in 1971. Compare the percentage change in price since then with the percentage change in the general price level measured in the C.P.I.

There is no single cause of inflation. Not all observers would rank the importance of the factors noted above in a similar way. There would nonetheless be general agreement with the following conclusions:

1. Industrialized economies for the last three decades, but more particularly since the mid-1960s, have become increasingly vulnerable to a long-run, continuing increase in measured inflation rates.
2. Continuing inflation creates short-term problems—internal inequities and a possible reduction in the ability to compete in world markets. These, together with the longer-term disruptions that accompany behavior modified to anticipate inflation, exacerbate the inflationary process.
3. Once inflationary expectations have become entrenched, corrective policy measures can be offset—particularly in an economy as dependent on world trade as Canada's—by price increases that the government may not be able to control. The eradication of inflation can therefore be a long and painful process.
4. Continuing inflation, particularly in North America, has been accompanied by an increase in measured unemployment rates. Over the long term, continuing inflation is inconsistent with the maintenance of full employment. Fiscal and monetary policies directed at the control of inflation, unless associated with other measures, will have increasingly costly and socially disruptive unemployment consequences before they have a significant effect on inflation rates.
5. Continuing inflation inevitably results in greater public demand for government intervention in the economy, to offset the structural disabilities and inequities bred by the inflationary process. It is therefore imperative that inflation be controlled if governments are to be free, in responding to and serving social and economic objectives, to opt for less rather than more intervention in the economy.

From *The Way Ahead*, Ottawa: Government of Canada, 1976, pp. 8-10.

SUMMARY

Money facilitates the flow of real goods and services by acting as a unit of account, a medium of exchange, and a store of value. It is people's willingness to accept money in exchange for goods and services that gives money its value and permits us to realize the increased production which specialization, permitted by the use of money, can bring.

Almost anything can serve as money—as long as people are willing to accept it. The main types of money are currency (coins and bills) and checking deposits in the chartered banks. Of these, checking accounts deposits are the most important, accounting for a very high percentage of all financial transactions.

Just as the amount of money in existence will change with the passage of time, so may the value of money. To record changes in the value of money, various price indexes are maintained to relate present price trends to those of a selected reference point, the base year.

Long run trends of either an inflationary or deflationary nature are among the most important basic economic problems. Either, if serious, can have catastrophic effects on an economy; hence reasonable price stability has become one of the prime goals of all economics. The policies which may be used in the quest for price stability are a crucial part of Unit 4, in particular, chapters 26 to 30.

KEY CONCEPTS

barter
medium of exchange
store of value
currency
price index
inflation

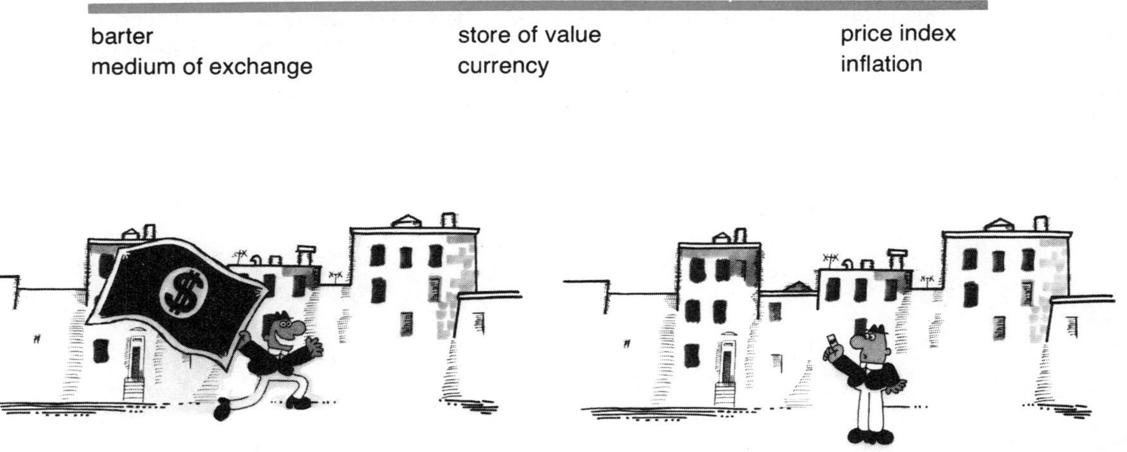

Courtesy of the Prices and Incomes Commission

The Man Who Got a Raise: The illustrations are from a short animated cartoon used as an advertisement on Canadian television as part of an anti-inflation campaign. The man who got a raise may, by getting higher wages, have contributed to the rising prices which reduced his own increase purchasing power. If the inflation were caused by increased costs of labor, raw materials, capital, taxes, or other items which producers might pass on in higher prices, this would be called "cost-push inflation." "Demand-pull" inflation is inflation which can be attributed to an excessive rate of growth in the money supply or in the amount of credit available in contrast to the rate of growth in the supply of actual goods and services.

QUESTIONS FOR REVIEW AND DISCUSSION

1. What are the major functions of money?
   Explain each with examples.
2. What is the most important factor in determining the value of money? What are the major parts of our money supply?
3. What is a price index? What steps are taken to prepare and maintain a price index?
4. Why is it incorrect to call The Consumer Price Index a cost-of-living index?

PROBLEMS AND EXERCISES TO SHARPEN YOUR UNDERSTANDING

1. Assume that you are one of a large group marooned on the proverbial deserted island. You have been chosen to develop a monetary system. In addition to acceptability, what other features should your monetary system have? Explain the need for each.
2. Outline, with explanatory comments, those in our society who gain (a) in an inflationary period, (b) in a deflationary period.
3. Obtain data and examine it to see what conclusions may be drawn from the patterns over the last ten years in:
   (a) the annual percentage change in the money supply, (M1);
   (b) the annual percentage change in the CPI;
   (c) the annual rate of change in the average level of wages and salaries.
4. Describe what you think would be the effect on you, your family, the community, and the nation if Canada were to experience a situation like the German "hyperinflation" of the early 1920s. Before undertaking this "what if" question, you should do some reading on the collapse of the German currency and its effects. The section on either German history, or general European history, will likely be the best place to go looking in your library.

CHAPTER 17

THE BANKING SYSTEM IN OUR ECONOMY

■ THE ROLE OF BANKS ■ THE FRACTIONAL RESERVE PRINCIPLE ■ THE EXPANSION AND CONTRACTION OF CHECKING ACCOUNTS ■ SUMMARY ■ APPENDIX: THE ECONOMIC ORGANIZATION OF A PRISONER OF WAR CAMP (PART 2)

Having examined the nature and functions of money in the previous chapter, the topic of banking must have run through your mind. "Money," of course, is the business of banks, and though many other types of financial institutions deal primarily with money, as opposed to goods, it is with banks that you are most likely to be somewhat familiar. This is fortunate for, as the references in Chapter 16 indicate, the banks play a crucial role in maintaining, transferring and helping to create, yes create, a major part of our money supply.

■ THE ROLE OF BANKS

If time and space permitted, at this point we could take a complex and fascinating historical digression into the evolution of the banking system we have today. If this were done, we would find that banks have been fulfilling the same basic functions for many centuries. Granted, techniques have been changed by many forces, but a trip back in time to, let us say, Renaissance Florence, would perhaps surprise us. Banking institutions there would be found engaged in handling foreign currencies, providing safe keeping facilities, transferring funds on behalf of clients and many other services in addition to the two primary functions which are still the most important activities of banks, accepting deposits (and honoring drawn checks on them) and granting credit to the many borrowers, individual or institutional, who seek the interim use of borrowed money. Unfortunately, the pressure of priorities prevents a detailed historical study of the evolution of banking—though some personal research might be undertaken. Beyond several basic points, we are limited to an examination of the primary functions referred to above. Before this, however, the basic points to keep in mind must be mentioned.

What specifically are banks? They are corporations, privately owned, who deal in the provision of financial services. What is their objective? Like other privately owned firms, the objective is to make a profit for the owners as a result of the provision of services to their customers.[1] Are they free to operate as they wish, as many firms are? Definitely not. Due to the importance of the banks as custodians of the largest part of deposits and also their role in the overall functioning of the economy, they are carefully regulated by Federal legislation, the Bank Act and by the central bank, the Bank of Canada. Let us now turn to the primary roles of the banks in the economy.

■ THE FRACTIONAL RESERVE PRINCIPLE

If you were to stand outside the teller's window of a chartered bank on a business day,

[1]For more detailed information on the development of banking in Canada in an historical perspective, see: "Banking in Canada" and "A Brief History of the Bank of Montreal," contained in the book of readings correlated with this text, A. H. MacDonald, (ed.), *Readings in the World of Economics*, Toronto: McGraw-Hill Ryerson, 1973.

FIG. 17-1. FRACTIONAL RESERVE BANKING

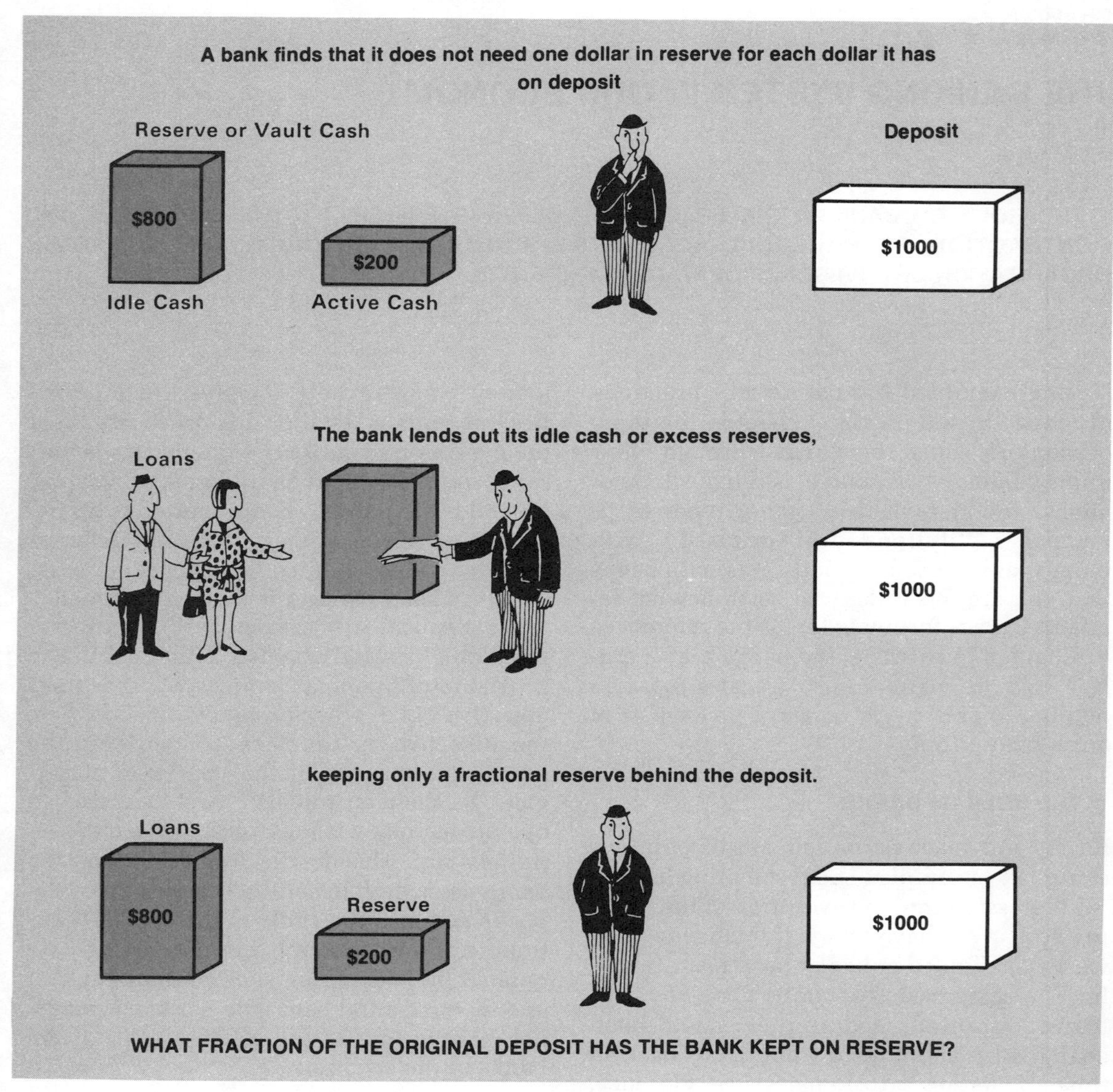

you would see people coming into the bank and depositing money with the teller, and other people coming into the bank and withdrawing money from accounts previously deposited. If you went back behind the teller's window, you would see other bank employees receiving checks written to people who had checking accounts in this bank, and checks written by the owners of these accounts to people who might or might not have accounts in this bank.

Now, notice a very important thing. On a typical day, it is quite likely that the total amount of money coming into the bank is very nearly equal to the total amount of money that the bank has to pay out. And, if you went into the bank vault, you might notice that the total amount of money in the vault did not change very much during the day, since the money coming in was very nearly equal to the money going out.

A banker noticing these things would begin to realize that, if the money coming in was very nearly equal to the money going out on a typical day, *it would not be necessary to keep every dollar deposited locked up in the vault.*

If a banker did this, it would be found that most of the cash in the vault would remain idle. Instead of allowing this money to stand idle, it would make sense to lend some of it out and earn interest on the otherwise idle funds. The funds could be invested in bonds from various levels of government or corporations, or could be loaned to a business which promises to pay interest on the loan and return the money at a future date.

Thus, as long as all those who have money deposited in a bank do not want to withdraw all their money at the same time, the bank finds it does not need to keep 100 percent of its deposits in cash to protect itself against withdrawals. Rather it will keep only a *fraction* of its total deposits in cash in reserve against possible withdrawals in excess of new deposits. This is where the term **fractional reserve** comes from. By lending out *excess reserves*, the bank keeps only *fractional reserves* against account deposits.

In the case of bank accounts, the term *deposits* is thus somewhat of a misnomer. The bank does not hold all the funds placed in deposit accounts in safekeeping as they would if the funds were locked up in a safety deposit box. Rather, the bank takes some of the funds deposited in customers' accounts and uses them, leaving an IOU in the depositors' accounts. If all goes well (as it usually does), all of the IOU's are not cashed at once. When any depositor at the bank or borrower from the bank wants to exercise the right to claim cash in exchange for the IOU, the bank

The Changing Face Of Banking

Chambers in the Halifax Chronicle-Herald. Reprinted by permission.

This cartoon, which appeared at the time of the revision of the Bank Act in 1967, pokes fun at the austere "old days" when Canadian banks were almost notoriously conservative and also at the rash of activities of the banks at the time in their quest for new business under some of the more liberal revisions in the Act.

will pay the desired cash out of the fractional reserves it keeps in the vault or with funds from new deposits coming into the bank.

Fractional reserve banking may seem a little strange or maybe even a little shady to you at first glance, but it is not. Fractional reserve banking is legal and perfectly respectable. Once you understand the process, it involves no deception. If banks did not earn interest by lending out their temporarily idle funds, they would probably have to charge more for providing their services than they now do, for banks are in business to earn profits just like other business firms that deal in commodities less mysterious than money and credit.

In view of this situation, what keeps this potentially shaky banking system stable? The answer to this question has a number of different parts.

The first consideration is the nature of our banking system—a branch banking system. Despite the large number of "banks," over seven thousand, these are simply branches of our ten chartered banks, five of which dominate Canadian banking.[2] With a branch system, withdrawals or losses in one bank branch or in an area may be offset by events (or access to funds) in other areas. Large banking chains are much more protected against unanticipated drains than would be a large number of small banks.

Other measures promoting stability come from the various restrictions and regulations of the banking system. Bank charters are difficult to obtain. Large amounts of capital must be put up by the would-be founders and close scrutiny is applied. Protection is given depositors by provisions of the Canada Deposit Insurance Corporation, which insures deposits up to $20 000 per depositor in banks and some other financial institutions.

Finally, the most important in several ways, are the reserve requirements, provided by the Bank Act and enforced or regulated by the Bank of Canada. When last amended in 1967, (the Act is reviewed approximately every decade) the Act revised the previous provision for a minimum cash or **primary reserve** of 8% of all deposits to a dual system requiring 12% of demand or checking deposits and 4% of other deposits, these being primarily savings accounts. This produces an average which runs approximately 6% of all deposits. Most of this cash reserve is actually in the forms of deposits the chartered banks have held by the Bank of Canada. Only about one-third is in currency within the banks.

In addition to the primary reserves, the banks must also maintain a **secondary reserve** in excess cash or "liquid securities." These are securities which may be quickly turned into cash and where there is negligible risk of losses in the event of quick disposal. The chief component of this reserve is usually a bank's investment in Treasury Bills, Federal Government Securities which usually mature 90 days after they are issued. The secondary reserve may be set as high as 12% of a bank's total of deposits. Increases may be made monthly by the Bank of Canada but only at a maximum rate of increase of 1% per month. Decreases may be made by the central bank at any time. Between the revision of the Bank Act in mid-1967, and mid-1978, the level of the secondary reserve requirement has ranged between 5% and 9%.[3]

Although these required reserves may add additional security and safety to the banking system, the Canadian experience has been such that they have not really been necessary—at least for the purpose of safety. They are, however, important tools at the disposal of the government and the central bank should they wish to influence crucial trends in the economy and in the banking system. One of the primary targets for such influence may be the role of the banking system as creator or destroyer of a large portion of our money supply.

[2]This is as of mid-1978. Have there been changes since then?

[3]As of mid-1978, revision of the Bank Act was scheduled to be carried out in 1979. When this is done, be sure to check for changes in any key areas.

Norris in Vancouver Sun

"In keeping with the spirit of restraint we will try to manage without raising our interest rates and trust that you will manage without the loan."

Consider the subject matter of the cartoon in relation to our references to reserve requirements. What action on the part of the Bank of Canada could have induced the spirit of restraint? When the policies of the central bank are dealt with in detail in Chapter 27, the potential power of interest rates can be compared with the influence of reserve requirements.

THE EXPANSION AND CONTRACTION OF CHECKING ACCOUNTS

Once you understand the basic principle of fractional reserve banking, you can see how the lending activities of banks can expand or contract the nation's money supply. When banks make loans they, in effect, create checking accounts—that is, the business or person receiving the loan is advised that he now has on deposit at the lending bank such-and-such amount of money. When bank loans are paid off, or called in, checking accounts are, in effect, destroyed—that is, the deposit created by the loan is wiped out. Furthermore, in a fractional reserve system, a loan of $1000 can expand the money supply by more than $1000. And calling in a loan of $1000 can reduce the money supply by more than that amount.

Let us see how this works. Say that a bank gets $1000 in deposits and does not have to keep all $1000 in the form of vault cash to cover withdrawals of these deposits. Assuming the bank has to keep 15 percent of its deposits in reserve to cover temporary imbalances between withdrawals and new deposits, it can lend $850 to Joe Smith, who needs a loan to finance an expansion in his business. The bank could lend Joe $850 of its vault cash, but it is more likely to just open a checking account in Joe Smith's name for $850. In either case, in return for the loan, the bank would get an IOU from Joe, promising to repay the loan (plus interest) at some specified future date.

Now what happens once Joe gets the $850 loan? Let us say that Joe writes a check for $850 on his account at the bank and gives it to Bill Jones, the building contractor who is expanding Joe Smith's store. Bill will now deposit the check in his own bank, whose reserves are now increased by $850. This increase in its reserves, in turn, increases the lending power of Bill Jones' bank. And if it lends out 85 percent of the increase of its reserves—$722—this further expands the amount of money in the economy. Then, Mary White borrows the $722 from Bill Jones' bank and spends it on goods sold by Joe Smith, who will deposit the funds in his bank, helping to build up its reserves, and so on.

As long as the money lent out by one bank is redeposited in another bank, this permits additional loans to be made and expands the total amount of check money in the economy. The exact amount of expansion depends on the fraction of its reserves that a bank lends out and on how much of the money lent out is redeposited in the banking system. If each bank lends out 85 percent of its reserves, for example, and all loans are redeposited, the entire money supply (demand deposits) will grow by a total of 6 2/3 times the original deposit of $1000. How this works is shown in Table 17-1.

This process also works the other way. Money withdrawn from checking accounts and not redeposited in a bank, reduces bank reserves. The reduction in a bank's reserves, in turn, may force it to call in some loans. If the repayment of these loans results in withdrawals from another bank, its reserves fall, and it may have to call in some loans, and so on. The amount of contraction depends on

Table 17-1: EXPANSION OF BANK DEPOSITS IN A FRACTIONAL RESERVE SYSTEM

Growth of initial deposit as new deposits created by loans are added.[4]

Stage	Deposits	Reserves (15%)	Loans
1	1000.00	150.00	850.00
2	850.00	127.50	722.50
3	722.50	108.38	614.12
4	614.12	92.12	522.00
All other stages together	3480.05	522.00	2958.05
TOTAL	6666.67	1000.00	5666.67

But Note: In the real world, the actual expansion of deposits is unlikely to reach the theoretical limit indicated above—because some banks in fact will use their reserves incompletely and only after a considerable time lag.

how many loans the banks call in to build up their reserves and on how many of these loans are repaid by withdrawals from other banks.

Thus, by calling in loans, banks can contract checking deposits, just as they can expand checking deposits by making loans. When the banks increase loans and deposits, they create money; when they call in loans and reduce deposits, they destroy money.

The central point to bear in mind is that the checking accounts held by the public in the nation's chartered banks are the most important part of our nation's money supply. Indeed, these checking accounts are such an important part of our money supply that the Bank of Canada keeps a weather eye on how the lending activities of the banking system are changing the size of the nation's money supply.[5]

[4]Those inclined to math problems will be able to determine what formula is needed to calculate the total of deposits which could be created from an initial deposit of X dollars and a reserve rate of Y%.

[5]As an extension of the topic of banking, see the sections on interest rates from the perspective of the Canadian Imperial Bank of Commerce, and also the "Wizard of Id," in the book of readings correlated with this text, A. H. MacDonald, (ed.), *Readings in the World of Economics,* Toronto: McGraw-Hill Ryerson, 1973.

SUMMARY

Since our banking system operates on the fractional reserve principle, banks can use their lending activities to expand or contract the amount of check money that might be in existence at any given time. If a bank lends out temporarily idle funds, the amount of checking accounts in the whole banking system can expand by more than the amount of the original loan. If a bank calls in a loan, the amount in checking accounts can contract by more than the amount of the loan originally called in. The amount of expansion or contraction that actually takes place depends on what fraction of their reserves banks can lend out and on how much of the money loaned out is re-deposited in the banking system.

To protect against bank runs in a fractional reserve system, the Canada Deposit Insurance Corporation insures deposits up to $20 000 per depositor. To keep some control on how much check money the private banking system creates or destroys through its lending activities, the Bank of Canada is empowered to supervise and regulate the reserve requirements.

KEY CONCEPTS

fractional reserve
branch banking system
primary reserve
secondary reserve

QUESTIONS FOR REVIEW AND DISCUSSION

1. What are the major forms of money used in Canada's economy today? Which form of money accounts for the largest part of our money supply?
2. What is meant by the fractional reserve principle? Explain in your own words how this principle affects the lending activities of chartered banks, and how it is related to the total amount of check money in the economy.
3. What is the greatest threat to a fractional reserve banking system? How does the CDIC help to protect against this threat?
4. Explain how an increase in the secondary reserve could decrease the total money supply.

PROBLEMS AND EXERCISES TO SHARPEN YOUR UNDERSTANDING

1. Research revisions to the Bank Act to determine if there are any changes in:
   (a) the structures of the range of Reserve Rates;
   (b) limits on types of investments or loans banks can make;
   (c) requirements to start a new chartered bank.
2. Research recent developments in computer payments systems, which are in experimental use in some areas now. If/when such a system replaces the use of checks, what effects will it have and on whom?

APPENDIX:

THE ECONOMIC ORGANIZATION OF A PRISONER OF WAR CAMP (Part 2)

This appendix completes the study introduced in the appendix to Chapter 13. This segment deals with the development of monetary systems, several institutions rather like banks, price fluctuations and other more complex aspects of the "economy" within the camp.

THE CIGARETTE CURRENCY

Although cigarettes as currency exhibited certain peculiarities, they performed all the functions of a metallic currency as a unit of account, as a measure of value, and as a store of value, and shared most of its characteristics. They were homogeneous, reasonably durable, and of convenient size for the smallest or, in packets, for the largest transactions. Incidentally, they could be clipped or sweated by rolling them between the fingers so that tobacco fell out.

Cigarettes were also subject to the working of Gresham's Law. Certain brands were more popular than others as smokes, but for currency purposes a cigarette was a cigarette. Consequently buyers used the poorer qualities and the Shop rarely saw the more popular brands: cigarettes such as Churchman's No. 1 were rarely used for trading. At one time cigarettes hand-rolled from pipe tobacco began to circulate. Pipe tobacco was issued in lieu of cigarettes by the Red Cross at a rate of 25 cigarettes to the ounce and this rate was standard in exchanges, but an ounce would produce 30 home-made cigarettes. Naturally, people with machine-made cigarettes broke them down and re-rolled the tobacco, and the real cigarette virtually disappeared from the market. Hand-rolled cigarettes were not homogeneous and prices could no longer be quoted in them with safety: each cigarette was examined before it was accepted and thin ones were rejected, or extra demanded as a makeweight. For a time we suffered all the inconveniences of a debased currency.

Machine-made cigarettes were always universally acceptable, both for what they would buy and for themselves. It was this intrinsic value which gave rise to their principal disadvantage as currency, a disadvantage which exists, but to a far smaller extent, in the case of metallic currency; that is, a strong demand for non-monetary purposes. Consequently our economy was repeatedly subject to deflation and to periods of monetary stringency. While the Red Cross issue of 50 or 25 cigarettes per man per week came in regularly, and while there were fair stocks held, the cigarette currency suited its purpose admirably. But when the issue was interrupted, stocks soon ran out, prices fell, trading declined in volume and became increasingly a matter of barter. This deflationary tendency was periodically offset by the sudden injection of new currency. Private cigarette parcels arrived in a trickle throughout the year, but the big numbers came in quarterly when the Red Cross received its allocation of transport. Several hundred thousand cigarettes might arrive in the space of a fortnight. Prices soared, and then began to fall, slowly at first but with increasing rapidity as stocks ran out, until the next big delivery. Most of our economic troubles could be attributed to this fundamental instability.

PRICE MOVEMENTS

Many factors affected prices, the strongest and most noticeable being the periodical currency inflation and deflation described in the last paragraphs. The periodicity of this price cycle depended on cigarette and, to a far lesser extent, on food deliveries. At one time in the early days, before any private parcels had arrived and when there were no individual stocks, the weekly issue of cigarettes and food parcels occurred on a Monday. The non-monetary demand for cigarettes was great, and less elastic than the demand for food: consequently prices fluctuated weekly, falling toward Sunday night and rising sharply on Monday morning. Later, when many people held reserves, the weekly issue had no such effect, being too small a proportion of the total available. Credit allowed people with no reserves to meet their non-monetary demand over the weekend.

The general price level was affected by other factors. An influx of new prisoners, proverbially hungry, raised it. Heavy air raids in the vicinity of the camp probably increased the non-monetary demand for cigarettes and accentuated deflation. Good and bad war news certainly had its effect, and the general waves of optimism and pessimism which swept the camp were reflected in prices. Before breakfast one morning in March of this year [1945], a rumour of the arrival of parcels and cigarettes was circulated. Within ten minutes I sold a treacle ration, for four cigarettes (hitherto offered in vain for three), and many similar deals went through. By 10 o'clock the rumour was denied, and treacle that day found no more buyers even at two cigarettes.

More interesting than changes in the general price level were changes in the price structure. Changes in the supply of a commodity in the German ration scale or in the makeup of Red Cross parcels, would raise the price of one commodity relative to others. Tins of oatmeal, once a rare and much sought after luxury in the parcels, became a commonplace in 1943, and the price fell. In hot weather the demand for cocoa fell, and that for soap rose. A new recipe would be reflected in the price level: the discovery that raisins and sugar could be turned into an alcoholic liquor of remarkable potency reacted permanently on the dried fruit market. The invention of electric immersion heaters run off the power points made tea, a drug on the market in Italy, a certain seller in Germany.

In August, 1944, the supplies of parcels and cigarettes were both halved. Since both sides of the equation were changed in the same degree, changes in prices were not anticipated. But this was not the case: the non-monetary demand for cigarettes was less elastic than the demand for food, and food prices fell a little. More important however were the changes in the price structure. German margarine and jam, hitherto valueless owing to adequate supplies of Canadian butter and marmalade, acquired a new value. Chocolate, popular and a certain seller, and sugar, fell. Bread rose; several standing contracts of bread for cigarettes were broken, especially when the bread ration was reduced a few weeks later.

In February, 1945, the German soldier who drove the ration wagon was found to be willing to exchange loaves of bread at the rate of one loaf for a bar of chocolate. Those in the know began selling bread and buying chocolate, by then almost unsaleable in a period of serious deflation. Bread, at about 40, fell slightly; chocolate rose from 15; the supply of bread was not enough for the two commodities to reach parity, but the tendency was unmistakable.

The substitution of German margarine for Canadian butter when parcels were halved naturally affected their relative values, margarine appreciating at the expense of butter. Similarly, two brands of dried milk, hitherto differing in quality and therefore in price by five cigarettes a tin, came together in price as the wider substitution of the cheaper raised its relative value.

Enough has been cited to show that any change in conditions affected both the general price level and the price structure. It was this latter phenomenon which wrecked our planned economy.

PAPER CURRENCY—BULLY MARKS

Around D-Day, food and cigarettes were plentiful, business was brisk and the camp in an optimistic mood. Consequently the Entertainments Committee felt the moment opportune to launch a restaurant, where food and hot drinks were sold while a band and variety teams performed. Earlier experiments, both public and private, had pointed the way, and the scheme was a great success. Food was bought at market prices to provide the meals and the small profits were devoted to a reserve fund and used to bribe Germans to provide grease-paints and other necessities for the camp theater. Originally meals were sold for cigarettes but this meant that the whole scheme was vulnerable to the periodic deflationary waves, and furthermore heavy smokers were unlikely to attend much. The whole success of the scheme depended on an adequate amount of food being offered for sale in the normal manner.

To increase and facilitate trade, and to stimulate supplies and customers therefore, and secondarily to avoid the worst effects of deflation when it should come, a paper currency was organized by the Restaurant and the Shop. The Shop bought food on behalf of the Restaurant with paper notes and the paper was accepted equally with the cigarettes in the Restaurant or Shop, and passed back to the Shop to purchase more food. The Shop acted as a bank of issue. The paper money was backed 100 percent by food; hence its name, the Bully Mark. The BMk. was backed 100 percent by food; there could be no overissues, as is permissible with a normal bank of issue, since the eventual dispersal of the camp and consequent redemption of all BMk.s was anticipated in the near future.

Originally one BMk. was worth one cigarette and for a short time both circulated freely inside and outside the Restaurant. Prices were quoted in BMk.s and cigarettes with equal freedom—and for a short time the BMk. showed signs of replacing the cigarette as currency. The BMk. was tied to food, but not to cigarettes; as it was issued against food, say 45 for a tin of milk and so on, any reduction in the BMk. prices of food would have meant that there were unbacked BMk.s in circulation. But the price of both food and BMk.s could and did fluctuate with the supply of cigarettes.

While the Restaurant flourished, the scheme was a success; the Restaurant bought heavily, all foods were saleable and prices were stable.

In August parcels and cigarettes were halved and the Camp was bombed. The Restaurant closed for a short while and sales of food became difficult. Even when the Restaurant reopened, the food and cigarette shortage became increasingly acute and people were unwilling to convert such valuable goods into paper and to hold them for luxuries like snacks and tea. Less of the right kinds of food for the Restaurant were sold, and the Shop became glutted with dried fruit, chocolate, sugar, etc., which the Restaurant could not buy. The price level and the price structure changed. The BMk. fell to four-fifths of a cigarette and eventually farther still, and it became unacceptable save in the Restaurant. There was a flight from the BMk., no longer convertible into cigarettes or popular foods. The cigarette re-established itself.

But the BMk. was sound! The Restaurant closed in the New Year with a progressive food shortage and the long evenings without lights due to intensified Allied air raids, and BMk.s could only be spent in the Coffee Bar—a remnant of the Restaurant—or on the few unpopular foods in the Shop, the owners of which were prepared to accept them. In the end all holders of BMk.s were paid in full, in cups of coffee or in prunes. People who had bought BMk.s for cigarettes or valuable jam or biscuits in their heyday were aggrieved that they should have stood the loss involved by their restricted choice, but they suffered no actual loss of market value.

PRICE FIXING

Along with this scheme came a determined attempt at a planned economy, at price fixing. The Medical Officer had long been anxious to control food sales, for fear of some people selling too much, to the detriment of their health. The deflationary waves and their effects on prices were inconvenient to all and would be dangerous to the Restaurant which had to carry stocks. Furthermore, unless the BMk. was convertible into cigarettes at about par it had little chance of gaining confidence and of succeeding as a currency. As has been explained, the BMk. was tied to food but could not be tied to cigarettes, which fluctuated in value. Hence, while BMk. prices of food were fixed for all time, cigarette prices of food and BMk.s varied.

The Shop, backed by the Senior British Officer, was now in a position to enforce price control both inside and outside its walls. Hitherto a standard price had been fixed for food left for sale in the Shop, and prices outside were roughly in conformity with this scale, which was recommended as a "guide" to sellers, but fluctuated a good deal around it. Sales in the Shop at recommended prices were apt to be slow, though a good price might be obtained: sales outside could be made more quickly at lower prices. (If sales outside were to be at higher prices, goods were withdrawn from the Shop until the recommended price rose: but the recommended price was sluggish and could not follow the market closely by reason of its very purpose, which was stability.) The Exchange and Mart notice boards came under the control of the Shop: advertisements which exceeded a 5 percent departure from the recommended scale were liable to be crossed out by authority: unauthorized sales were discouraged by authority and also by public opinion, strongly in favour of a just and stable price. (Recommended prices were fixed partly from market data, partly on the advice of the Medical Officer.)

At first the recommended scale was a success: the Restaurant, a big buyer, kept prices stable around this level: opinion and the 5 percent tolerance helped. But when the price level fell with the August cuts and the price structure changed, the recommended scale was too rigid. Unchanged at first, as no deflation was expected, the scale was tardily lowered, but the prices of goods on the new scale remained in the same relation to one another, owing to the BMk., while on the market the price structure had changed. And the modifying influence of the Restaurant had gone. The scale was moved up and down several times, slowly following the inflationary and deflationary waves, but it was rarely adjusted to changes in the price structure. More and more advertisements were crossed off the board, and black market sales at unauthorized prices increased: eventually public opinion turned against the recommended scale and authority gave up the struggle. In the last few weeks, with unparalleled deflation, prices fell with alarming rapidity, no scales existed, and supply and demand, alone and unmellowed, determined prices.

PUBLIC OPINION

Public opinion on the subject of trading was vocal if confused and changeable, and generalizations as to its direction are difficult and dangerous. A tiny minority held that all trading was undesirable as it engendered an unsavory atmosphere; occasional frauds and sharp practices were cited as proof. Certain forms of trading were more generally condemned; trade with the Germans was criticized by many. Red Cross toilet articles, which were in short supply and only issued in cases of actual need, were excluded from trade by law and opinion working in unshakable harmony. At one time, when there had been several cases of malnutrition reported among the more devoted smokers, no trade in German rations was permitted, as the victims became an additional burden on the depleted food reserves of the Hospital. But while certain activities were condemned as anti-social, trade itself was practiced, and its utility appreciated, by almost everyone in the camp.

More interesting was opinion on middlemen and prices. Taken as a whole, opinion was hostile to the middleman. His function, and his hard work in bringing buyer and seller together, were ignored; profits were not regarded as a reward for labour, but as the result of sharp practices. Despite the fact that his very existence was proof to the contrary, the middleman was held to be redundant in view of the existence of an official Shop and the Exchange and Mart. Appreciation only came his way when he was willing to advance the price of a sugar ration, or to buy goods on the spot and carry them against a future sale. In these cases the element of risk was obvious to all, and the convenience of the service was felt to merit some reward. Particularly unpopular was the middleman with an element of monopoly, the man who contacted the ration wagon driver, or the man who utilized his knowledge of Urdu. And middlemen as a group were blamed for reducing prices. Opinion notwithstanding, most people dealt with a middleman, whether consciously or unconsciously, at some time or another.

There was a strong feeling that everything had its "just price" in cigarettes. While the assessment of the just price, which incidentally varied between camps, was impossible of explanation, this price was nevertheless pretty closely known. It can best be defined as the price usually fetched by an article in good times when cigarettes were plentiful. The "just price" changed slowly; it was unaffected by short-term variations in supply, and while opinion might be resigned to departures from the "just price," a strong feeling of resentment persisted. A more satisfactory definition of the "just price" is impossible. Everyone knew what it was, though no one could explain why it should be so.

As soon as prices began to fall with a cigarette shortage, a clamor arose, particularly against those who held reserves and who bought at reduced prices. Sellers at cut prices were criticized and their activities referred to as the black market. In every period of dearth the explosive question of "should non-smokers receive a cigarette ration?" was discussed to profitless length. Unfortunately, it was the non-smoker, or the light smoker with his reserves, along with the hated middleman, who weathered the storm most easily.

The popularity of the price-fixing scheme, and such success as it enjoyed, were undoubtedly the result of this body of opinion. On several occasions the fall of prices was delayed by the general support given to the recommended scale. The onset of deflation was marked by a period of sluggish trade; prices stayed up, but no one bought. Then prices fell on the black market, and the volume of trade revived in that quarter. Even when the recommended scale was revised, the volume of trade in the Shop would remain low. Opinion was always overruled by the hard facts of the market.

Curious arguments were advanced to justify price fixing. The recommended prices were in some way related to the calorific values of the foods offered: hence some were overvalued and never sold at these prices. One argument ran as follows:—not everyone has private cigarette parcels: thus, when prices were high and trade good in the summer of 1944, only the lucky rich could buy. This was unfair to the man with few cigarettes. When prices fell in the following winter, prices should be pegged high so that the rich, who had enjoyed life in the summer, should put many cigarettes into circulation. The fact that those who sold to the rich in the summer had also enjoyed life then, and the fact that in the winter there was always someone willing to sell at low prices, were ignored. Such arguments were hotly debated each night after the approach of Allied aircraft extinguished all lights at 8 p.m. But prices moved with the supply of cigarettes, and refused to stay fixed in accordance with a theory of ethics.

CONCLUSION

The economic organization described was both elaborate and smooth-working in the summer of 1944. Then came the August cuts and deflation. Prices fell, rallied with deliveries of cigarette parcels in September and December, and fell again. In January, 1945, supplies of Red Cross cigarettes ran out and prices slumped still further; in February the supplies of food parcels were exhausted and the depression became a blizzard. Food, itself scarce, was almost given away in order to meet the non-monetary demand for cigarettes. Laundries ceased to operate, or worked for £s or RMk.s: food and cigarettes sold for fancy prices in £s, hitherto unheard of. The Restaurant was a memory and the BMk. a joke. The Shop was empty and the Exchange increased in volume, becoming a larger proportion of a smaller volume of trade. This, the first serious and prolonged food shortage in the writer's experience, caused the price structure to change again, partly because German rations were not easily divisible. A margarine ration gradually sank in value until it exchanged directly for a treacle ration. Sugar slumped sadly. Only bread retained its value. Several thousand cigarettes, the capital of the Shop, were distributed without any effect. A few fractional parcel and cigarette issues, such as one-sixth of a parcel and twelve cigarettes each, led to momentary price recoveries and feverish trade, especially when they coincided with good news from the Western Front, but the general position remained unaltered.

By April, 1945, chaos had replaced order in the economic sphere; sales were difficult, prices lacked stability. Economics has been defined as the science of distributing limited means among unlimited and competing ends. On 12th April, with the arrival of elements of the 30th U.S. Infantry Division, the ushering in of an age of plenty demonstrated the hypothesis that with infinite means economic organization and activity would be redundant, as every want could be satisfied without effort.

R. A. Radford, "The Economic Organization of a P.O.W. Camp", *Economica,* vol. XII, No. 48, November, 1945, pp. 194-201. Reprinted by permission of the London School of Economics and Political Science.

CHAPTER 18

LABOR AND THE ECONOMY

■ THE OBJECTIVES OF UNIONS ■ THE GROWTH OF THE CANADIAN LABOR MOVEMENT ■ THE STRUCTURE OF THE UNION MOVEMENT ■ COLLECTIVE BARGAINING ■ UNIONS NOW AND IN THE FUTURE ■ SUMMARY

During the past century, organized labor has emerged through a stormy history to become one of the most important forces in our economy. The crucial role of labor and the controversy it frequently generates even today warrant an examination of unions, which in actual practice should go far beyond the scope of this chapter—especially if the student is concerned with the study of Canadian history, economic or otherwise.

■ THE OBJECTIVES OF UNIONS

When it first emerged, the union movement was in major part a byproduct of the industrial revolution. More specifically, like cooperatives, socialism, and the growing governmental regulation of and intervention in the economy, it was a reaction to the many immediately adverse effects of the growth of industrial society. Examination of life, especially economic and social conditions, in the early nineteenth century will indicate many valid grievances. Unions developed as one attempt to rectify the problems of workers through the application of the old motto "united we stand; divided we fall."

The primary concern of unions has been, and still is for action to ensure acceptable working conditions. Initially, wages and hours were the paramount issues. With the passing of time, more and more items emerged as points for concern and action by unions. "Fringe benefits" have expanded to include vacations, sickness and accident insurance, pensions, job security, training plans, grievance procedure, and a host of other items. Perhaps the best example would be to obtain a copy of a complete contract between a union and an employer, either corporate or governmental. Examination of such a document will illustrate more clearly the range of concerns than all the generalizations in a text could ever do. In addition, discuss the issue with some people who are members of unions to gain some insight into a union's role as seen by its members. (About one third of the members of our labor force belong to unions, so you should not have too much difficulty in finding someone.)

■ THE STRUCTURE OF THE UNION MOVEMENT

The reading that begins on page 211 indicates the existence of a multi-tiered system within the structure of organized labor. Let us examine this structure, working from the national level down to the local level. Then, in the next section, we will look at the establishment and operation of unions at the local level.

In Canada there are two large federations of labor—in effect, unions made up of unions. These are the Canadian Labor Congress, with which over 75 percent of Canadian union members are affiliated, and the Confederation of National Trade Unions, primarily Quebec-oriented, with about 10 percent of the total Canadian union membership. The federations, which have

The Growth Of The Canadian Labor Movement

This reading, which is in itself a chapter subsection, outlines the historical development of labor organizations in Canada. Its author, Dr. J. K. Eaton, is with the Economics and Research Branch of Labor Canada.

Trade union locals were in existence in Canada in the early part of the 19th century, and the first Canadian labor centre—the Canadian Labor Union (CLU)—was founded in 1873. The CLU lasted only four years, but its successor, the Trades and Labor Congress of Canada (TLC), which was founded in 1883, had a continuous existence until 1956. By 1900, the movement was nation-wide; locals existed in all provinces, and the main urban centres had a nucleus of locals, in some cases affiliated to a local trades and labor council. It was also a united movement in that only one national centre, the TLC, existed; although there were unions outside the TLC there was nothing in the constitution of that body which would have excluded their future affiliation.

Official union statistics do not exist prior to 1900, when the Department of Labor was established. The first union membership figures were not published until 1911, but prior to that, the Department reported on the number of locals formed, and these give some indication of union growth prior to 1911. From 1900 to 1920 the movement grew steadily, with only a slight interruption in the early war years; stagnation occurred during the inter-war period; and from 1940, growth has been fairly continuous.

The movement had a chequered existence for the first part of the century, beset by internal divisions and external factors such as depression and unemployment. The first internal division occurred in 1902, when the TLC amended its constitution in such a way as to exclude unions in competition with the international unions. This led to the formation of the National Trades and Labor Congress, which in 1909 became the Canadian Federation of Labor, and sought to represent those unions, mainly national, excluded from the TLC.

Also Divisive Factor

The establishment of revolutionary union centres was also a divisive factor. The Industrial Workers of the World, or "Wobblies," had its main influence in the western United States and Canada in the period prior to World War I. Although it continued to exist after the lifting of a 1918 ban on its activities, its influence after the war was minimal. Its place in Canada was taken by the One Big Union, an indigenous organization, formed in 1919 mainly under the impetus of the Winnipeg General Strike. The

The Public Archives of Canada

This photo shows a march during the tumultuous events during the Winnipeg General Strike of 1919. See the last problem at the end of this chapter for some suggestions for detailed examination of these stormy days in Canada's labor history.

OBU's main influence was also in the West, and at its peak in 1919, it claimed a membership of 40 000. Its membership dropped, however, and its sphere of activity became limited to Winnipeg; in 1956, it joined the Canadian Labor Congress.

Another division in labor's ranks was the foundation in 1922 of the Canadian and Catholic Confederation of Labor. The seeds of this movement were sown in 1900 when Archbishop Bégin acted as arbitrator in a lockout of boot and shoe workers in Québec City. The willingness of the employers and workers to accept his judgment, based on the Papal encyclical *Rerum Novarum,* indicated that the province was fertile ground for Catholic unionism. The first specifically Catholic union was formed in 1907 among pulp makers in northern Québec. This foundered, but was reformed in 1912, and with assistance from the Catholic clergy, the movement spread throughout the province. Attempts were made in 1918 at Québec City and in 1919 at Trois-Rivières to establish a province-wide federation, but it was not until 1922 that this was achieved in a founding convention in Hull. The CCCL continued in existence until 1960, when it underwent a change of name and ideology, discussed later.

Largest Union Expelled

Expulsions from the TLC benefited the Canadian Federation of Labor and its successors. The largest Canadian union, the Canadian Brotherhood of Railway Employees (CBRE), which was founded in 1908, was expelled from the TLC in 1921 because it was a dual union to the Brotherhood of Railway Clerks. In 1939 seven unions were expelled, on instructions from the American Federation of Labor, because of their connection with the Congress of Industrial Organizations, an organization of industrial unions that had broken away from the AFL. In 1927, the CBRE combined with the CFL, the OBU and several other national unions to found the All-Canadian Congress of Labor (ACCL). This body suffered from divisions in the thirties but in 1940 merged with the expelled CIO unions to form the Canadian Congress of Labor (CCL).

Consequently, at the outbreak of World War II, the Canadian labor movement was divided among three main centres: the TLC, the CCL and CCCL; and several important unions, among them the railway running trades brotherhoods, outside of these centres. The forties and early fifties, however, saw the growth of a united and more effective movement.

The period from the outbreak of war to the mid-fifties was one of growth and consolidation; membership between 1939 and 1956, when the Canadian Labor Congress was formed, increased fourfold, from 359 000 to 1 386 000. Growth was steady. During the Second World War, as in the First, the membership increased considerably; but, contrary to the previous experience, there was no falling-off in membership in the postwar period. This can be partly accounted for by the fact that there was no postwar depression as in the 1920s and unemployment did not deplete the ranks of potential recruits. At the same time, the union movement was better organized and better able to take advantage of the favourable labor market situation. While the civilian labor force showed an increase, the percentage of the civilian labor force organized into unions showed an increase also, so that in 1956 the movement represented almost a quarter of the civilian labor force and almost one third of the paid workers in that civilian labor force.

Same Euphoria Absent

Although the same euphoria was not present after 1956 and more particularly in the sixties, the upward trend of membership continued. But, whereas in the previous 15 years, membership had almost quadrupled, there was only a 90 per cent increase in the 17 years between 1956 and 1973; in fact, between 1959 and 1962, there was an actual decline.

In the late fifties and early sixties, union growth did not keep pace with the increase in paid workers, and the degree of unionization declined. Although it began to improve after

1964, it was not until 1972 that the 1958 level was again attained.

This decline in the degree of unionization can be accounted for by the growth in the proportion of white-collar workers, and the high rate of unemployment in the latter part of the period, particularly among the new entrants to the labor force. The small but gradual increase in union membership, and in the degree of unionization after 1966, can be attributed mainly to advances made in the public service, largely as a result of the introduction by the federal and several provincial governments of collective bargaining procedures for public servants.

Trend to Unity Begins

The year 1940 marked the beginning of the trend toward labor unity. In that year, the fusion of the national unions in the All-Canadian Congress of Labor with the industrial unions expelled by the Trades and Labor Congress brought into existence the Canadian Congress of Labor. The dominant union in the ACCL had been the Canadian Brotherhood of Railway Employees, which was itself mainly an industrial union; therefore, the new organization was inspired with the spirit of industrial unionism. Being a new organization and allied with the more dynamic CIO in the United States, the CCL took a more active role in organizing the unorganized than did the TLC.

The TLC also showed a considerable increase in membership during this period. Although it consisted mainly of craft unions, its doors had always been open to other types of unions (the United Mine Workers is an outstanding example) and under the impact of modern technical developments, its craft union affiliates had modified their purely craft character and allowed membership to semi-skilled workers.

The TLC also showed indications of a greater independence from the AFL. This was particularly noticeable in the conflict over the expulsion of the Canadian Seamen's Union. When, in 1944, the AFL decided to grant jurisdiction over all seamen to the Seafarers' International Union, the TLC told the AFL that the SIU was a dual union to the Canadian Seamen's Union, which already had jurisdiction in Canada. In 1948, when a further effort was made to undermine the CSU by the formation of the Canadian Lake Seamen's Union, with which the shipping companies had signed an agreement, the TLC again supported the CSU and suspended the Brotherhood of Railway and Steamship Clerks for supporting the dual union.

TLC Prepared to Co-operate

In subsequent discussions with the AFL, the TLC made it clear that it was prepared to cooperate with, but was not prepared to be dominated by, the international unions. This victory, however, was partially reversed in the following year when the CSU was expelled from the TLC for organizing a seamen's strike that was seen by the TLC as part of a world Communist conspiracy.

The conflict with the Communists in the postwar period was one factor that brought the TLC and the CCL closer together. They had both been active in support of the Second World War; in the postwar period they supported the plans for postwar reconstruction, and also gave their support to the Korean War. It was in these two latter instances that the differences with the Communists arose. Apart from expelling the CSU, the TLC at its 1949 and 1950 conventions passed resolutions which to all intents and purposes made it impossible for Communists to work within the Congress or its affiliated unions. In 1949, the CCL, along with the CIO, the British Trades Union Congress and several other western European national union centres, left the Communist-dominated World Federation of Trade Unions. (The TLC, like the AFL, had never joined the WFTU.) At the same time, the CCL carried out its own purge of Communist unions, among them the United Electrical Workers; the Mine, Mill and Smelter Workers; and the International Fur and Leather Workers Union.

Further Unifying Factor
A further factor bringing the two centres together was their desire to influence government policy. Their experiences in this field were not always satisfactory; during the war the TLC complained of "government by order in council". However, after pressure against an order in council dealing with wartime wage controls in December 1943, the labor movement was consulted more frequently by the Government about legislation affecting labor.

The eventual union in 1956 of these two centres into the Canadian Labor Congress was assisted by the amalgamation in 1955 of their counterparts in the United States, the AFL and the CIO. In both cases, the mergers had been preceded by a period of cooperation in which one of the most important features was agreement on no-raiding pacts. The TLC and the CCL at their 1953 conventions decided to form a committee of trade union unity. This committee drew up the no-raiding pact and established a procedure for independent arbitration as its final step. The unification congress was held in April 1956 in Toronto, attended by 1600 delegates from 120 unions representing just over one million members. The congress rejected clearly any subordination to the AFL-CIO and the latter agreed that its officers working in Canada would be transferred to the CLC.

The One Big Union, which left the ACCL in 1936 and from 1946 onward claimed an annual membership of about 12 000, merged with the CLC in 1956 and agreed to the taking-over of its locals by CLC affiliates.

Steady Membership Increase
The Canadian Labor Congress enjoyed a steady increase in membership. Although there was a decline in membership between 1959 and 1962, by 1956 its membership was higher than it had been previously and by 1973 was 74 per cent higher than the 1957 figure. The affiliation of all but one of the railway running trades brotherhoods boosted CLC membership, but expulsion of the Teamsters and the SIU had the opposite effect. The CLC was particularly concerned during this period with the organization of white-collar workers, and in 1962 established a committee and a department for this purpose. The 1966 convention demanded a review of the structure of the organization, and in 1968 a report was presented to the convention dealing with the review of structure and laying down a code of ethics. The latter was motivated to some extent by the desire to avoid the government intervention that had taken place in the United States. In the review of structure, the main recommendation was with regard to mergers, but apart from making a general request for the merging of suitable units, no specific recommendations were made. The code of ethics dealt with corruption and with the rights of members, and recommended the establishment of public review boards.

Mergers did take place, but it is unlikely that the committee on structure had much influence on them, because in most of the cases the impetus came from the United States. As a result of mergers of national Canadian unions, however, two large public service unions were formed: the Canadian Union of Public Employees and the Public Service Alliance of Canada.

Canadian Autonomy
The influence of the old CCL was shown in the increased importance given to social and political action. Although the CLC did not affiliate to the New Democratic Party, which was formed in 1961 out of the old Co-operative Commonwealth Federation, it did encourage its affiliated bodies to do so. At its 1970 convention, the CLC also pledged itself to "a new sense of direction . . . in the area of social action" and a reform caucus at this convention sought to push the CLC in a more social and political direction. Later conventions have given attention to the status of Canadian sections of international unions, and sought to increase their autonomy. Arising from a convention decision in 1970, a questionnaire requesting information on Canadian autonomy was sent to the international affiliates operating in Canada and guide-

lines were subsequently established.

The presence of international unions in Canada was opposed by the Confederation of Canadian Unions, a federation of independent Canadian unions founded in 1968. It had a membership of 22 000 in 1973.

The Canadian and Catholic Confederation of Labor also increased its membership. Between 1940 and 1956, membership more than doubled to 101 000, and in 1973 the membership of the CCCL's successor, the Confederation of National Trade Unions, had increased to 164 000. During the 1940-1956 period, and particularly just after the war, a series of conflicts, the most important being the Asbestos strike in 1949, compelled it to modify its sectarian attitude toward the non-Catholic unions. In 1950, during the Korean War, it collaborated with the TLC, the CCL and the Railway Brotherhoods in making representation to the Government over control of prices. The former policy of passivity was tending to give way to recognition that social peace without justice was not satisfactory, and that it was necessary to give workers support in their struggle against capital. The previous *entente* between the Catholic unions and the State was disrupted under the Duplessis régime. In these circumstances, the CCCL was more favourably disposed to cooperation with the other centres. At its 1955 congress, it declared itself favourable to trade union unity and ready to undertake a study of the best methods for accomplishing complete trade union unity in Canada while at the same time safeguarding the spirit of independence of the Canadian labor movement. Although not prepared to merge with the CLC, it was prepared to seek affiliation to that body as a single union, with constituent bodies safeguarded from raiding by the other unions in the CLC.

Alters Name

In 1960 the CCCL dropped "Catholic" from its name and became the Confederation of National Trade Unions (CNTU). The leadership of the church was increasingly being replaced by that of university-trained leaders whose influence was reflected in the increasing militancy of the organization. The CNTU divested itself of its ideological outlook, and until the late sixties could be considered as a modern business union. Since then, there has been a greater influence of Québec nationalism on the leadership and the ties with the Government have loosened considerably. The efforts toward unity with the CLC failed, but the CNTU collaborated more closely with the Québec Federation of Labor (the provincial body of the CLC). There were probably underlying philosophical and political reasons for the failure of the unity talks, but ostensibly the reason was the reluctance of the CLC to accept the CNTU as an affiliate without any change in its basic structure. The CLC believed that some of the locals and even federations of the CNTU should be prepared to merge with the appropriate unions affiliated to the CLC, but this was not acceptable to the CNTU. Unity talks between the two organizations were eventually broken off in 1964 and a period of inter-union rivalry in Québec ensued.

Friction developed also between the CNTU and the international unions over the former's efforts to organize groups of French-speaking workers who were part of nation-wide bargaining units. Eventually, the Canada Labor Relations Board allowed separate bargaining units for certain groups in Québec, such as the Canadian Broadcasting Corporation newsmen. Inter-union raiding reached such proportions that the CNTU, the QFL and the Québec Teachers' Corporation opened negotiations to formulate a no-raiding pact. This brought the QFL into conflict with its parent body, the CLC; the conflict was resolved at the 1968 CLC convention, where it was agreed that the CLC would also be a party to any negotiations conducted in Québec with regard to a no-raiding pact. Since then, there has been collaboration between the three organizations in a "Common Front" against the Québec Government, although differences between them have appeared from time to time. The dispute with the Government resulted in jail sentences in the spring of 1972 for the leaders of the three organizations.

Several Unions Secede
The involvement in the "Common Front" and defiance of the Québec Government by its leaders led in 1972 to the secession of several CNTU unions to form the *Centrale des syndicats démocratiques.* This organization reported a membership of 41 000 in 1973.

There are so many imponderables about the Canadian labor movement that to predict its future development would be a hazardous enterprise. In terms of membership growth, it is just emerging from a period of stagnation comparable to that which existed in the inter-war period. The movement rose out of that stagnation due to the organization of semi-skilled workers by the new industrial unions, and the assistance of more beneficial legislation. Since the mid-sixties, the growth has been largely attributable to the organization of government employees, assisted mainly by the extension to them of collective bargaining rights.

Today there still remains potential for growth in that almost two-thirds of the non-agricultural paid workers are unorganized. But these are in a different job situation than were the unorganized in the thirties. They are not semi-skilled workers in mass production units, but are mainly white-collar workers and workers in small establishments. Their organization will be a much slower process than was the organization of the semi-skilled workers.

Furthermore, there has been a deterioration in the image of unionism since the thirties. Apart from the fact that labor is no longer regarded as an underdog, the high incidence of strikes, and certain instances of corruption in the unions have not done the movement much good.

The future of organized labor in Canada depends on whether it can improve this unfavourable image and adapt itself to the task of organizing the increasing number of white-collar workers.

From *The Labor Gazette,* Labor Canada, Ottawa, Vol. 75, Number 9, September, 1975, pp 643-648.

permanent structures, research bodies, legislative advisory committees, educational sections, etc., in addition to regular congresses, promote the common interests and concerns of member unions and their individual members. They are financed by payments of dues ultimately coming from individual members.

Within the federations are found the individual unions, running from the very large (the largest being the Canadian Union of Public Employees, C.L.C., with over 200 000 members) to the very small (some individual locals which are directly chartered by the C.L.C.). There are two basic types of unions within this system. One group is referred to as "national" unions (such as C.U.P.E.) which have no links as such with groups outside Canada except through the C.L.C. Found within the C.L.C. are the members of the second group, the "international" unions[1], where Canadian locals are a part of unions which are essentially American in total operation. Canadian locals are affiliated with the C.L.C. and, through the union headquarters, with the A.F.L.-C.I.O. in the United States.

Most unions have a number of locals. The **local** is ordinarily based on locality in the geographical sense and also on the basis of place of employment. For example in Anytown, Canada, there may be two firms producing widgets, Canadian Widget Corp. Ltd. and Super-Duper Widget Ltd. The Widget Workers Union would normally have two

[1] About two-thirds of all union members belong to international unions.

locals, one for the employees in each firm.

In the promotion of common interests, community welfare, and the many other objectives of unions, inter-union cooperation below the national level (i.e., the federation) is important. There are over 100 district labor councils where local conditions and community affairs are the chief matters of concern. Each province has a federation of labor structured much like the national federations. At the provincial levels, one of the most significant interests is in the existing structure and process of change of provincial labor legislation. Other items, such as minimum wage laws, workmens' compensation, vocational training programs which come, in whole or in part, under provincial jurisdiction, receive constant attention from provincial federations. At this level, as at the national, lobbying the government is one of the primary activities. (The same is true of course of many business and commercial organizations and associations.)

COLLECTIVE BARGAINING

It is at the local level that organizational activity must be first carried out and where the most important function, **collective bargaining,** goes on. Collective bargaining is the process of negotiating and agreeing on terms of a contract with an employer through a group or organization established for that purpose.

Before this can be done, a union must be properly established in a way provided for by law.[2] For the sake of illustration, let us assume that a third widget plant is opened in Anytown, that well-known widget manufacturing center.

The employees may proceed to organize themselves or may be approached by members of the Widget Workers Union. The initial organization is established with those wishing to join making application, paying dues or an initiation fee, and electing a provisional executive under a provisional constitution.

When the body has the support of the majority of the employees within the proposed bargaining unit, application is then made to the appropriate governmental Labor Relations Board for **certification.** Certification means that the union is given legal recognition and rights, is entitled to bargain for those in the unit, and must be treated in good faith by the employer. The local, thus established, would become a part of the union, let us say Local 313 of the Canadian Union of Widget Workers. The constitution, executive and structure would now be finalized on terms compatible with the requirements of provincial law and the national union's constitution. The stage is now set for collective bargaining to take place.

The basic procedure is for members to meet, draw up proposed terms for a contract, select a bargaining committee, and perhaps seek special advisors or advice on negotiations, pension provisions, etc. from the national union.

The actual process of bargaining is usually a slow process involving degrees of modification of positions by both sides in promotion of eventual agreement. In most cases, agreement is reached. When this is approved (ratified) by the union members and the employer, it then becomes the binding contract for the specified period which usually runs from one to three years. In the event that agreement can not be reached at this stage, the sequence of events then follows a format covered by the applicable legislation, either federal or provincial.

Once governmental authorities have determined that a deadlock exists, the first stage frequently involves the appointment of an outside mediator by or conciliation officer from the appropriate Department of Labor, whose function it is to try and bring the two

[2] Most employees are in fields where labor legislation is under provincial jurisdiction. Some are under federal regulation. The provisions are essentially the same across Canada.

Table 18-1. UNION MEMBERSHIP IN CANADA, 1927-1977

Year	Union Members in Thousands	Union Members as % of	
		Total Labor Force	Non-agricultural Labor Force
1927	275	7.5	12.0
1932	311	7.5	15.3
1937	323	7.2	16.2
1942	462	10.3	18.0
1947	832	17.1	27.9
1952	1146	21.4	30.2
1957	1386	24.3	32.4
1962	1423	22.2	30.2
1967	1921	26.1	32.3
1972	2371	27.6	34.4
1977	3149	31.0	38.2

Note: After 1949, data are as of January 1 of the year given. Prior to 1949, data are as of December 31 of the previous year.

Source: The Labour Gazette, vol. 75, No. 9, September, 1975, and vol. 77, No. 9, September, 1977.

sides to an agreement. If agreement is not reached here, the **conciliation** process may then go to (or in some cases start with) the appointment of a conciliation board. This board normally has three members, one selected by each side and a Chairman selected by the first two members. In the event agreement on a chairman cannot be reached, he may then be appointed by the Minister of Labor or the Labor Relations Board. After hearing representations, the conciliation board presents recommendations which it hopes can form the basis for an agreement. These are not mandatory on either side; and, if unacceptable to either or both, the dispute goes to the next stages.

After a mandatory "cooling-off period", the workers must decide between alternate courses of action, a strike or **arbitration.** In some instances, particularly the public service's vital areas, arbitration may be the only course. If it is chosen or required, the results of the arbitrator or arbitration board become binding on both sides. In the event of a strike, presumably the effect will be to weaken one side or both to produce a willingness to reopen negotiations and reach a solution.[3]

Once the parties have reached their agreement, at whatever stage, the collective agreement determines the contract for the bargaining unit.[4]

UNIONS NOW AND IN THE FUTURE

The union movement has achieved much, both for its membership and for society. For members, tremendous improvements in total patterns of working conditions and stan-

[3] For a debate on the issue of strikes, see the essays by R. P. Riggin and Bernard Brody, reprinted in Unit 3 of A. M. MacDonald, (ed.), *Readings In The World of Economics,* Toronto: McGraw-Hill Ryerson, 1973.

[4] In some cases, all individuals must be union members. This is a "union shop." In other cases, some may not belong to the union or pay dues to it. This is an "open shop." As a result of efforts by unions to overcome the existence of these union-weakening situations, most non-"union shop" situations are now covered by the **Rand Formula,** named after the former Supreme Court Justice. Devised in 1946, this states, in essence, that those who benefit from union negotiations need not join, but should have to pay dues to the union automatically.

Collins in the Montreal Gazette

John Collins' cartoon contains a label crediting Canada with the "world's worst strike record." This is, in fact, a debatable point. International data are not always comparable, and different data may be used to judge a nation's "strike record." For further examination of this controversy, see Walter Stewart, *Strike,* Toronto: McClelland and Stewart, 1977, pp. 44-48, and the Canadian Foundation for Economic Education's Newsletter *Rapport,* No. 9, Winter-Spring, 1978, pp. 2-3. Regardless of the statistical differences and debates, one point will emerge from an examination of our strike record and that is what Collins is aiming at: Canada's recent record is not a good one.

dards of living have been achieved. Unions have brought an increased degree of order and organization to labor-management relations and have contributed much in promoting beneficial economic and social action by governments and businesses alike.

At the same time, unions still have a less than perfect public image among many people and groups. Power, once acquired, may be used wisely, or may be abused. In this respect, unions have proved to be less than perfect—like all other human institutions. Let us recall the concept of countervailing economic power referred to in Chapter 13. Just as unions were a reaction to unrestrained business, so may voices calling for more rational action by unions or government controls over them be a reaction to the emergence of union power and the abuse of power in some cases. The crucial thing to remember is that there are no simple "good-bad" labels which can be applied, despite the fact that many would have us believe this is the case. All specific incidents must be examined on the basis of the case itself and rational judgements must be formed on the basis of the circumstances there.

Some specific topics which have gained

The Trend To Industrial Democracy In Canada

The acquisition by labor of the right to participate in a number of aspects of decision-making is sometimes referred to as "industrial democracy." This reading provides a synopsis of a study on the subject sponsored by the Economic Council of Canada. The trend to industrial democracy is very likely to be prominent among topics involving organized labor as we move into the 1980s.

Industrial democracy is one area of labor relations in which there is no clear-cut ideological split between management and labor. Broadly defined, this concept consists of breaking down the traditional dichotomy between labor and management to allow workers more authority and involvement in structuring and controlling their work environment.

Neither group has embraced this notion wholeheartedly. Some managers contend that such an institution would be too unwieldy and that, far from improving productivity, it could actually lead to greater inefficiency because lengthy consultation sessions would cut into time spent on the job. Union leaders have argued that participation is merely another management ploy to exploit workers and to undermine the role of unions. Even workers themselves have expressed misgivings about their ability and desire to participate in such a system.

Growing interest

But advocates of this new system of worker-management relations are gaining ground in Canada. Keith Newton, an economist with the Council, notes the increasing interest in industrial democracy in a recent paper.[a] He attributes it in part to the unhealthy state of the Canadian economy. Faced with continuing high inflation and unemployment, lagging growth rates, and industrial disputes, many Canadians regard industrial democracy as a means toward a more cooperative and hence more productive relationship between labor and management.

As well, the Canadian Labor Congress has focused public attention on participation with its demand for a tripartite planning body at the national level. Although the government has not agreed to the specific CLC proposal—a Social and Economic Planning Council, comprised of business, labor, and government representatives—there have since been a series of tripartite meetings and the government seems to be considering some form of multipartite consultation. The introduction of joint decision-making at the national level[b] would probably set an example for the private sector.

Even though attitudes are changing, Dr. Newton expects that industrial democracy is not likely to find widespread acceptance without considerable debate. Canada has been relatively slow to reach this stage of management-labor relations. In most European countries, worker participation occurred more than two decades ago either through voluntary initiatives, as in Britain and Denmark, or through legislation, as in Germany. Consequently, Canada now has a wide range of varied experience to assess and draw upon.

Forms of industrial democracy

In Dr. Newton's opinion, industrial democracy can and should be tailored to meet the unique needs of each environment. He cautions that Canada should not try to duplicate a form of industrial democracy simply because it has proven successful elsewhere. He points out that participation can take many forms in practice. For example, there are differences in how industrial democracy is initiated and operated. It may be the result of statutory provisions, as with works councils and safety committees. Or

[a] Keith Newton, *The Theory and Practice of Industrial Democracy: A Canadian Perspective,* Economic Council of Canada, Discussion Paper No. 94.

[b] Note the Council's recommendation on this subject in its *Fourteenth Annual Review: Into the 1980s,* Ottawa: Supply and Services Canada, 1977, p. 91.

contractual agreements or informal arrangements may give rise to voluntary institutions, such as committees for joint consultation and negotiation. Whether they are legal or voluntary, these arrangements may be instituted at several levels: the factory, the firm, or the industry.

The characteristics of the work place decide its potential for worker participation. In the case of the firm, Dr. Newton describes four determinants: the autonomy of the enterprise, its size, technology, and organizational structure. For example, smaller firms may be more conducive to communication and cooperation than larger firms, which are likely to have more rigid regulations and more remote, impersonal supervision.

Whether or not the firm reaches its potential depends on what Dr. Newton calls "human factors." That is, how willing workers are to participate and how amenable management is to their participation.

Already, many firms across Canada are implementing innovative work arrangements, such as job enrichment and flexible hours, which give workers more control over their work environment. Dr. Newton believes that such innovations will become more frequent. At the plant level, there seems to be a clear preference for an evolutionary and voluntary growth of industrial democracy, so that it meets the particular requirements of individual organizations.

Reprinted from: Economic Council of Canada, *Bulletin,* vol. 2, No. 1, December, 1977, p. 3. For further reference, see also G. Sanderson and R. Stapenhurst, (eds.), *Industrial Democracy Today: A New Role For Labour,* McGraw-Hill Ryerson, Toronto, 1979.

much more attention in recent years may attain even greater prominence between the time of writing and the time of reading.

One is the role of unions in the public service. It has now become common practice for public servants to have collective bargaining rights. Concern is mounting, however, about how far these rights should go. Specifically, the question of the right to strike in the public service (or at least in vital sectors) is a subject of growing debate. However, in this instance, all positions must finally involve the question of compromise between the rights of particular groups, and of society as a whole.

A second issue is one which is only part of a broader pattern—that of Canadian nationalism with its many facets. As with issues involving government policy, culture, ownership of business, etc., the close relationship between the Canadian labor movement and that in the United States is coming under closer scrutiny. More voices can be heard both inside and outside the labor movement for a more truly Canadian union structure.

A third issue is the relationship between organized labor and political parties. Unlike the British case where the Trade Union Congress is officially connected with the Labor Party, the C.L.C. has not developed comparable direct ties with the New Democratic Party in Canada. The C.L.C. does generally support the N.D.P. and many Canadian unions are affiliated with the N.D.P. and make contributions to election efforts. Many within the N.D.P. and the labor movement advocate closer ties between the two, and more specifically political activity on the part of organized labor. Frequently, political analysts attribute many of the N.D.P.'s problems to the lack of an effective relationship between the party and organized labor which could perhaps, as it appears to do in the U.K., deliver decisive results at the ballot box. The direction taken by organized labor in this respect may be a crucial one for the whole of Canadian society.

From organized labor's own perspective,

"I forget. . . . Is it the company's turn to go for a price increase, or is it our turn to try for a raise?"

Al Kaufman with permission from *The Saturday Review*

This cartoon indicates a basic element in "cost-push" inflation, where cost increases may drive up prices. Wage increases, frequently labeled "excessive," have led to mounting concern about the use (or abuse) of bargaining power by very strong unions. In some cases, there appears to be grounds for criticism. In others, however, wage demands may simply be responses to increases in the cost of living. As is usually the case, sweeping generalizations, regardless of content, are not found to be satisfactory in dealing with wage-price relationships.

several issues have become matters of increasing concern. During recent years, both inflation and unemployment have been unusually high. While this situation exists (or threatens to exist, or grows even worse), unions will place the priority on the protection of their members from the effects of either of these economic problems. Job security is often difficult to ensure, especially in the face of economic downturns. As a result, more attention will likely be paid to protecting existing jobs in an age when one trend is that of increasing automation. (This topic will be explored in Chapter 31.)

Attempting to maintain real income is often a recurring problem and, as the Kaufman cartoon illustrates, may in reality be part of the vicious circle of a wage-price spiral. "Cost-of-living" clauses are becoming increasingly common in contracts[5] and "COLA" (cost-of-living allowance) provisions in pensions are also growing more widespread.

This whole area of protecting jobs and real income levels is a highly controversial one. In reality, what is good (or necessary) for one individual or group may have undesirable effects on society as a whole. The basic problem thus is one of conflicting interests. To put this more precisely, let us consider the implications of the Kaufman cartoon. Should the workers get their raise (even if they might not be more productive), with the cost carried by the firm, and/or the consumers of their output, or should they face reductions in real income in the interest of more general price stability? The answer is very likely to depend on who is asked—the workers and their families, the employers, or the consumers of the goods. The solution that is deemed "correct" will be strongly influenced by value judgments and vested interests.

Another focal point of union activity in the immediate future seems likely to be in "organizing" sectors of the labor force where unions do not presently exist. Table 18-1 clearly shows that a large proportion of the labor force still is not unionized. These sectors are primarily in "white collar" and "service" industries. Banks are one sector where unions have just started to appear and are likely to be making major efforts to expand in the decade of the 1980s.

One more and, in Canada, a relatively recent concern is that of attaining some degree of power or influence over management. The reading "The Trend to Industrial Democracy" highlights this issue.

The objectives outlined in the reading, along with the first three points mentioned above, plus wider public concern about the use of power by unions, seem likely to be the issues concerning organized labor and its role in the 1980s. As you see and/or hear current stories about labor-management relations, try to analyse them to see to what extent the points raised here are significant factors.

[5] See data in Table 30-5.

SUMMARY

Labor unions play an important role in the determination of wages and working conditions in the economy. While only about one third of all employed persons in the labor force in this country are members of labor unions, these organizations or workers nevertheless occupy a strategic position in many industries such as manufacturing, mining, construction, and transportation. They also have an indirect effect on the returns to labor in many other fields.

Labor unions are more than simply economic bargaining units designed to put pressure on employers to pay higher wages. They are also social organizations and, to a degree, political organizations, both of which help to determine the character of the society. Workers who might otherwise feel like insignificant cogs in a great business or industrial machine often join unions as a means of becoming part of a group that will stand up for their rights and interests. Thus, even beyond the monetary rewards that the union may help them to get, workers often join unions in order to achieve a sense of self respect and a feeling that they are human beings who count for something and cannot be pushed around by the great impersonal forces of an industrial society. Less remotely, workers want their union to stand up for them against their immediate supervisors or foremen, to protect them from being personally humiliated.

Of course, unions are themselves large organizations, and the degree to which they satisfy these needs and aspirations of workers vary considerably from one union to another. The quality of leadership in different unions has a great deal to do with how effectively unions play their economic and social role in this country. The society itself has sought to ensure, through legislation, that unions do not, in the name of the protection of individual worker's rights, coerce their individual members or transgress the rights and legitimate interests of employers.

Within the labor movement, a complex structure has emerged. Unions band together in federations to promote common interests. In organizing, expanding, or bargaining, the key units are union locals. It is at the local level where the primary function of collective bargaining is carried out under the ground rules laid down by laws of either the federal or provincial governments. The future of unions, like their past, may prove to be a stormy one. Growing concern over strikes and inflation may lead public opinion toward steps to regulate the use of union power. Questions about the political role of unions and the independence of unions related to U.S. labor organizations also loom on the horizon as major points of contention, while unions on the other hand see an increased need to provide protection for their members in an era of historically high inflation and unemployment.

KEY CONCEPTS

local	collective bargaining	arbitration
certification	conciliation	Rand Formula

QUESTIONS FOR REVIEW AND DISCUSSION

1. Why did unions first appear? How have their objectives changed over the years?
2. How did the development of the union movement in Canada parallel trends in the United States?
3. How is a union formed? What is collective bargaining? What power does a union have to promote its objectives?

PROBLEMS AND EXERCISES TO SHARPEN YOUR UNDERSTANDING

1. Should all public employees have the right to strike? Firemen? Nurses? Teachers? If they are not to be permitted to strike, how do you propose to protect them?
2. What are the disadvantages of locals being locals of international unions? What are the possible advantages? What changes in the *status quo* do you recommend?
3. What do you feel unions stand to gain and to lose by increasing political activity in general? Through closer ties with the N.D.P. specifically? What might be the result for the country as a whole?
4. Can automatic increases in wages to keep pace with general increases in prices be justified? Examine this issue through a debate format, with one side representing labor and the other side representing management or the general public.
5. Following the polarization of opinions in the debate above, establish a "conciliation board" to try to bring the two sides to a compromise. In what areas will concessions be likely or necessary? When a compromise is reached, try to assess who would carry any ultimate costs contained in it.
6. Undertake a research project into one of the significant labor disputes in Canada's history. Strong contenders might be:
   (a) the Winnipeg General Strike of 1919;
   (b) Labor relations in Cape Breton in the 1920s;
   (c) the Asbestos strike of 1949.
   Some preliminary references for these would be:
   (a) Kenneth McNaught and David Bercuson, *The Winnipeg General Strike,* Toronto: Longman, 1974; Peter Kidd, *The Winnipeg General Strike,* (Jackdaw #C29) Toronto: Clarke, Irwin, 1972.
   (b) Paul MacEwan, *Miners and Steelworkers,* Toronto: Hakkert, 1976; Dawn Fraser, *Echoes From Labor's War,* Toronto: New Hogtown Press, 1976.
   (c) Pierre Elliott Trudeau, *The Asbestos Strike,* trans. James Boake, Toronto: James Lorimer, 1974.

CHAPTER 19

FUNCTIONS OF GOVERNMENT IN A MARKET ECONOMY

■ ECONOMIC FUNCTIONS OF GOVERNMENT ■ FINANCING GOVERNMENT ACTIVITIES ■ THE GOVERNMENT IN THE MARKET ECONOMY ■ SUMMARY ■ APPENDIX: THREE REACTIONS TO A ROYAL COMMISSION

There is always a great temptation to oversimplify one's own—or, even more, someone else's—position in economic matters. Adam Smith, for instance, certainly advocated a general policy of **laissez faire** (or let things alone), contending that there was too much government interference in private economic affairs. But while Smith was strongly against government meddling with free markets, he did not argue that there was *no* role for government in the economy. On the contrary, in *The Wealth of Nations,* Smith specifically stated what he thought the role of government in a free society should be:

> According to the system of natural liberty, the sovereign [government] has only three duties to attend to; three duties of great importance, indeed, but plain and intelligible to common understandings: first, the duty of protecting the society from the violence and invasion of other independent societies; secondly, the duty of protecting, as far as possible, every member of the society from the injustice or oppression of every other member of it, or the duty of establishing an exact administration of justice; and thirdly, the duty of erecting and maintaining certain public works and certain public institutions, which it can never be for the interest of any individual, or small number of individuals, to erect and maintain; because the profit could never repay the expense to any individual or small number of individuals, though it may frequently do much more than repay it to a great society.[1]

Very few champions of *laissez faire* today would deny Smith's contention that government, at minimum, should provide for the national defense, administration of justice, law and order, and the maintenance of certain socially desirable public works.

Many people today would argue that government must have a much larger role, even in free societies, than that recommended by Adam Smith. They would contend that the technological, social, and political changes that have swept this country and the world since 1776[2] inevitably have greatly expanded the necessary role of government. Canada has been transformed from a small-scale, essentially rural economy to a massive, industrial, urban economy, vulnerable to depression and mass unemployment, which government can and should try to counteract.

The evolution of democracy and growing demands for an improved standard of living

[1] Adam Smith, *The Wealth of Nations,* New York: Random House, Modern Library edition, 1937, p. 651.

[2] Remember that, to economists, 1776 is important as a publishing date. *The Wealth of Nations* was first printed in that year. An interesting perspective is given by Milton Friedman, an influential American economist, in a survey called "Adam Smith's Relevance For Today," which appeared in a U.S. journal called *Challenge,* March/April, 1977, Vol. 20, No. 1, p. 6.

GOVERNMENTS IN THE ECONOMY

Transport Canada

A. H. MacDonald

Government of Saskatchewan Photo

The St. Lawrence Seaway Authority

Governments are major providers of goods and services. As indicators, this group of photos includes major facilities. The first, Mirabel Airport at Montreal, is operated by the Federal government. The second photo shows the hydro-electric plant at Mactaquac, operated by the provincially-owned power corporation in New Brunswick. The third photo shows the potash mine at Lanigan, Saskatchewan. This mine was originally owned by a European-controlled company and in 1977 was taken over by the provincially-owned Potash Corporation of Saskatchewan. The last photo shows the St. Lambert lock of the St. Lawrence Seaway Authority. The Seaway was built as a joint project of the Canadian and American governments, the Province of Ontario, and the State of New York.

have increased pressures for welfare programs to improve the lot of the common man, and this has also served to expand the role of government. Nevertheless, few issues continue to excite more controversy than how large a role government should play in our economic life.

ECONOMIC FUNCTIONS OF GOVERNMENT

Government as an economic institution has had a unique evolution in Canada, some aspects of which will be examined in subsequent chapters. In this chapter we will examine the principal economic functions played by our government today, and compare the role of the *government* with that of the *market* as a means of allocating and developing the nation's scarce resources.

Establishing and Enforcing the Rules of the Game

All societies must establish some framework of law and order to exist at all. A market economy, as we have seen, could not exist without some protection of private property and enforcement of contracts. But, once this general point is made, there is room for debate as to just which rules are necessary or desirable. Do we need standard weights and measures? Meat inspection? Laws to forbid child labor? Laws to protect people from working long hours? Zoning regulations? Smoke prevention laws? Blue laws to keep stores closed on Sunday? Minimum wage laws? Laws to prevent retail stores from selling products at less than the manufacturer's advertised price? Each of these areas requires careful analysis, on economic as well as social grounds. Some you may accept, other you may reject.

Providing Information and Services to Help the Market Work Better

Many government agencies today are concerned with gathering and publishing information on all sorts of things from the weather to the price of retail goods and services. An important service of the federal government is to try to help bring together people looking for work and employers seeking employees. Special depreciation allowances and tax write-offs are sometimes provided to firms in a particular type of industry or area within the country. Special retraining programs are provided by some governmental agencies to help workers acquire the skills needed in the market place. Such services are usually provided by the government in hopes that the adjustments required in a market economy can take place faster and more efficiently than would otherwise be the case.

Fostering Competition

Beginning in 1889, the federal government has attempted to strengthen the economy through legislation aimed at providing free and open competition. In that year, an amendment to the criminal code made it illegal for any producer to "prevent, limit, or lessen unduly" his supply or to "enhance unreasonably" its price. However, the terminology, as a whole, was vague. No specific enforcement staff was set up, and the net effect of the law was slight.

Later, in 1910, a separate Combines Investigation Act was passed. This prohibited any form of monopoly, combine or oligopoly which "has acted or is likely to operate to the detriment of the public".

In 1923, a new act was passed, providing for the establishment of administrative and investigational staff. Later revisions to this act and to the criminal code have added rulings against various specific business practices to the original prohibitions of monopolies which were not "in the public interest."

The legislation, which was all consolidated in 1960 into a single act, has long been a target for criticism from several points of view. Those who seek more vigorous enforcement criticize the vague wording and its ensuing legal difficulties, the lack of vigorous government action in many oligopolistic situations where price fixing is done

Governments and the Preservation of the Market System

In this excerpt from The New Industrial State, *Professor Galbraith suggests that the effect of government action in this field may actually be little more than the perpetuation of the* status quo, *preserving the power of corporations who have it while limiting the growth of those who seek to acquire it—and, in the process, minimizing the degree of effective competition. Though Galbraith was primarily concerned with the U.S. economy, many would claim that the proposition does also apply to Canada*

The law is very severe on any overt collusion in the setting of prices. Such collusion simplifies the task of the oligopolists in seeking to arrive at the most advantageous price for all. And the government scrutinizes closely mergers which might have the effect of increasing the market power of the individual oligopolist. The most important effect is to deny market power to those who do not have it, or have difficulty in exercising it, while according immunity to those who already have such power.

Thus, the three majors in the automobile industry, as the result of long and intimate study of each other's behavior within the confines of one city, are able to establish prices which reflect the common interest. And they can do so with precision. No consultation is required. The procedure is legally secure. Not much would be changed were the companies allowed, in fact, the consult and agree on prices.

A group of smaller suppliers of parts or subassemblies to the automobile industry will not have the same capacity for estimating each other's needs and intentions. They may also be more numerous—that is to say they will have less market power. Should it become known that in response to their weaker (and more competitive) position they have come together to discuss prices, and thus to win some of the ability to control prices that the automobile majors possess as a matter of course, the law would be upon them like a tiger. It exempts the market power of the strong. And it partly disguises this exemption by attacking efforts by the weak to acquire like power.

From: J. K. Galbraith, *The New Industrial State,* Boston: Houghton, Mifflin Co., 1967, pg. 186. Reprinted by permission of the publisher.

openly, and the sometimes ridiculous penalties which come from convictions, sometimes being fines of only a few thousand dollars against corporations whose annual profits run in the tens of millions.

From the other side, critics from the business world say that often the law is so imprecise that it is impossible to tell whether or not an offense is being committed. It is also pointed out that to be able to make the necessary capital investment and attain the economies of large scale production, while operating in a country with a small population, the existence of only a small number of firms in many fields is an inevitable result. In many instances, this is certainly a reasonable point which cannot be overlooked.

In the final analysis, one must always be on guard to separate facts from value judgments. To many, what "is not in the public interest" is all too often "what is not good for me."[3]

In many areas of the economy, where competing services or products would be inefficient and/or prohibitively expensive, we are faced with a natural situation for a monopoly. Various public services and utilities provide the best examples and here we may find

[3] At the time of writing, legislation to revise the Competition Act was still before Parliament, and had been for some time. Its fate was obscured, however, by the potential effect of the report of the Royal Commission on Corporate Concentration. See the Appendix to this chapter for some initial comments about the report.

varying degrees of regulation from all three levels of government. At the federal level, railways, air transport, and pipelines are under controls which affect prices to the consumer, rates of return to the companies, routes used, and regularity or maintenance of service. On a provincial level, we frequently find controls running from regulation of telephone charges to milk prices. City governments also frequently establish monopolies, through franchises, for such services as bus transportation, and regulate routes and fares. Regulatory authority may range from city contracts and bylaws, through general public utilities commissions at the provincial level, to specialized agencies such as the Canadian Transport Commission at the federal level.

Public Enterprises

In many obvious cases, governments operate directly in the economy through departments or government owned "Crown Corporations" to provide services or fulfill functions which are necessary and would not necessarily be fully provided if left to the free markets. Leading examples are defense, fire and police protection, education, highways, public health services, and the many others which you can name.

Some of these, such as defense or education, are financed out of tax revenues while others cover part of their own costs. Autonomous crown corporations may depend on some form of financial aid or they may, like Air Canada, be self-supporting.

Promoting Economic Security

In a free market economy, individuals are dependent upon their own resources. However, political, social, and moral values may frequently find themselves in conflict with the economic values of "free enterprise." It is now accepted by all that society has an obligation to help those who cannot fully look after themselves.

These adjustments in the effects of normal market forces may take many different forms. Minimum wage laws, subsidies to certain types of producers, family allowances, various categories of pensions, subsidized housing or health services, direct welfare payments, lower tax rates for lower income levels, and unemployment insurance are some of the more important forms of government action to lessen burdens for those who are deemed in need of government assistance. An overall classification system would, of course, be very complex. Some measures are associated with one level of government, while others involve more than one level, with costs being shared. Some measures, such as family allowances, are automatic, payments being received by all, regardless of "need"; whereas others involve some type of eligibility or means test. Some programs are financed out of tax revenues while some, such as the Unemployment Insurance Fund, are, to a considerable degree, financed out of "contributions" from potential recipients of benefits.

A wide range of views about the provision of benefits and distribution of costs may be found. Options frequently are directly related to ideological or political stance: the "left" or NDP favoring more programs with greater emphasis on relating benefits to needs; the "right," the business view, being more hesitant about the further expansion of social service and welfare programs. No specific position has been given to either of the two major political parties, for both contain members with a fairly wide range of viewpoints, with the consensus of each being somewhat "middle of the road," the Liberals (federal) perhaps leaning somewhat more to the "left." The same divergence of viewpoint can be seen within both the Democratic and Republican parties in the U.S. If anything, the extremities of opinion found under single political labels are even more pronounced there.

What is the future role of governments in this area? If historical trends are in any way significant,[4] the expansion of services and programs in the "welfare state" can be expected to continue, perhaps with more atten-

[4] See Tables 19-1 and 19-3.

Table 19-1. GOVERNMENT TRANSFERS TO INDIVIDUALS AND PERSONAL INCOME, 1947-1977[4]

	1947	1952	1957	1962	1967	1972	1977
Total Personal Income	$10 926	18 592	25 170	32 788	50 579	83 767	171 485
Federal Transfers to Individuals[1]	$ 611	975	1460	2110	2918	6376	13 970
Provincial/Local Transfers to Individuals[2]	$ 223	368	592	802	1749	3542	8334
Total Transfers[3]	$ 834	1343	2052	2912	4667	9918	22 304
Transfers as % of Personal Income	7.6%	7.2%	8.2%	8.9%	9.2%	11.8%	13.0%

Notes: [1] Includes payments from Canada Pension Plan after 1967; excludes interest on public debt.
[2] Includes payments from Quebec Pension Plan 1967; excludes interest on public debt.
[3] Excluded also are payments to non-residents, payments in the form of subsidies or assistance to individually-owned businesses or farms, or payments as they go to another level of government en route to an individual recipient.
[4] All dollar data are in millions of current dollars.

Sources: Statistics Canada: *National Income and Expenditure Accounts, 1926-1974*, vol. 1, cat. 13-531; *National Income and Expenditure Accounts, 1962-1976*, cat. 13-201; and *National Income and Expenditure Accounts, Fourth Quarter, 1977*, cat. 13-001.

The data presented here indicate the growing role of government transfers in personal income. In addition to the direct transfers, we must also remember the provision of more and more services of many types. For example, in 1947 who would have paid for the texts you are now using? Who made the payment to enable you to use this text now? The same basic pattern of an increasingly important role by government in personal income and services may be seen in almost all developed economies during the same time period.

tion to relating payments to needs and with more emphasis given to distributing costs in relation to ability to pay.[5]

Providing a Sound Monetary System

The process of specialization and exchange lies at the heart of a market economy, and money plays a key role in this process. As Figure 13-2 indicated, it is the exchange of real goods and services for money payments that enables a system of market prices to answer a society's basic economic questions.

For money to perform its function as a *medium of exchange*, people must have confidence in it and be willing to accept it as a basis for economic transactions. But, by the same test, anything that people are willing to accept as a medium of exchange can serve as money, and keep a market economy rolling. Chapter 17 indicated some of the government's potential power over banks and the money supply. Chapter 27 will refer in considerable detail to the role of the Bank of Canada in our economic system. On an historical basis, Section 91 of the British North America Act gives the federal government power over "Banking, Incorporation of Banks, and the Issue of Paper Money." Until 1934, Ottawa shared its power to issue paper money with the chartered banks. Prior to this date, due to lack of machinery and techniques, the ability of the government to regulate the money supply or to prevent changes in the value of money was limited. Since its foundation in 1934, however, the Bank of Canada has been an important instrument through which the government can and does try to directly influence and regulate the economy to maintain a desirable level of price and monetary stability.

[5] An excellent area for research in political and economic history is the evolution of many of these concepts and programs from "dangerous radicalism" in the 1920s to "sound policies" in the more recent period. See: D. Owen Carrigan, *Canadian Party Platforms, 1867-1968*, Toronto: Copp Clark, 1968.

Employment and Income with Special Reference to The Initial Period of Reconstruction

In April, 1945, the Canadian government tabled a White Paper on Employment and Income in the House of Commons. Canada had gone through almost a decade of severe depression in the thirties. During World War II, the role of the government in the economy had changed drastically. The state had assumed control over all aspects of the economy in conjunction with the war effort.

In addition to the changes caused by the wartime situation, changes had started to take place in general thinking about economics. One catalyst for change was the trauma brought about by the severe problems which had existed between the wars. The other was the impact of the work of some economists, especially John Maynard Keynes of Cambridge University. You will encounter numerous references to Keynes' ideas and impact throughout Unit 4. It is sufficient to say at this stage that he provided a new approach to cycles in the economy and suggested these could and should be offset by government action. The 1945 White Paper reflected a general acceptance of this thesis, that government action in peacetime (as opposed to wartime) to promote economic stability and growth is a wise and desirable course of action.

In the reading in Chapter 13, "Is Fear of Corporate Growth Declining?", you encountered initial reference to Robert Bryce in the context of a Royal Commission in the mid-1970s. Bryce had studied at Cambridge under Keynes, went to Harvard where he played an important role in introducing Keynes' ideas and, in 1938, came to Ottawa where he was to hold many key posts in the public service, including that of Deputy Minister of Finance from 1963 to 1970. Bryce played a major role in influencing government policy in a direction that was to make Canada, in the words of J. K. Galbraith, "the first country to commit itself to a firmly Keynesian economic policy."

Following is the initial section of the Foreword of the White Paper on Employment and Income, and then an introduction to another section which indicates in a general way, the approach to economic analysis and policy which will be covered throughout Unit 4.

Foreword

The ultimate aim of all reconstruction policies is the extension of opportunity, welfare and security among the Canadian people. Reconstruction must start from the circumstances which result from nearly six years of war; circumstances in which, at the peak, not far from half of the Canadian people derived their occupation and their incomes directly, or indirectly, from government expenditures. The program of reconstruction is, therefore, not a simple matter of striking out for new goals, but a complicated task of combining the demobilization of the armed services and war industry with the rebuilding of an ampler and more stable Canadian economy.

Comprehensive provisions have been made for the demobilization and reestablishment of the members of the armed forces. These provisions will depend for their success on the conditions of civilian life, in which such persons are finally reestablished, and particularly on the availability of employment or other gainful occupation.

The central task of reconstruction, in the interest of the armed services and civilians alike, must be to accomplish a smooth, orderly transition from the economic conditions of war to those of peace and to maintain a high and stable level of employment and income. The Government adopts this as a primary object of policy.

This goal cannot be achieved by legislation alone, nor by a single device or plan. In this, it is like the wartime stabilization program. Its attainment will require the effective working of a number of compatible policies, all directed to the same end, and each contributing to the success of the others. It will not be enough that it is an object of government policy. It must be an object of national endeavor. The active cooperation of all governments and groups in the country will be essential to success.

In setting as its aim a high and stable level of employment and income, the Government is not selecting a lower target than "full employment". Rather, the Government is mindful that employment and incomes will be subject to fluctuations in the sphere of international trade, which cannot be wholly and instantaneously offset, and that seasonal fluctuations, resulting from climate and buying habits, are not to be overcome without much patient and resourceful work. The Government is inaugurating policies which break new ground, and is confident that these policies, with full public understanding and support, will achieve, in the immediate postwar period, satisfactory results of decisive importance. In later years, as experience grows, they can be made to yield ever-improving results which will mark a new era in Canadian development.

II. The Sources of Employment and Income

Remunerative employment and income in any economy are provided by the expenditures which are made. These expenditures are best classified according to the channels through which the expenditures flow, viz., *(a)* export trade, in which the decision to spend is made outside the country; *(b)* private investment in plant, equipment and other durable goods and goods in stock, in which the decision is governed largely by prospective earnings in relation to cost; *(c)* consumption expenditures, the level of which is mainly dependent on the level of incomes; *(d)* public investment in useful works for improving the productiveness of resources, and the welfare and opportunities of the people. Public expenditures for current goods and services also provide employment, but cannot to any large degree be determined with reference to the needs of employment, except in terms of reasonable stability. In maintaining a high and stable level of employment and income, the Government proposes to use appropriate means to influence expenditures in all these channels with particular emphasis on those which are most susceptible of encouragement and control.

From *Employment and Income*, Ottawa: King's Printer, 1945, pp. 1-2, 4. (House of Commons Sessional Paper #90, 1945.) For additional reading on the historical background to and personalities of the advent of Keynesian economics in Canada, see Peter Newman's *The Canadian Establishment*, vol. 1, Chapter 10, especially pp. 329-339. See also references (b) and (c) in the last problem at the end of Chapter 28. In the reading "All Around the Merry-Go-Round" in Chapter 26, you will encounter some strong views about the extent to which the spirit of the White Paper has been put into effect.

Promoting Economic Stability

Government stabilization policies, whether aimed at slowing down inflation or overcoming a recession, have now become a major part of our economic life. Use of government fiscal policy (taxing and spending patterns) and monetary policy (controlling the money supply, credit conditions, and interest rates) is, however, a relatively recent phenomenon in Canada as in other "free enterprise" societies. The development of the basic techniques and the acceptance of the responsibility of the state in this area together mark one of the most important developments in the whole field of economics. Unit 4, dealing with the performance of the economy as a whole, will examine in detail the significance of the emergence of this new role for governments in recent decades.

Table 19-2: TOTAL GOVERNMENT REVENUES (NATIONAL ACCOUNTS BASIS), 1941-1977[1, 3]

Year	Direct Taxes		Taxes From Non-residents	Indirect Taxes	Investment Income	Other Transfers From Individuals	Total
	Individuals[2]	Business					
	(millions of dollars)						
1941	332	510	24	1164	140	28	2198
1943	792	640	27	1381	259	29	3128
1945	909	599	29	1346	310	29	3222
1947	927	702	35	1855	261	35	3815
1949	956	723	47	1955	242	57	3980
1951	1279	1431	56	2677	285	77	5805
1953	1748	1244	54	3107	378	84	6615
1955	1855	1310	67	3407	420	79	7138
1957	2350	1378	83	4095	490	106	8502
1959	2444	1615	74	4651	604	224	9612
1961	2944	1649	116	5159	710	256	10 834
1963	3387	1891	127	6115	885	274	12 679
1965	4431	2197	167	7741	1080	377	15 993
1967	7009	2396	218	9489	1495	447	21 054
1969	10 055	3221	234	11 423	2257	838	28 028
1971	13 042	3346	278	13 048	3180	1107	34 001
1973	17 041	5080	322	16 686	4386	1072	44 587
1975	24 058	7891	465	21 518	7104	1153	62 189
1977	30 629	7930	533	26 714	9444	1591	76 841

Notes: [1] Excluding all categories of intergovernmental transfers; including all other receipts of all three levels of government.
[2] Includes Canada and Quebec Pension Plan receipts after 1967.
[3] All data are in millions of current dollars.

Sources: Statistics Canada: *National Income and Expenditure Accounts, 1926-1974,* vol 1, cat. 13-531; *National Income and Expenditure Accounts, 1962-1976,* cat. 13-201; and *National Income and Expenditure Accounts, Fourth Quarter, 1977,* cat. 13-001.

Table 19-2 provides a general breakdown of all revenues for the three levels of government. For details on the relative importance of different types of taxes or non-tax revenue for the various levels of government, see up-to-date data in the #13-001 accounts or the section on Government Finance in the latest *Canada Yearbook*. Table 19-3 treats the expenditures of the three levels of government in a comparable way. For a detailed analysis of directions of government spending, again see a source such as that recommended above.

FINANCING GOVERNMENT ACTIVITIES

How does government get the real resources, goods, and services needed to perform the economic functions described above? In a market economy, government taxes or borrows money from individuals and firms. This reduces demand in the private sector of the economy and frees real resources, goods, and services for use in the public or government sector of the economy.

Table 19-2 gives a breakdown of Federal, provincial, and local government revenues since 1941. The difference between the total government receipts shown in Table 19-2 and the total government expenditures shown in Table 19-3 was made up by government borrowing.

Since the benefits of most government programs are generally available to all citizens, regardless of the amount of taxes they pay, people tend to take government goods and services for granted. Yet the same people generally view the taxes necessary to

Table 19-3: TOTAL GOVERNMENT EXPENDITURE (NATIONAL ACCOUNTS BASIS), 1941-1977[1,4]

Year	Current Goods and Services	Transfers To Individuals[2]	Interest on Public Debt	Subsidies and Capital Assistance	Transfers to Non-Residents	Total	Current Surplus or Deficit	National Account Surplus or Deficit[3]
				(millions of dollars)				
1941	1576	191	291	75	6	2139	59	62
1943	4093	207	371	213	7	4891	−1763	−1781
1945	3576	542	512	264	7	4901	−1679	−1691
1947	1343	834	559	183	46	2965	850	763
1949	1722	942	572	90	15	3341	639	343
1951	2811	1024	609	142	21	4607	1198	826
1953	3824	1449	620	127	37	6057	558	83
1955	4036	1719	664	94	36	6549	589	−40
1957	4573	2052	774	149	52	7600	902	−19
1959	4976	2721	1023	272	85	9077	535	−601
1961	6206	2709	1184	342	77	10 518	316	−835
1963	6982	2979	1431	478	89	11 959	720	−624
1965	8358	3423	1675	549	119	14 124	1869	207
1967	11 153	4667	2081	728	217	18 846	2208	148
1969	14 241	6161	2767	811	185	24 165	3863	1915
1971	18 368	8255	3622	997	249	31 491	2510	130
1973	23 037	11 198	4788	1414	318	40 755	3832	1252
1975	33 553	17 059	6548	4335	591	62 086	103	−3768
1977	42 516	22 304	8990	3853	629	78 292	−1451	−5551

Notes: [1] Excluding all categories of intergovernmental transfers; including all other expenditures of all three levels of government.
[2] Includes Canada and Quebec Pension Plan payments after 1967.
[3] Based on the current surplus/deficit position plus depreciation allowances in government accounts less government investment spending. This is the ultimate measure of the public sector's overall surplus or deficit position.
[4] All data are in millions of current dollars.

Sources: Statistics Canada: *National Income and Expenditure Accounts, 1926-1974,* vol 1, cat. 13-531; *National Income and Expenditure Accounts, 1962-1976,* cat. 13-201; and *National Income and Expenditure Accounts, Fourth Quarter, 1977,* cat. 13-001.

provide these benefits as a burden.[6] Once the range of government activities has been determined at the ballot box, however, *someone* has to pay the bills. And in deciding who this someone should be, various principles of taxation have been put forward at various times. Most of our present taxes, however, involve some balance between considerations of **equity** or fairness and considerations of *expediency* or ease of collection (the largest amount of feathers plucked from a goose, with the least amount of squawking).

We shall now look at some of the equity considerations involved in taxation, and see how some of the different taxes listed in Table 19-2 compare on this score.

The Benefits-received Principle

The benefits-received principle of taxation says that taxes should be levied on people in proportion to the benefits they receive from the government activities supported by these taxes. The logic of this principle is carried over from the logic of the marketplace, where the benefit received from any given

[6] On this point, Yale economist Henry Wallich has made this interesting observation: "The nation as a whole pays taxes to buy public services, as it pays grocery bills to buy groceries. The tax burden may be heavier for some individuals than for others. But the nation as a whole has no more reason to complain about the 'burden' of taxes than about the 'burden' of grocery bills—and no more reason to hope for relief." (Quoted from E. S. Phelps, (ed.), *Private Wants and Public Needs,* New York: W. W. Norton, 1962, pp. 54-55.)

Collins in Montreal Gazette

Financial Nightmare

This view of trends in government finance is shared by all those who face the prospect of higher taxes. We should remember the other side of the ledger, however, for hopefully the costs will be balanced by services.

purchase is assumed to be related to the price people are willing to pay for it.

The license fees collected by various provincial and local governments can be considered as taxes based on the benefits-received principle. The use of excise taxes on gasoline to pay for building and maintaining highways is another example of how such current taxes in Canada are related to this principle. The social insurance taxes[7] received for the Canada Pension Plan and unemployment insurance are also kept in separate funds for these specific purposes. But most government revenues today are not kept in separate funds according to the taxes levied to collect them. It is usually impossible to measure the separate benefits received by individual persons from most government services.

In addition to the practical problems of administration, the benefits-received principle of taxation also runs in direct opposition to the widely held notion that the government should provide some things to all of its citizens, whether they can pay for them on an individual basis or not.

The Ability-to-pay Principle

The ability-to-pay principle of taxation says that the cost of government should be assessed according to what different people can afford to pay. While slogans such as "the broadest backs should carry the heaviest burdens" may sound simple, there are many difficult problems involved in determining ability to pay. People with the same current incomes, for example, may differ in many other ways, such as the amount of wealth they have saved or inherited in the past, the number of children or aged or sickly relatives they have to support, and so on.

Despite the problems involved, however, current income is the single measure most often used in considering ability to pay. *Vertical equity* is concerned with the amount of taxes paid by people in different income classes, while *horizontal equity* is concerned with the amount of taxes paid by the people in the same income class. If horizontal equity assumes that equals should be taxed equally, it logically follows that vertical equity must assume that unequals should be taxed unequally.

The Problem of Tax Incidence

One of the thorniest questions in tax analysis is figuring out who really carries the burden of a tax. If a tax is placed on one person and he passes it on to someone else in the form of higher prices or lower wages, rents, interest, or profits, who really pays the tax? Answering this type of question is called figuring the incidence of a tax. It is not easy.

[7] These are nominally described as "contributions" but they are, in fact, specified forms of taxes.

If the true burden of a tax can be passed on to someone else other than the person required to turn over the money to the government, it is called an **indirect tax**. Excise taxes (those levied on the sale of specific commodities such as gasoline, tobacco, or alcoholic beverages) and federal sales taxes are often cited as examples of indirect taxes. These taxes are usually treated as a cost of doing business, and thus get included in the purchase price of the taxed goods or services. Other examples of indirect taxes that are usually considered as costs of doing business and so are included in purchase prices are taxes on business-owned property and the part of social security taxes paid by employers.

If a tax cannot be shifted from the person who pays the revenue to the government, it is called a **direct tax**. A personal income tax is a good example of a direct tax that cannot be shifted. Once your income is earned, it is yours, and the reduction in your income as the result of the tax directly reduces the amount of money you have left for consumption and savings. Property taxes paid by individuals on their homes or other personal property, and the part of social insurance taxes paid by employees are frequently cited as other examples of direct taxes whose true burden cannot be shifted from the person who pays the tax to the government. However, a landlord whose property taxes go up may shift the tax to the tenants in the form of higher rent.

Corporate income taxes or corporate profit taxes, which are levied on the profits remaining after all the costs of doing business are deducted from a corporation's receipts, can also be considered as direct taxes. This is possible if a corporation is unable to increase its prices enough to make its after-tax profit equal to what its profit would be in the absence of the tax. Most economists today feel that these corporate income taxes are partly direct and partly indirect, with some of the burden being borne by corporate owners or stockholders and some of it borne by consumers.

Progressive, Proportional, and Regressive Taxes

Once the true incidence of a tax has been figured, a tax is called *progressive* if it takes a larger percentage of high incomes than it does of low incomes. A proportional tax takes the same percentage of incomes from different income groups. And a regressive tax takes a larger percentage of low incomes than it does of high incomes.

With these definitions of vertical tax incidence in mind, let us look at one of the taxes included in Table 19-2.

The Federal government's personal income tax, which accounted for almost 50 percent of Ottawa's tax revenue collected in 1977, is a clear example of a progressive tax. After standard adjustments are made to determine taxable income, the 1977 Federal income tax rate for a wage earner with $5000 a year in taxable income was 15.8 percent. This compares with an average rate of 18.0 percent if the same taxpayer had a taxable income of $10 000 a year, and a rate of 21.9 percent if the taxable income was $20 000, and so on up to a maximum rate of 43 percent on taxable income above $85 000 a year.[8]

To the extent that it is not shifted forward to consumers, the Federal corporate profits tax is a progressive tax. This is so because the tax tends to reduce the amount of profit a corporation can pay to its stockholders in the form of dividends, and most stockholders are from higher income groups.

Excise taxes and sales taxes placed on retail goods are regressive in nature, since low-income groups usually spend a larger portion of their incomes on such goods than high-income groups, who tend to spend a larger part of their incomes on untaxed ser-

[8] However, since some forms of income are not counted as taxable income, and since some forms of income are taxed at special rates lower than the regular rates for income from wages and salaries, very few people ever pay the top Federal income tax rates. The rates given are those initially effective before a tax reduction was introduced in the Federal budget.

FIG. 19-1. GOVERNMENT IN THE CIRCULAR FLOW OF MONEY, GOODS AND SERVICES

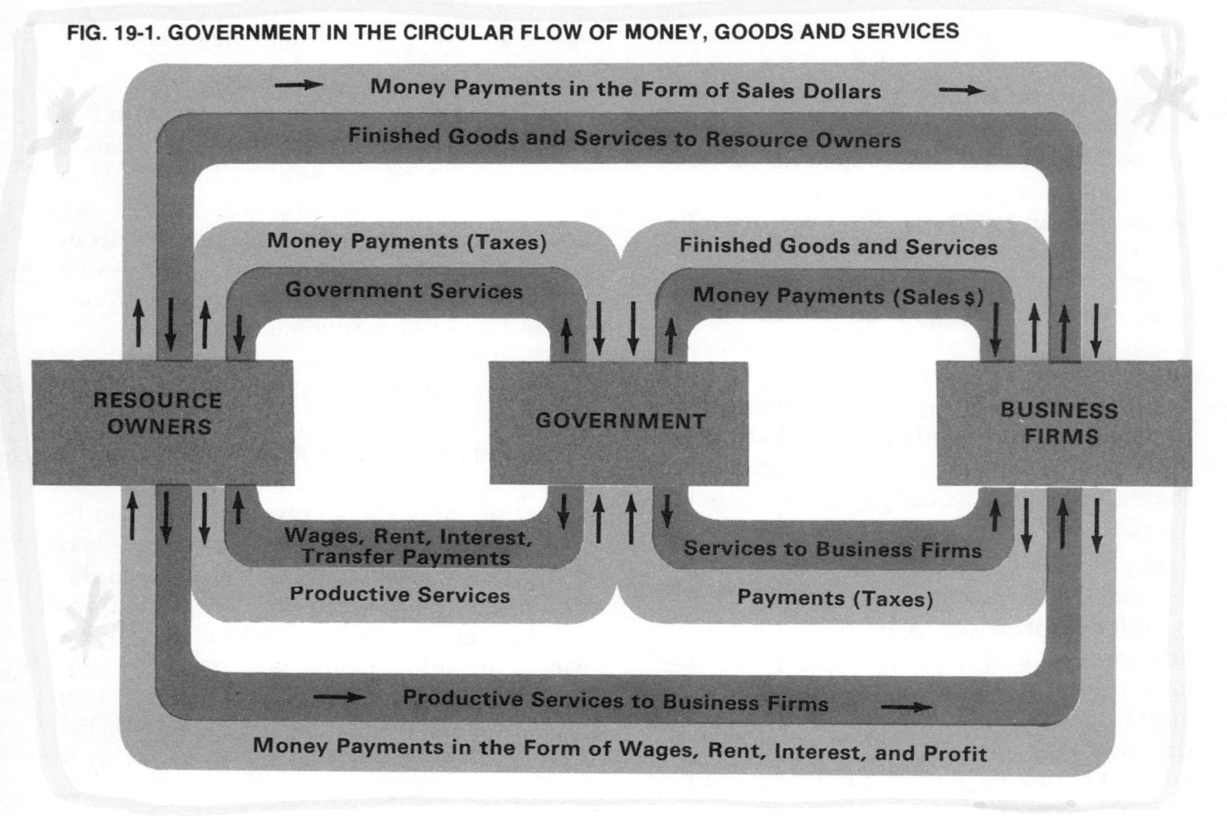

vices and savings.[9] Some provincial sales taxes, however, exempt food purchases and other necessities. These exemptions make these taxes less regressive than they would otherwise be. Putting excise taxes on luxury items, usually purchased only by high income groups, might even make some excise taxes progressive in nature. On balance, however, most economists agree that the total package of indirect Federal and provincial sales and excise taxes covered in Table 19-2 is basically regressive.

[9] A $.25 tax on a litre of gasoline is the same *amount* for all income groups, but this amount represents a different *percentage* of different incomes. Consider, for example, two men who have used 1000 litres of gasoline in a year. If one man has an annual income of $10 000 a year, his gasoline tax bill of $250 represents 2.5 percent of his income. If the second man has an annual income of $50 000 a year, his gasoline tax bill of $250 would represent only 0.5 percent of his income. The second man would have to use 5000 litres of gasoline before the fixed gasoline tax would take the same percentage of his income as it took from the first man. A richer man might use more gasoline than a poorer man, but chances are he would not use 5 times as much. Thus this excise tax is a regressive one.

THE GOVERNMENT IN THE MARKET ECONOMY

We have seen in this chapter that the government is itself a major element in a market economy in the modern world. It provides a broad range of services to the private economy and uses its taxing powers to obtain command over resources, goods, and services from the rest of the economy. In Figure 19-1, we have added government to our diagrammatic representation of the flow of goods and services, and the counterflow of money, in a market economy.

You should compare this diagram with Figure 13-2 to see how resource owners now sell some of their productive services to the government (as well as to business firms), while business firms also sell part of their

THE PERILS OF BEING MINISTER OF FINANCE

McNally in Montreal Star

"I can't make them out . . . they're all shouting something different."

Reprinted by permission

"You have a choice. I can destroy you painlessly, or I can make you Minister of Finance." (Attributed to P. E. Trudeau in a sketch by the Royal Canadian Air Farce, CBC Radio, December 24, 1977.)

Kamienski in Winnipeg Tribune

"Darn it! No matter how hard I try to look like Robin Hood, I still look like the Sheriff of Nottingham."

Reprinted by permission

UNDERSTATEMENT OF THE WEEK

Collins in Montreal Gazette

Being Minister of Finance may leave one open to occasional criticism. These observations should make us feel a bit of sympathy with whomever might hold this unenviable position. Jan Kamienski's sketch could be valid for almost any time. McNally's could be in the same category, though, as the documents on the desk indicate, it refers specifically to the original proposals on tax reform released in November 1969. Note the "menu" in Collins' cartoon. What happened to the two Ministers to hold the post between Benson and Chrétien?

"I know they don't work, but they're the only potions your witch-doctor's got!"

Cummings: Sunday Express, London (April 13, 1969) Reprinted by Permission

Government as Economic Witch Doctor. This less than flattering portrayal of Roy Jenkins, at the time Chancellor of the Exchequer (Minister of Finance) in the British government, indicates one view of the policies which governments may follow in trying to stabilize economic conditions. (What clues might there be in the cartoon regarding the political sympathies of the cartoonist? Jenkins was in a Labour party government.)

finished goods and services to government (as well as to individual resource owners). Notice too, that the government collects money from both businesses and individuals but also pays money out to both of these groups. You should be able to fit all government spending or tax programs into one or another of these streams of activity. Government regulatory activities will not, however, show as such on this diagram. Rather, they would modify the activities of private business firms and individuals in our diagram.

Why is There Growing Public Disenchantment with Government?

While it is doubtful that we are witnessing the beginnings of a trend back to the free-market ideal envisioned by Adam Smith, there have recently been signs of a growing public disenchantment with the present extent of government intervention. In a paper completed for the Council,[a] Professor H. Scott Gordon observes that this phenomenon is not peculiar to Canada alone. It reflects a widespread belief in many countries that the benefits gained from the growing role of government in the modern state are not sufficient to outweigh the disadvantages.

Gordon identifies economic welfare, social justice, and personal freedom as the three major objectives toward which government activities are directed. However, he finds that these three "social goods" are not complementary. Almost inevitably, gains in welfare and justice are achieved at the expense of freedom. For example, seat belt legislation is enacted to reduce the probability that people in car accidents will be seriously injured or killed. However, it also limits the individual's freedom to choose whether or not he wants to assume the risk of driving unencumbered by a seat belt.

He believes that the root of the current anti-

[a] H. Scott Gordon, *The Demand and Supply of Government: What We Want and What We Get*, Economic Council of Canada, Discussion Paper No. 79.

government sentiment is that the public does not find that this sacrifice is warranted; there is a general belief that the improvements in welfare and justice have not been sufficient to justify the concomitant loss in freedom.

Complex goals difficult to attain . . .

In part, this disenchantment reflects the great complexity of all three social goods. Public dissatisfaction stems largely from the failure to understand that the main task of politics is to deal with problems that are not technically soluble.

According to Gordon, there are a number of reasons why government has not been more effective in promoting justice and economic welfare. It is difficult for government to make constructive use of its own mistakes in policy. If legislation does not achieve its intended objective, a political admission of this failure could well mean defeat in the next election. Hence, the policy remains. Even when the opposition party forms the new government, it is difficult for it to undertake sweeping reforms because the civil servants which it inherits are similarly reluctant to acknowledge mistakes.

If the government tries to rectify an ineffective policy, it may only succeed in causing the legislation to become progressively more coercive. Gordon cites the steps leading up to seat belt legislation as an illustration. Once a government is persuaded of the value of seat belts, it requires car manufacturers to offer them as options. However, as many people still do not use them the government makes their installation obligatory. When this does not work, it requires manufacturers to add seat belt buzzers. Finally it becomes mandatory for people to wear seat belts when driving in a car.

without increasing constraints on freedom

Gordon finds that perhaps the greatest threat to personal freedom resides in the extraordinary, even extra-legal, powers of government in a situation which it conceives to be a serious emergency. There is the risk that these powers will be exercised even when the danger is not sufficiently great to warrant such stern measures. According to Gordon, this has occurred at four different times in Canada, most recently when emergency powers were used to establish control over wages and prices. In his opinion, an even greater danger arises if the public acquiesces in this misuse of power.

Successful policies can create a different sort of problem for the government in that they may be difficult to end once their usefulness is over. It is difficult to disband an established administrative mechanism and to relocate or dismiss personnel. Consequently, policies tend to stay in place even when they have become merely redundant or "make-work" projects.

Gordon notes that a general climate of disaffection with the role of government will be strengthened by discoveries of gross inefficiency on the part of a government department or agency. Similarly, the feeling that the government is acting to further the interests of a particular group rather than working for the good of the general public can heighten dissatisfaction, particularly if the group is already well favored or if it is being benefited in a cladestine manner.

While the current disaffection with government is still moderate, he sees it as a positive force, potentially providing stimulus for the most comprehensive reform of the modern state so far. It is important, however, that it not persist unheeded by government. In Gordon's view the solution is not a return to a "laissez-faire" society, nor a change in governing parties, but a reassessment of the proper scope of government in the national economy.

Reprinted from Economic Council of Canada, *Bulletin*, vol. 1, no. 3, Spring, 1977, p. 3. A segment from Gordon's paper plus a number of excellent additional readings will be found in *Government and the Economy—How Much?*, Toronto: Canadian Foundation for Economic Education, 1977.

SUMMARY

We have expanded our account of how our economy functions, by incorporating government into the system. In a "mixed" economy, such as that of Canada, government performs many economic functions. These include administering the rules of the game, protecting property, and enforcing contracts; providing information and services to individuals and businesses; encouraging and supporting research and development; preserving competition in the market—and regulating monopolies when there is no competition; providing a broad range of public goods, such as parks, highways, and schools; improving the economic security of individuals; creating a sound monetary system; and promoting national economic stability and growth.

To pay for all such activities, government units at the Federal, provincial, and local levels levy a wide variety of taxes on individuals and businesses. Some taxes, such as license fees, excises, and social insurance taxes are based on a benefits-received principle. Others, such as personal or corporate income taxes, are based on an ability-to-pay principle. Taxes often appear to be a compromise between *equity* (equality of treatment for people in about the same financial situation) and *expediency* (ease of collection).

It is sometimes difficult to figure out just who bears the real burden of a particular tax, the person who pays it or someone else to whom the tax might be shifted. In general, taxes that cannot be shifted, such as personal income taxes, are called direct taxes; and taxes that can be shifted, such as excises or sales taxes, are called indirect taxes. A tax that increases proportionately as the taxpayer's income rises is called *progressive*; one that declines relatively as income rises is *regressive*; and one that claims a constant percentage share of rising income is *proportional*. Federal taxes in Canada are, on balance, progressive; provincial and local taxes are generally regressive.

Through its siphoning off of taxes, its payments of money to the public, its use of private resources, goods, and services, and its production of public goods and services, government has become a major element in the production of goods and the provision of services. This, along with the development of a more regulatory role for government has led our economy to evolve from a market system in the literal sense of the term to what is often described as a "mixed market system."

KEY CONCEPTS

direct tax
equity
indirect tax
laissez faire

QUESTIONS FOR REVIEW AND DISCUSSION

1. What were the three roles Adam Smith assigned to the government in a market economy? In what way has the government of Canada today gone beyond these three roles? Do you think that this trend is good or bad? Why?
2. Do you think that the government strengthens or weakens the market system when it enforces laws regarding competition? Why?
3. Do you think that the benefits-received principle or the ability-to-pay principle is the best principle of taxation? Why? What are some problems involved in applying each of these principles? What is to be done when the two conflict?
4. Define in your own words a progressive, proportional, and regressive tax, and give a specific example of each. Is the Federal or provincial and local tax system more regressive in nature? Why?

RESEARCH PROBLEMS TO EXPAND YOUR UNDERSTANDING[10]

1. When and why were personal and corporate income taxes introduced in Canada?
2. What general division of taxing power among the three levels of government took place at the time of Confederation?
3. Prepare a sketch of the Rowell—Sirois Commission, briefly outlining the background of its establishment, its recommendations, and their effects.
4. During recent years, financial powers and responsibilities have dominated many of the meetings of federal-provincial leaders. Try to determine some of the fiscal changes sought by the larger provinces and the reasons for their positions. What has been the response of Ottawa? Of the smaller or poorer provinces?

[10] Some initial reference sources for all of the above research problems would be:
(a) the latest *Canada Yearbook*;
(b) publications from the Canadian Foundation for Economic Education, in the series *Government and the Economy*, especially J. H. Perry and Gwyneth McGregor, *Government and the Economy—Taxation*, Toronto: CFEE, 1977, and a title in preparation dealing with Federal-Provincial fiscal relations;
(c) publications from the Canadian Tax Foundation (these are much more detailed studies!).

THREE REACTIONS TO A ROYAL COMMISSION

Following are three selections from *The Financial Times* of Canada giving reactions to the *Report of the Royal Commission on Corporate Concentration*, which appeared in May, 1978. The first by Don McGillivray, who is a Contributing Editor of the *Times* and Economics Editor of Southam News Service is a straight-forward factual survey of the *Report*. The editorial from the *Times* provides a favorable reaction to the study. The final selection by George Radwanski, author of a major biography entitled *Trudeau*, (Toronto: Macmillan, 1978), provides a strongly critical perspective. Given the views presented in the two final selections, you should be able to make some reasonable projections about reactions from the trade union movement, from political sources (at least a "right" and "left" alignment), and from the corporate sector. Reaction from small business has been mixed. For an initial assessment, see the comments by John Bulloch, President of the Canadian Federation of Independent Business, in the *Financial Post*, May 27, 1978, p. 7. At the time of writing, there has been no firm indication of government action on the *Report's* recommendations. Investigation of what effect the *Report* has had on government policy would be an appropriate topic for further research.

DON McGILLIVRAY:

Commission advocates updated laissez-faire

Can "workable competition" get Canada moving again without a new bout of government intervention?

This key concept of the Royal Commission on Corporate Concentration, obscured and often ignored in first-glance reporting last week, is an attempt to use market forces on Canada's peculiar problems.

It is Adam Smith for the 1980s. But in the updated version of laissez-faire, the "let it go" idea would be better expressed as "let it grow."

The royal commission concluded, after a three-year, $3-million study of the private sector, that further intervention in the economy by government would not help any problems it found: inflation, unemployment, an apparent failure to be competitive and efficient, high domestic production costs, and weak export performance.

Instead it called for "workable competition"—in essence a plan to encourage growth and efficiency by a deliberate halt to government intervention and a lowering of trade barriers.

This was the core of its other major recommendations:

• Abolition of taxes on reinvested profits, coupled with a distribution tax on paid-out dividends; removal of capital gains taxation. Both these moves would be aimed at cutting costs, improving competitiveness and opening up sources of capital for small and medium-sized companies.

• Enactment of Bill C-13, the proposed Competition Act, with two significant changes. Mergers would not require preclearance from the "competition policy advocate" and the Competition Board, but would be judged harmful or harmless on their later record according to rules set out by the board. And conscious parallelism—identical pricing without formation of an overt combine—would require something else, such as a circulated price memo, to be illegal.

• Retention of the Foreign Investment Review Agency and vigilant enforcement of Canadian law, including the new Competition Act, to see that foreign-controlled firms do not misuse their position to the detriment of Canadian-owned firms or yield to pressures of other governments to withhold jobs and technology from Canada.

• Moves to strengthen and diversify corporate boards of directors. The commission said companies can help overcome public suspicion if they "leaven their boards of directors with more people whose backgrounds are not in corporate business" and break the tight control over director nominations by management. Bank boards, in particular, should have a reasonable number of directors who are not advisers, officers or customers of the bank.

• Prohibition of any merger among Canada's "Big Five" banks along with encouragement to the entry of other institutions, with primary stress on consumer loans and loans to small business.

• Removal of tariff and non-tariff barriers to encourage growth and competition, along with approval for specialization agreements which would enable fragmented Canadian industries to compete at home and abroad against large-scale foreign companies.

• Disclosure of more information on corporate operations, particularly by large, provincially-chartered private companies not now required to file financial statements. But this would be accompanied by a lightening of the reporting load on companies as the government eliminated overlaps and duplications in the information to be filed with agencies.

• Critical study of government regulations which contribute to inefficiency and which have been promulgated without thought for their costs or implications for democracy.

Workable Competition

The royal commission's concept of workable competition developed from its analysis of the Canadian economy in which "the structure and conduct of firms and industries differ greatly from economic models of pure competition" where firms are supposed to be able to move freely in and out of industries as profits rise and fall.

The commission set out four conditions for workable competition:

• First, small and middle-sized firms must not be unfairly prevented from operating and expanding, or restricted by artificial barriers from entering an industry.

• Second, the trade barriers which protect most Canadian manufacturing must be selectively reduced, and Canadian firms—as an offset—allowed to enter specialization agreements to get the economies resulting from longer production runs.

• Third, conglomerates must be required to disclose accounting and profit data to prevent them from hiding areas of high profit and growth which might attract competition if the full facts were known.

• Fourth, competition policy must be strong and vigorously enforced. The commission made a special note of the fact that its criticism of some aspects of the new Competition Act did not mean that it thought competition policy unimportant.

"On the contrary, a strong and vigorously enforced competition law is necessary to prevent dominant firms from entrenching a monopoly or quasi-monopoly position or exploiting tariff protection, to provide a check on abuses of market power, and to increase the likelihood of entry and competition from small and medium-sized firms."

The commission recommended no specific action on the situation which caused it to be set up in the first place—the proposed takeover of Argus Corp. Ltd., Toronto, by Power Corp. of Canada Ltd., Montreal. Such conglomorate mergers, it said, should be considered by Parliament and the government when they occur.

THE FINANCIAL TIMES OF CANADA:

An Agenda for Action

Some people made up their minds long ago that business is guilty of ripping off consumers, stifling competition and exerting inordinate power over governments.

These people see no need of sifting the evidence or distinguishing between one business and another. All are guilty as charged. All that remains is to pass sentence.

Last week's Report of the Royal Commission on Corporate Concentration was, naturally enough, a big disappointment to such people. Anything would have been a disappointment except a forthright indictment of business and all its works.

This accounts for the sour, negative reception of the report by some commentators. It deserves a better hearing. Even people who think the verdict is wrong should look at the evidence on which the commission based its conclusions. And this evidence is so voluminous, more than 5000 pages of main report and special studies, that anything said immediately after its release was bound to be based on a quick skim rather than a careful study.

Anyone who takes the time to look at it, will discover that the report is far from being a knee-jerk, "big is good" verdict. It is, instead, a thoughtful attempt to deal with a Canadian paradox.

The paradox is this—Canadian industry is already highly concentrated but it will have to become more concentrated if Canadian companies are to compete in the big world outside this country.

It is not that Canadian plants are too small; it is that they are not specialized enough. And the size of the companies themselves is too small, in relation to their non-Canadian competitors, to allow them to be fully efficient, able to take risks and to carry on an adequate program of research and development.

So Canadian companies should be encouraged to grow to world scale. That means they may be even more dominant than they are now in the Canadian market. How can consumers and potential competitors be protected from the results of this dominance?

The commission puts its faith in a strong, efficiently enforced competition law. It applauded, as the *Times* has previously, the general direction of the second-stage competition bill now before Parliament. But it said mergers should be judged by results, not on the basis of forecasts.

The commission also advocated selective reduction of tariff and non-tariff barriers to let foreign competitors balance the growth in the dominance of Canadian firms. It added the usual caution about keeping an eye on the social costs of freer trade. But it said tariff walls should be dismantled first as an incentive to consolidation of fragmented Canadian industries and socialization agreements.

The report turns a much needed searchlight on the anti-competitive policies of government, the regulations, interventions and Crown corporations which promote inefficiency and monopoly profits.

There is a good case, which this newspaper has stated, for dismantling the Foreign Investment Review Agency. The royal commission stopped short of that but it recommended against any extension of the review process.

Company executives as well as government policy makers need to read carefully the sections on public disclosure. The commission leaned strongly towards openness, which it saw as being in the long-run interest of business as well as of the public. And this policy has a much wider implication. Pension funds, for example, should tell members of the pension plans as much about their investments and activities as companies tell their shareholders. And government, as the commission says, needs trust even more than private companies do and should operate with more candor.

One way companies can earn more public trust is to have their "outside" directors more truly represent the interests of shareholders as distinct from management. The recommendations of the commission on this point are no sure cure. Company executives, determined to have a board which does not ask awkward questions, can find their way around any system of independent nomination. But such executives should reflect that a "troublesome" board member has often saved a company from a major disaster.

An aspect of the commission's work likely to have permanent value is the enormous amount of documentation, constituting the most careful look ever taken at corporations in Canada.

Then there are the tax recommendations. The abolition of taxation on reinvested profits (with certain safeguards) is a good idea whose time has not yet come. It is a political nonstarter at this time but it is useful to have it in the report.

In the 1960s, the Carter commission on taxation toyed with the idea and decided it was too radical to urge in its report. In the 1970s, the idea advanced to the status of a royal commission recommendation. Perhaps in the 1980s it will be considered objectively by a public free of the illusion that taxing corporations is a way of "soaking the rich." There are already, of course, a good many economic studies to show that it is a way of soaking the poor.

The abolition of the capital gains tax should have more chance. It was put into the Income Tax Act to plug a supposed loophole, but it was part of a "reform" which made the tax law so complex that more loopholes were created than plugged. Abolishing the tax would cost the government little in terms of revenue, simplify the law, and eliminate the bias toward real-estate investment which results from the principal-residence exemption.

There are arguments, of course, on both sides of this question as well as on other recommendations of the commission. But the commission has done a useful job and its report should be considered seriously as an agenda for action, not dismissed on the basis of anti-business prejudice.

From *Financial Times of Canada,* May 22, 1978, p. 8. Reprinted by permission.

GEORGE RADWANSKI:

Commission Report a Colossal Bust

OTTAWA—In the spring of 1975, faced with the proposed take-over of Argus Corp. Ltd. by Power Corp. of Canada Ltd., the Trudeau government had a serious and embarrassing problem.

It simply didn't know whether the creation of corporate size and power on that scale—the super-conglomerate resulting from the deal would have had control over assets worth an estimated $7 billion—was desirable in Canada. It had no policy and no yardsticks by which to judge at what point, if any, "big" becomes "too big."

Three years and a $3 million royal commission later, it still doesn't know. And business leaders, whose first reaction was delight at the pro-business findings of last week's report of the Royal Commission on Corporate Concentration, really have less cause to be enthused than might appear at first glance.

The inquiry was established to study, as Prime Minister Trudeau put it at the time, "whether and to what extent such concentrations of corporate power confer sufficient social and economic benefit to Canadian society as to be in the public interest."

Instead, the commissioners proceeded on the implicit assumption that what's good for the corporations is probably good for everyone and in the public interest. They sidestepped the most fundamental questions, and they produced what amounts less to an inquiry report than to a brief from the corporate community.

The result is to make the report a colossal bust, a document of negligible credibility and less utility that so totally adopts the corporate viewpoints as its own in purportedly considering the public interest that one reporter aptly described it as reading "like a wolf's report on sheep welfare."

Two brief excerpts, one from the beginning and the other from the end of the report, illustrate just how badly the commission derailed itself from the investigative track on which it had been set by its mandate.

In the introduction, addressing itself to the problem of defining the "public interest" which corporate concentration either serves or subverts, it says:

"A corporation, or indeed any institution, has no single 'public interest,' but rather has many publics, with many competing interests. The 'publics' of a corporation include shareholders, creditors, employees, customers, suppliers, governments, and local, national and even international communities. We do not imply in this report that there is any best allocation of corporate resources among competing publics . . . We make no *a priori* assumption that any given allocation is superior from a public interest sense."

If this means anything at all when translated from royal commissionese, it must surely be that the "public interest" can be defined as narrowly as what is good for the shareholders of a corporation, or as broadly as what is good for the nation as a whole—and that the commissioners consider one definition as valid as another.

Having thus refused to define the concept of "public interest" which is so central to their mandate—or, perhaps, having deliberately sought to obscure its definition—the commissioners nevertheless do not shrink from boldly concluding in the final sentence of their report: "No radical changes in the laws governing corporate activity are necessary at this time to protect the public interest."

While this lapse in logic is characteristic of the intellectual aridity that afflicts the entire 413-page study, what is even more serious is the report's almost total failure to confront the most fundamental issue raised by corporate concentration: the resulting increase in corporate power.

No Cause for Concern

The commissioners examine the effects of concentration on competition, pricing and working conditions, and they devote an entire chapter to its impact on corporate influence in the sense of corporations attempting to persuade the government to carry out their wishes. In each instance, they conclude that there is no real cause for concern.

But what they barely touch on is the question not of mere influence but of the direct and actual *power* that can result from sheer size.

All substantial business enterprises, whatever their size, wield a certain amount of economic, political and social power: Every time any company makes a decision to expand or cut back, to hire more workers or lay off, to invest at once or lay off, to pour more resources into one part of the country or another, it is having some impact on the economy and society in general.

When such decisions are made independently by a large number of relatively small corporations, the impact is diffused and the power is fragmented. But when huge chunks of the economy are in the hands of a few giant corporations, the power of these corporations and the individuals who control them can become awesome—and perhaps too much for governments to control.

In such instances, the corporations may in effect move from "micro" to "macro" economic decision-making; instead of relying on mere influence, they may have the power to directly affect the overall course of the economy through their own allocative decisions and thereby to actually rival government as an economic policy maker.

Instead of assessing the magnitude of this danger and suggesting at what level of bigness, if any, it should be considered a serious concern, the commissioners dismiss the matter in a passage that borders on the flippant:

"It is often difficult to say what the foreign or any other 'policy' of the Canadian or any government is, and even more difficult to test particular conduct or action against it. A government 'policy' is often no more than the expression of a hope or sentiment, and a particular policy or an aspect of it frequently conflicts with another. It will seldom be possible to draw useful conclusions about corporate responsibility by weighing a corporation's notions against government policy."

Marvelous. There's no such thing as government policy, and therefore we needn't worry whether corporations can grow large and powerful enough to defy it. Next question?

While insisting that corporate concentration really isn't a serious problem, the commission does concede that there may be certain isolated mergers which are not in the public interest and should be blocked by the government. But that, it says, is for the cabinet to determine on a case-by-case basis.

And, in what constitutes the ultimate failure of the whole exercise, the inquiry—originally established precisely for the purpose of advising the government on how to make such decisions—does not suggest any guidelines or criteria for the cabinet to use in making these case-by-case determinations.

Having thus declined to carry out its central task, the commission then goes out of its way to echo the corporate viewpoints on a variety of issues. Proposed screening of mergers under the Competition Act would be both unnecessary and disruptive, it says. And the notion of corporate social responsibility mustn't be carried too far, it warns, in long passages that read like the words of a 19th-century boss trying unsuccessfully to sound enlightened. Consider this gem, for instance:

"Although the corporation producing . . . products may be said to have a responsibility to reduce the dangers, that responsibility cannot be taken to the point where the corporation could guarantee them to be absolutely safe."

The commissioners even manage to throw in a recommendation that corporate income tax and capital gains tax be abolished. What has that got to do with corporate concentration? Nothing, obviously—but once you're putting in a good word for your friends, why not go all the way?

But despite these obvious effects, the business community really has no reason to feel particularly well served. Whatever the merits of the commission's basic judgments about the innocuousness of corporate concentration, they are so inadequately justified, so clumsily stated and presented with such evident bias that their credibility is nil.

No Criteria for Mergers

In failing to suggest workable criteria for evaluating the case-by-case acceptability of mergers, moreover, the commission does not so much help the business community as leave it open to the likelihood that these evaluations will be made on an arbitrary, political basis more related to the mood of the day than to objective considerations.

Though the commissioners are the principal perpetrators of this fiasco, the Trudeau government deserves a large share of the blame for setting it in motion through the choice of appointees. Seeking a "safe" inquiry, it composed the commission of veteran mandarin Robert Bryce—who was supposed to do the bulk of the work and steer the inquiry—and two relative lightweights with strong business ties.

With those three commissioners, critics expected from the outset that the inquiry would have a conservative, pro-corporate bias. When Mr. Bryce resigned for health reasons, the inquiry was shorn of much of its intellectual vigor, and we are left with a report on corporate concentration written by a corporation president and a corporate lawyer.

The pity of it is that this is an important subject that deserved serious, tough-minded study—and still does.

From *Financial Times of Canada*, May 22, 1978, p. 9. Reprinted by permission.

CHAPTER 20

THE MARKET SYSTEM—A SYNOPSIS

Throughout Units 2 and 3, we have been looking at the basic elements and forces in market systems in general and the Canadian economy in particular. Before going on to examine aspects of the performance of the economy as a whole, it would be appropriate to review these essential elements.

Our market system is frequently referred to as capitalism, free enterprise, or private enterprise. Within such a system, regardless of which name we choose to describe it, there are a number of fundamental principles which apply to the basic productive factors, resources, capital, labor, and management. One of these is most directly referred to within the term "private enterprise." This is, of course, the concept of private property, the fact that the factors of production may be (and usually are) owned by individuals, either separately or in voluntarily formed groups. As a result, the returns which accrue to these factors of production, wages, rent, interest, and profit go to these individual owners. What motivates the persons who own or have access to the productive factors? The answer to this question is a second fundamental part of our market system: self-interest or the profit motive. Attainment of maximum personal benefit is recognized as the primary objective and the driving force of a market economy. Within what context do these two principles operate? Another of the synonyms for our system, "free enterprise," refers to a third principle: freedom of individuals to use the factors at their disposal as they see fit. Absence of external controls or restrictions on utilization of factors at one's disposal is considered a crucial part of the market system and is the primary distinction between a market economy and a command economy. Finally, within this unregulated system, we assume that competition, a logical product of the profit motive, will exist and will affect all participants in the various specific markets of the economy.

How will these principles come into play in the many individual markets which make up our economy? Through transformation into the forces of supply and demand, the complementary and conflicting elements of these principles will affect the actions and reactions of buyers and sellers, consumers and producers. The interrelationship of these two essential groups forms the primary part of the mechanism of each individual market, the constantly changing pressures which influence prices and output levels. A second crucial product of this inter-relationship of market participants is the generation of the unending flow of money, goods, and services, which was illustrated in Figure 13-1.

Such, then, are the essentials of the market system, a method of answering the basic economic questions in a way which, it is hoped, will provide the maximum possible benefit for the greatest possible number, with minimal interference or restriction for the individual participants in the economy. The advantages and potential advantages of a system guided by "the invisible hand," as Adam Smith called it, should now be apparent, not just in theoretical terms but in real terms based on your own experience.

We must, however, be realistic in any summary of the market system. As it functions in our economy, or any other economy, it is not perfect—to put it mildly!

One element crucial to the validity of our

Here is an amusing view of our economy at work. The King's special powers obviously impose some constraints on freedom within his "free enterprise" system. But, as we have seen, in the real world "free enterprise" has had many limiting or modifying forces emerge or evolve within it.

supply and demand theory is competition. An absence or reduction of competition, on either side of a market, can counter the traditional nature of the market mechanism. Concentration of market power, in any hands, may produce many undesirable results. The acquisition of sufficient power to regulate a market tends to produce a quest for greater power by those at a disadvantage. This may lead to the restoration of balance, or it may not reach this goal, or it may lead to the passing of the disadvantage to a third party.

Another problem which exists is that of poverty and its perpetuation. This, as seen in Chapter 14, may be the product of a number of different forces. Regardless of cause, its continued existence amidst great wealth points out the result of the conflict of interest between personal interest and the common good in a self-interest oriented society.

Still another key problem may emerge as a result of the interdependence upon which our economic system is built. The tendency for the economy to fluctuate was originally regarded as a necessary evil. The harsh effects of this cyclical tendency and the other two problems just referred to have provided the basis for many categories of criticism of the market system and proposals for alternatives to it.

These weaknesses have all had their effects on the nature of the market system. The chief one has been to act as a catalyst for evolution within the market economy. As indicated in Chapter 19, government has become a powerful force in the market system, playing a number of different roles with different objectives. The net result has been the evolution of what many call the "mixed economy" or the "modified market system." Here again, the term chosen to describe the situation is of little ultimate significance. The important thing is to recognize that the way our basic questions (what and how much? by whom? for whom?) are answered is now dependent in most instances on the total relationship between the traditional market forces and the restrictions we have put upon them, especially through the medium of government.

The Framework For The Market System

This reading provides an overview comment about the nature of the market system and the role of government within it. It is taken from a federal government "discussion paper" outlining potential policies for the federal government in the period following the termination of "wage and price controls" at the end of 1978. Try and get access to the complete paper to examine the more specific policy options outlined in the document.

The market system is an efficient mechanism for allocating resources. Moreover it has great advantages in terms of the freedom of choice and the scope for initiative that it offers. For these reasons it makes sense to rely as fully as we can on markets as a core of our economic structure.

However, the market system as we know it is not some simple textbook abstraction. It embraces the whole set of arrangements and circumstances within which buyers and sellers meet. It includes the legal framework, the institutional practices, the incentives offered by taxes and subsidies, the degrees of economic power exercised by various participants, and the information available to them as they make their decisions. Governments have a responsibility to see that the framework within which markets work supports their efficiency and flexibility rather than inhibiting them. They have a responsibility to see that the incentives offered in the marketplace will lead to individual decisions that are consistent with the common good.

Governments set the framework of laws and regulations within which markets operate. In a narrow sense the laws may simply protect the integrity of the marketplace, for example through fair advertising and fraudulency regulations. More generally the legal framework can influence the economic power of people on the two sides of a market. Governments must be concerned to see that the laws and their application do not lead to unbalanced markets that tend to favor one side or the other. This is relevant in the labor market as well as in the markets for goods and services.

Governments can influence the choices that people make by regulations that limit or prohibit market freedom, for example through regulations to control pollution, through safety rules, or through prohibition of unsafe products. Indeed this is often the best way for governments to fulfill their responsibilities in these areas. However there is a risk that the number of regulations and regulatory bodies may proliferate needlessly, adding to costs and creating rigidities that impair innovation. This area is being reviewed by the government to see whether the objectives of regulation can be achieved in less costly ways.

An alternative to regulation is to alter, through taxes and subsidies, the incentives facing people in markets. Markets work with great efficiency in response to the incentives offered and it is therefore important that the incentives encourage the desired result. For instance, rather than, or in addition to, combating pollution by regulation, we should ensure that the costs of industrial pollution are borne by producers and consumers of the offending products.

The functioning of the marketplace can be improved by increasing the information available to participants. We have made some progress in recent years in opening up information flows, but we have a long way to go. The government is prepared to open itself more fully to public discussion of its policies. In this paper some concrete suggestions are made with respect to the management of the economy. If we expect individuals to accept responsibility for their actions, we will need to develop a more open private sector as well. Openness dispels misconceptions and mistrust. In the labor market, for example, a freer flow of information at the bargaining table would often assist the parties in coming to mutually acceptable settlements.

Markets that work well, within an appropriate balance of incentives, will be able to respond to the changing opportunities and challenges that will arise in a dynamic society. Some people may gain and some may lose as the economy goes through these adjustments and governments have a responsibility to see that the costs of change do not fall too heavily on a particular group. This is an important responsibility, but it must be recognized that an effort to "cushion" everyone against every adjustment would prevent necessary and desirable changes.

From Government of Canada, *Agenda For Cooperation,* A Discussion Paper on Decontrol and Post-Control Issues, Ottawa: Government of Canada, 1977, pp. 15-17.

UNIT 3 REVIEW

1. What are the basic types of private business organization in Canada? Outline the primary characteristics of each type. What are the advantages and disadvantages of each?
2. What is money? What are the main components of the money supply in Canada?
3. What is the function of a price index? Explain how a price index is compiled. What is a COLA clause?
4. Explain how a system of fractional reserve banking can produce expansions or contractions in the money supply.
5. What do labor unions do for their members? Describe the process of collective bargaining.
6. What are the chief economic roles of governments in Canada?
7. Explain the difference between a progressive tax and a regressive tax.
8. Should taxes be imposed on the basis of the "ability-to-pay" or "benefits received" principle? Explain your choice.

THE ECONOMIC SYSTEM AS A WHOLE

The analysis of particular markets—such as the market for shoes or steel—does not provide us with a comprehensive or correct view of the functioning of the national economy as a whole. To achieve such a view, we must create a model of the total economy, especially through the concept of *gross national product.* This will enable us to see the relations among all the major parts of the economic system—and thereby to discover how, through fiscal, monetary and other policies, we attempt to achieve such vital national goals as full employment, price stability, and economic growth.

CHAPTER 21

WHAT IS MACROECONOMICS?

■ MACROECONOMICS ■ FALLACIES OF COMPOSITION ■ NATIONAL ECONOMIC OBJECTIVES ■ THE CONCEPT OF A NATIONAL ECONOMIC SYSTEM ■ SUMMARY

Our study of economics up to this point has focused largely on individual markets and institutions and on the behavior of buyers and sellers in this framework. This branch of economics is called **microeconomics** (*micro* is derived from the Greek word for *small*) because it is concerned with small sections of the national economic system.

■ MACROECONOMICS

In Unit 4 of this book we shall widen our focus to include the national economy as a whole. This branch of economics is called **macroeconomics** (*macro* is derived from the Greek word for *long* or *large*) because it is concerned with the entire economic system and with such huge aggregates as total consumption or investment or the general level of prices.

Some of the most important economic issues are found in the *macro* area. What causes total national production of goods and services to increase or decrease? What causes unemployment in the nation as a whole to rise or decline? Is it possible to avoid booms and busts in the national economy? Why does the general level of prices sometimes rise, sometimes decline? What causes the entire national economy to grow slowly or rapidly? Answering such questions requires that we have a sense of the economic system as a whole, not just of the factors that may cause the price of butter to rise or decline, jobs for musicians to expand or contract, or the production of economics texts to increase or decrease.

One does not pass from one discipline to another when one moves from microeconomics to macroeconomics; they are two interrelated aspects of economics as a unified body of ideas. Changes in the level of the national economy (macro) affect the market for, say, potatoes (micro). On the other hand, the national economy (macro) will be either stimulated or retarded by an upswing or downswing in the market for automobiles (micro). Just as particular parts of industry affect the national economy, so do expansions or contractions of the national economy affect its particular parts, such as the market for automobiles, housing, or refrigerators.

However, there are some important differences that occur when one shifts one's perspective from individual markets to the national economy as a whole.

One must be wary, therefore, of making false analogies about the behavior of the economy as a whole on the basis of the actions of individual buyers and sellers. This sort of false analogy between the parts of a system and the whole system is frequently encountered in other fields besides economics.

■ FALLACIES OF COMPOSITION

Let us consider a few examples of these so-called fallacies of composition.

One person who stands up at a football game can see better. But if everybody stands up, nobody can see better—and, in fact, most may find their view blocked.

Settlers who clear land quickly by burning off a forest may grow richer. But if all settlers

FIG. 21-1. MICROECONOMICS AND MACROECONOMICS

MICROECONOMICS STUDIES PARTICULAR PARTS OF THE ECONOMY

Prices and Employment in the Market for Potatoes

Prices and Employment in the Market for Economists

MACROECONOMICS STUDIES THE ECONOMY AS A WHOLE

Potato Market +

Economist Market +

All Other Markets +

The Role of Government

Price Level for the *Whole* Economy

Employment Level for the *Whole* Economy

BOTH ARE *RELATED* ASPECTS OF THE SAME SCIENCE—THE SCIENCE OF ECONOMICS

clear the land by burning forests down, they—and the nation—will become poorer.

One person who runs for an exit when a fire breaks out in a theater will get out faster. But if all people rush for the exit when fire breaks out, they may block each other's way and the toll of lives may be greater than if they had waited and moved more slowly.

In economics, it is just as important as in the previous cases to avoid making false analogies between what is likely to be the outcome of a particular course of individual behavior and what will result from such behavior if the nation as a whole follows that course. For instance, if in a particular year one individual person saves a larger share of his or her income, that individual's total personal wealth will increase. But if, in a particular year, all people in a nation save a larger share of their income this may or may not increase the national wealth. The reason is that if everyone's increased savings (reduced spending on goods and services) should have the effect of reducing the total sales of goods, reducing the number of jobs, and reducing everyone's income, then the effort on the part of all to save more may result in less employment, production, and total wealth. Paradoxically, the effort to save more may even cause the actual amount saved to decline—because people might have less income from which to save before the year is over.

Similarly, we have seen that, in a particular market, a rise in the price of a product is likely to ration the quantity demanded—that is, cause people to buy less of that product. However, at the national level, a rise in all prices may or may not cause people to buy less of all goods. Whether they buy more or less of all goods when prices rise generally will depend on whether total incomes are rising more or less rapidly than prices and on whether people expect the price rise to continue or not. If they expect prices to go still higher soon, they may rush to buy immediately, as prices start to move up.

If a particular business succeeds in laying off workers and saving money in that way, it may increase its profits. But if all industries lay off workers, all may suffer declining sales and profits.

In our effort to understand the workings of our national economy, we must be alert to the danger of committing such fallacies of composition, based on false analogies between the particular parts of the economy and the economy as a whole.

NATIONAL ECONOMIC OBJECTIVES

In Unit 4 then, we shall be developing some new concepts that will help us to understand the functioning of the national economy. Our aim will be to get a sense of the factors that cause the economy to grow (or shrink) and of the types of policies that can be used to help the national economy to achieve certain fundamental objectives. Some of the most important of these national objectives are:

1. *A growing level of national output and income,* which will enable individuals to improve their standard of living and the nation as a whole to maintain its strength and international standing;
2. *A high level of employment opportunities* for all those who seek jobs;
3. *A stable economy* that does not undergo sharp rises in prices **(inflation)** nor price collapses **(deflation).**[1]

These economic objectives are so important that the problems of how to achieve them often become highly controversial political issues. They arouse intense emotions in the people involved. Until you have experienced unemployment—especially if there are others dependent upon you for their support—you can scarcely imagine how distressing it is to be jobless. This is a personal tragedy, and it is difficult for the affected individuals to regard unemployment as a basic malfunctioning of the economic system.

During the Great Depression of the 1930s—which affected all Western countries—the brilliant English writer George Orwell wrote of the unemployed workers he saw:

> They simply could not understand what was happening to them. They had been brought up to work, and behold! it seemed as if they were never going to have the chance of working again. In their circumstances it was inevitable, at first, that they should be haunted by a feeling of personal degradation. That was the attitude toward unemployment in those days: it was a disaster which happened to *you* as an individual and for which *you* were to blame.
>
> When a quarter of a million miners are unemployed, it is part of the order of things that Alf Smith, a miner living in the back streets of Newcastle, should be out of work. Alf Smith is merely one of the quarter million, a statistical unit. But no human being finds it easy to regard himself as a statistical unit. So long as Bert Jones across the street is still at work, Alf Smith is bound to feel himself dishonored and a failure. Hence that frightening feeling of impotence and despair which is almost the worst evil of unemploy-

[1] See the Introduction to Economic Council of Canada, *1st Annual Review,* Ottawa: Queen's Printer, 1964.

> ment—far worse than any hardship, worse than the demoralization of enforced idleness, and only less bad than the physical degeneracy of Alf Smith's children . . .[2]

Eventually, however, it is inevitable that those who are unemployed will grow bitter against *somebody*—against those people, government officials or businessmen or bankers, whom they come to regard as responsible for their own desperate condition and the misery of their families.

But the workers are not the only ones who personalize their bitterness over depressions. Owners of businesses, seeing their businesses fail, may blame "greedy" trade unions, "lazy" workers, or "stupid" politicians; government leaders or politicians may blame "malefactors of great wealth," "economic royalists," or "self-seeking" foreigners.

THE CONCEPT OF A NATIONAL ECONOMIC SYSTEM

But such problems as unemployment, business failures, steeply falling or climbing prices result from a malfunctioning of the economic system rather than from the wickedness of particular persons or groups in society. To be sure, economic ignorance or incompetence of government policy makers can hurt the performance of the national economy. Our aim in the study of macroeconomics is to understand objectively what causes malfunctions of our economic system—and to discover what, if anything, can be done to prevent them or alleviate them.

It is understandably difficult for most people to conceive of that complex abstraction, a national economic system. Obviously, no one can really *see* the system as a whole. Individual human beings come in contact only with particular parts of the system.

Thus, consumers will know the word *inflation* and realize that there is, in some vague way, something wrong with the national economy. But what they can see with their own eyes is the increase in the price of food at the supermarket or gas at the service station.

It is then only a quick step for consumers to put the blame for rising prices on the immediate sources of the goods they buy. That was why on occasions when food prices were rising sharply, consumers in many cities throughout the United States and Canada organized buying strikes and picketed outside supermarkets, carrying placards denouncing the owners of the stores for raising prices and hurting their family budgets.

The consumers did not accept the fact that the owners of the supermarkets were themselves often caught in a web of rising prices that they could not completely control. Even though producers and retailers were increasing their prices, in many cases, their own costs were increasing just as rapidly.

The real cause of rising prices was to be found in the overall functioning of the economic system—and in the mistakes that had been made by all buyers in the economy and by governmental economic and monetary officials, who had permitted the total demand for goods and services to grow more rapidly than the capacity of the economy to satisfy those demands. The result was general price inflation—although some sectors, such as food, were more sharply affected than others, such as the prices of automobiles or housing.

Developing a concept of the economic system as a whole is one of the most important purposes of the study of economics. This concept must not be merely vague and general, but quite specific and detailed. Economists have a number of different ways of describing the national economy, but the most important of these from the standpoint of the beginning student (and the mature analyst) is based on the concept of the gross national product. This approach was developed in the USA by the National Bureau of Economic Research and the U.S. Federal Department of Commerce in the 1930s. It has been continuously refined and has been adopted in many countries, including Canada, since that time. We shall turn to a study of gross national product in the next chapter.

[2] George Orwell, *The Road to Wigan Pier*, Berkeley edition, New York: 1961, p. 81.

SUMMARY

Units 2 and 3 of this book were concerned with microeconomics, the study of separate parts of the economic system. In Unit 4, we shall study macroeconomics, the study of the economic system as a whole.

While microeconomics and macroeconomics are interrelated parts of economics as a complete discipline, it is important to realize that fallacies of composition may be committed if one assumes that what holds for the separate parts of the economy holds equally for the economy as a whole. For instance, a fall in the price of one commodity may cause more units of it to be purchased; but generally falling prices in the economy as a whole may not lead to an increase in overall consumption.

The purpose of studying macroeconomics is to help us achieve such fundamental national objectives as: (1) a growing level of output and income, (2) a high level of employment opportunities, and (3) a stable economy that avoids either sharply falling or sharply rising prices.

To gain such objectives, economic policy makers—and the public generally—should have a clear concept of the national economic system and what causes it to function effectively or poorly. To advance such understanding, we shall turn in the next chapter to the study of the gross national product.

KEY CONCEPTS

microeconomics
macroeconomics
inflation
deflation

QUESTIONS FOR REVIEW AND DISCUSSION

1. Define microeconomics and macroeconomics. In what ways are they similar, and in what ways do they differ?
2. Define the fallacy of composition, and give two specific examples of this fallacy in areas other than economics. How might this fallacy apply to the study of economics?
3. What is the danger of personalizing national economic problems? How can the study of macroeconomics help you overcome this danger?
4. What national economic objectives are most closely related to the study of macroeconomics? What are some specific reasons why each of these objectives is important for the Canadian economy?

PROBLEMS AND EXERCISES TO SHARPEN YOUR UNDERSTANDING

1. From current newspapers or magazines, watch for articles, editorials or detailed stories dealing with the overall performance of the Canadian economy. From these, try to find examples of:
   (a) differing opinions about primary objectives or goals for the Canadian economy;
   (b) personalization of an explanation of, or opinion about economic conditions;
   (c) influences from outside Canada on economic events within Canada.
2. From the selections used for the problem above, note which specific measures of performance of the economy are most frequently referred to.
3. Upon completion of problem 2 above, using either the same reference material or other sources of information about the U.S. economy, try to make observations about:
   (a) the indicators of performance used to measure what is happening in the U.S.A.;
   (b) any significant similarities or differences between actual economic trends in the U.S. and those in Canada.

CHAPTER 22

THE CONCEPT OF GROSS NATIONAL PRODUCT

■ STOCKS AND FLOWS ■ FINAL GOODS AND SERVICES ■ MONEY AS A UNIT OF ACCOUNT ■ GROSS NATIONAL PRODUCT ■ THE FLOW OF PRODUCT APPROACH TO GNP ■ THE EARNINGS AND COST APPROACH TO GNP ■ SUMMARY

Before we can make much progress in macroeconomics, we must have some way of measuring the performance of our economic system as a whole. This chapter will be devoted to this problem of *measurement*. Later chapters will be devoted to *explaining* changes in total economic activity and to ways of *alleviating* macroeconomic problems.

■ STOCKS AND FLOWS

The problem of measurement is not an easy one. How does one go about measuring a national economic system? We could count the number of factories. We could add up the number of people working. Or we could add up all the money people have in banks. Should we perhaps count the number of kilometres of railroad tracks or highways? Or the number of telephones? Or a host of other things or events? And how should all these facts be combined and arranged?

Economists grappled with this problem of measuring total economic performance for a long time before Dr. Simon Kuznets, an economist on the staff of the National Bureau of Economic Research in Washington, finally worked out the technique that has become widely accepted as the best *single* measure of the performance of the economy as a whole.[1] A key point in Kuznets' system is the distinction between the *stock* of wealth in an economy at any given point in time and the *rate of flow* at which an economy is adding to its wealth over a period of time.

In measuring economic performance, which fact is more important: (1) that the nation has almost x million cars on the road (the stock) or (2) that it is producing new cars at a rate of almost y million a year (the flow)? Is our current economic activity best measured by the fact that we have perhaps m million telephones at the present time, or the fact that we are perhaps producing n million new telephones every year?

By and large economists have come to agree that the stock of assets (should they be telephones, automobiles, railroads, presses, private houses, or all these and others combined) in existence at a point in time reflects *past* economic performance. A better measure of *current* economic performance is the *rate* at which we are producing *new* assets to add to our present wealth. *Flows* measure current economic activity far better than *stocks*, which represent a conglomeration of the results of economic activity over a long period of time.

If an economy is performing well, it will be producing *new* goods and services at a high *rate*. If it is performing badly, the *rate* at which it is producing *new* goods and services will be low.

The period of time over which an economy's rate of production is usually measured is *one year*. If shorter periods of time are

[1] In 1971, Kuznets was awarded the Nobel Prize in Economics for this work.

used, the output during this period is usually converted to an annual rate. Thus, the production of 10 cars in one week is expressed as an annual rate of 520 cars a year.

Once we distinguish between a stock of output at a given point in time and the rate of production over a year's time, however, we still have some measurement problems remaining. What goods and services should we count in our flow measurements and which, if any, should we leave out? And, once we decide which goods and services to count, how do we add automobiles, baseball bats, chewing gum, teachers' services, haircuts, and the myriad of other goods and services produced in our economy during a year?

■ FINAL GOODS AND SERVICES

In counting the flow of output in the economy we must avoid **double counting**. If a farmer grows wheat and sells it to a miller who grinds it into flour and sells it to a baker, who bakes it into bread and sells it to a hungry newspaper boy, how much has the economy produced? The answer is: "It has produced one loaf of bread." The bread is the *final product* of all the economic activity described above. It would be a mistake to add the wheat *and* the flour *and* the bread—this would be double (or triple) counting. We do not count **intermediate products**—the products that are used up at a later stage of production. Instead, we just count the *final product*—the bread—since the value (price) of the bread already includes the value (price) of the wheat and the flour, as well as the value of the farmer's and the baker's services.

In measuring the rate of output for the total economy, just as in this example of one product, we must be careful to count only the production of **final goods and services**—those goods and services that go to their ultimate consumers and are not included in a later stage of production. A haircut the day before a high school dance and a Boeing 747 purchased by C.P. Air are both examples of final goods and services; they are goods and services that have been purchased by their ultimate consumer.

Coal and iron ore used in making steel, and steel used in making automobiles, on the other hand, are all intermediate goods—they have not been purchased by their final consumer. The value of these goods will be included in the price paid by the final consumer of the goods they are used to produce.

■ MONEY AS A UNIT OF ACCOUNT

Once we have agreed to count only the *flow of final goods and services*, however, we are still faced with the problem of adding up haircuts, hockey sticks, bubble gum, flowers, and 747s. We obviously cannot add hockey sticks and 747s directly. But, if we consume 100 hockey sticks that are sold for $13 apiece and two 747s are sold for $20 million apiece, we can add $1300 and $40 million and say that we have consumed $40 001 300 worth of output. We thus use money (in this case dollars) as a **unit of account** to compare and add the value of different things. It is important to remember that the total of goods and services produced is a *dollar* total, not a *physical* total measured in any other type of units.

■ GROSS NATIONAL PRODUCT

We now have the basic tools needed to construct a single measure of total economic performance. Using dollars as a unit of account, we can add up the market value (sales prices) of all the final goods and services produced during one year. This measure is called the **gross national product**.

The gross national product, GNP for short, expresses the value of the final goods and services produced in one year. In terms of Figure 13-1 in Chapter 13, it measures the *rate* at which final goods and services are *flowing* through the economy. Think of this as clocking our total economic performance. To make a comparison, when you drive a car, you may shift from a rate of 95 km/h to 60 km/h and then up to 90 km/h. Similarly, the rate of GNP may slow down or speed up.

The GNP is such an important concept in modern economics that Statistics Canada, which calculates the official GNP estimates for our economy, measures it in *two* different ways—two ways that logic says should yield the same total and that therefore offer a practical way of checking the results of very complicated estimates.

If we want to measure the value of final goods and services by using money as our unit of account, we can count: (1) *the money spent to buy the output*, or (2) *the money received for producing the output*. If we had a record of all transactions in the economy, the amount spent would obviously equal the amount *received*, and both would measure the amount of real goods and services *produced* and *sold*.

The method of estimating GNP by counting the money spent to buy it is called the *flow of product* approach. The method of estimating GNP by counting the money received for producing it is called the *earnings and cost* approach.

THE FLOW OF PRODUCT APPROACH TO GNP

In measuring the output of final goods and services by counting the money spent to buy it, Statistics Canada divides buyers into four broad categories. By grouping together large classes of buyers who behave in roughly the same way, we can get some good insights into how different parts of the total economy behave over different periods of time. The four broad categories of total spending used are: (1) personal consumption expenditures, (2) business (and some individual and government) investment for real capital goods, (3) government expenditures for currently produced goods and services, and (4) our net exports of goods and services. This total, when reached, is usually referred to as GNE, Gross National Expenditure.

FIG. 22-1. PERSONAL CONSUMPTION EXPENDITURES IN CANADA, 1977

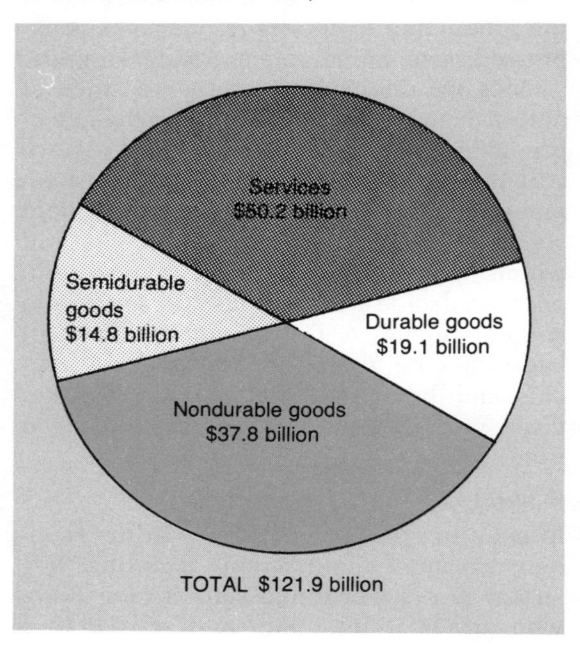

Consumer Spending

By far the largest part of our nation's output in any given year is purchased by individual consumers. In 1977 personal consumption expenditures for currently produced final goods and services in Canada totalled $121.955 billion or about 59 percent of total GNP.

Remember that this figure counts only consumer expenditures on *currently* produced *final* goods and services. It does not count expenditures on intermediate goods that go into the making of final consumer goods and services. And it does not count expenditures on goods produced in previous years, unless some current service is involved in bringing the old good to a consumer. If a consumer buys a *used* car, for example, only the difference between what the used car dealer paid for it and sells it for would represent an addition to GNP. (This difference represents a payment by the consumer to the used car dealer for the *services* in obtaining and marketing the car.)

Personal consumption expenditures fall into four general categories: *durable goods*, such as new cars or refrigerators; *nondurable goods*, such as food and clothing; *semidurable goods*, and finally, *services*.[2] Figure 22-1 gives the relative breakdown among the four sub-groups for 1977.

Investment Spending

The investment category in the GNP accounts is one of the most difficult to understand at first glance. The main reason for this difficulty is that *investment*, as used by economists in estimating GNP expenditures, has a special meaning that often differs from the usual man-in-the-street use of this term. In ordinary speech people often talk of buying shares of corporate stock as investing. Or they speak of investing in a life insurance policy or investing in the purchase of government bonds. From the standpoint of a product flow, however, these activities are not investment but only *transfers* of assets from one form (money) to another form (pieces of paper, such as stocks or bonds or life insurance policies). These transfers do not involve the production of any new economic goods, and they are not counted in GNP (except for any sales commissions that are involved for the *services* of the broker or salesman who arranges these transfers).

[2] One unusual aspect of the definition of consumer expenditures is that it does not include purchases of new houses; payment for the construction of a house or apartment building is counted as an *investment* expenditure (discussed later) rather than as a *consumption* outlay. Many houses and apartments are built and owned by commercial builders or real estate firms. Rather than trying to divide housing into two categories, consumption outlays and business investments, economists put all new housing construction under *investment*. The purchase or sale of an *old* house is not included in GNP, since it is not part of this year's production; it presumably was counted in GNP the year it was built. Only the payment for the services of the real-estate firm that currently handled the sale of the old house is included in this year's GNP.

Investment in GNP terms occurs only when money is spent to buy *real capital goods* such as a new factory, a new power generator, or any other capital good whose final use is to aid in the production of other goods and services.

As discussed later, changes in inventory are also counted in figuring investment spending. You may want to review Chapter 3 for the definition of real capital goods. Capital goods (with the possible exception of some inventories) are not intermediate goods such as the wheat or the steel mentioned in the double counting examples. Intermediate goods are quickly used up in the production process; and their final use is not determined until they are embodied in other goods and services. Real capital goods, however, usually last a long time in aiding in the production of other goods and services, and their final use is to give this aid in the production process.

Most investment expenditures in our economy are made by business firms; but, as noted above, individuals' home purchases are also counted as investment rather than as consumption spending. Businesses invest in real capital goods for many purposes; to meet a growing demand for their products, to produce new products requiring new equipment, to operate more efficiently, or to replace worn out equipment. Within Canada's GNP accounts, a separate section includes investment by various levels of government.

Investment in GNP terminology is called **gross fixed capital formation** if it includes all expenditures for new capital goods, with no allowances being made for the wearing out of existing capital equipment during the year. If some allowance is made for the wearing out of existing capital goods, as well as the production of new capital goods, the resulting figure would be called **net fixed capital formation**. In fact, the word *gross* in the term gross national product is used to signify that economists decided to use a figure

COMPONENTS OF GNP

Hudson's Bay Co.

C P Air

Hydro Quebec photo by Jacques Lambert

National Harbours Board and Wamboldt-Waterfield Photography Ltd.

The four pictures on these pages symbolize the four major components of gross national product. The first picture, of shoppers, represents the largest component—*consumer spending on goods and services.* The second picture stands for *investment* (or, formally, Gross Fixed Capital Formation)—the airplane is a capital good which has been produced for use by the airline. The third picture, representing *government expenditure,* shows the dam at Manicouagan built by Hydro Quebec. This represents investment by government as opposed to a case of current spending on goods and services, such as the salary of your economics teacher (unless you are in a private school). The last photo, showing cargo being handled at the port of Halifax, stands for net exports.

for all the capital goods made, regardless of how much wearing out (depreciation) of capital goods took place. By deducting from GNP a figure to represent the depreciation of capital equipment, however, economists can give an estimate of the so-called **net national product (NNP)**. But, ordinarily, economists employ the gross national product as the basic figure to show the total output of goods and services in the economy in a year.

Gross private domestic investment (invested by the private sector) includes four major categories:

1. *Business investments in structures:* (factories, warehouses, office buildings, etc.);
2. *Machinery and equipment:* (machinery, machine tools, electronic computers, office equipment, trucks, ships, airplanes, and so forth);
3. *Residential structures* including, as noted above, all new housing built during the time period covered, whether intended for rental, cooperative, or individual family ownership;
4. *Changes in inventories,* additions to or subtractions from the stock of raw materials, semifinished or finished goods in the hands of business or farmers. Businesses obviously could not operate without inventories; changes in the level of their inventories reflect changes in the total level of production.

If all businesses and farms held inventories of $7 billion at the beginning of the year, for example, and if, at the end of the year, all businesses held inventories of $8 billion, the change in inventories during the year would be an increase of $1 billion; this would be added to GNP. If, on the other hand, the level of inventories during the year were to drop $1 billion, GNP would be reduced by that amount.

One may compare the changes in business inventories to the water in a bathtub, into which water is simultaneously flowing in through the tap and pouring out through the drain. When water is pouring in faster than it leaves, the water level rises. This is also true with production that boosts the level of inventories and raises GNP—remember it is the *rate of flow* of output (water), not the *stock* of goods and services (the water in the bathtub at any given time), that we want GNP to measure.

FIG. 22-2. GROSS PRIVATE DOMESTIC INVESTMENT IN CANADA, 1977

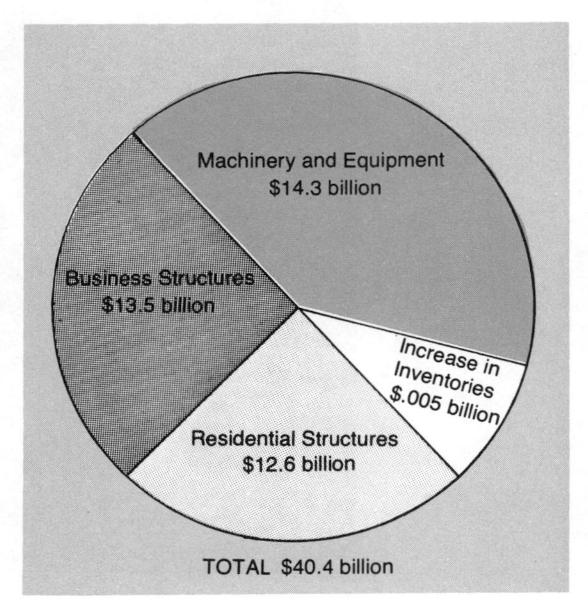

Swings in inventories can have a significant effect in changing total GNP. For instance, if one year businessmen were *adding* to inventories by $1 billion and in the next *reducing* inventories by $1 billion, the swing of $2 *billion in inventory accumulation* would be very important in changing the course of the economy.

In 1977 gross private domestic investment totalled $40.429 billion. Figure 22-2 gives the relative breakdown among the four subgroups.

Because investment is the category of spending which determines the capacity of the economy to generate goods and services in future time periods, the level of investment spending within GNP is one of the most closely watched economic indicators.

Spending by governments on things like new highways in Ontario, new power pro-

Table 22-1. GROSS GOVERNMENT INVESTMENT IN CANADA, 1977.

	(billions of dollars)		
Government Structures	6.148	1.373	Federal
Machinery and Equipment	1.052	2.816	Provincial
Residential Structures	.026	2.721	Municipal
Changes in Inventories	.043	.359	Hospitals
Total	7.269	7.269	Total

Source: Statistics Canada, *National Income and Expenditure Accounts, Fourth Quarter, 1977,* cat. 13-001.

duction facilities in Quebec, new rail cars for CN to carry western wheat, or a new ferry to run between Nova Scotia and Newfoundland is also spending of a type which will help determine future production and distribution capacity. As a result, government investment is included along with private investment within the total of gross fixed capital formation as computed by Statistics Canada.

For 1977, the government sector contributed a total of $7.269 billion in investment spending. This total, broken down in two ways within Table 22-1, added to the private sector figures, produces a total for gross fixed capital formation in 1977 of $47.7 billion.[3]

Government Current Spending

In the GNP accounts, government purchases of goods and services include Federal, provincial, and local government purchases. But we should remember that government outlays for goods and services do *not* include all government expenditures. As noted above, investment is excluded.

Like consumer expenditures or total investment, government spending in the GNP accounts includes only outlays for currently produced goods or services. *It does not include transfer payments.* Much of the money that government pays out actually represents transfer payments, as in the case of family allowances, unemployment insurance and similar cases. When the government sends pension checks to retired persons, this is a transfer of funds rather than a payment for any current service performed by recipients. This is also true of payments to unemployed workers, disabled persons, widows, and orphans. If persons receiving these transfer payments use their checks to buy food and clothing, this shows up as a personal consumption expenditure, not as a government expenditure.

Current spending on goods and services, as recorded in the GNP accounts, includes payments for the work done by the Prime Minister and all other public officials and for the services of soldiers, sailors, civil servants, and postal workers. Government spending in GNP also includes payments for a great variety of goods purchased for government current use at all levels of administration.

Excluding the amounts invested in 1977, the three levels of government paid out about $102.5 billion in all forms, but only $42.5 billion of that amount represented current expenditures on goods and services; the rest was accounted for by transfer payments to individuals, businesses or other levels of government.

Foreign Spending

Many goods and services produced in Canada are sold abroad, and much consumption, investment, and government spending in Canada is for products that are not produced

[3] For a variety of reasons, there is some inconsistency in the use of the term "investment" in economic newswriting and reporting. If it is not clearly indicated, be careful to watch to determine if a reference to "investment" refers just to private investment or to the total of private plus public amounts, i.e. to gross fixed capital formation as reported in the GNP accounts of Statistics Canada.

in this country. So that all the final goods and services produced in Canada are counted, and so that only the purchases of goods and services produced in this country are counted in GNP, we add up total Canadian exports of goods and services and subtract the total imports of goods and services to get a figure for net exports of goods and services. This figure is usually negative since Canada usually exports less than it imports, but in some years the figure has been positive. In 1977 the total exports of Canada were $52.49 billion and the imports were $57.09 billion. The net exports of Canada were, therefore $−4.6 billion. This is also added to GNP

FIG. 22-3. NET EXPORTS OF CANADA

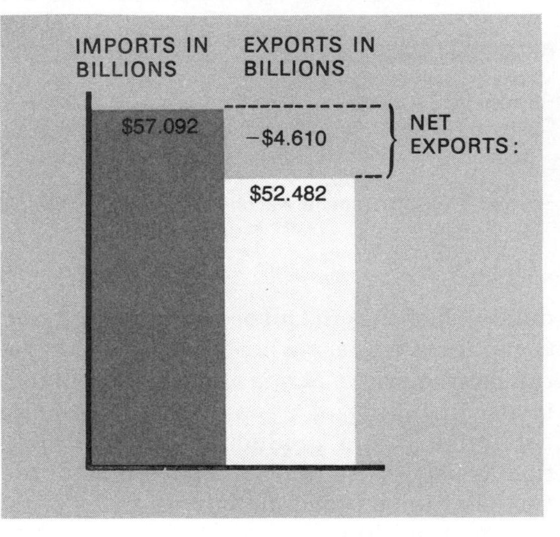

Adding Up Expenditures to Get GNP

We now can sum consumer spending, total investment spending, total government spending, and net exports to get the GNP for one year. In 1977 the preliminary figures, with an adjustment item of $+.155 billion, totalled $207.7 billion.

THE EARNINGS AND COST APPROACH TO GNP

The GNP for 1977 can now be checked by the earnings and cost approach (that is, by measuring the money received by all those responsible for producing GNP).

When we use the earnings and cost approach to measure GNP, we find that there are six main categories to be covered:

1. Depreciation—money put aside to cover the wearing out of equipment or plants;
2. Indirect excise and sales taxes—paid to Federal, provincial, or local governments;
3. Wages and salaries—paid to workers and managers;
4. Rents—paid to landlords or others who hire out their property for use;
5. Interest—paid to banks or other lenders of money;
6. Profits—the sums retained by businesses when there is a surplus of earnings over costs of doing business. In the national accounts, profits are further broken down by separating the income of unincorporated businesses from corporate profits, and then dividing corporate profits into the part used to pay corporate income taxes, the part used to pay dividends to stockholders, and the part retained for use in the business (undistributed corporate profits or corporate savings).

These six categories will now be discussed in greater detail.

Depreciation

Part of the money a business receives for selling its products will be put aside as a **depreciation reserve**. This recognizes that the businesses' existing capital equipment will wear out some day and will have to be replaced. It is hard to measure the wear and tear on capital goods, but if a company did not set aside some funds for the eventual replacement of worn-out equipment, it would be understating its true cost of doing business. A company that paid out all its income to its suppliers of productive services, the government, and its stockholders, with nothing left over to replace its capital equipment, would be behaving dangerously from the standpoint of survival. Bakeries must replace their ovens, steel companies their furnaces, taxicab companies their cars, newspaper companies their printing presses, and so on. In 1977 the total amount of depreciation reserves or *capital consumption allowances* put aside by Canadian businesses equalled $19.4 billion, or over 9 percent of GNP after provision has been made for adjustments in the value of inventories.

Indirect Taxes

Some of the money business firms receive for the sale of their products must be turned over to the government to cover sales and excise taxes that have been levied on particular goods. Indirect tax payments, as figured in the GNP accounts, include all the sales and excise taxes levied by the different levels of government. In 1977 the total amount of indirect taxes turned over to the government by business firms totalled $23.4 billion, or about 11 percent of GNP.

Once a company has set aside part of its income for depreciation allowances and turned over to the government whatever excise and sales tax revenue it has collected, the rest of its receipts (not counting the part used to purchase intermediate goods) is available for payment to those who provide productive services to the company. Anything left over after the suppliers of productive services have been paid is counted as profit.

Wages and Salaries

The payments for the labor and managerial services of a company's employees usually take the form of wage and salary payments. The GNP accounts, however, use a broad category of *compensation of employees* to include tips, bonuses, commissions and employer's payments of all categories of wages and salaries. In 1977, wage and salary payments totalled $119.9 billion, making this the largest single item on the earnings and cost side of GNP. It accounted for over 57 percent of the total.

This total employee compensation figure of $119.9 billion, however, does not tell us how many different people shared in its distribution, or how the total was distributed among them. But we already know from Chapter 14 that, in a market economy, an employee's compensation or income is largely determined by the value of the service he has to sell in the marketplace. Corporate executives, with very scarce managerial skills, often receive very large salaries, bonuses, and stock options compared to other employees who have less scarce skills to sell.

Interest and Investment Income

People receive interest for lending their savings and capital funds to businesses, and people pay interest on funds they have borrowed to finance their economic activities. Statistics Canada takes total interest payments received by individuals and subtracts the interest payments made by individuals to arrive at a figure for total *net* interest income. Total net interest plus certain other investment incomes was $12.4 billion in 1977, just under 6 percent of GNP.

Profits

Profits are a residual item. They represent what is left over after all the other payments have been made. If a firm does well, there may be a lot left over. If a firm does poorly, profits may be low or even negative (losses).

As we noted earlier, there are basically two kinds of profits, profits of corporations and profits of unincorporated businesses. Statistics Canada accounts call unincorporated profits *income of unincorporated enterprises*, since many small business owners do not pay themselves wages, rent, or interest on their own resources that they have put into their businesses. Therefore, the money left over after they pay all their other expenses really cannot be considered profit in a pure sense of the word. Hence, the government uses the term *income of unincorporated enterprises*, with a subdivision to show a total for farm product receipts. In 1977 the total income of unincorporated businesses plus rental incomes equalled $12 billion, or 5.8 percent of GNP.

Total corporate profits in 1977 were $20.5

FIG. 22-4. TWO WAYS OF LOOKING AT GROSS NATIONAL PRODUCT (1977 FIGURES IN BILLIONS OF DOLLARS)

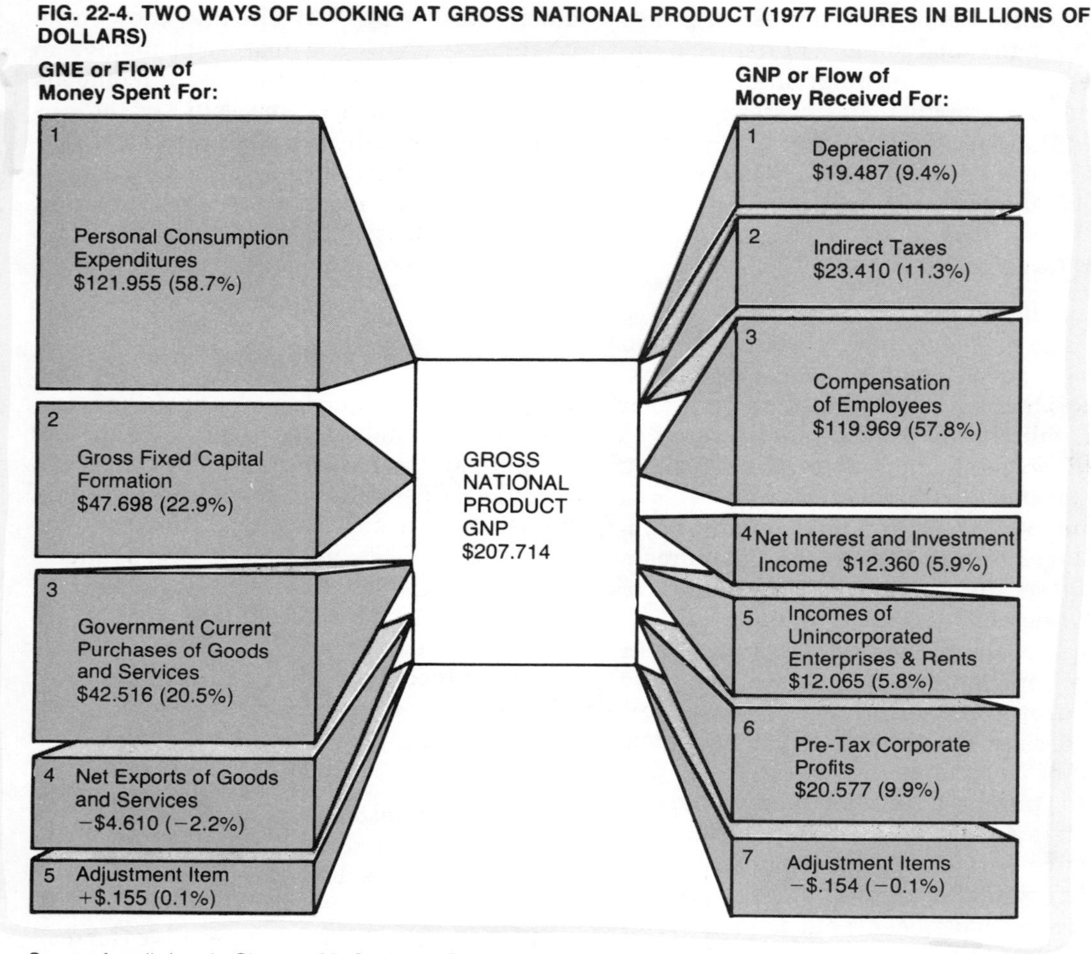

Source for all data in Chapter 22: Statistics Canada, *National Income and Expenditure Accounts, Fourth Quarter, 1977,* cat. 13-001. Data are seasonally adjusted at annual rates. Note: these data are the first reported for the year 1977, and may be altered slightly for future reporting or quotation.

billion or just under 10 percent of GNP. Since corporations have to pay part of their profits out to the government in the form of corporate profit taxes, however, and since not all of their after-tax profits are paid out to the stockholders as dividends, total corporate profits are subdivided into: corporate income taxes, dividends, and undistributed corporate profit or corporate savings.

Adding Up Money Received to Get GNP

Adding up depreciation, indirect taxes, employee compensation, investment income and net interest, unincorporated business and rental income, and gross corporate profits, we get a total GNP of $207.6 billion dollars for Canada in 1977.

This total from the earnings and cost approach is basically the same total we previously obtained using the flow of product approach to measuring GNP.

Figure 22-4 provides a good summary indicating how both approaches to measuring GNP add up to the same total figure representing the flow of final goods and services in our economy during the year 1977.

SUMMARY

This chapter has introduced the concept of gross national product as the most comprehensive single measure of an economy's total economic performance. The gross national product measures the *rate* at which an economy is producing final goods and services. Since it is difficult to add the flow of different final goods and services directly, money is used as a measuring device, called a unit of account. By adding up the amount of money spent to buy final goods and services (the flow of product approach), or by adding up the amount of money received for selling final goods and services (the earnings and cost approach), we can get a good estimate of the total amount of goods and services produced during any given time period (usually one year).

The GNP is such an important concept in modern economics that we will devote the next chapter to refining our understanding of this concept so that we can use it more intelligently in analysing the total performance of an economy.

KEY CONCEPTS

double counting	unit of account	gross fixed capital formation
intermediate products	GNP/GNE	net national product
final goods and services	investment	depreciation reserve

QUESTIONS FOR REVIEW AND DISCUSSION

1. Distinguish between a stock and a flow. Give an example of each from an area outside of economics (such as water in a bathtub) and then give an example from the area of economics.
2. Give an example of an intermediate product and a final product. How does the concept of final products help us avoid the problem of double counting? Why is it important to avoid the problem of double counting in economics?
3. "You can't add apples, oranges, and pears." In what sense is this statement true? Is there also a sense in which the statement is false? Explain how money can be used as a unit of account to add the *value* of apples, oranges, and pears.
4. Explain in your own words exactly what is it that the gross national product is designed to measure. Explain the flow of product approach to GNP, and explain the earnings and cost approach to GNP. Why must the GNP obtained by the flow of product approach always logically be equal to the GNP obtained by the earnings and cost approach?

PROBLEMS AND EXERCISES TO SHARPEN YOUR UNDERSTANDING

1. Below is an alphabetical listing of the annual rates of expenditures and receipts for 13 items in the gross national product accounts of a particular country.

   Use these data to determine the GNP from *both* the flow of product approach and the earnings and cost approach. What is the GNP of this country?

Compensation of Employees	50
Corporate Profits Before Taxes	10
Depreciation	8
Dividends	3
Gross Fixed Capital Formation	12
Current Government Purchases of Goods and Services	14
Incomes of Unincorporated Enterprises	9
Indirect Taxes	11
Net Exports of Goods and Services	20
Net Interest and Investment Income	2
Personal Consumption Expenditures	44
Undistributed Corporate Profits	3

2. Use an economic publication such as the Canadian Statistical Review to obtain current GNP data for the Canadian economy. Do you see any major changes in (a) the absolute amounts or (b) the relative percentages in any of the basic components?

CHAPTER 23

REFINING THE CONCEPT OF GROSS NATIONAL PRODUCT

■ ADJUSTING FOR PRICE CHANGES ■ ADJUSTING FOR POPULATION CHANGES ■ REMEMBERING WHAT IS NOT INCLUDED IN GNP ■ SOME KEY COMPONENTS OF GNP ■ THE CIRCULAR FLOW OF GNP ■ SUMMARY

When you think of total national production for a year, you almost inevitably think of things like the millions of automobiles or hamburgers turned out. But, as we saw in Chapter 22, all the different physical outputs can be added up only by converting them into money values. And, when you measure national output in money terms, a problem that immediately arises is how to take account of the price changes that affect the value of individual goods or services and the value of total national output. If GNP increases 5 percent in one year, but the average level of prices also increases 5 percent, the real increase in physical output of goods and services is zero.

In addition to price changes, another problem that arises in using GNP figures to measure the growth in the nation's standard of living has to do with population change. If *real* GNP increases 2 percent in one year (that is, if the physical output of goods and services increases 2 percent), and if the population of the country also increases 2 percent in that year, then the improvement in the average person's standard of living will be zero. The extra goods and services produced will just go to take care of more people.

GNP is not, in any case, a perfect measure of a nation's standard of living. There are some things that many people consider important in determining their standard of living—such as leisure or free time—that are not measured by real GNP, even in *per capita* terms. GNP does not record certain types of productive activities—such as the services provided by individuals to their families. If a mother cooks and bakes and cleans for her own family, the recorded impact on GNP is zero. But if she goes out and works for another family, cooking, baking, and cleaning, the recorded effect on GNP is equal to her annual earnings.

In this chapter we shall consider some of the refinements in the concept of GNP that are necessary if we want to use GNP data as an index of a nation's standard of living or as a measure of the economic well-being of a nation's people.

We shall also consider how GNP can be broken into various subcomponents that will be useful in analysing total economic activity.

■ ADJUSTING FOR PRICE CHANGES

Over long periods of time, marked by major increases or decreases in prices, the difference between **real GNP**, as measured in *constant* prices, and **nominal GNP**, as measured in *current* prices, can be huge. Over shorter periods of time, with reasonably stable prices, the difference between these two measures may not be so dramatic. But that has not been Canada's experience in the

Table 23-1. GNP IN CURRENT AND CONSTANT (1971) PRICES, 1962-1977

Year	GNP Current Prices (billions of dollars)	Implicit Price Index for Total GNP (1971 = 100)	GNP in 1971 Prices (billions of dollars)
1962	42.927	73.4	58.475
1963	45.978	74.8	61.487
1964	50.280	76.6	65.610
1965	55.364	79.1	69.981
1966	61.828	82.6	74.844
1967	66.409	85.9	77.344
1968	72.586	88.7	81.864
1969	79.815	92.6	86.225
1970	85.685	96.9	88.390
1971	94.450	100.0	94.450
1972	105.234	105.0	100.248
1973	123.560	114.6	107.812
1974	147.175	131.7	111.766
1975	165.445	146.5	112.955
1976	190.027	160.4	118.484
1977	207.714	170.9	121.566

Sources: Statistics Canada, *National Income and Expenditure Accounts, 1962-1976,* cat. 13-201, and *National Income and Expenditure Accounts, Fourth Quarter, 1977,* cat. 13-001.

seventies. Hence, it is an important distinction to be aware of.

Economists say the *nominal* GNP is measured in **current prices** if they measure the physical output during a given year with the prices that prevailed in *the same year. Real* GNP is measured in **constant prices**, if a *price index* is used to convert or deflate current prices into prices that prevailed during a given *base year.*[1] Statistics Canada has a composite price index which is designed to reflect changes in the prices of all the goods and services contained in GNP. This index, which is shown as the second column in Table 23-1, uses 1971 as the base year, and it compares prices in other years to the prices that prevailed in 1971.

Once we have a reliable price index like the GNP deflator, it is possible to show the difference between measuring *real* GNP in *constant* prices and measuring *nominal* GNP in *current* prices. It is possible to separate changes in physical output from changes in the prices at which real output is bought and sold. This is done in Table 23-1 for the years from 1962 through 1977. Figure 23-1 shows this information in graphic form.

[1] A review of the section dealing with price indexes in Chapter 16 may be advisable.

ADJUSTING FOR POPULATION CHANGES

After adjusting for price changes, a two-fold increase in our annual rate of real output is still a significant achievement. But, if one also takes into account the increase in population over the period from 1962 to 1977, even the increase in real GNP gives an exaggerated picture of the improvement in the economic well-being of the average Canadian.

FIG. 23-1. GNP IN CURRENT AND CONSTANT (1971) PRICES, 1962-1977 (BILLIONS OF DOLLARS)

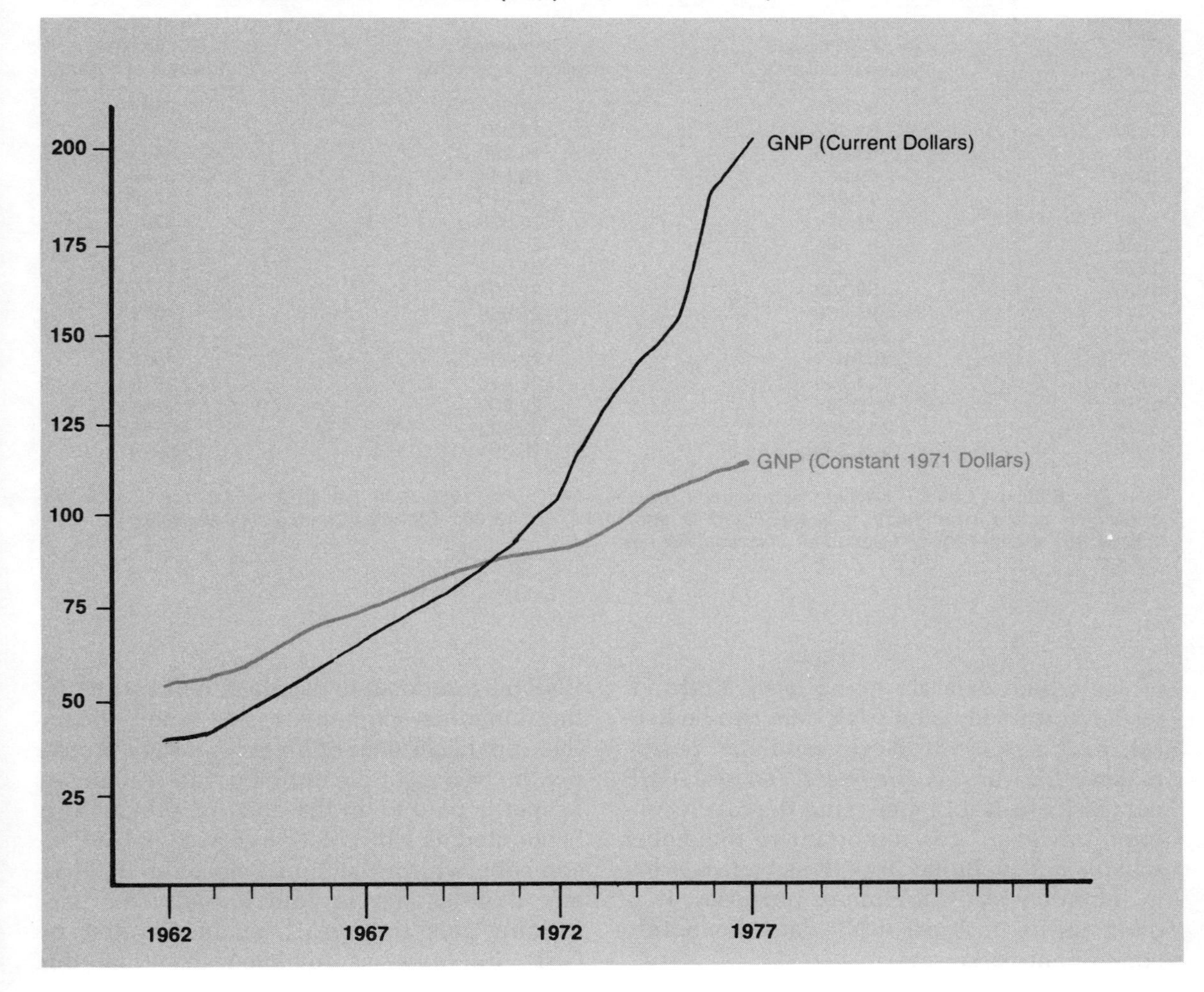

Table 23-2 on page 278 gives real GNP data in 1971 prices and population data from 1962 through 1977. If we divide the real GNP figures by the population figures, we get a figure for *real* GNP *per capita*. This is probably the best single figure that can be obtained for measuring the performance of an economic system—it gives the annual rate of real output for each person in the economy.

Thus, in using GNP data to make comparisons over long periods of time, it is important to adjust for both changes in prices and changes in population. Yet, in dealing with changes in GNP over short periods of time, such as from one quarter to another, or even from one year to another, some sources may use nominal, or current-price GNP, unadjusted for changes in prices or population. When you read stories about increases or decreases in GNP in the newspapers, take care

Table 23-2. TOTAL AND PER CAPITA GNP IN CONSTANT (1971) PRICES, 1962-1977

Year	Real GNP in 1971 Prices (billions of dollars)	Population (millions of persons)	Real GNP Per Capita (thousands of dollars)
1962	58.475	18.583	3147
1963	61.487	18.931	3248
1964	65.610	19.290	3401
1965	69.981	19.644	3562
1966	74.844	20.015	3739
1967	77.344	20.378	3795
1968	81.864	20.701	3955
1969	86.225	21.001	4106
1970	88.390	21.297	4150
1971	94.450	21.569	4379
1972	100.248	21.820	4594
1973	107.812	22.095	4879
1974	111.766	22.446	4979
1975	112.955	22.800	4954
1976	118.484	22.993	5153
1977	121.566	23.291	5219

Sources: Statistics Canada, *National Income and Expenditure Accounts, 1962-1976,* cat. 13-201; Statistics Canada, *National Income and Expenditure Accounts, Fourth Quarter, 1977,* cat. 13-001; Statistics Canada, *Vital Statistics,* cat. 84-201 and 84-001; and *Canadian Statistical Review.*

to see which data are being used. Both adjusted and unadjusted GNP data can be useful to business and government policy makers for various purposes. To use GNP data to its fullest in analysing the total economy, however, it is important to remember what is *not* included in GNP as well as what is included. And, for many purposes, it is often useful to break GNP data down into component parts.

REMEMBERING WHAT IS NOT INCLUDED IN GNP

While we have said that *real* GNP *per capita* is the best *single* measure of total economic performance over any significant period of time, even this figure must be interpreted with care. Remember that, except for only very minor exceptions, GNP counts only the purchase and sale of final goods and services *in the marketplace.* If an economy has a lot of nonmarket production and consumption, GNP may understate its rate of real output. In the Canadian economy, as we noted above, the unpaid services of housewives are probably the best example of this point. If a housekeeper is paid to do the dusting, the dusting is counted as a productive service in GNP. If someone within the family does the dusting and if no money is paid formally for performing this service, it is not counted in GNP. But more is involved than just the value of dusting. To the extent that do-it-yourself furniture gets made, fences get built, lawns get mowed, houses get painted, and so on—with no money paid to hired hands in the marketplace—GNP understates the actual rate of economic activity.

The exclusion of nonmarket transactions is a less serious consideration in a highly specialized, interdependent, urban economy like ours than it is for less specialized, more self-sufficient, largely rural economies. It is important to keep this point in mind, therefore, when making GNP comparisons between countries.

In addition to problems with nonmarket production, the GNP concept places no value on leisure or free time. If two countries both had the same real GNP per capita, but one nation had an average work week of 60 hours while the second had an average work week of only 30 hours, most people would say the second nation was clearly better off. In Canada, the average work week has been cut in half over the past century or so, and vacations have been lengthened. No accurate measure of such gains in leisure time can be included in our GNP estimates, but we should be aware of this point in noting the increase in real GNP per capita over time.

Despite the qualifications and refinements we have made in the basic GNP concept, however, the fundamental point remains—GNP data provide an excellent measure of total economic performance. If used with care, these data give us many valuable insights into the workings of our economic system. And their usefulness can often be enhanced even further if we subdivide GNP into certain subcomponents that illustrate and measure the basic circular flow of our economic system.

SOME KEY COMPONENTS OF GNP

On the money spent (flow of product) side of GNP we have seen that the major components are consumer spending, private investment, and government spending on goods and services. On the money received side, however, economists have found it useful to combine and refine some of the categories discussed in the last chapter into three basic subcomponents. These subcomponents, for which Statistics Canada publishes separate figures on an annual basis, are: *net national income, personal income,* and *disposable personal income.*

Net National income can be defined as GNP *minus* depreciation allowances and indirect taxes.

Personal income can be defined in two ways. One definition is: National income *minus* the sum of social insurance taxes, corporate income taxes, and undistributed corporate profits, *plus* transfer payments. Another definition of personal income is: The sum of compensation of employees, rents, interest, unincorporated income, and dividends, *plus* transfer payments (including interest paid by government), *minus* social insurance taxes. Either definition gives the same total, if the proper adjustments are made.

Disposable personal income is simply personal income *minus* personal income taxes.

Table 23-3 outlines the relationship between these major components and total GNP, but does not use actual data.[2]

The flow of spending, output, and income are thus interrelated in the GNP measurement of our market economy. Indeed, some economists find it useful to use a diagram such as Figure 23-2 to illustrate how the money spent for GNP flows into income and how this income flows *back* into GNP.[3]

Table 23-3. GNP AND SOME KEY COMPONENTS[2]

GROSS NATIONAL PRODUCT
  Less: Depreciation
  Less: Indirect Taxes
Equals: NATIONAL INCOME
  Less: Social Insurance Taxes
  Less: Corporate Income Taxes and Undistributed Corporate Profits
  Plus: Transfer receipts
Equals: PERSONAL INCOME
  Less: Personal Income Taxes
Equals: DISPOSABLE PERSONAL INCOME
  Less: Personal Consumption
Equals: PERSONAL SAVING

[2] Condensation of data into the basic elements is a task which makes the result difficult to reconcile with the original data. For a challenging experience, using Stat Can #13-001, try to work this table out. It will be a difficult task.

[3] Net exports, which were discussed in the last chapter and which constitute a small part of GNP, are not shown as a separate item in Figure 23-2.

FIG. 23-2. THE CIRCULAR FLOW OF INCOME

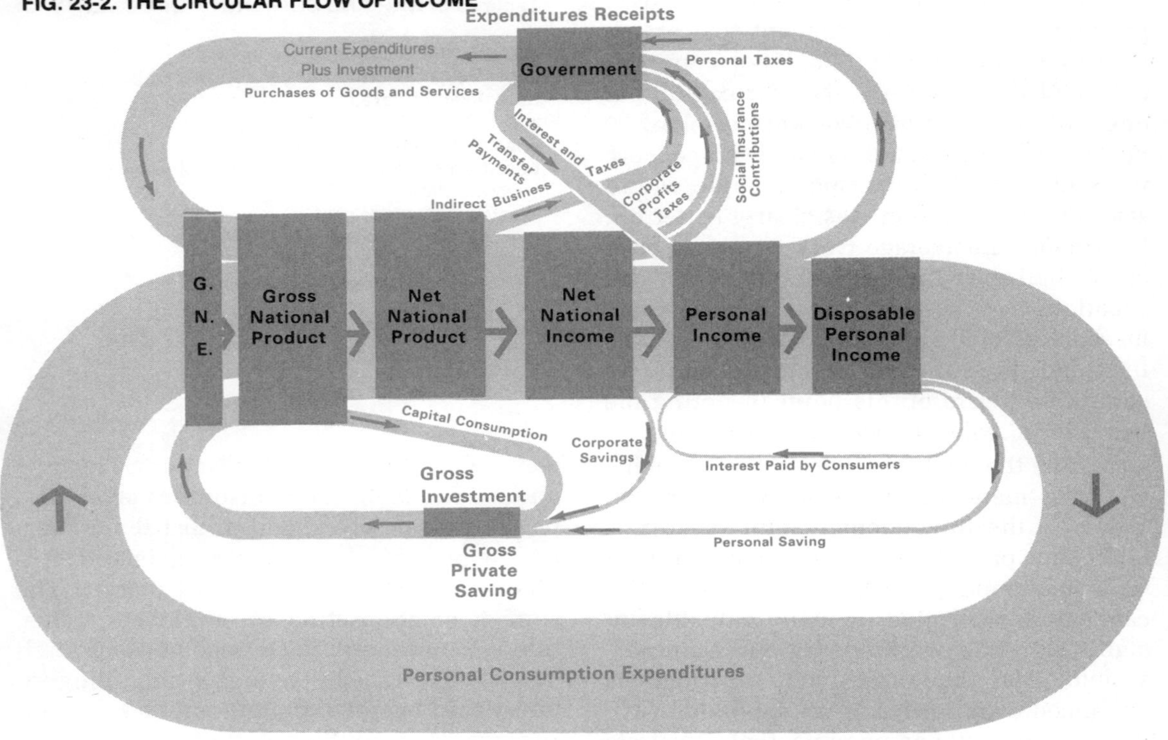

THE CIRCULAR FLOW OF GNP

At first glance, Figure 23-2 may appear to be a "plumber's nightmare," but let's try to summarize our measurements of total economic activity by following the flow in Figure 23-2, stage by stage.

1. Start with the major spending components—government spending on goods and services, consumer spending, and private investment. The outflow of funds for the purchase of goods and services by all these groups equals GNP.

2. Two streams of money are then diverted from the initial flow of spending on goods and services. One of these is depreciation charges and other allowances for the wearing out of capital goods; these depreciation allowances flow back to private investment. The other diversion consists of indirect business taxes which add to the cost of the goods consumed, but which immediately flow back to government. When these deductions have been made for depreciation and indirect business taxes, all the money that flows on becomes the net national income.

3. Net national income goes to businesses in the form of corporate profits and unincorporated income, and to individuals in the form of employee compensation, rent, interest, and dividends. Government transfer payments also enter the flow at this stage. Transfer payments increase peoples' incomes, but they do not represent payments for final goods or services. Therefore they are shown bypassing the GNP and national income meters.

4. Before we can add up personal income, however, we must remember that part of the compensation of employees goes straight to the government in the form of social insurance taxes. And business corporations pay taxes on their profits to government. Corporations also retain part of their earnings as undistributed profits, which flow back to private investment.

Only after these payments have been made does the rest of the income stream flow on to the public, which has sold business the use

FIG. 23-3. THE CIRCULAR FLOW OF INCOME — ANOTHER PRESENTATION

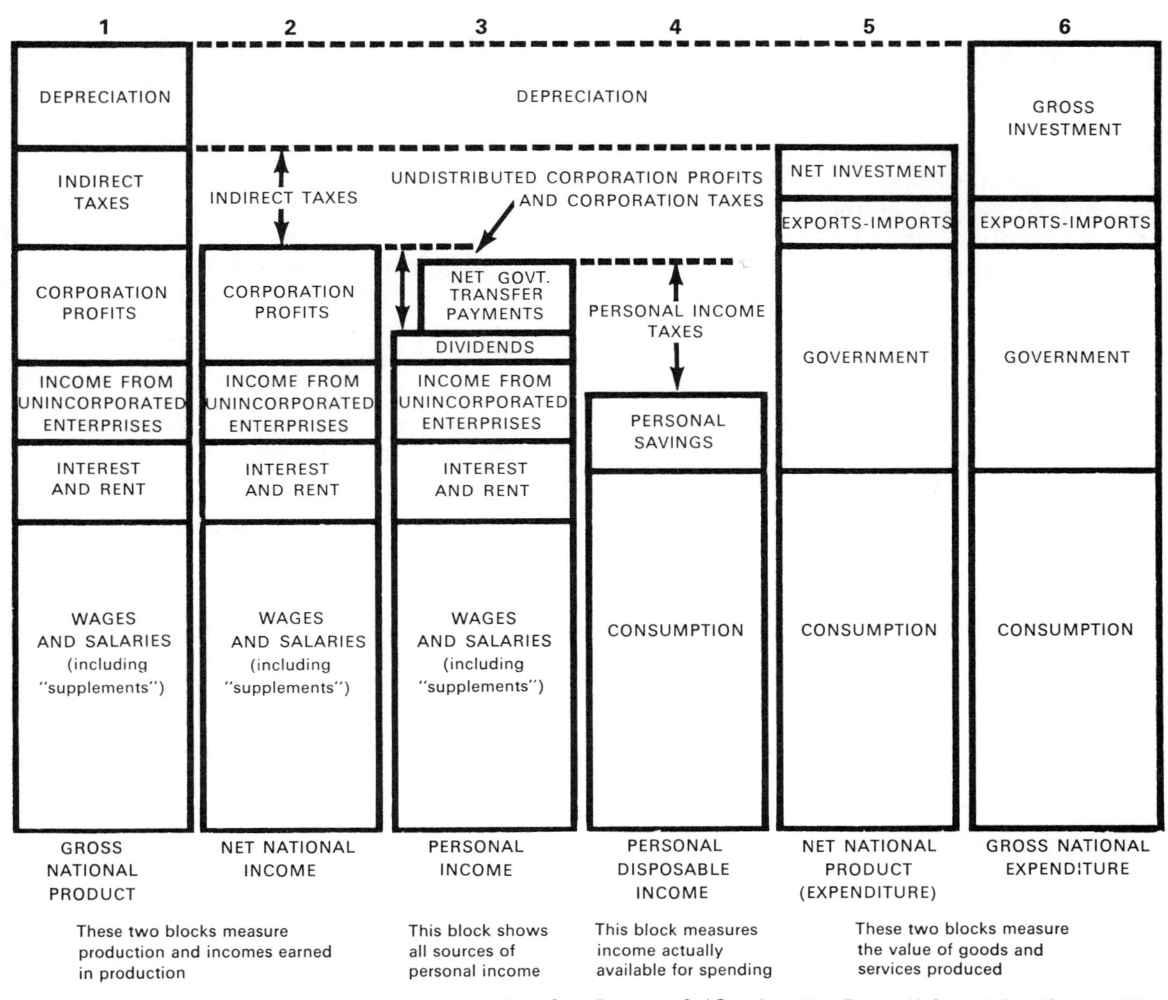

Paul A. Samuelson and Anthony Scott, *Economics*, 2nd Canadian edition, Toronto: McGraw-Hill Co. of Canada, 1968.

of its management and labor services, capital, and natural resources, and to individuals who have conducted professions, unincorporated small businesses, and farms. This part of the flow now represents personal income.

5. After paying part of its personal income to the government in the form of personal taxes, the public divides its disposable personal income into two parts: one part goes into personal savings and helps finance private investment; and the second part, by far the biggest, is used to pay for consumer goods and services. Private investors put their money into capital goods, housing, and inventories. And government buys more goods and services.

Thus, the circular flow of GNP and national income goes on and on, with its total rate sometimes rising, sometimes falling.

We have now finished our task of showing how to measure total economic performance. Now we must turn to the next task of *explaining* changes in total economic performance. Why is it that the circular flow of spending, output, and income sometimes spins at a rapid rate and sometimes slows down? Explaining the rate of total economic performance will be the task of the next chapter.

■ SUMMARY

In using money GNP figures to measure an economy's total rate of performance, one must be careful to consider price changes and changes in population and to remember that some things such as nonmarket transactions and leisure time are not included in GNP.

This chapter has shown how a price index can be used to convert GNP data from current prices to constant prices in terms of a given base year. If constant price data are then divided by population data, the resulting figures for real GNP per capita represent the best single measure of changes in economic performance and living standards currently available.

In order to analyse total economic performance, it is helpful to trace the relations between the major spending components of GNP and the major income components. Figure 23-2 showed how money expenditures by government, business, and consumers became income payments in the form of wages and salaries, rents, interest, dividends, profits, and transfer payments. The flow of these payments, which compensate productive elements in the economy for their contributions, can be measured to record changes in the level of GNP, national income, personal income, and disposable personal income.[4]

[4] Figure 23-3 presents the same basic structures as 23-2, except that details of composition of GNP, NNI, etc. are shown.

KEY CONCEPTS

real GNP
nominal GNP
disposable personal income
current prices
constant prices
national income
personal income

QUESTIONS FOR REVIEW AND DISCUSSION

1. Is GNP a good index of a nation's standard of living? Why? What are some of the refinements in the GNP concept that can improve its usefulness as an index of a nation's standard of living?
2. How can a price index be used to convert nominal GNP in current prices into real GNP in constant prices? Why is such a conversion useful?
3. Explain the concept of *real* GNP *per capita.* How is it obtained?
4. What types of economic transactions are *not* counted in a nation's GNP accounts? Why are these omissions important in comparing GNP figures between countries?
5. What are the differences between the concepts of gross national product, national income, personal income, and disposable personal income? Which concept would be most useful if you were:
   (a) an economist trying to estimate the total output of a nation's economy?
   (b) a tax collector trying to estimate future government revenues?
   (c) a buyer for a large department store trying to decide how many dresses might be sold this spring?

PROBLEMS AND EXERCISES TO SHARPEN YOUR UNDERSTANDING

1. Use the data at the end of Chapter 22 and your understanding from this Chapter to determine the national income of the economy shown. Cross-check your answer. Adding the following data, also determine the personal income and the disposable personal income for this economy.

social insurance taxes	8
transfer receipts	14
personal income taxes	20

2. Use the same sources you used at the end of Chapter 22 to determine recent figures for national income, personal income, and disposable personal income in the Canadian economy.

CHAPTER 24

EXPLAINING TOTAL ECONOMIC PERFORMANCE

■ THE RELATIONSHIP BETWEEN SPENDING, OUTPUT, AND INCOME ■ THE CONCEPT OF EQUILIBRIUM FOR THE ECONOMY AS A WHOLE ■ TOTAL INCOME ■ TOTAL DEMAND ■ POTENTIAL OUTPUT ■ SUMMARY

To explain the performance of the national economy, we must analyse total spending, total output, and total income. In Chapter 22 we have noted that total output could be measured by (1) adding up all the expenditures on final goods and services of consumers, businesses, and government or (2) adding up all income received by those responsible for producing the same goods and services. In this chapter we shall take a more detailed look at the actual data on spending, output, and income of the economy during the years 1962-1977.

■ THE RELATIONSHIP BETWEEN SPENDING, OUTPUT, AND INCOME

The data on total spending from 1962 to 1977 are presented in Table 24-1A. This shows how the outlays of consumers, businesses, government, and the trade sector varied from year to year in buying the national output. All of the amounts in Table 24-1A are in billions of dollars at constant prices; separate price deflators have been used to express each of the components of total spending in terms of 1971 prices.

For each year shown in these tables, total spending equals total output, which also equals total income, as we have defined these terms. On first sight, the statement that spending equals output equals income may not impress you as being particularly significant; it may seem like a mere definition.

Yet this statement contains a concept that is crucial to any comprehension of the functioning of the total economic system—the concept that *spending is constantly being transformed into output, and output into income, and income into spending, and so on.* This is the concept of the *circular flow* of spending, production, and income in a national economic system. If one wished to dramatize this concept, one might say that it is, in a sense, the economic equivalent of Einstein's famous formula, $E = MC^2$, which describes the transformations between energy and matter in physics.

Like Einstein's physics equation, the economic equation is much more than a truism that simply asserts that spending, output, and income are really the same thing looked at in different ways. Rather, the equation implies a *functional relationship* in which spending, output, and income are *interdependent*—that is, changes in spending *cause* changes in output, and changes in output *cause* changes in income, and changes in income *cause* changes in spending.

The truth of this statement should be visible to anyone. If you go to a large industrial center and notice that all the chimneys of the mills and factories are smoking, that masses of workers come out of the plant gates when shifts change, that the factories are working overtime, and that trains of freight cars hauling goods away are very long and full, you can be quite sure that the restaurants and

Table 24-1. (Part A): GROSS NATIONAL EXPENDITURE IN CONSTANT (1971) DOLLARS —1962-1977

Years	Personal Expend-iture on Consumer Goods and Services	Govern-ment Current Expen-diture on Goods and Services	Gross Fixed Capital Formation		Inventory Changes[1]	Exports of Goods and Services	Imports of Goods and Services	Residual Error of Esti-mate	Gross National Expen-diture in Constant (1971) Dollars
			Government	Business					
	(billions of dollars)								
1962	35.272	10.911	2.664	9.625	.745	9.744	−10.769	+.283	58.475
1963	36.992	11.070	2.682	10.167	.756	10.631	−11.125	+.314	61.487
1964	39.218	11.637	2.652	11.898	.654	12.058	−12.595	+.088	65.610
1965	41.606	12.253	3.003	13.261	1.436	12.606	−14.140	−.044	69.981
1966	43.778	13.388	3.307	14.716	1.377	14.315	−15.989	−.048	74.844
1967	45.863	14.343	3.403	14.543	.249	15.770	−16.805	−.022	77.344
1968	48.138	15.429	3.430	14.537	.768	17.727	−18.284	+.119	81.864
1969	50.353	15.993	3.350	15.501	1.517	19.462	−20.727	+.776	86.225
1970	51.526	17.650	3.329	15.581	.078	21.223	−20.588	−.409	88.390
1971	55.616	18.368	3.754	17.046	.392	22.181	−22.016	−.891	94.450
1972	59.841	18.930	3.772	18.183	.515	23.655	−24.489	−.159	100.248
1973	63.879	19.795	3.751	20.633	1.346	26.156	−27.824	+.076	107.812
1974	67.375	20.656	3.957	21.775	2.334	25.570	−30.453	+.570	111.766
1975	70.784	21.571	4.131	22.613	−.526	23.930	−29.707	+.159	112.955
1976	75.105	21.757	3.899	23.050	1.257	26.060	−32.132	−.512	118.484
1977	77.186	22.225	4.023	22.777	−.064	28.067	−32.760	+.112	121.566

Source: Statistics Canada, *National Income and Expenditure Accounts, 1962-1976,* cat. 13-201; and *National Income and Expenditure Accounts, Fourth Quarter, 1977,* cat. 13-001.

Table 24.1 (Part B): PERCENT DISTRIBUTION OF GROSS NATIONAL EXPENDITURE IN CONSTANT (1971) DOLLARS BY COMPONENTS—1962-1977

Years and Quarters	Personal Expend-diture on Consumer Goods and Services	Govern-ment Current Expendi-ture on Goods and Services	Gross Fixed Capital Formation		Inventory[1] Changes	Exports of Goods and Services	Imports of Goods and Services	Residual Error of Esti-mate	Gross National Expendi-ture
			Government	Business					
1962	60.3	18.7	4.6	16.4	1.3	16.7	−18.2	+0.2	100.0
1963	60.2	18.0	4.4	16.5	1.2	17.3	−17.8	+0.2	100.0
1964	59.8	17.7	4.0	18.2	1.0	18.4	−19.1	—	100.0
1965	59.5	17.5	4.3	19.0	2.1	18.0	−20.4	—	100.0
1966	58.5	17.9	4.4	19.6	1.9	19.1	−21.4	—	100.0
1967	59.3	18.5	4.4	18.8	0.3	20.4	−21.7	—	100.0
1968	58.8	18.8	4.2	17.7	0.9	21.7	−22.2	+0.1	100.0
1969	58.4	18.5	3.9	17.9	1.8	22.6	−24.0	+0.9	100.0
1970	58.3	20.0	3.8	17.6	—	24.0	−23.3	−0.4	100.0
1971	58.9	19.4	3.9	18.0	0.4	23.5	−23.2	−0.9	100.0
1972	59.7	18.9	3.7	18.2	0.5	23.6	−24.5	−0.1	100.0
1973	59.3	18.4	3.6	19.1	1.1	24.3	−25.8	—	100.0
1974	60.3	18.5	3.6	19.5	1.9	22.9	−27.2	+0.5	100.0
1975	62.7	19.1	3.7	20.0	−0.4	21.2	−26.4	+0.2	100.0
1976	63.4	18.4	3.3	19.5	1.1	22.0	−27.3	−0.4	100.0
1977	63.5	18.3	3.3	18.7	—	23.1	−27.0	+0.1	100.0

Source: Calculated from Table 24-1A.

Note: [1]Inventory changes are primarily in the private sector. The figure however consolidates both private and government inventory accounts. The first two investment figures exclude the category of inventory changes.

movies and stores in that region will be crowded with people spending money; that families, getting bigger paychecks, will not only be putting money into more goods and services but also will be paying more taxes and putting more money into savings—savings which can be used by businessmen to buy more capital goods.

On the other hand, if when you look around an industrial center you notice that many chimneys are smokeless, that many plants are idle, that few workers are coming off the shifts, that the trains of freight are short, you can be quite sure that, with output down, the income of the industrial center will have fallen—and that the restaurants and movies and stores will be less crowded, that tax payments will be lower, that savings accounts will be dwindling at the banks, that sales of new cars and new houses and many other goods will be down. Less output means less income, and less income means less spending.

What is true for a large industrial area generally holds for the national economy as a whole. It does *not* hold for a *single* producer or industry. A shoe manufacturing firm which produces more shoes will not necessarily sell more shoes; it may have miscalculated the market. The income its own workers receive will not be spent primarily on the shoes made. But, for the economy as a whole, output, income, and spending affect each other and rise and fall together.

The relation between output and income in the total economy is *reciprocal*. The more goods produced, the more income paid out; and the more income paid out, the more goods demanded and produced. Conversely, the less that is produced, the less income is paid out; and the lower the income and spending, the lower the output. These relationships can be called the *induced* aspects of total economic performance.

But changes in spending, output, and income may also be due to *autonomous* forces that affect the economy independently. Such autonomous forces include wars, sharp changes in the international economic situation, the discovery of new inventions or production techniques, changes in population or numbers of people entering the labor force, changes in the public's confidence or businessmen's expectations about the future, changes in tax laws or government spending and floods, storms, or other natural disturbances.

THE CONCEPT OF EQUILIBRIUM FOR THE ECONOMY AS A WHOLE

In our discussion of supply and demand in Unit 2 of this book, we introduced you to the idea of **equilibrium**— a balance that occurred between supply and demand when the market price was established. At that price, there was no desire on the part of sellers to offer more units, nor any desire on the part of buyers to purchase more units. Thus, the market was for the time being at rest, with no tendency to change. Some new factor—such as a bumper crop of a farm product which greatly increased the supply—might disturb this equilibrium and cause price to fall until the microeconomic system (that is, the market for that farm product) was again in equilibrium.

One can conceive of the national economic system (the macroeconomy) as also constantly going through a process of adjustment in order to achieve a state of equilibrium, with no tendency toward further change. For instance, if government increases its spending, this will cause production to increase and income payments to rise, until the macroeconomic system is in a new state of balance. Or, if businesses become greatly apprehensive about the future and reduce their expenditures for new plants and equipment, they will cause the output of capital goods to fall and less income to reach those who would have produced those capital goods—and those others to whom the capital-goods producers would have paid

THE CIRCULAR FLOW OF SPENDING, PRODUCTION, AND INCOME

Lynn Pelham from Rapho-Guillumette

George W. Martin from DPI

In our complex economy, money flows round and round, and output is constantly transformed into income—then back again into output. Thus . . .

1. When everyone is working, as this parking lot near a big industrial plant shows, . . .
2. Then everyone has more wages to spend . . .
3. And the goods keep pouring forth to meet their demands.

Hays from Monkmeyer

Grant White from Monkmeyer

Table 24-2: GNP, PERSONAL INCOME, AND EXPENDITURE, 1962-1977

	GNP	Personal Income	Personal Disposable Income	Personal Expenditure	Personal Saving
			In billions of current dollars		
1962	42.927	32.788	29.340	27.452	1.647
1963	45.978	34.829	31.168	29.225	1.691
1964	50.280	37.282	33.049	31.389	1.383
1965	55.364	41.071	36.263	33.947	2.001
1966	61.828	46.094	39.901	36.890	2.662
1967	66.409	50.579	43.123	39.972	2.736
1968	72.586	55.677	46.820	43.704	2.639
1969	79.815	61.804	50.911	47.492	2.730
1970	85.685	66.633	54.009	50.327	2.872
1971	94.450	74.092	59.943	55.616	3.509
1972	105.234	83.767	68.100	62.208	5.015
1973	123.560	97.832	79.719	71.278	7.230
1974	147.175	117.055	94.731	83.441	9.568
1975	165.445	136.345	111.134	97.016	12.246
1976	190.027	155.795	126.029	110.543	13.398
1977	207.714	171.485	139.265	121.955	14.928

Sources: Statistics Canada, *National Income and Expenditure Accounts, 1962-76,* cat. 13-201; *National Income and Expenditure Accounts, 4th Quarter, 1977,* cat. 13-001.

Note: all data in this table are in current, not constant (1971) dollars.

their income for other goods and services—until the macro-system is again in equilibrium at a lower level.

Of course, the national economy is never really at rest; events will always be occurring that cause it to make new adjustments. However, for purposes of analysis, we may conceive of total spending, total output, and total income as temporarily achieving a state of equilibrium, with no tendency to change, *at various rates of economic activity.* Spending, output, and income can be in equilibrium at high rates of economic activity, with all (or almost all) of a nation's productive resources fully employed. Or they can be in equilibrium at low rates of economic activity, with many of a nation's scarce resources unemployed, or wasted in forced idleness. And it is possible for the flow of spending, output, and income to be in equilibrium at a rate of economic activity that can be sustained only at the expense of the type of widespread general price increases we call inflation.

Why is this so? Why is our total economy sometimes in equilibrium with large amounts of unemployment? Why is it sometimes in equilibrium with prices rising on every front? Why does it seem so difficult to obtain a nice steady equilibrium with both full employment and stable prices *at the same time?* To help answer these questions, this chapter will focus on the basic factors that determine our economy's (1) total income, (2) total demand for goods and services, and (3) total productive capacity.

As we mentioned previously, all of these things are related to each other. But each of them is also related to other (and different) autonomous, independent, or outside factors as well. Separating internal or induced relations from external or autonomous relations is important in explaining total economic equilibrium. We will start with the factors that influence total income. Then we will consider the determinants of total demand and the determinants of total productive capacity, in that order.

TOTAL INCOME

Total income is probably the most passive of our three main factors of total income, total demand, and total productive capacity. Total income depends more on the internal or *induced* relationship between output and income than it does on external or *autonomous* factors that occur regardless of the state of current economic performance. To produce output, factors of production must be hired and paid. The amount paid out as disposable personal income, however, does depend on the amount businesses put aside for depreciation allowances and undistributed corporate profits, on the amount people pay in taxes, and on the amount they receive in transfer payments. Some of these factors are, however, influenced by autonomous forces that are not necessarily related to the current rate of economic performance.

At any given time, depreciation charges are pretty much fixed by the necessity of paying off the costs of existing capital equipment, and tax rates are fixed by political bodies not directly connected with the economic system. Undistributed corporate profits and transfer payments, however, are more sensitive to changes in the rate of economic activity.

Examine data presented in Table 24-2. The consistency of the patterns is quite apparent. Would the figures be closer or further apart if the data were converted to constant 1971 dollars?

Since 1960 DPI has moved in a fairly narrow range of about 64 to 67 percent of GNP; this illustrates our point that increases in the disposable income of our citizens are closely related to increases in real output.

TOTAL DEMAND

We have already seen in Table 24-1A that **total demand** (or total spending) can be divided into the basic components of consumption, investment, and government spending on current goods and services. Each of these components is influenced by different factors, and over time they behave in different ways. Thus, total demand is a mixture whose composition as well as total size is influenced by a variety of internal and external economic factors.

Consumer Spending

Consumer outlays on final goods and services are sometimes affected by external factors such as style changes or the development of new products. The availability and cost of credit from banks and other lending institutions, expectations about future prices, the stock of goods currently available, and the stock of goods and wealth already owned by consumers can also affect consumers' spending habits. But, during recent years, data from the economy clearly indicate that *the single most important influence on the volume of consumption spending has been the amount of disposable personal income being received by consumers.*

Table 24-2 indicates how consumers have divided their real disposable personal income between consumption spending and personal savings over the years from 1962 to 1977.

Since we have already seen that DPI is strongly related to GNP, the fact that consumer spending is strongly related to DPI means that consumer spending has been one of the most predictable components as well as the largest single component of total demand. Since the early 1960s, consumer spending has stayed in a range of about 60 percent of total demand.

Business needs inventories—stocks of goods—on hand, in order to keep the flow of production going and to have goods available to meet consumer demands. Here is a warehouse full of inventories awaiting shipment. When the economy is rising, businesses tend to build up their inventories in order to be prepared to handle bigger orders—and to avoid having to pay higher prices that may seem to lie ahead. But when the economy slumps, orders fall off, and prices soften, businesses try to work down their inventories—by slowing production and filling incoming orders by reducing the level of their inventories. Inventories represent a part of business investment.

Norman Mansfield

Investment Spending

Investment spending on plant, equipment, and inventories seems to jump around more than consumer spending. When we turn to investment spending, there is no single factor that has the same overriding importance that disposable income has in the case of consumption spending. Investment decisions are much more autonomous with respect to current rates of economic activity than are consumption decisions. True, high sales and high profits may induce businesses to invest in more capital goods and more inventory, but since capital goods purchased now will have to be used for some time before they fully pay for themselves and return a profit on the investment, expectations about *future* sales and *future* profits may be more important than current figures.

In addition to confidence and attitudes about the future (which may or may not be

Table 24-3: GROSS PRIVATE BUSINESS INVESTMENT IN CONSTANT (1971) DOLLARS, 1962-1977.

	Investment	Inventory Change	Total	Total as % of GNP
		(Millions of 1971 dollars)		
1962	$ 9625	$ 759	$10 384	17.7%
1963	10 167	782	10 949	17.8%
1964	11 898	721	12 619	19.2%
1965	13 261	1461	14 722	21.1%
1966	14 716	1493	16 209	21.7%
1967	14 543	238	14 781	19.1%
1968	14 537	751	15 288	18.7%
1969	15 501	1519	17 020	19.7%
1970	15 581	103	15 684	17.6%
1971	17 046	432	17 478	18.5%
1972	18 183	500	18 683	18.7%
1973	20 633	1362	21 995	20.2%
1974	21 775	2316	24 091	21.5%
1975	22 613	−542	22 071	19.5%
1976	23 050	1235	24 285	20.5%
1977	22 777	−86	22 691	18.7%

Source: Statistics Canada, *National Income and Expenditure Accounts, 1962-1976,* cat. 13-201; and *National Income and Expenditure Accounts, Fourth Quarter, 1977,* cat. 13-001.

Note: It may be observed that there are some slight deviations between the % totals here and the sum of the business investment % plus the inventory change % figures in Table 24-1 (Part B). This is because the inventory figures here are those solely for the private sector whereas, in the other table, the inventory figures are both private and public sector accounts. (A comparison of the two or the original sources will indicate just how small the inventory factor is within the government sector.)

related to the current rate of economic activity) changes in technology, the invention of new machines or production techniques, the discovery of new natural resources, and other external factors also influence investment decisions. Since much of business investment in real capital goods is financed by borrowing the savings of others, the amount and cost of credit may also have an influence on the rate of investment spending. So, all in all, the rate of investment spending is more variable and unpredictable than the rate of consumption spending.

The data on total private investment spending in Table 24-3 show the levels of total private investment and the percentage of GNP that this represents over a sixteen year period. Take note of the variability in both of these figures over the time period shown. There were even sharper breaks in the rate of investment spending during the Great Depression of the 1930s than in the slowdowns centered around the years 1962 and 1970. In these cases it seems safe to say that autonomous drops in investment spending caused the drops in total economic activity, rather than the other way around.

Government Current Spending

In a democratic society, the amount of government spending is determined by the elected representatives of the people. Sometimes these spending decisions may be related to the current rate of economic activity; but it is probably fair to say that too many government spending decisions have traditionally been dictated by autonomous political forces, rather than by any strong internal economic relationships. Despite the increase in the total amount of government spending in recent years, since 1960, current government spending has remained very close to 20 percent of GNP.[1]

We must now turn our attention to what determines an economy's *total productive capacity*—or, as economists frequently call it, the **potential output** of the national economy. This simply means the total amount of goods and services that could be produced at any given time if the human and material resources of the economy were fully employed.

POTENTIAL OUTPUT

An economy's total productive capacity is set by the quantity and quality of its scarce productive resources. As the quantity or quality of productive resources change over time, the economy's capacity or potential output changes. At any given time, then, the economy's potential output depends on the quantity and quality of its:

1. Human resources—the number, health, strength, education, and skills of its people, including their ability to organize economic activity and get things done;
2. Natural resources—the gifts of nature that are used in producing goods and services;
3. Real capital resources—the plant and equipment needed to make other goods and services;
4. Technology—the technical knowledge of how to combine other resources in a way that facilitates production;
5. The environment for enterprise—the basic social, economic, and political values and other institutions that aid or hinder production.

Both internal and external factors can affect the above determinants of the economy's productive capacity. At first sight, such basic external factors as population change or technological discoveries may appear to be quite independent of internal economic developments. But a closer look would reveal that, as a country is industrialized and grows richer, its birth rate and death rate may change significantly. With rising wealth, birth rates and death rates both may decline—and, depending on the exact rate at which they fall, population may grow either faster or slower. Similarly, a country may, as it grows richer, devote a larger proportion of scarce resources to education and research—and this may lead to a more rapid rate of technological change.

Just because an economy has the extra capacity to produce more, however, does not mean that it actually *will* produce more; actual output may fall far below potential output. In a market economy, there must be enough total demand—spending by consumers, business, and government—to call forth all the output that the economy is capable of producing. If there is not, there will be unemployment, industrial excess capacity, and business stagnation or decline.

On the other side, if total demand is too great—that is, if consumers, business, and government are trying to buy more goods and services than the economy is capable of producing at full employment—then the excess total demand will simply bid up prices, and inflation will take place.

The way to achieve stable economic expansion is to keep the growth of total demand for goods and services in line with the growth of total capacity or potential output. But this is not always easy to do. In Chapter 26, we will focus on this problem of keeping total demand and total supply in balance in order to attain both a high level of employment and stable prices. In the following chapter, we will briefly examine techniques of forecasting future economic trends.

[1] The role of government spending to fit special economic circumstances such as inflation or unemployment will be discussed in Chapter 28.

SUMMARY

The balance or equilibrium of a nation's economy is determined by the internal relationships among total spending, total output, and total income—and by such external forces as wars, the discovery of new resources, technological change, or population increases. The internal economic relationships are affected by these external forces; and the external forces may also be affected by internal economic developments.

The amount of goods and services produced by a national economy at any time, the level of employment, and the stability of prices depend basically on (1) the total demand of consumers, business, and government for goods and services and (2) the productive capacity or potential output of the economy.

If total demand is less than total productive capacity, there will be unemployment and idle resources. If total demand exceeds total capacity, there will be rising prices and inflation. To achieve full employment and stable prices, the makers of economic policy have the difficult job of trying to bring different forces into balance at just the right point.

KEY CONCEPTS

equilibrium | total demand | potential output

QUESTIONS FOR REVIEW AND DISCUSSION

1. What is the difference between *induced* and *autonomous* economic forces? Give a specific example of each, and explain why both types of forces are important in explaining total economic performance.
2. Would you say that disposable personal income is largely determined by induced or autonomous forces? What actual evidence can you cite to support your answer?
3. What are the three main components of total demand? Which of the components is closely related to disposable personal income? What actual evidence can you cite to support your answer?
4. Which component of total demand is the most unstable? Explain this instability.
5. What are the main determinants of an economy's total productive capacity or its potential output? Has our actual output always been equal to our potential output? Why or why not?
6. If total demand exceeds total capacity, what is the most likely result? What is the most likely result if total demand is less than total output at the current rate of economic activity?

PROBLEMS AND EXERCISES TO SHARPEN YOUR UNDERSTANDING

1. Use sources of recent data to update the figures in Table 24-1 for personal consumption expenditures, gross fixed capital formation, net exports and government current purchases of goods and services, *all in constant dollars.*
   (a) How have personal consumption expenditures changed as a percentage of GNP since 1977? How do you explain the change or lack of change?
   (b) How have gross investment and net exports changed in terms of 1971 dollars and as a percentage of GNP since 1977? How do you explain this change or lack of change?
   (c) How have government current purchases of goods and services changed in terms of 1971 dollars and as a percentage of GNP since 1977? How do you explain this change or lack of change?
   (d) Which component of total demand has remained most stable since 1977? Which component of total demand has fluctuated the most since 1977? What explanations do you offer for this behavior of these components of total demand?
2. Your teacher may wish to have you move one stage further into macroeconomic analysis of the determination of national income and output—or you may be interested in doing so on your own. At the next level of detailed study is an examination of the relationship between total savings from the income flow and total investment within the expenditure flow. The savings-investment relationship and its impact was a key component of what is, to this point in time, the most influential work in economics in this century. John Maynard Keynes *General Theory,* published in 1936, was a milestone in economic analysis and has had a major impact on the policies of governments among "developed" economies since the 1940s. Your teacher can refer you to more advanced texts dealing with the S-I relationship. Some recommended starting points, looking at it from the personal link to Keynes, are: Silk's *The Economists,* Heilbroner's *The Worldly Philosophers,* or Chapter 16 of Galbraith's *Money,* or Chapter 7 of his *The Age of Uncertainty.* (See bibliography for full information on these titles.) Frequent references to the influence of Keynes will be encountered in Chapters 26-30.

CHAPTER 25

ECONOMIC FORECASTING

■ THE THREE TRICKS OF FORECASTING ■ ECONOMIC INDICATORS ■ SYSTEMATIC FORECASTING ■ BUILDING AN ECONOMETRIC MODEL ■ OTHER ECONOMETRIC MODELS ■ SUMMARY

We noted earlier that one of the reasons for seeking to establish principles and laws in any science is to be able to predict the future course of events. However, we noted that such sciences as economics and meteorology, which deal with open systems (in which outside disturbances cannot be excluded nor wholly understood) are less dependable in their predictions than sciences such as physics or chemistry, which deal with closed systems. The problem of prediction in economics is also increased by the fact that economic data are likely to be less precise than those in the natural sciences.

Nevertheless, economists cannot avoid the task of making predictions (often called forecasts), if they are to be useful to business, government, and the society generally. Every business and government policy maker knows that, like it or not, one must seek to look into the future; every decision made must be based on some explicit or implicit forecast of future conditions. If a business decides to build a new factory, it is because of a judgment that the state of the business in the future will require increased capacity to meet the demand for its products.

This holds for all other business decisions with respect to increasing output, changing prices, building up inventories, borrowing funds, hiring or laying off workers, introducing new products; or government decisions with respect to changing expenditures, tightening credit conditions, building additional public facilities, expanding highway systems, and so on. All such decisions are based on some forecast of future conditions.

All those involved realize only too well that perfect economic forecasting will always be beyond the ability of mortals, since economic events are part of the chance-ridden movement of history. But the advance of economics as a science has strengthened the basis for making forecasts and thereby has at least reduced the risks in making economic decisions and long-range plans. We should, therefore, think of forecasting as the analysis of statistical data and other economic, political, and market information for the purpose of reducing those risks that decision makers cannot avoid.

■ THE THREE TRICKS OF FORECASTING

Just as every stage magician has certain techniques for working miracles, the economist has certain forecasting tricks that can be logically explained to anyone. There are three basic tricks or techniques for economic forecasting; these may be nicknamed (1) loaded deck, (2) oaks-from-acorns, and (3) test-tube.

The Loaded Deck

The loaded-deck technique may look fraudu-

Chas. Addams

Foretelling the future involves the analysis of statistical data and other economic, political, and market information.

lent, but it is extremely important in economic forecasting. If you know how a deck of cards is stacked, then you know how the cards will be dealt (in such a case, the present is really identical with the future, though the future has not yet been revealed to all). In economic forecasting, this technique will not work without fast, accurate reporting. But when these are available the results can be impressive. For instance, advance news of the outcome of the Battle of Waterloo, brought through their own carrier pigeons, gave the Rothschilds their chance to make a fortune on the London Stock Exchange in 1815. Similarly, this technique could be used to predict expenditures on the construction of buildings by a knowledge of the construction contract awards that already had been made.

Oaks from Acorns

This technique is based on the concept that the future is not identical with the present, but is an outgrowth of it. So, if you know how the present is germinating or growing, you can figure out what the future probably will be. Closely related to this idea is the notion that change through time is rhythmic or cyclic—and that, like the life and death cycles of plants and animals, economic activity also has its rises and declines. With this approach, economists seek to predict changes in business conditions by detecting the *symptoms* of a coming change of phase in the economy. Thus, just as a falling barometer may reveal a coming storm, or a rising body temperature a developing illness, falling stock-market prices or other leading economic indicators *may* foreshadow a coming decline in general business activity.

The Test Tube

This technique stems from the idea that, although changes in the real world may seem confusing and chaotic, scientific analysis can reveal certain underlying regularities. The way to find these regularities (or laws, principles, or theories) is to black out much of reality and hold only to the abstractions. Though the theories that result will be unreal, in the sense of being too simple, they will still possess the power to explain and hence predict real-world events—provided that they are valid theories. To be sure, as we have said before, economic theories or laws generally lack the consistency of those in the physical sciences. Nevertheless, economic relations or theories, derived from a study of the past, may be useful tools for prediction within some acceptable range of probable error.

All scientific or rational economic forecasting depends on one or another combination of the above three techniques. Even those who make forecasting an art and cloak it in mysticism probably depend on them, too—even if somewhat unconsciously. A businessperson who feels that business in his city is going to get worse because it is expected on good authority that the government is closing a big defense base there is really using a loaded-deck technique. A manager who "intuits" that business is going to improve because of news that the companies in the area are filling up their order books and starting to raise their prices is really using an oaks-from-acorns technique. And a manager who expects the economy to decline because of news that money is getting much harder to borrow and interest rates are rising is really using a test-tube approach—that is, implicitly accepting the theory that changes in the cost and availability of money will affect, with a lag, the general state of the economy.

Thus, there is little philosophical difference between the way the businessperson or the consumer goes about trying to foresee economic conditions and the way the economist does it. However, the economist tries to do forecasting more systematically and thoroughly, not basing the forecast on one or two pieces of information or hunches, but rather on as much relevant information as can be assimilated. The economist also tries to integrate this information in a way that is consistent with past performances and that may, therefore, have a good chance of holding true for the future.

Economic forecasters aim at being first-class reporters. They put the loaded-deck technique to work by trying to gather and analyse as much accurate information as they can, as fast as they can. Sometimes, this information gathering is done by broad surveys—for instance, surveys of businesses' intentions to invest in new plant and equipment. Sometimes, it is done by consulting official government statistics as soon as they appear or by maintaining close contact with other economists, to have a sense of what the official statistics will show even before they are published. Information gathering also requires the economist to get around—to meet with businesspeople, bankers, government officials, as well as with their colleagues in the forecasting business. A forecast has a better chance of succeeding if it is based on a firm and detailed knowledge of the present.

ECONOMIC INDICATORS

For many years, economic analysts have searched for a single indicator or set of indicators that would always predict general business developments. Some thought they had found such indicators in stock market prices, interest rates, iron production, railroad car-loadings, or business failures. Debate over which of the many possible indicators are really sufficiently dependable for forecasting purposes still continues.

The National Bureau of Economic Research, a private nonprofit center of economic studies in the United States, has been conducting statistical analyses of business cycles for more than three decades and has done an exhaustive job of screening time series with forecasting value for the USA. Before World War II, two leading National Bureau economists, Wesley C. Mitchell and Arthur F. Burns,[1] after analysing approximately 500 monthly or quarterly series, selected 70 which regularly traced the business cycle, of which 21 indicators were judged to be the most trustworthy. After the war, it seemed advisable for the National Bureau to screen all the series again, both because later information was available and because political and economic changes might have made the Mitchell-Burns studies obsolete. The task of updating the Bureau's indi-

[1] Burns was appointed Chairman of The Federal Reserve Board, The U.S. Central Bank, in 1970 and held that post for seven years.

cators was undertaken by Geoffrey H. Moore.

Moore again found that it was possible to select a series of indicators which typically turned up or turned down in advance of turning points in general business activity; these were called **leading indicators**. There were also indicators that turned up or down roughly at the same time as general turns in business activity; these were called **coincident indicators**. And, finally, there was again found to be a set of indicators whose upturns or downturns typically followed after upturns or downturns in general business; these were called **lagging indicators**.

In the group of leading indicators, the National Bureau put 12 series; the average work week in manufacturing, the gross accession rate (that is, the number of workers added to employment rolls) in manufacturing, the layoff rate in manufacturing, new orders for durable goods, the number of new housing units started, contracts for industrial and commercial building, the net change in the number of operating businesses, the liabilities of business failures, corporate profits after taxes, the common stock price index, changes in business inventories, and the price index of industrial raw materials.

In the category of coincident indicators, the National Bureau included 9 series: employment in nonagricultural businesses, the unemployment rate, the industrial production index, the GNP in current dollars, the GNP in constant dollars, bank debits outside of New York City, personal income, sales by retail stores, and the wholesale price index, excluding farm products and foods.

In the lagging group, the National Bureau put 5 series: plant and equipment expenditures by business, the wage and salary cost per unit of output in manufacturing, the value of manufacturers' inventories, consumer installment debt, and bank interest rates on business loans.

When an upturn in general economic activity is approaching, the leading indicators should typically turn up. But the leading indicators sometimes give off false signals. Therefore, National Bureau economists warn that, even if the leading indicators show a turn, one cannot be sure of it until this is confirmed by a rise in the coincident indicators; and this will be further reinforced by a rise in the lagging indicators.

To be sure, this makes the leading indicators somewhat unreliable forecasting tools. The chief trouble with them is that they are extremely sensitive. They oscillate a great deal from month to month, and it is therefore hard to know, when making a forecast, whether an up or downturn in one of the leading series is genuine and serious or only a temporary wiggle.

This is why it is necessary for economists to look not at one but at many leading indicators and to seek to evaluate the underlying factors that are causing any of the indicators to move up or down.

Comparable indicators have proved to be generally reliable for Canada as well, and frequent reference can be found in all discussions and comments on our economy.[2]

SYSTEMATIC FORECASTING

To go beyond the simple observation of economic indicators, economists seek to discover enduring *relationships* among economic factors and to apply these to situations in the past, present, or future. An-

[2] Detailed reference has been given to the original NBER indicators because they represent the pioneer work in this field, work which has been extended in the U.S., Canada, and elsewhere. The NBER presently identifies 36 leading, 25 coincident, and 11 lagging indicators. The major ones, along with much other current U.S. data, may be found in the U.S. Department of Commerce's monthly *Survey of Current Business*. Canada does not use any single set or source of indicators which are regarded as "standard", as the NBER indexes are in the U.S. A number of different sources, many of which plot some of the same indicators, issue indexes in Canada. See Problem 1 for readily available sources.

alysing the general business picture and making quantitative estimates of what conditions may be like a year or more ahead requires all the theoretical training, knowledge of statistical and institutional facts, technical skill, and political insight that an economist can command.

In dealing with comprehensive forecasting problems, economists today have two tremendous advantages over those who worked a generation or more ago. The first is the advance of macroeconomic theory, which we have discussed in earlier chapters. The greater understanding of how all parts of the economy are interrelated enables the economist to get a better sense of the way changes in government policies, business profits, consumer income, or foreign trade will affect the economy as a whole. The second advantage economists now have is the system of national income and product accounts developed since the early 1930s. These, as explained in Chapters 22 and 23 of this book, give the economist a detailed and comprehensive statistical picture of the national economy.

From macroeconomic theory and national income accounting stem the two most important techniques for systematic economic forecasting.

Chas. Addams

Lost-horse forecasting: Where would you go if you were the gross national product?

Judgmental Forecasts

The first of these techniques is the judgmental approach or, to give its nickname, the *lost horse* technique. That, at any rate, is what it was named by Professor Sidney Alexander, of the Massachusetts Institute of Technology. He took the name from an old joke about how to find a lost horse. You do it by going to where the lost horse was last seen and asking yourself where you would go from there if you were a horse.

When you apply that theory to business forecasting, each component of the GNP (consumption, private domestic investment, government expenditures, and net foreign investment) plays the part of a lost horse. The analyst first finds out where each of these was when last reported. But how the economist answers the question of where each section of GNP is going from there depends on skill, patience, insight, and information.

Competent economists will go deeply behind each component of GNP in preparing their forecasts. They will study government plans and policies, analyse budget estimates, weigh the likelihood of the passage of important legislation, and attempt to estimate the price tags the various bills will bear.

They will look behind private investment at the factors affecting the capital goods industries and study ratios of inventories to sales and of production to capacity. They will look at the factors that affect building construction, such as credit terms, availability of mortgage money, vacancy rates, rents, and price movements. They will measure their analyses against the findings of capital spending surveys and those of authorities in the construction field.

They will try to gauge the effect of government taxing and spending policies on private investment and consumption and estimate the relationship between the growth of investment and consumption. Then they will see how money and credit conditions may affect people's spending or saving. They will study the main categories of durable goods, such as automobiles, appliances, home furnishings and try to get a sense of the market for these goods. They will study trends in population and family formation to try to develop estimates of the consumption of food and other soft goods. And they will measure their estimates against the findings of consumer intention-to-buy surveys.

Economic forecasters must put all of these parts together to make a whole—but they must also carry in their minds an image of how the whole will affect the parts. They will also have to sense how noneconomic factors—such as international relations, military events, and national elections—may affect the economic picture.

Since the task of preparing a forecast of the national economy can be almost endless, the economist must figure out the point at which no further information can be accepted. But, at best, the time available for these analyses is pretty short, since forecasts must be based on the most current information. If one takes too long, facts will grow cold. The best course for the forecaster is to stay at the task continuously, constantly modifying the forecast on the basis of new information.

The only way to judge whether an economist has done a thorough and sensitive forecast is to examine the details of the analysis and reasoning. Of course, a lost horse analysis depends a lot on the economist's subjective judgments about the data available and on a somewhat intuitive perception of relationships. So all of the analysis may not show on paper. The good economist must possess a sureness of judgment essentially like that of the good scientist.

Econometric Forecasting[3]

The more rigorously systematic way of tackling the problem of predicting what will happen to the national economy is to build an **econometric model**. This involves combining economic theory, economic statistics, and mathematics.

An economist starts to build an econometric model by first selecting an economic theory, or set of theories, that can be expected to take into account all the significant factors likely to affect the general business picture or particular industry situation that is being studied.

The next step is to translate the theory or theories into a set of mathematical equations that make up an econometric model. The equations relate the factors to be discovered (the dependent variables) to the factors already known or that can be estimated (the independent variables). These independent variables can be of two types: first, those that are historical facts, such as last year's profits or the current rate of spending on inventories; and, second, future elements, such as government spending, that can be estimated from advance information. All the elements in the econometric model will be interrelated; all the separate equations must be solved simultaneously.

[3] The importance of this field can be noted by the awarding of the first Nobel Prize in Economics in 1969 for pioneer work in Econometrics. The recipients were Dr. Jan Tinbergen of The Netherlands and Dr. Ragnar Frisch of Norway, who pioneered the Econometric approach with joint work in the 1930s.

The economist bases the forecasting model on the past relations between the dependent and independent variables. It must be assumed that relationships which existed in the past will hold for the future.

BUILDING AN ECONOMETRIC MODEL

The way systematic forecasting is done can best be shown if we actually build an econometric model—even a very simple one. The model will be designed to forecast the Canadian economy one year ahead. This is how to do it:

1. Make up a theory of the forecast.
   We might theorize, for instance, that (1) next year's investment will depend on this year's profits; (2) next year's government spending can be projected from this year's spending; and (3) next year's personal consumption will depend on the levels of investment and government spending next year. We also know, by definition, that (4) *gross national product* will equal the sum of *investment, government spending,* and *consumption.*
2. Use symbols for words.
   Let us call next year's private investment, I; this year's profits, P_{-1}; next year's total government spending, G; this year's government spending, G_{-1}; consumption, C; and gross national product, the familiar GNP.
3. Translate the theory of the forecast into mathematical equations, and add some small letters (a, b, c, and d) to represent *constant relationships* which have been found to exist in the past.
   In other words, every statement, (1) to (4), in paragraph 1 above, must be expressed as an equation—as follows:[4]

(1) $I=aP_{-1}$
(2) $G=bG_{-1}$
(3) $C=c\,(G+I)$
(4) $GNP=I+G+C$

This is our forecasting model. The small letters, a, b, c, and d, represent the constant terms, whose values do not change. For instance, since the number of legs on a horse is always four, we can say horses (H) have four legs (L). In the form of an equation this would be: $H=4L$, or more abstractly, $H=aL$, which simply indicates what we said before—the number of legs and the number of horses are always related by some constant term, *a* or 4.

4. Calculate the constants. Look up previous years' statistics on consumption, investment, profits, government spending. From these find values for a, b, and c that reflect the previously existing relationships between factors either in 1977 or from 1976 to 1977.[5]
5. Now we are ready to forecast.
   As of May, 1978, we have just received preliminary data for 1977 and we are forecasting the economy for 1978. So, to solve equation (1), we must look up corporate profits in 1977; these actually totaled $20.6 billion. Now we must find data for total government spending in 1977. The current and investment components totaled $49.8 billion.
6. Put all available figures into your model. (We have put in the constants for you, a=2.200; b=1.102; c=1.352.)

   (1) $I=2.200 \times \$20.6$ billion
   (2) $G=1.102 \times \$49.8$ billion
   (3) $C=1.352 \times (G+I)$
   (4) $GNP=C+I+G$
7. Solve the equations.
   We want values for I, G, C, and GNP. Complete the equations in sequential order, putting the values you get in the

[4] For the sake of simplicity, our model here assumes that I represents only private investment, G includes both government current and investment expenditures, and, finally, the exports and imports will be equal and can be excluded.

[5] These computed are from data in Chapter 22 and comparable data for 1976.

first two into (3) and the values from all three into equation (4).

8. *Establish the results* (see if yours are the same).

For 1978, private investment will be $45.32 billion; government current plus investment spending will total $54.87 billion and consumption will be $135.46 billion. For a total for GNP, our estimate becomes a figure of $235.65 billion market or current dollars.[6] These results are guaranteed—provided that the theories on which they are based are valid, and provided some outside catastrophe does not upset the system.

Of course, the relationship between large economic aggregates, such as consumption, investment, and government spending, will not be completely stable; they will vary to some degree from one year to the next. The question the forecaster must answer is whether the selected relations are stable *enough* to be useful—within some range of probable error—for forecasting purposes.

OTHER ECONOMETRIC MODELS

Econometricians are constantly trying to find better and more stable relations among variables and to develop series of equations that will prove to be reasonably dependable models of the economy. Real models, infinitely more complex than the example we have set forth above, have been developed, involving many dozens of intricate equations. The use of electronic computers has greatly facilitated the solution of these highly complicated econometric models. A number of business corporations and governments are seriously employing econometric models in their forecasting.[7]

Models can also be used for forecasting, not only the economy as a whole, but also the market for specific products. For instance, equations can be worked out to show the demand for wheat, which can be made to depend essentially on the price of wheat—or the demand for milk, which might be taken to depend on (1) the price of milk, (2) the income of consumers, and (3) the average retail price level of all commodities.

Similarly, one might build an econometric model to forecast sales of automobiles that would depend on (1) the income of consumers in excess of basic living costs, (2) the number of households, (3) the number of existing automobiles already owned by consumers, (4) the age of the existing stock of automobiles, (5) prices of cars, and (6) credit conditions, especially the average number of months it takes to pay off an automobile loan. Equations of this type might be worked out, on the basis of historical data, to forecast the demand for refrigerators, washing machines, housing, or other durable goods.

Likewise, many other business forecasting problems—such as future changes in costs, prices, interest rates, inventories, and so on—may be handled by using econometric techniques similar to those mentioned earlier. In every case, the problem is one of selecting factors upon which the element being forecast appears likely to depend, and of then testing the past relationships of factors to produce a formula that will have forecasting value.[8]

[6] Since it is assumed exports-imports = O, a check on this forecast should be made using an adjustment for the foreign trade factor.

[7] Probably the most commonly referred to major econometric model in Canada is known as CANDIDE and constructed and run by the Economic Council of Canada.

[8] As an additional indication of the importance of work in this area, it might be noted that another Nobel Prize was awarded in 1975 for work in this field. The recipient (who shared the 1975 award) was Leonid Kantorovich. The first Soviet citizen to be awarded a Nobel Prize in Economics, Kantorovich is presently head of a mathematical-economics laboratory at the Institute of Economic Management in Moscow.

For further details on the nature of econometrics, see Ira Kominow, "A Noneconomists' Nonmathematical Guide to Econometric Forecasting" reprinted in A. H. MacDonald, (ed.), *Readings in the World of Economics*, Toronto: McGraw-Hill Ryerson, 1973.

SUMMARY

To be useful to policy makers in business or government, whose decisions must be based on some conception of what the future will be, economists have sought to improve the powers of prediction of their science. Inherently, economics, which deals with an open system of events and all the uncertainties of human behavior, cannot be expected to be as dependable in its predictions as such sciences as physics or chemistry, which deal with closed systems. However, economics has proved useful in reducing the risks involved in making decisions, and economic forecasting is increasingly used in business and government.

In this chapter we characterized the basic techniques of forecasting as *loaded deck, oaks from acorns,* and *test tube* approaches. The loaded-deck approach primarily means fast, accurate, and thorough reporting of existing facts which will have some significance for the future. The oaks-from-acorns approach means an effort to discover those symptoms—or leading indicators—which suggest the changes that are occurring in the economy and that can be expected to continue into the future; the leading indicators are especially useful for trying to catch turning points in the business cycle, though they sometimes give false signals. The test-tube or scientific approach to forecasting involves model building, based on economic theory, statistical data, the forecaster's judgment, and mathematical techniques.

In general, forecasting models may be thought of as judgmental or as econometric. The judgmental models give much more scope for the intuitions or guesses of the forecaster; the econometric models involve the setting up of rigorous mathematical equations, with the relationships among variables derived from historical data. Of course, judgmental models also require analysts to use theory and statistics, and econometric models require analysts to use their judgment—especially in the construction of the model and its modification to take account of new developments. Econometric models are useful not only for forecasting the general economy but for predicting the demand for many types of products, prices, costs, interest rates, and other elements important to decision-makers.

We are all aware that any guess about the future is, to some degree, a gamble. But decision-makers try to get the best odds they can in that gamble. Their odds are likely to improve if they act on the basis of full information, detailed knowledge of changes in the economy, and careful analyses of the implications of those changes for the future prospects of individual businesses and the national economy.

KEY CONCEPTS

leading indicators
coincident indicators
lagging indicators
econometric model

QUESTIONS FOR REVIEW AND DISCUSSION

1. What are some of the problems that make predictions difficult in economics? Why are predictions or forecasts nevertheless still necessary?
2. What are the differences between the loaded-deck, oaks-from-acorns, and the test-tube techniques of economic forecasting? Which techniques do you think would most likely be used by each of the following?
   a stock broker
   a company sales manager
   a company purchasing agent
3. In forecasting what will happen to the national economy, how does econometric forecasting differ from judgmental forecasting? Can these methods be combined? Can they ever be separated completely? Explain.
4. Explain how economic forecasting can be used to reduce the risk involved in making certain decisions. Can these risks ever be eliminated completely?

PROBLEMS AND EXERCISES TO SHARPEN YOUR UNDERSTANDING

1. Examine newspapers and magazines for references to various recent indicators for the Canadian economy and its apparent direction.

   The Financial Post is an excellent source of regular references in the "Chartwatch" column and many news articles.

   A frequently quoted index called the "Trendicator," composed of a number of leading indicators, is maintained by the Royal Bank of Canada. Any branch should have up-to-date information about this index and its components.
2. Using data for the two most recent year's GNP/GNE accounts, calculate constants comparable to those used in the illustration of an econometric model in this chapter. From the constants and required data, project the GNP for the next year in the way set out in the illustration. What might improve the reliability of your forecast?

CHAPTER 26

THE GOALS OF TOTAL ECONOMIC PERFORMANCE

■ HIGH-LEVEL EMPLOYMENT ■ THE COMPOSITION OF UNEMPLOYMENT ■ PRICE STABILITY ■ INFLATION AND UNEMPLOYMENT: AN INEVITABLE TRADE-OFF? ■ THE DILEMMA OF STAGFLATION ■ SUMMARY

In Chapter 21, we referred to three fundamental economic goals which have emerged for Canada and other modern, industrial economies: (1) a growing level of output and income, which permits the people of a nation to improve the material conditions of their life; (2) a high level of employment, which enables all those who want to work to find work; and (3) a stable price level, which ensures that the value of one's money or other assets does not change wildly or erratically through no fault of one's own.[1]

In Chapter 31, we shall discuss the goal of economic growth. In this chapter and the four following, we shall consider the other two goals, high employment and price stability.

■ HIGH-LEVEL EMPLOYMENT

Unemployment is obviously a serious problem, not only for those who are vainly seeking jobs, but also for their family dependents and for the society at large. Businesses lose sales when workers have no jobs or incomes with which to pay for goods. And the society loses the goods or services that the unemployed might have produced if they were working. Those who are working and paying taxes will have to help support the unemployed. Unemployment is only one aspect of the total economic waste to the society. When there are unemployed workers, there will usually also be unemployed plants and machinery, and the entire nation will enjoy less output and income than it might otherwise have had.

Unemployment does not mean the disappearance of the basic scarcity of productive resources; rather, it means that the nation is not using its scarce resources in the most productive way. Unemployment is the worst possible way to use scarce resources—because they are producing nothing. The real cost of unemployed resources is the loss of goods and services that these resources would be turning out if they were employed. Since we do not have enough resources to produce all the goods and services we would like in the first place, this is a real cost indeed.

To measure the economic cost of unemployment, then, we must measure the gap between the amount of work actually being done and the amount that would be done if the economy were operating at a high rate. However, we must recognize that **full employment**—in the sense that literally no one is out of a job and the unemployment rate is zero—is not a realistic goal. In an economy such as ours, some workers are always changing their jobs; some people are entering the labor force while others are retiring; some workers or managers are doing a poor job and getting fired; some industries are losing out in the marketplace and having to cut back their work forces; some industries are suffering seasonal slowdowns; and so on. Even when our national economy is very

[1] See Economic Council of Canada, *First Annual Review*, Ottawa: Queen's Printer, 1964, Chapters 1 and 2.

FIG. 26-1. UNEMPLOYMENT RATES AS A PERCENTAGE OF THE CIVILIAN LABOR FORCE, 1926-1978

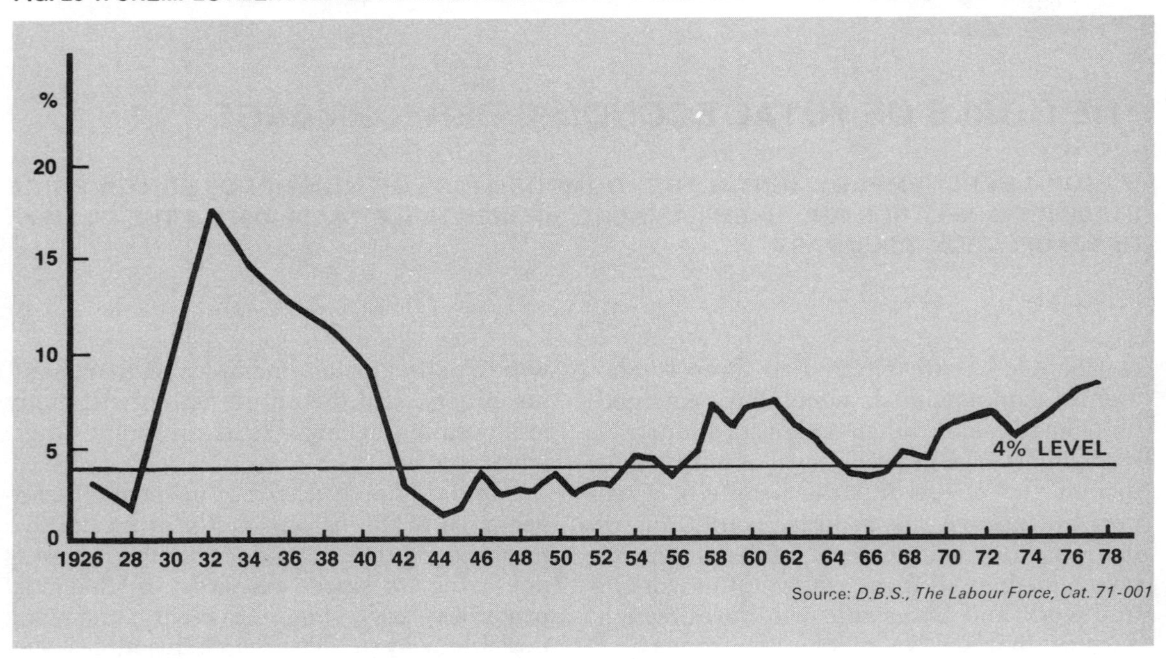

Patterns here show a trend of a rising unemployment rate after the mid 1960s. Along with this fact, however, other related facts should be recognized. The proportion of people in the labor force (the participation rate) was increasing significantly and though unemployment rates were rising, the rate of increase in the number of people working was also quite high when contrasted with either historical trends in Canada or trends in the same time period in other industrial nations. As an entry into this complex area, an excellent starting point would be an Economic Council of Canada study entitled *People and Jobs, A Study of the Canadian Labour Market,* Ottawa: 1976.

Table 26-1. SELECTED UNEMPLOYMENT RATES, MONTH OF FEBRUARY, 1978.

Overall Monthly Unemployment Rate			=	8.3%
Men (All) =	7.5%	Women	=	9.6%
Age 15-24 =	15.5%	Age 15-24	=	13.8%
Age 25+ =	5.0%	Age 25+	=	7.0%

Note: data are preliminary seasonally adjusted estimates.
Source: Statistics Canada, *The Labour Force,* cat. 71-001, February, 1978.

healthy and prosperous, between 3 and 4 percent of the labor force will be normally or unavoidably unemployed.

Even if we take 4 percent unemployment as the goal of our high-employment policy, however, the record shows that we have often fallen far short of reaching this objective. Figure 26-1 shows that the most dramatic failure in this respect took place during the Great Depression of the 1930s. Recently, we have seen unemployment rates rise to a level not experienced since the 1930s.

THE COMPOSITION OF UNEMPLOYMENT

So far we have been talking of employment and unemployment as averages for the entire civilian labor force. Average unemployment rates, however, often conceal differences in unemployment rates among different groups in the labor force. Table 26-1 indicates that the unemployment rates for young people is much higher than the average rate for all workers. Levels vary from one region of Can-

Reprinted by permission of Yardley Jones

"The latest figure? You could try the 17th floor . . ."

Growing levels and rates of unemployment have provoked a lot of bitter humor from Canadian cartoonists in recent years. This one appeared in 1973. If, in 1973, when the average yearly rate was 5.3%, the 17th floor was the "location" of the latest figure, where would the chart have reached by 1977, when the yearly average was over 8%?

ada to another (see Table 31-2). Significant differences are also found if the labor force is divided into groups by industrial category or educational level. Once unemployment rates become high enough to affect a large percentage of any given group within the labor force, it can give rise to serious social problems because large numbers of these groups are shut out from the mainstream of our economic life.

All Around the Merry-Go-Round

A short but not very jolly trip on the economic carrousel with Peter Sadlier-Brown, an economist who believes that our view of unemployment changes because economics changes. Today, he says, Ottawa economists talk about "new"—or voluntary—unemployment, but this concept merely shifts the blame for unemployment from government to employers and workers, as did neo-classical economics. Around and around we go. Hang on tight!

They say the Inuit have eight words for snow because it plays such an important part in their lives. We must have twice as many ways to describe unemployment, descriptions which are constantly changing. Just as Keynesian "cyclical" or "involuntary" unemployment replaced neoclassical "voluntary" unemployment, so later economists identified "structural" unemployment and, more recently, "new" unemployment.

Today economics is still reacting to the shock of the first "limits to growth" revelations. It seems to be struggling to define for itself a new fundamental question, and when it does, another view of unemployment will undoubtedly emerge.

It is too easy to explain this proliferation of shifting definitions entirely as a natural result of changes in the actual causes of the problem. Our view of unemployment changes because economics changes.

Obviously, how much unemployment we have has a lot to do with it too. When unemployment is high it is subjected to microscopic examination by economists. Many new subspecies are discovered, named, and treated. (Sometimes you get the impression that they can't see the snow for the flakes.) Thus, frictional unemployment and structural unemployment always capture more attention during cyclical downturns than they do during booms, when presumably they are the only type of unemployment left.

But a brief look at our changing perceptions of unemployment in this century reveals how powerfully our definitions of unemployment determine our policies for coping with it.

Before the Great Depression, economists of the day considered that *the* question of economics was the optimal allocation of scarce resources among competing ends. Economic theorists were primarily concerned with how prices and market forces solved the allocation question.

Neo-classical economists, as they came to be called, considered the labor market a market just like the others. Their theories told them that the higher the price—in this case the wage—the more labor time workers would be willing to supply. A higher wage also meant that employers would demand a lesser amount of labor time. To rid the world of unemployment, all one had to do was persuade workers to accept lower wages until all of the available labor supply was employed.

Any remaining unemployment was called "frictional." It resulted from a number of short-term imbalances which are a normal part of the functioning of a dynamic economy—for example, individuals moving between jobs.

According to the neo-classicists, improving foresight and information would reduce frictional unemployment. Any unemployment above the frictional level was the result of workers refusing to work for lower wages or being prevented from doing so by legislative, social or institutional barriers. The neo-classical remedy was to remove the barriers or prevent them from being erected in the first place.

In the thirties, Keynes offered an alternative view of unemployment. During the Depression the basic question facing economists could no longer be considered the optimal allocation of scarce resources among competing ends. Massive unemployment and unused capacity shifted the focus of economics to a concern about making use of overabundant resources.

Keynes' argument was that there were circumstances in which the overall level of economic activity would not be high enough to fully employ the available labor supply. His solution was to stimulate the economy to a higher level of activity by using the borrowing and spending powers of government.

This view of unemployment clearly put the onus for doing something about it on governments—a point about which earlier economists had equivocated.

The neo-classical idea of reducing wages to cure unemployment was rejected by Keynes as positively harmful. Lower wages and incomes would result in a lower level of economic activity, just the opposite of what was required to bring about higher levels of employment. In making this point Keynes said: "It is fortunate that workers, though unconsciously, are instinctively more reasonable economists than the classical school, inasmuch as they resist reductions in the money wage."

As the Second World War drew to a close, there was widespread concern that a depression would follow. Almost everyone believed that the combination of integrating returning soldiers into the labor market and transforming a war economy into a peace economy would lead to high unemployment.

The Keynesian approach was accepted by the Government of Canada in a White Paper presented to Parliament in 1945. This paper marked a turning point. The government accepted the responsibility for maintaining a "high and stable" level of employment and endorsed the view that techniques for the government to do something about it were available, if it chose to use them.

But the White Paper did not take responsibility for all unemployment. The paper explained that, while "high and stable" was not really a lower target than full employment, one must be mindful of unemployment resulting from fluctuations in international trade and those associated with the seasons.

No one paid any attention. Action on seasonal unemployment was demanded, and by the fifties winter works programs were under way. Seasonal unemployment is less of a concern now because we have high unemployment throughout the year. It is only slightly higher in winter.

The focus of economics changed again in the period following World War II. Attention began to center on economic growth; the structure of the economy and the barriers to economic growth began to be recognized as major problems.

During the recession of the late fifties, structural unemployment moved to center stage. Subtly, the emphasis began to shift away from the Keynesian concern about the overall level of economic activity. Instead, problems were attributed to the supply side of the labor market and to a mismatch of supply and demand. As far as getting jobs was concerned, workers either lacked the required skills or lived in the wrong places.

Training, re-training and matching workers with jobs through government-run employment services was the prescribed solution. An expanding number of these programs were finally housed under one roof when the Department of Manpower was formed in 1967. It soon became the "glamor" department in the Ottawa bureaucracy.

Another front on the war against structural unemployment was the "special case" of slow growth regions. Tactical weapons in this war were subsidies for direct job creation. In 1969 the various existing programs were brought together and upgraded in the new Department of Regional Economic Expansion, headed by the former Minister of Manpower, Jean Marchand, and run by many of the same bureaucrats. It too had its brief moment in the spotlight.

With the seventies came disillusionment about the growth orientation of post-war economics and serious challenges to the growth hegemony. The world was faced with the prospect of oil and food shortages. People became concerned about the limits to growth. It was a perfect opportunity to return to the comfort of the fundamental question of neo-classical economics: the optimal allocation of scarce resources among competing ends.

In keeping with the times, contemporary classical economists have revived the concept of "voluntary" unemployment. There is, after all, a lot of evidence to support the case for what they call the "new" unemployment. There are job vacancies and people without jobs at the same time. The volunteer army of unemployed is not refusing to accept lower paid jobs, as in the earlier version of the theory; this time, the volunteers are refusing to accept unpleasant, unattractive jobs, or jobs with no career prospects.

Proponents of the "new" unemployment cite two major explanations. First, that a growing number of people are entering the labor force who can afford to be choosy. Since they are young (the children of the baby boom) or "secondary" earners (mainly women) they can afford to wait it out. Second, that a too-generous unemployment insurance program not only draws marginal workers into the labor force but makes being jobless a less painful state than it has been before.

Most available evidence suggests that Ottawa economists still firmly clutch the notion of the "new" unemployment. To the extent that unemployment is of this "new" type, stimulating the economy as Keynes prescribed is considered inappropriate. It will not change the "volunteer's" behavior and it might be inflationary.

Consistent with this view, the solution outlined in the Employment Strategy presented to Cabinet some months ago by Employment and Immigration Minister Bud Cullen called for direct, short-term job creation, subsidized longer-term job creation, and upgraded manpower policies. A downgrading of the unemployment insurance program was evident in the winter P.R. campaign against U.I. cheaters.

Ottawa has taken a step back from the commitment to high and stable levels of employment advocated in the 1945 White Paper. Official statements shift the onus away from government to employers (who are accused of not living up to their responsibilities) and to workers (who are charged with expecting too much). The circle seems complete.

Reprinted with permission from "Perception", The Canadian Council on Social Development, March-April, 1978, pp. 29-31.

PRICE STABILITY

As discussed in Chapter 16, inflation may impose severe hardships on many people and may, if rapid enough, disrupt the whole economic system. As a result, reasonable price stability has become a prime objective. What, however, is reasonable price stability? Is two percent inflation the maximum? Five percent? Ten percent? The answer, unfortunately, is simply that there is no precise answer. Comparison with other countries and against other factors within the economy will determine when, as Chambers' cartoon in Chapter 30 illustrates, the economic policeman may descend to slow down inflationary patterns. An excerpt from an annual report of the Governor of the Bank of Canada which follows spells out more clearly the dangers of inflation and indicates the strong feeling of monetary authorities for the need to maintain price stability.

In the pursuit of the goal, however, many problems exist. Ultimately, prime causes must be found; otherwise, we would be dealing with the symptoms of the disease and

Collins in Montreal Gazette

If the public mood is as this cartoon illustrates, anti-inflationary action by government will of course be almost inevitable. Not guaranteed, however, is complete satisfaction with the cost of the return trip.

not the disease itself. In the pursuit of causes, many conflicting views are heard, all too often with sufficient degrees of validity to make it extremely difficult to know where the truth lies. Art Buchwald's delightful piece of satire has only too many elements of reality in it (for all its exaggeration) for the sake of humor. In Canada, an additional problem is the extent to which we import inflation from the USA through the impact of prices of finished products or components, wage rates, and interest rates, or from other sources such as the great jump in international prices for oil since 1973.

The Dangers of Inflation

This selection, from the 1969 report of the Bank of Canada which appeared early in 1970, indicates the position of the bank regarding the prospective dangers of excessive inflation. At a point in time when these dangers actually exist, what specific policies would the Bank of Canada implement?

The overriding consideration is of course that failure to control inflation could eventually lead to a serious recession and disruption of the economy. Maladjustments and distortions accumulate during a period of inflation which, if neglected, would ultimately produce a severe adjustment from which all would suffer. If, moreover, it ever became clear that inflation would not be controlled by official policies, or even if there were serious doubts about the will of the authorities on this matter, there would be a great multiplication of efforts to protect against inflation, including demands for larger and more frequent income adjustments. The wage and salary settlements in recent years at levels far in excess of the long-term trend of productivity increase must reflect in large part an attempt to compensate for inflation which has occurred and to protect against further inflation which is anticipated. This process could become cumulative and result in severely restrictive policies being needed just to keep the price rise from accelerating.

A second reason is that we simply cannot ignore the inequities of inflation, its serious impact on the poor, the retired, and other elements in the community who because of their weak bargaining position are unable to keep up in the race with rising prices. Even those who manage to maintain their position fairly well on a current basis suffer greatly when the time comes to retire on fixed pensions. The life expectancy of a man retiring at sixty-five is just long enough for him to see the real value of his pension cut in half by an average price rise of 5 percent a year.

Third, inflation militates against economic growth. It introduces an additional element of uncertainty about the future which diverts people's energies and skills away from constructive activities towards trying to outguess the course of the inflation. It rewards economic initiatives on the basis of how well they happen to fit the progress of the inflation rather than on their economic contribution. Such temporary stimulating effects as inflation can have on the level of economic activity depend on its not being expected: if inflation is pushed to the point where it is generally expected and constant efforts are being made to adjust to it, then the stimulating effects are lost.

Fourth, inflation is extremely damaging to capital markets. The less confidence there is in the maintenance of the value of money, the more reluctant investors are to commit their funds for long periods of time. Economic growth cannot fail to be retarded if it becomes extremely difficult to borrow long-term funds for projects that take many years to yield their full return. It is true that some borrowers, notably business corporations, can continue to obtain a portion of the funds they require by giving up equity in some form or other, for example, through convertible debentures. But this is not possible for homeowners or for provincial or municipal governments borrowing to provide social capital, including funds for schools, universities, and hospitals.

Finally, inflation can undermine our international competitive position. It is true that other countries are also having a difficult time in controlling inflation, but we should not assume that they will fail to do so. And if we could make some gains in our competitive position by doing somewhat better than others in controlling inflation, the long-term rewards in the form of increased output and employment, and an improved trade balance would be tangible and worthwhile.

Source: Bank of Canada, *Annual Report of the Governor to the Minister of Finance for the year 1969*, pp. 9-10. Reproduced by permission of the Bank of Canada.

Inflation And The Good Guys

WASHINGTON—Since everyone seems to be interested in what will happen to the economy of the United States in the Seventies, I invited a distinguished panel of the nation's leading businessmen, labor leaders, economists and government forecasters to a meeting in Washington, D.C., to discuss the subject. The meeting was held in the shadow of the White House: In a booth at a Walgreen's Drugstore, to be exact. Here are some excerpts from the discussion:

Elias Endicott of the Banking Institute of Compounded Quarterly Interest was very optimistic—"The challenge of the Seventies will be closely tied to the monetary policies of the government. If Washington gives the banks permission to raise the rates of interest on money borrowed, to a reasonable 18-1/3 per cent, and at the same time permits us to pay no more than 2-1/8 per cent interest on money deposited by our clients, we could send the inflationary spiral into a downtrend by 1975."

Sheldon Carbon, president of the Recall Motor Co., believes the key to the fight against inflation is labor's attitude toward wage increases. "Labor must be responsible and realize that any demands for wage increases will only heat up the economy.

"No one is more sympathetic to the rise of the cost of living of the average worker than management. At the same time, labor is only hurting itself when it makes unreasonable wage demands at a time when everyone should tighten his belt. To show that Recall Motors is serious about wanting to keep inflation from getting out of hand, the Recall board of directors has voted to increase the price of their new 1971 models by only $891.50 which still makes a two-door, four-cylinder 'Recall' at $10,980 one of the best buys in the country."

Rock Sloboda, president of the United Typewriter, Sandstone, Match, and Picture-Framing Federation of Labor, felt that the Seventies would be an opportunity for everyone to show good faith. "We want to keep our demands in the ball park," Sloboda told the panel. "Therefore we will not ask for a three-hour, four-day week, with double time for coffee breaks. We will stick to the same demands we made last year: A four-hour, three-day week with a two-month paid vacation every year. If management agrees to what we believe is the absolute minimum our members will accept, we see no reason for industry to increase its prices in the next 10 years."

Alexander Bell the XII, the telephone company's vice-president in charge of public relations, said the phone company was working on more efficient and cheaper phone service than the American public had ever had before. To provide this cheaper service the phone company was asking for an increase in rates for the early Seventies of only 33-1/3 per cent.

Charles Fairweather, President Nixon's adviser on inflationary trends, said the Administration still felt the solution to inflation was a "full unemployment program."

"Without belaboring the point," he told the panel, "the basic reason for inflation is that people have too much money to spend. If they are not working, the problem of inflation will take care of itself."

While the panel members came to no hard conclusions, they all agreed that the causes of inflation were other irresponsible forces at work in the country, who unlike them did not have the best interests of the United States at heart.

INFLATION AND UNEMPLOYMENT: AN INEVITABLE TRADE-OFF?

In recent years, while the problems of inflation and/or unemployment have been common ingredients of the daily news, much emphasis has been placed on the relationship or **trade-off** which had seemed to exist between the two. What precisely does this mean, and what are the implications for our two economic goals?

Table 26-2 and Figure 26-2 plot the data in Canada from 1960 to 1977. What do the data seem to indicate? The answer is apparently a degree of an inverse relationship between the two. When one considers the forces which promote each, such is not really surprising. The patterns shown in Figure 26-2

Table 26-2. INFLATION AND UNEMPLOYMENT RATES, 1960-1977.

	Yearly Average Percentage	
Year	Unemployment Rate[1]	Inflation Rate[2]
1960	6.7	1.2
1961	6.8	0.9
1962	5.6	1.2
1963	5.3	1.8
1964	4.5	1.8
1965	3.6	2.4
1966	3.4	3.7
1967	3.8	3.6
1968	4.5	4.0
1969	4.4	4.6
1970	5.7	3.3
1971	6.2	2.9
1972	6.2	4.8
1973	5.6	7.6
1974	5.3	10.8
1975	6.9	10.8
1976	7.1	7.5
1977	8.1	8.0

Notes: [1] Statistics Canada altered its survey of the labor force at the beginning of 1976. The data provided here have been revised from the original Statistics Canada data to produce estimates for 1960-75 inclusive, which will be comparable with post-1975 labor force survey data. Estimates for 1960-1965 are those of the authors. Estimates for 1966-1975 have been calculated by Statistics Canada. Official revised estimates for the pre-1966 period may appear in the future. (If you are using any unemployment rate data from before 1966, try to determine if your figures can be directly compared with those for 1966 and later.)

[2] As reflected by the Consumer Price Index's percentage rate of change from year to year.

Sources: Statistics Canada; *The Labour Force,* cat. 71-001; *Historical Labour Force Statistics,* (1977), cat. 71-201; *The Consumer Price Index,* cat. 62-001; *Prices and Price Indexes,* cat. 62-002.

FIG. 26-2. INFLATION AND UNEMPLOYMENT RATES, 1960-1977

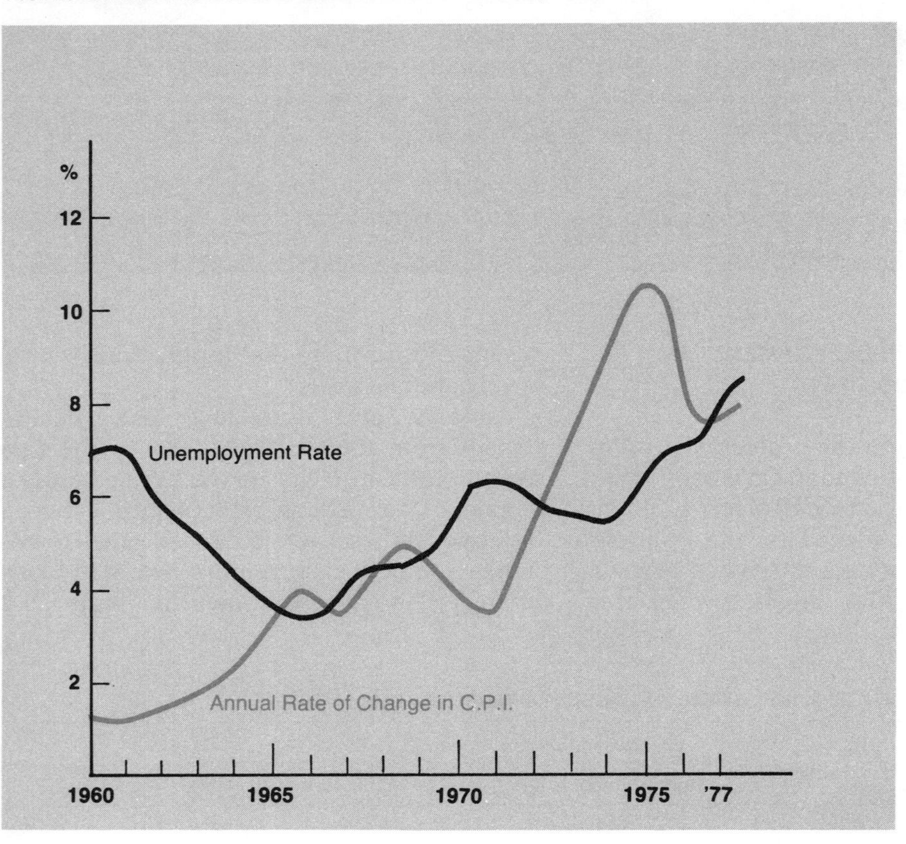

This figure illustrates the data contained in Table 26-2. The patterns here indicate the tendency from 1960-1973 to an inverse relationship between the two trends and how this tendency seems to have been altered since 1973.

are frequently illustrated in (or referred to as) a diagram called a **Phillips Curve**. It is named after Professor A. W. Phillips of The London School of Economics. The relationship, if valid, could be used in measuring the potential cost of any anti-inflationary or anti-unemployment policy by projecting the undesirable impact on the other factor.

Figure 26-3 shows the Phillips Curve approach,[2] though this diagram illustrates a range rather than a specific curve which would be based on the scatter of dots showing the combinations for years, quarters, or months over a fairly long term. An examination of the scatter on a chronological sequence would show shifts back and forth between the inner and outer edges of the range. Recent data (1972-1977) indicate a movement of the curve to the right, a less desirable situation. Why less desirable? Simply because, as you can test with a ruler, a given percentage decline in inflation is accompanied by higher increases (in both absolute and relative terms) in unemployment. Such is one of the fundamental problems for economic policy makers. The Phillips Curve is a simple little diagram, but the concepts in-

[2] As shown by the full title of the original study, which is referred to in problem 2 at the end of the chapter, the original Phillips Curve measured the trade-off between unemployment and rates of wage increases. It has become common to use other valid measures of inflation in place of rates of wage increases, and hence the use of the most widely used Canadian measure, the rate of change in the C.P.I.

Kuch in the Winnipeg Free Press. Reprinted by permission

This cartoon, which appeared in 1971, illustrates perfectly the concept of the "normal" Phillips Curve relationship as we experienced it in Canada through the decade of the 1960s.

FIG. 26-3. THE SHIFT IN THE PHILLIPS CURVE, CANADA, 1960-1977

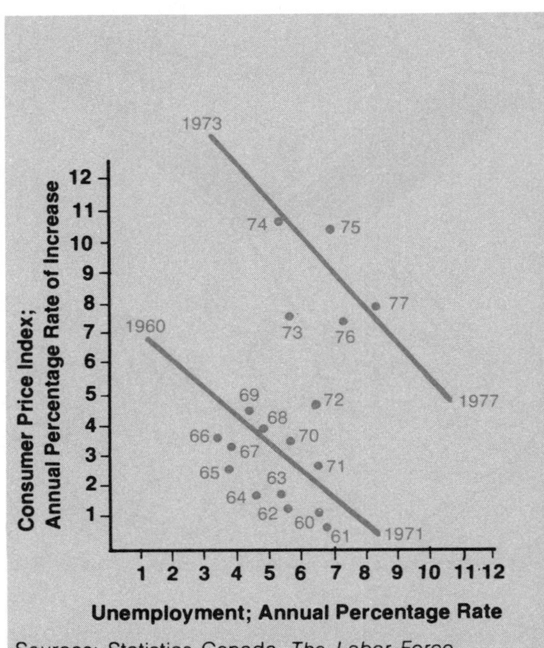

Sources: Statistics Canada, *The Labor Force*, cat. 71-001; *Historical Labor Force Statistics*, (1977), cat. 71-201; *The Consumer Price Index*, cat. 62-001; *Prices and Price Indexes*, cat. 62-002.

volved rank among the most important in an introduction to economics.

The nature of the relationship that the curve seems to illustrate brings us back to a fundamental aspect of economics—the necessity of choice. Examination of the data for the period from 1972, however, provides an additional complication when it is contrasted with the pre-1972 relationships.

THE DILEMMA OF STAGFLATION

Observation of the pre-1972 data indicates what appears to be an inverse relationship, which is most clearly visible within Figure 26-2. From this, and similar patterns for other time periods and other developed economies, we have tended to think of inflationary surges or increases in rates of unemployment as somewhat either-or situations, as symbolized in the cartoon by Kuch which preceded this section.

The data for the period from 1972 on, however, presents some unattractive patterns. We have experienced relatively high inflation and unemployment at the same time.

What historical trends had seemed to show as a potential see-saw has either started acting strangely, or else it did not really exist earlier, except as a statistical coincidence. Collins' cartoon (page 316), based on the see-saw analogy, illustrates in a different way the same phenomena as the content of Figure 26-3.

The unpleasant situation which the cartoon and Figure 26-3 document is one about which economists are uncertain. The problem has three potential explanations.

The first possibility is that the trends of the 1970s, sometimes referred to as **stagflation,** i.e. a stagnant economy with rising unemployment but also high inflation, are temporary. The essence of this is the belief or hope that various factors such as the impact of oil price hikes by the OPEC nations just happened to come at a time of slowing economic growth; in other words, that abnormal or unusual forces coincided to produce an abnormal situation which in time will revert to normality. The hope here is simply that the rightward shift in the curve in Figure

Collins in the Montreal Gazette

This cartoon indicates the essence of the data from Table 26-2, or the patterns shown in Figure 26-3.

the rightward shift in the curve in Figure 26-3 will reverse itself. To many economists, however, this appears overly optimistic. If this is not the basic explanation, we face even less appealing alternatives.

The first of these is that the shift in the curve is likely to be more or less permanent as a result of trends like increasing participation in the labor force, or the expectation of continued higher rates of inflation either imported from abroad or generated within Canada. If such a permanent shift in the curve has taken place, the implication is that either we must collectively endure a greater degree of both inflation and unemployment or, should we choose to try to bring one down, the trade-off cost will be even greater than in the past. Neither of these has much appeal to anyone but, if this explanation is valid to any significant degree, all segments in our society are faced with some bitter choices.

The other alternative is not particularly promising either. If the curve has not shifted, temporarily or permanently, then it has either ceased to exist or else it was an illusion in the first place. Either of these options forces us to admit that there is something inherently wrong with some critical parts of our understanding of how the economy functions, because the general premises of the curve as a model (as well as a measure of what happened in the past) are linked to what has become the accepted wisdom of economics since the 1930s. The implication of this possibility is quite plain. If we don't really know what makes it run, the chances of being able to effect repairs on the economy are not especially good.

This assessment of the contemporary situation may seem pessimistic. If so, it is because the situation is a highly unattractive one with not too much hope for either clear policy options or a short-run resolution.

What then of our goals, high employment levels, and price stability? The importance of both in government policy is a reflection of the post-1930s view that government in-traditional "boom to bust" swings in the total performance of the economy. If, as seems to be the case, goals do clash, then a balance or compromise must be sought, hopefully meeting the short and long term needs of conflicting interests as well as any compromise can. Such may not be completely satisfactory, but the alternatives are even less desirable. And if the traditional premises on which our understanding and our policies are based, are, in fact, in the process of being proved faulty, the significance of the whole problem is that much greater—as may be the costs to our society if the problem can not be solved.

SUMMARY

For this chapter alone, the normal summary is non-existent. The concepts and their significance are too crucial to abbreviate further. The four subsequent chapters deal with the ways in which action may be attempted to modify the direction of the economy once policy choices have been made, or a given combination of goals accepted. As has been shown, both our capacity to direct the economy and our confidence in our future ability to do so have been put under serious strain in recent years.

KEY CONCEPTS

full employment
reasonable price stability
trade-off
Phillips Curve
stagflation

QUESTIONS FOR REVIEW AND DISCUSSION

1. Does unemployment mean that economic scarcity has ceased to exist?
2. What is the cost of unemployment to the individual who is unemployed? What is the cost of unemployment to the total economy, including those who are working? What is a reasonable way of stating a high employment goal for an economy? Explain.
3. What is generally meant by the term *inflation?* What groups in society are most hurt by inflation? Are any groups helped by inflation? If so, which groups are they?
4. What forces which might tend to counteract high unemployment might also induce inflation? Why?

PROBLEMS AND EXERCISES TO SHARPEN YOUR UNDERSTANDING

1. Examine the data for your region and the nation for the latest twelve months. What are the locations within the range of the Phillips Curve in Figure 26-3? What are the most appropriate short-run objectives on a regional level? On a national level? Justify your positions.
2. If you have access to a library containing *Economica,* the monthly journal from the London School of Economics, you might examine the original study of the British economy on which the concept of the Phillips Curve is based. See: A. W. Phillips, "The Relationship Between Unemployment and the Rate of Change in Money Wage Rates in the United Kingdom, 1862-1957," *Economica,* November, 1959, pp. 283-299.
3. Examine newspapers and magazines to establish present opinions about priorities that should be followed by government in the conduct of economic policy. Choose comments reflecting the opinions of organized labor, the business com-

munity, the federal government, different regions of the country and other such specialized points of view. In particular, watch for conflicts of opinion over the immediate importance of unemployment and inflation as major problems.

Comparision of present points of view with those a year ago, or several years ago, might prove interesting. The Montreal Star editorial "Unemployment and National Priorities" and Christopher Young's piece "Jobs For All A Lost Dream?", both reprinted in A. H. MacDonald, (ed.), *Readings In The World of Economics,* Toronto: McGraw-Hill Ryerson, 1973, provide a perspective from the beginning of the decade of the 1970s which could be used as one point of contrast.

4. Under your teacher's direction, research some more detailed aspect of either historical or analytical perspectives on inflation, unemployment, and the relationship between them. Some references might be:
   (a) John Young, "Interpretations of Inflation and Their Implications", reprinted in *Readings In The World of Economics.*
   (b) "Inflation", Canadian Imperial Bank of Commerce *Commercial Letter,* Issue #4, 1975.
   (c) John Young, "Toward A Consensus on Inflation?" *Finance and Development,* vol. 14, no. 1, March, 1977.
   (d) Economic Council of Canada, *Thirteenth Annual Review,* "The Inflation Dilemma," Ottawa: Supply and Services Canada, 1976.
   (e) *Understanding Unemployment,* Toronto: Canadian Foundation for Economic Education, 1976.
   (f) Canadian Labour Congress, Statement on "Unemployment", reprinted in *Readings In The World of Economics.*
   (g) H. L. Robinson, *Rising Prices,* Toronto: James Lorimer, 1978.
   (h) Cy Gonick, *Out of Work*, Toronto: James Lorimer, 1978.

   The latter two titles may be used also as references in the following four chapters as well.

Should your research or the topic you have chosen move you ahead into the areas of monetary, fiscal and other stabilization policies, and the problems we have been encountering with these, check coverage of these topics in the next four chapters and watch there for other references which will be of use to you.

CHAPTER 27

THE BANK OF CANADA AND MONETARY POLICY

■ ORGANIZATION OF THE BANK OF CANADA ■ MONEY AND ECONOMIC ACTIVITY ■ RESERVE REQUIREMENTS ■ OPEN MARKET OPERATIONS ■ THE BANK RATE ■ MORAL SUASION ■ MONETARY POLICY IN PRACTICE ■ SUMMARY

"Whereas it is desirable to establish a central bank in Canada to regulate credit and currency in the best interests of the economic life of the nation, to control and protect the external value of the national monetary unit, and to mitigate by its influence fluctuations in the general level of production, trade, prices and employment, so far as may be possible within the scope of monetary action. . . ."

So reads the preamble to the Bank of Canada Act, which governs one of the most crucial institutions in our economy. In this chapter we will examine the functions and impact of the central bank within our economy.

Central Banking Functions

This excerpt is taken from an article entitled "Why A Central Bank?" by J. K. Horsefield, who, at the time of its publication, was Chief Editor for the International Monetary Fund. This portion deals with the basic functions of central banks, examining them briefly in the order of their chronological emergence.

Nowadays it is customary to describe a central bank as one that (1) acts as banker and fiscal agent for the government, (2) holds part of the commercial banks' reserves, (3) holds or manages the country's gold and foreign exchange reserves, (4) has a monopoly of the banknote issue, and (5) can regulate credit. (These responsibilities are listed here not in order of importance but in the order in which they came to be exercised as central banking grew up.) In practice, not all central banks exercise all five functions, but in combination they represent what might be thought to be the job of the ideal central bank.

Central banking in this sense—as an activity separate from ordinary commercial banking—is generally considered to have emerged first in England. When the Bank of England was created in 1694, however, no one thought that it would have even one of the five responsibilities listed above. Its banking powers were, indeed, quite subsidiary; its main purpose was to lend £1,200,000 to the Government. It differed from other banks of the time only in being much larger than most, and in having its capital in the form of a semipermanent government debt rather than in the personal resources of its partners.

The first central banking job (as we now think of it) that came the Bank of England's way was to act as fiscal agent for the Government. The Bank's close relations with the Government on the one hand and the City of London on the other made it easy and convenient for the Government to use it, from about 1700 onward, to circulate Treasury bills (short-term government securities), and later to handle the government debt generally. This in turn added to the Bank's

Bank of Canada

Like the Bank of England, the Bank of Canada has a monopoly of banknote issues. Here old bills meet the "end of the road."

reputation for stability, and encouraged other bankers to keep deposits with it. Because the Bank came to realize that the deposits of other bankers were more volatile than private deposits, it began, early in the nineteenth century, to hold a larger reserve of gold, in proportion to its liabilities, than other banks did; and this led to its third function, that of holding the gold (and later the foreign exchange) reserves of the country as a whole.

The acquisition by the Bank of England of the monopoly of banknote issue (the fourth function listed above) was in a sense the result of a misunderstanding. In the 1830s it was thought that by controlling the note issue it would be possible to avoid the recurrence of financial crises, but it was not understood at the time that similar crises could be produced by the credit policies of banks whose demand obligations assumed the shape of deposits. Accordingly, steps were taken to concentrate note issuing powers in the Bank of England—though the process was not complete even in England until 1912, and still does not apply to Scotland.

This brings us to the fifth, and obviously the most significant, function of a central bank—the control of credit. For a long time the Bank of England was reluctant to accept responsibility for exercising any control over the other financial institutions, but it gradually learned to use appropriately the powers that it possessed. By the time of World War I, the idea that such control was the proper function of a central bank was widely advocated. In 1920 it led the International Financial Conference, convened by the League of Nations at Brussels, to urge that every country should set up a central bank.

Reprinted from *Finance and Development,* Vol. II, No. 3, Sept. 1965, pp. 159-160. Published by International Monetary Fund and The International Bank For Reconstruction And Development.

ORGANIZATION OF THE BANK OF CANADA

Canada was relatively late among developed nations in the creation of a central bank. Prior to 1934, when the Bank of Canada Act was passed, the functions of a central bank were carried out either by the federal government or were more or less left to market forces.

The impact of the Great Depression of the early 1930s was a major one. There was considerable division of opinion about just what a central bank could do to alleviate existing conditions or prevent their recurrence, but there was agreement on one point from most quarters. The banking and monetary system, with its automatic responses to market forces, had proven itself to be less than satisfactory.

Initially, the Bank of Canada was privately owned with a government-appointed Governor. This original arrangement was in part a recognition of the desirability of having central banks free from governmental interference, and in part a concession to the principle of private enterprise in banking. The latter aspect did not endure long, for by 1938 the Bank of Canada had become a Crown Corporation. The potential problem associated with the former proposition did not emerge until 1960-1961 when a dispute between the Governor of the Bank, James Coyne, and the Minister of Finance, Donald Fleming, turned into one of the major political and economic crises of the Diefenbaker administration. One result was the confirmation of the fact that, ultimately, the wishes of the government of the day must prevail and the Bank of Canada must implement policy fundamentally acceptable to the government. The successor to Coyne (who did resign—on the day that a government bill dismissing him was turned down in the Senate[1]) was Louis Rasminsky whose views on the relationship between the Bank and the government were the direct opposite of those held by Coyne.

This marked a restoration to the positions taken by governments from the late 1930s. The primary reason for concern that this should be the case is the need to have policies of the government and the central bank working toward the same goals. If they are in conflict, then the one may neutralize the other.

Beyond this key question of the relationship between the Bank and the government, we need not concern ourselves about details of internal structure or questions related to operations outside the realm of monetary policy.

What precisely is **monetary policy?** In brief, it is the management of the money supply and the availability and cost of credit to promote fundamental economic goals.

What is the relationship between the money supply, credit and its cost, and these goals? Before proceeding with an examination of how the Bank of Canada goes about implementing monetary policies, we should briefly examine the targets.

[1] For a detailed, though politically oriented account, see Peter C. Newman: *Renegade in Power: The Diefenbaker Years*, Toronto: McClelland and Stewart, 1963, Chapter 21.

The Bank and the Government

Louis Rasminsky was appointed Governor of the Bank of Canada in 1961, following what Peter Newman called "The Carnage of the Coyne Affair." Shortly after his appointment, he released a statement, the first part of which follows, in which he dealt with the question of the extent to which the Bank of Canada was or was not independent of the wishes of the government of the day.

I have been greatly encouraged by the many public expressions of goodwill which have appeared since the announcement of my appointment as Governor of the Bank of Canada. I have decided to make public at this time my views on certain matters connected with the administration of this office. These views had been made known to the Directors and to the Government in the following form when my appointment was being considered.

I believe that it is essential that the responsibilities in relation to monetary policy should be clarified in the public mind and in the legislation. I do not suggest a precise formula but have in mind two main principles to be established: (1) in the ordinary course of events, the Bank has the responsibility for monetary policy, and (2) if the Government disapproves of the monetary policy being carried out by the Bank it has the right and the responsibility to direct the Bank as to the policy which the Bank is to carry out.

The first principle is designed to ensure that the Bank has the degree of independence and responsibility necessary if it is, in the language of the Bank of Canada Act, "to regulate credit and currency in the best interests of the economic life of the nation." To discharge this duty the Bank must be sufficiently independent and responsible in its operations to be able to withstand day-to-day pressures from any source. But in the longer run, if there should develop a serious and persistent conflict between the views of the Government and the views of the central bank with regard to monetary policy which, after prolonged and conscientious efforts on both sides, cannot be resolved, the Government should be able formally to instruct the Bank what monetary policy it wishes carried out and the Bank should have the duty to comply with these instructions. The exercise of this authority by Government would place on Government direct responsibility for the monetary policy to be followed. If this policy, as communicated to the Bank, was one which the Governor felt he could not in good conscience carry out, his duty would be to resign and to make way for someone who took a different view.

Source: *Evidence of the Governor Before The Royal Commission on Banking and Finance,* Ottawa: Bank of Canada, 1964, p. 131. Text reproduced by permission of the Bank of Canada.

MONEY AND ECONOMIC ACTIVITY

How do changes in the money supply affect the rate of total economic activity? Remember that the money supply is a *stock* of currency and checking accounts. And our GNP measure of total economic activity is a *flow* of goods and services. How do changes in the *stock* of money affect the *flow* of economic activity? This is done largely by the effect of these changes on total demand or total spending.

Changes in the money supply affect total spending in the economy. In part, changes in the money supply influence total spending *directly*—by putting more funds in the hands of consumers, businesses, or government units. In part, however, increases in the money supply influence total spending *indirectly*—by reducing rates of interest and thereby making it cheaper and more attractive for businesses, consumers, and government units (especially at the provincial and local level) to borrow funds and increase their spending on goods and services. On the other hand, reductions in the money supply will cause reductions in total spending both directly (by making less money available) and indirectly (by increasing rates of interest, which then makes money more costly and deters consumers, businesses, or government from borrowing and spending).

If there is idle capacity in the economy, increases in total spending can increase output

Bank of Canada

Gerald Bouey, Governor of the Bank of Canada in the late 1970s.

and employment without putting much upward pressure on the price level. But, if the economy is already at full capacity, and there are not many unemployed resources around, an increase in total demand will tend to bid up prices. Under these conditions, a cut in total spending is called for, and we would want to reduce the rate of growth of the money supply in hopes that the restraints upon spending would prevent prices from rising further, without changing the level of output and employment.

The relationships among total spending, total output of goods and services, and the general price level can be set forth in a simple equation known as the **equation of exchange:** $MV = PQ$. M denotes the money supply; V denotes the velocity of money; P denotes the general price level; and Q denotes the quantity of goods and services produced.[2]

The terms in this equation may require some further explanation. Let us start with the right side of the equation where PQ refers to the quantity of goods and services produced at a given price level. This is none other than our definition of GNP used in Chapter 22, where GNP was defined as the current market value of final goods and services. So we can change the right side of the above equation to make it read: MV = GNP (again, see footnote 2).

We know M stands for the money supply—all the money in checking accounts in commercial banks plus all the currency in circulation. This leaves us with just one more key term to look at—the V which refers to the **velocity of money.** In very brief terms, the velocity of money represents the number of times a year the money supply, M, turns over.

We may best explain this term by starting with an individual person, whom we will call Citizen Cash, who maintains an average balance of $1000 in a checking account during the year and usually has $100 in currency on hand.

But in the course of a year Cash actually spends $13 200 (this is done by constantly replenishing the amount in Cash's bank account and wallet out of income). Thus we can say that the velocity of Cash's money supply during a year is 12 (the number of times he or she turns over the $1100 in the checking account and wallet). The turnover of the money supply for the nation as a whole is not as rapid, generally being in the range of 2.5 to 3.5, the ratio being based on GNP divided by total money supply. This might appear to be a very minor and insig-

[2] The components within the equation indicate general relationships which tend to exist, but are not to be considered as literal in a mathematical sense. By this we mean that the equations are not to be read as having a precise relationship such as exists in an equation like: $2 \times 3 = 1 \times 6$.

nificant range for fluctuation, but remember that a shift in the ratio from 2.5 to 3.75 is an increase of 50 percent.

The velocity of money is what relates the stock of money to the flow of economic activities as measured by GNP. As the equation of exchange tells us, the money supply times the velocity of money equals GNP (which is composed of current output, Q, times current prices, P). With the terms defined as we have defined them the equation of exchange can be a useful device in understanding monetary policy.

If the velocity of circulation were constant, the Bank of Canada could change GNP by simply changing the stock of money. And if the price level remained constant, all of the changes in GNP would be the result of changes in physical output (Q). But if we were already at full capacity, and output remained constant, all of the changes in GNP would be the result of changes in prices (P).

With a constant velocity in times of full employment and inflation, a cut in the money supply could pull down the price level without changing physical output. With a constant velocity in times of unemployment and stable prices, an increase in the money supply could increase output without changing the price level.

Unfortunately, the job is not that easy. Velocity does vary over time. In periods of business slumps and periods of falling interest rates, velocity tends to slow down. In periods of business booms and rising interest rates, velocity tends to speed up. Thus, there is no direct stable relationship between the stock of money and the flow of GNP. If there were a stable relationship, the job of monetary policy would be considerably easier than it really is. Since the relationship is not always stable, however, the Central Bank must exercise its best judgment in using monetary policy to influence the total rate of economic activity.

Let us now turn to the specific tools used by (or available to) the Bank of Canada to affect M and V and through these, to influence P and Q. (Before continuing in this chapter, it might be advisable to do a quick review of Chapter 17, which deals with the operations of the chartered banks, since it is primarily through the chartered banks that the central bank influences the economy as a whole.)

RESERVE REQUIREMENTS

As Chapter 17 stressed, the foundation of the banking structure is the fractional reserve system and, built on this, the process by which the total of bank deposits (the prime component of the money supply) may expand or contract.

As we have seen, there are two categories of actual reserves, primary and secondary. Until 1967, the Bank of Canada held power by statute over the primary rate but never used this power. In 1967, direct control over the primary rate was returned to Parliament. The secondary reserves, which were set not by statute but by general agreement with the chartered banks, were written into the revision of the Bank Act in 1967 so that this is now a formal, legal power held by the central bank.

Up to the present, however, direct use of power over reserve requirements has been more a potential weapon than anything else. The Bank of Canada has chosen to use other techniques in actually affecting the level and composition of chartered bank reserves and, through this, M and V.

OPEN MARKET OPERATIONS

In practice, the most important technique of monetary policy has been the use of the Bank's role in the market for Federal government bonds. The phrase "open market operations" in fact refers to bond market activity. The market for bonds, government and corporate, differs considerably from the stock market, which was examined in Chapter 10.

The Bank of Canada, as a part of its role in administering the sale and redemption of government securities, is also the primary

A KEY TO THE RELATIONSHIPS BETWEEN INTEREST RATES AND BOND VALUES

Bond Values and Yields

Time to Maturity Date

Coupon Rates
i.e. % of Par Value
Paid in Interest Per Year

YIELDS

i.e. % rate of return for security of given coupon rate and time to maturity if purchased second-hand at given price per $100.00 par value.

MARKET VALUES

i.e. selling value of second-hand security per $100.00 par value given time to maturity, coupon rate, and yield as an expression of present borrowing cost or level of return demanded for the security.

1 YEAR

PER CENT PER AN.	3%	3½%	4%	4¼%	4½%
6⅛	97.01	97.49	97.97	98.21	98.45
6.20	96.94	97.42	97.90	98.14	98.38
6¼	96.90	97.37	97.85	98.09	98.33
6.30	96.85	97.33	97.80	98.04	98.28
6⅜	96.78	97.26	97.73	97.97	98.21
6.40	96.76	97.23	97.71	97.95	98.19
6½	96.66	97.14	97.62	97.86	98.09
6.60	96.57	97.05	97.52	97.76	98.00
6⅝	96.55	97.02	97.50	97.74	97.98
6.70	96.48	96.95	97.43	97.67	97.91
6¾	96.43	96.91	97.38	97.62	97.86
6.80	96.39	96.86	97.34	97.57	97.81
6⅞	96.32	96.79	97.27	97.50	97.74
6.90	96.29	96.77	97.24	97.48	97.72
7.	96.20	96.68	97.15	97.39	97.63
7.10	96.11	96.58	97.06	97.29	97.53
7.20	96.02	96.49	96.96	97.20	97.44
7¼	95.97	96.44	96.92	97.16	97.39
7.30	95.92	96.40	96.87	97.11	97.35
7.40	95.83	96.31	96.78	97.02	97.25
7½	95.74	96.21	96.69	96.92	97.16
7.60	95.65	96.12	96.60	96.83	97.07
7.70	95.56	96.03	96.50	96.74	96.98
7¾	95.51	95.98	96.46	96.69	96.93
7.80	95.47	95.94	96.41	96.65	96.88
7.90	95.38	95.85	96.32	96.56	96.79
8.	95.28	95.76	96.23	96.46	96.70
8.10	95.19	95.67	96.14	96.37	96.61
8.20	95.10	95.57	96.04	96.28	96.52
8¼	95.06	95.53	96.00	96.23	96.47
8.30	95.01	95.48	95.95	96.19	96.42
8.40	94.92	95.39	95.86	96.10	96.33
8½	94.83	95.30	95.77	96.01	96.24
8.60	94.74	95.21	95.68	95.92	96.15
8.70	94.65	95.12	95.59	95.82	96.06
8¾	94.61	95.08	95.54	95.78	96.01
8.80	94.56	95.03	95.50	95.73	95.97
8.90	94.47	94.94	95.41	95.64	95.88
9.	94.38	94.85	95.32	95.55	95.79
9.10	94.29	94.76	95.23	95.46	95.70
9.20	94.20	94.67	95.14	95.37	95.61
9¼	94.16	94.63	95.09	95.33	95.56
9.30	94.11	94.58	95.05	95.28	95.52
9.40	94.02	94.49	94.96	95.19	95.43
9½	93.94	94.40	94.87	95.10	95.34
9.60	93.85	94.31	94.78	95.01	95.25
9.70	93.76	94.22	94.69	94.92	95.16
9¾	93.71	94.18	94.64	94.88	95.11
9.80	93.67	94.13	94.60	94.83	95.07
9.90	93.58	94.05	94.51	94.74	94.98
10.00	93.49	93.96	94.42	94.65	94.89

2 YEARS

PER CENT PER AN.	3%	3½%	4%	4¼%	4½%
6⅛	94.20	95.13	96.06	96.52	96.98
6.20	94.07	94.99	95.92	96.38	96.85
6¼	93.98	94.90	95.83	96.29	96.76
6.30	93.89	94.81	95.74	96.20	96.67
6⅜	93.76	94.68	95.61	96.07	96.53
6.40	93.71	94.64	95.56	96.02	96.49
6½	93.53	94.46	95.38	95.84	96.31
6.60	93.36	94.28	95.20	95.66	96.12
6⅝	93.31	94.24	95.16	95.62	96.08
6.70	93.18	94.10	95.02	95.48	95.95
6¾	93.09	94.01	94.93	95.39	95.86
6.80	93.00	93.93	94.85	95.31	95.77
6⅞	92.87	93.79	94.71	95.17	95.63
6.90	92.83	93.75	94.67	95.13	95.59
7.	92.65	93.57	94.49	94.95	95.41
7.10	92.48	93.40	94.31	94.77	95.23
7.20	92.30	93.22	94.14	94.60	95.05
7¼	92.22	93.13	94.05	94.51	94.96
7.30	92.13	93.05	93.96	94.42	94.88
7.40	91.96	92.87	93.79	94.24	94.70
7½	91.78	92.70	93.61	94.07	94.52
7.60	91.61	92.52	93.44	93.89	94.35
7.70	91.44	92.35	93.26	93.72	94.17
7¾	91.35	92.26	93.17	93.63	94.08
7.80	91.27	92.18	93.09	93.54	94.00
7.90	91.10	92.00	92.91	93.37	93.82
8.	90.93	91.83	92.74	93.19	93.65
8.10	90.75	91.66	92.57	93.02	93.47
8.20	90.58	91.49	92.40	92.85	93.30
8¼	90.50	91.40	92.31	92.76	93.21
8.30	90.41	91.32	92.22	92.68	93.13
8.40	90.25	91.15	92.05	92.50	92.95
8½	90.08	90.98	91.88	92.33	92.78
8.60	89.91	90.81	91.71	92.16	92.61
8.70	89.74	90.64	91.54	91.99	92.44
8¾	89.66	90.56	91.45	91.90	92.35
8.80	89.57	90.47	91.37	91.82	92.27
8.90	89.40	90.30	91.20	91.65	92.10
9.	89.24	90.13	91.03	91.48	91.93
9.10	89.07	89.97	90.86	91.31	91.76
9.20	88.90	89.80	90.69	91.14	91.59
9¼	88.82	89.72	90.61	91.06	91.50
9.30	88.74	89.63	90.53	90.97	91.42
9.40	88.57	89.47	90.36	90.81	91.25
9½	88.41	89.30	90.19	90.64	91.08
9.60	88.24	89.13	90.03	90.47	90.92
9.70	88.08	88.97	89.86	90.30	90.75
9¾	88.00	88.89	89.78	90.22	90.66
9.80	87.92	88.80	89.69	90.14	90.58
9.90	87.75	88.64	89.53	89.97	90.41
10.00	87.59	88.48	89.36	89.81	90.25

Source: *Consolidated Tables of Bond Values*, copyright Financial Publishing Company, Boston, Mass., U.S.A.: reprinted by permission.

The tables from a bond-yield book, as it is usually called, shows the mathematical nature of price determination in the bond market. Two factors are predetermined, the maturity date and the coupon rate which are fixed when bonds are issued. Interest rate changes alter the yield level which in turn alter the market value of the bond. For example, let us imagine you want to sell a 4% bond of XYP Corp. maturing two years from today. The present yield on the company for this maturity date is 7.6%. Your $1000.00 par value bond thus has a market value of about $934.40. If you decide not to sell but in twenty-four hours interest rates and yields take a dramatic drop of a full percentage point, the yield falls to 6.6% and the value goes up to $952.00.

As comparison of the tables would show, market values go up as yield or prevailing interest rates decline and as time to maturity (when the bond is redeemed at par value) draws closer. All bonds except "Parity Bonds" (Canada Savings Bonds being the prime example of this type—cashable at full face or par value at any time) are liable to fluctuate like this if interest rates change after they are issued. Given these relationships, what could you do if you were "strong" enough to alter price levels on bonds whose yields affect the yields on other issues. The significance of reversing the "yield dictates price" relationship should be apparent.

FIG. 27-1. THE INTEREST RATE SCALE

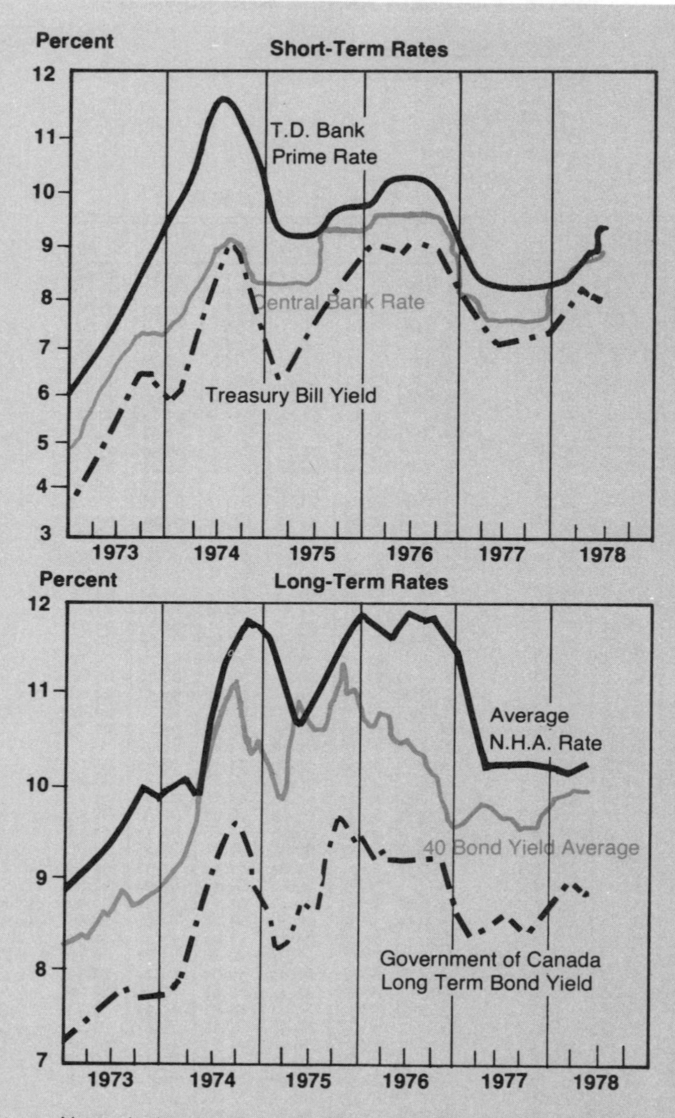

Notes: In the short-term group, the Treasury Bill Yield is that on Federal Treasury Bills (See account following); the Bank Rate is just that (see the next section in this chapter); the T-D Prime Rate is the rate for Toronto-Dominion's "best customers," i.e. those eligible for the lowest interest rate.

In the long-term group, the N.H.A. rate is that on N.H.A. mortgages, the 40 Bond Yield Average is made up of yields on selected provincial, municipal, public utility, and corporate issues.

Source: "Canada's Business Climate," The Toronto-Dominion Bank, Summer Issue, 1978. Reprinted by permission of the Toronto-Dominion Bank.

The parallel patterns of interest rates paid by borrowers on new loans or received by buyers of second-hand bonds is clearly indicated in these graphs. Governments, corporations and individuals all fit into the scale at a fixed point in time. If rates move, it then means that all rates will change, though not always by the same degree.

participant in the market for unmatured bonds. One of the reasons is simply to help maintain the market for new issues by assuring the existence of a "buyer of last resort" in case holders of bonds want or need to sell them before maturity date. This role permits the bank to have a considerable impact on the market prices and hence on the yield which buyers of second-hand bonds would receive if they were to purchase the securities and hold them to maturity. This influence is primarily on the yield of unmatured federal issues. Another influence on the yield on outstanding bonds is through deliberate positioning of the rate of interest on new federal issues. For example, if outstanding long term bonds presently offer a yield, at market price, of 7 percent and a new issue is offered with an 8 percent interest rate, who would buy second-hand ones? Answer—no one, until the price drops to increase the rate of return to the 8 percent level.

Why is the overall scale of interest rates for all borrowers important? The graphs in Figure 27-1 indicate that when the return on federal issues goes up, other interest rates go up. Is it coincidental? Of course not. Interest rates, at any given moment, are based on a comparative credit rating, that of the Federal government being the foundation—if the foundation of a house is lifted up, the house is likely to move as well. (This does not imply that other factors do not affect interest rates as well. Supply and demand, as well as the competitive pressure of rates in the United States, directly influence rates, as does the existing level of inflation. These are persistent forces, regardless of Bank of Canada activities.)

In this way, the Bank, by influencing interest rates, can affect *V* specifically by affecting the cost of credit, hence the general inclination to borrow and spend or invest.

But even more important, these activities will also affect *M* by having an effect on the reserves of the chartered banks, hence on the capacity of the banking system to expand deposits. How does this take place?

Outside the Bank of Canada, the chartered banks rank among the major holders of government securities, especially the Treasury Bills which are held as the major part of the secondary reserves. If the Bank of Canada sells securities from its holdings to the chartered banks, (perhaps including this with an increased yield), the payment is ordinarily made by a check drawn against the chartered bank's deposit with the Bank of Canada, a part of its primary reserve. If this reserve is depleted, it must either not increase deposits (assuming it had excess reserves) or it must decrease its deposits (to meet the reserves-deposits ratio required). This is most readily done by calling in demand loans and not renewing them. When one remembers how deposit contraction-expansion affects the banking system, it should be apparent that a decrease in reserves of $1.00, assuming total reserve requirements of 10 percent, could bring a $10.00 contraction in total deposit capacity. The same process works in reverse. If the central bank wishes to expand *M*, it then buys securities, increases reserves, and thus the deposit creation capacity of the banking system. This combined tool has been the one used thus far, as the primary means of affecting reserve levels, money supply and interest rates, i.e. key elements of *M* and *V* in our equation.

THE BANK RATE

The bank rate is the rate at which the chartered banks could borrow from the Bank of Canada. Let us assume that this is done to increase cash reserves and loan-deposits capacity. What would happen if the bank rate went up? The chartered banks would either have to pay more and increase their lending rate to maintain profitability or, facing the possibility of less demand at higher interest rates, curtail the borrowing and thus reduce their lending-deposit creation capacity. If the bank rate went down, it would tend to reverse the pattern. (Remember, however, one can lead one to credit, but cannot force him or her to borrow.) Such is the primary possible role of the bank rate.

In practice, however, it is of relatively lit-

FIG. 27-2. INTEREST RATES: CANADA-UNITED STATES

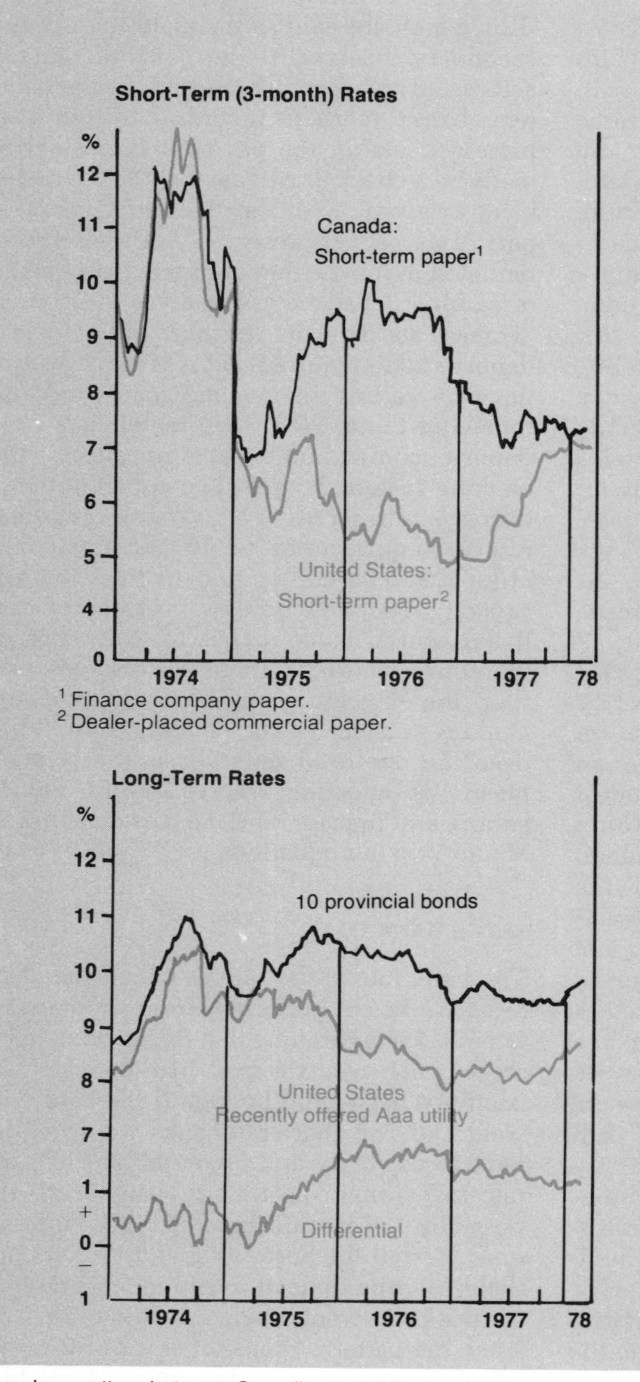

The close pattern between Canadian and American interest rates is quite apparent in these two graphs. In fact, these examples were selected because they show the trend somewhat better than normal. One can find movements in opposite directions. Such is generally rare, however, and is usually a short-run situation. Needless to say, U.S. rates are, to a considerable degree, a major determinant of the level of Canadian rates and will continue to be as long as a significant amount of borrowing is done in the U.S.

tle significance; for the chartered banks do not borrow, except on very rare occasions, nor are they encouraged to do so. Why then is the bank rate given so much attention if it is changed? Primarily, because it is an indicator of policy regarding interest rates, though, as Figure 27-1 illustrates, changes in the bank rate are generally a reflection of what is happening to interest rates and bond market yields. For a time, the rate was tied directly to the Treasury Bill yield rate. This is no longer the case, but it tends to reflect short-term interest rates, especially the yield on Treasury Bills.

MORAL SUASION

In addition to the forces or possible forces mentioned previously, one other aspect of policy should be mentioned. This is generally referred to as **moral suasion**. It is simply the promotion of the point of view of the Central Bank in its regular or perhaps special contacts with the administrators of the chartered banks. It of course does not get attention because it is not public, but the result of direct personal contacts and correspondence which is not released. Is it effective? In answer to a question about it when appearing before the Royal Commission on Banking and Finance, Governor Rasminsky said:

> "I think the general experience is that the public interest is recognized by the chartered banks, and after the discussion the cooperation of the chartered banks is forthcoming."[3]

In practice, moral suasion continues to rank after bond market operations as the most commonly utilized tool of monetary policy.

MONETARY POLICY IN PRACTICE

In recent years, the effectiveness of the Bank of Canada and many other central banks has been called into question as inflation rates have surged higher and higher. Some criticisms have been directed chiefly at governmental neglect of monetary policy in favor of other approaches to try to curb inflation. Others point out that many counter-inflationary policies of central banks have either been too "half-hearted" or have been negated by other aspects of either their own monetary policies—or other governmental actions/inactions. One of the most frequent forms of attack on the Bank of Canada was that its "tight money" policies were insufficiently tough or were defeated by Bank-created loopholes. As Figures 27-1 and 27-2 indicate, in the 70's interest rates have been high, partly as a result of deliberate Bank policy. At the same time, however, extremely high rates of growth in the money supply were taking place. The essence of this was that while V was being restrained, M was expanding rapidly. The latter, when taking place at a high rate, was not at all appropriate if one wished to see the product, MV, restrained. Figure 27-4 indicates the patterns of change in the money supply in conjunction with inflation rates over the past half-century.

FIG. 27-3. INFLATION AND INTEREST RATES

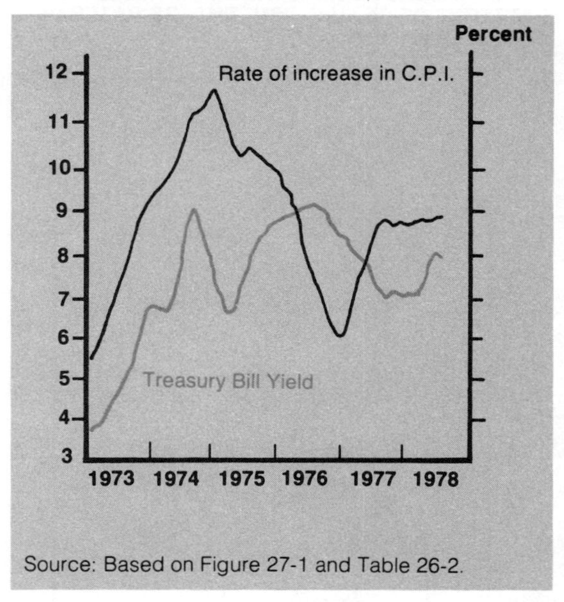

Source: Based on Figure 27-1 and Table 26-2.

The patterns here show a close relationship between interest rates (represented by the Treasury Bill Yield) and inflation (based on the C.P.I.). What can you offer as an explanation of this? If it is cause-effect, which is which and why?

[3] Bank of Canada, *Evidence of the Governor Before the Royal Commission on Banking and Finance*, Ottawa: Bank of Canada, 1964, p. 54.

FIG. 27-4. MONEY SUPPLY AND INFLATION; PATTERNS OF ANNUAL PERCENTAGE RATES OF CHANGE, 1921-1977

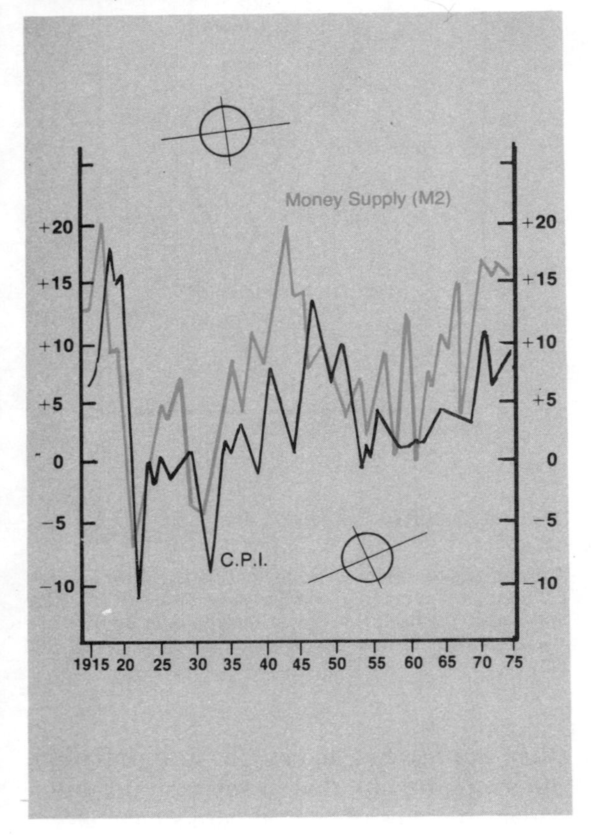

This figure plots the patterns of the annual rate of change for the money supply (measured by M2) and inflation (measured by the C.P.I.). The tendency to a strong direct relationship should be obvious. Note during the last decade shown, when the inflation rate was building, the rate of increase in the money supply was high as well. This has been the basis for much of the criticism directed at the Bank of Canada during the inflationary spiral of the 70s.

Sources: Statistics Canada and Bank of Canada

The call for more and better monetary policy has led since 1976 to more conscious (and more publicized) action by the Bank of Canada to exercise greater control over the rate of growth in the money supply.[4] Daily reading about Bank of Canada policy should lead you to references to this.

The following reading provides—through a summary of a recent study, some of the elements of the criticism of monetary policy in Canada in recent years. References will be found to some other counter-inflationary policies which will be discussed in Chapters 28 and 29.

In addition to the debates and conflicts of opinion over what central banks actually are or should be doing, the role of the money supply and monetary policy has also been receiving more attention among economists. Their concern is often as much directed toward long-term fundamental and historical relationships (i.e. economic theory) as it is to issues of day-to-day policy. Growing economic problems, plus more research into monetary and monetary policy issues, have led to the emergence of what has come to be referred to as a "monetarist school" of economists.

Probably the most prominent figure among these is Milton Friedman of the University of Chicago, who received the Nobel Prize in Economics in 1976. The "monetarists" see monetary issues as much more important than was generally accepted during much of the three decades or so following the publication of Keynes' *General Theory* in 1936. (Check the references accompanying the reading from the 1945 White Paper in Canada in Chapter 19, the reading "All Around the Merry-Go-Round" in Chapter 26, and finally, references (b)-(d) in Problem 2 at the end of Chapter 28.) The increasing inability of governments, generally depending on Keynesian policies related to government taxing, spending, and borrowing (which will be treated in Chapter 28), to cope with stagflation, has helped bring monetarism much more consideration at both theoretical and policy levels.

In addition to academic conflict with the Keynesian school, monetarists have also become embroiled in debate with what might be described as the "concentration of market

[4] For some initial perspective, see the Economic Council of Canada's *Fourteenth Annual Review*, Ottawa: Supply and Services, 1977, pp. 21-24, or the section in J. W. Popkin's *Government and the Economy—Stabilization Policies*, Toronto: Canadian Foundation for Economic Education, 1977, pp. 25-27.

Monetary Policy And The War Against Inflation

When wage and price controls were imposed almost two years ago, many supported them as a necessary step in combating inflation, since traditional monetary and fiscal measures had failed to maintain a stable economy. Others contended that even if a tighter monetary policy proved effective in halting inflation, by limiting consumer demand or reducing wage increases, it would entail unacceptable costs in terms of unemployment.

In a paper done for the Economic Council, George Lermer, an economist with the Department of Consumer and Corporate Affairs, disputes these claims.* He argues that in a situation of world-wide inflation, a well-designed monetary policy is a weapon of paramount importance. However, in Canada, it is a tool which has been sadly misused. He advocates that the Canadian government dismantle controls—except perhaps for specific programs controlling wage negotiations in the public sector—and return to sound monetary management.

If monetary policy is now being judged inadequate for the task of fighting inflation, it is because in recent years, particularly in 1974 and 1975, it has not been effectively deployed. That is, in an inflationary situation when growth in the money supply should have been restricted to slow consumer spending and hence ease the upward pressure on prices, the contrary occurred. According to Lermer, monetary growth in Canada has been so expansionary that we have actually been fortunate to avoid even higher rates of inflation.

Temporarily Higher Unemployment is Inevitable

Although an anti-inflation program comprised solely of tight monetary policy would likely worsen unemployment, Lermer views this as a temporary and necessary price to pay. He credits the restrictive monetary policy in the United States with reducing inflation in that country from 12 per cent in 1974 to 7 per cent in 1975—a record not matched by Canada. This was achieved at the cost of a one per cent increase in unemployment during this period. In Lermer's opinion, this is not too high a cost for such a drop in inflation. Although Canada has not suffered such severe inflation, he feels similar action was warranted here.

Inflation has now been incorporated into the planning of households and firms and therefore it is more difficult to halt the spiral of wages and prices now than it would have been when the first inflationary shock occurred. Participants in the economy have adjusted their behavior in line with their inflationary expectations. For example, employees who were on long-term contracts when inflation began bargain for future wage increases large enough to compensate them both for earlier and anticipated losses in purchasing income. Employers have little reason to refuse these increases since lower wage rates could result in higher turnover rates and a lower quality labor force which could force labor costs even higher in the end.

The Dangers of Controls

Controls, together with a tight monetary policy, can help to break this chain of inflationary expectations and ease the adjustment period. They demonstrate the government's commitment to an anti-inflationary policy for as long as it is required—a commitment that may not be as evident to union and company leaders with a restrictive monetary policy alone. Nevertheless, Lermer warns that controls are a dangerous instrument. By limiting price movements, they interfere with the means by which resources are allocated and goods are directed to domestic and foreign markets. Moreover, they can adversely affect productivity levels, thereby causing a drop in real per capita incomes which may be as serious a cause of social discontent as inflation itself.

Although inflationary expectations may now be sufficiently strongly entrenched to warrant this kind of intervention, Lermer advocates a

* George Lermer, *Has Monetary Policy Failed?* Economic Council of Canada, Discussion Paper No. 86.

return to monetary policy as the main means of achieving price stability as soon as possible. Monetary policy should be redesigned, with the Bank of Canada permitting the exchange rate to fluctuate in response to world prices. One alternative that he suggests is to limit devaluations in the exchange rate to a maximum of one per cent a year, but to allow unlimited appreciation of the Canadian dollar. Consequently, if inflationary shocks occur within Canada, they will be checked quickly before they can be reflected in wage negotiations, since the Bank would be unable to facilitate excessive wage hikes by increasing the supply of money. A firm commitment by the Bank of Canada to such a policy would reduce the likelihood of monetary policy contributing to any future inflationary pressure.

Reprinted from Economic Council of Canada, *Bulletin*, vol. 1, no. 3, Spring, 1977, p. 7.

—Roschkov in Windsor Star

"They raised the interest rates to slow down borrowing because they're worried about inflation."

Roschkov in Windsor Star

In a period when an "expansionary" policy is called for, lower interest rates and easier credit may be promoted to try to stimulate the economy. Under these conditions, however, the validity of the old saying "You can lead a horse to water but you cannot make it drink" may show up. People may not respond in the desired way quickly enough.

Likewise, in times of "restraint," higher interest rates may not affect either potential borrowers or the banking system, as Roschkov's cartoon aptly shows.

power" school. Their most prominent spokesman is John Kenneth Galbraith, whose name and ideas you have encountered before. The "market power" advocates reject the monetarist view, stating that, in modern economies, trends are set by a small number of very powerful forces who are more-or-less immune to traditional monetary moves (and many fiscal policies as well). Galbraith's position is that, to offset concentrated power, the ultimate weapon which governments will likely find necessary will be the use of direct controls over wages and prices to impose stability. This is unacceptable to most monetarists who tend, like Friedman, to be "small c" conservatives, proponents of less rather than more government action and advocates of a return to a more truly private, "private enterprise" system. Leonard Silk's book, *The Economists*, uses the chapter title "Prophet of the Old-time Religion," (i.e. Adam Smith) for his chapter on Friedman, while the chapter on Galbraith is entitled "Socialism Without Tears." The two titles say a great deal about the fundamental positions of these two men, who rank among the most visible economists in the world today. Given Canada's recent experience with controls, this aspect of Galbraith's approach to stagflation will emerge in Chapter 30 where controls are discussed. (As a minor concluding point, it may be of interest to some that Galbraith grew up in Elgin County, Ontario.)

SUMMARY

The Bank of Canada seeks to use monetary policy—variations in the money supply—to promote high employment and price stability. When the bank is worried about a business decline and unemployment, it adopts an easy money policy. It increases the reserves in the banking system, increases the money supply, and seeks to push down interest rates in order to increase borrowing and spending by the public.

But, when the bank is worried about inflation, because it fears that excessive spending is over-straining the real resources of the economy, it adopts a tight money policy. It restricts or reduces the reserves of the banking system and tends to push up interest rates. This policy is aimed at reducing total spending, but it may affect some sectors of the economy much more than others. For instance, higher interest charges may have a major effect in deterring consumers from buying houses or automobiles, where interest charges constitute a good part of the cost of buying a house or a car over a long period of time.

This is especially true of the demand for housing. The amount of a home loan (or mortgage) is usually quite large (the largest single debt that most families ever incur), and the payments may

FIG. 27-5. THE CHAIN OF MONETARY POLICY AND ECONOMIC ACTIVITY

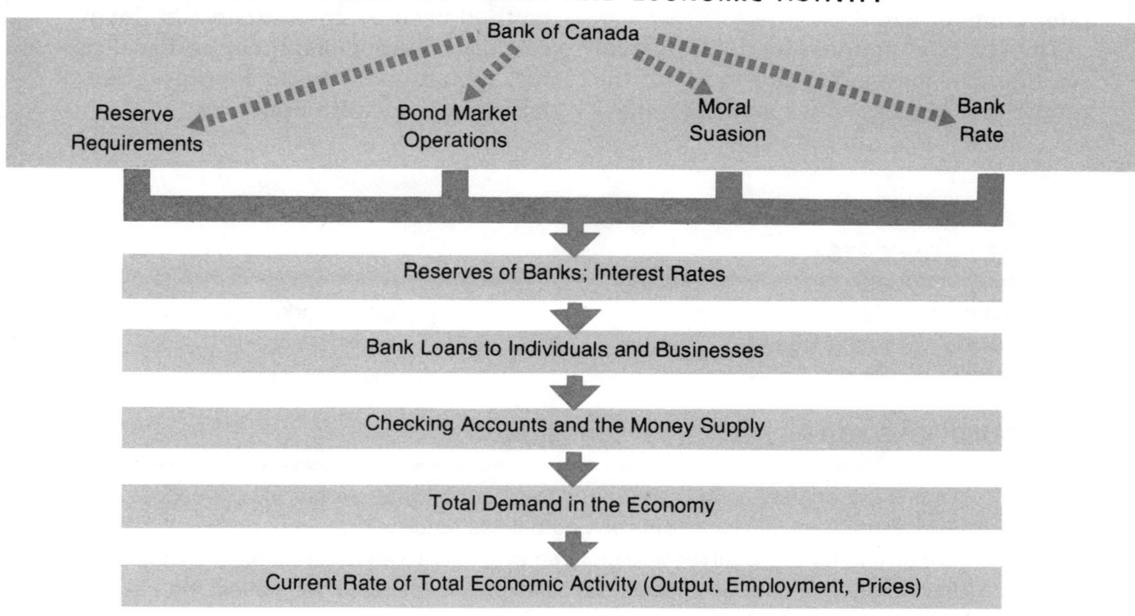

This gives a brief summary picture of how the main tools of monetary policy are related to the total level of economic activity. Influence over interest rates and bank reserves stimulates or retards bank loans. This, in turn, affects the amount of check money in the economy. And the amount of money in the hands of the public and business is related to the total level of demand in the economy. Total demand, in turn, influences the rate of economic activity in the economy in terms of output, employment, and prices.

stretch out for 20 years or more. If money is hard to get (and is expensive), many families will hold off from buying a new house—in part, also, because they will find it hard to get rid of their present house, since potential customers for their old house will also find it difficult and costly to get a new mortgage loan on it.

Some businesses may also be deterred from buying new capital equipment by tight money and high interest rates. If they think they can save interest costs by waiting until money is cheaper, they may postpone capital outlays. Provincial and local governments may decide to postpone outlays on new school buildings, highways, hospitals, or transit systems, if the cost of borrowed funds is high and they think they can save a great deal of money by waiting until interest rates come down.

The bank's actions—and its verbal statements—may affect the mood of the public and possibly its spending behavior. If the Governor of the Bank of Canada makes worried speeches about the outlook for inflation and implies that he will take action against it, this may make businesses and the general public more cautious about their spending. Or if he advertises determination to ease money and spur business activity, this may improve public optimism and increase the willingness of businesses to borrow and invest in plant and equipment. But public statements do not necessarily work; the public sometimes disregards the warnings and sometimes over-reacts. Monetary policy is only one element—though an extremely important one—in influencing the ups and downs of the economy. Its effectiveness and importance is a subject for vigorous debate among some economists. In the next chapter, we will turn to another key method used by governments in the pursuit of economic stabilization-fiscal policy, which involves the manipulation of taxing and spending patterns.

KEY CONCEPTS

monetary policy
equation of exchange
velocity of money
open market operations
bank rate
moral suasion

QUESTIONS FOR REVIEW AND DISCUSSION

1. What is the primary function of the central bank? What are the main weapons used by the Bank of Canada in carrying out this function?
2. How do changes in legal reserve requirements affect the nation's money supply? How do open market purchases and sales of government bonds affect the nation's money supply? How do changes in the Bank rate affect the nation's money supply? Which of these changes would you recommend for large and quick changes in the money supply? Which type of change gives us the most flexibility in influencing the money supply?
3. If you thought that there was a great deal of excess demand in the economy and a serious threat of inflation, what monetary policy would you recommend? Why? What if you thought there was only a little excess demand and only a possibility

of inflation? What if you thought there was not enough demand in the economy, and felt there might be a drop in production and an increase in unemployment?

4. What is meant by the *velocity of money*? How does this concept help us relate changes in the money supply to changes in the rate of total economic activity?

PROBLEMS AND EXERCISES TO SHARPEN YOUR UNDERSTANDING

1. Take a sheet of paper and make a list labeled *a* through *h* to correspond to the following policies. Then make columns with the following headings: Reserves of Banks, Bank Loans to Individuals and Businesses, Checking Accounts and the Money Supply, and Total Demand in the Economy.

   Assume that there is no change in the velocity of money. Under each column and beside each letter place a plus sign (to indicate an increase), a minus sign (to indicate a decrease), or a zero (to indicate no change) to show the most likely change in each of these areas caused by each of the following policies.
   (a) The Bank of Canada buys government bonds on the open market.
   (b) The Bank of Canada sells government bonds on the open market.
   (c) The Bank of Canada increases the Bank Rate.
   (d) The Bank of Canada decreases the Bank Rate.
   (e) The Bank of Canada lowers secondary reserve requirements.
   (f) The Bank of Canada raises secondary reserve requirements.
   (g) The Governor of the Bank of Canada makes a speech saying that he feels that inflation is becoming a serious problem for the economy.
   (h) The Governor of the Bank of Canada makes a speech saying that he feels that unemployment is becoming a serious problem for the economy.
2. Examine current newspapers, especially the financial press and other recent sources, for indications of current Bank of Canada policy and particular methods being used to implement the Bank's policies.
3. Some research into the debate on the usefulness of monetary policy would be both interesting and worthwhile. Some preliminary references might be:
   (a) J. H. Wood, "Money and Output, Keynes and Friedman In Historical Perspective," in *Business Review,* Federal Reserve Bank of Philadelphia, September, 1972.
   (b) Leonard Silk, *The Economists,* New York: Discus Books, 1978. (See Chapters 2 and 3 on Friedman and Galbraith.)
   (c) J. K. Galbraith, *Money, Whence It Came, Where It Went,* New York: Bantam, 1976. (See particularly chapter XIX, "The New Economics At High Noon.")
   (d) M. Friedman, *On Galbraith and on Curing The British Disease,* Vancouver: The Fraser Institute, 1977. (Part I deals with Galbraith; Part II outlines his approach to the problem of "too much government" in the economy.)

CHAPTER 28

FISCAL POLICY

■ THE PRINCIPLES OF FISCAL POLICY ■ ANALYSING FEDERAL FISCAL POLICY ■ TAX RATES VERSUS TAX REVENUES ■ THE FULL EMPLOYMENT BUDGET ■ GRAPHING THE FULL EMPLOYMENT BUDGET ■ TAX CHANGES VERSUS CHANGES IN GOVERNMENT SPENDING ■ SUMMARY ■ APPENDIX: AN APPLICATION OF THE PRINCIPLES OF FISCAL POLICY

There is a famous passage about the importance of balanced budgets in Charles Dickens' *David Copperfield* that goes, "Annual income twenty pounds, annual expenditure nineteen six, result happiness. Annual income twenty pounds, annual expenditure twenty pounds ought and six, result misery." This piece of wisdom applies to an individual family or business. But it does *not* apply to the government budget of a nation.

If your family's expenditures indeed exceed the money coming in, your father and mother will in all probability be desperately worried. They will try to figure out how to cut back on your food bills or clothing expenditures or something else; they will ask themselves whether some bills can be deferred, for example whether the bank will be willing to accept a postponement of the payment due on the mortgage on your house; they may even try to think of something to sell (such as a family heirloom or the car or some stocks) in order to bring in some additional money. They know that if expenditures cannot be brought down to equal income, or income increased to meet expenditures, something unpleasant will happen—a court action from creditors, the loss of your house, or whatever. But notice that, whatever happens, it will basically be your own family's misery—your neighbors (if they do not happen to be your creditors) and the nation at large will not be hurt by one family's failure to balance its budget.

National governments must keep budgets, which record all the money they pay out (for everything from armies to the services of mailmen), and all the money they collect (especially through taxes). These government budgets have a superficial similarity to the budgets of families or businesses in recording income and expenditure. But there is an enormous difference between a government's budget and that of an individual family or business. Whether a government's budget is in balance, deficit, or surplus does not primarily affect the welfare of the government itself, but does have a major bearing upon the welfare of the nation as a whole.

If we were to paraphrase the quotation from *David Copperfield* above to apply to the national budget, we might write: "*Annual income ten billion dollars, annual expenditure nine billion, result happiness or misery, depending upon circumstances. Annual income ten billion dollars, annual expenditure eleven billion, result misery or happiness, depending upon circumstances.*"

The making of decisions on how much money government should spend and how much it should try to collect in taxes (and the relationship between these two sums) is the job of **fiscal policy** just as the making of decisions about changes in the size of the money supply is the essence of monetary policy. Remember that the purpose of both fiscal and monetary policy is always to increase production of real goods and services while maintaining high employment and stable prices.

In Canada, monetary policy is primarily the responsibility of the Bank of Canada, though ultimately the bank must accept the wishes of the government of the day. Fiscal policy, on the other hand, is the direct responsibility of governments as they determine their revenues and expenditures.

THE PRINCIPLES OF FISCAL POLICY

The main points about fiscal policy can be briefly developed:

1. Increases in government spending—other conditions being equal—add to the total demand for goods and services. Hence they stimulate the economy. Cuts in government spending conversely reduce total demand and restrain the economy.[1]
2. Increases in tax rates—other conditions being equal—cut total demand for goods and services and hence restrain the economy. Reductions in tax rates conversely increase total demand and stimulate the economy.[2]

Therefore, fiscal policy decisions about whether to increase or reduce government expenditures and about whether to increase or reduce tax rates depend primarily upon the actual and anticipated state of the national economy and upon the judgment of economic policy makers as to whether the economy needs stimulation, restraint, or neither one.

The three basic conditions of the national economy, with the appropriate fiscal policy actions, would then be as follows:

1. If the economy is at less than full employment and a continuation or worsening of unemployment and recession is expected, then an increase in total demand by additional government spending, by a tax cut, or by a combination of the two, can stimulate the economy and increase employment.[3]
2. If, on the other hand, the economy is already at or close to full employment, the general price level is rising, and this situation is expected to continue and inflation to worsen, then a reduction in total demand by reduced government expenditure, by a tax increase, or by some combination of the two, can restrain the economy and check inflation.
3. But if the economy is considered to be in reasonably good balance, with relatively high employment and price stability, then no change in the existing relationship between government spending and taxes may be called for. Or, if the government must increase its expenditures in order to meet some important national need (such as wage a war or educate more people), then such an increase in expenditures should be offset by higher taxes, if necessary to keep the economy in balance. Or, conversely, if the government is able to cut its total expenditures significantly (perhaps because major construction programs are completed), then the government should reduce tax rates accordingly, in order to offset the decline in government spending by a rise in private consumption and investment, thereby preserving a balanced economy with both high employment and stable prices.

The above points briefly cover the principal findings of modern economic analysis concerning fiscal policy. However, these

[1] In terms of the simple equation that $C + I + G = GNP$, an increase in G (government expenditures) will increase GNP—both because G itself is larger and also because the money government spends will reach consumers and business, who in turn will also increase both C (consumption) and I (investment). Cuts in government spending will have the opposite effect, by reducing first G and then, as the government pays out less money, both C and I.

[2] Increases in tax rates will, in terms of the same equation, reduce C and I by taking more income away from consumers and businesses, while cuts in taxes will increase C and I by leaving more income in the hands of consumers and business. Lower taxes, therefore, will tend to stimulate GNP; higher taxes will tend to restrain GNP.

[3] See the cartoon by John Collins, "Forgotten Fiscal Techniques" in A. H. MacDonald, (ed.), *Readings In the World of Economics*, Toronto: McGraw-Hill Ryerson, 1973.

conclusions of the large majority of modern economists still excite much public emotion and concern, especially because of fears about unbalanced budgets (based on false analogies with family or business budgets) and worries about the size of the national debt.

To economists it is not the absolute size of the national debt that is likely to hurt or help the economy but rather the *changes* in the size of the national debt—that is, whether in particular years the government increases or decreases the surplus or the deficit in the budget.

The effort to run a big surplus in the budget (should the government be so foolish as to try this when the country is already suffering from much unemployment) by raising tax rates, cutting expenditures, or both would hurt the national economy. It would reduce total demand, deepen the recession or depression, and aggravate unemployment. However, the running of a surplus in the government budget (which would reduce the national debt) would be wise fiscal policy if the economy were at full employment and suffering from inflation because of excess total demand.

Conversely, the decision to run a budget deficit (thereby increasing the national debt) when the economy is suffering from inflation would be foolish fiscal policy, since it would further increase total demand and aggravate inflationary strains. But the decision to run a deficit (increasing the national debt) when there is widespread unemployment and a business slump may improve business conditions and national welfare by increasing total demand for goods and services.

Thus we see that neither government budget surpluses nor deficits are inherently good or bad. They are good or bad as fiscal policy measures only in relation to the needs of the national economy for stimulation or restraint or continuing balance. Thus, it is changes in the national debt, resulting from current deficits or surpluses, that are important, rather than the absolute size of the national debt.

FIG. 28-1. FISCAL POLICY WEATHER VANES

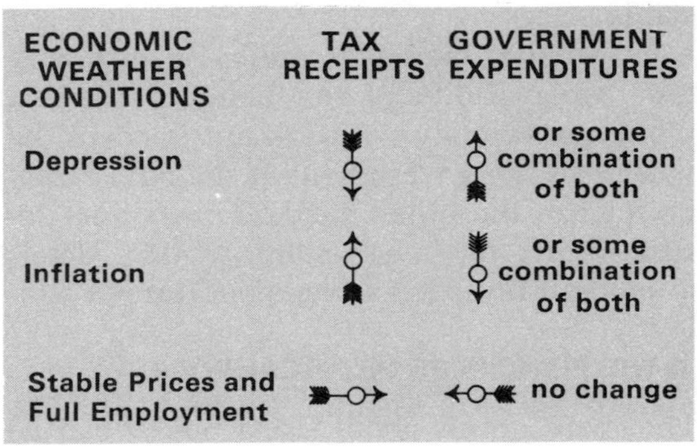

ECONOMIC WEATHER CONDITIONS	TAX RECEIPTS	GOVERNMENT EXPENDITURES
Depression	↓	↑ or some combination of both
Inflation	↑	↓ or some combination of both
Stable Prices and Full Employment	→	← no change

ANALYSING FEDERAL FISCAL POLICY

You will recall from Chapter 19 that total government spending and taxing involve many different types of expenditures and taxes, at different levels of government (including the provincial, local, and Federal levels). In considering fiscal policy, however, we shall focus on the Federal government, because it is difficult, if not impossible, for the individual provinces to follow fiscal policies deliberately designed to stimulate or restrain their own economies.

Even at the Federal level, the whole notion of using taxes and expenditures for the explicit purpose of influencing the rate of total economic activity is a relatively new one. This is not to say, however, that we have not always had a fiscal policy; in fact, we have. Any government expenditure or tax, regardless of its intended purpose, has some effect on the economy. And *doing nothing* to change taxes or expenditures is just as much a policy decision as one to change them, for doing nothing will also have its economic effects, which may or may not be appropriate to meet the existing needs of the economy.

For instance, suppose the government budget is in balance and the government decides not to change it. If total demand in the economy is very strong and prices are being bid up, a government budget that just balances receipts and expenditures will add more to total demand and aggravate inflation

Much of the confusion over national budget-making comes from a false analogy with individual family budgets—which, if not in balance, can lead to great misery. Here is a scene in an 18th century English debtors' prison, as drawn by Hogarth. For nations, however, efforts to balance the national budget at the wrong time may lead to general economic misery.

Prints Division, The New York Public Library

than the budget would if expenditures were cut or taxes increased to yield a surplus.

Or, if total demand is very low and lots of resources and people are unemployed, then a balanced budget will hold down demand and contribute to the persistence of unemployment, where a decision to raise expenditures or reduce taxes, or both, would step up total economic activity and improve the unemployment situation. In fiscal policy, even inaction is a policy decision.

Changes in government spending or taxation will affect the economy in a stimulative or restrictive way, whether or not they actually produce surpluses or deficits. Cutting a government budget surplus from $1 billion to $½ billion can expand the economy just as much as a change from a balanced budget to a deficit of $½ billion. The reason is that, in either case, total demand will be increased by that amount in the first instance in the government (G) sector, with additional stimulative effects upon private consumption (C) and investment (I).

Similarly, cutting a government deficit from $1 billion to $½ billion or increasing a surplus from $½ billion to $1 billion will both have a restraining effect upon the economy of the same degree.

TAX RATES VERSUS TAX REVENUES

In analysing the economic effects of changes in the government's fiscal programs, most economists use the data on Federal receipts and expenditures compiled for the national income and product accounts. Here, one deals with all receipts and expenditures, not just the regular "Budget Accounts," which do not include many categories of transfers in and out of the flow of income. (Recall Table 19-3 and Figure 23-3.) How can the government cut tax rates and still increase its revenue? The answer is that *the rate of economic activity* also changes. And, as economic activity changes, the amount of revenues collected by any given set of tax rates also changes.

If our Federal tax system were a *proportional* tax system, tax revenues would change in direct relation to changes in economic activity or earned incomes. An increase of 10 percent in GNP or personal income, for example, would increase tax

FIG. 28-2. TAX RATES AND TAX RECEIPTS AT DIFFERENT GNP LEVELS

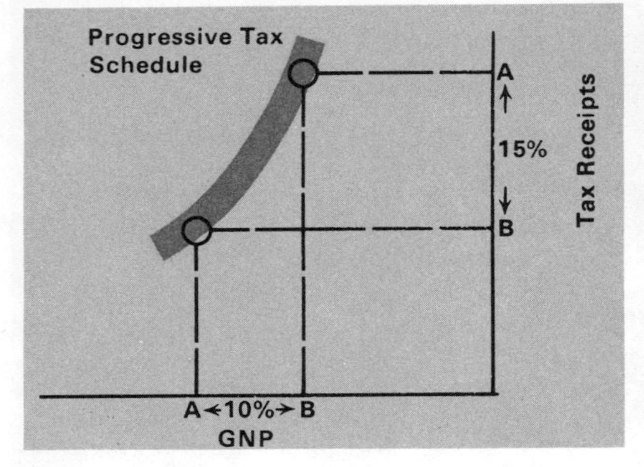

FIG. 28-3. EFFECT OF A TAX CUT AT DIFFERENT GNP LEVELS

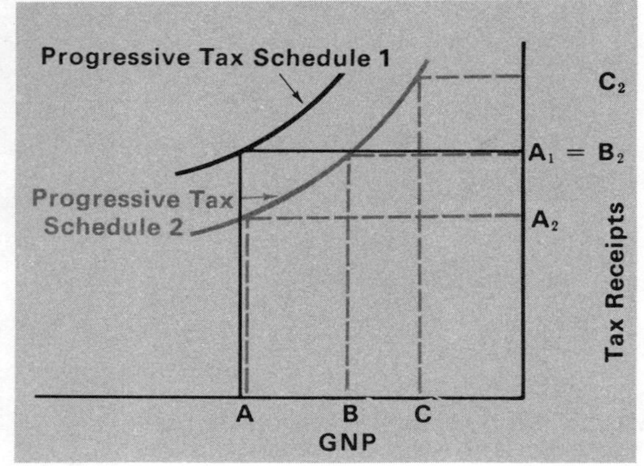

receipts by 10 percent in a proportional tax system. But, as you should recall from Chapter 19, our *Federal* tax system, on balance, tends to be *progressive* in nature. Thus, as the economy expands and incomes increase, tax revenues tend to expand even more rapidly than incomes—a 10 percent increase in incomes, for example, might result in a 15 percent increase in tax receipts. Conversely, if the economy contracts and incomes fall, tax receipts tend to fall even faster than the decline in incomes—a 10 percent decrease in incomes, for example, might result in a 15 percent reduction in tax receipts.

Figure 28-2 illustrates how such a progressive tax structure would operate. The curve labeled "progressive tax schedule" gets steeper as it goes to the right because as GNP increases, tax receipts increase faster than the changes in GNP. The schedule gets less steep as you move to the left because, as GNP declines, tax receipts fall faster than the changes in GNP. This is illustrated by the fact that a move of 10 percent between A and B on the GNP axis results in a larger move of 15 percent between A and B on the tax receipts axis.

Figure 28-3 illustrates how a reduction in tax *rates* at any given level of GNP can actually yield higher tax *receipts*, if GNP expands enough. If taxes are cut from the black progressive tax schedule 1 in Figure 28-3 to the colored progressive tax schedule 2 (a downward shift in tax collections at every level of GNP), tax receipts would fall from A_1 to A_2 at the level of GNP marked A. But, if GNP increases to the level of GNP marked B, tax receipts at the new level of GNP would be as great with the reduced tax rates (B_2) as they were with the old tax rates at the old GNP level (A_1). And, if GNP would increase to the level marked C as a result of the stimulative effect of lower tax rates, then the tax receipts on the reduced tax schedule (C_2) would actually exceed the tax receipts at the old GNP level with the old tax rates (C_2 is larger than A_1).

The important point is that, with progressive tax rates, actual tax *receipts* depend not only upon tax rates but also upon the level of economic activity.

THE FULL EMPLOYMENT BUDGET

It is no easy task to decide just how much stimulation or restraint the budget should contain, since this involves forecasting the state of the economy in the fiscal year ahead. Looking at budget surpluses or deficits can be misleading. These actual surpluses or deficits do not really tell you whether a given fiscal policy was stimulative or restrictive.

Many economists argue that, rather than looking at actual government budget surpluses or deficits after the fact (given the actual level at which the economy operated during the period covered), they should look at what the government budget surplus or deficit would be at full employment[4] levels of GNP, before they determine the fiscal policy for the year ahead.

If the economy is not operating at full employment, however, the economists' job of estimating what the Federal budget would look like at full employment is very difficult. First, the full employment level of GNP changes each year, as the economy and labor force grow. And changes in GNP change the amount of tax receipts—even if tax rates remain the same. Secondly, both government spending and tax rates change in ways that the administration itself cannot wholly control.

GRAPHING THE FULL EMPLOYMENT BUDGET

The concept of a **full employment budget** can be simply illustrated with a graph, as in Figure 28-4 for a hypothetical situation.

Suppose that government expenditures are at a level of $10 billion for a given year and that there is a progressive tax system which yields more tax receipts as GNP rises.

At the point where the line representing government expenditures intersects the line representing the tax schedule, the Federal budget will be in balance. This point in our diagram is found at B, where GNP is equal to $63 billion and tax receipts are equal to $10 billion, exactly the same as government expenditures. Assuming that a GNP level of

FIG. 28-4. THE FULL EMPLOYMENT BUDGET

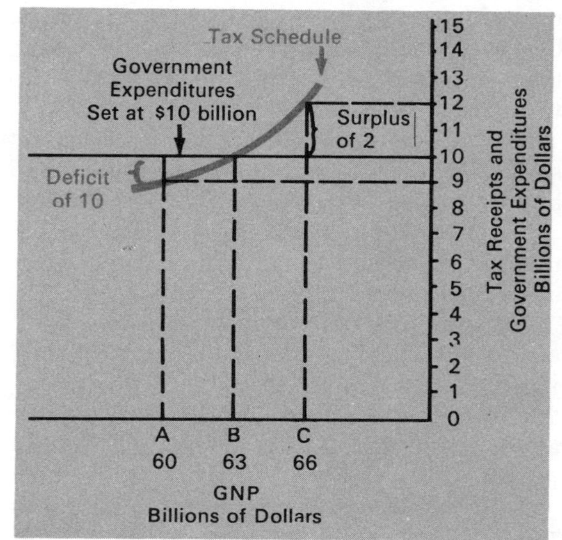

$63 billion corresponds to full employment (96 percent of the civilian labor force) at existing price levels, the national budget is now set at a level that will provide no further stimulus to the economy once full employment is reached.

Suppose, however, that the pressures of demand are so strong that GNP in current dollars keeps rising to point C, where GNP equals $66 billion. Due to our progressive tax system, tax receipts at that GNP level will rise to $12 billion, thereby producing a $2 billion surplus in the Federal budget. This large surplus will help to restrain the boom and prevent inflation.

What if, on the other hand, GNP is running at an annual rate of only $60 billion—as at point A on the diagram? At that level, there are unemployed resources in the economy; let us say that the unemployment rate is 5 percent, instead of the 4 percent rate we desire. At that level of GNP, our tax system is yielding tax receipts of only $9 billion, so the Federal budget is $1 billion in deficit. The budget then exerts a stimulative effect on the economy and helps to move it toward point B, where the budget will be in balance and unemployment will be down to 4 percent.

[4] In Chapter 26, we used 4% unemployment as a rough indicator of "full employment." It should be recalled that in the real world, there is considerable debate over what is a reasonable goal. Goals for employment or the definition of "full employment" will be found to vary from time to time and user to user.

Thus it is apparent that our full employment budget represented in Figure 28-4 is designed to stimulate the economy when there is unemployment and to restrain it when there is excess demand and inflation.

Let us change our assumptions now to show how the concept of a full employment budget might help us to make intelligent changes in our tax system, if it were clear that the economy was suffering from chronic unemployment.

Assume now that at point C, where GNP equals $66 billion, unemployment totals 4 percent; that at point B, with GNP equal to $63 billion, unemployment is 5 percent; and at point A, with GNP at $60 billion, unemployment is 6 percent.

This would mean that our full employment budget would yield a surplus of $2 billion at point C, since tax receipts would rise at the $66 billion GNP level to $12 billion, with government expenditures set at $10 billion. But a full employment budget set to yield so high a surplus might, in fact, prevent the economy from ever attaining full employment. For, whenever GNP starts to increase, a larger and larger share of the expansion is drained off by heavy taxes (two-thirds of the rise in GNP from B to C would go to taxes) and this **fiscal drag**[5] may curtail total demand to the extent that the economy never reaches point C. Indeed, if the economy reaches equilibrium anywhere below point B, the government's *actual* budget would show a deficit—despite the fact that a full employment budget would yield a surplus of $2 billion.

One remedy for this unduly repressive full employment budget would be to cut taxes. Such a tax cut is represented in Figure 28-5 by tax schedule 2, which now brings the budget into balance at C rather than B, thereby removing excess fiscal drag from the budget.

Another remedy would be to increase government expenditures from $10 billion to

[5] This phrase is used to refer to an excessive amount of income being drawn into government revenue, restraining demand and preventing it from increasing enough to generate full employment.

FIG. 28-5. A CUT IN TAXES TO CHANGE THE FULL EMPLOYMENT BUDGET

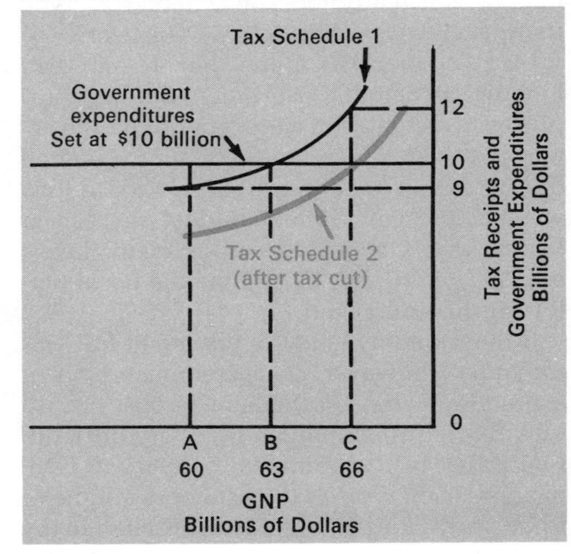

$12 billion, where they would equal tax receipts at the C, or full employment, level of GNP.

Or one might achieve the same objective of setting the full employment budget into balance at point C, by some combination of lower tax rates and higher government expenditures.

TAX CHANGES VERSUS CHANGES IN GOVERNMENT SPENDING

The earliest advocates of using fiscal policy to influence the total level of economic activity usually focused on changes in government spending as the main weapon for affecting total demand. In recent years, however, more attention has been given to changing taxes rather than expenditures as the basic fiscal policy tool.

While either cuts in government spending or tax increases will reduce total demand and while either increases in spending or tax cuts will increase total demand, there are some important differences in these two weapons—even when their effect on total demand is the same.

Some of these will emerge in the more detailed considerations in the next chapter.

SUMMARY

Beware of false analogies between the budgets of individual families or businesses and the government budget. If the individual family or business does not balance its budget, it may suffer because of an inability to pay its debts, without benefiting anyone, or the economy as a whole. But the national budget is primarily important for its effect on the national economy. For instance, a planned government budget deficit, coming in a time of heavy unemployment, may help to stimulate economic activity and raise employment without hurting the government itself. And a planned surplus, coming in a time of rapidly rising prices, may help restrain the economy and promote price stability.

Fiscal policy involves the making of decisions about government expenditures and taxes. Put most simply, increases in government spending increase total demand and increases in taxes cut total demand; vice versa, cuts in government spending cut total demand and cuts in taxes increase total demand. Therefore, if the economy is suffering from unemployment (too little total demand), government should increase its spending, reduce tax rates, or both. If the economy is suffering from inflation (excess total demand resulting in rising prices), then government should reduce its spending, increase taxes, or both.

An important problem in analysing fiscal policy is to distinguish between tax rates and actual tax receipts. Lower tax rates, by helping to produce a higher level of total economic activity (GNP), may actually result in higher tax receipts; or the reverse may occur, with higher tax rates resulting in lower tax receipts, if GNP is dragged down by too heavy a tax burden.

To determine the probable effects of a particular fiscal policy, it is useful to employ the concept of the *full employment budget*. This shows how much the government's national income accounts budget would be in surplus or deficit, if the economy were operating at full employment.

If the full employment surplus is too large (though there is currently widespread unemployment and an actual budget deficit), the size of the full employment surplus may hamper the economy and prevent it from achieving full employment and an actual budget surplus. But if the full employment surplus is too small (or if the budget is even set to yield a deficit at full employment), the combination of too much government spending in relation to too low tax rates may—especially in a period of actual full employment—cause inflation.

KEY CONCEPTS

fiscal policy | fiscal drag | full employment budget

QUESTIONS FOR REVIEW AND DISCUSSION

1. What is government fiscal policy? How does it differ from monetary policy? How is it similar to monetary policy?
2. Under what conditions would a government surplus be wise? Under what conditions would a surplus be unwise? Under what conditions would a government deficit be wise? Under what conditions would a deficit be unwise?

3. Explain the statements: "We always have a fiscal policy" and "A decision not to change taxes and spending is just as much of a policy choice as a decision to change either taxes or spending."
4. How would you use the full employment budget as a guide to fiscal policy decisions?
5. Why is it possible to cut tax rates and still have subsequent increase in the tax receipts?
6. Explain the term *fiscal drag.*

FOR FURTHER RESEARCH

1. Examine the policy implications of the most recent Federal budget. Sources would include the actual budget statement of the Minister of Finance and its supporting papers, press coverage of reactions to the budget, the most recent annual *Economic Review* of the Department of Finance, and the most recent edition of an annual analysis, *The National Finances,* published by the Canadian Tax Foundation.
2. Historical research on the evolution of general approaches to fiscal policy will help broaden your perspective. Some references could be:
   (a) Henry Murphy, "Fiscal Policy: What Does It Really Mean?" and J. K. Galbraith, "The Keynesian Revolution", both reprinted in A. H. MacDonald, (ed.), *Readings In The World of Economics,* Toronto: McGraw-Hill Ryerson, 1973.
   (b) J. K. Galbraith, "How Keynes Came To America," in *Economics, Peace and Laughter,* Boston: Houghton Mifflin, 1971.
   (c) J. K. Galbraith, *Age of Uncertainty,* Boston: Houghton Mifflin, 1977. (See particularly Chapter 7, "The Mandarin Revolution".)

   The references given for the final research topic at the end of C ιapter 27 would also be of use here.

APPENDIX:

AN APPLICATION OF THE PRINCIPLES OF FISCAL POLICY

The king in the *Wizard of Id* cartoons reproduced here seems to be unaware of the benefits of a counter-cyclical fiscal policy in a recession. Fortunately, as it always is in imaginary worlds, a hero is at hand to exercise his own initiative.

Reproduced by permission of Johnny Hart

the WIZARD of ID
by Brant parker and Johnny hart
SO LONG, GENTS... THANK YOU FOR THE GOLD!
ROBBING HOOD LEPT HERE
GADS!.. ANOTHER RECESSION! WHAT'S HAPPENING AROUND HERE?
© Field Enterprises, Inc., 1971
...WHERE DOES ALL THE MONEY GO?
MUST BE ROUGH ON THOSE POOR DEVILS DOWN THERE.
SIRE... A PEASANT TO SEE YOU.
9-12
WOULD YOU CARE TO RENT OUT THAT EAST WING, SIRE... IT'S JUST WHAT I'M LOOKING FOR.
ARE YOU MAD?
...WE'RE IN A RECESSION, STUPID! HOW COULD YOU POSSIBLY AFFORD TO.....
...OH, MONEY'S NO PROBLEM, SIRE....
...MY "ROBBING HOOD" CHECKS KEEP COMING IN LIKE CLOCKWORK.

ADDITIONAL ASPECTS OF MONETARY AND FISCAL POLICY

■ SOME PROBLEMS OF ECONOMIC POLICY MAKING ■ THE COMPLEXITIES OF BUSINESS FLUCTUATIONS ■ THE MULTIPLIER AND THE ACCELERATOR ■ AUTOMATIC VERSUS DISCRETIONARY ECONOMIC POLICY MAKING ■ SUMMARY

In the preceding chapters, we have studied how monetary and fiscal policy can be directed against either unemployment or inflation. Monetary and fiscal policy are not mutually exclusive instruments. They can be used together in various mixes, depending on many practical considerations, and can be supplemented by other possible policies.

■ SOME PROBLEMS OF ECONOMIC POLICY MAKING

One of the hardest tasks in writing an introductory textbook about any subject is trying to figure out how to make difficult matters clear—without making the reader think they are simpler, easier, and more conclusively solved by members of the profession than they really are. This is certainly true of economics. In particular, the making of economic policy is anything but simple and definitively solved today. Chapter 26 hopefully has made that quite clear. In addition to the major quandary discussed there, a number of other more specific problems haunt those who make economic policy decisions.

Problems of Information Lags and Forecasting

A most urgent requirement for economic policy making is timely and accurate information about where our economy is and where it appears to be heading. Our data have, in some areas, serious inadequacies. Even with good statistics, however, it takes time to collect and analyse the data. Often we must base decisions on information about where we were a month or two ago and where we think we might be next month, next year, or even a year and a half from now.

Economic forecasting is still, as you have seen, an imperfect art, although economists are hard at work trying to improve it. But economic prediction can never be as sure as prediction in some of the physical sciences. Therefore economic policy making must always be done with considerable uncertainty about the future.

Problems of Lags in Decision Making

Even after the relevant information is in and analysed, how long does it take to get a policy decision made? Here we find some important differences between monetary and fiscal policy. The Bank of Canada often makes decisions on monetary policy much more quickly than the government can make up its mind and coordinate the policy recommendations of many different agencies of government.

Political considerations doubtless play a bigger role in delaying fiscal policy decisions, although monetary policy is by no means immune from political pressures.

Problems of Lags in Affecting the Economy

Once a monetary or fiscal policy decision

has been made and action taken, how long does it take for its total effect to reach the economy?

Here again there are differences between monetary and fiscal policy. Just within the area of fiscal policy, there are differences between the lagged impacts resulting from changes in different tax changes and different government expenditure programs. For instance, a change in the personal income tax which immediately shows up in people's paychecks will quickly affect consumer spending; but a change in tax credits for business investment in new plant and equipment may be considerably delayed because the decisions about how much to invest in the near future have already been taken and cannot be altered quickly.

Monetary policy actions may affect the economy with a considerable lag. Once the Bank of Canada has decided to stimulate the economy by buying securities and bonds in the open market, bank reserves will go up almost immediately. But it may be three to six months, or even longer, before the full process of the multiple expansion of checking accounts has worked its way through the economy and increased consumer and business demand in the marketplace.

Similar delays are associated with changes in government expenditures. For instance, contract negotiations over a large government program may stretch out over a period of months, and, even after the programs are launched, there may be all sorts of delays resulting from slow delivery of equipment, shortages of skilled manpower, or controversies over design. Some programs may be delayed in their impact by political or administrative problems at the provincial and local levels as well as at the federal level. Blaine's cartoon, "The Problem of Time Lags," reprinted in A. H. MacDonald, (ed.), *Readings In The World Of Economics*, Toronto: McGraw-Hill Ryerson, 1973, aptly summarizes the potential impact of time lags.

Problems of Initial Impact

The Canadian economy consists of a host of different groups, industries, regions, and individuals whose interests may be differently affected—especially initially—by particular policy actions. Even policies that have the same impact on total demand will have quite different effects on particular elements within the economy. For instance, a tax cut of the same amount, say $1 billion, will be very differently regarded if it is distributed evenly to all income groups, or if it goes mainly to the poor or mainly to the rich. Arguments over initial impact will, therefore, often delay and complicate tax decisions.

Monetary policy, which strongly influences interest rates, may have most of its effect in those areas where borrowing plays a large role. Most people do not borrow money to buy groceries or go to the movies, but they do frequently borrow to buy homes, automobiles, and other durable goods. Hence, these sectors may suffer more heavily than others from a tightening of monetary policy and a hike in interest rates.

Changes in government spending also tend to have a concentrated initial impact. Some programs will benefit the residents of a particular province (as in a big water resource development program); others may affect a particular industry (as in programs to expand airports, or improve merchant shipping); and other government programs may benefit particular groups in the economy (such as the poor, farmers, or old people). One simple cannot make overall fiscal and monetary policy without considering the political complications resulting from these questions of initial impact.

Problems of Public Versus Private Decision Making

In deciding which combination of monetary and fiscal policy to use, some people are also concerned with whether the changes in total spending required are carried out by private individuals and businesses or by government agencies.

Monetary policy works almost exclusively through the private banking system. If the central bank decides to increase demand by increasing bank reserves, the actual loans and spending decisions will be made by the

Collins in Montreal Gazette

For governments in the 1970s, economic policy making was very much of a juggling act.

private sector of the economy. Similarly, in using fiscal policy to increase demand, tax cuts will mean leaving more income in the hands of private individuals and businesses who will then decide where the extra income they have should be spent.

However, if we increase total demand, not by cutting taxes but rather by raising government expenditures, then government officials and politicians will make the initial spending decisions. Even though most of the money spent in this way goes to private firms that sell to the government, the types of goods and services that the government buys will be quite different from the goods and services that would be purchased if the same amount of money were spent by private individuals or businesses. The choice of whether to boost government spending, cut taxes, increase bank reserves, or to aim at some combination of these measures thus involves economics; but whether you favor one method or another is also a matter of your political and social preferences. Political conservatives are more likely to prefer tax cuts and monetary actions to increase bank reserves; political liberals are more likely to prefer increases in government expenditure for particular social programs.

Clearly, personal or group interests are bound to affect the choice of economic policies arrived at in the political arena. But economic policies will also depend on the character and wisdom of political leaders and citizens who seek to develop economic policies that will serve the interests of the nation as a whole, not just the aims of one particular group or other.

Problems in Balancing Political and Economic Considerations

Since fiscal policy decisions, for the most part, must pass through The Commons whose members periodically stand for election, their actions are usually more visible than monetary policy decisions made by the central bank whose Governor is appointed for a long term and whose operations are usually invisible to the general public. This may make it somewhat easier for the central bank to act when politically unpopular economic restraint is necessary than it is for the Government. While many M.P.'s may be in favor of cutting some government spending in principle, very few are for enacting cuts in government programs within their own ridings. Nor, barring major emergencies, do many relish running on a program of raising taxes. Hence, there are often some practical limitations on the use of fiscal policy to combat the threat of excess demand that may develop during periods of prosperity. Who wants to take a chance of killing off a boom and being blamed for causing a recession and unemployment?

Thus, political as well as economic considerations must be weighed—and are weighed in making economic policy decisions. Whether or not this is the best way to make sound economic decisions is beside the point; it is simply a fact of life in a free and democratic society. This is why the economic understanding of the general public is so important in the economy. Given the nature of our political and economic system, it is the people who, through their votes and other influences, determine within broad limits the scope and nature of government policies.

In the Canadian situation, the economic impact of the division of power in our federal system provides a further complication.

Partisan political differences between Ottawa and the provinces may arise, though hopefully never in a way as blatant as a notorious example from 1930. Mackenzie King was being pressured to indicate what federal aid would be given to the provinces to assist them in providing relief to the unemployed—a field from which Ottawa's direct participation was barred in those pre-Keynesian days. In the course of his reply, the Liberal Prime Minister made the blunt statement that some measures might be taken . . . "but I would not give a single cent to any Tory government!" Hansard records a polite response of "Shame!" from R. B. Bennett and H. H. Stevens. This and several similar comments the same day helped defeat the government in an election later that year. (See the House of Commons Debates, April 3,

1930, pp. 1227 ff. for this famous exchange.)

More likely to be of significance than partisan quarrels are disputes based on different economic priorities in different parts of the country, some of which may be in conflict with the broader view of national conditions which Ottawa must focus upon.

"Constitutional" issues based on both law and politics about whether Ottawa or the provinces have or should exercise power in certain areas may also produce complications. As Canada appears to be moving toward constitutional reform, the distribution of economic responsibilities is certain to become a more prominent issue. Advocates of a reduced role for Ottawa seem to come generally from the "have" provinces, who want more authority and have the resources to pay for it, from Quebec where the economic issue is more closely tied to the broader philosophical quest for either more autonomy or outright independence, and from those parts of the private sector who see a reduced Federal role as the first stage of a general reduction in the role of government in the economy. Those most fearful of reductions in Federal power are the "have-not" provinces, who fear decreases in the rate of transfer of funds through Ottawa, and those in the private sector who are more inclined to a greater role for government as a transfer or regulatory force in the economy.

One final basic complication results simply from the fact that our federal structure exists. Ignoring debates over priorities, policies or changes in the distribution of power, a major portion of the total of governmental expenditures and revenues are decentralized; that is, they are in the hands of the provinces and municipalities. To the extent this exists, there cannot be a single fiscal policy in the orthodox sense. Localized policies will be developed and it is more than likely that some of these may have effects which are in conflict with the nationally-directed policies from Ottawa. At present, about half of the dollars being raised or spent in the "government" sector are at the provincial and local levels. As a result, the impact of this situation could be significant. Table 30-6, which covers a very short time period under examination in Chapter 30, provides an illustration of this in measuring the relative surplus-deficit positions of various levels of government.

THE COMPLEXITIES OF BUSINESS FLUCTUATIONS

One of the problems that makes the life of an economic policy maker difficult, important, and exciting in a free society, where private business and individuals play so large a role, is that the economy may expand or contract in ways that are difficult to anticipate, but which the policy maker must seek to moderate.

Since the emergence of modern, market economies, there have been recurrent periods of prosperity with close to full employment and recession, or deep depression with large scale unemployment. Some observers have professed to see a regularity in these movements of business, which they choose to call *business cycles,* similar to cycles in light waves, sound waves, or planetary cycles.

Economists have offered a great many theories of such business cycles. But no one has been able to offer a theory to explain all upswings and downswings in economic activity in a consistent way that economists generally are willing to accept.

Actually, a close look at economic activity over the years shows that upswings and downswings have varied greatly both in *amplitude* (how high or low they go) and in *duration* (how long they last). Although the economy as a whole may expand or contract, different industries or sectors grow (or shrink) at different rates in every expansion or contraction. Some industries even grow while most are shrinking or shrink while most are growing.

Many modern economists prefer to talk of business *fluctuations* rather than cycles because they take the word *cycle* to imply a greater smoothness and regularity than seems to exist.

While detailed studies of past fluctuations reveal that upswings or downswings do not result from any single cause, the following generalization does appear valid: *Most upswings appear to come to an end and turn into a downswing because of imbalances that develop between the rate at which the productive capacity of the economy is growing and the rate at which total demand for the uses of that capacity is growing.*

Imbalances can develop in many ways. Businesspeople may invest a great deal in new plants and equipment and then not find a market for all the goods they are capable of producing. This may then cause them to cut back on their capital spending. As they stop spending money on plants and equipment, total demand will be reduced, workers will be laid off, and the general economy will decline.

Or businesspeople may invest a great deal of money in accumulating inventories—stocks of goods and raw materials needed in production. They may do this because they think prices will rise or because they think goods are going to be in short supply and that they will therefore be unable to fill all the orders they can obtain. But if the demand for their products fails to grow rapidly enough to permit them to use those inventories, this will cost businesspeople money. They may then cut production in order to lower their inventories. This will mean less demand for products of other industries. Again, the general economy may decline—if the inventory cutting is sufficiently widespread—and unemployment may increase.

Imbalances may also come about because there has been an overproduction of homes and consumer goods, relative to what the public wants to buy and can afford to buy. Or imbalances may result from heavy reductions in government ordering and spending—for instance, on goods produced by defense industries.

If the imbalance is great enough and the downward pull of some important factor, such as capital spending on new plant and equipment, inventories, housing, or defense goods is large enough, then other sectors of the economy will be affected. The drop in payments of money to some workers (for instance, those formerly employed on construction projects and other investment programs) will cause those workers to reduce their spending for autos, refrigerators, clothing, and other goods. Employers and workers in those industries will, in turn, reduce their spending on consumer goods. This *multiple* effect upon consumption resulting from an initial drop in spending is very much like the process which we described in Chapter 17, in discussing the contraction and expansion of checking accounts and the money supply.

THE MULTIPLIER AND THE ACCELERATOR

The process that we have been describing works in reverse when the economy is moving upward. Then, a given increase in government spending or in business investment will put more money in the hands of consumers, who will in turn spend part of it for additional goods and services, whose providers will respend part of what they receive, and so on. The process does not go on indefinitely because those receiving extra income do not spend the whole of it, but rather save some. Thus, the initial impulse resulting from increased outlays by government or business will gradually fade away.

Economists have two terms to describe the process by which an initial increase in expenditures affects the economy.

They refer to (1) the **multiplier effect** when a given increase in spending causes an addition to national income and *consumption* greater than the original amount spent.[1]

And they refer to (2) the **acceleration principle** when a rise in the demand for consumer goods causes a more than proportionate increase in the demand for *investment goods* (new plant and equipment) required to produce those additional consumer goods.

Since industries will be able to fill orders without additions to their existing plants and equipment when they are operating well below capacity, a surge in orders for their goods beyond their existing capacity will cause them to increase their investment spending sharply. This speed-up in capital investment (the accelerator principle) then feeds more income to consumers, who help to swell national income by spending and re-spending their extra income (the multiplier effect).

Since the multiplier effect and the acceleration principle will magnify and intensify the effects of either a boom or a recession, the problem facing policy makers is to prevent the start of sharp departures from steady growth. It is much harder and more painful to cure inflation or unemployment once they have taken hold and have begun to affect the economic system as a whole.

The confidence of economists that serious inflation or unemployment can be avoided emerged from their finding that modern fiscal and monetary policy had proved their effectiveness and that these economic measures have been accepted, in their general outline, by political leaders of the major parties and by the leaders of influential groups among business and labor.

As indicated in Chapter 26, however, our recent experience has shown that our capacity to regulate the economy is less than perfect, and both the confidence of economists and the intensity of debate among them has increased as a result.

[1] For a more detailed examination, see "The Multiplier Process" by Shu-Chin Yang in A. H. MacDonald, (ed.), *Readings In the World of Economics*, Toronto: McGraw-Hill Ryerson, 1973.

AUTOMATIC VERSUS DISCRETIONARY ECONOMIC POLICY MAKING

There have been strong differences among economists on how to apply fiscal and monetary policy to keep the economy steady and at a high rate of employment. Because of all the difficulties of forecasting the course of the economy, getting policies adopted in time, and not knowing whether the measures adopted will be too much or too little to deal with conditions as they emerge, some economists believe that we should not rely too much on the discretion of policy makers. Rather, they argue that we should follow certain fiscal and monetary rules to keep the system steadily growing. They would build automatic stabilizing devices into our system that would prevent massive changes in economic activity, while permitting us to take our chances with smaller fluctuations.

Economists favoring automatic rules hold that this would avoid the risk of poorly timed discretionary changes, which might do more to upset rather than to stabilize the economy. Economists favoring automatic rules over shifting human judgments feel that much can be done with monetary and fiscal policy.

Automatic Monetary Policy

In the area of monetary policy, for instance, one school of thought advocates that central banks should adopt the simple rule of automatically increasing the money supply at the same rate as the sustainable growth of the full-employment capacity of the economy (about 3½ percent to 4 percent a year) and then forget about attempting to offset every real or imagined fluctuation in economic activity.[2] They contend that if the economy slumps, the automatic increase in the money supply will buoy the economy up; or if an inflationary boom gets going, increasing the money supply only at the predetermined rate of 3½ percent to 4 percent a year will restrain, if not eliminate, the increase in prices.

Most economists, however, do not believe that it is possible—or wise—to try to automate fully the rate of growth of the money supply. They fear that this would tie the bank's hands and prevent it from dealing effectively with unforeseen emergencies or unusually sharp upswings or downswings in the economy. There is, however, a growing agreement among the economists that, normally, the money supply ought to be made to grow at about the same rate as the productive capacity of the economy.

Automatic Fiscal Policy

In the area of fiscal policy, there is widespread agreement among economists that we have been wise to add certain automatic stabilizers to our system. For instance, our unemployment insurance system, which increases receipts in good times and increases benefit payments when unemployment increases, is an important built-in stabilizer. Most important of all, though, is our progressive tax system, which takes more money out of the economy when business is booming and employment high and takes much less (in percentage as well as absolute terms) out of the economy when business sags and unemployment rises.

Proponents of automatic, as opposed to discretionary fiscal policy, would go still further; they argue that if we set tax rates to balance the budget at full employment, the government should then not worry about changing taxes or government expenditures to offset changes in economic activity. They contend that the delays and distortions involved in such discretionary changes in taxes or spending might result in more harm than good.

Even proponents of such a full-employment budget policy as an automatic rule recognize, however, that it would provide only partial offsets to the big swings in business activity that can occur in a free-enterprise economy. The problem of using the full-employment budget as a guide to policy making is far greater when the economy has reached full employment than when there are many unemployed resources. There is greater hesitancy about braking an expansion than about curing unemployment.

Adopting the full-employment budget as a guiding rule to fiscal policy would not, in any case, eliminate the need for human judgment and periodic changes in tax rates or government expenditures. For one thing, the full-employment level of GNP changes over time, as the productive capacity of industry and the quantity and quality of the labor force change. For another, government spending may shift markedly up or down for reasons independent of economic considerations. For instance, a war will push government spending up sharply, and the end of a war may push it down. Hence, the job of setting tax rates to balance the budget at full employment will need to be done periodically, *after careful review of the actual and prospective conditions of the natural economy and the expenditure side of the government budget.*

As with the automatic monetary rule, few economists really want to tie the hands of policy makers by making them give up completely the ability to make discretionary changes in fiscal policy to combat substantial inflations or depressions, should they develop. During the period of increased economic difficulty in the 1970s, there has been an increase in the scope of the debate over both realms of automatic policies, perhaps as a result of a feeling that had options or discretionary policies not been permitted to follow the directions they did, the emergence of stagflation might have been avoided.

[2] The principal advocate of this rule is Professor Milton Friedman, whose name should be familiar from the references to him in Chapter 27.

SUMMARY

The making of economic policy in the real world is complicated by many problems: the time lags in making policy decisions because of uncertainty about the existing and future state of the economy; the time lags before changes in government spending, taxes, or monetary policy will have their effect upon the economy; controversies over the initial impact of particular policy actions, which may benefit or hurt different sectors or groups within the economy in varying degrees; controversies over whether general economic actions should be taken in a way to increase the private or public sector of the economy—and other complexities involving both political and economic considerations.

A major economic obstacle to wise policy making is the limited state of knowledge as to the causes of business fluctuations (sometimes inappropriately called business cycles). In general, these fluctuations appear to result from imbalances that develop in a free economy between the growth in total demand and the growth in total productive capacity of the economy. But every upswing and downswing appears to have its own peculiarities and its own specific causes and complications.

Because of the many complexities facing economic policy makers that make it possible for their actions sometimes to aggravate rather than moderate business fluctuations, some economists favor automatic rules for economic policy, rather than discretionary changes made by fallible human beings. In the monetary area, the principle automatic rule recommended would be to increase automatically the money supply at the same rate as the economy's full-em-ployment productive capacity—a rate of 3½ percent to 4 percent a year. In the fiscal area, the principal rule would be to adjust tax rates to a level that would produce a balanced budget when the economy is at or near full employment.

Most economists believe, however, that while these two monetary and fiscal rules are good general guides to policy, there are too many uncertainties—with respect to swings in private business and to political forces affecting government spending—to automate either fiscal or monetary policy. On the contrary, most economists think it would be unwise to tie the hands of either the Bank of Canada or the government in dealing with unforeseen economic conditions as they develop. Indeed, many economists think we need more, rather than less, flexibility in economic policy making because of the difficulties of economic forecasting.

KEY CONCEPTS

multiplier effect

acceleration principle

QUESTIONS FOR REVIEW AND DISCUSSION

1. Would you say that the problem of lags in decision making were more serious for monetary policy or fiscal policy? Why? How does the problem of lags affect the economy once a decision has been made?

2. What type of monetary or fiscal policy would you advocate if you were primarily interested in distributing the impact of your policy as widely as possible throughout the economy? Why?
3. Why do economists now talk more about business *fluctuations* rather than business *cycles*?
4. What is the multiplier? What is the accelerator? How do these forces interact to make the problem of business fluctuations more severe?
5. Would you favor making our monetary and fiscal policy decisions more automatic or more discretionary than they are at the present time? Give specific examples and support your argument.

FOR FURTHER RESEARCH

1. Examine current policies and opinions about the distribution of economic power between Ottawa and the provinces from the perspective of the Federal government, the government of your province and, if you are not a resident of Quebec, the provincial government in Quebec.
2. In the spring of 1978, Federal Finance Minister Jean Chrétien introduced a short run program of tax cuts, federally funded, but implemented selectively by some provinces. This was an innovative way of promoting Federal policy through a method which permitted different effects in different parts of the country. Research the way the program was put into effect and the major conflict which developed between Chrétien and Quebec Finance Minister, Jacques Parizeau.

THE AGE OF CONTROLS

■ A BACKGROUND PERSPECTIVE ■ CONTROLS COME TO CANADA ■ GENERAL POSITIONS ON CONTROLS ■ SUMMARY ■ APPENDIX: ATTACK ON INFLATION

■ A BACKGROUND PERSPECTIVE

As we have seen, during the post-1945 era, governments of most developed market economies had to a considerable degree been attempting to modify cyclical swings through the use of fiscal and monetary policies.

The turbulent decade of the seventies has seen drastic changes in the approaches of both the Canadian and American governments in their attempts to stabilize their economies. Both have experimented with the use of direct controls over a wide range of wages and prices. These moves mark the first uses of such power other than in time of war—steps which may be important precedents for the future. To put the introduction of controls in Canada in some perspective, a bit of historical background is appropriate.

The American Scene, 1960-1969

During the sixties, both the Kennedy and Johnson administrations in the U.S. tried to reinforce traditional policies by getting voluntary support for restraint from key sectors of the economy. This technique was comparable in some ways to the "moral suasion" used by the Bank of Canada, but differed in that, behind requests for compliance was the full range of power of the Presidency. **Voluntary restraint** produced under such circumstances was considered by some to be little more than compliance to coercion or blackmail. As the Vietnam War escalated, the attempt was made to sustain a "guns *and* butter" approach within the economy. A high rate of growth was sustained in the private sector while government policies added potential inflationary pressures. Up to 1966, "jawboning," as the persuasive power of the Presidency had come to be known, along with the more orthodox policies, had some degree of effect. "Guideposts" or "guidelines" served as indicators of maximum desirable levels of increases in prices and wages in key sectors. Behind the guideposts stood the apparent willingness of Jack Kennedy and Lyndon Johnson to use the power they had. Both were strong-willed Democrats and neither was philosophically committed to avoiding the use of government power in the marketplace.

By 1968, however, this phase of voluntary restraint started to crumble. Taxes moved up to help finance the war, price increases started to intensify, and demands for wage increases grew more than proportionally. Perhaps most important, the resolve of the government to keep a grip on the economy showed signs of weakening. The Johnson administration had come under increasing military siege in Southeast Asia and political siege at home. The presidential elections looming in the fall of 1968 may have added to the pressures against taking the tough moves which were called for. By mid-1968, the guideposts had been broken so many times without government reaction that they became ineffective. The capture of the White House by the Republicans that fall signaled an end to the Democrats' experiments in pro-

"See—I warned you that if you didn't stop screaming you'd bring the cops down on us."

Chambers, The Halifax Chronicle-Herald, reprinted by permission

This cartoon from the late 1960s predicts that government would ultimately have to play the role of policeman in response to rising inflationary pressures.

moting voluntary restraint. President-elect Nixon indicated the new administration would rely on monetary and fiscal techniques. Guideposts were to be abandoned and compulsory controls were obviously unthinkable to the more conservative Republicans.

Canada: An Initial Experiment

As inflationary pressures here started to advance in the late sixties, Canada adopted the technique of promoting voluntary restraint. The Trudeau government established a Prices and Incomes Commission which was to monitor trends and act as an economic "conscience." It did not, however, have any power of enforcement and during its existence between 1969 and 1972, it was forced to play the role of observer rather than of policeman. Between 1969 and 1971, the orthodox situation seemed to prevail in Canada. In response to various policies, and perhaps to some degree to the influence of the Prices and Incomes Commission, inflation rates moved down from a 1969 "peak" of 4.6% to 2.9% in 1971 while during the same period unemployment climbed from 4.4% to 6.2%. By 1972, it was declared that the battle against inflation had been won. Attention turned to unemployment. The Phillips Curve seemed to still be applicable.

The Nixon Experiment

In the United States, however, the same period showed unsettling signs. In response to orthodox measures to curtail inflationary pressures, unemployment rose from 3.5% in 1969 to 4.9% in 1970 and 5.9% in 1971. But, unexpectedly, throughout 1969-71, prices continued to increase and did so at rates in the range of 5%, a higher level than the U.S. economy had experienced for two decades. The traditional policies were generating the anticipated cost in higher unemployment levels but were not slowing price increases as had been expected. By 1971, it was becoming clear that either tougher orthodox policies or changes in fundamental approach were required. The first option, with the strong probability of even higher unemployment rates, was not an appealing prospect when the economic and social costs were considered. A further complication was the fact that by mid-1971, presidential elections were, again, just a year away. The administration was already under fire because of the growing unemployment (as well as the rate of inflation) and tougher orthodox anti-inflationary policies would likely identify the Republicans in an election year as "the party which brought on the recession."

The motives which produced many of the startling policy shifts in the ill-fated Nixon

White House will long remain subjects for intense debate. For our purposes here, the nature of the alteration in policy in August, 1971 is more significant than detailed speculation about just why it was carried out. On August 15, 1971, Nixon introduced a series of moves to try and stimulate the economy through tax cuts and investment tax credits. To avoid the inflationary effects of the new fiscal measures and bring existing price and wage pressures under control, a complete freeze on wages, prices and rents was imposed. A government which had been noted for at least nominal adherence to a policy of minimizing interference in the marketplace took the peacetime power of government in the American economy to a new peak.

It must be noted that the imposition of **direct controls** did not mark a conversion of Nixon to what, only ten days before, he had described as the "Galbraith scheme," a set of policies to which he was "unalterably opposed" and which he said were supported only by "extremists of the left."[1] It was indicated from the outset that controls were to be a temporary emergency measure to permit the orthodox medicine to work (and presumably to help overcome the inflationary psychology which had started to develop).

The time limit on the controls program was followed. Gradual loosening took place during 1972 and by early 1973 the program was deemed to have done its job and controls were ended. At the outset, it seemed to have worked. In 1972 and 1973, unemployment declined to 5.6% and 4.9% respectively. The annual rate of inflation for the full year 1971 averaged out at 4.3% compared to 1970's 5.9%. In 1972, the rate was down to 3.3%. In 1973, however, as the last stages of the program were being dismantled, the initial indicators of success vanished in an economic whirlwind which almost equaled the intensity of the political and judicial firestorm which drove Nixon out of the White House in 1974.

[1] *The New York Times*, August 5, 1971.

Inflationary Storms, 1973-1975

During the period from early 1973 through 1975, the dam broke. Prices surged upward on a worldwide basis and in many instances, the rapid upward jumps in the rate of price increases were accompanied by rising unemployment. The data outlined in Tables 30-1 through 30-3 on page 360 indicate briefly the scale of the outbreak of stagflation on an international basis.

Causes were complex and are not yet fully agreed upon. Individually, most of the industrialized nations encountered combinations of problems which helped contribute to the total picture. In Canada, for example, rising labor participation rates helped push up the rate of unemployment. As the economy weakened, corporate profits stagnated during 1974-76 and business investment slowed down, with a resulting effect on the creation of jobs. Rapid rates of expansion in the money supply and large governmental deficits in 1974 and 1975 contributed to inflationary pressure. In the face of rising inflation, with the expectation of more to come, wage demands surged, in many cases far exceeding increases in productivity. Food prices leaped upward, many in response to increases in international price patterns.

In Canada and elsewhere, the extent to which both inflation and unemployment might be imported or exported became apparent to all. In the initial stages of this period, the impact of trends in the U.S. was especially important to Canada. In addition to just importing problems from the U.S., Canada and other nations experienced several other international shocks. One result of the Middle East War of 1973 was an increase in the price of Middle East crude oil from $3.00 a barrel in 1973 to $14.00 in 1977. This was due to the power exerted over oil supplies by major Arab producers (who were quickly joined by other oil-exporting nations). Other energy prices moved up accordingly in international and domestic markets and these pushed other price pressures into the economic structure. A further

Table 30-1. INTERNATIONAL CONSUMER PRICE TRENDS, 1970-1977.

	Annual Percentage Rate of Increase							
	1970	1971	1972	1973	1974	1975	1976	1977
Canada	3.3	2.9	4.8	7.6	10.8	10.8	7.5	8.0
United States	5.9	4.3	3.3	6.2	12.2	7.0	4.8	6.8
United Kingdom	6.4	9.5	6.8	8.3	19.2	24.9	15.1	12.1
Italy	5.0	5.0	5.6	10.4	24.5	11.2	22.0	15.0
Germany (F.R.)	3.7	5.3	5.5	6.9	5.9	5.4	3.9	3.5
Japan	7.6	6.3	4.9	11.7	21.9	7.7	10.4	4.9

Sources: For Canada, see Table 26-2; for others: *United Nations Statistical Yearbook, 1976,* New York: United Nations, 1977; *Bank of Canada Review,* February, 1978.

Table 30-2. INTERNATIONAL WAGE TRENDS IN THE MANUFACTURING SECTOR, 1971-1977.

	Annual Average Percentage Rate of Increase						
	1971	1972	1973	1974	1975	1976	1977
Canada	9.0	8.3	9.4	13.1	13.9	13.7	11.0
United States	6.1	6.6	7.1	8.3	9.2	7.7	9.1
United Kingdom	13.2	13.3	10.9	20.4	26.9	17.1	9.5
Italy	14.4	9.6	24.8	22.4	26.2	21.2	27.8
Germany (F.R.)	10.9	9.0	10.7	10.5	8.1	6.3	7.6
Japan	16.1	16.4	24.4	32.1	14.9	8.2	9.5

Source: *National Institute Economic Review,* (National Institute of Economic and Social Research, London), Number 84, May, 1978.

Table 30-3. INTERNATIONAL UNEMPLOYMENT RATES, 1970-1977.

	Average Annual Rate (%)							
	1970	1971	1972	1973	1974	1975	1976	1977
Canada	5.7	6.2	6.2	5.6	5.3	6.9	7.1	8.1
United States	4.9	5.9	5.6	4.9	5.6	8.5	7.7	6.9
United Kingdom	3.1	3.8	4.1	2.8	2.9	5.1	6.9	7.6
Italy	3.4	3.4	3.9	3.7	3.1	6.4	6.4	7.5
Germany (F.R.)	0.6	0.8	0.8	0.9	1.5	3.6	3.6	3.5
Japan	1.1	1.2	1.4	1.3	1.4	2.0	2.1	2.1

Sources: For Canada, see Table 26-2; for others, *National Institute Economic Review,* (National Institute of Economic and Social Research, London), Number 84, May, 1978.

unsettling effect was produced by growing instability in the international system of exchange rates—the relationships among various national currencies. Crises had been recurring in world money markets since 1967 and by the mid-seventies, the old orderly system which had worked reasonably well for two decades was breaking down. (This phenomenon will be examined within Chapter 33.)

To many it appeared that the three decades of general stability and prosperity which had followed World War II were about to end. Such was the broad background to Canada's experiment with controls.

CONTROLS COME TO CANADA

The inflationary surge in Canada from 1972-1974 helped to create a sense of national crisis. The Federal government saw a surge of inflation in the U.S. which came to exceed our own rate—an unusual set of circumstances. At the same time unemployment in the U.S. was rising and by 1974 the U.S. rate also was higher than that in Canada. Many in this country doubted whether our rising inflation could be controlled in the face of what was happening to the south—unless we were prepared to pay a very high price in terms of unemployment. Until July, 1974, the government party was a minority in Parliament, which had some effect on its capacity to act. It was in fact more than a year after the July, 1974 election before, in the face of worsening circumstances, the Trudeau government took significant action.

The election campaign of 1974, especially in retrospect, proved an interesting affair. The Progressive Conservatives under Robert Stanfield had, for a year before the election was called, advocated a program of emergency controls along the line of those used by the Nixon administration in the U.S. The policy was not well received and, in the face of obvious resistance from business, labor, public opinion polls and within the party itself, the Conservatives attempted to moderate their position. During the election campaign, the Liberals openly attacked the proposals for controls and took a "no controls" position. The return of the government with a clear majority was interpreted by many observers as due in major part to a rejection by the voters of direct controls over the economy—despite the rising rate of inflation.

Trends between the election in 1974 and October 1975 can be quickly summarized from Tables 30-1 and 30-3. In the U.S., the inflation rate peaked and started down but, by 1975, unemployment had risen to 8.5%. In Canada, inflation continued unabated at over 10% while unemployment rose from 5.3% in 1974 to 6.9% in 1975. Even more ominous was the spectre of worse to come as further pressures were obviously building. One of those (though it was not the only one) which was apparently very significant in pushing the government to more drastic action was the trend in wage settlements. Wage demands were rising even more sharply than present price increases, contract lifetimes were shrinking, and cost-of-living clauses were multiplying rapidly. These guaranteed that future inflation would automatically generate compensating wage boosts which could drive prices even higher. The shadow which loomed on this horizon is summarized in Tables 30-4 and 30-5 on page 362. This was, to use a Galbraithian phrase, "the tyranny of circumstance" which led to the Thanksgiving Day present received by Canadians in 1975. With Prime Minister Trudeau's announcement on that day, the age of direct wage and price controls had arrived in Canada.

The A.I.B.

The Appendix to this chapter reproduces a major segment of the initial policy statement regarding the Anti-Inflation Board—the A.I.B., as it quickly became known. Examination of this will provide an introduction to the details of its structure.

The major features of the program included the following points. The controls were directed toward prices of output from major corporations. The impact on prices was to come primarily through controls on profit margins. Dividends were also regulated. Some specific exemptions were made, including food prices at the producer level, energy prices, and imports (which, of course, could not be controlled). Wages and fee increases were to be restricted under a system of ceilings—with some extra provision for groups whose incomes had lagged relative to prices, and an initial exception was made for groups covered under contracts which had been signed prior to January 1, 1974. Initially, raises below $600 per annum were to be exempt and an upper ceiling of $2400 as a maximum increase was imposed. The controls directly covered about 45% of the labor force. In addition, Ottawa

Table 30-4. AVERAGE ANNUAL WAGE CHANGES IMPLICIT IN MAJOR NEW CONTRACTS, BY SECTORS, CANADA, 1973-1975.

	Average Percentage Increase		
	1973	1974	1975
Private Sector	10.5	14.3	14.7
Manufacturing	9.4	13.1	13.9
Public Sector	10.0	14.2	19.1
Federal	9.0	11.3	13.6
Provincial	10.0	14.6	19.3
Municipal	9.9	12.5	17.6
Overall Weighted Average	10.3	14.3	16.9

Source: Economic Council of Canada, *Thirteenth Annual Review,* Ottawa: Supply and Services, 1977, p. 28.

Table 30-5. MAJOR NEW CONTRACTS: COLA CLAUSES AND TIME SPANS, CANADA, 1970-1975.

	Percentage of Contracts		
	With COLA Clauses	With 12 months Duration (or Less)	With 3 years (or More) Duration
1970	(not available)	14.2	31.8
1971	4.4	18.2	32.6
1972	11.8	17.6	30.9
1973	19.4	13.8	30.8
1974	33.7	27.3	13.3
1975	41.0	47.0	10.9

Source: Economic Council of Canada, *Thirteenth Annual Review,* Ottawa: Supply and Services, 1977, p. 29.

requested (and generally received) provincial compliance to enforce the ranges in sectors under direct provincial jurisdiction. The basic structure of the ceilings and guidelines was set up in such a way that rates of increase would diminish over time. The actual average targets developed for salary increases, for example, were 9.1% for the first year of the program, 7.3% for the second year, and 5.7% for the third year. The basic objectives were to bring the rate of inflation down to 8% in 1976, 6% in 1977, and 4% for 1978. In contrast to the Prices and Incomes Commission, the A.I.B. had teeth, in the form of authority to overrule or decrease requests for increases under its jurisdiction, though there was a procedure for appeal of A.I.B. decisions.

In contrast to the Nixon experiment, the Canadian system was to operate over a longer period of time in the hope that the additional time period would permit not just better results but also lasting effects. Another significant contrast with the American control program was that, while the U.S. experienced an initial freeze which gradually relaxed, the Canadian program started with more realistic levels and aimed at tightening these over time. Like the U.S. experience, Canada attempted to back the controls program up with policies affecting other parts of the economy.

Problems of the Control Era

As has been noted, monetary policy limited the growth of the money supply. In the realm of fiscal policy, the call went out for restraints of expenditure and growth in the civil service. However, the ability of the government to take drastic action in fiscal policy was constrained by problems associated with a severe slowdown in the rate of growth in the economy. In the face of economic lags,

Table 30-6: GOVERNMENTS' SURPLUS-DEFICIT POSITIONS, CANADA, (NATIONAL ACCOUNTS BASIS), 1974-1978.

	(in billions of current dollars)				
	1974	1975	1976	1977	1978 [1]
Federal	1.083	−3.551	−2.879	−7.343	−11.660
Provincial	.570	−1.427	−1.365	.271	.220
Municipal	−.812	−.727	−1.119	−.882	.200
Hospital	.082	−.058	−.171	.142	.008
Canada Pension Plan	1.310	1.473	1.561	1.677	1.596
Quebec Pension Plan	.461	.522	.609	.584	.640
Total	2.694	−3.768	−3.364	−5.551	−8.996

Note: [1] Data for 1978 represent the preliminary estimates for the annual rate of flows as at the end of the first quarter, 1978.

Source: Statistics Canada, *National Income and Expenditure Accounts, 4th Quarter, 1977,* cat. 13-001, and advance preliminary data for 1st Quarter, 1978.

The data above record the total impact of all government spending flows into GNE accounts. For a concise debate on the merits of what has been happening in this period, particularly in Federal fiscal policy, see two commentaries in the *Financial Post* in mid-1978. John McCallum of the Economics Department of the University of Manitoba made a strong defense of the wisdom of Federal policy (*Financial Post,* May 13, 1978, p. 8). Ronald Wilson of the Commerce Department of Mount Allison University in New Brunswick, made a contrasting analysis, maintaining that the deficits have been harmful to the economy (*Financial Post,* June 24, 1978, p. 8.).

tax revenues did not keep up to expectations. 1977 saw declines in total receipts of both personal and corporate direct tax revenues, though this was partly attributable to tax cuts. At the same time, payments in a number of areas went up significantly. Some of these were automatic products of the cycle. As unemployment rose, so did unemployment insurance expenditures. Other areas of increase were discretionary—but many of these were called for by circumstance. For example, Federal expenditure on direct job creation increased by almost 200% between 1976 and 1977, from $107 million to $314 million. The total impact of fiscal policy, as measured by the surplus-deficit position, is outlined in Table 30-6. At this time, it might be appropriate to look again at the cartoon portfolio in Chapter 19. You should now have a better grasp of the nature of the tiger which awaited Jean Chrétien when he assumed the portfolio of Finance.

Future chapters on trade and exchange rates will throw more light on these events. For immediate purposes, the key point is that rising prices continued to be imported in a number of forms and, to further complicate the scene, a significant decline in the value of the Canadian dollar took place between 1974 and 1978. U.S. dollars during this period became 15% more expensive. The German mark appreciated by over 50% and the Japanese yen by 80% against the Canadian dollar. Prices on many imported goods rose rapidly in response to this situation.

And Then—?

As a result of the impact of such forces, as the economy in 1978 withdrew from controls, the results were far from those hoped for in October, 1975. Re-examination of the data in Tables 30-1 to 30-3 shows that our performance, measured against other major industrial nations, has not been especially good. The net position seems ominously like that in the U.S. during their late stages of controls, for our price and wage patterns in 1977-78 started moving up while unemployment remained extremely high. Some of the key statistics for the last stage of the era of

Table 30-7. SELECTED TRENDS, CANADA, APRIL, 1977—July, 1978.

	1977			1978		
	April	July	October	January	April	July
Unemployment (thousands)[1]	868	866	887	891	935	927
Unemployment Rate[1]	8.2%	8.2%	8.3%	8.3%	8.6%	8.4%
Consumer Price Index	157.9	161.8	165.0	167.8	171.2	177.7
Rate of Increase Over Previous 12 Months	7.7%	8.4%	8.7%	9.0%	8.4%	9.8%
Food Component, C.P.I.	174.7	182.9	186.9	193.0	200.4	219.7
Rate of Increase Over Previous 12 Months	6.2%	9.0%	12.7%	14.9%	14.7%	20.1%
General Wholesale Price Index	560.4	563.8	567.0	579.7	600.4	603.4
Rate of Increase Over Previous 12 Months	9.6%	9.0%	11.1%	8.8%	7.1%	7.0%
Average Weekly Wage/Salary	$246.43	$251.62	$257.53	$256.00	$261.08	$266.77
Rate of Increase Over Previous 12 Months	9.8%	9.3%	9.6%	6.9%	5.9%	6.0%
Average Hourly Wage in Manufacturing[1]	$6.25	$6.41	$6.54	$6.63	$6.72	$6.84
Rate of Increase Over Previous 12 Months	11.0%	10.5%	10.6%	8.5%	7.5%	6.7%
Average Hourly Wage in Construction	$9.63	$9.75	$10.05	$10.17	$10.21	$10.09
Rate of Increase Over Previous 12 Months	13.6%	14.0%	12.0%	7.8%	6.0%	3.5%

Note: [1] These series are seasonally adjusted.

Source: Statistics Canada, *Canadian Statistical Review,* cat. 11-003E, September, 1978, vol. 56, number 9, and *Canadian Statistical Review, Weekly Supplement,* cat. 11-004, October 13, 1978.

controls (or at least this particular era of controls) are outlined in Table 30-7. The A.I.B. is worth studying, however, because it was the single largest government incursion into Canadian economic activity ever experienced in peacetime.

GENERAL POSITIONS ON CONTROLS

Experience in Canada and the U.S. with **incomes policies**, both voluntary and direct, has been briefly outlined. In addition, a number of Western European nations have used various combinations of similar policies.[2] Observations based on these policies in practice have helped clarify judgments which had been previously based on theory or the use of controls in wartime situations. The result has been the emergence of fundamental disagreements about the use of incomes policies. Given the fact that direct controls move farthest away from the presently accepted views of the appropriate roles for government in a market system,[3] debate about direct controls has been the most intense—and, of course, involves all sectors in society, not just economists.

The Case For Controls

Supporters of controls cite the following:

1. *The Pressure of Inflationary Psychology.* The expectation that there will be inflation or that it will get worse obviously has an influence on all sectors of the economy. With such expectations, protection of one's own position is obviously the "necessary" course of action. Such self-defense is normally most effective if one's

[2] See Economic Council of Canada, *Thirteenth Annual Review,* Ottawa: Supply and Services, 1976, pp. 150-54 for a concise survey of trends in the U.S., U.K., Netherlands, Germany and Scandinavia to 1976.

[3] In comments at a conference in Toronto, J. K. Galbraith described the use of direct controls as "a far greater change in economic policy than anything the Keynesian Revolution involved" (*Financial Post,* October 16, 1976, p. 6).

own income (be that wages, salary, rent, investment income, prices or profits received) is moved up so as to keep in line with the price increases to be faced. As a result, general supporters of the use of controls see benefits here. This point seems even more important to those who see controls as the lesser of a number of evils and suggest that a prolonged "breathing space,"[4] which controls could provide, would help to restore confidence and decrease the psychological pressure which could otherwise produce greater inflation. The hope that this could be achieved was a key element in both the American and Canadian experiments. Examination of almost any detailed comments about why Canada adopted controls, whether from the Prime Minister, the incumbent Ministers of Finance, 1975-78, the A.I.B., or other official sources, will inevitably turn up references to the need to diminish inflationary expectations.

2. *Alterations in the Market System.* Some economists have become increasingly concerned about the dilution of competition in market economies. You have already encountered references to the prominence of John Kenneth Galbraith within this school of thought. Concentration of power in the corporate sector increases the likelihood that prices will be set in relation to desired profits, or what it is believed the market will bear, rather than reflecting costs and the impact of supply and demand. The same trend, it is contended, exists in the wage sector. The increased power of organized labor in both the public and private sectors increases the abuse of this power, resulting in increased inflationary pressure. Strong advocates of controls usually cite this as the basis for the inevitable use of controls.
3. *The Circumstances of Stagflation.* During the period of the seventies, when unemployment became a trend, the use of anti-inflationary policies of the traditional variety became more and more risky as a result of the fear of generating massive unemployment in the quest for price stability. In this situation, it became common to accept temporary controls. Many of those who have been "forced converts," however, see controls as something to be used only as a last resort, for as limited a period of time as possible in order to bolster monetary and fiscal policy. Despite some lapses which might indicate the contrary,[5] it would appear that Prime Minister Pierre Trudeau was in this category. An even better example of a short-run emergency convert is Simon Reisman. Reisman had served as Deputy Minister of Finance and was one of the key economic advisors to the government for a number of years until his resignation in December, 1974. During the tenure of the A.I.B. program, he was one of the strongest critics of the control program in practice, and of controls in principle. During early 1975, however, Reisman urged the adoption of mandatory controls "because we had reached the point where monetary and fiscal policies acting alone could only have been effective in curbing inflation at very heavy cost in terms of lost output and employment."[6]

[4] Pierre Trudeau, in an interview with CTV, December 28, 1975, said: "I view this control period as a breathing space." See also footnote 5.

[5] One of the most notable of these lapses was in an interview with CTV, December 28, 1975. For coverage of this interview and the storms it raised, one good source is Anthony Westell's *The New Society*, pp. 111-114.

[6] *Financial Post*, October 16, 1976, p. 7. There was considerable speculation about the reason(s) for Reisman's resignation. One interpretation was that it was the result of the unwillingness of the government and the then Minister, John Turner, to take a sufficiently strong (using emergency controls?) position against inflation. Turner's view was that controls were still in the realm of the unneeded and/or unacceptable. Turner resigned from the Cabinet less than a month before controls were imposed. At the time of his resignation, and especially after the control program was introduced, the question was then raised: did he leave for the exactly opposite reason for Reisman's departure: i.e., because the decision had then been made to adopt controls and he would not accept the policy? (Both Reisman and Turner have denied these speculations.)

Virtually all supporters of controls, either temporary or long-run ones, see them as the only alternative in the face of the existence of one or more of these three pressures. The feeling of inevitability is often expressed by Galbraith, who sees them as the only alternative to a system where the "market" has ceased to exist in many key sectors. In an October, 1976 conference in Toronto, he observed:

> I've long believed that an incomes and associated price policy is inescapable. This is not the result of any experience I look back on with any pleasure or ideological preference, something which we often imagine to rule in economics. It is the tyranny of circumstance. What foolish men blame on wilful politicians or misguided economists is usually attributable to force of circumstance, or, as in this case, to poverty of alternatives.[7]

The Case Against Controls

Detractors maintain that:

1. *Controls are not effective.* The evidence of experiences in the U.S., Britain and some other economies indicates that controls tend to have effects only while in force. The objective of using them as a breathing space, after which more "normal" conditions will prevail, thus seems futile. Experience with inflation after controls is likely, if anything, to be worse than before controls were imposed.
2. *Controls maintain inequalities during their existence and create increased unrest for the future.* Without many exemptions or loopholes, a system of controls is likely to restrict some groups or sectors which had fallen behind. Resentment about this and general opposition to governmental restriction of market freedom will produce a pressure-cooker situation awaiting the end of controls for an explosion.
3. *Controls divert attention from other needs, or serve as a disincentive.*
   (a) In the government sector, the breathing space may produce a degree of complacency which inhibits the use of other needed policies to assist in restraining inflationary pressures once controls are ended.[8]
   (b) In the private sector, controls may lead to distortion and disruptions. Overall output, productivity and profitability may be stifled or business may move elsewhere to avoid the problems. Growth in employment may be inhibited. Inappropriate decisions may be made about investment or resource allocation as a result of artificial data rather than the signals of an unrestrained marketplace. Labor is not rewarded for improvements in productivity which could take place in a control-free environment, so that productivity is more likely to lag.[9]
4. *Controls are too difficult to bring to an end.* As noted above, post-control experience is likely to be unsettling. It will be difficult to balance needs against apparent fairness in determining what sectors to free from controls and when. Indications of an end to controls will lead to demands to "make up for lost ground." At this stage, virtually any alternate government policies are likely to appear weak, consequently inducing more inflationary pressures.[10] Governments may be

[7] *Financial Post,* October 16, 1976, p. 6. The "looking back" presumably refers to his experience as director of price control programs in the United States during World War II. In one passing reference to this experience, he makes the wry observation: "Previously I had argued against a general ceiling on prices with great conviction; now I argued for it with equal passion. Almost no one noticed this change of mind. No one at all criticized it. In economics it is a far, far wiser thing to be right than to be consistent." (*The Age of Uncertainty,* p. 222.)

[8] Simon Reisman, in the source cited in footnote 6 above, sharply criticized government inaction in the early stages of the period of controls.

[9] See Trudeau's recognition of these arguments from the private sector in the digest of his remarks to the Toronto conference on controls, *Financial Post,* October 16, 1976, p. 7.

[10] Note carefully the impression conveyed in the Collins' cartoon regarding Macdonald's announcements about plans for the post-control period.

tempted to continue the use of controls to avoid the problems inherent in ending them.

5. *Controls, even for a limited period, tend to lead to more use of government power.* Having used controls once and set the precedent, it will be much easier for government to use them again—or to resort to other forms of increased regulation of the economy. The possibility and fear of this further weakens the private sector and could have implications far beyond the realm of economic affairs. At the Toronto conference to which previous references have been made, Simon Reisman went so far as to state that:

   > More important than the damage to economic efficiency is the loss of freedom which a control system entails. Over the years we have witnessed increasing state encroachment in many aspects of society.
   >
   > . . . Their [controls'] permanent use would deliver a vital blow to the very innards of our free society. Indeed the ultimate result would, in my view, be an authoritarian political system ruled by force.[11]

6. *Controls do not have any effect on price increases on products imported into Canada.* Approximately 25% of our spending is on imported goods and services and thus a quarter of our purchases cannot be reached by a system of controls.

"WE'RE WORKING ON A NEW MODEL"

Collins in The Montreal Gazette

Initial indications from Ottawa, as the end of formal wage and price controls came close, were that a new program of voluntary restraint would take the place of the AIB controls. John Collins' cartoon, like many other responses to the lack of firm indications of Ottawa's intent, showed something less than enthusiasm for the "new model" when plans were announced by the Minister of Finance, Donald Macdonald. (Actual implementation was to pass to other hands. Macdonald resigned from the Finance portfolio and from Parliament not long after the initial announcements about the post-control plans were made. Unlike the resignations referred to in footnote 6 in this chapter, Macdonald's resignation did not appear to have been influenced by policy issues.)

A Hint of Common Ground

The above summaries indicate the general range of the lines of battle in the debate. There are, however, some points concerning either general principles or specific practice about which a degree of agreement seems to exist. Each of the following points of "agreement", however, must be regarded as assuming several things. General supporters of controls would preface each proposition with: "As controls are used." Many opponents "in principle" would qualify their acceptance with: "If controls cannot possibly be avoided." Some opponents of controls would not accept any of the points made below because of unalterable opposition to controls—except in time of war. The key points where a degree of common ground exists are the following:

1. During any period of controls, monetary and fiscal policies must be utilized as well and not neglected in favor of the power of controls. As indicators, note the following observations:

   Galbraith: "An incomes and price policy does not replace monetary and fiscal

[11] *Financial Post,* October 16, 1976, p. 7.

policy. It supplements it in that part of the modern economy where market control of prices has given way to private administration . . . ."[12]

Reisman: "Controls should only be imposed for a limited time and for a limited purpose, as a temporary supplement to demand management policy. . . . Controls can provide time in which to reestablish sound monetary and fiscal policies."[13]

2. Controls should be applied only to sectors in the economy where power is most concentrated and where competition does not exist to keep prices down. (Our two witnesses would both accept this statement. However, since they are not in agreement about just what sectors contain too much concentration of power, they would not mean exactly the same thing if they were each writing or saying this.)

Reisman: "Some of them [large corporations] possess a greater measure of discretionary power to influence costs and prices than smaller enterprises. The difference is more one of degree and of timing, than of basic operating conditions in the marketplace."[14]

Reisman, again: "[Controls establish] a framework in which governments can constrain wage pressures from their own large and growing unions."[15]

Galbraith: "I wouldn't urge, as the recent experience of Canada affirms, that it [the power of controls] should cover the whole economy. It is occasioned by the power that particular groups in the economy possess to affect their own salaries, wages, prices and profits. Where . . . the market is still a force, it should continue to regulate prices and incomes."[16]

[12] *Financial Post*, October 16, 1976, pp. 6-7.
[13] *Ibid.*
[14] *Ibid.*
[15] *Ibid.*
[16] *Ibid.*

And One Final Fundamental Clash

As has been indicated above, many of those who have accepted the use of controls under duress have done so only with the qualification that such action is acceptable only if it is temporary.[17] The use of controls, in a temporary form, is generally the option associated with those who have accepted them under the pressures of inflationary psychology or stagflation. There is no debate over the issue of how long to retain controls between this group and those who say: "NO—under any circumstances!"[18] The issue here is the existence of controls, not their longevity. Given the fact that controls have become a part of our system once, and may well be used again, the other side of the triangle appears more important.

Those who advocate controls as a necessary response to the deterioration of the market system generally do not see anything temporary about the situation. The Galbraithian edict on this point has been clear and was restated at the Toronto conference on controls, when he said:

> The choice between unemployment and a price and incomes policy may not be forever. In economics few things are. But the choice will exist for so long as there are strong corporations, strong unions, and both are motivated as now.[19]

Supporters of the short-run approach to controls had been described several years previously by Galbraith as

> men of established faith [who] still defend the controls not as an intrinsic feature of the system, but as a temporary expedient. This will lead them, when there are controls, to urge a return to the free market, as it is right-

[17] Refer again, as examples, to footnotes 4 and 13.
[18] For a perspective on the period 1975-78 from a more committed anti-controls position, see the columns of Richard Lipsey of Queen's University in the *Financial Post*, June 17 and June 24, 1978, page 7 in each issue.
[19] *The Financial Post*, October 16, 1976, p. 6.

eously termed. And if their advice is heeded, renewed inflation will force renewed controls.[20]

This division of opinion could not be more clear: Controls only under temporary circumstances, versus controls in some sectors as a more or less permanent feature. Many, in fact, would suggest that this may be the basic question about controls in Canada in the future. If this does emerge as the fundamental question, how it is answered is critical for us all.

[20] J. K. Galbraith, *Economics and the Public Purpose,* Boston: Houghton Mifflin, 1973, pp. 212-213. (This is probably the best work of Galbraith's to examine for his views on controls.)

Reprinted with the permission of Rusin Kaufmanis, *Ottawa Citizen*, June 13, 1977

This cartoon will perhaps bring back memories of the one by John Collins on page 349. It effectively summarizes the basic issues facing governments as they attempt to influence the economy: namely, where do we want to go, and how do we actually get there. It is crucial to recall that the issue affects the "passengers" just as much and, perhaps even more than, the "driver."

SUMMARY

This chapter represents the completion of a block of five chapters dealing with our quest for economic stability. As a result of the extreme importance of the material in Chapter 30 to an understanding of current economic issues, it must be regarded as a basic starting-point for further study, not as a comprehensive analysis to be neatly summarized in a more abbreviated form. To understand the development of economic affairs in the 1980s, the student of economics will have to have a basic appreciation of what the decade of the seventies has brought in terms of problems and policies, and the dilemmas we continue to face as the decade ends. As the cartoon by Rusin Kaufmanis indicates, there is considerable conflict of opinion about where we should go—and even more about what route is most appropriate to get us there.

Amidst uncertainty about appropriate policy choices, one fact seems very clear. The advent of controls marked, at the very least, a major change in the rules of the game, though many people thus far seem to have overlooked or avoided this fact. Galbraith described the implementation of controls as "a far greater change in economic policy than anything the Keynesian Revolution involved." The Keynesian alterations in economic policy making were designed to stabilize an existing system. Should we find ourselves resorting to controls again, we are going to have to face the reality that what we are doing amounts to more than changing the rules. It will amount to fundamental changes in the basic nature of the system.

KEY CONCEPTS

voluntary restraint | direct controls | incomes policies

QUESTIONS FOR REVIEW AND DISCUSSION

1. What pressures led the United States to controls in 1971? What were the short-run effects? the long-run effects?
2. How did the Canadian scene just prior to controls (1973-75) compare with the American pattern in 1969-71?
3. How did the Canadian program of controls (1975-78) compare with that in the U.S. (1971-73) in terms of approach? effect?
4. What are the general arguments for and against controls in a developed market economy?

FOR FURTHER RESEARCH

1. Do some detailed research on the operation and effectiveness of the program of wage and price controls directed by the Anti-Inflation Board between 1975 and 1978. Be prepared to use various sources, such as the Economic Council of Canada's *Annual Reviews* (see the 1977 Review, chapter 2), or do some "chasing" for major coverage, such as that in *The Financial Post,* October 16, 1977,

pp. 6-7, and S1-12, which dealt with a conference on controls featuring Prime Minister Trudeau, J. K. Galbraith, and Simon Reisman, a former Deputy Minister of Finance and outspoken critic of the controls program. Some publications from the A.I.B. itself may be found in your school or local library. Some specific additional titles are:

(a) W. D. Wood and P. Kumar, (eds.), *Canadian Perspectives on Wage-Price Guidelines, A Book of Readings,* Kingston: Industrial Relations Centre, Queens University, 1976.

(b) M. Walker, (ed.), *Which Way Ahead? Canada After Wage and Price Control,* Vancouver: The Fraser Institute, 1977.

These two titles are both given with some reservation. The first appeared very soon after the program was implemented and has a very heavy proportion of international and historical content. The second contains the perspectives of a number of prominent contributors (including Simon Reisman) and, though a range of points of view are expressed, there is a strong "anti-controls" position implicit in the book. In the absence of a Canadian counterbalance to (b), at least at this time, it might be appropriate to either remind you of Galbraith, *Economics and the Public Purpose,* Boston: Houghton Mifflin, 1973, and also suggest an examination of *The Economic System in an Age of Discontinuity,* by Wassily Leontief and Herbert Stein, New York: New York University Press, 1976. (Leontief was the recipient of the Nobel Prize in Economics in 1973). Either of these two sources provides the "pro-controls" side of the discussion.

2. For additional broad background reading on theory or policy in practice, you may not have utilized all the references contained within Chapters 26-28. Review these for sources not yet examined. Search out other broad assessments of economic problems and practice from both a Canadian and a wider perspective. Additional suggestions:

   (a) J. W. Popkin, *Government and the Economy—Stabilization Policies,* Toronto: Canadian Foundation for Economic Education, 1977.

   (b) Anthony Westell, *The New Society,* Toronto: McClelland & Stewart, 1977. (A prominent Canadian journalist takes a look at economic, social and political trends; see Chapter 5 in particular.)

   (c) John Seater, "A Perspective on Stagflation," in *Business Review,* Federal Reserve Bank of Philadelphia, May, 1975.

   (d) Anne R. Braun, "Inflation and Stagflation in the International Economy," in *Finance and Development,* the World Bank/IMF, September, 1976.

   (e) Gunnar Myrdal, *Against The Stream: Critical Essays in Economics,* New York: Vintage Books, 1975. (See Chapters 1 and 2, "Crises and Cycles in the Development of Economics," and "Stagflation". Myrdal was the recipient of the Nobel Prize in Economics in 1974.)

3. Some observers of the stagflationary scene have suggested using a "discomfort index" to measure the degree of the combined impact of inflation and unemployment. One straight-forward approach to this would be simply adding the two percentage figures together. For example, the 1965 inflation rate of 2.4% and unemployment rate of 3.6% would have produced a "discomfort index" rating of 7.0.

   Based on the data available in Table 26-3, plus more recent data, prepare such an "index" and examine the pattern of events in Canada against it. (If you are using the *Study Guide and Workbook* to go with this text, you will have done the calculation in conjunction with Chapter 26. You may then move on to examine the data in relation to other events.

Working from data in Tables 30-1 and 30-3, and current data you can obtain, a similar exercise could be carried out for other nations as a contrast with Canada. Of particular interest should be our performance measured against that in the U.S.

Collins in The Montreal Gazette

"A COUPLE OF PETS THAT GO WITH THE PROPERTY"

4. During the 1974 election campaign, the Progressive Conservatives promoted a policy of controls but lost the election. The Liberals, who had opposed controls during the campaign, won the election and then brought controls into effect during the period 1975-1978. In the 1979 election campaign, the question of controls in the future did not emerge as a key issue. Collins' cartoon points out, however, that Joe Clark acquired the same problems which had faced the nation earlier in the decade. What has been Progressive Conservative policy since 1979 about the use of direct controls in Canada?

APPENDIX:

ATTACK ON INFLATION: A Program of National Action

Following are three sections from the Policy Statement tabled in the House of Commons by the Minister of Finance, Donald Macdonald, on October 14, 1975. Reproduced are an initial summary of why the program was introduced, a concise outline of the four areas where government action was to be implemented, and, finally, the sections dealing with prices and incomes, i.e., the controls program.

The Problem Confronting Us

The problems that inflation creates were clearly spelled out in the budget of June 23, 1975:

> In its present cost-push form, inflation threatens to price our goods out of world markets and to lessen the capacity of our business firms to expand their operations. It disrupts financial markets and impairs rational planning by business and government. It undermines the effectiveness of the traditional instruments of demand management policy to keep the economy on course. When inflation reaches a certain point, the stimulation of spending may simply lead to higher prices rather than more goods and more jobs; in the longer run, it actually makes unemployment worse.
>
> Not only that, but inflation ultimately inflicts grievous damage to the fabric of society. It lowers the living standards of those on fixed incomes, including pensioners. It leaves people without reliable, understandable guideposts by which to arrange their economic affairs. It injects grave uncertainty into decisions on family budgets, housing, savings and provision for old age. It provokes deep frustration, social tension and mistrust of private and public institutions. Collective bargaining is embittered. Industrial relations are damaged. We in Canada are already beginning to live some of these experiences.

Inflation is a dynamic process which feeds upon itself. In the absence of strong measures to bring it under control, the kind of severe and prolonged inflation we have been experiencing tends to generate expectations of further inflation and defensive responses to these expectations which, unfortunately, serve only to confirm them later on.

The risk has mounted that both the rate of inflation and the rate of unemployment will rise in the months and years ahead if no decisive action is taken. This is unacceptable to the government. The evidence of widespread and deep-seated concern in the country shows that it is unacceptable to all Canadians.

The severity of the problem is compounded by the need for further increases in the relative prices of some forms of energy, of some commodities, and perhaps of some classes of rents if necessary supplies of energy, commodities and rental housing are to be forthcoming. In addition, the steepness of the increase of average wages over the recent past means that those groups that have not had recent adjustment have tended to fall seriously behind. They will have to have some chance to catch up. Thus, we have to get the average rate of increase of prices and incomes down while allowing these particular increases in prices and incomes to occur.

Faced with this situation, the problem is not just to get over the worst of our current troubles, difficult as that is likely to prove. It is to reduce inflation in ways that do not store up further trouble for the future, and to find ways of improving the structure of our economy so that the same troubles do not recur.

The Government's Program for Attacking Inflation

The program that the government is setting in motion has four main elements:

(1) *Fiscal and monetary policies* aimed at increasing total demand and production at a rate consistent with declining inflation.
(2) *Government expenditure policies* aimed at limiting the growth of public expenditures and the rate of increase in public service employment.
(3) *Structural policies* to deal with the special problems of energy, food and housing, to ensure a more efficient and competitive economy and to improve labor-management relations.
(4) *A prices and incomes policy* which establishes guidelines for responsible social behavior in determining prices and incomes of groups, together with machinery for administering these guidelines and ensuring compliance where necessary.

The government is convinced that the full participation of provincial governments and of the major interest groups in the community will be essential to the success of this program of action. As an integral part of the program, intensive consultations with the provinces and with representatives of business, labor and other interest groups are being arranged. The government is entering into these consultations anxious to hear the views and suggestions of others for improving the program.

Prices and Incomes Policy

The government has concluded that the time has come to implement a prices and incomes policy in Canada with the following main characteristics:

1. Maximum emphasis on voluntary compliance with price and income guidelines.
2. The fullest possible degree of consultation both with the provincial governments, whose joint participation is being sought, and with business, labor and other groups.
3. Provision for statutory enforcement of guidelines in respect of key groups.
4. A determined effort to keep to a minimum the need for detailed regulation, reporting, and surveillance, and thereby to keep to a minimum the size of the administrative staff involved.

A description of the principal features of the legislation, administrative machinery and guidelines is contained in the following two sections.

Legislation, Administration and Provincial Participation

The government intends to introduce legislation to provide authority to require specified groups to restrain prices and profit margins, compensation and dividends. While the emphasis of the government's approach toward these specified groups will be to seek voluntary compliance through consultation and negotiation, authority will be available to ensure that the public interest will prevail.

The specified groups subject to the legal enforcement of restraint under the legislation include the following:

(a) firms which employ more than 500 employees. For this purpose, firms are defined to include any group of corporations which would be treated as associated corporations under the Income Tax Act of Canada.
(b) firms, any or all of whose employees bargain in association with employees of other firms.
(c) firms in the construction industry which employ more than 20 employees.
(d) the federal government and all its emanations.

(e) participating provincial governments and their emanations, including municipal institutions.
(f) employees of the entities referred to above.
(g) individuals or other firms that are carrying on a business that is a profession.

The legislation will also provide authority for the Governor-in-Council to add to the groups that are subject to the legislation. This power may be exercised only if the Anti-Inflation Board referred to below, upon being asked by the Governor-in-Council to consider the matter, determines that a group is of strategic importance to Canada and recommends that the group be added.

In order to clarify the guidelines, to monitor their observance and, where necessary, to begin the process of bringing certain organized groups or individuals under a system of restraint, the government will establish an Anti-Inflation Board, initially by Order-in-Council under the *Inquiries Act* and later in the proposed legislation. The terms of reference of the Board will be set out in the legislation and will involve:

—monitoring movements in prices, profits, compensation and dividends in relation to the guidelines;
—identifying actual or proposed movements that would contravene the guidelines in fact or in spirit;
—endeavoring through consultations and negotiations with the parties involved to modify actual or proposed increases to bring them within the limits and spirit of the guidelines or to reduce their inflationary effect;
—referring to an official with the authority of enforcement, to be called the Administrator in the proposed legislation, the actual or proposed movement of prices, profits, compensation and dividends if the consultations and negotiations do not lead to their modification; and
—promoting greater public understanding of the inflationary process by publishing reports, arranging public hearings and meetings, and by other means.

The Board, therefore, is designed to permit both flexibility and maximum cooperation. The Board will exercise all of the powers of a person appointed as a commissioner under Part I of the *Inquiries Act* and will, once the legislation is in force, have additional powers to obtain relevant information.

Where the Board or the responsible Minister determines that there are reasonable grounds for believing that an actual or proposed movement of prices, profits, compensation and dividends has contravened or is likely to contravene the guidelines, the Board or Minister may advise the Administrator to this effect. The Administrator, an official to be appointed by the Governor-in-Council, will attempt to establish whether the supplier or employer has contravened or is likely to contravene the guidelines. He will also attempt to determine whether there are circumstances that justify the supplier or employer in contravening the guidelines.

In those cases where the Administrator finds that the guidelines will be or have been contravened without good reason, the Act will empower the Administrator to order that:

—the person be enjoined from contravening or continuing to contravene the guidelines; and
—the person be required to pay to the government, or back to the buyer, as appropriate, the whole or any portion of excess payment or receipt, as the case may be, arising from that contravention of the guidelines.

Those persons against whom the Administrator has acted will, during a period of sixty days, have a right of appeal. The legislation will establish an Anti-Inflation Appeal Tribunal, consisting of a chairman and others to be appointed by the government. The Tribunal will dispose of appeals by either dismissing them or by allowing them in one of three ways. The order of the Administrator may be entirely rescinded, the order may be varied, or the matter may be referred back to the Administrator for reconsideration. An appellant will be able to appeal the decision of the Appeal Tribunal to the Federal Court of Appeal. Further, the Cabinet within thirty days of an order by the Administrator, will be permitted under the terms of the legislation to rescind the order of the Administrator or instruct him to vary his order.

The Federal government is obliging itself and all its crown corporations and agencies to follow the guidelines with respect both to prices and compensation. The Federal government is inviting the provincial governments to participate in the program by adhering to the guidelines and submitting to the legislation in the same way as the Federal government, both with regard to their own operations and the operations of provincial enterprises and agencies and municipalities. It is being proposed to the provinces that the Anti-Inflation Board would establish a distinct public sector panel to deal with prices and compensation in the public sector, and they would be invited to nominate some of the members of such a panel. Participating provinces would be expected to enact such legislation as may be required. Any province not prepared to participate would be asked to enact legislation essentially similar to the national regime.

In addition to participating in the program in these ways, the provincial governments are being asked to undertake responsibility for a program of rent control and to regulate professional fees in accordance with the guidelines. It is expected that federal-provincial consultative machinery will be established in these important areas of the program.

The Initial Guidelines

Introduction

This section sets out the broad guidelines which all Canadians are being asked to follow. The government fully anticipates that the great majority of Canadians will be prepared to conduct their affairs in accord with the guidelines. It therefore expects that the powers of enforcement applicable to specified groups identified under the legislation will have to be used only rarely and in exceptional cases.

These guidelines are based on the principles proposed by the government in the consensus discussions of last winter, a description of which was tabled in the House of Commons by the Minister of Finance on May 8. These proposals had benefited greatly from the discussions with representatives of business, labor and the provincial governments.

In this policy statement the guidelines are referred to as "initial" guidelines. They have deliberately been so labeled in order to emphasize the willingness of the government to modify them in their technical aspects, in the light of considerations advanced in Parliament or Committees of Parliament, in the consultations with provinces, business and labor, by the Anti-Inflation Board or by other interested parties. In moving into an unfamiliar field of administration, it is inevitable that important considerations will have been overlooked. The government in addition wishes to have the flexibility to modify the guidelines as the program proceeds, the state of expectations in the economy returns to more normal levels, and structural changes in the economy take place.

The guidelines will be effective October 14. For purpose of those specified groups subject to legal enforcement of restraint, the guidelines will be issued as regulations under the legislation. Those regulations will be deemed to be effective October 14.

Guidelines for Price and Profits

General Principle

The general principle is that increases in prices should be limited to amounts no more than required to cover net increases in costs. The precise form of the objective will be adapted to the different circumstances of different kinds of suppliers, but should lead to broadly equivalent behavior when these differences are taken into account.

Firms Which are Able to Allocate Costs to Individual Products

Firms which are able to allocate costs to individual products are expected to increase prices of these products by no more than increases in costs allocated to this product. Similarly firms are expected to reduce prices if costs decrease. If the firm can establish that the price in effect at the time of the announcement of the program was not typical, it may select another price which was in effect during the previous thirty days.

Simple Numerical Example

	Prior to October 14, 1975		After October 14, 1975	
	Per Unit	Total	Per Unit	Total
Volume		5 000		5 200
Employment		5		5
Sales	$20.00	$100 000	$21.05	$109 472
Less Costs:				
Materials	$ 6.00	$ 30 000	$ 6.36	$ 33 072
Labor	$12.00	$ 60 000	$12.69	$ 66 000
Total Costs	$18.00	$ 90 000	$19.05	$ 99 072
Profit	$ 2.00	$ 10 000	$ 2.00	$ 10 400
Profit Margin		10%		9.5%

In the example shown on the table, material costs rise by 6 per cent or 36 cents per unit of output. Wage rates rise 10 per cent, but the increase in output from 5000 units to 5200 units is obtained with the same labor force, due to an increase of productivity. Thus labor costs per unit of output rise only 5.8 per cent or 69 cents. Taking labor and material costs together, the net increase in costs per unit is $1.05. Thus, the firm is entitled to increase its price by $1.05. Its profit per unit of output remains the same, but with larger volume total profits rise by 4 per cent. In relation to sales, however, the margin of profit declines from 10 per cent to 9.5 per cent.

In setting prices which will be in effect for some period of time ahead, firms may make increases in prices on the basis of forecasts of cost increases.

These forecasts, however, should be based on known changes, or changes which can be expected to occur within the period for which the firms normally set prices in advance and which can be foreseen with a reasonable degree of assurance.

To compute the increase in costs which may be passed on, it will be necessary to estimate the cost of a product on or near October 14, 1975. A similar estimate of the cost of the product in question must be made at the date the selling price is to be increased. The difference between the two cost estimates is the maximum amount by which prices should be changed.

Costs may vary considerably from day to day and many firms may not customarily compute their costs on a daily basis. Therefore the two required cost estimates should be made on a reasonable basis, and both should be consistent with the firm's usual accounting practices. Future cost increases that have been recognized in the October 14, 1975 selling price should be treated as if they had already occurred. They will therefore form part of the October 14 estimate of product cost.

Firms Which are Unable to Allocate Costs to Individual Products

If a firm finds it impossible to allocate costs to individual products, it should price its products in such a way as to leave its percentage pre-tax net profit margin no higher than 95 per cent of its average percentage pre-tax net profit margin in the last five completed fiscal years. The Anti-Inflation Board will be prepared to provide information on appropriate net margins to firms which have not existed long enough to have a five-year average.

For the purposes of the percentage net profit margin guideline, profit will be defined as total operating *revenue* (computed in accordance with generally accepted accounting principles applied on a consistent basis) which can be reasonably regarded as having been earned in the normal course of business by the firm *minus* the *costs* allowable for the purpose of justifying price increases. The percentage net profit margin will be defined as profits divided by total operating revenue.

Definition of Costs

The definition of costs allowable for purposes of justifying an increase in any price is that portion of the unavoidable outlays and expenses of the supplier (computed in accordance with generally accepted accounting principles applied on a consistent basis) that can be reasonably regarded as having been made or incurred for the purpose of gaining revenue from the sale. The regulations will include a detailed list of items which should be excluded from allowable costs. Included in this list will be such items as losses resulting from occurrences which are not typical of the normal business activities of the supplier, capital losses incurred by the supplier, certain expenses which are incurred at the discretion of management, and the excess over the fair market value of goods purchased in non-arm's-length transactions.

Frequency of Price Changes

Firms are expected to refrain from increasing the price of any individual product more frequently than once every three months, except where this would impose severe hardship on the firm. Retailers and wholesalers will be exempt from this requirement.

Distribution Sector

In the distribution sector customary pricing policies are generally based on gross margins. Retail and wholesale firms should not increase markups on their various merchandise categories. Where the nature of the trade makes the application of this limitation impracticable, such firms should not exceed the percentage gross profit margin realized during the last complete fiscal year before October 14, 1975. The latter proposal would permit firms to follow their customary pricing practices and vary markups on particular products in line with market forces but restrict the gross profit margin expressed as a percentage of total sales. If a firm finds it necessary to follow the more general percentage gross profit margin rule, it should ensure that no one product line has an excessive increase in its markup.

Under the guidelines for the distribution sector, percentage net profit margins would not change significantly if operating costs rose at the same rate as material costs. If operating costs rose faster than the costs of goods sold, profit margins would be reduced. In some cases, operating costs may rise so quickly that absolute profits would fall. In such a situation firms would be justified in raising prices to restore the level of absolute profits to the level in the last complete fiscal year. If the costs of goods sold rose appreciably faster than operating costs, net profit margins would increase. In such cases, the firm should reduce markups in order to reduce its percentage net profit margin to the level in the last complete fiscal year.

Food Prices

Prices received by farmers and fishermen for their products are exempt from the guidelines. The operations of marketing boards will be discussed with the provincial governments to ensure that they are consistent with the guidelines.

The general obligations related to prices and profits would apply to processors and distributors of foodstuffs.

Exports

Firms supplying the international market will be expected to sell abroad at international market prices and to ensure that, in selling products or services to a person or firm with whom they do not deal at arm's length within the meaning of subsection 251(1) of the Income Tax Act, the product or service is sold at its fair market value. In general, firms also supplying the domestic market will be expected to ensure that the domestic market is fully satisfied in terms of quantity, at a price consistent with the general guidelines. If a firm can demonstrate that it is setting its domestic prices in accordance with the cost-pass-through rule, and that its overall net margin on all sales satisfies the percentage pre-tax net margin rule, it will be regarded as having followed the guidelines.

If, however, a firm can demonstrate to the Anti-Inflation Board the impracticality of or hardship entailed in following the general guidelines, the following arrangements are proposed. The firm would price its domestic sales in a way consistent with the guidelines, and would be subject to a special levy on the profits derived from its export sales. If a firm can demonstrate to the Anti-Inflation Board that it would be impractical or harmful to the national interest for it to price in the domestic market differently than in the international market, the firm will not be regarded as having failed to follow the guidelines if it prices all its products at international prices, but would be subject to the special levy on all its profits. Once firms have received permission to be treated in a particular way, they will continue to be treated that way for the whole of the program.

The nature and form of this special levy will be announced following consultations with interested parties.

Financial Institutions and Interest Rates

Banks and other financial institutions are expected to conform to the general principle: that is to say, increases in service charges and interest rates charged by these institutions should be justified by increases in the interest rates which they pay and increases in their operating and other expenses. It would not be feasible to control interest rates determined in financial markets given their nature and the importance of international capital flows to Canada. It should be stressed, however, that interest rates may be lower on average if the program is successful in establishing a widespread expectation that the rate of inflation will steadily decline. Insurance premiums should be increased only by the amounts required to cover net increases in the cost of claims and operating expenses.

Regulated Industries

Where industries are subject to regulation under existing statutes, as in transportation and communications, Federal regulatory agencies are to use their powers over prices and the quality of service in order to ensure conformity with the program. The provincial governments are being asked to instruct their regulatory agencies to do likewise.

Construction Industry

Whenever possible the cost-pass-through principle will apply to firms in the construction industry. For example, a contractor continuing to build houses of a similar standard and quality to those which he has been building in the recent past should increase the price per square foot only by the amount required to cover increased costs. Where cost allocation is not possible, the percentage net profit margin rule will apply, but there will be consultations with the industry to adapt it to the special circumstances which may prevail. Construction, engineering and other firms bidding on individual contracts for custom designed structures, projects and products are requested to follow their customary tendering procedures. Monitoring will take place to ensure that competitive conditions are being maintained.

Rents

The provincial governments are being asked to undertake responsibility for implementing a program of rent control based upon the following principles (a) increases up to a certain percentage would be permissible; (b) increases above this percentage must be justified on the basis of increased costs; (c) new structures where rents have not yet been established would be exempt from control for at least five years after completion of the building, in the event that rent control should be in effect for that length of time. This is to ensure an adequate incentive for construction of new rental accommodation.

Selection of Guidelines

The Anti-Inflation Board will have the right to advise firms which guidelines they should follow. Thus, the Board may represent to a firm that it can allocate costs to individual products and therefore should follow the cost-pass-through guideline rather than the percentage net profit margin guideline. It may advise a firm engaged in production as well as distribution that it should follow a single guideline or apply different guidelines to the different operations.

Exceptions

None of the guidelines requires a firm to price in a way which will perpetuate or create a loss in its overall operations.

A firm will be regarded as having acted in accordance with the program if its profit per unit of output or percentage net profit margin exceeded the guidelines as a result of unusual productivity gains resulting from the efforts of the firm, or of favorable cost developments which could not reasonably have been anticipated.

Guidelines for Incomes

Compensation: General Principles

There are four elements in the guidelines for wages and salaries and other forms of compensation. These are:

1. The basic protection factor.
2. Share in increases in national productivity.
3. Adjustment for past wage and salary experience.
4. Minimum and maximum dollar increases.

These guidelines set the upper limits to increases in compensation which should be paid. Employees and employers will be free to negotiate new collective agreements and employers to increase pay scales for non-unionized employees, but these upper limits should not be exceeded. Future increases provided for in contracts and agreements in force as of October 14, 1975, including cost-of-living adjustments, will be exempt from the guidelines. Where agreement has been reached by October 14, 1975 on compensation increases to be incorporated in new contracts, such increases will also be exempt from the guidelines. Special consideration will be given to those cases where contracts have expired and negotiations are underway, where the expired contract was signed prior to the beginning of 1974.

Existing contracts may not be reopened without the consent of the Anti-Inflation Board. Employers are not allowed to agree during the program to pay increases after the termination of the program for services rendered during the program.

The Basic Protection Factor

The basic protection factor provides a substantial degree of the protection that will be afforded to workers against price rises in the future. It will be supplemented, as the program proceeds, by the application of a retrospective provision that any excess of the cost of living increase over the increase provided for in the basic protection factor for that year may be included in the allowable compensation increase of the following year.

In order to give guidance to those who wish to conclude multi-year contracts as well as to those who wish to make agreements for one year only, the basic protection factor will consist of three numbers, applicable to the first, second and third years of the contract, agreement or award. The initial set of numbers comprising the basic protection factor will be 8 per cent for the first year of a new contract, 6 per cent for the second year, and 4 per cent for the third year. These basic numbers may be changed from time to time, probably more often than once a year, as the program proceeds and the rate of inflation in the economy changes.

By way of amplification, it may be explained how this feature of the guidelines would operate in the second year of the program. Suppose that the cost of living index had risen by 9 per cent in the first year by comparison with the basic protection factor for that year of 8 per cent. Workers under two-year contracts would be allowed a 1 per cent increase to allow for the difference in the first year between the cost-of-living increase and the basic protection factor of that year, plus the 6 per cent basic protection factor provided in their two-year contract. Workers entering into new contracts at the conclusion of contracts negotiated under the guidelines would also be allowed the 1 per cent increase that provides the retrospective protection plus whatever is the current basic protection factor pertaining to the first year of new contracts.

If the consumer price index has increased by less than the basic protection factor, no adjustment need be made.

Share in Increases in National Productivity

In addition to the basic protection factor, the guidelines provide for a share in increases in national productivity. The standard amount provided for in the initial period of the program is 2 per cent per annum. This compares with the average increase in productivity, defined as the real gross national product divided by the number of employed persons, of 2.08 per cent for the period 1954-74.

Adjustment for Past Wage and Salary Experience

A further element in the compensation guidelines is related to the past experience of each group. Some groups have fallen behind in the last two or three years because of the time at which their contracts were negotiated or for other reasons. It is essential that they should be provided with an opportunity to catch up. On the other hand, some groups have obtained relatively large increases in this period, and some element of adjustment for this situation is necessary if the program is to succeed.

The adjustment for past experience is to be calculated as follows. The average annual increase in a group's compensation in the last two years or over the life of the existing contract, whichever is the greater, is compared to the average annual increase in the consumer price index over the same period plus 2 per cent. If the group's increase was the same as the national benchmark, no adjustment is made. If its increase was 1 per cent smaller, then 1 per cent is added to the basic protection factor, plus the share in increased national productivity. If its increase was 2 per cent smaller,

Allowable Increases in the Initial Period

Difference between group's average gain and the national benchmark	−4	−3	−2	−1	0	1	2	3	4
Basic protection factor	8	8	8	8	8	8	8	8	8
Share in national productivity	2	2	2	2	2	2	2	2	2
Past wage experience factor	2	2	2	1	0	−1	−2	−2	−2
Allowable increase	12	12	12	11	10	9	8	8	8

then 2 per cent is added. If its increase was 1 per cent larger, the 1 per cent is subtracted from the basic protection factor plus the share in increased national productivity. If its increase was 2 per cent larger, then 2 per cent is subtracted. This adjustment factor cannot exceed plus or minus 2 per cent.

Thus, groups that have fallen behind may not recover all their losses in the first year. Losses will be carried forward into the future so that groups which incurred substantial losses in the recent past may achieve above-average gains in subsequent years. On the other hand, no group is asked to accept less than the basic protection factor as a result of this guideline.

Minimum and Maximum Dollar Increases

The fourth element in the compensation guidelines places minimum and maximum dollar

Allowable Increases by Income Level and Past Wage and Salary Experience

Difference between group's average gain in last two years and national benchmark	−4	−3	−2	−1	0	1	2	3	4
Income—$	Percentage and Dollar Increases								
5000	12%	12%	12%	12%	12%	12%	12%	12%	12%
	600	600	600	600	600	600	600	600	600
7000	12%	12%	12%	11%	10%	9%	8.6%	8.6%	8.6%
	840	840	840	770	700	630	600	600	600
10 000	12%	12%	12%	11%	10%	9%	8%	8%	8%
	1200	1200	1200	1100	1000	900	800	800	800
25 000	9.6%	9.6%	9.6%	9.6%	9.6%	9%	8%	8%	8%
	2400	2400	2400	2400	2400	2250	2000	2000	2000
50 000	4.8%	4.8%	4.8%	4.8%	4.8%	4.8%	4.8%	4.8%	4.8%
	2400	2400	2400	2400	2400	2400	2400	2400	2400

limits on permissible increases. At the lower end of the scale, increases of $600 may be paid in any event, and regardless of the size of the increases received in the past two years. The $600 figure represents a 12 per cent increase for those earning $5000 a year, about the minimum wage. At the upper end of the scale, no group, no matter what the change in compensation over the last two years, should have an average increase for its members of more than $2400. This represents 8 per cent, the initial basic protection factor, of a salary of $30 000. The table below illustrates the effect of this guideline rule on different income groups. Someone earning $7000 a year could get an increase of 8.6 per cent even if he had obtained large increases in recent years while someone earning $50 000 a year could get only a 4.8 per cent increase in any circumstance. The proportion of employees who will benefit from the minimum dollar provision will increase as the rate of inflation declines.

Groups Covered

The guidelines apply to "groups" defined either as bargaining units or as combinations of employees which employers have established for the unilateral determination and administration of pay. Although the principles apply to groups rather than individuals, some groups such as executive groups may be very small, and some in very particular circumstances may even have only one member. The $2400 maximum rule means that the average increase to all executives in a certain category cannot exceed $2400, but some executives may receive more than $2400 providing others receive less.

Forms of Compensation Covered

All forms of compensation, including for example fringe benefits, bonuses and stock options, are to be included in compensation for the purposes of the guidelines. Where it is administratively impossible to include any of these elements in compensation for purposes of calculating the past wage experience factor, these elements may be excluded from that calculation.

Promotions and Reclassification

Increases in wages and salaries resulting from promotions from one established level to another are not covered by the guidelines. Employers should not, however, modify their existing promotion policies or their systems of job classification currently in force for the purpose of evading the guidelines. It should be pointed out that employers are obliged not only to limit the increases in pay scales for each category of employees in a group, but to avoid changing the proportion of employees in the various categories in a way which would result in an increase in average pay for the group in excess of the guidelines.

Piece Rates and Commissions

The guidelines are not intended to prevent individuals from increasing their earnings under existing piece work, commission or production pay plans. When changes are made in such plans the effect will be determined by assuming the same amounts and kinds of output achieved in the past. The effect of changes in the plan will be subject to the guidelines. No limit will be placed on increases in earnings, under the new or revised plan, resulting from greater output. Changes in premium rates, such as overtime, must be included as a form of compensation.

Cases Where Groups Cover Wide Ranges in Incomes

If a group has members some of whom would be eligible for the $600 minimum rule, and others who would not, members eligible for the $600 may be excluded in determining the average increase.

Exceptions

It is difficult to develop a set of rules covering

wages which are wholly equitable and capable of allowing wages to continue to play their important role in the allocation of resources. There will, therefore, be exceptions to the above guidelines. If an employer can demonstrate that he cannot attract or hold workers at existing wages and that an increase above the guidelines is necessary, the employer will not be regarded as having breached the guidelines.

There may also be other grounds for exceptions, such as increases necessary to maintain long-established historical relationships between wages in closely related groups and other special cases of equity. Employers may also grant increases in compensation above the guidelines if such increases result from taking measures to improve the health or safety of the employees while at work, to eliminate restrictive work practices, to offset experience deficiencies in pension funds, or to eliminate sex discrimination in pay practices.

Professional Income

Increases in fees for professional services, such as the services of doctors, lawyers and accountants should be governed by the same general principles as apply to other prices and incomes. Specifically, professional fees should be increased only by the amounts required to cover the increased costs of providing the services and to improve the net income of the self-employed professional person by the same amount as would be available to the salaried professional person. Thus the $2400 maximum increase would apply in the determination of professional fees. Professionals would, of course, have the right to increase their incomes by more than $2400 if that increase reflected increases in workload. The basic fee schedule must not be increased, however, in a way which would allow the average professional working the same amount as in the base year to increase his income by more than the guidelines permit.

The provincial governments are being asked to use the guidelines as the basis for setting fee schedules in areas such as health where they have direct control, and to use their powers and influence to ensure that in other areas fee schedule changes are in conformity with the guidelines.

Dividends

The general principle will be that there will be no increases in the first year in the dollar level of dividends per share from the last completed fiscal year. Exemptions may be granted in some cases, such as where a firm could show that an increase was necessary in order to raise new equity capital, or a firm could show that last year's dividend was clearly atypically low.

Reprinted from *Attack on Inflation*, Policy Statement tabled in the House of Commons by the Honourable Donald S. Macdonald, Minister of Finance, October 14, 1975, Government of Canada, 1975, pp. 2-3, 12-24.

The document *Attack on Inflation* should be examined in its entirety to see the intent in other areas of policy. During the period of controls, two working papers were issued to indicate something of the problems ahead and the plans of the government. The first of these was entitled *The Way Ahead* and was issued in October, 1976. The second was *Agenda for Cooperation* and appeared in May, 1977. An excerpt from *The Way Ahead* on causes of inflation appeared in Chapter 16. It might now be appropriate to go back and reexamine this, taking into account the period during which it was produced and the nature of government policy at the time, to see how the view here reflects the period and the source. An excerpt from *Agenda for Cooperation* on the market system and the role of government appeared in Chapter 20. The suggestion made above concerning *Attack on Inflation* should also be applied to this reading.

CHAPTER 31

ECONOMIC GROWTH

■ WHAT IS GROWTH? ■ REAL VERSUS APPARENT GROWTH ■ THE TWO FORCES OF GROWTH ■ THE CENTRAL ROLE OF INVESTMENT ■ THE RESEARCH AGE ■ MEASURING ECONOMIC GROWTH ■ WHAT IS AUTOMATION? ■ AN OPTIMISTIC VIEW OF AUTOMATION ■ A PESSIMISTIC VIEW OF AUTOMATION ■ PROBLEMS OF REGIONAL ECONOMIC GROWTH ■ THE LIMITS TO GROWTH ■ SUMMARY

Economic growth has become a major objective of national economic policy in all countries. The relatively rich market economies recognize that their economies must continue to grow, if they are to provide for their increasing populations, to have sufficient jobs for their growing labor forces, to improve living standards for their people as a whole, to keep social tensions from worsening, and to maintain their position in the world. The developing nations of the world have been undergoing a revolution of rising expectations, in which their people are demanding a better life that cannot be attained except through economic growth. Despite these needs, we have also become more aware of the limits of resources and other problems which may impose a ceiling on economic growth.

■ WHAT IS GROWTH?

The concept of growth is one of the more subtle and elusive in economics. The concept is really based upon an analogy derived from biology. To get a clearer idea of what economic growth really means, it may be useful to take a closer look at the concept of growth in biology. One leading biologist, D'Arcy Thompson, defined growth as "a process, indirectly resulting from chemical, osmotic, and other forces, by which material is introduced into the organism and transferred from one part to another."

Economic growth ought, then, to involve similar processes in economic organisms. But what is an economic organism? Clearly it is not the flow of goods and services that issue from the economy each year; that is, the economic organism is not the gross national product. Rather, the economic organism is the complex of people, factories, stores, farms, forests and rivers, dams and highways, autos and trucks, ships and planes, airports and harbors, houses, schools, banks, oil wells and oil refineries, and mines and smelters that *produce* the stream of goods and services.

If you wanted to take a picture of that economic organism growing, you ought to do it the way a cameraman takes a picture of a flower growing. The motion picture cameraman would show you that process of biological growth from the beginning—first of all, the seed popping, the stem climbing out above ground and growing into the plant; then the bud forming and the flower bursting into bloom. The motion picture of an economic organism growing would show you, similarly, the changes that come to a dynamic industrial area over the years—rail lines spreading, factories building, new and more complex industrial equipment coming along. It would show you, too, some of the changes in the economic factors—the multiplying population, the expanding cities, the changes in occupations of the people as industrialism advances, even the changes in the faces of the people.

Such a pictorial representation of the

growth of an economic organism tells a dramatic story, but a somewhat superficial one. For it shows, quite effectively, the outer manifestations of growth, but it does not show the growth beneath the surface that has been making possible that outer transformation—the underlying growth in *ideas*. Recording the growth in ideas is impossible for the photographer; it is just as impossible for the economic statistician.

REAL VERSUS APPARENT GROWTH

It will not do to torture the analogy between economic and biological growth to illustrate the ways in which new material is taken in by biological or economic organisms and transferred throughout the organism (as, for instance, the idea of an assembly line was transferred to many parts of an industrial economy) so that the entire organism becomes enlarged. Nevertheless, there is one part of the analogy that deserves the greatest possible stress: That is the basic distinction in both cases between the growth of the organism—in economics, the growth of the system's productive capacity in the deepest sense—and the mere growth in its current rate of operation.

Just as a growing boy may, for a time, be sick and lie in bed, doing nothing, but still be growing, so may a nation's economy be in a temporary recession or depression, but still be growing.

West Germany After World War II

In World War II Germany was devastated by Allied bombing and ground fighting; the remaining German population, after the war, was embittered and demoralized. To anyone flying into Berlin or Frankfurt at the end of the war, the vast areas of shattered, hollow buildings looked like the remnants of a shattered civilization on some dead planet.

So it seemed. Yet only a few years later the new West Germany had become the economic powerhouse of Europe—not merely what it had been in 1939 before the war, but a still bigger and more powerful economy, crowded into a smaller space.

Everyone, including the economists, was astonished by the speed of that transformation from wreckage to powerhouse. "I always thought it was impossible for the German economy to recover," said Professor Theodore Schultz, who served with the Allied occupation authorities in Germany just after the war. But he added "We were dead wrong—British economists, American economists, and for that matter, Germans." They had all underestimated the real growth forces in West Germany. The plants and cities that had been destroyed, said Schultz, "were really quite secondary, minor details remedied in very short order." What was basic was the culture and economic growth potential of the nation.

Canada During the Great Depression

Was the German case something special? We may use our experience to show much the same thing. After the 1929 collapse, the Canadian economy stagnated for almost a decade of depression. In 1938 the Canadian economy was still producing less than in 1929.

But when war came and full employment was restored, did the output go back only to its 1929 level? On the contrary, the economy far surpassed it. By 1942 the nation's real output had already risen 50 percent above the mark set at the end of the boom of the 1920s. In a great rush the nation made up for the decade of depression; almost overnight it climbed up to where it might have been if there had been no long depression.

It was indeed as though the economy had been growing beneath the surface through the years while it was functioning at so low a level of output and employment.

THE TWO FORCES OF GROWTH

What, then, are the real forces that determine the growth of the economy? And to what extent can they be altered?

Public Archives of Canada

During the Great Depression, the swelling ranks of unemployed people moved across Canada in search of jobs and/or assistance. On several occasions, the economic hardships of life in the 1930s led to major protest movements directed at governments at all levels. This photo shows many of those participating in the "On to Ottawa" trek of 1935 arriving in Regina. The Regina riots of July 1, 1935, illustrated in Chapter 1, occurred several days after the arrival of the "march" in Regina.

Scraps of various theories of economic growth have been littering our libraries for hundreds of years. But during the 19th century economists generally had abandoned the effort to explain growth and instead tried to turn economics into a neat, precise, deductive science like Newtonian physics. Growth was too messy—too full of historical, sociological, technological, political, geographical, and institutional complexities.

The new interest in the growth field by economists after World War II started theories of growth multiplying again. The interest was spurred on by political factors—first, the drive of the poor nations for industrial and economic development and, second, the great thrust forward of the Soviet Union and the evolving competition between communism and capitalism. The result of this renewed interest in growth has been the rediscovery of what the earlier writers, philosophers, historians, and economists had already learned.

This was that there are basic sets of causes of growth:

One is the complex of cultural factors—including science, technology, population changes, religion, politics, social attitudes, class structure, and the intellectual and moral qualities of men—their skills, their imaginations, their drive, their courage.

The other is a set of economic factors affecting the possibility of accumulating capital funds and investing them in real capital equipment.

THE CENTRAL ROLE OF INVESTMENT

These two sets of factors, cultural and economic, must come together if growth is to occur. The two are joined in the act of investment; that is the crucial moment for economic growth. The act of investment embodies within the economic organism those technological and other cultural elements that make possible an expansion of output. Many statistical studies have shown that there is an important and direct link between the rate of investment and the rate of economic growth over time.

But if it is investment that plays so basic a role in economic growth, what causes investment to rise or to sink?

Broadly, in considering what spurs on the investment process, economists have come to split investment into two categories—**autonomous investment** and **induced investment**. Economists use both terms without much precision. What they mean approximately, though, is this:

Investment is autonomous when it moves independently or creates its own demand.

Investment is induced when it represents a response to pre-existing demand that forces producers to increase capacity.

Another way of stating the difference would be to say that autonomous investment results primarily from noneconomic causes, from forces outside the economic system itself—that is, from the action of the various cultural forces that help to bring about economic growth.

Induced investment, by contrast, results primarily from economic factors—from changes in business activity, from the relationship of costs, prices, interest rates, profit margins, the ratios between sales and capacity, and other forces within the economic system itself, in the case of the capitalist economies. In the Communist economies, the government planners substitute their orders and directions for the influences of prices and profits in a capitalist system, although Communist planners today are seeking to imitate these capitalist guides to improve the performance of their economies.

Autonomous investment is the heart of the long-term growth process. It comes chiefly from:

1. The discovery of new techniques of production, such as the assembly line or the steam engine; these cut production costs.
2. The development of new products, such as the automobile or the television set; these create new markets.
3. The development of new resources, such as petroleum or helium, a process usually stimulated by some technological advance (though at one time military conquest or exploration of distant lands played the leading role in bringing new resources to many nations).
4. Population growth and migration, which may stimulate investment in housing, public utilities, and social capital, such as schools and colleges, public health facilities, and so on.
5. Wars which necessitate expansion of plant and equipment to produce defense goods. Wars can also result in disinvestment if real capital goods are destroyed and wiped out by fighting.

The last two factors—population growth and migration, and war—may seem to come close to induced investment, or response to existing demands. But, essentially, they are noneconomic factors—cultural forces outside the operation of the economic system itself, and so are grouped with autonomous investment.

What has become increasingly clear is that the most important element in autonomous investment is the growth of scientific and technological knowledge which culminates in new products, new processes, and new resources. This is called *innovational* investment. There we find the great origin of economic growth.

In the past, Canada has had three great innovational pushes that have sent the economy climbing upward, each lasting about half a century. The first big push—based on agricultural and timber exports and sailing ships lasted from the end of the American Revolution until the 1840s. Then came the second push—based on the building of the railroads and on steel—lasting until close to the end of the 1890s. The third thrust—powered by electricity and the automobile—got under way around the turn of the century, and perhaps ended a few years ago.

THE RESEARCH AGE

It is going to be a lot harder, though, to fasten a label on the new innovational push that we have been experiencing since the end of World War II. That is because it has not been based on any one or two innovations that provide a convenient tag, but rather upon a whole flood of them.

These postwar innovations owe their origin to major scientific progress in nuclear and solid-state physics, organic and inorganic chemistry, electronics, engineering, the earth sciences, the biological sciences, and mathematics. The important scientific work that led to breakthroughs and innovations in those fields stretched back through the war years and on through the years of apparent economic stagnation in the 1930s (when the work of scientists such as Einstein, Lawrence, Fermi, and Meitner was far from stagnating).

What will this new epoch be called? It is clearly an understatement to call it the atomic age, as people did at the end of the war. It is too narrow to call it the age of automation. And it is much more than the space age. Because of its tremendous breadth, we might simply call it the *research age*.

The research age is characterized by the application of *organized* science to industry. Probably the greatest thing that sold industry on the new approach was the way organized research attacks paid off in World War II. By 1939 British scientists were moving into high places in their government and industry to attack a wide variety of problems. In the United States the Office of Scientific Research and Development performed much the same function and initiated many of the projects which have changed our world. Most dramatic and important of all was the Manhattan project, which enlisted and coordinated the talents of many specialists in the quest for the atom bomb. Similarly, in the chemical industry there was urgent need to find a way synthetically to replace natural rubber; a search was organized, it succeeded, and the United States was able to build enough rubber plants to ease its dependence on imported rubber during the war. With these and such other great technological achievements as radar and antibiotics, the realization dawned that the world had entered a new phase of the Industrial Revolution—a phase that might be called the Research Revolution.

This research revolution has deepened and widened since the war. Nor is it only the big, sensational things—headline-grabbers such as atomic reactors, hydrogen bombs, electronic computers, jet transports, atomic submarines, earth satellites—that have issued forth from this new innovational push. The list of new products that have staged a fast growth in the postwar period is long. Here are just some of the fastest-growing new products and new services, created by industrial research and development, that helped push the economy upward at a rapid pace from the late 1940s through the 1960s: transistors, titanium sponge, power steering and power brakes, antibiotics, television sets and later, color television, polyethylene, styrene plastics and resins, vitamins, helicopters, synthetic fibers and rubber, butadiene, synthetic detergents, commercial jet aircraft, electric driers, tape recorders, photocopy machines, and, of course, high-speed computers for business and scientific work.

There is another side to this picture, however. You find it in the list of products that have shown a declining trend through the postwar period. Lumped together in this group are sheepskins, local transit, lead, cast-iron boilers, railroad passenger cars, anthracite coal, radiators and convectors, steam locomotives, tin, brick, woolen goods, tractor moldboard plows, work shirts, domestic heating stoves, creamery butter, black blasting powder, natural soap, textile bags, and other victims of technological change. Many of these relatively declining products represented innovations in their day (if you go back far enough, all of them did). And like them, each of the multitude of postwar innovations has its own life to live. Some will have a long and pretty steady period of expansion before they taper off. Others shoot up like a rocket, hit a ceiling, then perhaps drop back. Still others will keep booming upward for a long time.

This falling off of obsolescent products as technology changes is the reverse side of the innovation process on which one distinguished economist, Joseph Schumpeter, built his theory of economic growth and business cycles. It is what Schumpeter called **creative destruction**—creative, because the ultimate effect of innovation is growth, not stagnation; capitalism is a system of economic change that, in his words, "not only never is but never can be stationary."

We do not know precisely what our laboratories will discover in the years ahead. But we do know that if we sponsor adequate research programs, they will make discoveries that call for new investment and generate greater production. Knowing this, we can, in a real sense, make innovation a deliberate program rather than a chance development and thus help ensure future growth.[1]

MEASURING ECONOMIC GROWTH

We have sought to make clear that economic growth means the increase in the capabilities of the economy for production; and, most fundamentally, this means growth in a nation's underlying ideas, skills, and technology. Since it is virtually impossible to put into numerical tables the underlying organic growth of an economy, economists seeking to measure growth must settle for the next best thing—current measures of economic *output* or *income*. From these performance records, they can derive long-term growth trends for the economy itself.

Economists do this on the assumption that there is some meaningful relationship between changes in output or income, and changes in the capacity of the underlying economy. And that does seem to be the case—over the long run. Provided that the time period covered is long enough to cancel out swings in business activity, and that the beginning and final dates of the period covered have nothing unusual about them (generally speaking, base and terminal dates should be at approximately the same rate of employment and capacity utilization), such time series are about the best means available of measuring economic growth.

Statistics on gross national product provide us with the data for measuring overall economic growth over long periods of time. Since we are really interested in the capacity of the economy to produce actual goods and services, rather than changes in the money value of the goods and services produced, GNP data must be adjusted for price changes over the period covered GNP must be expressed in constant dollars—that is, dollars translated into the value they had in purchasing goods and services in some particular base year. Also, adjustment for changes in population should be made as well. Discussion of these modifications of raw GNP data was provided in Chapter 23 and should be reviewed.

WHAT IS AUTOMATION?

There is no generally accepted definition of **automation**. Some who use the word give it a quite narrow definition, such as "a system by which many or all of the processes of pro-

[1] For further discussion of patterns of industrialization and forces of growth, see George Baldwin's essay "Industrialization—A Standard Pattern," which is reprinted in A. H. MacDonald, (ed.), *Readings In the World of Economics*, Toronto: McGraw-Hill Ryerson, 1973.

duction, movement, and inspection of parts and materials are automatically performed or controlled by self-operating machinery and electronic devices, including computers." Others, however, give the term *automation* a much broader definition, to cover every sort of technological progress which increases the productivity of labor.

Such a definition as the last would appear to be too broad. Much technological progress has nothing to do with automatic machinery. For instance, if farmers increase the yield of their land by using better seeds or more fertilizer, this would appear to have nothing to do with automation. Or, if retailers increase their sales while reducing their number of employees by letting customers wait on themselves, as in supermarkets or discount stores, this would not appear to have much to do with automation. Because there is no generally accepted definition of what automation is, nobody knows how much automation has contributed to increasing labor productivity—output per unit of labor. Obviously, only a small percentage of the nation's productive equipment, valued at hundreds of billions of dollars and including all sorts of capital equipment from airplanes and locomotives to hand drills and sledge hammers, has been automated in the sense of being subjected to non-human controls.

Further, even if automation were taken to be synonymous with all technological progress, it would still not be responsible for all increases in productivity. Productivity may be increased by operating the nation's existing factories, plants, and other productive equipment at higher levels of capacity, where they perform more efficiently. Or productivity may be increased by gains in the competence and efficiency of human management, by higher labor skills, or by scientific research that leads to the discovery of new resources or better ways of using old resources.

AN OPTIMISTIC VIEW OF AUTOMATION

However, even if we accept the growing custom of calling all technological progress automation, and if we assume that this automation is responsible for all increases in productivity, the statement that "automation replaces people" is incorrect as it stands. It contains a major concealed assumption that total output remains constant while worker productivity increases, and thus that fewer people will be needed to do the same amount of work.

But this is an assumption that does not correspond to the historical facts. Two centuries of technological progress show that total output does not remain constant, as mechanization advances. Since the mid-eighteenth century (if we may take that as the start of the Industrial Revolution) enormous increases in mechanization have produced enormous gains in productivity, in total output, and in income and employment. Gains in productivity and total output have been matched by growing demands—including demands for goods once non-existent—and, as a consequence, living standards have greatly increased.[2]

The automation scare, therefore, looks to many economists like nothing but a revival of *Luddism*. The Luddites—named after Ned Lud, a feeble-minded textile worker who smashed two frames belonging to a Leicestershire employer in England around 1780—were workers who, in the early nineteenth century, went around smashing new labor-saving machinery in protest against reduced wages and unemployment attributed to the introduction of the new machinery.

A PESSIMISTIC VIEW OF AUTOMATION

Those who nevertheless fear the effect of automation on employment (including some labor leaders and many workers in lines affected by rapid technological change, some social psychologists, engineers, mathematicians, and social reformers) contend that economists who regard automation as "simply the latest stage in the evolution of

[2] For a wider perspective, see the two papers from the Canadian Imperial Bank of Commerce dealing with "Automation" and "Leisure," which are reprinted in *Readings In the World of Economics*.

technological means for removing the burdens of work" just do not understand what the new automation revolution is all about.

One such social critic, Donald Michael, a social psychologist, asserts that, compared with earlier technological change, automation "is so different in degree as to be a profound difference in kind." The difference, according to Michael, is that automated machines do not simply *augment* man's muscle power but rather *replace* his hands, fingers, eyes, ears, nose, and brain. They can perform "with a precision and rapidity unmatched in humans."

Hence, it is claimed, the new machines can do everything that ordinary, and many extraordinary, workers can do, only better and faster. They can make and roll steel, mine coal, manufacture engine blocks, weave cloth, sort and grade oranges or bank checks, assemble typewriters, design and test rockets and airplanes, make machine tools, direct traffic, keep inventory records, etc.

The late Professor Norbert Wiener, a mathematician at the Massachusetts Institute of Technology, invented the name *cybernetics* for these new developments. Cybernetics is the theory of the science of automatic controls. (The name comes from the Greek word for *helmsman*.) With the large scale use of cybernetics by industry, masses of ordinary workers would be headed for unemployment, according to Wiener. The new cybernetic revolution, therefore, "will produce an unemployment situation in comparison with which . . . the depression of the 1930s will seem a pleasant joke."

Those who fear that the Wieners and Michaels are basically right and the optimists wrong can point to some dramatic shifts in industries that have been big manpower users but that are shedding workers or failing to increase employment, despite big gains in output. This, the pessimists say, will happen during the years ahead in every industry. This will not be like the past, when workers displaced from jobs in one industry shifted readily to jobs in another, as when marginal farmers left their plows by the millions and became factory hands. Instead, say the pessimists, all the big labor-using industries—the factories and offices of business, as well as the farms and the mines—will be hit simultaneously.

This, they contend, is already happening. The decline in agricultural jobs is an old story. What has happened in farming, argue the pessimists, can happen in every other major sector of the economy. Eventually, they say, electronic slaves will be everywhere, doing everything that is routine and many things that are not, and doing those jobs more cheaply than people can. Admittedly, they concede, some brainy types of humans will be needed to design and program the machines. But the mass of workers will not be able to shift to the new creative jobs, as they did from farm to factory in the past; the intellectual requirements will be too difficult.

AUTOMATION AND UNEMPLOYMENT

Despite such arguments, the majority of economists refuse to be alarmed over the alleged threat of mass unemployment resulting from automation.

For automation to produce mass unemployment, three developments would have to take place:

1. Automation would result in a rate of growth of **productivity**[3]—output per worker—far greater than anything that we have experienced in the past.
2. Human labor could not adapt to the new job requirements created by the new technology in the economy as a whole.
3. The overall growth in demand for all the goods and services produced would be too slow to create enough jobs for all the workers whose productivity would be greatly augmented by automation.

All three of these developments, the optimists about automation argue, are improbable. Wise social and economic policies, they

[3] For detailed coverage, see the study by Libby Joyce, *Understanding Productivity*, Canadian Foundation for Economic Education, Toronto, 1977.

Table 31-1. PROVINCIAL PERSONAL INCOMES PER CAPITA AS A PERCENTAGE OF NATIONAL LEVEL, 1949-1977

Years	Nfld.	P.E.I.	N.S.	N.B.	Que.	Ont.	Man.	Sask.	Alta.	B.C.	Y.T.& NWT	Canada
	(Personal income per capita, by province, as a percentage of personal income per capita at the national level)											
1949	50.9	55.5	74.5	69.4	85.1	119.2	103.4	96.8	105.4	118.7	—	100.0
1950	51.0	55.1	74.4	70.2	85.9	121.2	101.4	83.3	100.6	122.3	—	100.0
1951	48.3	54.5	69.2	67.1	84.0	118.3	100.9	107.2	111.1	119.2	86.8	100.0
1952	47.6	60.7	71.9	64.8	84.9	117.1	98.0	111.9	107.4	120.2	96.4	100.0
1953	50.8	48.9	73.0	63.7	86.5	118.0	95.0	100.4	106.3	120.2	103.3	100.0
1954	53.4	53.0	76.5	67.2	88.9	120.2	94.4	73.2	98.7	122.7	112.0	100.0
1955	53.1	49.5	73.8	66.0	86.6	119.5	94.4	89.0	99.8	123.3	109.5	100.0
1956	53.5	58.7	72.0	65.8	86.2	117.8	97.0	93.5	104.6	121.2	130.1	100.0
1957	54.5	51.3	73.9	65.3	88.1	119.6	93.6	77.8	99.2	121.5	125.6	100.0
1958	53.6	53.2	74.1	65.7	87.0	118.9	99.0	83.2	104.1	116.1	114.6	100.0
1959	54.0	59.1	75.6	66.9	86.7	118.9	99.0	82.3	101.6	117.0	111.6	100.0
1960	55.5	56.9	76.4	68.1	87.2	117.8	99.4	89.2	99.8	115.3	105.7	100.0
1961	58.2	58.9	77.8	68.0	90.2	118.4	94.4	71.0	100.0	115.0	96.6	100.0
1962	56.0	60.4	75.6	66.2	89.1	116.9	97.6	93.2	99.8	112.0	87.9	100.0
1963	56.3	58.4	75.5	67.0	88.6	117.2	94.3	98.2	98.2	112.3	88.8	100.0
1964	56.9	60.8	75.9	68.5	90.3	117.3	95.8	84.5	96.0	113.3	86.2	100.0
1965	59.2	60.1	74.7	68.4	89.9	116.5	93.8	90.1	97.0	113.7	80.5	100.0
1966	59.9	60.2	74.8	68.9	89.2	116.4	91.9	93.1	100.1	111.6	80.8	100.0
1967	61.0	62.1	76.7	69.3	90.5	116.2	95.4	81.3	99.1	110.8	82.4	100.0
1968	61.5	63.9	76.6	70.4	89.0	117.0	96.6	84.7	100.3	108.4	85.9	100.0
1969	61.0	62.7	77.4	70.1	88.4	117.9	93.9	80.5	100.0	109.6	88.2	100.0
1970	63.4	66.5	77.5	72.0	88.7	118.4	92.9	72.5	99.3	108.8	94.6	100.0
1971	63.8	63.2	77.5	72.3	88.7	117.0	94.1	80.3	99.0	109.0	86.8	100.0
1972	63.7	66.2	79.9	73.3	89.6	115.9	93.6	78.7	98.7	109.2	91.4	100.0
1973	63.7	69.7	79.9	72.9	89.4	113.5	96.0	91.4	100.2	110.5	91.5	100.0
1974	67.3	66.6	79.5	74.3	90.6	111.8	94.7	96.1	100.2	110.2	93.4	100.0
1975	68.5	70.2	79.1	77.0	91.1	109.8	96.6	103.2	103.8	108.4	91.7	100.0
1976	67.8	68.7	78.4	75.7	92.6	109.2	94.1	100.8	103.8	109.3	90.8	100.0
1977	68.2	67.2	79.5	75.1	93.2	109.3	93.0	92.4	104.3	110.1	94.2	100.0

Note: Data for the Yukon and N.W.T. prior to 1951 were consolidated with data for British Columbia.

Source: Based on data in Statistics Canada, *National Income and Expenditure Accounts*, cat. 13-531, (1949-1970) and cat. 13-201, (1970-77).

contend, can make automation a vast benefit, rather than a hardship, for the Canadian people.

PROBLEMS OF REGIONAL ECONOMIC GROWTH

Since the decade of the 1960s, one specific topic which has attracted unprecedented attention is the problem of **regional disparity**. Regional inequalities plague most nations, less developed as well as industrialized. It is within the developed nations such as Canada, however, where inequalities tend to stand out more and frequently create additional social and political tensions. Throughout the 1960s, perhaps the crucial point of concern was the realization that, despite efforts to overcome the existing disparities which had been long recognized, the degree of change in the situation was relatively slight. The degree of change, using personal income per capita as a measure, may be seen by examining the data in Table 31-1.

The data in this table indicates some nar-

Table 31-2. REGIONAL UNEMPLOYMENT RATES, 1966-1977

	Canada	Atlantic region	Quebec	Ontario	Prairie region	British Columbia
			(Per cent)			
1966	3.4	5.4	4.1	2.6	2.4	4.6
1967	3.8	5.3	4.6	3.2	2.5	5.1
1968	4.5	6.0	5.6	3.6	3.3	5.9
1969	4.4	6.2	6.1	3.2	3.3	5.1
1970	5.7	6.1	7.0	4.4	4.9	7.7
1971	6.2	6.8	7.3	5.4	5.2	7.2
1972	6.2	7.7	7.5	5.0	5.3	7.9
1973	5.6	7.8	6.8	4.3	4.7	6.7
1974	5.3	8.6	6.6	4.4	3.3	6.2
1975	6.9	9.9	8.1	6.3	3.9	8.5
1976	7.1	10.9	8.7	6.2	4.2	8.6
1977	8.1	12.7	10.3	7.0	4.8	8.5

Note: See footnote 1, Table 26-2.

Source: Data have been calculated from provincial rates in sources shown in Table 26-2 by the Federal Department of Finance.

rowing of the gaps, the largest upward movements in the direction of the national average being those in Newfoundland and P.E.I., with downward movements of ten percentage points in Ontario and B.C. There are still wide gaps, especially for the Atlantic region.

Regional inequities are also indicated in the patterns of employment and unemployment. The information shown in Table 31-2 indicates that, in the area of unemployment, the gaps between regions have not been altered in a significant way.

As a result of the continued existence of such wide gaps, considerable attention has been given to the causes of regional disparity. A detailed examination of regional conditions would reveal what, by this time, you might be inclined to suspect as at least partial explanations of the problem.

In addition to the two primary features illustrated in the tables, what are other common characteristics of Canada's poorer regions? Within such a list would appear items such as the following: a higher rural element in the population; more dependence on seasonal jobs or employment in primary industry as opposed to manufacturing; more limited natural resource bases; smaller local markets; longer distances from larger markets; lower rates of investment; and lower skill or educational levels within the labor force. This group of characteristics is not an exhaustive one, nor is it completely valid for all "depressed" regions. Within it, however, are a number of keys to many of the regional problems in Canada.

An obvious question regarding these factors is: which are causes and which are results? Obviously, the nature of the factors and the interrelationships among them are such that, to a degree, we are facing a "chicken or egg" problem. Despite this, however, some root causes may be isolated.

The resource factors, natural and human, are in part in this category. Limited natural resources place many restrictions on an economy. Small populations, i.e., local markets, decrease the potential benefits of large-scale production. Exporting could offset this, but distance factors may be imposed by forces external to man. A frequent result of these forces is the nature of what may be called the sectoral balance between primary and secondary industry. Value produced per worker in small-scale or primary industries is frequently lower and this may account for many income differentials. Less use of potential collective bargaining power is also regarded as a possible factor in some income gaps where productivity does not provide an explanation. The income factor in turn affects the *C* component of total expenditure on a local or regional basis. In addition, lower incomes and less industry reduce the ability of provincial and municipal governments to contribute appreciably more within the *G* component. Existing problems in turn tend to lead to relatively lower *I* levels from existing industries and may deter new investment in a region.

The preceding is only a brief introduction to a complex set of problems. It should be sufficient, however, to indicate factors which may impede completely balanced growth in Canada or elsewhere.[4]

If these then are the types of problems, what has been done and what is required in the future? An examination of the goals of policies related to regional growth shows a complex and not always compatible mix. Frequent changes in goals and the direction of policies emerge.[5] The federal role, however, has become a very strong one and many efforts have been made to coordinate programs and bring a greater degree of planning to bear. The establishment of the Department of Regional Economic Expansion in 1968 was designed to promote this aim while incorporating many agencies and programs under its direction.

Early in the 1960s, much attention was paid to rural areas under the program of the Agricultural Rehabilitation and Development Act of 1961 and the Fund for Rural Economic Development of 1966. Known as ARDA and FRED, both became involved in rural growth projects and also in aiding in the shift of population out of marginally productive farming areas.

In the field of industrial development, the Area Development Agency, created in 1963, became prominent, though many of its early aims regarding planning seemed to be abandoned as it concentrated on providing capital assistance to new industries.

The ADA program was replaced by the provisions of the Regional Development Incentives Act of 1969. This Act provided for grants to new or expanding industries in the private sector, scaled in relation to the number of new jobs created. Eligible areas originally included the Atlantic Provinces and sections of the other six provinces where unemployment was especially high. Changes in the **designated areas** increased the applicability of the Act during the 1970s.

In 1973, a policy review called for a more decentralized approach by DREE. A more regionalized structure was established and new "umbrella agreements," each called a "General Development Agreement" (**GDA**), were signed with each of the provinces except Prince Edward Island, which has a special long-term Development Plan under a FRED agreement. The GDAs seem designed to permit a more flexible approach to DREE assistance and coordination efforts, and it appears likely that the GDAs will become the core element in Federal policy.

Within the total pattern, many problems and grounds for criticism emerge. Governments at the local and provincial level frequently seem to compete more than they co-

[4] For further views on the causes of disparities among regions, see: Economic Council of Canada, *Second Annual Review*, Ottawa: Queen's Printer, 1965, chapter 5; T. N. Brewis, *Regional Economic Policies in Canada*, Toronto: Macmillan, 1969, especially chapters 2 and 4; T. N. Brewis, ed., *Growth and the Canadian Economy*, Carlton Library Series, Number 39, Toronto: McClelland and Stewart, 1968, chapter 6; and, finally, an Economic Council of Canada study, *Living Together, A Study of Regional Disparities*, Ottawa: 1977. This Economic Council study is a "must" for this topic!

[5] For perceptive comments on the early period, see the essay by Brewis on "Regional Economic Disparities and Policies," in Officer and Smith, eds., *Canadian Economic Problems and Policies*, Toronto: McGraw-Hill of Canada, 1970; and by Green, "Regional Economic Disparities," in Officer and Smith, eds., *Issues In Canadian Economics*, Toronto: McGraw-Hill Ryerson Ltd., 1974.

operate. Industries may take advantage of this. Political problems and rivalries may be significant. More than one disaster has occurred in areas where such can not be afforded. Examples are the cases of the initial heavy water project at Glace Bay, Nova Scotia, the Bricklin sports car venture in New Brunswick, an oil refinery at Come-By-Chance, Newfoundland, and the forest products complex at The Pas, Manitoba.[6]

[6] For some case studies of major projects of the type which often fail, see Philip Mathias' *Forced Growth*, Toronto: James Lewis and Samuel, 1971.

Given the best of management and good fortune, overnight miracles cannot be expected. Capital investment in infra-structure (such as transportation facilities) and education takes time to bear fruit. It must also be accepted that many of the poor in poor areas are not necessarily going to be helped by industrial growth—as should be recalled from ideas discussed in Chapter 14. The objectives of growth must also be related to the other categories of policies needed to reduce the burden of disparity at the personal as well as the regional level.

General Development Agreements and Subsidiary Agreements

The following is a general outline of the GDAs which evolved from a major review of DREE policies in 1973. (To examine this newer approach to DREE policy, it is recommended that you get information about the GDA for your province—except in P.E.I., where the GDA role is filled by the "Island Development Plan.")

The present approach to regional development is both multi-disciplinary and "multi-dimensional". It calls for the identification and pursuit of major developmental opportunities by means of a coordinated application of public policies and programs, both federal and provincial, in cooperation with elements of the private sector where appropriate. There are three principal objectives:

- to encourage the formulation and implementation of federal and provincial policies which will provide general support for the development of slow-growth regions;
- to identify obstacles to economic development in slow-growth regions and modify or provide the necessary programs to reduce or remove these obstacles; and
- to identify specific opportunities for development in slow-growth regions and assist in the realization of these opportunities.

The framework for implementing this strategy is established by a General Development Agreement (GDA), and its Subsidiary Agreements, between the federal government and each province.

General Development Agreements

The GDAs provide a formal means to encourage coordinated federal and provincial action aimed at the realization of the potential of each region and province for economic and social development. These agreements provide a statement of objectives to be pursued and describe the extent of activity to be coordinated, the types of support to be provided, and the mechanism by which joint decisions can be taken. The agreements are enabling and flexible so that specific actions by both levels of government can be tailored to the specific needs of each area and its people, and to opportunities as they are identified. The specific programs carried out under the agreements will therefore vary from time to time and from place to place.

The General Development Agreements in themselves do not provide for specific commitments of resources for the implementation of programs or projects, but set up the formal framework within which such commitments are to be made under Subsidiary Agreements over a 10-year period. As such, each GDA includes objectives, a broad strategy to reach them on the basis of an analysis of the province's socioeconomic circumstances, authority to enter into Subsidiary Agreements, and an outline of the guidelines and criteria for the implementation of the strategy through the Subsidiary Agreements.

Although there are significant variations in the objectives from one province to another, they all generally include objectives along the lines of improving the opportunities for productive employment, and access to those opportunities, in those areas which require special measures to facilitate economic expansion and social adjustment. Depending on the particular economic circumstances of a province, the emphasis in the objectives is on the standards of living, especially in relation to the national average; or alternatively on a more equitable distribution of socioeconomic development among geographic, industrial or social sectors within the province.

The GDA strategies are basically similar. Each notes that Canada and the province will seek to achieve a coordinated application of relevant federal and provincial policies and programs through continuing:

- analysis and review of the economic and social circumstances of the province, and the province's relationship to the regional and national economy, as these may be relevant to achieving the stated objectives;
- identification of development opportunities and assistance in their realization through coordinated application of relevant federal and provincial policies and programs, including the provision and specialized measures required for such realization.

A broad strategy to apply this general approach to varying conditions and opportunities in the province is provided in the Schedule A appended to each GDA. Schedule A contains a brief analysis of the province's socioeconomic circumstances, on which is based a more elaborate statement of development objectives for the province. It also presents a general outline of priorities for federal-provincial initiatives.

The GDAs provide for Subsidiary Agreements to be entered into for the implementation of development initiatives agreed upon by the federal and provincial governments. These parts of the agreements also identify the criteria that should be taken into consideration in the formulation of Subsidiary Agreements in respect to the impact and cost of the initiatives: direct job creation, spin-off effects, implications for quality of life and environment, effect on immediate and future expenditures, and so forth.

The development strategy and activities outlined in the GDAs can be implemented through three types of Subsidiary Agreements:

Those which coordinate existing federal and provincial programs in support of a particular development opportunity. For example, if the objective is to increase meat processing in southern Manitoba, a Subsidiary Agreement could incorporate assistance from established programs of the federal Departments of Agriculture, Industry, Trade and Commerce, and Regional Economic Expansion, and of the Province of Manitoba. The coordinated application of these existing programs could, without any new authority and funds, achieve the objective.

Those which provide specific support not available through other government programs. For example, in order to realize increased forestry development in northern New Brunswick, it may be necessary to provide a large industrial incentive or finance a special site for industrial facilities and also to improve programs for forest management, manpower training and forest access roads. A Subsidiary Agreement could provide for the special assistance only, or for both the special assistance and the other requirements.

Those which establish continuing programs to fill gaps in the existing range of government development programs. For example, there may be a need for continuing long-term programs for such developmental requirements as planning, resource management or general infrastructure. The GDAs authorize DREE to enter into Subsidiary Agreements with the provinces for such long-term support programs.

The GDAs also call for annual meetings of relevant federal and provincial departments and of the federal and provincial ministers.

GDAs have now been signed with all provinces except Prince Edward Island, which already has a 15-year comprehensive development plan covering 1969 to 1984.

Subsidiary Agreements

By the end of December 1975, 37 Subsidiary Agreements had been formulated and signed; others were in an advanced state of analysis and formulation. Most of these Subsidiary Agreements are of the second category noted above, although some or parts of some are of the first and third type.

As these Subsidiary Agreements appear, they demonstrate the multi-dimensional and flexible nature of DREE's new approach (New Brunswick Forestry, Manitoba Northlands, Saskatchewan Steel). Yet at the same time, there is still considerable reliance on selected infrastructure support (Cornwall, Gros Morne, Newfoundland and New Brunswick Highways) and very basic resource and rural development (Newfoundland Forestry, Saskatchewan Mineral Development).

The cost-sharing for the Subsidiary Agreements varies from province to province, and, within a province, from Sub-Agreement to Sub-Agreement. The department is authorized to share in the cost of a Sub-Agreement with a province up to 90 per cent for Newfoundland, 80 per cent for Nova Scotia and New Brunswick, 60 per cent for Quebec, Manitoba and Saskatchewan, and 50 per cent for Ontario, Alberta and British Columbia. The average federal share runs below these maximum levels, at least in those provinces where the maximum level is above 50 per cent.

The projects to be implemented under Subsidiary Agreements involve an estimated total investment of approximately $1040 million. Current plans indicate that the federal and provincial shares will amount to about $541 million and $211 million respectively during the life of the agreements. It is expected that these development activities will also generate investment by the private sector amounting to some $288 million in the establishment of new industrial and commercial ventures or in the expansion and modernization of existing facilities.

From: Department of Regional Economic Expansion, *The New Approach*, Ottawa: 1976, pp. 19-22.

THE LIMITS TO GROWTH

During the two decades following the end of World War II, economic growth was a virtually unchallenged goal for most nations and was accepted by most people without question. In more recent years, however, conflicting opinions have started to emerge.

Several factors appear to have played major roles in raising questions about either the desirability or even the possibility of continual economic growth.

One of the factors certainly has been the significant increase in ecological consciousness. The effects of expanding urbanization and industrialization on the environment have made us aware of how high some of our third party costs have been. Some critics of growth suggest that the extent of environmental destruction associated with economic development is such that we must curtail our rates of growth and drastically modify many aspects of industrial society to prevent further irrepairable environmental damage.

A second factor has been increasing concern about the uneven distribution of what we produce, nationally or internationally. It is also suggested by some that our priorities should be directed toward more equitable distribution of existing output than the production of more goods and services in absolute terms.

Related to this has been a reconsideration of some of our other values. Some observers advocate that there is much more need to be concerned with improving the quality of life in non-material terms than emphasizing quantitative improvements based on expanded output.

A less philosophical factor has been rising oil and other energy costs and the growing realization that many of our resources, nationally or worldwide, are in fact limited. Shortages of gasoline and heating oil in some parts of the United States in the winter of 1973-74 and questions about the size of Canada's oil and gas reserves have certainly made people realize this. The result has been an increase in the concern about the wise use of resources and the development of alternatives for meeting our needs. An obvious question is: to what extent may we have to reduce our needs in the future, for energy and, perhaps many other things presently taken for granted?

These concerns are hotly debated. Strong cases can be made for the need for continued growth, and for the case that most of the problems associated with growth can be solved or prevented as long as we are willing to absorb the costs of either cure or prevention.

Within the framework of the debate about growth, you are quite likely to encounter references to some of the projections which have sometimes been referred to as the **Doomsday Models**. These are projections which indicate that continued uncontrolled growth will ultimately produce a total collapse of the economic and social systems on our planet.

Perhaps the most widely known model of this category is that contained in a study, *The Limits To Growth*, sponsored by the Massachusetts Institute of Technology, and the "Club of Rome", an international group of academics, business, and government leaders. The M.I.T. team led by Dennis Meadows extended an elaborate econometric computer model begun by Professor Jay Forrester of M.I.T. Working from historical data and trends, they ran a number of computer projections, all of which indicated that if past and present trends continued, the result would be disaster. The patterns which the model projects are all based on the assumption of continued exponential growth. Every new year's growth is a larger absolute increase because it builds on a larger base, just as compound interest builds up a savings account. The final conclusions of the M.I.T. models indicated that resources would ultimately be exhausted by growing demand and population, with catastrophic effects on human society. The one escape from this "Doomsday" situation was indicated as the adoption of zero rates of growth in population and economic output by the end of this century. Figure 31-1 on page 400 contains one of the simple basic graphs showing the projected key trends.

The Limits To Growth, which was published in 1972, raised much controversy.

Related Reading—The Limits To Growth

For other critiques of growth, less catastrophic in their projections, see Schumacher, E. F., *Small Is Beautiful*, London: Sphere Books, 1974, and Ehrlich, Paul R. and Anne H., *The End of Affluence*, New York: Ballantine Books, 1974. For a wider perspective, see Weintraub, Schwartz and Aronson, eds., *The Economic Growth Controversy*, White Plains, N.Y.: International Arts and Sciences Press, 1973. For a Canadian perspective on resource conservation, see Science Council Committee, *Toward A Conserver Society: A Statement of Concern*, Ottawa: Supply and Services Canada, 1976.

FIG. 31-1. GROWTH AND COLLAPSE: A DOOMSDAY MODEL

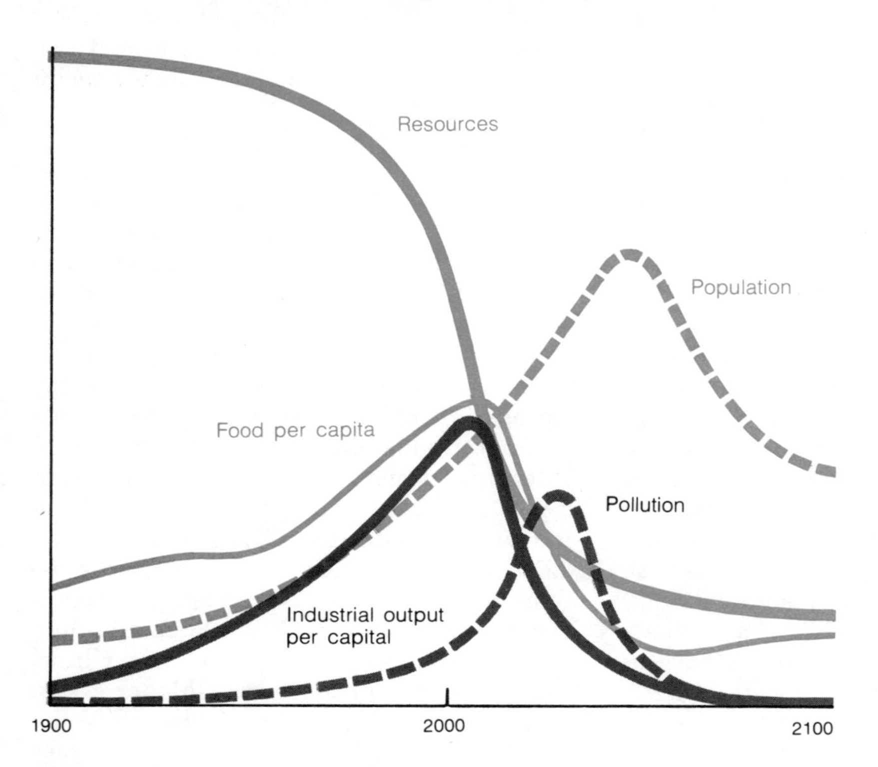

This computer model "assumes no major change in the physical, economic, or social relationships that have historically governed the development of the world system . . . Food, industrial output, and population grow exponentially until the rapidly diminishing resource base forces a slowdown in industrial growth. Because of natural delays in the system, both population and pollution continue to increase for some time after the peak of industrialization. Population growth is finally halted by a rise in the death rate due to decreased food and medical services." (Dennis L. Meadows and others, *The Limits to Growth (Washington: Potomac Associates, 1972), p. 129.)*

Many economists argued that many of the assumptions in the model were inaccurate. For example, the assumption that existing trends will continue was considered inappropriate. The failure to consider the effects of growing scarcities on prices, and this in turn on the use of resources, was regarded as a key weakness. These various criticisms indicated that the Doomsday scenario was not inevitable, and that modifications could be made in the future economic structure without resorting to a "no-growth" approach.

Despite all its limitations, this first "Report to the Club of Rome" had a significant effect. Even if the report contains inaccuracies, it called attention to the catastrophic problems which could emerge if nations do not carefully monitor their growth. It indicated the need for careful long-range planning, and the recognition of the growing interdependencies in our economic system on a world-wide basis. If such considerations are not given their proper attention, the Doomsday scenarios could become a reality.

SUMMARY

Economic growth fundamentally means the increase in the capabilities of a national economy for producing goods and services. It therefore refers to changes in the size of the labor force, the quantity of capital (real plant and equipment), usable national resources, and, most importantly, the ability of the nation to employ these resources with increasing effectiveness. At bottom, then, increases in productive efficiency depend upon the growth of knowledge; on new processes, products, and resources; and on the effective operation of the entire economic system.

But growth is not automatic. It demands the continuous efforts of the people to improve their productivity and a sound national economy in which both material and human resources will be fully and effectively utilized. It requires investment in capital equipment and investment in people and knowledge. And it means that there must also be strong incentives for efforts to increase productivity and to invest in growth. In recent years, fears have been raised over automation—the replacement of human labor by automatic machinery and other technological changes. Those who are worried that automation will lead to mass unemployment argue that once workers displaced by new technologies that increase productivity could move from one industry to another (as from farming to industrial production), but that soon the new machines will be so efficient and adaptable that they will infiltrate the whole of industry and leave few jobs for unskilled or semi-skilled labor, and even reduce the number of jobs for those with higher skills.

Others feel that these fears appear to be greatly exaggerated. Gains in productivity resulting from automation have not produced overall rates of gain for the nation remarkably faster than in some earlier periods of prosperity, although they have helped productivity to advance somewhat faster since World War II than the long-run average annual gain. This more rapid rate of productivity gain is, however, a blessing, since it means faster economic growth and higher individual incomes—provided that full employment can be maintained. Modern economic theory indicates that, despite more rapid productivity gains, this can, in fact, be done if appropriate fiscal and monetary policies are employed to raise total demand for goods and services, and hence for labor.

Unemployment results, not from rising productivity, but from permitting a gap to develop between the potential and actual output of the economy. The policy solution to the so-called automation problem is, therefore, basically, to use general economic policy to close the full-employment gap.

Despite growth in the economy as a whole, interregional gaps have remained a major problem in Canada. Wide differences in incomes and unemployment rates are among primary indicators of regional differences. Many other features of depressed regions are found, some being causes of disparities, some being results, and some being in both categories.

Limited resources, smaller local markets, the distance factor, lack of secondary industry, and lower investment levels appear to rank high among the prime causes of the problem. Much emphasis has been given to the problem by all levels of government.

Does growth have limits? This complex issue is examined briefly with particular attention paid to some of the gloomier projections which have been made. Here, questions related to values have a strong influence and should be closely examined. Our national and world-wide response to this issue will have vital effects on us and future generations.

KEY CONCEPTS

economic growth
autonomous investment
induced investment
Doomsday Models
creative destruction
automation
productivity
regional disparity
designated area
GDA

QUESTIONS FOR REVIEW AND DISCUSSION

1. How would you define economic growth? Why is economic growth important for the Canadian economy?
2. Distinguish between autonomous investment and induced investment. Why are both types of investment important in promoting economic growth?
3. What is meant by an innovational push? Give three examples of innovational pushes that have occurred in Canadian economic history.
4. What is meant by the term *research revolution*? How does the post-World War II research revolution differ from earlier applications of science and technology to industry? What implications does it have for the growth of the total economy? What implications does it have for the growth—and decline—of particular industries?
5. Can all increases in the productivity of our economy (as measured, say, by changes in output per manhour worked) be attributed to automation? Why?
6. Has technological unemployment led to mass unemployment in the economy in the past? Do you think that it will in the future? What three conditions would have to occur for automation or technological change to lead to mass unemployment? Do you think that these conditions are likely or unlikely to occur in the near future? Why?
7. What leads to the existence of regional disparities within Canada? What difficulties are involved in attempting to reduce interregional disparities?
8. What factors may limit the capacity of a nation's economy to continue to grow indefinitely?

PROBLEMS AND EXERCISES TO SHARPEN YOUR UNDERSTANDING

1. Write a brief essay evaluating the following statement.

   In discussing technological unemployment resulting from automation, too many people look backward and ask, "Why did these people lose their jobs?" A more appropriate view would be to look ahead and ask. "What can we do to create new jobs for them?"

In your essay try to mention as many specific policies as you can that might be employed to insure that we will be able to create enough new jobs to enjoy the increased productivity that results from automation.

2. Organize a class debate on the topic: Resolved that strong continued economic growth is vital to the well-being of all people.
3. Organize a class debate on the topic: Resolved that zero economic growth or moves in that direction will do more to protect the well-off in Canada, or the developed nations of the world, than to help the poor, either in our own society or elsewhere.

APPENDIX:

REGIONAL DISPARITY: ONE APPROACH TO POLICY

Reference has been made to a major Economic Council of Canada study on regional disparity published in 1977. The following sections on general policy proposals and specific recommendations come from a concise summary of the large original study.

Proposals for Policy

A number of implications flow fron this study of the causes of regional economic disparities, which in turn have led us to a number of proposals that the Council hopes might contribute in a significant way over time to alleviating the problems those disparities create. These proposals are grouped under two main headings. The first includes recommendations aimed at increasing the level of productivity in the less-prosperous regions, which lies at the heart of their disparity of total income and, more particularly, of earned income. The second grouping covers policies aimed at reducing disparities in unemployment. The distinction between productivity and unemployment is by no means mutually exclusive, however, and measures to deal with one problem can under different circumstances serve to ease or compound the other. An improvement in productivity and in competitiveness, for example, could lead to an increase in employment. On the other hand, a reduction in wage and salary levels might lead to an increase in employment as a result of its effect in increasing a region's competitiveness, but also result in an increase in disparities of income on a per capita basis.

Measures to Increase Productivity

Our studies have attempted to demonstrate that three of the major factors commonly assumed to be primarily responsible for the large differences that exist in productivity between regions—industrial structure, capital per worker, and transportation costs—actually play a comparatively less important role. Lower output per worker emerges as the main factor lying behind productivity differences. While insufficient capital is undoubtedly one factor accounting for differences in worker productivity in some sectors of the various regions, it is evident that other elements such as the quality of the labor force, the speed of adoption of technological improvements, and urban structure also play a crucial role. Managerial competence may be a further important factor, but this is difficult to establish conclusively.

Labor Force Education and Training

As a result of the substantially increased emphasis since the early 1960s on the importance of "human capital" and the contribution of education to its enrichment, there has been a significant improvement in Canada generally in educational facilities, teacher qualifications and the average number of years that students devote to education in school and in post secondary institutions.

The substantial disparities that used to exist in educational achievement between provinces have been considerably reduced, but important gaps still remain in teacher qualifications and the number of years of compulsory schooling. In the case of the latter, there is, for example, a 20 per cent difference between Newfoundland

and Ontario. Furthermore, nearly half of the present labor force did not enjoy the benefits of the better educational opportunities now available.

The Council suggests that, in some of the slow-growth provinces in particular, a greater potential for growth would be yielded by altering spending priorities so as to reduce the share of funds devoted to physical development and industrial assistance and increase that available for education. Within the field of education itself, we believe there should also be a shift of emphasis away from spending on facilities and on maintenance of small classes so that more funds can be earmarked to improving teacher qualifications and upgrading the education and training not only of existing students, but also mature members of the labor force. While the federal government manpower training program is making an important contribution to improving the qualifications of those now in the labor force, access to it is confined almost exclusively to those who are unemployed, and its focus is concentrated on the development of particular skills. We consider, therefore, that the provinces could very usefully supplement this scheme with programs of their own to upgrade the educational levels of those in the work force generally—employed and unemployed.

Knowledge and Technology

While it is not conclusive, there is compelling evidence to indicate that lags in the adoption of new technology is an important factor in accounting for low productivity in some sectors of the regional economies. In some cases, this may be due to lack of awareness of new technologies being introduced elsewhere and, in others, to a lack of appreciation of their potential contribution to improving productivity. In an effort to reduce this lag, we propose that each provincial minister responsible for industrial development join forces with private industry associations and trade unions in keeping abreast of new technological developments relevant to industries within the provinces—including service industries—and encouraging adoption of those that hold promise of increasing productivity.

Increased awareness of new technological developments represents only a part of the wider knowledge that should be sought out to find the means of reducing differences in productiveness between regions. We urge that the resources of regional industry associations, labor organizations and institutions be mobilized to amass detailed knowledge about the causes of productivity differences from wherever it is to be gleaned and to apply that knowledge to finding the means of reducing those disparities. We believe that such an undertaking would broaden the scope for entrepreneurship in the slower-growth provinces. Such an effort should be coupled with the introduction of new and better programs to upgrade the education and training of present and potential business managers so as to enhance their ability to seek out ways of improving efficiency and productivity. We consider that the federal government could play a very useful role in contributing its own knowledge and expertise to both of these undertakings at little additional cost.

The Process of Urbanization

Earlier in the report, reference was made to the role played by urban centres with a population of up to at least 1½ million in facilitating the growth of productivity and of real incomes. Larger centres serve to reduce the cost of common facilities because of economies of scale, and they provide the critical mass required for the introduction of a wide range of business and community services that are not supportable in smaller communities. It was for that reason that we warned about the adverse economic consequences that could flow from provincial policies aimed at retarding this development. The Council goes further and suggests that in those provinces where improvement in productivity and incomes is a primary goal, consideration should be given to the adoption of policies and programs aimed at encouraging the development of urban centres to the extent that is possible within the limits imposed by the industrial structure of various regions. Governments can exercise a positive influence through such means as the development of highway networks, public transportation facilities and the location of airports. Metropolitan centres such as Toronto and Montreal may already be close to or beyond the limits of advantage offered by large-scale urban communities because of increasing costs resulting from pollution, congestion and social disorder. We suggest that in those cases provincial policy should be aimed at encouraging the development of satellite cities of intermediate size within their vicinity.

Measures to Reduce Unemployment

Regionally Oriented Fiscal Policy

We have already stressed our conviction that unemployment in the slow-growth regions could be significantly reduced by the adoption of both federal and provincial fiscal policies aimed in a concerted way at achieving a better balance between aggregate demand for goods and services and productive capacity of those areas over the course of the business cycle.

The Council proposes that the provinces, particularly those with high unemployment, approach the task of budget-making through calculation of the budget position that would result in circumstances of "full employment"—that is, full employment in relation to prevailing levels of unemployment within a given province in the past. In seeking to maintain an adequate level of aggregate demand through adjustment of the budgetary position, it is important for the provinces to be realistic in assessing to what extent unemployment is due to deficient demand and to what extent it is due to other factors that are not amenable to correction by fiscal policies.

The federal government could and should play an important role in achieving the objective we have outlined. It is our recommendation that the federal government seek to adjust its fiscal policies so that they will have the most favorable impact possible on the high-unemployment regions. In addition, however, we consider that Ottawa could take steps to increase the feasibility of provincial fiscal measures aimed at achieving a better balance of aggregate demand. As we have pointed out, the federal government would be a beneficiary of provincial fiscal policies to the extent that they were successful in increasing output, employment and incomes. Its tax revenues would be increased and its share of the cost of providing unemployment insurance benefits and social assistance would be reduced. It should not be impossible for the federal government to devise a means of turning back at least a part of those gains to the provinces. Ottawa could further facilitate the implementation of regional fiscal policy by acting as a guarantor of some portion of new provincial bond issues.

Distribution of Federal Taxation, Spending and Employment

Because of its very size, federal government policies on taxation, spending and location of its facilities have a massive but varied impact on the regional economies of the country. The extent of that impact is hard to measure, however, because of the present lack of detailed information. It is, for example, difficult to assess whether the interaction between federal taxation policies and its expenditures on goods and services best serve the objective of reducing regional disparities within the limits necessarily set by the need to achieve other important objectives.

Recently, increased emphasis has been placed on relocating certain federal activities in high-unemployment areas in an effort to generate jobs both directly and indirectly. An important unanswered question, however, is whether the net costs of the additional jobs created by transfers to locations that are often far removed from the centre of demand for such services exceed those to create jobs by other, more direct means—such as the subsidization of private firms by DREE to encourage increased employment.

The Council recommends, therefore, that the federal government carefully consider the comparative costs of creating jobs by relocation of its services and by other alternative means. And we also propose that every two to five years it publish a detailed breakdown of the location of its spending and tax receipts by provinces and territories so that their regional impact can be more adequately assessed.

Migration

Increased mobility of workers—either on a temporary or permanent basis—can improve the capacity of the labor market to better match demand and supply, thus increasing the efficiency of the economy as a whole. At present the federal government has a program in effect to help underwrite the costs of temporary moves by workers to available jobs in other locations. We believe this program should be expanded on an experimental basis to cover part of the cost of shifting workers that is now borne alone by companies and unions in certain industries, notably construction.

Permanent migration is no panacea for the problem of regional disparities, but within limits it can benefit the financial position of individuals and help to reduce problems in slow-growth areas without too severe side effects. While the federal government has an excellent program in place to assist workers and their families in making such a transition, relatively little use is made of it. The Council suggests that a survey should be undertaken to determine to what extent workers are aware of the assistance available to them to migrate to other areas and to what extent they are familiar with the existence of job opportunities elsewhere. In the event that knowledge about these two elements proves to be inadequate, we consider that it would pay to put more effort into publicizing the facts both about job vacancies and transfer assistance programs.

Wages Levels, Productivity and Unemployment

If wage levels do not bear a realistic relationship to productivity, competitiveness will be reduced, sales and output and employment will be lower than otherwise, and unemployment will necessarily be higher. We have already put forward a number of proposals aimed at increasing productivity in an effort to increase the real income that can be derived from productive employment. But where it comes to a trade-off between higher wages and greater unemployment, we are in no doubt that the balance should be struck in favor of reducing unemployment at the expense of somewhat higher incomes for those fortunate enough to have jobs.

While pay levels for different occupations in different industries and different parts of the country are determined by a myriad of factors that lie outside the realm of government, they may be influenced in an important way by government policies. The minimum wage levels established by provincial governments, for example, have a bearing on many other related wage and salary scales. At the present time, three provinces with unemployment rates considerably above the national average—New Brunswick, Nova Scotia and Quebec—require the payment of minimum wages that are above those in Ontario and Alberta, both of which have relatively low unemployment. We urge that over time those provinces with high unemployment and high minimum wages allow their minimum pay level to come into better balance with those prevailing in provinces with below-average unemployment so as to better the prospects for increasing employment and reducing the number of those without jobs.

The federal government's policy of paying the same wage rate for all workers in the same occupation, regardless of local or regional wage levels and regardless of the rate required to attract the required number of workers, also has an adverse impact on wage levels generally in the slow-growth regions, thus aggravating the problem of regional unemployment. We believe the individual inequities and economic distortions that result from such a policy could and should be overcome by basing wage scales generally in a given area on the prevailing rates in the private sector. Recognizing that such an approach could create adjustment problems initially, we suggest that it should be gradually phased in over a period of five years or more.

Conclusion

"What is past is prologue," Shakespeare wrote in *The Tempest.* Our determined objective in Canada must be to see that gross disparities in living standards and opportunities over the long distant past do not become a prologue to the indefinite future. The triumph of medical science over so many devastating human diseases is a story of long, arduous, painstaking and often frustrating experiment and research. We still have a long way to go in our experiments and research before we can expect to overcome the problems of economic disparity, which are also a source of considerable human misery. Notwithstanding our own frustrations at the doors of knowledge that still remain locked to us, we remain convinced they will eventually open to us if we have enough persistence and patience. We are hopeful that our most recent studies will prove useful in adding to the store of knowledge we urgently need in order to hasten our understanding of the problems and that that knowledge might provide a basis for formulating new policies that will contribute to the reduction of regional disparities. The Council believes the vicious circle can be broken if there is the will, particularly among those trapped within it, to do so.

Recommendations

1

We recommend that the governments of the provinces where incomes and educational attainment are lower than the national average examine ways of improving the educational attainment of new entrants to the labor force and of increasing the ease with which mature members of the labor force can upgrade their education.

2

We recommend that, in the provinces where incomes are lower than the national average, each minister of industrial development or his equivalent, in co-operation whenever possible with private industry associations and trade unions, investigate what is the best applicable technology in each provincial industry, including service industries, with a view to encouraging its adoption where it is not yet in use.

3

We recommend that, in provinces where incomes are lower than the national average, any existing or future urban strategy give full consideration to the productivity advantages in manufacturing that may be gained by working with, rather than against, the tendency for population to drift from rural to urban areas and from smaller to medium-sized urban settlements.

4

We recommend that the growth of satellite cities of intermediate size, in the vicinity of Montreal and Toronto, be encouraged by the provincial governments concerned.

5

We recommend that industry trade associations, trade unions, and other appropriate institutions undertake formal studies to determine why productivity levels in their own industry differ from province to province and that they disseminate the results together with appropriate recommendations.

6

We recommend that all provincial governments, but especially those in low-income provinces, consult with appropriate educational institutions on ways to expand training in formal techniques of management available to existing and potential managers in the province.

7

We recommend that the governments of all provinces, but especially those where unemployment rates are above the national average, calculate each year the amount by which the provincial budget would be in surplus or deficit if the provincial economy were operating at full capacity.

8

We recommend that, in all the provinces where unemployment rates are usually higher than the national average, except Newfoundland, each provincial government continuously assess how much of its unemployment is due to demand deficiency and stimulate demand by increasing the full-employment budget deficit or decreasing the full-employment budget surplus, as the case may be.

9

We recommend that the governments of New Brunswick, Nova Scotia, and Prince Edward Island attempt to agree among themselves, each year, on appropriate joint changes in the full-employment budget surplus or deficit.

10

We recommend that the mix of fiscal policy instruments used by the federal government for cyclical stabilization purposes be chosen in such a way as to increase the proportion of national demand going to high-unemployment regions.

11

We recommend that the cost of relocating any particular federal activity for the purpose of creating jobs rather than achieving better local provision of federal services be always compared with the cost of creating a similar number of jobs through other programs involving direct subsidies.

12

We recommend that the federal government publish, every two to three years, a breakdown, by province and territory, of the location of its cash expenditures and tax receipts.

13

We recommend that the federal government review the terms under which assistance is available for moving workers to temporary jobs and consider undertaking a social experiment to discover whether the benefits of financial assistance to temporary mobility initiatives by the private sector would exceed the costs to the taxpayer.

14

We recommend that a survey, or surveys, be taken to determine the degree of awareness among the unemployed of job opportunities outside their province of residence, as well as their degree of knowledge about federal programs of mobility assistance.

15

We recommend that, as part of a strategy of full employment, the ministers of labor in high-unemployment provinces gradually move to a situation where their minimum wages are not higher than in any province where unemployment is lower than the national average.

16

We recommend that the federal government very gradually move to a situation where the wages of its own employees in each province are more closely related to wages for comparable workers in the private sector.

From: Economic Council of Canada, *Living Together; A Study of Regional Disparity, Highlights,* Ottawa: 1977, pp. 32-37.

UNIT 4 REVIEW

1. What are the major elements of GNP? Why do we describe GNP as a "circular flow"? What causes GNP to increase or decrease?
2. Why is economic forecasting vital? What are the limits imposed upon any forecaster?
3. What are the major goals for our economy? To what extent are they in conflict with each other? Would different groups in our society disagree about the relative importance of these goals? Why?
4. What are the functions of a central bank? How may a central bank use its powers to influence the direction of the economy?
5. Distinguish between fiscal and monetary policies. What factors limit the ability of governments to use fiscal policies to influence the direction of the economy?
6. What factors encourage or inhibit economic growth? What factors limit the ability of either the public or private sectors to increase growth in distressed regions?

THE INTERNATIONAL ECONOMY

Economic contacts between societies or nations are almost as old as human society itself. In relatively modern times, however, economic interdependence has increased by almost astronomic proportions. The flows of goods and services, people, ideas and also of problems has led us to realize that we do live in a "global village." This unit will examine some aspects of the economic life of our global village and look at some of the key issues in Canada's international economic life.

CHAPTER 32

INTERNATIONAL TRADE

■ THE BASIC CASE FOR TRADE ■ ABSOLUTE ADVANTAGE ■ COMPARATIVE ADVANTAGE ■ PROBLEMS OF TRADE RESTRICTIONS ■ THE IMPORTANCE OF PRODUCTIVITY ■ PROMOTING INTERNATIONAL TRADE ■ ARGUMENTS FOR PROTECTIVE TARIFFS ■ SUMMARY ■ APPENDIX: MULTINATIONAL CORPORATIONS

■ THE BASIC CASE FOR TRADE

The case for international trade among nations is the same as the case for trade among individuals, cities, provinces, or regions within the same nation. It is the case for specialization and exchange. Rather than trying to produce everything, people improve their standard of living by specializing in certain types of production and trading their products for goods in which they do not specialize.

You could perhaps grow your own food, make your own clothes, build your own house, provide your own entertainment, your own police and fire protection, your own education, and so on—if you were very industrious, clever, and lucky. Perhaps others could also learn to be self-sufficient. But what would an economy of entirely self-sufficient individuals be like? The chances are that it would turn out to be an economy of primitive living standards. Obviously, individuals working all alone could not produce automobiles, television sets, calculators, airplanes or many of the other goods and services we want. Living standards would drop drastically if you tried to replace specialization and exchange among individuals with self-sufficiency.

The same holds for cities. It would make no sense for the citizens of any city to buy and consume only goods and services produced in that city. In fact, there would probably be no cities able to do that.

How about provinces? Why should Ontario try to grow its own oranges, or Newfoundland grow its own wheat, or Saskatchewan catch its own fish? Just as individuals have different strengths and skills, so do geographic areas differ in their natural, human, capital, and technological resources. It is these differences in scarce productive resources that make specialization and trade profitable for *both* sides in interregional or international trade.

While the basic case for international trade rests on the increase in total output which results from specialization and exchange, there are certain differences that arise when trade takes place across international boundaries rather than within the same country. These differences are the result of man-made rules and conventions dealing with money and foreign trade, rather than of economic principles. But the fact that nations use different currencies and pass laws about international shipping of goods and services does raise some special problems that justify treating international trade as a topic in itself. Nationalism—the spirit of giving priority to the interests of your own country—also makes the subject of international trade worth closer analysis. In this chapter we shall review the basic case for international trade in more detail and discuss the issues

THE UNENDING FLOW OF TRADE

The Port of Vancouver, National Harbours Board

National Harbours Board and Wamboldt Waterfield Photography Ltd.

The data on port activity points out the growing flow of Canadian trade. The upper photo shows Vanterm, a container facility in Vancouver. The lower photo shows containers being loaded at the port of Halifax. These two photos have been selected to point out the growing use of containers in international shipping.

FIG. 32-1. CANADA'S SEABORNE EXPORTS, 1961-1977

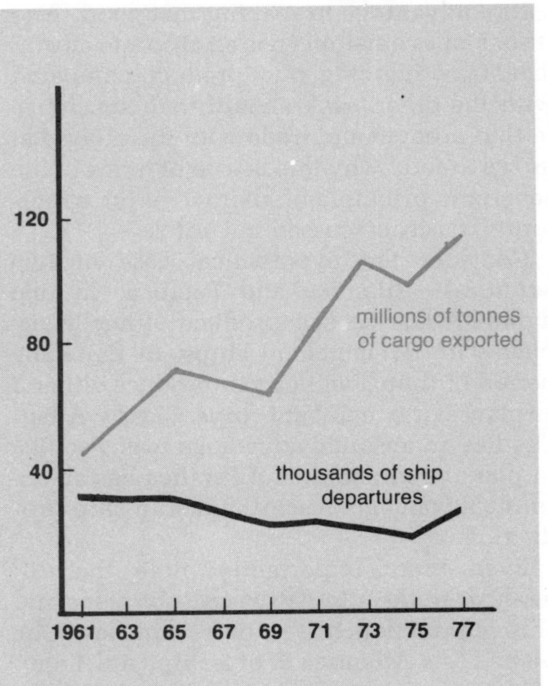

Table 32-1. 30 DAYS' OUTPUT OF PLANES AND SHIPS WITH ABSOLUTE ADVANTAGE AND NO SPECIALIZATION

	Planes (10 days)	Ships (20 days)
Atlantica	2	1
Pacifica	1	4
Total	3	5

Table 32-2. 30 DAYS' OUTPUT OF PLANES AND SHIPS WITH ABSOLUTE ADVANTAGE AND WITH SPECIALIZATION

	Planes (30 days)	Ships (30 days)
Atlantica	6	—
Pacifica	—	6
Total	6	6

raised by national attempts to restrict the flow of goods and services from abroad.

It is easy to see that, measured by the *absolute advantage* of the production of a certain good by one country rather than another, more goods and services can be produced by specialization than by self-sufficiency. This is more difficult to see, but equally true, in the case of *comparative advantage*. Let us consider these cases in turn.

ABSOLUTE ADVANTAGE

If one nation can produce a good more efficiently than another, it is said to have an **absolute advantage** in making that good. And if each of two nations has an absolute advantage in producing one product compared with the other, each should then specialize in that product and trade with the other. Let us see exactly why this is true in terms of the economic principle of alternative (or opportunity) costs, discussed in Unit 2.

Consider the hypothetical case of two countries, Atlantica and Pacifica. In one month Atlantica can produce either 6 airplanes or 1½ merchant ships. In the same period of time, Pacifica can produce either 3 airplanes or 6 merchant ships. Clearly Atlantica has an absolute advantage over Pacifica in plane production, and Pacifica has an absolute advantage over Atlantica in ship production.

Even more importantly, note the differences in the alternative costs of plane and ship production to the two countries. One plane costs Atlantica ¼ of a ship, and 1 ship costs Atlantica 4 planes (given the ratio of 6 planes to 1½ ships).

On the other side, 1 plane costs Pacifica 2 ships, or 1 ship costs Pacifica ½ plane (given the 3 planes to 6 ships ratio).

These alternative cost figures show that it is cheaper (in terms of ships given up) for Atlantica to make planes; and cheaper (in terms of planes given up) for Pacifica to make ships.

If there is no specialization, the total output of planes and ships at the end of one month in which both nations spend 10 days building planes and 20 days building ships will be as shown in Table 32-1.

Now, if both nations decide to specialize in the product in which each has an absolute advantage, output at the end of a month will be as shown in Table 32-2.

Thus, total output has risen from 3 planes and 5 ships in Table 32-1 to 6 planes and 6 ships in Table 32-2. How will this extra output be divided between the two nations? That depends on the exact rate of exchange between planes and ships that the two nations work out. But there are several different rates of exchange that can make both nations better off after specialization.

Remember that before specialization, Atlantica had an alternative cost ratio of 4:1 between planes and ships. If Atlantica now traded 4 of its 6 planes to Pacifica for 1 ship, Atlantica would be no worse off than before specialization, and Pacifica would be considerably better off, as Table 32-3 shows.

However, remember that before specialization, Pacifica had an alternative cost ratio of 1:2 between planes and ships. If Pacifica now traded 2 of its 6 ships to Atlantica for 1 plane, it would be no worse off than before specialization, but Atlantica would reap all

Table 32-3. 30 DAYS' OUTPUT OF PLANES AND SHIPS AFTER SPECIALIZATION DISTRIBUTED AT ATLANTICA'S OLD RATIO OF 4 PLANES TO 1 SHIP

	Planes	Ships
Atlantica	2	1
Pacifica	4	5
Total	6	6

the gains from specialization and trade and would be much better off, as shown in Table 32-4.

Probably neither of the extreme cases of Tables 32-3 and 32-4 would occur, since neither nation would want to let the other reap all of the gains from specialization. At any ratio between 4 planes to 1 ship and 1 plane to 2 ships, both nations would gain. Let us take an intermediate ratio of 1 plane to 1 ship, which is better than either Atlantica and Pacifica could have done on its own. The outcome of trade at that ratio is shown in Table 32-5, after Atlantica and Pacifica trade 2 planes for 2 ships.

Thus, *both* nations are better off than they were in Table 32-1, when each nation was self-sufficient, and Atlantica got only 2 planes and 1 ship for a month's work, while Pacifica got only 1 plane and 4 ships for a month's work.

This example of two nations and two goods illustrates the basic analysis underlying international trade. You can change Atlantica and Pacifica to Brazil and Chile or to the United States and Canada, and change planes and ships to bulldozers, food, clothing, or typewriters, but the basic analysis will not change. Specialization is more productive than self-sufficiency, and both sides gain from trade.[1] In the real world, however, the exchange rates set up between different goods and services are not set as arbitrarily as we have done in the 1:1 ratio of Table 32-5. The forces of supply and demand for different goods in different markets, the relative sizes of different nations, the forces of political influence, and other factors may also affect the ultimate ratio.

COMPARATIVE ADVANTAGE

But what about cases where one nation has an absolute advantage in producing *all* goods compared to a second nation? Can trade now profitably occur between these two countries? Surprisingly enough, the answer is yes. This answer is based on the principle of **comparative advantage.** Even if one country has an absolute advantage in every field of production, the chances are that it has a *greater* advantage in some fields than in others. These differences in relative efficiency (or comparative advantage) are all that it requires to make specialization and international trade profitable. Again, this holds for nations as for individuals.

Suppose that X is both the best lawyer and the best typist in town. Since a higher income is earned as a lawyer than as a typist, X would be wise to concentrate on the

[1] Advanced texts in international trade extend the simple two-country, two-good case to many countries and many goods. But the essential points made in our simple example still hold true.

Table 32-4. 30 DAYS' OUTPUT OF PLANES AND SHIPS AFTER SPECIALIZATION DISTRIBUTED AT PACIFICA'S OLD RATIO OF 1 PLANE TO 2 SHIPS

	Planes	Ships
Atlantica	5	2
Pacifica	1	4
Total	6	6

Table 32-5. 30 DAYS' OUTPUT OF PLANES AND SHIPS AFTER SPECIALIZATION DISTRIBUTED AT A RATIO OF 1 PLANE TO 1 SHIP

	Planes	Ships
Atlantica	4	2
Pacifica	2	4
Total	6	6

Table 32-6. 30 DAYS' OUTPUT OF PLANES AND SHIPS WITH COMPARATIVE ADVANTAGE AND NO SPECIALIZATION

	Planes (10 days)	Ships (20 days)
Atlantica	2	4
Pacifica	1	1
Total	3	5

Table 32-7. 30 DAYS' OUTPUT OF PLANES AND SHIPS WITH COMPARATIVE ADVANTAGE AND WITH SPECIALIZATION

	Planes (30 days)	Ships (30 days)
Atlantica	—	6
Pacifica	3	—
Total	3	6

practice of law and hire someone to do the typing. An hour spent typing is an hour that cannot be spent in the court room, and the alternative (or opportunity) cost for typing is too high to make it wise to attempt to be self-sufficient in both areas. So, too, with nations; comparative advantage results from a difference among nations in the rate at which one good must be sacrificed in order to increase production of some other good.

To illustrate the principle, let us go back to our example of the hypothetical nations of Atlantica and Pacifica. But this time we shall give Atlantica an absolute advantage in making *both* planes and ships. Suppose that in one month Atlantica can make either 6 planes or 6 ships, while Pacifica can make either 3 planes or 1½ ships. Clearly, Atlantica now has an absolute advantage in both products. But Atlantica's advantage is greater in ships than in planes (2:1 in planes, and 6:1½ in ships). Contrarily, we may say that Pacifica's comparative disadvantage is less in planes than ships, or that Pacifica has a comparative advantage in planes.

Under the new conditions, Atlantica's alternative costs show that to produce 1 plane, it must give up 1 ship. But Pacifica has a different set of alternative cost ratios. To produce 1 plane, Pacifica must give up ½ ship, or to produce 1 ship, Pacifica must give up 2 planes.

To see that increased output is possible through specialization along these lines, we shall first set forth Table 32-6, which summarizes production in one month in which there is no specialization and in which both nations spend 10 days on plane production and 20 days on ship production.

When each nation specializes in that product in which it has a comparative advantage (Atlantica in ships, Pacifica in planes), the result is as seen in Table 32-7.

Thus, total output increases, through specialization, with both comparative and absolute advantage. And, as long as planes can be traded for ships, both nations will gain from the increased output.

How will the gain in total output be divided between the nations? As in the preceding case, the final distribution of the gains will depend on the exact trading ratio worked out by the nations. At a ratio of 1 plane to 1 ship (Atlantica's alternative cost ratio), all of the gains will go to Pacifica. At a ratio of 2 planes to 1 ship (Pacifica's alternative cost ratio), all the gains will go to Atlantica. But if the final ratio is set between these two ratios (say, 1½ planes to 1 ship), both nations will gain from specialization and trade.

The gains from comparative advantage were first discovered by the British economist David Ricardo (1772-1823) about 150 years ago. But the fact that many people still have difficulty with this important principle indicates that it is not easy for the beginner to master. Therefore, be willing to reread the preceding sections several times if necessary. You may also want to test your understanding at this point by trying to work out the example at the end of the chapter.

PROBLEMS OF TRADE RESTRICTIONS

In view of the strong case made for specialization and exchange, the existence of various barriers to trade between nations is hard to justify on economic grounds. There are some economic and some noneconomic considerations that indicate that trade barriers may be necessary and even desirable in a few limited cases to be discussed later. But, for the most part, trade barriers in the form of **tariffs** (taxes on imports), **quotas** (physical limits on the amounts of certain goods that can be imported into a country), and *administrative red tape* tend to hurt consumers and to protect certain inefficient producers.

As the result of tariffs and other trade barriers, consumers must pay higher prices or do without certain goods. In addition, industries that are not able to compete without special protection tie up scarce productive resources that could be better used elsewhere. One of the most famous arguments against tariffs and trade restrictions is the following satire, in which a French popularizer of classical economic thought, Frederic Bastiat (1801-1850), takes some typical protectionists' arguments and carries them to a devastating extreme. Bastiat's argument takes the form of a petition by a mythical group of candlemakers:

> We are subjected to the intolerable competition of a foreign rival, who enjoys, it would seem, such superior facilities for the production of light, that he is enabled to *inundate our national market* at so exceedingly reduced a price, that, the moment he makes his appearance, he draws off all custom for us. This rival is no other than the sun.
>
> Our petition is, that it would please your honorable body to pass a law whereby shall be directed the shutting up of all windows, dormers, skylights, shutters, curtains, in a word, all openings, holes, chinks, and fissures through which the light of the sun is used to penetrate into our dwellings to the prejudice of the profitable manufactures which we flatter ourselves we have been enabled to bestow upon the country; which country cannot, therefore, without ingratitude, leave us now to struggle unprotected through so unequal a contest.[2]

What about this argument? If you are a candlemaker, it may not sound bad. But if you are a consumer of light, it does not sound good at all. From the standpoint of the total economy's use of scarce resources, it does not make any sense to use resources to produce artificial light at considerable expense if natural sunlight is available. Why not use these resources in other industries, where they can contribute more to increasing the total amount of goods available for consumption? This is the essence of the argument against tariffs that result in using domestic resources to produce goods which it would be more efficient to import.

If there is unemployment in a country, it makes more sense to use domestic monetary and fiscal policy to increase total demand and put the country's resources to work in this way than it does to try to keep out foreign products and then produce the same goods at much greater expense at home. At full employment, increased consumer expenditures on protected goods simply reduce expenditures on other goods and services and lower the standard of living.

Economically, competition stimulates efficiency; it keeps producers on their toes, forces them to find ways of reducing costs and better serving consumers' wants. For these purposes, there is no difference between foreign competition and domestic competition. In terms of pure economic efficiency, "buy Canada" makes no more sense than "buy Quebec" or "buy Montreal, Quebec" or "buy Place Ville Marie in Montreal, Quebec." Each of these slogans, if enforced, would limit the opportunity for increased total production and income resulting from specialization and exchange.

[2] Frederic Bastiat, *Economic Sophisms*, New York: G. P. Putnam's Sons, 1922, p. 60.

Table 32-8. CANADA'S BALANCE OF MERCHANDISE TRADE (BILLIONS OF DOLLARS), 1970-1977.

Year	Exports	Imports	Balance
1970	$16.921	$13.869	+$3.052
1971	17.877	15.314	+ 2.563
1972	20.129	18.272	+ 1.857
1973	25.461	22.726	+ 2.735
1974	32.591	30.902	+ 1.689
1975	33.511	33.962	− .451
1976	38.132	36.793	+ 1.339
1977	44.628	41.712	+ 2.916

Notes: Data are in current dollars; 1977 data are preliminary and subject to revision.
Source: Statistics Canada, *Quarterly Estimates of the Canadian Balance of International Payments*, cat. 67-001, First Quarter, Ottawa: 1978.

THE IMPORTANCE OF PRODUCTIVITY

But, you may ask, what about such factors as cheap labor? If we remove all barriers to free trade between countries, will not foreigners, who may pay their workers much less than we do, take over all of our markets? There are several principal points to consider in weighing that issue. First, on logical grounds, do not confuse absolute advantage with comparative advantage. Second, remember that labor costs are only one part of the total costs of production.

Even if cheap labor would make it possible for other countries to produce *every* good more cheaply than we could in Canada (which is untrue), this would simply mean that we should have an absolute disadvantage in all areas. But, even with an absolute disadvantage in all areas, we would still have a *comparative* advantage in some areas. Hence, it would still pay others to specialize and trade with us rather than try to produce everything for all markets.

More important than this theoretical argument, however, is the fact that superior technology, capital equipment, management and labor productivity make it possible for us to pay very high wages and still compete effectively in many world markets. Our high-paid workers produce more than do many low-paid workers. Therefore, our *cost per unit of output* is very competitive. We may worry about cheap labor, but many other producers are worrying about highly productive technology and capital equipment.

A look at the record of Canadian exports and imports clearly proves that if a country's productivity is high, a high-wage country can still be very successful in world markets. Table 32-8 shows that in recent years we have consistently exported more than we have imported. In 1977, for instance, Canada had a surplus of $2.9 billion in merchandise trade.[3] Table 32-9 shows the geographic areas to which we sold our exports and from which we bought our imports.

If we look at particular categories of merchandise items, as set forth in Table 32-10, we see that our most important export cate-

[3] You may wonder how a nation can continually export more than it imports. If we do not buy foreign goods, where do the people in foreign countries get the dollars they need to buy Canadian goods? The answer is that the *balance of trade* in merchandise items (such as wheat or automobiles) is only part of a country's *balance of payments*. Tourists traveling in foreign countries, businessmen investing abroad, the government paying troops stationed abroad, and private and government loans or grants to foreign governments or businesses all make dollars available to foreigners to buy Canadian goods. If these other sources of payments were not available to foreign countries, we could not indefinitely export more merchandise than we import. The next chapter explores the difference between the balance of merchandise trade and the balance of payments in more detail.

Table 32-9. CANADA'S FLOW OF MERCHANDISE TRADE (BILLIONS OF DOLLARS), 1977.

	Exports To	Imports From	Balance on Merchandise Trade
United States	$31.016	$29.323	+$1.693
Japan	2.461	1.782	+ .679
United Kingdom	2.221	1.588	+ .633
Other E.E.C.	2.718	2.374	+ .344
All Others	6.212	6.645	− .433
Total	$44.628	$41.712	+$2.916

Note: Data are preliminary totals for 1977 and are subject to revision.
Source: Statistics Canada, *Quarterly Estimates of the Canadian Balance of International Payments,* cat. 67-001, First Quarter, Ottawa: 1978.

gories were from our country's high-wage industries. Agriculture, which also earns many dollars from the export of Canadian farm produce, is one of our low-wage industries. But much of our agriculture is highly capitalized and mechanized, especially in the area of grain production, and Canadian farmers generally have much higher incomes than farmers in other countries.

Thus we see that it is not the cost of labor *per unit of time* but rather the cost of labor *per unit of output* that is important in competing in world markets. If such factors as our labor cost per unit of output get out of line, then our ability to compete will be endangered, just as it will if our technological advantages fall behind others.

Table 32-10. MAJOR CANADIAN MERCHANDISE EXPORTS, 1977

Category	Value in Billions of Dollars
Passenger automobiles and chassis	$4.268
Motor vehicle engines and parts	3.618
Newsprint	2.381
Softwood lumber	2.338
Other motor vehicles and chassis	2.248
Wood pulp	2.156
Natural gas	2.028
Wheat and wheat flour	1.941
Crude oil	1.751

Note: Data are preliminary current dollar totals for the year.
Source: Statistics Canada, *Summary of External Trade,* cat. 65-001, Ottawa: 1977.

Technology and Trade

This commentary, from the 6th Annual Review of the Economic Council of Canada, clearly points out the importance of technological advancement and specialization for development of Canadian trade.

It is increasingly recognized that an important link exists between a country's trade performance and its technological and innovative capability. The application of "best practice" techniques in Canadian industry, whether developed in Canada or abroad, is an essential part of the strategy for improving productivity performance and competitiveness in world markets. Moreover, as has been indicated in previous Annual Reviews, the products of the science-based industries are now the fastest growing elements in world trade, and the evidence is accumulating that countries which acquire leadership capabilities in such industries can, in some cases, also gain important competitive advantages based on a technological head start. It should therefore also be an important part of our strategy to seek out and exploit areas of technology where the possibility exists for developing strong leadership capabilities—for carving out specialized niches in selected areas.

Canada is too small, however, to be a leader across the board, and there is a clear need for measures to adapt and diffuse foreign advances in technology *rapidly* for the purposes of Canadian production. The economies of small countries are becoming more and more integrated with those of large industrial countries. This process involves increasingly the exchange of parts and accessories used in the production of complex products, or product systems. The ability of a relatively small country to share in the growth of trade and productivity in this way depends largely on the degree to which efficient technology is being applied in its industries. Canadian industry must be able to meet *rising* standards of specification and quality, if it is to participate adequately in the growth of trade in manufactured products.

But there is clearly also room for some truly Canadian specialties in manufactured exports, whether such "unique" products appear from the ingenuity of manufacturers employing well-known technology in a new way, or from innovations based on really new discoveries. To carry out these processes successfully requires entrepreneurial capacities, able management, skilled labor, and effective application of technology, as well as a general environment conducive to practical innovation. A substantial involvement in international trade in many of these "new product" areas may be especially important for a country such as Canada, in order to spread the costs of innovative activities over a sufficient volume of production to justify the expenditures required to bring such technologies into production and use.

Finally, it must be stressed that the application of advanced technology to the resource industries is a matter of real and continuing importance in a Canadian trade context. This is a vast and varied subject, ranging from aerial prospecting for exploitable raw materials all the way to measures to reduce unit costs in transporting, processing, and manufacturing resource materials.

Source: Economic Council of Canada, *Perspective 1975,* (6th Annual Review), 1969, p. 77-78. Reproduced with the permission of Information Canada.

PROMOTING INTERNATIONAL TRADE

Our whole economy is better off if we can move resources from industries where we have no comparative advantage, rather than try to protect noncompetitive areas of our economy through restricting trade practices. But here a political problem arises. We have to balance the immediate harm or adjustment problems created in some industries or regions against the long-run benefits to the economy as a whole.

The adjustment problems and opportunities created by removing trade restrictions do create a need for domestic changes. In the international trade area, however, it seems to be politically easier to mount an attack against foreign competition than it is to launch technological change. Free trade helps everyone a little, but protection may help some people a lot. The beneficiaries of protection are in a good position to organize and exert political pressures for protection because their interests are easy to see. It is far more difficult to organize the many who benefit from freer trade—they may be scarcely aware of how much their interests are affected. Well organized groups representing a particular sector in the economy or a particular geographic area are frequently heard promoting the cause of trade restriction.

Moves Toward Trade Liberalization

Major changes in the direction of freer trade have been made since World War II. In 1947 Canada and 22 other countries met in Gen-

IMPORTS ARE EXPORTS AND EXPORTS ARE IMPORTS

Alcan Products Canada Limited

These two photographs explain the apparently contradictory title. The first shows bauxite, mined in Guinea, West Africa. From there, some is imported to Canada to smelters at the town of Arvida, Quebec, shown in the lower photo. Here, aluminum is made and—you guessed it—most of it is exported!

Alcan Products Canada Limited

TOWARD EUROPEAN ECONOMIC INTEGRATION

European Communities Photo—Cliche Phototheque

1. The European Economic Community was established by the Treaties of Rome in 1957. The six original members were France, Italy, Belgium, Luxembourg, the Netherlands and the Federal Republic of Germany. In 1973, the United Kingdom, Eire and Denmark joined as well. Membership for Norway had been approved but was rejected by the Norwegian voters in a referendum.

2. In addition to the E.E.C., a second group of European nations, the members of E.F.T.A., have been promoting freer trade without the commitment to the broader economic and political unity shared by countries signing the Treaties of Rome. E.F.T.A. was formed in 1958 and originally included the UK, Denmark (which have both "moved" to the E.E.C.), Sweden, Norway, Switzerland, Austria, and Portugal. The map, which shows the groups as of 1978, should be considered subject to change. Greece, Portugal and Spain have all applied for full membership in the E.E.C.

Reprinted with permission of *Toronto Daily Star*

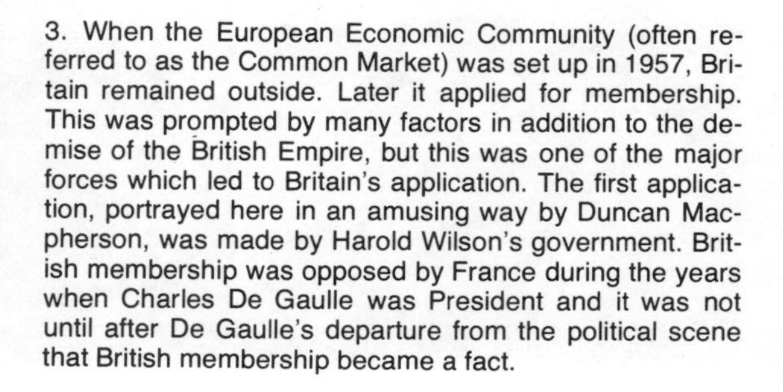

3. When the European Economic Community (often referred to as the Common Market) was set up in 1957, Britain remained outside. Later it applied for membership. This was prompted by many factors in addition to the demise of the British Empire, but this was one of the major forces which led to Britain's application. The first application, portrayed here in an amusing way by Duncan Macpherson, was made by Harold Wilson's government. British membership was opposed by France during the years when Charles De Gaulle was President and it was not until after De Gaulle's departure from the political scene that British membership became a fact.

4. In 1972, Britain accepted the terms for membership which had been negotiated with the E.E.C. Shown here signing the Treaty of Accession for British membership is Edward Heath, the British Prime Minister at that time.

British Official Photograph; By permission of British Information Service, Ottawa

Signs of Economic Integration

A short note published in a Canadian paper in 1977 provided an interesting perspective on economic integration in the E.E.C. The writer described a flight to London from Amsterdam. The aircraft was leased to British Airways by a Dutch company and flown by a Dutch crew. The quick breakfast, served by a British cabin crew, included Danish butter, West German orange juice, French jam, and rolls of unknown origin. Plastic cutlery from Britain was included.

Peterson in the Vancouver Sun

The cornered store

5. Peterson's cartoon effectively summarizes the potential impact of the rise of major trading blocks. Other nations may have increasing difficulty gaining access to markets within these multinational blocks. Needless to say, this is a particularly significant matter for a nation such as Canada, since 25% of our GNP is earned with our merchandise exports.

eva, Switzerland, and signed the General Agreement on Tariffs and Trade (GATT). Since then, many other nations have signed the GATT treaty. This treaty established a mechanism through which nations have bargained with each other for tariff reductions. The results have been a series of programs of tariff reductions which have helped to increase trade all over the world. The most recent set of agreements, the "Tokyo Round," was being negotiated in 1978.

Opposition to Freer Trade

Nevertheless, opposition to increasing liberalization of trade remains strong among many producer groups in this country and in other countries. Basically, this opposition stems from the unwillingness of particular producers to shift to other lines of production and their distaste for facing rugged foreign competition. The situation is often complicated by charges that foreign competitors are **dumping** their products in the Canadian market—that is, charging a lower price here than they charge at home or in some other markets. Producers also frequently assert that we should not let foreign goods into our country if our goods are excluded (whether by tariffs or other restrictive practices, open or concealed) from foreign markets. Similar arguments are often heard from foreigners who wish to exclude our goods from their markets—only the foreigners are more likely to stress the alleged unfair competition of firms which results from their huge size, their heavy investment in research and development, their superior technology, or similar factors.

ARGUMENTS FOR PROTECTIVE TARIFFS

There are, however, some arguments that may support protective tariffs in a few situations that are less important for Canada than for some foreign countries. One of these is the argument that developing nations need to build more *diversified* economies and cannot do this without protecting certain home industries. If a country finds that its comparative advantage is limited to one or two goods, the argument runs, the country might not want to risk putting all its eggs in one basket by specializing in just those one or two products. For, if the world market price of these goods should drop, this might put great strains on the overly specialized economy—and make it impossible for the country to import the goods it needs. Therefore, even at the price of protecting some industries in which it has no comparative advantage, a country may choose to work for economic diversity and stability at the cost of efficiency. However, the cost in lost efficiency may be very high and so may be the cost in economic growth—without corresponding gains in economic stability. Many developing countries are too small (with populations ranging from only ½ million to 10 million) to develop really diversified economies.

A somewhat similar argument is called the *infant industry* argument. Here the case is that, even though a new industry does not presently have a comparative advantage, it is likely to develop one in the future, if it can be protected during its infancy. This argument implies that a country should put the development of new industries, in hopes of future economic growth, ahead of getting goods as cheaply as possible immediately. (This argument has often been used in Canada during our own industrial development.) The argument also implies that protection is only temporary and will be removed in the future.

Finally, political considerations and the need for *wartime self-sufficiency* in certain areas vital to a nation's defence may dictate protecting certain industries as a necessary cost of living in a hostile world. But here it is necessary to decide just what industries are really *vital* for defence purposes. It is surprising how many industries faced by foreign competition think that they are vital to our defence.

Free Trade and Industrial Adaptation

This reading is taken from the 1977 Annual Review of the Economic Council of Canada. It points out some of the adjustments which would have to take place in the economy within a wider pattern of freer trade. Despite the concentration of concern in this selection on adjustment problems, the overall approach of the Council has been to consistently call for reduced trade barriers. The second paragraph within this material clearly points this out.

The Canadian government has been reasonably forthright in describing its export objectives, but its conditional offers to reduce trade barriers have not been as fully described in public. The element that appears to be lacking is a clear plan to foster the adaptation of Canadian industry to the trade concessions to which Canada would agree. Although various adjustment schemes exist, they are neither comprehensive nor extensive. From the viewpoint of Canadians in general, the long-run opportunities to be gained from reduced trade barriers and increased specialization, productivity, and real income are enormous. From the viewpoint of firms, labor groups, and communities that must face increased competition, however, the overall gains may appear irrelevant or unwarranted unless the ensuing hardship and economic loss are somehow offset or compensated and unless the new opportunities are quite concrete.

It is worth repeating that any increased protectionism by itself would very likely be self-defeating. Canada would find itself subsidizing its weakly competitive industries at the expense of its more competitive, largely export-oriented sectors. Consumers, as well as firms, labor groups, and communities that rely on competitive industries, would be the victims of policies that raised costs and inhibited the accessibility of Canadian products to large markets. The realities of the economic situation dictate that efforts for stronger participation in an open world economy must be accompanied by effective policies for industrial adaptation.

In a report published two years ago,* we concluded that, during a period of relative buoyancy, the economy as a whole should be able to absorb or offset transitional employment problems created by the move to freer trade. We remain convinced of this. In recent years, however, the Canadian economy has performed poorly with respect to growth and employment objectives. In part, this reflects a substantial decline in the competitiveness of Canadian industry in international trade on both the export and import sides—a decline that goes beyond the normal cyclical malaise associated with a world recession. The need for Canadian industry to readjust along the lines of its most productive endeavors is now greater than ever, and it will persist whether the degree of trade liberalization agreed upon by GATT is large or small.

It must be noted, however, that the difficulties of adjustment have also increased. The problem of limited resource mobility in some industries must be recognized as a special factor requiring innovative measures to overcome it in the long run. The textile and garment trades, for instance, employ many married women who cannot simply pick up and move to jobs elsewhere. Workers with strong family and cultural affiliations, such as those in smaller Quebec centres, are unlikely to want to migrate even if there are advantageous job opportunities elsewhere. Efforts to avoid, or at least ameliorate, problems of this type are surely desirable.

A discussion of the problems associated with the rearranging of Canada's industrial structure runs the risk of leaving the impression that only problems exist. Canadian industries that suffer from elements of comparative disadvantage would not necessarily disappear under freer trade arrangements, although their relative size in the economy would be reduced. Encourage-

* Economic Council, *Looking Outward,* Chapter 12.

ment by the federal government has already steered some industries—such as food processing—away from specialized lines that would bring them the severest competition. There are, however, industries with a clear comparative disadvantage in Canada—labor-intensive industries that even now are marked by lower-than-average wages and productivity and that would become even worse off under conditions of freer trade. Even after years of special protective measures and incentives to rationalize and modernize, the problems of orderly contraction will be difficult. In virtually all these enterprises, the value added per employee is well below the national average for manufacturing, which clearly suggests a need to improve productivity and/or shift resources to more rewarding activities.

The foregoing attempts to put the adaptation problem into its proper perspective, particularly when adaptation requires reorganization and various degrees of contraction rather than the total disappearance of such industries. Manufacturing accounts for only 20 per cent of total employment. The sectors most vulnerable to competition from developing countries are leather goods, textiles, hosiery and knitted goods, clothing, and selected electronics products.† Many of the enterprises in these industries are located in or around Montreal, Hamilton, Toronto, and Winnipeg. They represent a substantial proportion of manufacturing employment—about a third in Quebec and a fifth in Ontario—but only about 7 per cent of total employment in Quebec and less than 5 per cent in Ontario.** The situation appears to be particularly acute in Montreal, where a large proportion of the work force consists of married women with relatively poor education, who would likely find it difficult to readapt to either other locations or other occupations. It is rather less severe, on the other hand, in the Toronto-Hamilton-Niagara region and southwestern Ontario in general, where the proximity of many small and medium-sized towns to a large number of industrial firms facilitates movement to better jobs in more promising industries.

The situation is very critical in some of the smaller cities in Quebec and Ontario where, in general, alternative employment opportunities are less readily available. Many small towns and villages are threatened because of their greater dependence on the economic viability of one or a few firms. These communities are scattered all over the central provinces but are also numerous in other parts of the country. Their heaviest concentration, however, is in Quebec, especially in the Eastern Townships and the central and western regions of the province, as well as in the Ottawa Valley and other areas of eastern Ontario.

Given the already high levels of unemployment, especially in Quebec, it is clear that the achievement of an acceptable tariff and adjustment strategy will depend on a number of factors, including a return to a better economic performance for the Canadian economy as a whole; expanding opportunities for employment in viable industries and occupations; industrial incentive and alternative job-creation programs aimed at easing the cultural and geographic adjustment of competitively displaced workers; and adequate provisions for upgrading labor skills, job retraining and labor mobility facilities.

† Admittedly, other sectors—such as furniture making—have come under increasing competition from U.S. and foreign producers. This problem has been exacerbated by the very rapid rise in Canadian labor costs relative to those in the United States. The recent depreciation of the Canadian dollar, along with greater Canadian wage restraint in the future, may hopefully increase Canada's competitiveness in this and other product lines.

** Roy A. Matthews (assisted by Frances Mowbray)' "Canadian Industry and the Developing Countries: A Preliminary Assessment of the Dependence of Employment on Manufacturing Sectors Vulnerable to Low-Wage Competition," Economic Council of Canada Conference on Industrial Adaptation, June 1977.

From: Economic Council of Canada, *Fourteenth Annual Review, Into the 1980's,* Ottawa: 1977, pp. 41-44.

SUMMARY

The case for international trade is the case for specialization and exchange. In the last analysis, *specialization* increases the total output of goods and services because of the principle of comparative advantage, and *exchange* increases the income of those nations that specialize.

Comparative advantage rests upon the principle of opportunity cost—that is, how much of an alternative good must be foregone in order to produce a particular good. It is the difference in opportunity costs between two goods within different countries that defines comparative advantage. A country will have a comparative advantage in one good if it must sacrifice fewer alternative goods to produce it than does another country.

Comparative advantage can exist between two countries even though one of them can produce all goods more efficiently than the other—that is, has an absolute advantage in all lines of production. The more fortunate country can still gain by producing what it can do best and importing the rest from other countries.

Tariffs, quotas, and administrative red tape interfere with the free flow of goods across international boundaries. This interference prevents the full benefits of specialization and exchange. Trade restrictions hurt consumers in order to protect particular producers from foreign competition. Although countries often decide to protect particular industries to prevent short-term damage to the industries, to diversify their economies, to develop their infant industries, or to assure themselves of a supply of certain goods in wartime, it is usually very difficult to justify trade restrictions on economic grounds (from the standpoint of a nation as a whole).

Nevertheless, political pressures within nations and nationalistic attitudes and antagonisms between different nations continue to place many barriers in the way of free international trade in the world today. This is true despite the solid arguments in favor of free trade laid down by Adam Smith, David Ricardo, and other founders of economics almost two centuries ago—and despite continuing support for more liberal international trade from the vast majority of economists today.

KEY CONCEPTS

absolute advantage
comparative advantage
tariffs
quotas
dumping

QUESTIONS FOR REVIEW AND DISCUSSION

1. In what ways is international trade the same as trade among individuals and regions within the same nation? In what ways is international trade different?
2. What is the difference between absolute advantage and comparative advantage? Can one nation have an absolute advantage in everything? Can one nation have a comparative advantage in everything? Why?

3. In light of the advantages of specialization and exchange, why do countries want trade barriers to cut down the amount of international trade? What forms do these trade barriers often take?
4. What groups in an economy are helped most by trade barriers? What groups are hurt most?
5. How can domestic monetary and fiscal policy be used to reduce pressures for restrictive trade barriers within a country?
6. What is the difference between wages *per hour* and wages *per unit of output*? How does this difference relate to the cheap foreign labor argument in international trade?
7. Are trade barriers always bad? When might trade barriers contribute to the health of a country's economy? Why?

PROBLEMS AND EXERCISES TO SHARPEN YOUR UNDERSTANDING

1. If the same amount of resources is used in each country, the following amounts of coal and steel can be produced in Brazil and Chile.

	tonnes of coal	tonnes of steel
Brazil	4	12
Chile	3	6

   Note that Brazil has an absolute advantage in each good, but where does its comparative advantage lie? Should Brazil specialize in producing coal or steel? Why?
2. Research the economic and political background to the U.K.'s relationship with the E.E.C. Why were the British originally uninterested? Why did they change their position? What opposition was there to British entry?
3. What have been the significant results of the Tokyo Round of negotiations on trade policies by the signatories of the General Agreement on Tariffs and Trade?
4. Carry out a research project on some aspect of Canadian trade policy. Some topics which might be especially interesting to examine are:
   —The "National Policy" of Sir John A. Macdonald
   —Moves toward free trade with the U.S.A. by Sir Wilfrid Laurier
   —The Canada-U.S. Auto Pact

APPENDIX:

MULTINATIONAL CORPORATIONS

One of the trends which has accompanied the rapid expansion of international trade in the period since the end of World War II has been the rise of multinational firms to a position of prominence in trade and in total output. Most simply defined, a multinational corporation is a firm which has subsidiary companies in one or more countries other than the nation where the parent firm is located. In international economic terms, however, the multinationals which draw most attention are those very large firms which have many subsidiary and associate firms in a great many countries around the world.

THE SCOPE AND SIZE OF MULTINATIONAL CORPORATIONS

To get some sense of the relative importance of the major multinationals, the following could be considered as general characteristics. Sales volumes internationally will be well over a billion dollars a year. Corporate profits will exceed one hundred million dollars a year and assets of the firm will be valued in the range of a billion dollars. National origin will be American, European, or Japanese. The number of subsidiary firms will likely be more than fifty and operations will probably reach into at least three continents.

Among the largest multinationals, the relative size increases greatly. Table 32A-1 on page 430 lists the ten largest industrial firms in the world based on 1977 sales volumes. If this list were to be extended to the top fifty, the firm ranking as number 50 would be found to be B.A.T. Industries, based in London, with sales volume of $6.6 billion. In total, the combined 1977 sales volume of the top fifty was $725 billion, over three times the total GNP of Canada.

This ranking is based on sales volume. After-tax profits, total assets, or other criteria would produce different ranks. For example, if after-tax profits were used, Mobil Oil, Texaco and BP would drop from the 1978 list and be replaced within the "top ten" by General Electric, Petróleos de Venezuela, and Petrobrás (Petróleo Brasileiro), and a new ranking would exist.

A second factor is built in here as well. Firms included are those with 50% or more of sales revenues coming from manufacturing and/or mining. Financial institutions such as banks and "utilities," including firms primarily involved in transportation and communications, are excluded.

The fact that seven are oil companies should not be surprising, nor should the fact that two of the other three are automotive manufacturers. If the "top ten" were extended to the "top twenty-five," five more oil companies and three more automotive firms would be included.

As of the late 1970s, it has been estimated that in the range of 20% of the total output of the non-Communist world is generated by about four hundred multinational firms. This proportion of output has been expanding and some projections see it reaching to a level of 50% of output by the end of the century.

Along with the rapid increase in the proportions of output, trade and employment generated by multinationals, the most conspicuous trend of recent years has been the rise of non-American multinationals. If one were to go back to 1960, one would find a much higher proportion of the largest firms was U.S. based. Within Table 32A-1, we can see that seven of the top ten are still American. If, however, we were to extend that list by forty more ranks, the dominance of Amer-

Table 32A-1. TEN LARGEST INDUSTRIAL COMPANIES IN THE WORLD—1978: RANKED BY SALES IN 1977

Rank	Company	National Base	Sales (Billions of U.S. Dollars)
1.	General Motors	U.S.A.	$55.0
2.	Exxon	U.S.A.	54.1
3.	Royal Dutch/Shell	UK/Netherlands	39.7
4.	Ford Motor	U.S.A.	37.8
5.	Mobil Oil	U.S.A.	32.1
6.	Texaco	U.S.A	27.9
7.	National Iranian Oil	Iran	22.3
8.	British Petroleum	U.K.	20.94
9.	Standard Oil-California	U.S.A.	20.92
10.	I.B.M.	U.S.A.	18.1

Source: As reported in *Fortune,* August 14, 1978, p. 184

ican firms drops. Only twenty-two of the top fifty are U.S. based.[1] Table 32A-2 indicates the breakdown of national bases of the fifty largest industrial firms, again based on the level of 1977 sales.

The multinational corporation can be traced to historic roots that in some cases predate the Industrial Revolution.

The revival of trade in Europe in the late Renaissance was accompanied by a resurgence of banking, which was initially centered in the Italian city-states. Very quickly, the activities of banking houses spread across international borders. In fact, as national states began to emerge in Europe, bankers who were often located in other countries were among the most important allies of some of the royal dynasties who presided over the consolidation of the emerging monarchies.

At the same time, another international type of firm was emerging. Trading companies, such as the East India Company or the Hudson's Bay Company, were generally established to develop trade based on the resources or raw materials of developing colo-

[1] For an earlier assessment of the rise of U.S. multinationals in Europe, see J. J. Servan-Schreiber, *The American Challenge,* (English edition), New York: Atheneum, 1969. For a more recent perspective on the large-scale entry of non-U.S. firms into the United States, see Kenneth Crowe, *America For Sale,* New York: Doubleday, 1978.

Table 32A-2. NATIONAL BASES OF THE FIFTY LARGEST INDUSTRIAL CORPORATIONS BASED ON 1977 SALES VOLUMES

Country	Number of Firms
United States	22
Germany	7
Japan	6
United Kingdom	4
France	4
Netherlands	2
Switzerland	1
Italy	1
Brazil	1
Venezuela	1
Iran	1

Notes: (1) Of these, six are owned by national governments; these include state oil companies in Iran, Italy, Venezuela, Brazil and France, plus Renault, the automobile firm, in France.
(2) Two firms, Royal Dutch/Shell Group and Unifever are both designated as being jointly British and Dutch based. In drawing up this table, each firm was considered to contribute one half to each of the two countries.

Source: As reported in *Fortune,* August 14, 1978, p. 184

Table 32A-3. TEN LARGEST INDUSTRIAL AND MERCHANDISING COMPANIES IN CANADA, 1978, RATED BY SALES

Rank	Company	Sales (Billions of Dollars)	National Base—(Parent Firm)	(%)
1.	General Motors of Canada	$6.115	U.S.—(General Motors)	100
2.	Ford of Canada	$5.725	U.S.—(Ford)	88
3.	Imperial Oil	$4.970	U.S.—(Exxon)	70
4.	Canadian Pacific	$4.700	Canada	
5.	George Weston	$4.590	Canada	
6.	Alcan Aluminium	$3.221	Canada	
7.	Chrysler Canada	$3.119	U.S.—(Chrysler)	100
8.	Massey-Ferguson	$2.936	Canada—(Argus)	
9.	Canada Safeway	$2.582	U.S.—(Safeway Stores)	100
10.	Shell Canada	$2.349	UK/Netherlands—(Shell Group)	68

Source: As reported in *The Financial Post 300,* 1978, pp. 8-20

nial empires in exchange for some of the output of the "mother country." These early trading firms tended to have close ties to governments and often operated to promote the military and political, as well as the economic, interests of the "mother country." In this respect, some of the recent revelations about some of the links between multinationals and the policies of their parent governments[2] might be regarded as little more than a continuation of historical tradition. These early trading companies tended to operate under some form of official monopoly in given areas. As a result, they did not spread out from a home base into a wide range of different foreign locations.

This pattern of having foreign activities, other than marketing of products, develop in a number of different countries was something which did not really start to emerge until about the end of the nineteenth century. The trend started to appear in the primary or resource sector in particular. Firms went out in pursuit of resources, either ore bodies, forest resources or, later, petroleum reserves. Initially, raw materials might come back to the parent for processing but, increasingly, firms started to spread the location of processing and manufacturing facilities into other countries where there were either resources or markets or both.

Various factors tended to promote this trend in other types of industries. For example, in Canada, the entry of foreign manufacturing firms into production in Canada was stimulated by the tariff policy we adopted in 1878. The "National Policy" was designed to stimulate manufacturing in Canada. It did so, though much of the activity it promoted was that of branch plants of American firms whose output from the U.S. itself would be less competitive due to the tariff system.

As a result of the early appearance of branches of American and British firms, Canada has had an unusually high level of experience with multinational firms. The policy ramifications of the extent of foreign ownership in Canada will be examined in detail in the Appendix to Chapter 33. At this stage, it is sufficient to underline the fact that multinationals are an especially important part of economic life in this country.

Canada is a home as well as a host for multinational enterprises. The data in Table 32A-3 point out that in the industrial and merchandising sectors, nine of the "top 10" firms in 1978 (these ranked by sales volumes) are in the category of multinational firms. Six of the ten are subsidiaries of

[2] One case which received considerable attention was the role of U.S. based firms in the downfall of the Allende government in Chile in 1973. For an introduction to this, see Anthony Sampson, *The Sovereign State of I.T.T.*, New York: Fawcett, 1974, chapters 11 and 12. For further examination of the role of other firms in Chile, see R. J. Barnet and R. E. Muller, *Global Reach: The Power of the Multinational Corporations*, New York: Simon and Schuster, 1974.

Figure 32A-1. MASSEY-FERGUSON LIMITED: CORPORATE SUBSIDIARIES IN THE UNITED STATES AND CONTINENTAL EUROPE

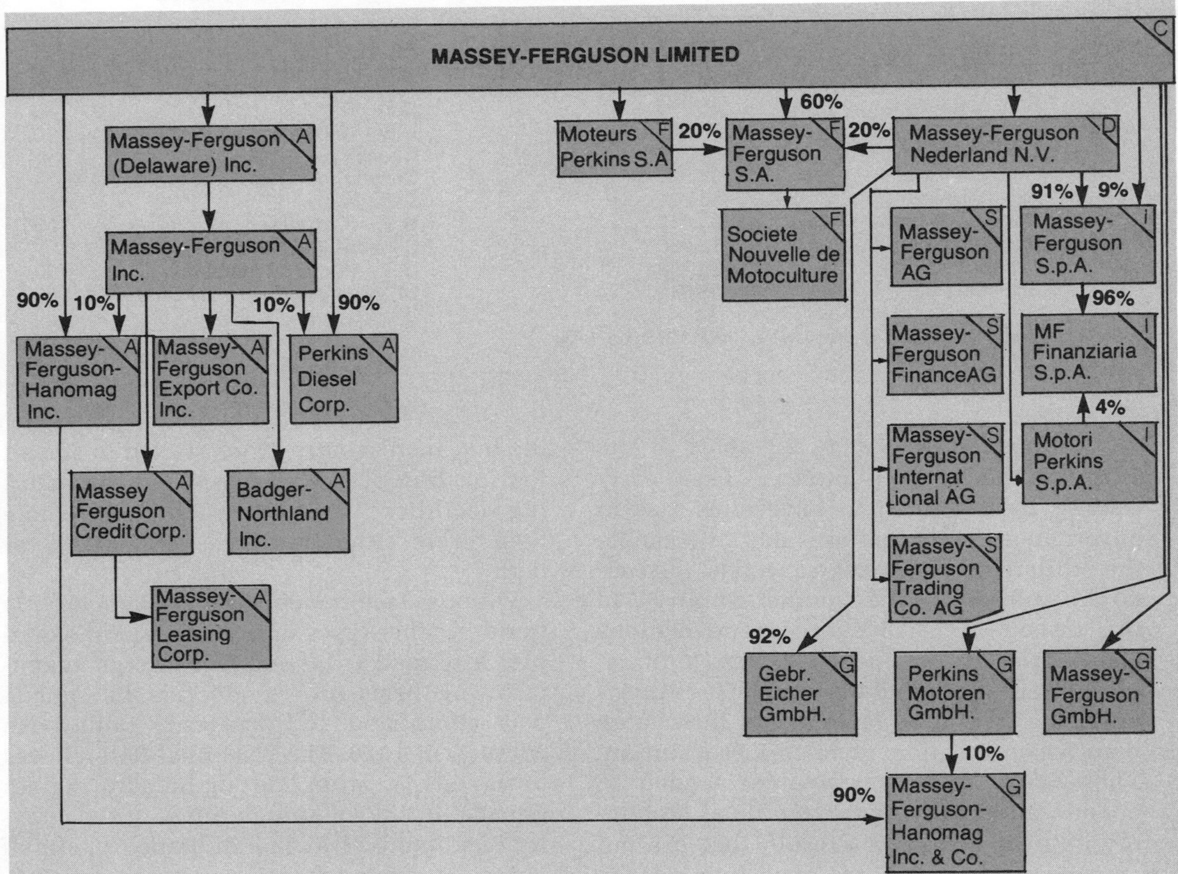

Based on data in Massey-Ferguson's "10-K" Annual Report for 1977 to the Securities and Exchange Commission, Washington, D.C.

This chart is limited to two geographical regions, the United States and continental Europe. It excludes interests in the United Kingdom, Eire, Australia, Africa and Latin America.

The arrows indicate lines of ownership and control. If no percentage is given, then the line of control is based on 100% ownership. The triangles inserted into the top right corners of each corporate block indicate nationality. The *C* in Massey-Ferguson Limited denotes "Canadian." *A* designates American incorporation. Within the European firms, the following codes are used: *D*—Dutch; *F*—French; *S*—Swiss; *I*—Italian; and *G*—German.

foreign-based multinationals. Three of the remaining four are Canadian-based multinationals which generate substantial portions of their business outside of Canada.

This listing indicates that, outside of financial and real estate corporations, six of the "top 10" in Canada in 1978 were subsidiaries of foreign-based multinationals. Of the four "Canadian" firms, three (Weston, Alcan and Massey-Ferguson) are definitely in the multinational category, having substantial proportions of their business done through subsidiaries in countries outside of Canada. See the diagram for an indication of part of the multinational structure of Massey-Ferguson.

Massey-Ferguson is one of the largest of the Canadian-based multinational firms. To put it into the context of the largest industrial firms in the world, within the sales rankings for 1977, it ranked as number 175 on a world-wide basis, with a sales volume

Table 32A-4. MASSEY-FERGUSON: 1976-77 NET SALES BY CONTINENT AND BY COUNTRY OR REGION

Continental Area	% of 1976-77 Net Sales	Country or Region	% of 1976-77 Net Sales
North America	29.9	United States	23.0
		Canada	6.9
Europe	37.6	United Kingdom	9.8
		Germany	7.8
Latin America	16.2	France	6.7
		Italy	4.9
Africa	6.0	Scandinavia	3.7
		Benelux	1.6
Asia	6.0	Brazil	9.9
		Argentina	3.9
Australasia	4.3	Turkey	1.8
		All Others	20.0
Total	100.0	Total	100.0

Source: Massey Ferguson Limited, *Annual Report,* 1977, reprinted by permission.

of just under $3 billion. The sales total is accounted for by subsidiary companies which range far over the globe. The diagram provides a chart of the structure of Massey's corporate organization in the U.S. and continental Europe, to provide an illustration of how such links are established. Figure 32A-1 can be linked in turn to Figure 15-1.

Another illustration of the scope of Massey's activities is given in Table 32A-4. This breaks down net sales for the fiscal year ending in 1977, first by continents and then by countries. The latter is not complete and attempts only to show some of the more significant of the national markets.

Given the illustrations of overall size and scope which have been introduced, you should by now have some sense of the extent to which large multinationals can and do pool resources, capital and technology in complex patterns. The result may see resources from countries A through D being processed and semi-finished in countries E-F, consolidated in the form of components for finished products, and assembled in countries A, E and G, for sale in countries A through Z. This pattern of direct participation in all stages of production from raw materials to the final form of a marketable product is sometimes referred to as vertical integration. Among the best examples of this are the "integrated" oil companies, whose activities span all stages from exploration for resources to the marketing of refined products.[3] Concentrating on one, or on a small number of stages within the entire production-marketing process, and expanding one's share of the market at these stages, is an approach referred to as horizontal integration. Massey-Ferguson, with its concentration on the manufacture and marketing of farm and construction machinery, is more of a horizontally integrated firm. These classifications can of course also be applied to firms which are not multinational in scope, but the patterns become more prominent among some major multinationals.

Still other multinationals have tended to diversify into a wide range of activities. Among the large multinationals, International Telephone and Telegraph, I.T.T., with 1977 sales of $13.1 billion, assets of $12.3 billion, and net profits of $550 million, is probably the most widely-diversified, with interests that include not only

[3] For a detailed account of the development of the world's major oil companies, see Anthony Sampson, *The Seven Sisters,* New York: Viking, 1975.

communications but wide holdings in such fields as electronics, insurance, hotels and real estate, book publishing, and food and bakery products. In 1977, I.T.T. ranked as the fifteenth largest industrial corporation in the world.

The range of interests of I.T.T., or the international scope of the activities of Massey-Ferguson, indicate the extent to which multinationals have evolved from their roots. One other significant change is beginning to emerge as well, and was hinted at in the first note accompanying Table 32A-2. This is the rise of publicly-owned firms within the ranks of multinationals. The largest government-owned firms have, to this point, not tended to be international in scope, but that is becoming less true. Within the "top fifty" in 1977, the only government-controlled firm which was truly a multinational was Renault. However, within the next fifty, one finds such firms as British Leyland, the automotive firm, and British Steel, a steel and metal refining firm, both of which are owned now by the British government. As a result of this trend, it is becoming more common to use the term "multinational enterprises", which provides for both private and public ownership.

THE EFFECTS OF MULTINATIONALS

As we have seen, one of the two reasons for the increase in the attention paid to multinationals has been the increase in their economic importance. Let us now turn to the second reason for increased attention—the rising concern about the effects of what has been happening, and the debate about the desirability of this situation.

As is the case with the more specialized issue of foreign ownership in Canada, which will be examined in the Appendix to the next chapter, the debate ranges beyond the limits of economics in the narrow sense and includes political, social and even ethical and philosophical aspects as well. The issues are complicated by the existence of different focal points. Some see the issues as ones which should be considered from an overall, that is a world-wide, perspective. Others examine the topic from the perspective of the "home countries," the nations out of which the multinationals spread. Still others, probably a majority of the critics, look more closely at the impact on the "host countries," the countries to which multinationals have spread their operations. Within the latter situation, one finds differing sets of potential problems in developed "host" nations, such as Canada, and less-developed "host" countries, such as the island nations of the Caribbean region.

Using the preceding structure, let us look briefly at some of the potential advantages and disadvantages which have emerged with the rise of multinationals.

From a world-wide perspective, four major benefits are associated with the growth of multinationals:

1. the overall expansion of output, income and employment;
2. an increase in the flow of international trade and a widening of access to goods and services;
3. a downward pressure on tariffs and other barriers to international trade;
4. the mutual recognition of interdependency which in turn tends to promote international stability and co-operation.

These are all generalizations for which some supporting evidence can be found, but against which other conflicting pieces of evidence can be offered. The same is true of the generalizations which are made regarding disadvantages or costs associated with the rise of multinationals.

Among the costs, greatest concern is voiced over these three problems in the international arena:

1. the rising rate of exploitation of limited world resources, with both the use of the resources and enjoyment of the wealth created being concentrated among a minority of the world's people;
2. the greater impact of large flows of funds associated with the activities of multinationals on international bal-

ance of payments patterns, and the stability of exchange rates;[4]

3. an increase in inter-governmental disputes as a result of attempts by individual governments to impose control over aspects of multinational operations within their jurisdictions.

These disadvantages are, to a considerable degree, the reverse sides of the advantages. The basic conflict between the first items in each list is, of course, the conflict of opinion over what is really happening in today's world. Are basic conditions of life becoming significantly better for significantly more people, or are the few benefiting more at the expense of the many? Regardless of how the question is answered, to attribute the result, even in part, to the impact of multinationals depends on one underlying assumption. That assumption is that the degree of impact made by the large multinationals is greater (either for better or for worse) than would have been the effect of smaller firms, presumably in greater numbers, whose operations have been more limited in terms of geography and possibly in economic scope as well. It should be pointed out that this assumption is often made, but is impossible to either prove or disprove.

For the "home country"—the national base from which a multinational operates—costs and benefits are somewhat easier to identify in general terms, and much easier to pinpoint in specific cases. The potential advantages are, in reality, comparable to the beneficial results which could come from having a colonial empire or from organizing patterns of trade along lines which will maximize benefits for one partner. The three chief advantages for a "home country" may be:

1. a more secure access to foreign resources, labor and perhaps to capital;
2. a regular inflow of funds as a return on investment;
3. the acquisition of allies and supporters in the international political arena.

[4] The impact of changes in any nation's balance of payments and how this may affect its exchange rate will be examined in detail in Chapter 33.

Conversely, the potential disadvantages to the "home country" may be the following:

1. the development of dependency on foreign resources or labor;
2. an outflow of capital, possibly to the detriment of the domestic economy, to make the "foreign investments;"
3. a possible outflow of jobs from the home economy which accompanies the outflow of capital;
4. the development of problems for the governments from whose jurisdictions multinationals spread in cases when the firms encounter difficulties abroad and call upon their parent governments for assistance;
5. the generation of resentment directed at a nation which has spawned multinationals, as a result of the power which the firms acquire and use or abuse abroad.

If we were to examine the five potential disadvantages above, and to look for some examples of these in practise, they are readily found.

As a case of dependency on foreign resources, the rise in the importance of cheaper imported oil in the United States prior to 1973 is a good example. Since then, the American government has promoted the idea (but not achieved the reality) of decreasing U.S. dependence on imported energy resources, which have become steadily more expensive and less secure. The basic source of the problem was the willingness of the United States to permit itself to become dependent on the system developed by the major U.S. oil firms and their international operations. We should note, however, that one need not be a "home country" for such a dependency to evolve. The eastern regions of Canada acquired an even greater degree of dependency based on the initial cost considerations which existed in the pre-1973 world, when a barrel of oil from Venezuela or the Middle East could be brought to Halifax or Montreal more cheaply than oil from Alberta.

An illustration of the outflow of jobs may be seen in the electronics industry. One of the more conspicuous areas is that of the manufacture of radio, stereo and television sets and components. In the two decades following 1960, the importance of this industry within both Canada and the United States has declined rapidly while actual sales volumes have increased greatly. Some of this can be explained by the competitive advantages of Asian producers, usually based in Japan, which center on labor costs and technological capacities. However, many North American manufacturers have shifted their own manufacturing facilities to the nations of the "Pacific Rim" to take advantage of similar cost savings. In Canada, we have seen comparable cases of production of goods such as hockey and baseball equipment being "relocated" in the West Indies. Again, it should be pointed out that such shifts could come about simply as a result of the factors of competition in a world without multinationals. However, the structure of multinationals does seem to increase the possibility of such relocations, which may often be at the expense of some sectors within the home economy.

As a final illustration, let us examine the last of the designated "costs" to the "home country." As a source of economic power which stretches beyond its own borders, the United States has been the dominant example in this century, as was Britain in the previous century. In the realm of international relations, the U.S.A., and its position of dominance, have come under increasing pressure and, in many cases, the economic causes have been significant ones. This is especially true in the case of less developed nations, many of which won political independence only after 1945. In such cases, economic nationalism has been closely tied to political nationalism. Powerful multinationals, which come to be regarded as a foreign "threat," may become targets for immense hostility. There are many instances where nationalistic pressures have helped to curb the economic and political influence of major powers such as the United States. Frequently, these pressures have been strongest when they have simultaneously been directed at the local abuse of political or economic power. Unfortunately, multinational firms and their parent governments have often become associated with dictatorial regimes, and the disparities these regimes support, with results which become almost inevitable.

The overthrow of the Batista government in Cuba by Fidel Castro is an example of such an association. The revolution which took place in Cuba was directed against the Batista government, and also at the extent of U.S. economic and political power in that country. The strong anti-American policies of the Castro government marked a reaction which should not have been surprising. Much more recently, events in Iran illustrate some similar elements. The movement against the Shah seems to have been based on a combination of political and social forces which were united in opposition to the political tyranny of the monarchy, the way in which the income from Iran's oil resources was being generally diverted from benefiting the majority of Iranians, the political influence of the United States as a result of its ties to the monarchy, the increasing influence of foreign businesses in Iran, and the growing intrusion of foreign culture.

In cases such as Iran or Cuba, complex mixtures of forces are at work. No two are ever quite the same, and any simple explanation is impossible. Even so, in much of the less developed world, any sign of foreign domination or exploitation, be it real or symbolic, may produce violent reactions.

This is something Canada should be aware of for, in a small way, we are potential targets for such reactions. We tend to see ourselves (and are generally viewed in the world) as one of a relatively small number of nations without enemies or critics. This is essentially the case with one significant exception—the Caribbean region.

In this area, Canada has been a foreign, dominating force in a number of sectors of the economy, through the operations of Canadian-based firms. Banking, real estate, and tourism and mining are three major sectors where Canadian firms have very influential positions—positions which have started breeding resentment. In Guyana, the Alcan subsidiaries have already been nationalized. In Trinidad, Jamaica, and some other islands, similar sentiments are being expressed. We should not be surprised if they come to the surface in the future.

"HOST COUNTRIES" AND MULTINATIONAL CORPORATIONS

In the preceding paragraphs referring to "home countries," there has been an emphasis on the potential links between economic and political forces. Such links are really the result of possible reactions, which spill back to "home countries" from "host countries": i.e. nations to which multinationals extend their operations. Let us turn now to look at multinationals from the perspective of "host countries"—the one which tends to be most complex of all.

For the "host nation," multinationals tend to provide the same potential advantages as the nation would derive from capital and technology from other sources. Developed and less developed hosts tend to benefit in similar ways, differing only in the degree of relative impact.

Needless to say, the more developed an economy is, the less impact any given investment or development will have. For the sake of simple illustration, let us consider the impact on the local economies of two communities, X and Y, of a new factory which would create twenty new jobs. If we know X is a city of two million people, we may assume the opening of the factory is not going to be an important event. On the other hand, if Y is a village of less than a thousand people, the generation of a new industry of that size could be a significant event for the community. So it is with the impact of multinationals on "host nations." Effects, especially the advantageous one, tend to be similar, differing in their degree of relative impact.

Imperial Oil Limited

This photo of a drilling site in the Beaufort Sea in the Canadian Arctic symbolizes the positive aspects of the impact of multinationals in Canada. Such firms have played and continue to play a leading role in developing resources in this country.

Among the primary potential benefits of major activity by multinational firms, the following are likely to be most important:

1. The increased capital investment will increase output, income and employment.
2. The increased access to technology will also tend to have beneficial impacts on output, income and employment, and may also increase the level of skills in the labor force.
3. The first two can also combine to increase research and development, which in turn can increase productivity.
4. Resources or labor or local entrepreneurial skills which might have remained idle may be developed.
5. The advent of activities related to 1. through 4. may generate opportunities for the development of additional locally-based economic activity.
6. All of the above will strengthen the tax base of governments.

7. The influx of new technology, skills and ideas can have wide-ranging multiplier effects on education, tastes and culture.

In summary, all of the above may promote economic growth, and cause improvements in the general standard of living to take place at a rate which is more rapid than would have been the case without the inflow of the foreign-based capital and technology. As has been indicated previously, Canada's economic growth has to a high degree been promoted by the activities of multinationals within Canada. There is no doubt about the fact that their presence has permitted us to develop more rapidly and extensively than if we had not had access to them, particularly to their capital. Benefits, however, generally have a price. Of late, we have been asking more frequently: just what has the price been, and what may it become in the future? Most "host nations" have been asking similar questions.

To the "host nation," the cost or potential cost of multinational activities is more complex. The extent to which potential disadvantages become real depends on a complicated mix of factors, including the degree of dependence on foreign firms, the extent to which they may dominate various sectors of the economy, the way(s) they use their economic power, the economic responses of the people, the private sector and the governments of the "host country," and a wide range of other political, social and cultural forces which may play a role in shaping responses to multinationals in any host country.

Among the primary concerns which tend to dominate "host nations" are these:

1. Dependence on foreign capital or technology, or permitting domination by foreign firms, may inhibit development of domestic enterprises and create a "branch-plant mentality" that saps domestic initiative or confidence.
2. Dependence creates vulnerability for jobs and economic stability, leaving the economy exposed to decisions being made elsewhere.
3. Long-run costs may include high outflows of profits to parent firms, or an increasing degree of foreign control that is financed by profits reinvested by foreign subsidiaries.
4. Multinationals may use purchasing and pricing policies which are designed to maximize their own benefits but, in so doing, may decrease prices being paid for a nation's exports, increase prices paid for imports, or minimize taxes being paid to governments.
5. The subsidiary status of "branch plants" may force them to place less emphasis on exports or on research and development, if such would conflict with activities in other divisions of the firm.
6. The subsidiary status of "branch plants" not only exposes them to direction by the parent firm itself, but indirectly to the requirements of the home government imposed on the parent firm.
7. The branches of multinationals may be less likely to act in accordance with the national needs or interests of the people, or the government, of the "host" than would enterprises native to the country.

All of these concerns, you will notice, deal with the possible effects on any economy of three factors: dependence on foreign capital, technology or decisions; the domestic performance of foreign-owned firms; and the control over one's own economy.[5]

What governments and populations of "host nations" generally have to come to terms with is the balance between potential costs and benefits they would like to achieve. This must ultimately reflect national priorities on the one hand and, on the other, the extent to which multinationals can

[5] Most of these will be examined in detail in a Canadian context in the Appendix to Chapter 33.

be persuaded to function within locally imposed controls and constraints. The quest for this balance, and for effective ways to regulate aspects of the operations of multinational firms, is one of the major challenges facing many nations today.[6]

In addition to the issues raised previously, two other concerns related to multinationals have come into sharper focus during the decade of the 1970s.

Within Chapter 31 dealing with economic growth, the question of the need for constraints on growth was introduced. Many observers see this closely connected to problems related to multinational firms. One of the general characteristics of these enterprises is a policy of expansion, both by acquisition of existing firms, and by the addition of new productive capacity. Many observers believe that such a concentration on increased output will simply reinforce the overemphasis on material progress at the expense of other significant social and ethical considerations.[7]

Another aspect of the power of multinationals which has come to the fore in the last decade is the broad issue of corporate morality as exercised or ignored by international firms. Revelations about the involvement of multinational firms in complex cases of political intrigue and bribery have increased fears about the potential for such behavior which accompanies the acquisition of great financial power and far-reaching economic interests.[8] It should be pointed out, however, that multinationals are institutions which are created by people and function through people. As a result, they are subject to the same weaknesses and the same problems which may emerge within any other human undertaking.

Within this framework of increasing scrutiny or criticism of their activity, multinationals have certainly come to feel threatened by government encroachment. As a result, they have frequently attempted to resolve or prevent problems and have become more active in promoting their "case," along with their specialized economic interests.[9]

There is little doubt that questions about the power of multinational firms form a major component of the debate over the relative roles and powers of big business, big labor, and big government which are going on in many countries, including Canada. The answers chosen and the policies adopted regarding multinationals will play a significant role in determining both the structure of economic society, and many of the approaches we will take to deal with economic problems and needs in the future.

BIBLIOGRAPHY

The following bibliography, which is the longest specialized bibliography contained within the text, contains a wide range of approaches in terms of content covered and the value judgments and opinions of authors. The scope indicates the vastness and complexity of the topic, and points out that the content of this appendix contains merely a few tips of a vast iceberg.

Antonides, Harry, *Multinationals and the Peaceable Kingdom*, Toronto: Clarke, Irwin, 1978.

Barnet, Richard J., and Muller, Ronald E., *Global Reach: The Power of the Multinational Corporations*, New York: Simon and Schuster, 1974.

Behrman, J. N., *Conflicting Constraints on the Multinational Enterprise*, New York: Council of the Americas, 1974.

[6] See Robert Hellman's *Transnational Control of Multinationals*, New York: Praeger, 1977, for a look at various methods which have been adopted by governments around the world.

[7] See Harry Antonides, *Multinationals and the Peaceable Kingdom*, Toronto: Clark Irwin, 1977, Chapter 6. For a similar Canadian perspective from a noted Canadian philosopher, see George Grant, *Technology and Empire*, Toronto: Anansi, 1969.

[8] One of the most notable cases involved Lockheed Aircraft. Information revealed about Lockheed's activities brought down a government in Japan, and promoted major crises in Italy and the Netherlands.

[9] For a more detailed presentation of cases "for" multinationals, see the books by C. H. Madden and E. H. Roach in the bibliography.

Clement, Wallace, *Continental Corporate Power*, Toronto: McClelland and Stewart, 1977.

Craig, J. G., *Multinational Co-operatives: An Alternative for World Development*, Saskatoon: Western Producer Prairie Books, 1976.

Crowe, Kenneth, *America For Sale*, New York: Doubleday, 1978.

Curzon, Gerald, and Curzon, Victoria, (eds.) *The Multinational Corporation in a Hostile World*, Toronto: Macmillan/McLean-Hunter, 1977.

Deverell, John, *Falconbridge: Portrait of a Canadian Mining Multinational*, Toronto: James Lorimer, 1975.

Franko, Lawrence G., *The European Multinationals*, Stamford: Greylock Publishers, 1976.

Hellman, Rainer, *Transnational Control of Multinationals*, New York: Praeger, 1977.

Hershfield, D. C., *The Multinational Union Challenges the Multinational Company*, New York: The Conference Board, 1975.

Madden, Carl H., (ed.) *The Case For the Multinational Corporation*, New York: Praeger, 1977.

Multinational Corporations in World Development, United Nations, Department of Economic and Social Affairs, New York: Praeger, 1974.

Neufeld, E. P., *A Global Corporation: A History of the International Development of Massey-Ferguson Limited*, Toronto: University of Toronto Press, 1969.

Paguet, Gilles, (ed.), *The Multinational Firm and the Nation State*, Don Mills: Collier-Macmillan, 1972.

Roach, E. Hugh, *In Defense of Multinationals: The Myths, the Realities and the Future*, Toronto: Canadian Institute of International Affairs, 1977.

Sampson, Anthony, *The Sovereign State of I.T.T.*, New York: Fawcett, 1974.

Sampson, Anthony, *The Seven Sisters*, New York: Bantam, 1976.

Servan-Schreiber, J. J., *The American Challenge*, New York: Atheneum, 1969.

Swift, Jamie, *The Big Nickel: Inco at Home and Abroad*, Kitchener: Between the Lines, 1977.

Vernon, Raymond, *Storm Over the Multinationals: The Real Issues*, Cambridge, Mass.: Harvard University Press, 1977.

Wilkins, Mira, *The Maturing of Multinational Enterprise: American Business Abroad from 1914 to 1970*, Cambridge, Mass.: Harvard University Press, 1974.

CHAPTER 33

THE BALANCE OF PAYMENTS

In the last chapter we discussed trade between nations pretty much in physical terms—that is, in terms of the exchange of real goods and services. It is this exchange of real goods and services that is important in determining people's consumption and living standards. But these physical transactions also have a financial side, which we shall consider in this chapter.

One of the main distinguishing—and complicating—features of international trade is that each nation has its own money. What happens when a French firm decides to buy Canadian newsprint? The French company earns money in the form of *francs*, but the Canadian paper manufacturer wants to be paid in money in the form of *dollars*. How does the French firm get dollars to pay for the goods it wants?

Or take the case of a Canadian who wants to buy a transistor radio made in Japan. The Canadian's money is in the form of dollars, but the Japanese radio manufacturer has to pay his workers and buy his equipment with yen. How does the Canadian (or the department store that sells the radio) get the yen needed to pay the Japanese manufacturer?

A superficial answer to these questions might be: "They go to a bank and trade their domestic money for foreign money." But how is it that the banks have foreign money to trade for domestic money? And what determines the rate at which francs can be traded for dollars or dollars for yen? The answers to these questions depend on *the balance of payments between nations*. Let us look first at the concept of exchange rates in more detail.

■ THE MEANING OF EXCHANGE RATES

There are several different ways that people, business firms, or the government of one country can get foreign money from other countries. They can sell goods and services to foreigners; they can receive interest and dividend payments on past loans and investments made in foreign countries; they can borrow or receive outright gifts from foreigners. All of these things bring in foreign money or foreign exchange.

Likewise, there are several ways in which the people, business firms, or the government of a country can make their currency available to other countries. They can buy goods and services produced in other countries; they can pay interest and dividends on past loans and investments received from foreigners; they can lend money to foreigners; or they can give them outright gifts and grants. All of these things make one country's money available to others and give them foreign exchange.

Most foreign exchange is deposited in various banks throughout the world. These banks keep balances in different national currencies to finance the exchange of real goods and services between nations. The French firm, which wants to buy the Canadian paper, deposits its francs and takes out dollars. The Canadian, who wants to buy a Japanese radio, deposits dollars and takes out yen, and so on. If, over a period of time, the banks find that they receive about five times as many francs as they do dollars, this tends to establish an *exchange rate* of 1 dollar to 5 francs. Or stated in the other way round, 1 franc equals 20 cents. If banks receive 100 times as many yen as they do dollars, this tends to establish an *exchange rate* of 1 dollar to 100 yen. Or, 1 yen equals 1 cent. An **exchange rate**, therefore, is the value of one country's currency in terms of another country's currency. Usually the exchange rate is quoted in terms of the domestic price of one unit of foreign currency, such as 1 franc equals 20 cents, 1 yen equals 1 cent, and so on.

Various methods of establishing exchange rates have been used at different times in the world. The most important cases to consider are: (1) free or floating exchange rates based on the free market supply and demand for different currencies, (2) fixed or stable exchange rates based on a gold standard and (3) regulated exchange rates based on some set of rules and controls created by the governments of the nations in the world.

FREE MARKET EXCHANGE RATES

In a completely free market, foreign exchange rates would move up and down in response to changes in basic supply and demand conditions in international money markets. Let us consider an example of dollars and francs, based on the supply and demand curves in Figures 33-1 and 33-2. Canadian consumers' demand for French clothes and vacations on the Riviera, Canadian business firms' desire to open sales offices in Paris, and the Canadian government's desire to pay Canadian personnel stationed in France in the kind of currency they can spend in the local grocery stores and cafes,

FIGS. 33-1 and 33-2. CANADIAN AND FRENCH EXCHANGE RATES

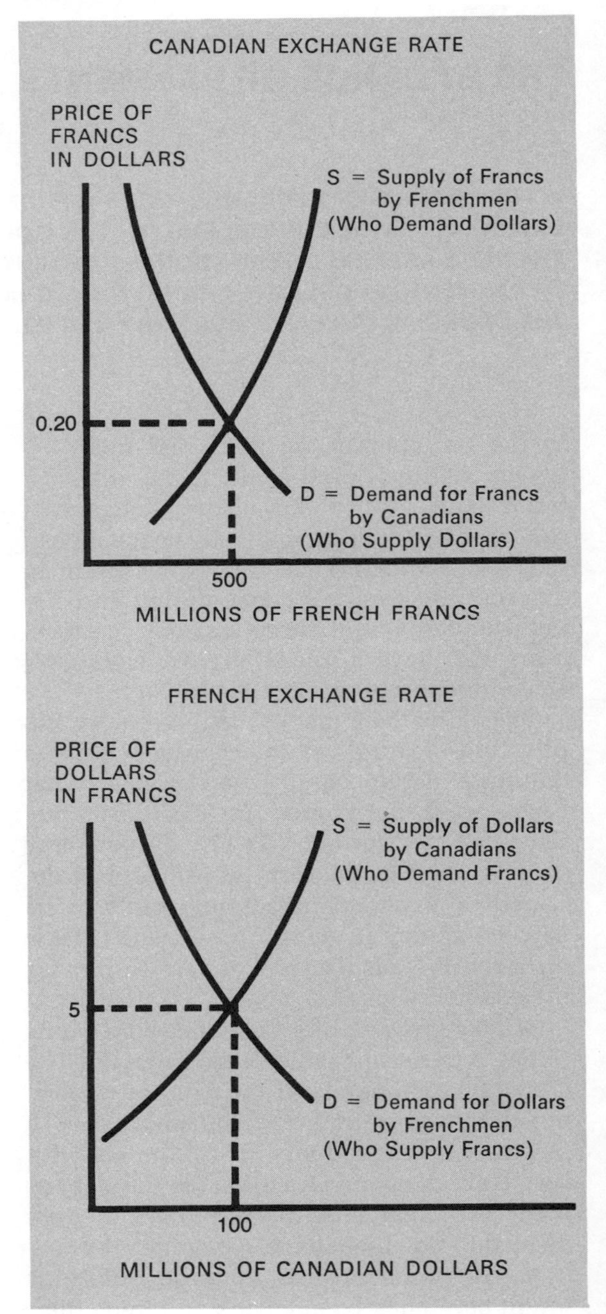

all create a demand for francs needed to pay the Frenchmen who provide these goods and services. In return Canadians must give up dollars. Likewise, Frenchmen who want to buy Canadian paper, see Quebec City, or open sales offices in Montreal, create a demand for dollars and a supply of francs.

The black curves in Figures 33-1 and 33-2 illustrate how these supply and demand conditions set up a Canadian exchange rate of 20 cents for 1 franc and a French exchange rate of 5 francs for 1 dollar. These are **equilibrium rates**. At these rates the 500 million francs that Frenchmen want to trade for dollars is exactly balanced by 100 million dollars that Canadians want to trade for francs. But what if these supply and demand conditions change?

The colored curves in Figures 33-1 and 33-2 indicate the results of an increase in the demand for francs (and an increase in the supply of dollars) by Canadians. If Canadians now want more francs than Frenchmen are willing to supply at the old equilibrium price, the dollar price of francs (the Canadian exchange rate) will be bid up. And, if Canadians are now willing to supply more dollars than Frenchmen are willing to buy at the old equilibrium price, then the franc price of dollars (the French exchange rate) will be driven down.[1] If the Canadian exchange rate moves up to 25 cents for a franc as shown in Figure 33-1, and the French exchange rate moves down to 4 francs for 1 dollar, as shown in Figure 33-2, a new equilibrium price is established in which 512 million francs are now traded for 128 million dollars.

There is much to be said for flexible exchange rates. They *automatically* keep the balance of payments between countries in equilibrium, so that the supply of different currencies is always equal to the demand for them. But freely floating exchange rates also have some disadvantages. If exchange rates go up and down by large amounts very often, international trade is much more risky, for these conditions might discourage traders and reduce the total volume of international trade.

How would you feel about going on a vacation in France if you had to live with uncertainty about the rate at which you could convert your dollars into francs? Suppose that the rate was 1 franc to 20 cents when you left for France; how would you feel if, by the time your plane got there, it had changed to 1 franc to 25 cents or 1 franc to 15 cents? Do you think the possibility of frequently changing exchange rates would encourage you or discourage you from taking your vacation in France, as opposed to taking it in Canada? What if you were an importer or exporter, how would you feel about freely floating exchange rates?[2]

GOLD STANDARD EXCHANGE RATES

Under the gold standard that prevailed throughout much of the world prior to the 1930s, each nation set a rate at which its currency could be converted into gold. Then it stood ready to buy and sell gold at this rate to any and all comers. These gold rates, then, set up stable exchange rates between different currencies. For, if Canada set its gold rate at 1 dollar an ounce, for example, and France set its gold rate at 5 francs to an ounce, then an ounce of gold could be bought and sold for either 1 dollar or 5 francs. And it can be seen that, ignoring the cost of shipping gold, this would ensure a

[1] In technical terms, it can be said that the dollar *depreciates* when the Canadian exchange rate (the dollar price of francs) rises. And it can be said that the franc *appreciates* when the French exchange rate (the franc price of dollars) falls. Under these conditions it takes more dollars to get a franc, and French goods become more expensive for Canadians. Likewise, it now takes fewer francs to get a dollar, and Canadian goods become cheaper for Frenchmen.

[2] Advanced texts discuss the possibility of hedging on the risk of rate changes by buying or selling in the *futures market* for foreign exchange. Hedging is a means of cancelling out a risk by betting on both sides at the same time. Thus, if you had placed a bet at even-money odds on the Montreal Canadiens to beat the Toronto Maple Leafs in a Stanley Cup Series and then grew nervous about your gamble, you could hedge your bet by putting an equal sum on Toronto at the same odds. No matter which team won you would lose (or gain) nothing. Similarly, you can hedge against the possibility of an exchange rate change by buying foreign exchange in the futures market.

stable exchange rate between the franc and the dollar of 1 dollar to 5 francs or 1 franc to 20 cents. If the exchange rate ever changed from the rate fixed by the gold standard, people would cease trading in foreign exchange and would instead ship gold to finance international trade.[3]

The stability of exchange rates under the gold standard eliminated uncertainty about the price of foreign currency. As long as the fixed rates were close to what the exchange rates would have been in a free market, adjustments were fairly easy to make, and there were few major problems.

Under this system, a country that found its currency slightly overvalued at the fixed rate would start to lose gold. Since its domestic money supply was closely tied to its gold stock under the gold standard, the loss of gold would tend to reduce its money supply, cut domestic demand, increase domestic unemployment, and hold down or maybe even reduce the domestic price level. These adjustments, in turn, would tend to reduce the country's demand for imports and to increase other countries' demand for its exports. With a reduced demand for foreign exchange and an increased supply of foreign exchange, these adjustments would then tend to increase the value of its currency in international money markets and stop the gold flow once the actual exchange rate was brought in line with the rate fixed by the gold standard. This process is illustrated graphically in Figure 33-3, which begins by assuming that the Canadian exchange rate for francs (22 cents) is higher than the rate fixed by the gold standard (20 cents).

FIG. 33-3. CANADIAN EXCHANGE RATE UNDER THE GOLD STANDARD WHEN THE DOLLAR IS INITIALLY OVERVALUED IN RELATION TO THE FRANC

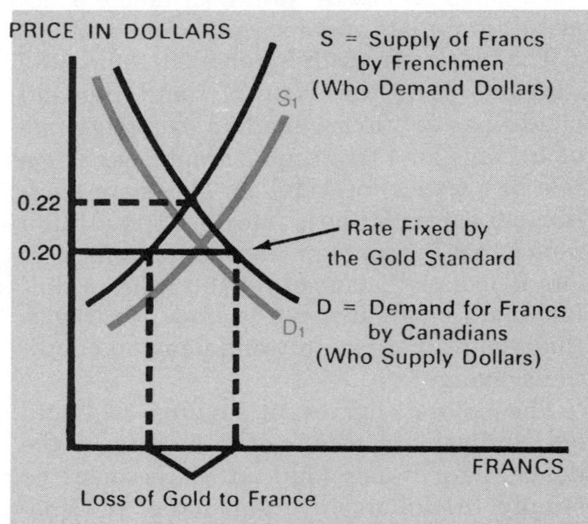

Canadian loss of gold to France reduced the money supply in Canada. This leads to reduced demand, increased unemployment, and stable or falling prices in Canada. This reduces Canadian demand for French goods and for francs (D_1). It also increases the French demand for Canadian goods and the supply of francs in Canada (S_1). The process continues until an equilibrium is established at the rate fixed by the gold standard, and no further gold movements are required.

Likewise, a country that found its currency undervalued at the exchange rate fixed by the gold standard would find itself gaining gold. If the influx of gold increased the domestic money supply, this would lead to an increase in demand, an increase in domestic employment, and perhaps an increase in the domestic price level. These factors would tend to increase the country's demand for imports and for foreign exchange and to reduce other countries' demand for its exports and its supply of foreign exchange. These adjustments, then, would eventually lead to a decline in the value of its currency until the actual exchange rate was again brought in line with the fixed rate established by the gold standard. This process is illustrated graphically in Figure 33-4, which begins by assuming that the Ca-

[3] In practice the exchange rate might vary within very narrow limits set by the cost of shipping gold. But, for simplicity, let us ignore shipping costs and assume that gold could be sent between countries at no cost. Under these conditions, the Canadian exchange rate would never rise above 20 cents a franc. If it did, no one would trade francs for dollars at this rate. Instead they would sell their dollars in Canada for gold, ship the gold to France, and then sell the gold for francs. They would get more francs this way than if they traded currency at an exchange rate above the rate of 20 cents a franc. Likewise, at Canadian exchange rates below 20 cents a franc it would pay to ship gold to Canada.

FIG. 33-4. CANADIAN EXCHANGE RATE UNDER THE GOLD STANDARD WHEN THE DOLLAR IS INITIALLY UNDERVALUED IN RELATION TO THE FRANC

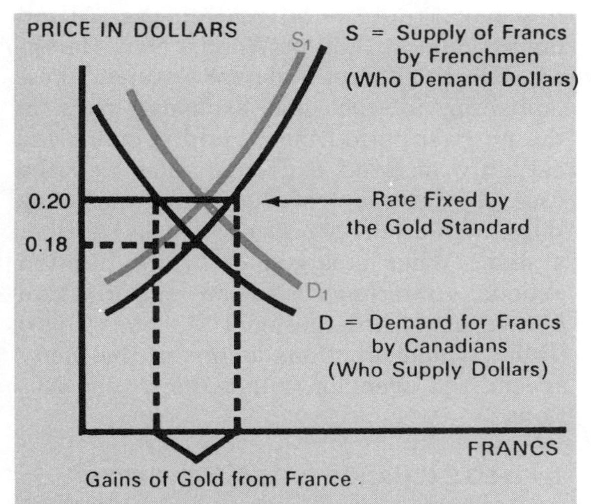

The gold shipped from France to Canada increases Canadian money supply under the gold standard. This leads to increased demand, increased employment and rising prices in Canada. This increases Canadian demand for French goods and for francs (D_1). It also reduces the French demand for Canadian goods and the supply of francs in Canada (S_1). The process continues until an equilibrium is established at the rate fixed by the gold standard, and no further gold movements are required.

nadian exchange rate for francs (18 cents) is lower than the rate fixed by the gold standard (20 cents).[4]

PROBLEMS OF THE GOLD STANDARD

Prior to World War I, the adjustments required to keep the fixed exchange rates set by the gold standard were not very great. But after different countries experienced different rates of inflation and economic disruption during that conflict, the postwar attempts to return to the pre-World War I gold standard in international trade failed completely. Then the stability of fixed exchange rates became like the stability of a straitjacket, imposing severe requirements on the domestic monetary policy of many nations in the world. These nations were plagued with internal economic problems, and they wanted to pursue an independent monetary policy. They did not want to base their domestic monetary decisions on the flow of gold in international payments. Countries receiving gold did not want to have domestic inflation just to preserve stable exchange rates, and countries losing large amounts of gold did not want to pay the severe cost of deflation and unemployment that was necessary if stable exchange rates were to be preserved under the rules of the game imposed by the international gold standard.

Matters were further complicated by the fact that, during the world-wide depression of the 1930s, there was no widespread understanding of how domestic monetary and fiscal policies could be used to combat domestic unemployment. Instead, one nation after another adopted trade policies that tried, in effect, to ship the domestic unemployment abroad to other countries by increasing its own exports and reducing its own imports. Tariffs were raised; import quotas were adopted; and countries devalued their currencies by changing the rates at which they would buy and sell gold.

The dollar would be *devalued* if the dollar price of an ounce of gold were increased from 1 dollar an ounce to 2 dollars an ounce. Each dollar would then buy less gold than it used to. If the gold rates of other currencies do not change, a country can make its exports cheaper and its imports more expensive by devaluing its currency.

If you can still get 5 francs for an ounce of gold, for example, and it takes 2 dollars to get an ounce of gold after devaluation, the exchange rate between dollars and francs would become 1 dollar to 2.5 francs or 1

[4] Orthodox gold standard systems also permitted free internal conversion of paper money into gold and vice versa. A gold standard thus regulated the domestic money supply. Problems associated with this, with trade flows and exchange rates compounded by the flow of much of the world's gold to the U.S.A. during and after World War I, brought an effective end to this system by the 1920s.

UPI

The basic plan for the postwar international financial system was hammered out at a monetary conference held at Bretton Woods, New Hampshire, in 1944. Here is a session in progress at the Mount Washington Hotel. Out of this conference emerged the International Monetary Fund and the International Bank for Reconstruction and Development.

franc to 40 cents. This would encourage Canadian exports to France and discourage Canadian imports from France compared to the old exchange rates of 1 dollar to 5 francs or 1 franc to 20 cents.

If only one country had devalued its currency under the gold standard, it might have succeeded in reducing domestic unemployment by increasing its exports and reducing its imports. But one country's exports are another country's imports, and every nation cannot increase its exports and decrease its imports by devaluing its currency at the same time, as the experience of the 1930s sadly demonstrated. As soon as one country would devalue its currency, others would follow suit in round after round of competitive devaluations that did little more than aggravate already worsening international tensions. Many countries abandoned the gold standard completely before the flames of World War II engulfed the world.

As World War II was drawing to a close, however, representatives of the Allied Powers met at Bretton Woods, New Hampshire, in an attempt to devise a system of establishing international exchange rates in the postwar period that would combine the certainty of fixed exchange rates and the ease of adjustment of fluctuating exchange rates, without the big disadvantages of either system. What emerged from the Bretton Woods conference was an organization known as the International Monetary Fund (IMF), which functions as one of the many specialized agencies within the United Nations.

FIXED EXCHANGE RATES AND THE IMF

The International Monetary Fund was established as an **exchange stabilization fund** designed to provide stable exchange rates along with reasonable flexibility in providing orderly adjustments if changes in existing rates become necessary. The system initially worked like this:

Each nation joining the fund selected a *par value*[5] for its currency in terms of gold, and gave the fund a supply of its own currency and gold reserves. The amount which each nation paid into the fund was set by a formula based on its national income and the volume of its international trade. The par values set up exchange rates very much like those under the old gold standard, but there was no need for a country to go through the cumbersome adjustment process required under the old gold standard if its currency *temporarily* changed in value.

If a currency was temporarily declining in value, the IMF loaned funds from its members' reserves to buy the currency and hold its price up. Likewise, if a currency was temporarily rising in value, the IMF could

[5] Within this system the market price could fluctuate within $\pm 1\%$ of the par value. This was the case for the Canadian dollar while it was pegged at $.925 U.S. during the period 1961-1970.

sell some of this currency from its reserves and help hold its price down. But the fund could stabilize exchange rates only if the changes were temporary. If there was a *fundamental disequilibrium*, even a large stabilization fund would eventually end up holding only weak currencies and find its supply of strong currencies exhausted. The term **fundamental disequilibrium** means that, at the existing exchange rate between a country's currency and the currencies of other nations, a country could never bring its payments to other countries into balance with its receipts from other countries. In such cases, the IMF abandoned its efforts to use its reserve funds to stabilize the existing exchange rate of a nation in trouble and permitted the official par value of its currency to be changed, according to previously agreed procedures.

Changes in par values of currencies under the IMF were relatively few, and they did not set off the rounds of competitive devaluations that were common before World War II. Several countries still resorted to their own forms of restrictive **exchange control** (that is, regulating which businesses and individuals may exchange the nation's currency for foreign currencies held by the nation's central bank—and in what amounts). Some countries changed the par value of their currencies without going through the official channels prescribed by the IMF. But, in general, the system of semi-stable, semi-flexible exchange rates worked reasonably well for over twenty-five years. In the 1970s, however, a combination of new problems, plus several old ones which had been growing steadily, forced a number of major changes in the international monetary system.

KEEPING INTERNATIONAL PAYMENTS IN BALANCE

However they are determined, the main function of exchange rates is to keep the payments between different nations in balance, so that all nations can achieve the maximum benefits from specialization and trade.

Table 33-1. A MODEL BALANCE OF PAYMENTS ACCOUNT

Item	Receipts	Expenditures	Totals
Exports	45.0		
Imports		42.0	+3.0
Balance on Merchandise Trade			+3.0
Tourist Account	2.0	3.5	−1.5
Interest and Dividends	.5	4.5	−4.0
Freight and Shipping	2.0	2.0	0
Other Current Items	4.0	6.0	−2.0
Balance on Non-Merchandise Trade			−7.5
Balance on Current Account			−4.5
Long Term Capital Account	+7.0	−2.5	+4.5
Short Term Capital Account	+2.0	−1.5	+0.5
Balance on Capital Account			+5.0
Unallocated Items			−2.0
Balance of Payments			−1.5

This is a grossly simplified account, but it indicates the basic structure. All that is needed to convert the model to reality is additional detail. The relative ratios are roughly those of Canada's 1977 accounts. The actual data for Canada are roughly these figures in billions of dollars. See Table 33-2.

The **balance of payments** of each nation is a statistical record of all the transactions which the individuals, businesses, and government of a nation have with the rest of the world during a year. The balance of payments thus records all outflows of the nation's money and all inflows of foreign money (foreign exchange).

If, during a given year, the individuals, businesses, and government of a nation spend more money abroad than they receive from foreign countries, that nation is said to have a balance of payments *deficit*. To finance the deficit, the nation will have to use up some of its foreign exchange holdings; or it may have to borrow money from other countries or from the IMF to cover the deficit; or it will have to sell gold that it owns to get the foreign exchange it requires to pay its debts.

Similarly, if during a given year, the individuals, businesses, and government of a nation pay out less of their money abroad than foreigners pay to them, that nation is said to have a balance of payments *surplus*. Through this surplus, the nation may accumulate the foreign exchange of other countries—or it may decide to buy gold from foreign central banks to cover the surplus.

Ideally, exchange rates in all nations of the world should be set so that different nations' international accounts balance without having to resort to very large shifts of holdings of any form of foreign exchange or gold in one direction. But in recent years, this goal has not been easy to attain. This has been due to the deficits of the United States in international trade and payments, and more recently to massive trade surpluses being achieved by some nations.

THE UNITED STATES BALANCE OF PAYMENTS PROBLEM

During the period 1914-1945, the United States accumulated a vast amount of the world's gold stock, in part as a result of surpluses from normal trade, but in major part as a result of payments for goods and services and repayments of loans during the wars and the post-World War I era.

At the end of World War II, in which the U.S. economy had to a high degree escaped the ravages of war while most others had not, other nations' demand for American goods was far beyond their ability to earn the American dollars needed to buy American goods—and their gold stocks had already been depleted. Throughout the world there was talk of a dollar shortage. Despite massive United States government loans and private investments abroad, the United States balance of payments continued to show a surplus—and it went on accumulating more of the world's gold until 1950.

After 1950 the United States began to run a persistent deficit in its balance of payments. For a while this deficit proved very useful in stimulating world trade because it began to redistribute the gold reserves that had accumulated in the United States. This strengthened the trading position of other countries, permitting them to relax trade restrictions and exchange controls.

But even a country as powerful as the United States cannot run a deficit in its balance of payments forever. If the deficit continued, eventually the vast stock of gold of the United States would be exhausted.[6] People throughout the world would lose confidence in the dollar, and world trade and foreign investment might be severely affected. As a result of the persistent deficits in the United States balance of payments from 1950 on, the United States gold supply had fallen from $24.5 billion in 1949 to less than $12 billion in the spring of 1967. These deficits continued to cause gold losses and caused a severe financial crisis in 1968, which started to undermine the international monetary system which had come out of the Bretton Woods conference.

How was the United States to stop its persistent balance of payments deficits? Should it consider changing the exchange rate between the dollar and other currencies—that is, devaluing the dollar, which would mean increasing the price of gold from its set value of $35 per ounce to some higher figure, such as $50 per ounce? When France was plagued by big balance of payments deficits in the years prior to 1958, it convinced the IMF that this was due to a fundamental disequilibrium, and it devalued the franc. This devaluation, and the subsequent changes in world exchange rates, made French exports cheaper to the rest of the world and made imports more expensive to Frenchmen and French businesses. The stimulus to French exports and curb to French imports thus stopped for a time the deficit in France's bal-

[6] An additional complication was that until March, 1968, the U.S. was obligated to have $1.00 in gold for every $4.00 of its paper money. At that time the requirement was abandoned.

THE BALANCE OF PAYMENTS

Alcan Products Canada Limited

Bank of Canada

How would each of these items fit into Table 33-1? Top left shows ore mined in Guinea for export to Canada. The mining and transportation equipment was installed with Canadian capital. Top right shows, hypothetically, recent gold acquisitions of the Bank of Canada. Lower left shows a number of CP Air planes at Vancouver. Assume the 747 in the foreground is departing for Tokyo with both Canadian and American passengers. Lower right shows Canadian troops on a NATO exercise in Germany.

CP Air

Canadian Forces Photo

ance of payments. (In 1969, however, the franc had to be devalued again.)

Similarly, in 1967, Great Britain found itself in serious international financial difficulties. Speculators believed that the British pound was overvalued at a rate of $2.80. They thought that Britain could not succeed in getting its balance of payments back into equilibrium—especially after a serious strike by the dock workers' union greatly worsened the trade deficit in the late summer and fall of 1967. As speculators, other businessmen, and official holders of sterling sensed that a devaluation of the pound was approaching, they began to convert their holdings of British pounds into gold in the London gold market. Britain did not have sufficient gold reserves to meet these heavy demands, and it had already borrowed heavily from other governments. So, on November 18, 1967, the British government, headed by Prime Minister Harold Wilson, cut the exchange rate of the pound from $2.80 to $2.40, a devaluation of 14.3 percent, as a means of cutting back imports (by making them more expensive) and stimulating exports (by making them cheaper), in order to restore equilibrium in the British balance of payments.

Why did the United States resist following the French and British examples and devalue the dollar? The answer is that the dollar had become the principal **reserve currency** in the world. World trade had expanded much more rapidly in recent years than had the world's gold supply. Therefore, many nations had been using dollars, as well as gold, to settle their international accounts. In effect, the dollar took the role of gold, and was regarded as being as good as gold. The U.S. did not want to shake the world's confidence in its money by a devaluation. Further, if the United States devalued the dollar, it would greatly reduce the reserves of many nations, and most people feel that this would create a more serious problem than the continuing deficit in the United States balance of payments.

Watch Out, Harold!

This cartoon, which appeared on Nov. 16, 1967, indicates the precarious position of the pound. The balancing act did not work. Three days later, on Nov. 19, Prime Minister Wilson devalued the pound.

Further, there was no assurance that a devaluation would get at the real causes of American deficits. The United States consistently showed a sizable surplus in its merchandise exports over its merchandise imports. If, through a devaluation, the United States were to make its goods still cheaper relative to those of other countries, in order to make its trade surplus still larger, it might find that other countries would simply raise tariffs or other artificial trade barriers against its exports. Or the United States might cause them to devalue their own currencies in order to protect their own balance of payments, and the United States would be no better off than it was in the first place. Indeed, all countries might be worse off if a

United States devaluation were to touch off a round of competitive devaluations, such as disturbed the world in the 1930s.

Much of the drain in the American payments situation came from the outflow of funds in foreign investment, aid and military expenditures. An easing of world tensions might permit a significant scaling down of that part of the deficit resulting from United States military programs overseas. A larger effort on the part of other countries to participate in foreign aid programs might reduce some of the American burden in that area. The United States might also curb its investment abroad. Voluntary programs between the United States government and business restrained the growth of private foreign investment after 1965. In 1968, these controls became compulsory for a time. Some interim measures were also to take place to reduce foreign lending by American banks and to discourage travel abroad by Americans.

The things which might have helped the U.S. payments problem didn't materialize. In fact, things were to get worse. At the same time, rigid controls which might have been used were opposed by many people in the U.S. and not put into place.

As observers watched the decade of the sixties advance without a solution to the U.S. payments problem, many economists feared a liquidity crisis in international trade unless new financial arrangements were created among the world's trading nations.

The growth of United States dollars as an international reserve and payments medium had been necessary to supplement the slow growth of the world's gold supply. Therefore, a shutting off of the supply of dollars—to end American balance of payments deficits—would check the growth of the international money supply. This could cause a stagnation in world trade. It might also lead more and more countries to resort to restrictive trade practices, thereby preventing nations from enjoying the real benefits of international specialization in terms of total output and total income. The result was the first of a number of monetary changes after 1967.

CHANGES IN THE INTERNATIONAL SYSTEM

In 1967 the member nations of the International Monetary Fund moved to create a new form of international money to bolster the world's monetary reserves and thereby prevent a stagnation of world trade and payments. The new medium was called a Special Drawing Right (SDR), because it would give nations the right to draw a limited amount of specially-created "paper gold" from the IMF.

In essence, the SDR is money created out of thin air, existing solely on the books of the IMF and member countries. It is used alongside the present world stock of gold, dollars, and pounds that central banks use as reserves to support their currencies and settle their accounts with each other. By expanding the total supply of such assets, the SDR could help eliminate not only the potential danger of a slowdown in international trade but even of a world depression of the kind touched off in the 1930s when nations began competing for scarce reserves and the gold standard collapsed.

Under the London agreement, the IMF could create any amount of Special Drawing Rights that the member nations agreed was needed to increase world reserves. Financial officers of the leading countries considered that initially a pool of $5 billion of SDRs would be created for a five-year period. The SDRs were distributed to IMF members in proportion to their quotas in IMF, that is the members' contributions to IMF's $21 billion pool of gold and currencies. The United States is the biggest contributor, with 24.6 percent of the total quotas. Thus, it got $246 million of every $1 billion in SDRs created. Canada's share of the first $9.5 billion was about $330 million.

SDRs are exchanged only between central

'Paper Gold' Boon To World Traders

The following editorial from The Vancouver Sun *points out the background to SDRs and optimism generated by their creation.*

Creating a new currency is not something done every day. When the International Monetary Fund launched its "paper gold," or special drawing rights, it did something never before done in history. It created a new kind of money—international money whose backing consists solely in the belief of governments in each other's responsibility.

The member-nations of the IMF have thus made a revolution—and something more.

They have in a sense created a world government, or at least a system of collective security in trade and finance which will in time affect all the nations, including those of the Communist bloc which do not now belong to the Fund.

Ordinary men and women should reflect on this, that here we have a group of men representing their governments it is true, but able to act largely on their own, who are placed in a position to inflate or deflate the world's economy as they see fit.

This too is something new in the world. The most patient efforts of great nations to create collective security in military and political matters have failed or been of doubtful success. But here we have an effort to create collective security in the economic sphere that shows signs of becoming a tremendous success.

To most people the new special drawing rights, or paper gold, is a mystery wrapped in an enigma. It is in fact a system of bookkeeping. No money exists except in the good faith of the member countries of IMF. The nations participating are given a quota of reserve "currency" on the books, in proportion, more or less, to the amount of real assets they have subscribed to the Fund.

Why is it necessary? Because for years world trade had been growing faster than a reliable reserve currency to settle international trading debts. Traditionally, gold has been used for this purpose. But gold as a percentage of total world monetary reserves has been on a declining curve for years. Experts fear these reserves cannot keep up with trade growth and as a result will cramp it.

In a sense, therefore, SDRs are a form of credit nations extend to each other.

The large element of faith on which the system will rest has skeptics shaking their heads. It will never work, they say.

Yet, 18 months ago, when speculation on the world's gold markets caused a desperate monetary situation, the world's central banks (that is, the Western world's) in desperation adopted the two-tier gold price system under which it was agreed that gold held in government reserves would not be sold on the open market at the handsome profits then possible, but should be used only to effect transfers between governments at the official price of $35 U.S. per ounce.

The same skepticism was voiced then. Governments would be unable to resist the attractive prices on the free gold markets. However, with very few exceptions, they have resisted. The two-tier system, intended to be only a holding operation until SDRs came into existence, has been a triumph.

It worked because most of the nations kept faith and in this world of chaotic international relations and failed hopes, that is something to cheer about.

It means, for one thing, that the world's economy has not broken down.

There is no automatic guarantee, of course, that it will not break down in the future. It could do so if great nations like France and Britain fail to put their economic houses in order and keep franc and pound on a healthy basis. There is renewed hope, however, from Bonn, Paris and London to Washington and Ottawa, that sounder fiscal and financial management will make this easier.

Being cost-free, SDRs should make possible substantial savings in real resources for the international community. It has been suggested in some quarters that these savings could be useful in the fight against poverty and stagnation in the underdeveloped countries if they were channelled through an agency such as the World Bank-affiliated International Development Association.

Significantly, it was to this association in effect that Lester Pearson's commission on economic development made its dramatic report. The burden of that report was that rich nations must do much more to help the poor ones in the 1970s.

SDRs will make the rich richer. They will in fact, make it that much easier for them to follow Mr. Pearson's pointing finger. If the poor nations cannot benefit directly, let them benefit indirectly.

Reprinted from *The Vancouver Sun,* October 6, 1969, with permission.

banks. They can be used by countries to buy back their own currencies from foreign nations that have accumulated them. For Canada, this means that the Bank of Canada can exchange SDRs for dollars turned in by participating foreign countries, or use them to buy foreign exchange.

The London agreement declared that the new plan could be "activated" only after an 85 percent majority of the votes of member nations was cast in favor of creating a pool of SDRs. The degree of agreement, reached in the fall of 1969, set up \$3.5 billion in SDRs on Jan. 1, 1970, and a further \$6 billion in 1971 and 1972.

The new scheme has opened up the opportunity for long-term stable growth of the world's monetary reserves. The agreement among the nations to supplement gold, dollars, and pounds with a created international reserve unit and to plan a steady increase in the total stock of world monetary reserves is truly revolutionary. Final approval of the plan in late 1969 was a landmark in international monetary history.

The new SDR system provided a solution to the potential shortage of international reserves on a world-wide basis. It could do nothing, however, about the pressures which were mounting to weaken the system of fixed exchange rates. A system of fixed rates, as we have seen, depends on general stability in the flows of payments of major nations. The decade of the 1970s saw more and more instability, a trend toward fundamental disequilibrium in the payments accounts of a number of important countries, most notably in the payments position of the United States.

In 1971, a series of crises finally produced a new set of agreements, the so-called "Smithsonian Agreements," within the International Monetary Fund. The United States formally devalued its dollar through an increase in the official price of gold. The United States also suspended its obligation to redeem U.S. dollars from foreign central banks with gold from its reserves. A number of strong currencies were increased in their official values. Finally, to permit more short-run flexibility in the system, the old provision of a ± 1% range within which a currency could move was replaced by a new and enlarged fluctuation band of ±4½%. These alterations, it was hoped, would permit a return to general stability and end the

Collins in The Montreal Gazette

Layman's guide to the floating currency situation.

upward and downward pressures in currency markets. Such proved to be far from the case.

Payments problems continued. Speculation in currencies continued and the crises continued. In little over a year, the Smithsonian system of new fixed rates was, in effect, abandoned. The U.S. dollar was devalued by a further 10%. The British pound and a number of other currencies were "floated," that is, official or fixed rates were abandoned. The European Economic Community tried to keep its members' currencies fixed in relation to each other while floating in relation to other currencies, but had to abandon this plan. Then in 1973, with the OPEC action which led to massive hikes in oil prices, further payments instabilities appeared as billions of dollars flowed out of the hands of oil importers into those of the oil-producing states. By 1975, the old Bretton Woods system with its Smithsonian patchwork was as dead as the proverbial doornail. The exchange rate structure for the worlds' major currencies had reverted to a floating rate system with values being determined by the flows of balance of payments accounts. In 1976, the IMF formally recognized the floating rates as being a permanent situation—at least until such time as payments flows moved toward some degree of equilibrium.

The latter half of the 1970s has seen little sign of any such move. Some nations such as the U.S. have continued to run large deficits and the U.S. dollar has fallen sharply in relation to most currencies. Other nations, most notably large oil exporters, Japan, Germany and Switzerland, have experienced large surpluses and their currencies have risen in value.[7] In the wake of uncertainty about exchange rates and inflationary pressures which have cut into the domestic purchasing power of most currencies, the speculative and investment demand for gold has increased and the free market price of gold has soared. Priced at under $60.00 per oz. in 1972, the value of gold had reached $250.00 per oz. by 1979.

For the foreseeable future, little change in the situation seems likely. Continued wide swings in payments balances seem likely to continue. Given this, no movement away from floating rates will be possible and currency "crises" under the pressure of market forces can be expected to continue as exchange rates move up and down. Canada, as our experience in the period 1975-1978 has shown, has no reason to expect to be isolated from these storms, which will continue in the realm of international finance.

[7] See Table 33-3 for one perspective on exchange rates during the period 1976-1978.

Table 33-2 CANADA'S BALANCE OF PAYMENTS, 1965-1979

Millions of Dollars, Surplus/Deficit Postion of Various Accounts

Year	Merchandise Trade	Non-Merchandise Trade	Current Account	Capital Account	Final Balance
1965	+118	−1248	−1130	+1288	+158
1966	+224	−1386	−1162	+803	−359
1967	+566	−1055	−499	+519	+20
1968	+1471	−1568	−97	+446	+349
1969	+964	−1881	−917	+982	+65
1970	+3052	−1946	+1106	+424	+1663[1]
1971	+2563	−2132	+431	+335	+885[1]
1972	+1857	−2243	−386	+605	+336[1]
1973	+2735	−2627	+108	−575	−467
1974	+1689	−3149	−1460	+1484	+24
1975	−451	−4306	−4757	+4352	−405
1976	+1339	−5140	−3801	+4323	+522
1977[2]	+2916	−7066	−4150	+2729	−1421
1978[3]	+3700	−7900	−4200	+1300	−2900

Notes: [1] Final balance is affected by acquisition of SBR credits; hence this year-end figure is not equal to the product of the current and capital account balances.
[2] 1977 data are preliminary and subject to revision.
[3] 1978 data are author's projections based on first nine months preliminary data.
Source: Statistics Canada, *Quarterly Estimates of the Canadian Balance of International Payments,* cat. 67-001, various issues, 1966-1978.

UPS AND DOWNS FOR THE CANADIAN DOLLAR

As we have observed, a country's exchange rate is ultimately determined by what is happening within its balance of payments account. If a floating rate system is in use, the impact of changes within the payments account will be seen quickly. If a fixed exchange rate exists, major changes in the payments flow will produce pressures which will eventually affect the exchange rate.

Let us first examine an example of the latter situation. Turn to the data in Table 33-2 and look at the final balances for the years 1966-1972. Recall that during this period (at least in the 1960s) the I.M.F.'s system of fixed rates was still in effect and Canada was a part of that system. With a pattern of moderate surpluses in 1967-69 inclusive, and then large surpluses in 1970 and 1971, we might expect there would have been upward pressure on the value of the Canadian dollar in relation to its fixed rate of $.925 U.S. in 1966. This pressure did develop and had an effect. After having greatly increased our holdings of foreign exchange, Canada in May, 1970, abandoned the fixed rate and permitted the dollar to "float," i.e., to have its value set by the forces of supply and demand. The value moved up from $.925 U.S. to $.99 U.S. by the end of 1970. During the next two years it continued to climb, peaking at $1.02 U.S. in mid-1972 before settling back to about parity with the U.S. dollar at the end of that year. What happened during that period is a good illustration of the types of pressures which were to undermine the system of fixed exchange rates on a worldwide basis. In fact, the Canadian dollar was the first major currency to adopt and maintain a floating rate as the old system gradually came apart.

Comparison of the 1970-1978 data in Table 33-2 with the 1970-1978 section of Figure 33-5 (page 456) should point out just how a floating rate system works. This should also indicate in a general way why

FIG. 33-5. CANADA'S EXCHANGE RATE TO THE U.S. DOLLAR, 1958-1978

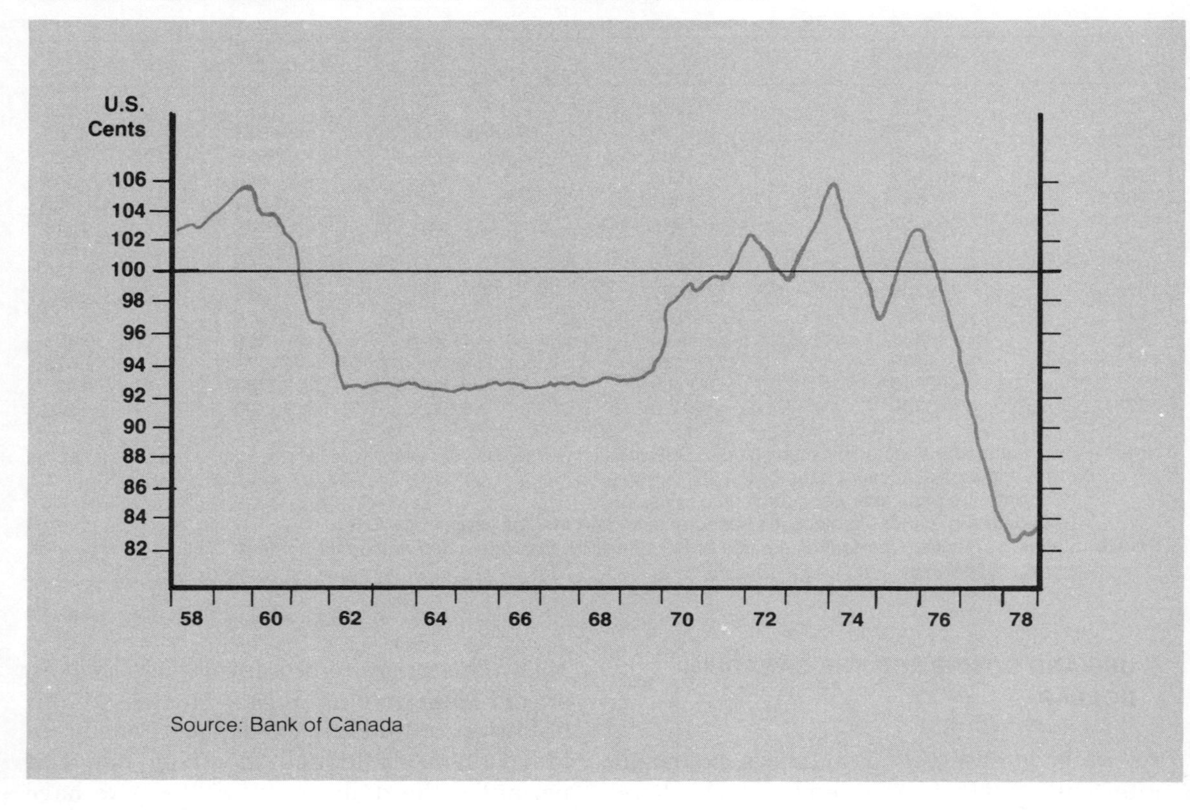

This figure shows our dollar's movement in relation to U.S. currency. A sharp slide took place in the late 50s when our dollar was floating, unlike most currencies. It was pegged at $.925 U.S. from 1961 to 1970. After 1970, it rose and then dropped to almost record lows. Since 1914, our dollar has been below $.85 on only two other occasions, in 1920-21 and then again in 1931-33.

the Canadian dollar fell as rapidly as it did between 1976 and 1978.

Before examining the 1976-1978 period in more detail, one point should be emphasized again to ensure clarity. Within a system where all currencies float in value, all exchange rates may change, but do not necessarily change by the same proportion. From Figure 33-5 we can see that the Canadian dollar dropped from about $1.02 U.S. in mid-1976 to about $.86 U.S. in mid-1978, a decline of roughly 16%. This can be rephrased to say that during this time period, the U.S. dollar increased in value by about 16% in relation to the Canadian dollar. Examine the data for 1976-1978 in Table 33-3 to compare this 16% gain by the U.S. dollar with the changes in some other currencies in relation to our own dollar.

Let us now turn to examine the 1976-1978 slide of the Canadian dollar more fully. Examining Table 33-2 in more detail, we can quickly spot some general trends. Canada has tended to run a surplus in merchandise trade, that is, in trade in goods. In only one year during the period 1965-1978 was such not the case. In non-merchandise trade, sometimes called the "service sector," we have consistently had deficits. These will be examined shortly. As a general rule, the non-

Table 33-3. EXCHANGE RATES FOR KEY CURRENCIES IN TERMS OF CANADIAN DOLLARS, 1968-1978

	Unit Value in Canadian Dollars					
Year	U.S. Dollar	British Pound	French Franc	German Mark	Swiss Franc	Japanese Yen
1968	$1.08	$2.58	.22	.27	.25	.003
1969	1.08	2.58	.21	.27	.25	.003
1970	1.04	2.50	.19	.29	.24	.003
1971	1.01	2.47	.18	.29	.25	.003
1972	.99	2.48	.20	.31	.26	.003
1973	1.00	2.45	.23	.38	.32	.004
1974	.98	2.29	.20	.38	.33	.003
1975	1.02	2.26	.24	.41	.39	.003
1976	.99	1.78	.21	.39	.40	.003
1977	1.06	1.86	.22	.46	.45	.004
1978	1.14	2.21	.26	.57	.68	.006

Note: Data for 1968-77 are average rates; data for 1978 are average rates during the month of August. All data have been rounded from original quotations, which are expressed at a minimum of four decimal places.
Source: Bank of Canada, *Monthly Review,* October, 1978

The table shows the cost of foreign currencies in terms of our dollar. For example, in 1968 it took $1.08 Canadian to buy $1.00 U.S. In 1974, $.98 Canadian would buy $1.00 U.S. In other words, the Canadian dollar was then worth 2% more. By mid-1978, the Canadian dollar dropped to a discount of 14% and we needed to pay $1.14 Canadian for $1.00 U.S. In other words, the Canadian dollar was then worth 2% more. By mid-1978, the Canadian dollar dropped to a discount of 14% and we needed to pay $1.14 Canadian for $1.00 U.S. Note the rise during 1976-78 in the German Mark, the Swiss Franc, and the Japanese Yen. How do the proportional increases of these three compare with the relative rise of the U.S. dollar against our own currency?

merchandise or service deficit has exceeded the merchandise surplus, producing a general pattern of "current account" deficits. Continuing with our generalizations, we can also see that we usually have a "capital account" surplus. Again, in the period 1965-1978, there was only one year where this was not the case. These capital account surpluses tend to be fairly close to the current account deficit[8] (though this is more often than not a coincidence).

Years when our final annual balances have been notably high or low have generally been the result of one of three things: an unusually high merchandise trade surplus such as in 1970-71, an abnormally large deficit in the service account, or a major drop in the inflow of capital (the latter two both occurred in 1977-78). In brief, we import a total of goods and services greater than we export, and we have depended on capital inflows to offset this and maintain the value of the Canadian dollar. But in 1977 and 1978, this did not happen.

During 1975 and the three years thereafter, our current account deficit was setting a new record each year. Various factors contributed to this, of which two were especially important and close to equally important in adding to the massive deficits in the service sector.

One of the problem areas is something which may well be familiar to you—foreign travel. The deficits in the travel and tourism account grew rapidly in the four problem years of 1975-1978. In prior years, 1969-1974 inclusive, the deficit in tourism had been fairly stable in the range of $200 million to $300 million. In 1975, the deficit increased to $727 million, in the following year it went over the billion dollar mark, and in 1977 reached $1.6 billion. During the winter re-

[8] An interesting observation might be made if you were to examine the cumulative totals of the current account and capital accounts for the period for which you have fairly accurate data, i.e. 1965-1977 inclusive. From that, compute the average current account deficit and average capital account surplus to see just how close we have been to long-run balance.

cesses of Parliament in 1977 and 1978, wry jokes made the rounds. On such sample of black humor went as follows:

Question: When is the Opposition going to get a policy statement from the government about the tourism deficits?

Answer: When the Opposition members get back from Florida and the Government members return from the Bahamas.

In reality, of course, many Canadians contributed to the rising deficit, for Canadians are among the most travel-hungry people in the world.

A look at the timing and direction of our overseas travel will show that the desire to gain brief escapes from our Canadian winters is a factor in this pattern. Perhaps you yourself or some member of your family has made a contribution to our rising tourism deficit in recent years.

In addition, not all of the problem can be attributed to more Canadians spending more money outside of Canada. The rate of growth in spending by foreign visitors, mostly from the United States, has slackened in recent years. The two forces combined, however, did contribute a deficit figure in 1977 which exceeded our final balance of payments deficit in that year.

During the same time period, a similar problem developed in the flow of interest and dividends, particularly in the realm of interest payments. As you should recall from Unit 4, levels of interest rates went up sharply during the decade of the 1970s. Also, Canada was paying a return on an ever-increasing level of foreign investments of various types. Between 1969 and 1974, unlike the tourist account deficit, the deficit on interest and dividends did increase, but not at an exceptional rate. It grew from $915 million in 1969 to $1.5 billion in 1974. In 1975 it reached $1.9 billion, the following year moved up to $2.4 billion, and in 1977 had reached $3.5 billion.

These two sectors contributed most of the increase in the growing current account deficit. But the current account situation does not tell the full story. After growth in the period 1973-1975, the capital account surplus contracted sharply in the period 1976-1978.

Several factors were at work here as well. One was certainly a general lag in investment which affected other countries as well as Canada. However, concern about rising inflationary pressures, problems with labor productivity, and lagging rates of growth have made Canada less attractive to potential private investors from outside Canada. Political factors have had effects as well. As will be seen in the Appendix to this chapter, the Canadian government has developed a process for monitoring new private foreign investment and in some cases may restrict new foreign investments. This can have psychological effects on would-be foreign investors, who may fear future extensions of government controls. A second political factor which had some effect was the victory of the Parti Quebeçois in the Quebec provincial election in 1976. The concern about the long-run stability of Canada which had started to spread outside our borders was not diminished by the P.Q. victory at the polls. For many, Canada, at least in the short term, is not regarded as a good place for investment.

In the capital account, as with the others, outflows are as important as inflows. In the capital sector, in addition to a slowdown in capital coming in, there has also been an increase in Canadian capital going out. Some of this marks expansion of Canadian firms into wider markets. Other examples mark more fundamental shifts. For example, some of our major nickel producers are moving resources to open new ore bodies outside of Canada while contracting operations in Canada. But capital moves at the behest of individuals, as well as corporations. Increasing numbers of Canadians are investing in real estate in more tropical climates and in the

Collins in The Montreal Gazette

This cartoon aptly summarizes the degree of economic interdependence in the world. Major changes in domestic economic conditions, flows of trade and investment, balances of payments and exchange rates are all forces which will spread their effects from one nation to another. Given the extremely high proportion of our GNP which comes from the international sector, Canadians should be especially conscious of economic trends on a world-wide basis.

southern United States. In many cases, this seems as much a reaction to our climate as anything else, but there is also some tentative evidence that some of the outflows may be strongly influenced by the mounting constitutional problems in Canada and the uncertainties about the political future.

The effect of all these shifts, inflows and outflows, both current account and capital account, was to produce increasingly large deficit figures in that last "final balance" column in Table 33-2. When that happens to a sufficient degree, there can be only one result: a sharp drop in the value of the nation's currency in relation to other currencies.

Still other rapid changes in our payments situation in the opposite direction could, of course, produce a rapid ascent in the value of the Canadian dollar, and this is not beyond the realm of the possible. It does, however, appear unlikely. Recent trends would seem to indicate that the dollar will remain well below parity in relation to the U.S. dollar for quite some time, and will probably be slow to move back even to the level of $.90 U.S. Projections of this type, however, are extremely risky and can be (and usually are) upset by unforeseen factors. Ultimately, the only guaranteed projection that ever can be made about payments accounts and exchange rates is that they will continue to fluctuate—just like the weather!

SUMMARY

A key reason for treating international specialization and exchange as a separate topic is that each nation has its own currency. Ways have to be devised to permit people who produce goods in one country to receive payment for those goods in their own currency from people who live in other countries. This complication also holds for individuals or businesses who want to loan or invest money abroad and for nations that wish to carry on military or economic programs abroad.

Hence, some means must be found for translating the currency of one nation into that of another. This means creating foreign exchange rates—ratios between the value of one currency and another. The determination of how much one currency is worth in terms of another depends basically on the supply and demand for particular currencies, among people, businesses, and governments who need it for international payments.

Different methods of determining exchange rates can be used. Some will aim at maximum flexibility; others at maximum stability of exchange rates. Floating exchange rates will result from permitting supply and demand alone to determine what any currency is worth. A fixed set of exchange rates can be chosen under the old-fashioned gold standard, according to which each nation will undertake to fix the value of its currency in terms of gold. After World War II, governments developed a fixed (or semistable) system of exchange rates under the International Monetary Fund. Through international borrowing, nations assisted each other to maintain stable exchange rates, without undergoing painful depressions as the price of adjustment. Only when nations were in fundamental disequilibrium could they devalue their currencies. This system worked tolerably well until the 1970s, and there was a large increase in the amount of world trade.

However, the expansion of world trade had depended in large degree on large and continuous deficits in the United States balance of payments. These deficits came from the fact that, although the United States had consistently exported more merchandise than it had imported, government spending overseas and private lending and investment abroad had exceeded American trade surpluses and resulted in overall deficits.

Recognition of the need for an ultimate end to U.S. deficits created a need for a new international reserve medium to supplement both gold and dollars and make possible the continuing growth of world reserves. In 1967, the leading financial nations agreed to create such a new form of international money—the so-called Special Drawing Rights. These SDRs, now being issued by the International Monetary Fund, promote the long-term growth of international trade and investment and ward off the dangers of a trend toward protectionism or collapse of the world's monetary system due to shortages of reserves.

The post World War II system of fixed rates of exchange finally broke down in the 1970s in the face of more and more instability in the payments balances of the world's major trading nations. The result has been a reversion to a system of floating rates where the value of a nation's currency is determined by supply and demand. Such is likely to continue to be the case until major powers such as the United States, Japan, the members of the E.E.C., and Canada bring their payments closer to fundamental balance.

Canada reverted to a floating rate in 1970. During the subsequent decade we initially saw a sharp rise in the value of our dollar from its old official level of $.925 U.S. Then, toward the end of the decade, as a result of mounting deficits in service account and declines in capital inflows, the dollar plunged by about 17% from $1.02 U.S. to $.84 U.S. between 1976 and 1978. With the short-term outlook for continued deficits, it seems likely the Canadian dollar will remain at a relatively low level.

KEY CONCEPTS

exchange rate	fundamental disequilibrium	balance of trade
equilibrium rates	exchange control	reserve currency
exchange stabilization fund	balance of payments	SDRs

QUESTIONS FOR REVIEW AND DISCUSSION

1. What is an exchange rate? What is a balance of payments? How are exchange rates related to the balance of payments between nations?
2. How are free market or floating exchange rates determined? What are the advantages and the disadvantages of floating exchange rates?
3. What are the advantages and disadvantages of using a gold standard to fix exchange rates at a set level?
4. What is an exchange stabilization fund? How does it attempt to achieve both the advantages of flexible exchange rates and the advantages of stable exchange rates?
5. Since a nation's balance of payments must always balance, what is the meaning of the terms surplus and deficit in a nation's balance of payments?
6. If a nation has a surplus in its balance of payments, how might it bring its balance of payments into balance? If a nation has a deficit in its balance of payments, how might it bring its balance of payments into balance?
7. What is the difference between the terms "balance of trade" and "balance of payments"? Explain how a country may have a deficit in the first but a surplus in the second, or a surplus in the first but a deficit in the second.
8. What are some of the possible long-run solutions to the deficit in the United States balance of payments?
9. How is a key currency or a reserve currency different from a regular or an ordinary currency? Why does a change in the value of a reserve currency have a different significance?

PROBLEMS AND EXERCISES TO SHARPEN YOUR UNDERSTANDING

1. Take a sheet of paper and make two columns. Label one column "Receipts from Foreigners." Label the other column "Payments to Foreigners." Then enter the amount of each of these following transactions in the proper column.

   a. A Canadian spends $1000 on a vacation in France.
   b. An American buys a $5000 automobile assembled in Canada.
   c. A Canadian buys $1000 worth of stocks in a new British electronics company.
   d. A Canadian firm buys a $90 million farm machinery plant in the Netherlands.
   e. A Swiss banking syndicate buys $10 million worth of CPR stock.
   f. CPR pays $10 000 in dividends to foreign owners of its stock.
   g. A Canadian restaurant buys $5000 worth of French wine.
   h. A French steel mill buys $500 000 worth of machinery from a Canadian factory.
   i. A Canadian sends his mother in Italy $300 for a Christmas gift.
   j. The Canadian government pays $5 000 000 to its troops stationed in Germany.
   k. The Italian government pays a Montreal hotel $20 000 to house its I.C.A.O. (International Civil Aviation Organization) delegation.
   l. A Canadian department store buys $500 000 worth of Japanese radios.
   m. A British electronics firm pays a dividend of $100 to a Canadian stockholder.

2. As a result of the preceding transactions, does Canada have a surplus or a deficit in its balance of payments? What is the size of this surplus or deficit? How might this surplus or deficit be financed to bring our balance of payments into balance?
3. Research in more detail the factors involved in the decline in the value of the Canadian dollar in the late 1970s.
4. What sectors or individuals in Canada benefited from the decline in the value of our dollar? What sectors or individuals were adversely affected by the decline in the value of our dollar? Explain why in each case.
5. What impact would a decline in the value of the dollar (such as that in the late 1970s) have on inflationary pressures in Canada?
6. What has happened to Canada's exchange rate since 1978? What can you offer as explanations for these recent events?

APPENDIX:

FOREIGN INVESTMENT IN CANADA

IN THE SHADOW OF THE EAGLE

In an address to the Canadian Parliament in 1961, John F. Kennedy, then President of the United States, summarized the relationship between his nation and ours in the following terms:

> "Geography made us neighbors. History has made us friends. Economics has made us partners. And necessity has made us allies."

Throughout the course of Canadian-American relations, the economic "partnership" has become a basis for concern on many occasions. During recent years, the relationship has come to be regarded from an increasingly nationalistic perspective on our side of the border.

The question of the economic relationship between the two nations is only part of a wider pattern, of course, and must be seen as such. There has been rising concern about Canadian sovereignty in the Arctic, growing dominance of "foreign" culture in films, television content, magazines on our newstands, protection of border waters (such as the Great Lakes) from further pollution (a major part of which is imported), apprehension about the increasing external influence on the young from non-Canadian professors and teachers, non-Canadian books and books (like this one) printed by foreign-controlled firms in the educational systems of the nation. These, and many other issues are portions of growing concern about Canadian independence and the Canadian identity. In many instances, the emergence is certainly based on a "pro-Canadian" feeling. On other occasions, it may be an "anti-American" expression. In more than a few cases, it may be hard to tell the difference.

Regardless of this fact, however, Canadian nationalism has definitely been on the rise and has affected many of our views of and dealings with our neighbors to the South. In the realm of economic matters, there are several crucial issues, each with many tangents.

From the time of Confederation on, Canada has been an extensive user of foreign capital. It has been said that "Canadians are as addicted to foreign capital as a drunkard is to his bottle." As a result of massive public and private need for capital in a nation with a relatively small population, this is not a surprising situation. Within this potentially beneficial addiction, however, there are several categories of problems which may accompany capital inflows.

If a country becomes dependent on foreign capital for growth, what happens if the tap is turned off? Growth could be impeded, of that we may be certain. By how much is another matter. Conflicting views about whether or not, if the need arose, Canada could take up the slack without suffering a major drop in growth and in our standard of living may be found from many quarters. To gain some idea of opinions on this point, do some research on the imposition of the Interest Equalization Tax, proposed in July 1963, and the "anti-Balance of Payments Deficit" measures of early 1968 by the U.S. government. Both were aimed at curtailing the outflow of investment from the United States. Canada did, to all intents and purposes, remain exempt from these measures, but the initial fears raised in Canada about the possible effects should such measures apply to us indicate the importance of capital inflows at that time.

Another problem which capital flow may create is due to the fact that it will influence a nation's balance of payments position and, if large enough, put pressure on a nation's exchange rates, be they based on free-floating or fixed-rate systems. During much of the post-World War II era, Canada's receipts of capital from the U.S.A. helped to counter the large trade deficit with that nation and the generally persistent current account deficit. However, as our total trade surplus increased, the continued capital inflow became a pressure-producing force rather than a stabilizing force; and the continued inflow of capital certainly helped lead to the unpegging of the dollar and its upward movement in 1970. Approximately a decade later, in 1976-1978, a rising current account deficit was accompanied by a decline in the capital account surplus. The result, as we have seen in Chapter 33, was a situation which helped intensify the sharp drop in the value of the Canadian dollar during this period.

In addition, however, to the impact of new investment, consideration must also be given to the outflow of interest and dividends to holders of previously invested funds. This may or may not offset plus or minus effects from the amounts involved in the Balance of Payments Capital Accounts. Again, referring to the 1976-1978 period, you should recall the role of the increase in our deficit in interest and dividends as a factor in the balance of payments problems Canada experienced at that time.

These variations in the possible effects of capital inflows on our balance of payments reinforce the old adage that everything has its cost or potential cost.

Despite these points, we must accept the fact that one very definite plus emerges from the inflow of capital, namely that of growth. The importance of investment to the economy was one of the main points of emphasis in Unit 4. Public and private investment levels have both been boosted through access to foreign capital. Now, when turning to the more crucial question of control, we must make a distinction, namely between capital which comes to Canada and is brought under control of Canadian firms or governments (for the most part debt capital on long-term loan) and direct investment involving the acquisition of ownership by outside interests. This may be done by the outright purchase of Canadian firms or by the formation of Canadian subsidiaries of foreign firms. (Refer back to Figure 32A-1 to see the extent to which one Canadian-based firm does this abroad.) This is the category of foreign investment which has received much more attention.

During the period since 1960, two men, Walter Gordon and Melville Watkins, have been especially prominent in the promotion of the proposition that steps must be taken to alter the growing external control over companies, industry groups, and the economy as a whole.

During the 10-year period, 1958-1968, when Lester Pearson was at the head of the Liberal party, Gordon was one of the more influential and more controversial figures within that party. His approach, one based on the assumption that growing American political, economic, and social influence had to be curtailed, led to a constant effort on his part to promote the establishment of restrictions on further takeovers of Canadian firms, to ensure that foreign-owned firms did comply with Canadian laws and interests and not those of the country holding control, and finally to begin a "buying-back" operation. He did succeed in opening up public debate but, with some piecemeal

A Choice for Canada—

We are fortunate that it is the Americans who are our neighbors and our friends. The dictates of geography require us to get along with them, and this is not difficult to do. They are likeable, tough-minded, business-like, and go after what they want. At the same time, on the whole, they do not resent people who have the courage to stick up for their rights and aspirations. Canadians are much more likely to be respected in the United States if they fight for their interests and their independence than if they give in silently and without protest every time Uncle Sam looks cross.

We have benefited greatly from the inflow of foreign capital. We shall continue to need more foreign capital. But the Canadian economy is now more mature than it used to be. As we continue to generate more capital ourselves, we should be careful not to disrupt our access to markets and technological know-how; we should encourage a larger proportion of the foreign capital that we still need to come in future in the form of debt and less in the form of direct investment. At the same time, we should take steps to reverse the present trend towards ever greater foreign control of the day-to-day operation of our economy.

It is alleged at times that if we do these things it will mean a reduction in our standard of living. I disagree. The greater production of goods and services in Canada, which would result from the proposals for improving our balance of payments and the lower costs of servicing foreign capital, would increase our living standards. If we were clumsy in the way we went about things, the rate of improvement in our standard of living might be slower than it would otherwise be. But if we do not do these things to reverse the present trends, we shall run a serious risk of new financial crises. The measures that would be necessary to meet them could well result in a reduction in our living standards. This is the situation we should face up to while there is still time.

The public should expect politicians in all parties, and leaders in all fields, to state what their position is on the broad question of foreign control of our economy. The future of our country depends upon what we decide to do about it. It is my hope that our leaders and a great majority of Canadians in all provinces will decide our independence is worth fighting for.

Source: Walter Gordon, *A Choice for Canada,* McClelland and Stewart, Toronto, 1966, pp. 124-125. Reprinted by permission of The Canadian Publishers, McClelland and Stewart Limited, Toronto.

exceptions, was not able to have his wishes turned into government policy during his period within the Cabinet.

The first reading contains a concluding section from a book of Gordon's printed between two periods of his membership in the Cabinet. It illustrates Gordon's concern and also the rather low-key approach he took to the issue of Canadian-American relations.

Gordon resigned from the Cabinet in early 1968 and did not seek re-election in the general election later that year. After leaving partisan political life, Gordon continued to promote his concerns about Canada's economic independence. He was one of the founders of the Committee for an Independent Canada and continued to speak and publish widely.

The reading from Peter Newman's book provides an assessment of Gordon's efforts.

A Political Obituary

Throughout the West and to a lesser degree in the Maritimes, Walter Gordon's theories of economic nationalism were regarded as a thinly disguised cover up for Toronto protectionism. The influx of foreign capital had done much to rid the citizens in both extremes of the country from the detested yoke of the Bay and St. James Streets brand of capitalism. In Gordon they thought they recognized the grip of the Toronto-Montreal industrial establishment which through its tariff and price-fixing policies had long exploited the resources of their areas with minimal returns to the inhabitants, and was now attempting to reassert its dominance. They feared Gordon's protectionist tendencies as a type of state socialism running directly counter to their idea of the open society and their longing for freer trade with the United States.

Neither was there any significant support for Gordon's policies in French Canada. The Quebec nationalist tradition, with its cultural and social roots, was not compatible with Gordon's economic thesis. The target of French-Canadian nationalists had never been American investment but the economic influence of Montreal's English-speaking managers. In fact, American dollars were welcomed in Quebec to offset the power of the province's own English-speaking community. Most of the Quebec ministers in Ottawa, particularly Pierre Elliott Trudeau and Maurice Sauvé, had been fighting Quebec nationalism all their political lives. They could not do battle against one kind of nationalism in their home province without at the same time opposing the Canadian nationalism implied in Gordon's economic doctrine.

Perhaps Walter Gordon's inability to move the nation in his direction was due to the historic accident that Canada matured into nationhood at a time when the human race was moving, as the eminent critic Northrop Frye pointed out, "towards a post-national world." In the long jostling of their history, Canadians had never been able to settle the nagging question whether their northern subcontinent could retain its political sovereignty while espousing only indistinct and not always compatible brands of nationalism. Still, despite the limited success of his nationalistic crusades, Walter Gordon's time in public life enlarged not just his party but the nation as a whole. He had three qualities rare in politicians—courage, simplicity, and selflessness; they made him for a time the conscience of his country.

Source: Peter Newman, *The Distemper of Our Times,* Toronto: McClelland and Stewart, 1968, p. 230. Reprinted by permission of The Canadian Publishers, McClelland and Stewart Limited, Toronto.

The passing of a decade since the comments were written has reinforced their basic validity. For a much more detailed examination of this important man, his ideas and his impact, it is strongly suggested you examine Denis Smith's book, *Gentle Patriot, A Political Biography of Walter Gordon,* Edmonton: Hurtig, 1973.

While Walter Gordon was still in the Cabinet, in February 1968, the report of a Gordon-sponsored task force entitled "Foreign Ownership and the Structure of Canadian Industry" was released with a Cabinet indication that it represented the views of those involved—not Cabinet policy. The appearance of this document, frequently referred to as the "Watkins Report," heralded the emergence of Professor Melville Watkins into a position of prominence. Watkins, an economist from the University of Toronto, and his panel of seven other university economists, produced a document which was much more specific in its warnings about and documentation of external domi-

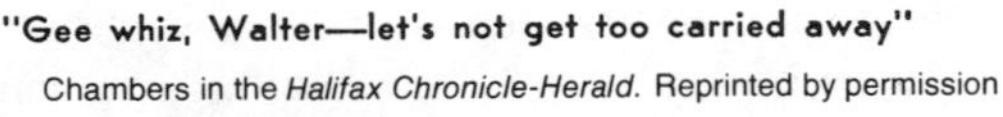
"Gee whiz, Walter—let's not get too carried away"

Chambers in the *Halifax Chronicle-Herald.* Reprinted by permission

Here is one cartoonist's view of Walter Gordon's nationalistic position. Is the impression conveyed in the cartoon consistent with the impression you get when reading the excerpt reprinted from *A Choice For Canada?*

nation of the economy. The Report produced much debate in the period immediately following its release, but there was no strong response to its recommendations by any of the major candidates in the race for the Liberal leadership in 1968. The new Trudeau Cabinet commissioned another study and the Watkins Report was consigned to the realm of archival material.

Of the many problems raised in the 1968 Report, Watkins focused attention on two. One was the question of "extra-territoriality"—the application of law beyond the borders of the nation where it is enacted. An example is the application of U.S. trading restrictions, through the control of the U.S. parent, to Canadian subsidiaries of U.S. firms. The other was the general political and social impact of the U.S. economic influence in Canada.

Walter Gordon was classed as a radical within the Liberal party, for he advocated many fundamental changes in the policies which had become firmly entrenched among his political peers.

In the wake of government inaction, Mel. Watkins took a more active role in the political area. In November, 1969, he and a number of political associates presented a document initially referred to as the "Watkins Manifesto" for consideration at an N.D.P. Policy Conference in Winnipeg. The terms of the policy proposals were much different in tone from the contents of the 1968 "Report." The policy suggestions, which came to be known as the "Waffle Manifesto" (page 468), were rejected at the Convention, probably because of their more openly anti-American sentiments and a greater emphasis on nationalization of industry by governments than the mainstream of the N.D.P. was willing to accept. Despite the differences which existed in their approaches, Watkins and Gordon shared a common concern about the fate of the country and in turn suffered similar fates themselves. They were both rejected by the political parties through which they wished to see their ideas promoted.

In 1970, the Commons Standing Committee on External Affairs and Defense carried out a review of foreign ownership. The result was another series of policy recommendations which came to be known as the "Wahn Report." The core proposal called for major subsidiaries of foreign companies to have at least 51% of shares held by Canadians. This was attacked from both sides. Some critics called it unwarranted interference in the private sector. Others said it wouldn't achieve

The Waffle Manifesto—1969

This document, as the excerpts indicate, clearly spoke in terms of the "New Left." Militantly socialistic and anti-American in tone, it was rejected by the N.D.P. by a 2-1 ratio. The "waffle" group ran a strong campaign against David Lewis for the party leadership in 1971. Since then, the leading figures have diversified their activities—generally outside the N.D.P.

The major threat to Canadian survival today is American control of the Canadian economy. The major issue of our times is not national unity but national survival, and the fundamental threat is external, not internal.

American corporate capitalism is the dominant factor shaping Canadian society. In Canada, American economic control operates through the formidable medium of the multinational corporation. The Canadian corporate elite has opted for a junior partnership with these American enterprises. Canada has been reduced to a resource base and consumer market within the American empire.

The American empire is the central reality for Canadians. It is an empire characterized by militarism abroad and racism at home. Canadian resources and diplomacy have been enlisted in the support of that empire. In the barbarous war in Vietnam, Canada has supported the United States through its membership on the International Control Commission and through sales of arms and strategic resources to the American military-industrial complex.

The American empire is held together through world-wide military alliances and by giant corporations. Canada's membership in the American alliance system and the ownership of the Canadian economy by American corporations precluded Canada's playing an independent role in the world. These bonds must be cut if corporate capitalism and the social priorities it creates, is to be effectively challenged. . . .

. . . Economic dependence must be replaced by independence, and capitalism by socialism. There can be no real independence without socialism, while socialism will create the basis, economic and political, for independence. Continental integration has become so pervasive that nationalists who value an independent Canada and socialists who reject the value of corporate capitalism now share a common agenda.

The immediate necessity is to support policies that compel foreign-based corporations to perform in the Canadian public interest. The ultimate goal is to build an independent economy where the priorities of social developments are set within Canada by Canadians. Therefore be it resolved that the New Democratic Party supports:

(1) Full disclosure of financial data by corporations (Canadian-owned as well as foreign-owned), and the immediate creation of a special agency to formulate policy toward multinational corporations.

(2) The immediate creation of a government export trade agency to block the intrusion into Canada of American law prohibiting trade with certain Communist countries through the medium of the American direct investment firm, and the extension of that agency to engage generally in state trading.

(3) Public control over foreign takeovers, so as to limit further loss of existing national firms by the prohibition of foreign ownership in key sectors (as at present in media and banking), by severely inhibiting mergers through a strengthened anti-monopoly policy, and by public ownership.

(4) The immediate creation of a Canada Development Corporation with full government ownership and control, financed in part through such means as taxation and directives to private financial institutions, and directed to pursue social, and not simply corporate, objectives, such as being an instrument of government planning and a

means of increasing Canadian independence.

(5) The selective nationalization of foreign-owned firms in the leading sectors of the economy (for example, the key resource industries) so as to replace foreign private ownership by Canadian public ownership.

(6) The creation of Crown corporations in new industries which would otherwise come under foreign control.

(7) The creation of an integrated set of national policies to stop the further slide of Canada into dependent status and to replace the present inefficient branch-plant economy with a national economy capable of generating its own growth and of being effectively controlled and directed by the national government.

anything, for firms are often controlled through ownership of less than 50% of the voting shares. This report, like the Watkins Report, was not acted upon by the government.

1972 saw the publication of the new Cabinet-sponsored study which came to be known as the "Gray Report," named after Herb Gray, the Minister who oversaw its preparation.

In its recommendations for policy, this report emphasized the need for a screening agency to have the power to permit or prevent new direct investments, indicated key sectors of the economy where foreign ownership would be regulated, and suggested the introduction of rules for foreign investment, including majority Canadian control of shares and directorships in companies.

After much debate, the Gray Report resulted in the creation of FIRA, the Foreign Investment Review Agency. The Agency, established in 1973, was given the power to review a wide range of types of new foreign investments, or purchases of control in existing Canadian firms. Final power of approval of FIRA recommendations is held by the Cabinet, but there appear to have been few instances of a Cabinet reversal of FIRA judgments. FIRA has, like all compromises, created dissatisfaction on both its flanks. Due to its limited use of power, and the extent to which it has permitted the continued inflow of direct investment, FIRA has been subject to especially harsh criticism from proponents of the "nationalist" position. The basis for the criticisms can be seen in the data in Table 33A-1.[1]

Table 33A-1. FIRA APPROVAL RATES,[1] 1974-1978

	1974	1975	1976	1977	1978[2]
Acquisition Cases	66%	71%	78%	91%	86%
New Investment Cases[3]	—	—	80%	89%	81%

Notes: [1] Approval Rate is the number of approved applications as a percentage of "resolved" cases. Applications "unapproved" are either turned down or withdrawn before a final ruling is made.
[2] 1978 data is for the first six months.
[3] Not subject to review before 1976.
Source: Foreign Investment Review Agency, *Foreign Investment Review*, vol. 2, no. 1, Autumn, 1978, page 30.

Another development which, like FIRA, had its roots in the ideas of Walter Gordon and the Watkins Report, was the establishment of the Canada Development Corporation. The concept of the C.D.C. originally was that it would serve as a vehicle through which Canada could "buy back" more control of key sectors. For example, the C.D.C. bought the Canadian oil and gas interest of Tenneco Ltd. One reversal of foreign control

[1] For a wider perspective, see "The Welcome Wagon," *MacLean's*, November 1, 1976, pp. 40 and ff.

took place in an unusual way. The C.D.C. acquired control of the base metal operation of Texas Gulf Ltd. in Canada by acquisition of 30% of the shares of Texas Gulf Inc., the American parent. In so doing, the C.D.C. became the major shareholder in the U.S. firm and acquired large interests outside Canada. The transfer of shares of the Crown Corporation, Polysar Ltd., has also provided C.D.C. with numerous interests outside Canada through Polysar's foreign, i.e. non-Canadian, investments. The C.D.C. has put some capital into small, Canadian, high-risk ventures but, in its initial years, it has followed a conservative policy in using most of its resources to purchase holdings in large, established firms.

Most of the other cases of definite government action have been somewhat comparable to the piecemeal approach to policy during the past. These *ad hoc* decisions by sector or by company go back to the late 1950s. For example, in 1958, amendments to the Broadcasting Act limited foreign participation in television undertakings to a maximum of 25%. In 1964, this percentage was extended to radio and cable television. In 1967, the revision of the Bank Act placed limits on foreign ownership of, as well as domestic concentration in, bank shares. That action was the culmination of a four-year (1963-1967) controversy over acquisition of control over the Mercantile Bank of Canada by an American bank from its previous Dutch owners.[2] In 1971, foreign ownership of federally incorporated sales finance companies was restricted to 25%.

In some instances, there has been federal action in cases involving specific firms. In 1970, Ottawa blocked the transfer of control of Denison Mines, the country's largest uranium producer, to U.S. interests. In 1971, action prevented U.S. acquisition of control over Home Oil Company. More recently, FIRA has provided a means to regulate takeovers. Reverse takeovers, that is, acquisition of Canadian control over foreign-owned or controlled firms have sometimes been carried out. The federal government purchased DeHavilland Aircraft of Canada and Canadair Ltd. from their foreign owners. Petro-Canada bought the Alberta holdings of Atlantic-Richfield, an American oil firm, and made a bid for Husky Oil, only to be outbid by the Alberta-based Alberta Gas Trunk Lines. However, most instances of reverse takeovers have come from the private sector.[3]

FACTORS RESPONSIBLE FOR THE HIGH LEVELS OF FOREIGN INVESTMENT IN CANADA

Having examined more recent aspects of the debate over foreign ownership, we should consider the question of what factors have led to the presence of such high levels of foreign capital in Canada. When we look back to the time of Confederation, or even prior to Confederation, it seems there were three basic factors at work.

The first of these is really a multi-faceted situation. In the period before the First World War in particular, Canada was a country with a small population in a vast area rich in resources. Our location, our historical and economic ties to both Britain and the United States, and our domestic situation described above all combined to produce a need for capital, opportunities for its use, access to potential sources of investment, and a willingness on the part of those investors to provide it. The inflow of funds was a natural one. Britain tended to be the primary source until after World War I and, it might be noted, British funds were channelled primarily into investment in bonds from either governments or the private sector, rather than into shares which conveyed ownership in the private sector. British capi-

[2] Newman's *Distemper of our Times* provides good coverage of the Mercantile Bank Case.

[3] There have also been several notable cases of takeovers by provincial governments. Saskatchewan acquired control of several major foreign-owned potash firms. Newfoundland purchased the power facilities at Churchill Falls and Quebec has started action to acquire major asbestos holdings.

tal in Canada in the period 1840-1920 played a role similar to the large-scale British investments in the United States in the era 1820-1860.

In the present century, as British investment declined, the flow of U.S. funds into Canada began to play an increasingly prominent role. The United States was and still is a market where Canadian governments or companies may borrow money by selling bonds. However, even in the pre-1900 period, U.S. funds coming into Canada tended to come in as direct investment into the private sector; in other words, the investors tended to come in as owners rather than as lenders.

One final observation about the earlier phases of foreign investment is that those funds coming into the private sector tended to be directed toward two areas—transportation and resource development. Resource development, again as a generalization, tended to be limited to initial stages and we evolved into a country heavily dependent on the export of raw materials and semi-finished products.

A second crucial factor which contributed to the inflow of foreign capital into the private sector was the tariff system. From the 1879 implementation of Sir John A. Macdonald's "National Policy," Canada has remained essentially a pro-tariff country, especially in the manufacturing sector. The tariff structure did help to promote the growth of a domestic manufacturing sector, but there were several by-products which were not expected and not especially desirable.[4] For an American manufacturer, the tariff wall provided two basic choices: either abandon the Canadian market, since U.S. produced output would be made uncompetitive after the cost of importation was added to the price, or get around the wall by opening a Canadian subsidiary to produce in Canada for the Canadian market. This explanation for the opening of a great many "branch plants" in Canada is very simplistic, but frequently valid. A related factor was that goods produced in Canada in the earlier part of this century received preferential tariff access to Britain and other parts of the British Empire and Commonwealth, regardless of whether the goods were produced by Canadian- or non-Canadian-owned firms. For some U.S. firms, this was even more important than simple access to the Canadian domestic market.

The resulting concentration of foreign direct investment in the resource sector and in manufacturing is emphatically indicated in the data on the private sector in Tables 33A-3 through 33A-5.

A final factor in the high degree of foreign control in Canada was our practice of maintaining an open door for capital within our tariff wall. This was more a result of an absence of government policy and the existence of a *laissez-faire* approach in the private sector than any overall plan to draw large amounts of foreign capital into specific sectors.

In short, we got to where we are as a result of a series of uncoordinated events, rather than from any general design. And, while getting there, we tended to be oblivious to what was happening. One of the earliest instances when questions were raised about the impact of foreign investment was a paper published in 1955 in the *International Journal* of the Canadian Institute of International Affairs. The author recommended a major study of the Canadian economy to examine this and other issues related to Canada's future economic growth. Such a commission was set up and the St. Laurent government appointed the author of the C.I.I.A. paper to serve as Chairman of the study—The Royal Commission on Canada's Economic Prospects. The author of the paper, who then served as Commission Chairman, was Walter Gordon.

[4] See J. M. Dales, *The Protective Tariff in Canada's Development*, Toronto: University of Toronto Press, 1966, for an assessment. Just one of the effects was the concentration of manufacturing in central Canada at the expense of the East and the West. Another was the proliferation of higher-cost, less competitive firms and higher prices for consumers.

Table 33A-2. FOREIGN LONG-TERM INVESTMENT IN CANADA, BY TYPE OF CLAIM, 1930-1975

Year-End Levels in Millions of Current Dollars

	Direct Investment	Government Securities	Other Portfolio	Other Categories	Total
1930	2427	1706	3186	295	7614
1939	2296	1703	2629	285	6913
1945	2713	1662	2433	284	7092
1950	3975	1962	2407	320	8664
1955	7728	1869	3289	641	13 527
1963	15 502	4207	4725	1771	26 205
1968	22 534	6822	6059	2564	37 979
1972	29 524	9387	7849	3163	49 933
1975	39 838	15 109	10 149	3553	68 649

Source: Statistics Canada, *Canada's International Investment Position,* Catalogue 67-002, various issues.

Table 33A-3. PERCENTAGE OF FOREIGN CONTROL OF CORPORATE ASSETS, BY MAJOR INDUSTRY GROUPS, 1968-1975

	1968	1969	1970	1971	1972	1973	1974	1975
Agriculture, Forestry and Fishing	12	15	13	13	10	10	9	9
Mining	64	68	68	69	61	58	59	67
Manufacturing	58	58	59	59	56	56	56	56
Construction	15	12	16	18	15	15	14	14
Transportation and Utilities	8	8	8	10	10	10	8	8
Wholesale Trade	28	26	27	33	34	32	29	28
Retail Trade	20	21	21	22	22	19	21	21
Services	20	23	23	23	24	26	27	23
Total, Non-Financial Industries	36	36	36	37	35	34	34	33

Note: Data are drawn from all corporations having gross revenues in excess of $500 000 and/or assets in excess of $250 000.

Sources: Statistics Canada, *Corporations and Labour Unions Returns Act, Part I*, Catalogue 61-210, various issues, 1970-1978. (Data from this source is frequently referred to with the acronym CALURA.)

Table 33A-4. PERCENTAGE OF FOREIGN CONTROL OF CORPORATE SALES BY MAJOR INDUSTRY GROUPS, 1968-1975

	1968	1969	1970	1971	1972	1973	1974	1975
Agriculture, Forestry and Fishing	9	9	7	8	8	8	7	7
Mining	63	69	73	76	65	61	64	67
Manufacturing	55	55	54	57	57	57	57	58
Construction	11	12	15	15	13	12	12	14
Transportation and Utilities	12	11	10	11	10	11	10	11
Wholesale Trade	27	25	25	29	29	29	29	28
Retail Trade	18	19	19	22	20	17	19	18
Services	16	18	19	18	19	24	23	21
Total, Non-Financial Industries	36	36	36	38	36	37	37	37

Note: See Note for Table 33A-3

Sources: As for Table 33A-3

Table 33A-5. PERCENTAGE OF FOREIGN CONTROL OF CORPORATE PROFITS, BY MAJOR INDUSTRY GROUPS, 1968-1975

	1968	1969	1970	1971	1972	1973	1974	1975
Agriculture, Forestry and Fishing	20	20	30	15	9	8	8	19
Mining	59	68	72	79	52	54	53	65
Manufacturing	63	63	62	66	66	61	61	66
Construction	13	17	14	13	23	18	14	15
Transportation and Utilities	17	17	18	21	19	22	17	18
Wholesale Trade	31	27	28	31	33	31	35	28
Retail Trade	18	17	15	14	20	9	13	12
Services	32	29	35	30	31	36	42	30
Total, Non-Financial Industries	45	47	45	46	44	44	45	46

Note: See Note for Table 33A-3

Sources: As for Table 33A-3

Table 33A-6. PERCENTAGE OF FOREIGN CONTROL OF CORPORATE ASSETS IN MINING AND MANUFACTURING, 1975

Sector	Percentage	Sector	Percentage
Mining:			
Metal Mining	44	Furniture Industries	23
Mineral Fuels	71	Paper and Allied Industries	41
Other Mining	55	Printing, Publishing	12
Total Mining	57	and Allied Industries	
		Primary Metals	14
Manufacturing:		Metal Fabricating	43
Food Products	50	Machinery	67
Beverages	30	Transport Equipment	78
Tobacco Products	100	Electrical Products	66
Rubber Products	93	Non-metallic Mineral Products	66
Leather Products	23	Petroleum and Coal Products	92
Textile Mills	59	Chemicals and Chemical Products	75
Knitting Mills	24	Miscell. Manufacturing	50
Clothing Industries	16		
Wood Industries	29	Total—Manufacturing	56

Notes: See Note for Table 33A-3
Source: Statistics Canada, *Corporations and Labour Unions Returns Act, Report for 1975,* Catalogue 61-210, 1978.

FOREIGN CONTROL OF THE CANADIAN ECONOMY: EXAMPLES AND TRENDS

Now that we have come full circle in an historical sense, let us now examine in more detail both some aspects of the degree to which the economy is foreign controlled, and some recent trends related to this control.

The data in Table 33A-2 show some measures of the rise in the levels of foreign investment in absolute terms. Perhaps more meaningful, however, are the relative data contained in Tables 33A-3 through 33A-5. Looking at the measure of control over proportions of corporate assets, sales and profits, these data indicate that for the most recent period, a degree of stabilization has set in. In fact, in some sectors, there have been shifts back toward proportionally more Canadian control.[5] The data point out clearly the high degree of foreign control in the mining and manufacturing sectors. Table 33A-6 (page 473) provides a further breakdown on these two sectors, based on CALURA (Corporations and Labour Unions Returns Act) data for 1975. One general pattern which may be noted is the tendency for foreign investment to be higher in those industrial areas where there tends to be more concentration, i.e. less competition. This is one issue raised in the reading from the FIRA review of the Report of the Royal Commission on Corporate Concentration. (The reading also examines the growth of the non-American portion of foreign investment in Canada in recent years.)

[5] One must be careful not to read too much into these figures, especially from year to year. A repurchase by Canadian interests of one big U.S. firm such as Alberta Gas Trunk's acquisition of Husky Oil can have significant statistical effect. Another factor may be reclassification of nationality as a result of smaller share transactions. Such reclassifications of Alcan and Inco took place in 1972 when both were designated as being Canadian-controlled.

Foreign Investment Review: The Concentration of Foreign Investment in Canada

Since many of the highly concentrated industries in Canada have a high degree of foreign ownership, the Royal Commission on Corporate Concentration devoted a chapter of its final report to the subject of foreign investment.

According to the Commission, the ownership structure of foreign direct investment in Canada has changed significantly in the past generation. For instance, in 1954, non-American investment represented only 4% of the book value of all foreign investment, but by 1973 this figure had increased to 9%, and all signs indicate that the percentage has continued to rise. The degree of control by American companies appears to have reached its peak during the late 1960s. The subsequent downtrend is expected by the Commission to continue, with the proportion of non-American foreign-controlled investment increasing. This is a trend that appears to be occurring internationally and is, according to the Commission, mainly due to the recent erosion of the comparative advantage inherent in the greater size of American firms and to the rising number of divestitures by American firms.

The Commission notes that, up until the mid-1960s, American firms benefitted from important economies of scale related partly to their larger size. But the size difference and the related advantages have been eroding in the past ten years to such a point that the sales of the world's 100 largest American corporations are now barely higher than the sales of the 100 largest non-American corporations—the average sales of the former being $5.6 billion and those of the latter $4.9 billion. The Commission cites several American studies which conclude that the growth of multinational corporations is linked to the growth of their national market base. This, of course, would favor the European multinationals, who have seen substantial growth occur in their home markets. The Commission also refers to the increase in competitive pressure placed upon American subsidiaries by European firms. The Commission's views are in accord with those of other studies concerning the relative size of American companies, which show that the rate of expansion of foreign investment by European companies is greater than that by American companies.

The second important factor which, according to the Commission, favors the relative growth of other-than-American investments in many countries is the number of divestitures by American corporations. One study shows that, around the world, the divestitures of foreign subsidiaries by American corporations was four times as high between 1971 and 1975 as between 1961 and 1965. Meanwhile, a relatively small and declining number of subsidiaries

Industrial Concentration, 1975

Major industries	*Percentage of industry controlled by largest firms*		*Rank of largest Canadian-owned firm in the industry*
	Top 4	*Top 8*	
Tobacco products	88.1	98.9	13
Petroleum and coal products	75.4	88.0	7
Communication (utilities)	72.4	79.6	1
Transport equipment	70.1	75.1	6
Rubber products	63.1	81.0	10
Primary metals	58.3	74.2	1
Storage	56.1	70.6	1
Metal mining	47.4	65.0	1
Public utilities	46.3	61.1	1
Mineral fuels	44.5	64.5	7
Beverages	44.4	65.8	1
Transportation (utilities)	41.4	48.3	1
Electrical products	39.3	51.7	1
Textile mills	36.1	44.3	2
Paper and allied industries	35.0	49.0	1
Machinery	28.8	37.5	2
Other mining	27.4	35.8	5
Non-metallic mineral products	27.2	39.5	3
Chemicals and chemical products	25.5	36.3	6
Wood industries	22.0	27.8	1
Printing, publishing and allied industries	21.9	31.6	1
Food	19.9	29.9	1
Leather products	17.3	28.5	1
Knitting mills	16.2	26.1	2
Metal fabricating	14.2	20.5	1
Miscellaneous manufacturing	13.9	20.3	3
Retail trade	12.9	22.4	1
Furniture industries	12.3	19.3	2
Finance	11.6	21.8	1
Wholesale trade	9.0	13.1	1
Services	8.2	11.2	4
Clothing industries	6.1	9.4	4
Construction	5.9	8.2	3
Agriculture, forestry and fishing	5.2	8.3	1

Source: Statistics Canada

were created between 1971 and 1975. Whereas in 1971 there were 3.3 new investments for each disinvestment, by 1975 the ratio had declined to only 1.4. The Commission reports that most of the divestitures were due to inadequate earnings, rather than to any pressures from host countries.

The patterns of international investment and

disinvestment had several repercussions for Canadian industries. According to studies prepared for the Commission, a relatively high proportion of the disinvestments of recent years have occurred in unconcentrated industries and few have taken place in concentrated sectors. This is consistent with another finding of numerous Canadian studies, which show that foreign firms are more likely to invest in concentrated industries. In fact, researchers have identified a "strong direct correlation" between the degree of foreign ownership, the degree of concentration, and the presence of large firms. The degree of foreign ownership is much greater in those industries in which an oligopoly of three or four firms controls a large percentage of total sales. By contrast, the degree of foreign ownership is relatively small in those sectors where there are many small firms and where no single firm has a significant share of the market.

According to the Commission, changes in recent years in the degrees to which various industries are foreign owned have by no means been haphazard, but rather have been related to the advantages that investments have in oligopolistic industries and the advantage of possessing certain core skills. The Commission notes that "the difficulties new firms face in acquiring these core skills contributed to the high concentration in these industries and the high level of foreign investment." The Commission also observes that foreign subsidiaries in Canada can often be more productive than Canadian-owned companies because of their access to the core skills of the foreign parent. Further along in the discussion of concentration in Canadian industries, the report observes that many of the oligopolistic structures in Canada had first been developed abroad and then brought to Canada by the direct investments of the firms involved in the oligopoly abroad. The dominant firm in the oligopoly is apt to be the first to invest in Canada—and is soon followed by the others who wish to protect their market share.

Despite the presence in Canada of many oligopolistic industries that have a high percentage of foreign firms, the Commission rejects the inference that foreign direct investment has *increased* the concentration in Canadian industries. For example, no relation was observed between the rate of foreign direct investment and changes in the level of concentration, and meanwhile it can be observed that Canadian industries with a high degree of foreign ownership are no more concentrated than the same industries in other countries where those industries have a lower degree of foreign ownership.

Reprinted from *Foreign Investment Review*, FIRA, Autumn, 1978, pp. 21-22.

Increasing concern has been expressed about the relationship which has developed between inflows of new direct investment on the one hand and levels of earnings from previous investment within Canada and the payment of returns on that investment to owners outside Canada. The net result is that, in the private sector, most of the new direct investment coming in could have been accounted for by the annual export of returns being paid out. In addition, retained earnings generated within Canada are financing the expansion of foreign control. In short, the increases in the level of direct investment since about 1960, as shown in Table 33A-2, have for the most part been carried out with funds generated on this side of the border. Table 33A-7 provides a range of data to illustrate what has been happening. This trend has also been accentuated by the extent to which government assistance to new industry through grants, loans, tax concessions and other types of assistance has been directed to foreign-owned firms.

In the decade of the seventies, as a part of trends extending far beyond Canada's

Table 33A-7. SELECTED INVESTMENT DATA, 1965-1975

	Annual Flows in Millions of Current Dollars					
	1965	1967	1969	1971	1973	1975
(a) Inflow of New Direct Investment	535	691	720	925	750	670
(2) Outflow of Income Paid on Direct Investment	587	627	592	792	905	1300(e)
(3) Difference Between (1) and (2): Net Annual Proceeds	−52	+64	+128	+133	−155	−630(e)
(4) Retained Earnings of Foreign-Controlled Firms Reinvested in Canada	735	845	1045	1380	2370	3500(e)
(5) Outflow of Canadian Foreign Direct Investment Abroad	125	125	370	230	785	795

Note: (e) = estimates
Sources: Statistics Canada, *Canada's International Investment Position,* Catalogue 67-202, various issues; and *Quarterly Estimates of International Payments,* Catalogue 67-001, various issues.

borders, there was an increase in both absolute and relative terms in investment coming in from non-American sources, particularly from Europe, Japan and, after 1973, from the Middle East. Petro-dollars (as they have come to be called) from the oil-producing states have tended to be invested in short-term debt securities. The total amounts coming to Canada have been insignificant in comparison to flows into Europe and the U.S.A., but they have been increasing.

Investment flows from Europe and Japan, on the other hand, have tended to flow into a wide range of industries and into real estate holdings.[6] Table 33A-8 presents the relative shares of profits in a number of industry groups in 1968 and 1974 to illustrate the increasing importance of non-U.S.-based

[6] For an indication of the flows into real estate in Canada, see the study on Montreal entitled *City for Sale* by Henry Aubin, Toronto: James Lorimer and Company, 1977.

Table 33A-8. PERCENTAGE OF NON-U.S. FOREIGN CONTROL OF CORPORATE PROFITS, SELECTED INDUSTRY GROUPS, 1968 AND 1974.

	1968	1974
Mining		
Metal Mining	2	8
Manufacturing		
Food Products	6	14
Tobacco Products	75	93
Textile Mills	2	8
Paper and Allied Industries	2	13
Machinery	1	12
Non-metallic Mineral Products	20	47
Petroleum and Coal Products	19	22
Total-All Manufacturing	8	14
Wholesale Trade	8	11
Services	4	12
Total-All Non-Financial Industries	6	9

Sources: Statistics Canada, *Corporations and Labour Unions Returns Act, Part I,* Catalogue 61-210, 1971 and 1978.

foreign firms operating in Canada. This increased flow of investment from Europe and Japan into Canada is not a unique trend. It has been developing in other parts of the world as well, including the United States, where funds from these sources are being joined by growing levels of Canadian dollars.[7]

CANADIAN FOREIGN INVESTMENT

This steady growth of Canada as a provider as well as receiver of capital flows is indicated by data within Table 33A-7. In reality, the only thing new here is the degree of the outflow. Canada has been a source from which investment capital has flowed out for many years. Canadian foreign investment has tended to be concentrated in the United States and the Caribbean region, and in such sectors such as banking and real estate interests in the West Indies.[8]

In the flow of funds to the United States, Canadians have been influenced by a variety of motives. The types of investment, and the sources of it, have been widening considerably, though real estate and manufacturing seem to be especially favored by Canadian capital going to the United States.

This outflow of Canadian capital has raised concern over the extent to which it is openly and directly transferring jobs, output and income out of Canada. Particular prominence was given in the late 1970s to the two large nickel producers, Falconbridge and Inco, who were both cutting back on activities in Canada while making major new investments in the Dominican Republic and Guatemala.[9] Note that, while Falconbridge is considered foreign-controlled, Inco is classed as a Canadian-controlled firm. The similarity in the actions by the two indicates that the nationality of a large corporation is often not a significant factor in the determination of corporate policy.

RECENT CONCERNS ABOUT FOREIGN INVESTMENT IN CANADA

Economic pressures and problems intensified in Canada in the 1970s. The growing rates of unemployment brought about increased awareness of the impact of either new investment coming in or Canadian investment generating jobs outside of Canada. Focusing on the short-term issue of jobs produces a split in judgments. If protection of existing jobs is the chief objective, then controls over capital, specifically to prevent its departure, would be called for. However, if such controls were imposed, they might well scare away potential investors and so prevent the creation of new jobs.

Consideration of the need for jobs has led to closer scrutiny of issues such as performance of research and development, attainment of competitive efficiency, and the quest for exports by foreign-owned firms operating in this country.

A number of studies seem to indicate that foreign-owned firms invest in research and development at levels at least comparable to, if not even higher than, Canadian-owned firms.[10] It has been suggested, however, that much of the research and development investment of foreign subsidiaries does not actually contribute to Canadian industry. The

[7] For some assessments of this, see Kenneth Crowe, *America For Sale*, New York: Doubleday, 1978. Of particular interest to us should be one chapter titled "The Ugly Canadian."

[8] The extent of Canadian economic power in the Caribbean has produced a growing level of concern among many in that area. Some instances of nationalization of Canadian assets, for example those of Alcan in Guyana, have already taken place. We should not be surprised if rising voices of economic nationalism directed against Canadian holdings become increasingly loud in the West Indies, especially Trinidad, Jamaica and the Bahamas.

[9] For some detailed examination of Inco's actions, see (and compare) "No, Not Our Inco!" by Ron Crocker in *The Last Post*, vol. 6, No. 8, June, 1978, pp. 34-39, and "The Great Inco Layoff Dilemma" by Guy Stanley and John Eichman, *The Financial Post*, November 4, 1978, pp. 40-41.

[10] See A. E. Safarian, *Foreign Ownership of Canadian Industry*, Toronto: McGraw-Hill, 1966, pp. 280-286, and N. H. Lithwick, *Canada's Science Policy and the Economy*, Toronto: Methuen, 1969, pp. 82-83. This fact was also confirmed in the research in the Watkins Report of 1968 and the Gray Report of 1972.

benefits often flow back to foreign parents and are put to use elsewhere.[11] Data indicate that Canada generally lags in spending on R and D in contrast to many other developed nations. As a percentage of GNP, we of late have been investing only about 1%, in contrast with rates in the range of 1.8% to 2.4% in France, Germany, Japan, the United States and a number of other European nations. Such lags in R and D have had detrimental effects on our productivity and capacity to compete, both at home and abroad. Foreign-controlled firms are partly to blame for this, but Canadian domestic investment in R and D have been every bit as deficient. This general deficiency has affected us in such basic areas as our capacity to expand exports of manufactured goods and, as a result, employment in Canada.[12]

To gain an idea of what has been happening, consider the following: in 1970, Canada's share of world trade was 5.4%; by 1975, it had declined to 3.8%. In the period 1973-1977, the economy overall expanded by a rate of 3.1% per year; Canadian manufacturing grew by a rate of 1.6% per year. In the twenty-five years between 1951 and 1976, the percentage of jobs within Canada provided by manufacturing declined from 25% to 20% of total employment. During this period, non-manufacturing sectors created 86% of new jobs; manufacturing accounted for only 14% of new jobs created.

[11] See A. J. Cordell, *The Multinational Firm, Foreign Direct Investment and Canadian Science Policy*, Ottawa: Science Council of Canada, Special Study #22, 1971, pp. 43-46.

[12] Canada's deficit in trade in manufactured goods was about $11 billion in 1977. This was more than covered by our surplus in trade in raw materials. However, among other things, this has implications for jobs and incomes. Numbers of jobs and income levels could generally be expected to be higher per million dollars worth of manufacturing output than would be the case in the resource industries. Also, the level of investment per new job is generally much lower in manufacturing, which is relatively labor intensive, than in many of the resource industries, which are more capital than labor intensive. To be more precise, investment per new job in manufacturing was running about $75 000 in the late 1970s, while in the resource industries, it was five times that per new job.

There is need to strengthen the manufacturing sector due to its potential to create better-paying jobs at much less investment per job than other sectors. However the presence of over 50% foreign control of assets raises questions about the capacity of much of our manufacturing industry to pursue export markets in case that direction brings them into competition with parent corporations. A case which gained considerable publicity in 1977 concerned a Toronto firm, Anaconda Brass, which was to be closed down with a loss of some 900 jobs. The U.S. parent firm had decided to supply the Canadian market from the United States. Implicit in this was an assumption that other markets would not be sought by the Canadian subsidiary to avoid competing with the parent. Instead of closing, the firm was purchased by its Canadian management and other interests, and prepared to fight for markets. The president of the firm, who had also held that position under the U.S. ownership, was quoted as saying: "There is an unwritten rule that if you're a subsidiary of a U.S. plant, you don't sell to the U.S. market. But our handcuffs have been removed and now we have the opportunity."[13]

The extent to which Canadian subsidiaries are so affected is difficult to study, or even to estimate. The very fact that such may be the case in a significant portion of our manufacturing sector is enough to make it an issue of national importance. How the potential problem can be avoided or overcome, however, is a complex problem indeed.[14]

Another prominent economic and political issue of the 1970s was the degree to which our energy resources have come under foreign control. Ever since the sale of Home Oil to U.S. interests was blocked in 1971, there have been signs of greater caution in the field of energy development and exports. The strong lobby for the more rapid

[13] *Saturday Night*, vol. 94, no. 2, March, 1979, p. 71.

[14] For a more detailed look at many of these concerns about manufacturing, see Richard Starks, *Industry in Decline*, Toronto: James Lorimer and Co., 1978.

development of our resources, and increases in oil and gas exports to the U.S., is certainly affected in part by the U.S. control over much of our oil and gas industry.

The fact that these controls and influences are strong was further emphasized in 1979 in the wake of cuts in world oil supplies following the overthrow of the Shah's government in Iran. Imperial Oil in Canada is a subsidiary of Exxon, and thus Imperial's imports into Eastern Canada were contracted through Exxon, and not negotiated independently. Exxon planned to divert 25 000 barrels of oil per day, originally contracted in Venezuela on behalf of Imperial Oil for its markets in Eastern Canada, to Exxon's own refineries in the United States. In response to strong reaction from the Canadian government, the planned diversion was compensated for by a series of swaps and substitutions.[15] However, the situation showed how vulnerable we are to decisions made outside the country, based on interests entirely different from the interests of Canada.

Despite such growing concern about foreign control over energy resources, Canadians also assumed, during the same period, that additional foreign funds would be necessary to further develop our resources and the necessary transportation systems, if only to cover our own projected consumption of these resources. In other words, the love-hate relationship with foreign capital continued. Amidst all the changes that have taken place, the fundamental situation remains.

The movement to promote economic nationalism is still confined to a small minority, whose views are seen as radical departures from Canada's traditional policies. If anything, the degree of concern about foreign control over the economy seemed to weaken in the 1970s in the face of other economic pressures and more lively political debate.

The ultimate resolution of the mounting political crises over the constitution and the status of Quebec may rekindle the issue of economic independence, for there is a fundamental philosophical link between them. If we do choose to keep the country together politically, we may well have to face also the question of whether we can maintain national independence in economic terms.

Many still do not believe that the question of foreign control over much of our economy is that important to Canadians. Others feel that the stabilization of the levels of foreign control has solved the problem. Some others feel that steps such as the establishment of FIRA have provided us with what is needed. And, finally, there are those who are still concerned about what is happening. Walter Gordon wrote:

> We seem destined to lose our independence and eventually become part of the United States. Most Canadians do not want this. But our leaders seem quite unable to comprehend the implications of trends that, if not soon reversed, will lead inevitably to the breakup of our country.[16]

This was a pessimistic view when it appeared in 1972. There are increasing numbers who feel that the outlook for Canada has not improved. As we move into the 1980s, we may have to meet head on the internal and external pressures which threaten our national survival. Our response to these will determine if Canada survives as a united country.

BIBLIOGRAPHY

Government Publications

Task Force on the Structure of Canadian Industry, *Foreign Ownership and the Structure of Canadian Industry,* Ottawa: Privy Council Office, 1978. (The Watkins Report)

Government of Canada. *Foreign Direct Investment in Canada,* Ottawa, 1972, (The Gray Report)

[15] See *MacLean's,* March 5, 1979, pp. 36-37.

[16] Walter L. Gordon, "Last Chance For Canada", *MacLean's,* September, 1972, p. 38.

Non-Government Viewpoints

Antonides, Harry, *Multinationals, and the Peaceable Kingdom*, Toronto: Clark Irwin, 1978.

Aubin, Henry, *City For Sale*, Toronto: James Lorimer & Company, 1977.

Clement, Wallace, *Continental Corporate Power*, Toronto: McClelland and Stewart, 1977.

Fayerweather, John, *Foreign Investment in Canada*, Toronto: Oxford University Press, 1974.

Gordon, Walter L., *A Choice For Canada*, Toronto: McClelland and Stewart, 1966.

Gordon, Walter, L., *Storm Signals*, Toronto: McClelland and Stewart, 1976.

Levitt, Kari, *Silent Surrender*, Toronto: Macmillan of Canada, 1970.

Litvak, I. A., et al., *Dual Loyalty*, Toronto: McGraw-Hill Ryerson, 1971.

Pope, W. H., *The Elephant and the Mouse*, Toronto: McClelland and Stewart, 1971.

Safarian, A. E., *Foreign Ownership of Canadian Industry*, Toronto: McGraw-Hill, 1966.

Smith, Denis, *Gentle Patriot, A Political Biography of Walter Gordon*, Edmonton: Hurtig, 1977.

CHAPTER 34

THE LESS DEVELOPED COUNTRIES

■ OBSTACLES TO GROWTH IN LOW-INCOME COUNTRIES ■ THE PROBLEM OF INFLATION ■ THE DIVERSITY OF LOW-INCOME COUNTRIES ■ A NEW INTERNATIONAL ECONOMIC ORDER? ■ SUMMARY

In an era when most North Americans and Western Europeans look forward to getting better housing, a wider variety of consumer goods, more entertainment, and more travel, the great majority of the world's population is still struggling to escape hunger, illiteracy, disease, and an early death. The average life span in the world's less developed or low-income countries is about 40 years. A high proportion of people in those countries have a per capita money income of $5 a week—or less. Hundreds of millions must try to exist on incomes as low as $1 or $2 a week. The location of the low-income countries of the world and the nature of some of their problems can be seen in Figures 34-1

FIG. 34-1. COUNTRIES WITH PERCENTAGE OF THE POPULATION IN AGRICULTURE ABOVE THE WORLD AVERAGE

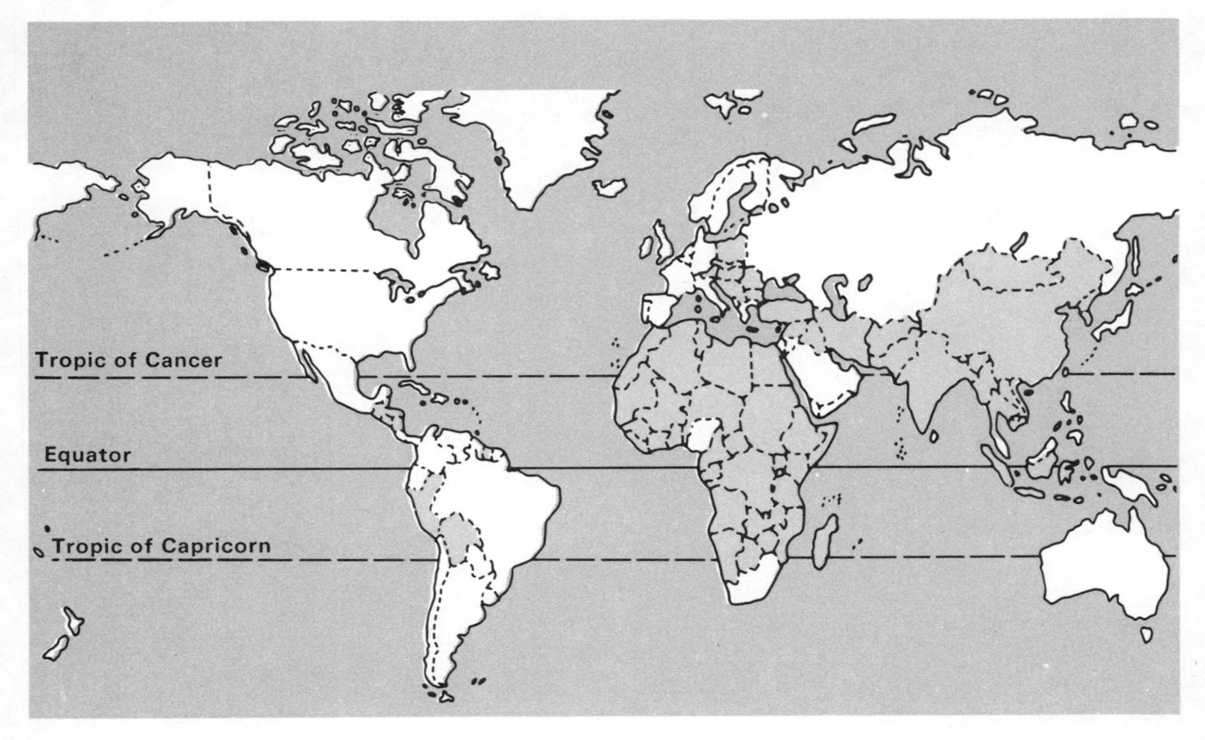

through 34-3. As can be seen from these maps, these countries tend to be concentrated in Asia, Africa, and Latin America and have a large percentage of their population employed in agriculture. They also have high infant mortality rates and very low rates of literacy.

The hardships endured by many in Asian, African and Latin American countries, and the growing political unrest which their misery creates, have forced the people of the developed countries to pay more attention to the low-income countries and to try to assist their development. From our standpoint, there are many reasons to try to help the poor nations to advance, based on humanitarian, political, and economic goals.[1] In the less developed countries themselves, the desire to achieve economic growth has become a veritable passion. But desiring economic growth and achieving it are two different things.

[1] See Section One of *Partners in Development*, the report of a special World Bank Commission on aid headed by former Prime Minister Lester Pearson, published by Praeger, New York, 1969.

OBSTACLES TO GROWTH IN LOW-INCOME COUNTRIES

The obstacles to growth in the low-income countries are complex, involving not only economic but also political, cultural, and emotional factors. One of the most difficult aspects is that their many problems aggravate each other and produce vicious cycles. For instance, there is the vicious cycle of inadequate saving. Poor people cannot afford to save because they live close to the margin of starvation. Because they cannot save, they cannot form capital—acquire plant, machinery, tools, or power sources. Because they cannot form capital, they cannot in-

FIG. 34-2. COUNTRIES WITH INFANT MORTALITY RATES ABOVE THE WORLD AVERAGE

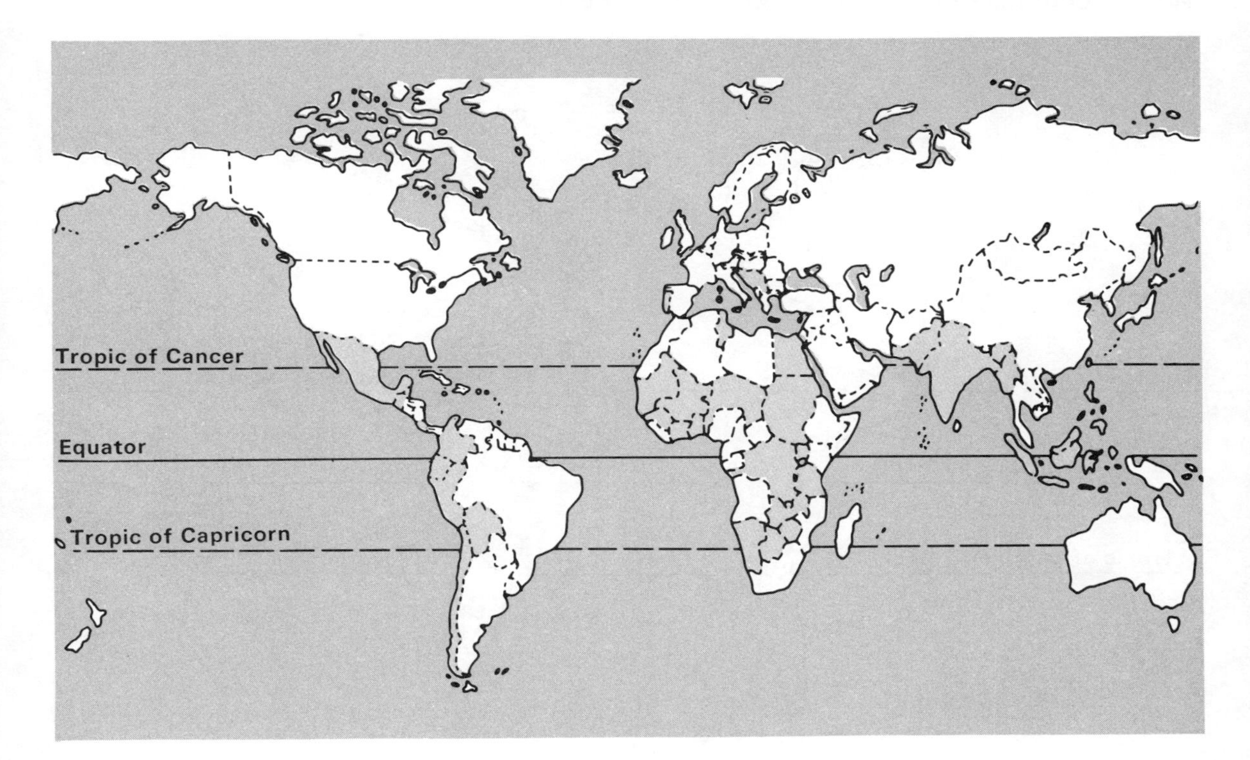

crease their productivity. Because they cannot increase productivity, they cannot raise their incomes. And because they cannot raise their incomes, they cannot increase their saving. The curse of the poor—as has often been said—is their poverty.

Nevertheless, poor countries must somehow try to break such vicious cycles by using their existing resources more effectively. Even though their natural resources, human resources (especially knowledge and technical skills), and capital resources may be severely limited, they do not impose absolute obstacles to economic growth.

Natural Resources

An abundance or a lack of natural resources will not, of itself, either ensure or prevent the economic development of a low-income country. In some cases, to be sure, a serious deficiency of overall natural resources may set a narrow limit on the rate of economic growth. Nations suffering from poor climate, infertile land, sparse mineral deposits, and a shortage of natural power sources will have to use a larger proportion of their scarce labor and capital than better-endowed nations to make up for their lack of natural resources.

But this lack will not be an absolute barrier to development. The example of Switzerland (this highly developed nation, one of the richest in the world, is situated in the midst of high mountains with few resources other than the ingenuity and skill of its people) shows that a lack of easily usable natural resources need not prevent growth. Conversely, cases such as that of Zaire, with its vast resources, show that an abundance of natural wealth is no automatic guarantee of economic growth.

A diversity of natural resources, such as we possess in Canada, undoubtedly makes

FIG. 34-3. COUNTRIES WITH LITERACY RATES BELOW THE WORLD AVERAGE

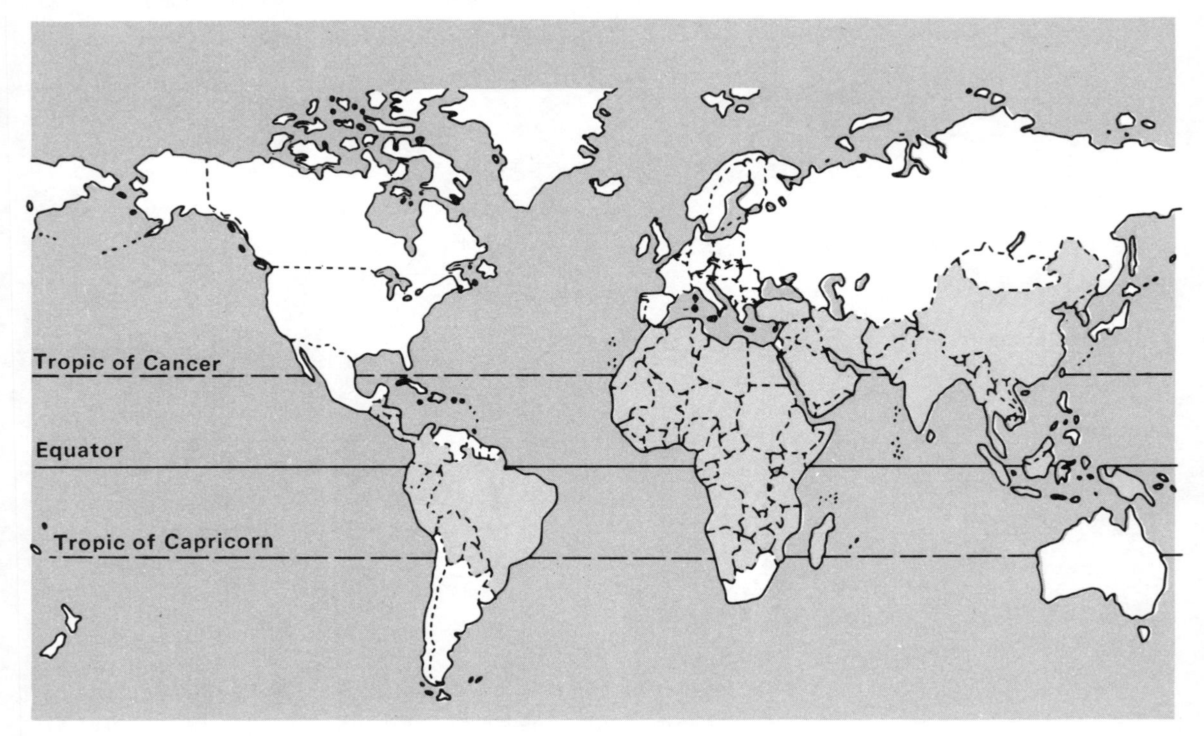

growth easier. But few nations are large enough or lucky enough to have such abundance and diversity. Many countries may have only one resource that is really in abundant supply—such as oil in Saudi Arabia, cocoa in Ghana, or natural rubber in Malaysia. Typically, the low-income countries are quite small, with populations ranging from ½ million to 10 million, but there are some exceptions as we will note later.

Many low-income countries are in fact too small to develop primarily in the self-sufficient way possible for a United States or a Soviet Union. They must trade their single surplus resource in world markets in order to obtain the other resources they require for their development. Their dependence on world demand for their single resource (or few resources) makes their development vulnerable to falling international prices. A drop in the price of their key export will cut the small country off from its external resources by reducing its ability to pay for them.

Small countries dependent on world trade may also suffer if technological changes elsewhere reduce foreign demand for their single resource export. This happened, for instance, to Malaysia, when the development of synthetic rubber, necessitated by World War II demands for a secure rubber supply, greatly cut the market for natural rubber. Similarly, Latin American coffee exports were hurt after World War II by the development of soluble coffee, which could be made from cheaper African varieties of coffee.

One-resource countries would like to stabilize the market and prices for their exports by international commodity agreements with their trading partners. These objectives have generally been opposed by the major

The conditions of life and work for many of the people in the less-developed countries make for a short and difficult existence. How can the people, like this child in a Manila shantytown, get out of the trap of poverty?

International Development Research Centre

How Guilty Are We?

Dr. Eric Williams, Prime Minister of Trinidad and Tobago, raises several crucial points about aid which should make us consider to what extent our "aid" is primarily in our own interest, rather than in the interests of the developing nations.

The demise of colonialism coincides with the birth of neo-colonialism. The emerging countries and the primary producers in general have repeatedly drawn attention to the increasing disparity between prices of raw materials and prices of manufactured goods. They have opposed also the growing restrictions in the markets of the developed countries on their own simpler industries. To develop, in these circumstances, a counter-program of economic aid to developing countries is simply to miss the whole point.

The evidence is devastating today of the pitfalls of economic aid. Canada's policies in respect of economic aid tend perhaps to be more liberal than those of other countries; but the fact remains that economic aid works often quite contrary to the best interests of the developing countries. It often forces them to buy the materials of the donor country, not infrequently competing with their own resources. The procedures associated with economic aid are cumbersome and time-consuming, and the opposition has been becoming more vigorous in respect of the Alliance for Progress in Latin America. The two most dangerous aspects of economic aid are: first, its military/political orientation; and, of perhaps even greater concern to the developing countries, the subordination of their own economic analyses and objectives to metropolitan emphasis and interests.

Source: *"The Developing Nation in the Modern World".* Encaenia Address by Dr. Williams at the University of New Brunswick, Fredericton, May 20, 1965. Reprinted with the permission of Dr. Williams and the University of New Brunswick.

consumer nations (which are for the most part the developed countries). From the perspective of the Third World countries, these remain unachieved goals. The one notable example of action which has been successful (from the perspective of producers) has been that of OPEC, the Organization of Petroleum-Exporting Countries, in obtaining massive increases in the price received for oil in the period since 1973.

Human Resources

Less developed countries often have the problem of too many people. **Overpopulation** gives rise to a vicious cycle of its own. Any significant increase in the standard of living—leading to a drop in the death rate—may result in an acceleration of the rate of population growth. This population upsurge may cause the standard of living to fall back to its former level of bare subsistence, thereby frustrating economic growth.

Efforts to limit population growth in low-income countries usually run up against religious, cultural, educational, and emotional barriers. Many religions and cultures attach a high value to large families, and the desire to have children is deeply rooted in mankind, psychologically as well as socially. Further, in poor countries, children may be seen—by the individual family—as additional sources of income. The children can soon help work on the family's plot of earth or go out to work elsewhere and bring money home. From the standpoint of the nation as a whole, however, these extra children may cause too heavy a burden upon total national resources and hence a decline in the living standards of the population as a whole.

Tied Aid:
The Case For and Against
in a Canadian Context

What is tied aid?

Assistance provided on the condition that goods and services will be supplied only by suppliers in the donor country

What is meant by "untying" aid?

Partial untying means allowing suppliers in all or a number of developing countries to compete against suppliers in the donor country for aid-financed orders. Full untying extends the opportunity to compete to suppliers in other developed countries as well

For

—Proponents of tied aid claim that it helps protect balance of payments and employment in Canada.
—Some individual Canadian suppliers who traditionally obtain aid-financed orders (e.g. locomotive manufacturers) might be caused short-term problems if Canada were to untie its aid.
—Where Canadian goods and services supplied under tied aid are not competitive, the terms under which such aid is provided may be sufficiently concessional to make the overall deal attractive.
—Politically-powerful domestic groups, such as exporters' associations, allege potential losses of orders leading to layoffs if aid is untied.
—If all or most other donors continue to tie their aid (which is the case, to varying degrees), Canada cannot be expected to step out of line.
—Tied aid can lead to more visibly Canadian projects in the Third World, which can generate support of aid by itinerant Canadian politicians and taxpayers.
—Tied aid is an opportunity to introduce goods and services into new markets.
—Canada has none of the colonial or historical links that give other donors a head start in untied commercial transactions with developing countries.
—In some areas of the world, tied Canadian aid may also confer an indirect commercial benefit on recipients—it may oblige suppliers in traditional donor countries to reduce their prices to meet the Canadian "competition".
—Untying can place a considerable burden both on recipients (not to mention the increased risk of corruption and other distortions), and on donors (to ensure that recipients can and do call tenders efficiently).

Against

—Strictly speaking, untied aid maximizes the real value of the aid by allowing the recipient to procure goods and services from the cheapest available source.
—Goods and services supplied under tied aid can cost from 15 to 30 per cent more than similar goods and services offered on the international market.
—The Economic Council of Canada says that halving the present amount of tied bilateral aid would not have a "noticeable" impact on Canada's balance of payments, besides reducing manufacturing employment and output in Canada by only about 0.2 per cent.
—Tied aid reinforces the tendency to provide goods and services that are technologically inappropriate, besides discouraging local solutions using local resources.
—Political advantages may be obtained from increased untying in terms of an enhanced international image, primarily in the eyes of the majority of the world's nations i.e. the developing countries.
—There is no evidence that tied aid has led to significant repeat orders—"one-of" orders (not leading to repeat business) may in fact be detrimental to Canada's reputation if suppliers are not interested in after-sales service.
—Untying can help to speed up the training of officials in developing countries capable of negotiating international tenders and procurement.

—Rigid adherence to tying regulations has been known to double the implementation time (as well as costs) of projects.

The Current Situation

Multilateral aid—Canadian multilateral aid is untied with the exception of multilateral food aid.
Bilateral aid—Up to 20 per cent of the dollar value of the bilateral program may be untied.

According to figures provisionally submitted to the Development Assistance Committee (DAC) of the Organization for Economic Cooperation and Development (OECD) as part of Canada's annual aid review exercise, 52 per cent of Canadian aid was estimated to be untied in 1977. The breakdown was estimated as follows:

	Total (a) ($million)	Untied (b) ($million)	(b) as per cent of (a)
bilateral aid	479.0	77.2	16
multilateral aid	517.2	436.7	84
	996.2	513.9	52

The International Situation

The latest available statistics from DAC indicate that the "best" performers in 1976 in respect of untying were Australia, Germany, Norway and Sweden (not to mention OPEC donors, usually totally untied). Only Belgium and Finland kept as large or a larger portion of aid disbursements fully tied than did Canada; however, France, Japan, Britain and the United States performed almost as "poorly" as Canada. Canada's performance showed a slight improvement in 1977.

Discussions on untying have taken place in the DAC forum and elsewhere almost continuously since 1970. Following relatively rapid agreement in 1973 on the untying of multilateral aid, much less progress has been made in respect of untying bilateral aid.

Reprinted from *Development Directions*, CIDA, Ottawa, August/September, 1978, p. 16.

While low-income countries generally have a surplus of labor, they also usually have a *scarcity of skilled labor*. This scarcity results from the lack of educational opportunities, formal and informal. A modern industrial nation needs large numbers of people with good educations and a wide variety of vocational skills, many of which have traditionally been learned on the job. A less-developed, rural nation lacks the human resources immediately suitable for economic and industrial advance.

At the level of higher education, many less developed countries have given insufficient emphasis to such fields as engineering, business administration, animal husbandry, and agriculture. Such fields, extremely important for economic development, are often neglected by students who regard them as lacking in social prestige.

The development problem in most poor countries is aggravated by the lack of a large, vigorous middle class. In developed countries, the middle class has traditionally provided the people who have served as organizers, leaders, and stimulators of national economic growth. If there is a shortage of entrepreneurs to play this role in low-income countries, it may be taken over by government officials or even army officers.

Capital Resources

Less developed countries are by definition short of real capital goods—everything from steel mills to farm implements. Accumulating capital goods is, as we noted above, difficult for low-income countries, whose people live close to the starvation level and who find it painful to increase savings.

Canadian International Development Agency and the National Film Board

Dependence on manual labor, illustrated by this photo of a dam under construction in India, may retard overall rates of growth by keeping total productivity down. However, such use of labor provides jobs which may be scarce. As with so many examples in our study of economics, it is a question of immediate goals and choices.

One way to try to crack this problem is by transferring surplus agricultural labor to industrial jobs where its output will be higher. In most less developed countries, there is widespread disguised unemployment in agriculture. Typically, in low-income countries, two-thirds to three-fourths of all workers are in agriculture; it has been estimated that the productivity of as much as one-third of these rural inhabitants is zero (possibly less than zero) because the fixed amount of land is hopelessly overmanned. The surplus labor does not increase the total output. Indeed, by breeding inefficiencies, it may even reduce total output. If these surplus agricultural workers could be transferred to other jobs, they could themselves make more capital goods—such as roads for dams—and, by increasing total output, increase national income and savings.

More capital could also be created, if existing natural, human, and capital resources could be used more efficiently. This might be done through special educational and training programs, through efforts to break traditional work habits, and through incentives for extra productive efforts on the part of both labor and management. Taxes on business are characteristically very high in low-income countries; this may act as a drag on productive business investment. Wealthy

IRAN: THE SHOCKS OF DEVELOPMENT

United Nations Photo

During the 1970s, Iran illustrated many of the conflicting forces and problems of the Third World. Its rich oil reserves supported an authoritarian state in which the gap between the rich and the poor grew ever wider, and western culture and political influence was increasingly dominant. With the collapse of this government, a new administration, dominated by conservative religious leaders, wished to pursue a more independent course, following traditional Islamic ways. The country seemed destined to increasing strife between groups divided over how best to use the nation's oil reserves, and whether to modernize rapidly, or maintain traditional ways.

United Nations Photo

people in less developed countries often put their money into luxuries, fancy homes, speculation in real estate; hoard it in private vaults; or send it abroad rather than invest it in productive uses in their own countries. In part, this may be a consequence of inflation, which as we shall see later, is often a problem in less developed nations.

However, private, productive investment in low-income countries may also be deterred by lack of **social overhead capital**—such as adequate means of transportation, communication, or power generation. It may not be profitable for a private investor to start a factory or mine or mill in the back country if there is no means of getting the products to market. Hence, government has a vital role to play in low-income countries in preparing the ground in which private investment and enterprise may flourish. But the governments of many less developed countries are suspicious or hostile toward private enterprise or private foreign investment. They often prefer to try to do the whole development job themselves and to gain the capital they need by gifts or loans from abroad on a government-to-government basis.

Nationalistic governments may pour their limited capital resources into monument building—that is, into such projects as huge plants, massive dams, nuclear reactors—which they think contribute to their national prestige. Such projects may be less useful to development than would many simpler, smaller scale investments, especially in sectors where productivity can be reasonably high and where significant numbers of jobs can be created.[2]

Nationalism

In their passionate nationalism, governments of low-income countries are only reflecting the emotions of their people. These emotions are very near the surface—and indeed sometimes erupt into internal revolutions, external wars, or even senseless slaughter of other ethnic or linguistic groups within the nation. The low-income countries are often still in the throes of trying to redress past grievances against their former rulers—whether their own traditional ruling class or foreign colonial rulers. This may color and distort their development thinking and planning with respect to both domestic and foreign investment.

THE PROBLEM OF INFLATION

The governments of low-income countries face special difficulties in handling their fiscal and monetary policies to promote rapid economic growth. New, unstable governments frequently hesitate to tax their people enough to cover the costs of all the development projects, educational programs, military activities, and welfare measures that they feel compelled to undertake.

As a result of this failure to tax as much as climbing government spending would warrant, inflation breaks out. It is often fed by the government's incompetence or inexperience in monetary matters. Once this inflation starts, it has a number of unhappy consequences. Inflation discourages productive investment and gives rise instead to speculation in land or commodities or causes capital flight to other countries. Secondly, inflation discourages people from saving because they fear that their savings will soon be valueless. Families may try to put all their savings into gold or tangibles that will be immune to inflation. Thirdly, inflation makes the goods produced in the low-income country uncompetitive in world markets—and simultaneously makes goods produced abroad relatively cheaper in terms of the poor nation's currency.

As the poor country's exports fall and its imports rise, its balance of payments falls into serious deficit. This makes it harder than ever for the poor country to borrow funds from abroad, since foreign financial institutions or businesses will be afraid that

[2] For a discussion of the problems of generating jobs along with economic growth in the LDCs, see A. G. Chandavarkar's study "More Growth—More Employment?" reprinted in *Readings In the World of Economics.*

World Bank Photo

One of the most common problems facing the typical less-developed nation is inadequate transportation and communication within the country. This photo shows road construction under way in Kenya with financial assistance from the World Bank.

they will never be able to get their money out of the low-income country, given all of its existing debts.

Therefore, poor countries experiencing balance-of-payments problems typically try to shut out imports and develop home-produced substitutes for imports. These policies usually aggravate the inefficiency of production in the poor country both because the foreign-made machinery is more efficient than the new domestic substitutes and because the production of the domestic substitutes may cause a shift of resources from relatively efficient to inefficient production.

Here we have another vicious cycle. Inflation leads to balance-of-payments deficits; this leads to cutting off imports; this leads to import substitution; this leads to greater inefficiency of production; this leads to more inflation; this leads to greater balance-of-payments deficits; and so on.[3]

At some point in this process, governments may devalue their currencies. They may do this openly or in a concealed way. If they decide—as they often do—to try to conceal the drop in the value of their money, they may try to do this by creating export subsidies (to reduce the price of their exports), by offering different exchange rates to

[3] Major increases in oil prices by OPEC countries have compounded the balance of payments and inflation problems of many of the oil-importing LDCs, where the capacity to absorb increased energy costs is much lower than in countries such as Canada.

foreigners to get them to buy particular goods, by offering special exchange rates to tourists from abroad, or by direct controls over particular imports and exports. They build up a complex system of licensing to control particular imports and exports, and this often breeds corruption—both among government officials and businessmen seeking special treatment or favors.

Thus, we see that once inflationary forces are set in motion, it becomes more and more difficult to eliminate them. If prices have gone up and wages have lagged, for instance, it may temporarily ease the problem by raising wages as much as prices have risen; but this may then squeeze profits and cause businesses to put their prices up further. The nation gets on an inflationary merry-go-round, and economic development is checked because of the poor use made of available natural, human, and capital resources.

THE DIVERSITY OF LOW-INCOME COUNTRIES[4]

We have made many generalizations in this chapter about the less developed countries. However, these countries differ widely among themselves in size, growth rates, inflationary behavior, and other respects.

Density of Population

Some low-income nations are huge—such as India with over 600 million people. Others are tiny—such as Gambia, with little more than 500 000 people. Some are densely populated—like Sri Lanka, with over 200 people per km^2. Others are sparsely settled—like Somalia, a desert land, with 5 people per km^2.

Income Differences

There are wide gradations between levels of income among the low-income countries. Brazil, for instance, is relatively an upper low-income country with a per capita GNP of $1140. Ethiopia is a lower low-income country with a per capita GNP of $100.[5]

Growth Rates

Some relatively low-income countries are growing fast—like Mexico with an average annual growth rate (in constant prices) of 5.5% during 1970-1976. Others are growing slowly or not at all. India had an annual average rate of 1.4% for the period 1970-1974. Barbados had an average of 1.7% during 1974-76. These rates were adjusted for inflation, but not for population growth.

Rates of Inflation

Inflation rates differ widely among the less developed countries, but are often quite high. The U.N. currently maintains price indexes based on 1970 = 100. Some measures of inflation are 1976 index readings of 267 in Bolivia, 200 in Haiti, 227 in Nigeria, and 285 in Burma. Some, however, are very low. For example, Egypt recorded 147, Guyana was 158, and the Indian index stood at 161. From the 1970 base, Canada had an index of 153 and many developed countries had much higher readings. As we can see, inflation is not a consistent factor in all less developed countries, and is not restricted to these countries.

Population Problems

In many countries, population increase is eating up most of the growth in total national output. Total output in Mexico, for example, increased by 5.5 percent annually from 1970 to 1976 but per capita growth increased by only 1.9 percent annually. During the same period, Pakistan's total output increased 3.6 percent annually but its per capita growth rate was 0.7 percent. In contrast,

[4] Statistical data in this section are from *The United Nations Statistical Yearbook-1977*, New York: United Nations, 1978, except for data transferred forward from Table 1-1.

[5] From Table 1-1; see this table again for international patterns.

Canadian International Development Agency

In many areas of the world, even a supply of water may be close to a luxury. Behind this Indian village well, a school under construction indicates the thirst for education which may exist along with physical thirst.

South Korea with a high growth rate of 10.9% and a relatively low rate of population growth saw its per capita output grow at an annual rate of 8.9% during the 1970-1976 period. (The above rates are all discounted so as to avoid inflationary effects on data.)

Despite tremendous efforts to raise living standards, many poor countries are barely able to increase the most important element in their people's living standard, food. Many low-income countries achieved a rate of increase of 1 percent per year or less in crop output per capita during much of the past decade. In some nations, major advances have been made, especially in Asia. Whether high rates of increase in food production can

Canada's Relations with Developing Countries

In 1978, the Economic Council of Canada released a major study on this topic. Reprinted here is a concise summary of that study which appeared in a journal of the Canadian International Development Agency.

A recently-released report by the Economic Council of Canada makes major recommendations concerning Canada's future relations with the developing countries. One of the major recommendations is that part of Canada's industrial sector be restructured to benefit some developing countries.

The 158-page report entitled *For a Common Future—A Study of Canada's Relations with Developing Countries* also assesses Canada's current trade, investment and aid relations with the Third World.

In the area of trade, the Economic Council points out that many developing countries possess a present or potential comparative advantage in the production of goods that are labor-intensive and based on standard technology. The Council recommends that Canada encourage the emergence of industrial capability in these nations through appropriate trade and investment policies.

One of the major recommendations of this advisory body to government, composed of academics and members of the business community, is that the federal government establish a fund of $4 billion devoted to a wide-ranging program of industrial reorganization within Canada that would benefit developing countries.

This adjustment fund would form part of a two-stage strategy aimed at restructuring some of Canada's industrial sectors threatened by imports from developing countries. The affected Canadian industries would be textiles, hosiery, clothing, leather products, some subsectors in the electrical and electronic equipment industry, sporting goods and toys.

A second stage of this strategy proposes that import barriers be lifted on these products. The aim would be to gradually liberalize trade with the Third World.

The Council estimates 250 000 Canadian jobs in industry would be lost—130 000 of them in Quebec and 100 000 in Ontario—about 15 per cent of the manufacturing labor force or 3 per cent of all Canadian jobs.

The Council says that an average of $16 000 per job created would be required to consolidate or replace the sectors threatened. The $4 billion fund spread over 15 years would reorganize the industrial sector in Ontario and Quebec for the eventual benefit of both Canada and the affected developing countries.

The Council also points out, however, that the opening of Canada's markets to industrial products from developing countries would benefit only the richest among them. For the poorest countries, development aid would remain the only form of assistance Canada could provide.

The Council recommends that Canada concentrate more of its aid budget on bilateral programs and reduce to 35 per cent the share of public funds going to multilateral non-food aid programs.

The Council notes that Canada devoted an important share—43.2 per cent in 1976-77—to multilateral bodies. The Council is not, however, convinced that organizations such as the UN General Fund and development banks use Canadian resources in the best manner compared with development activities Canada could itself carry out.

The Economic Council also believes that the Canadian government should establish a system for controlling the efficiency of aid in each of the 30 developing countries that become recipients and that an evaluation be carried out at least every five years.

The Council says that tied aid (now 85 per cent of all Canada's bilateral aid) which requires the recipient country to obtain goods and equipment from Canadian sources is inefficient, and concludes that lowering the proportion of tied aid in all bilateral programs from 85 per cent to 40 per cent would have no detrimental effect on Canada's balance of payments.

In order to ensure a gradual growth of development aid, the Council recommends the volume of Canadian assistance to developing countries never fall below 0.5 per cent of Canada's gross national product throughout the duration of the recommended industrial reorganization program.

The Report also touches on the issues of immigration to Canada of people from developing countries, the impact of Canadian investment in developing countries, and the effect of increasing costs of energy to both developing and developed countries.

In summary, the Council recommends that:

- the federal government establish, with affected provinces, an industrial adjustment and redeployment fund and a comprehensive joint regional development strategy in order to shift Canada's industrial structure away from highly protected, labor-intensive and standard-technology activities in favor of imports from Third World countries; the fund should be fixed at $4 billion and be spread over approximately 15 years;
- Canada's system of special quotas and other restraints on the import of manufactured goods be progressively dismantled over a period of approximately 10 years when economic conditions in Canada improve;
- Canada use the multilateral trade negotiation system to rationalize its own tariff structure, by reducing unusually high nominal tariffs to encourage the adjustment of highly protected industries vulnerable to developing-country competition;
- the rates of duty applicable under Canada's generalized system of preferences be halved in favor of developing countries whose national wealth and industrial capacity fall below an agreed-upon index;
- CIDA's Business and Industry Division, which supports preinvestment studies in developing countries, be transferred to the Department of Industry, Trade and Commerce or the Export Development Corporation;
- Canada limit its share of aid allocated to multilateral institutions in order to facilitate the reorganization of the bilateral program, and multilateral non-food aid constitute not more than 35 per cent of the total aid program;
- the total number of countries given aid by Canada on a bilateral basis be gradually reduced to about 30;
- Canada move progressively toward untying aid fully in respect of procurement in developing countries and that it allow procurement in other donor countries that would extend the same treatment to Canada;
- a system of aid-effectiveness monitoring be established for each of the 30 countries that would receive Canadian aid in the new bilateral program; the system would produce evaluations for each recipient country at least every five years;
- Canadian aid would not fall below 0.5 per cent of gross national product for the period from now until the end of the proposed adjustment and redeployment of industry program;
- the government finance the development of data related to ethnic adjustments in Canada and conduct studies to suggest ways to facilitate the adjustment of immigrants to Canada and foster racial harmony.

Although not a formal recommendation, the Council suggests that Canada's aid efficiency could be improved either by allowing the External Affairs Department to have full authority for coordinating policies dealing with development relations, or by creating a new department using CIDA as the core, with responsibility for integrating all aspects of development assistance to the Third World.

Reprinted from *Development Directions*, CIDA, Ottawa, August/September, 1978, pp. 8-9.

C.U.S.O. AT WORK

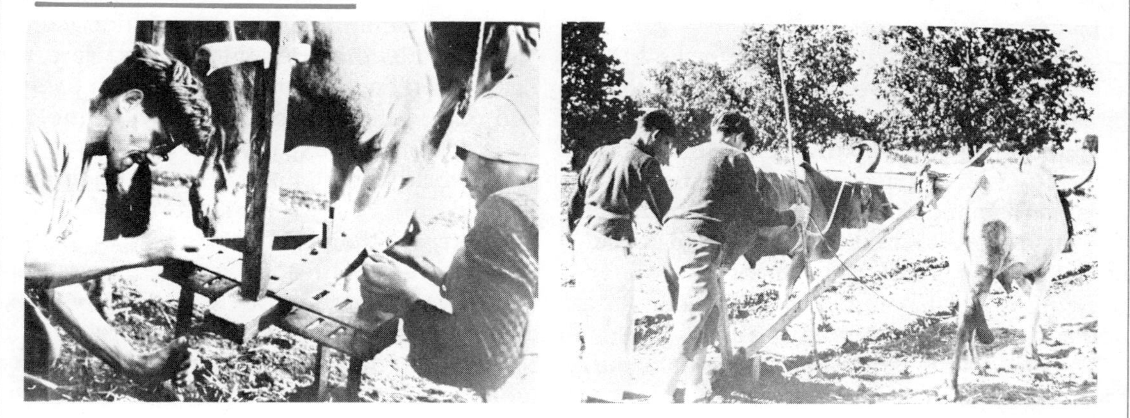

Canadian University Service Overseas and Jim Ward

"Agriculturist and nurse needed for work in private ashram institution devoted to the uplift of tribal people. Farm of thirteen acres and dispensary in isolated rural setting, three miles from nearest bus, no electricity and no running water. Head of ashram dominating (but interesting). Communal vegetarian food, two private rooms. Monthly salary ten dollars each. Lots of development work needed."
Reprinted from Man Deserves Man, *by Bill McWhinney and Dave Godfrey, by permission of McGraw-Hill Ryerson, Toronto.*
This was the assignment received by Jim and Sheila Ward who spent a number of years in India with Canadian University Service Overseas (C.U.S.O.). This body, typical of many volunteer organizations in the developed countries, was started in 1961, and in its years of growth, C.U.S.O. personnel overseas have increased from 17 to well over a thousand. The photographs of Jim Ward at work indicate what C.U.S.O. volunteers do—work at the local level. The book from which the material is taken provides fascinating accounts of the experiences and the opinions of C.U.S.O. volunteers who have served all over the developing world.

become general trends remains to be seen. Many observers fear that the relative rates of population increase and the low rates of growth of food production are setting the stage for a serious food crisis and widespread starvation. They regard the population problem, which we shall consider in greater detail in the next chapter, as one of the most serious facing the world today.

A NEW INTERNATIONAL ECONOMIC ORDER?

Experience in the decade of the 1970s has brought about changes in targets for development and in attitudes toward policies designed to promote development. Trends have indicated that the goals of the previous decade, which called for a narrowing of the gaps between the rich and poor nations, are very long-term at best. Such a view may be called either pessimistic or realistic. Regardless of which description is chosen, the emerging facts indicate that many short-term targets often involve little more than basic survival for many of the less developed countries and large proportions of their citizens.

In virtually all cases, aid from developed nations in its various forms has remained far below the accepted U.N. target of .7% of GNP of donor nations. Canada's aid effort has been running at about .5% of Canadian GNP, 30% below the target level, and our performance has been relatively good among the developed countries. As of the mid-

1970s, the comparative figures for the Federal Republic of Germany, the U.S.A. and Japan were, respectively, .34%, .27% and .21%.

Gains which have taken place in the LDCs as a result of aid have often been countered by other forces. Factors such as the impact of population growth, rising prices for necessary imports such as oil and machinery, depressed demand for and prices of many of the key exports from the LDCs, and major increases in the yearly burden of interest on growing debts have all inhibited economic and social progress in many nations.

The net result is a bleak immediate outlook. Concern is rising over the need for increases in aid from the developed world at a time when stagflation affects both the willingness and relative capacity of donors to maintain existing levels.

In addition to the need for more aid, increased attention is being given to other issues which have far-reaching implications for citizens of both the developed and less developed countries.

During the 70s, an important objective of the LDCs was to gain freer access to export markets in the developed world. The U.N. Conferences on Trade and Development (UNCTAD) gave this a high priority. Agreements reached within the General Agreements on Tariffs and Trade (GATT) have made some provisions for special trade preferences for LDCs, but there is no doubt about their need to have export opportunities increased. There is a question, however, about the extent to which this will be provided for, given the pressures facing the economies of the developed world and the rising frequency of calls for trade barriers to protect domestic jobs in many of the developed countries, including Canada.

There are other concerns of the LDCs in the area of trade. One of these is to stabilize prices received for many of their export staples. The example of what the OPEC nations have been able to do in increasing their earnings has stimulated other groups of commodity producers to promote similar programs of joint action to improve the prices of their exports. Another need is for freer access to technology in ways which can be controlled by the LDCs themselves. Here, the LDCs often encounter problems with patents and other forms of controls over technology by corporations (usually based in the developed world) which have led in technological advances.

Related to the problem of trade barriers is that of the balance of payments problem faced by many of the LDCs. Instability of exchange rates and shortages of foreign currency reserves have been increased by two mounting and interrelated problems. The OPEC price increases on oil have hit many LDCs even harder than countries such as Canada. In order to finance energy imports along with other needs, the rate of foreign borrowing by the LDCs increased significantly in the 1970s. Estimates are that, as of 1977, the level of repayable debt carried by the LDCs was about $225 billion, up from about $60 billion in 1970. The yearly burden of interest payments has increased even more for, despite the fact that many of the loans are at subsidized rates, virtually all interest rates have been going up during this period. In the face of these mounting burdens, the LDCs are certainly in need of reductions in the burden of both oil costs from OPEC, and debt charges from the lender nations and institutions. It would be risky to speculate about OPEC's policy, given the extent to which the factors influencing OPECs prices have been influenced by political rather than economic considerations. Relief from the pressures of debt charges is likely to come in many cases, though it often as not may be prompted by the lack of any alternative. Some nations have already reached a crisis over their debts. In 1976 and 1977, Zaire was unable to meet obligations on loans and a moratorium was granted while attempts were made under International Monetary Fund coordination to restore some degree of financial order. The heavy

The Failure of Aid and the Need to Find a Better Alternative

This article, written by Tim Brodhead, was printed in an opinion column in a journal published by CIDA, the Canadian International Development Agency. Its appearance there does not mean that it reflects in any way, CIDA's policy or the general attitude of the Canadian government toward aid. It does, in many ways, however, reflect the direction of the ideas raised in the section of the text "A New International Economic Order?"

The inadequacy of aid as a tool for effecting a more equitable distribution of the world's wealth has become increasingly apparent. The hopes of achievement on the scale of the massive and successful Marshall Plan for the post-Second World War reconstruction of Europe have faded.

Economic inequality is probably greater now than it ever has been: the lowest income countries, with 26 per cent of the world's population, have a per capita GNP which is only 4 per cent of that of the developed countries, which contain an approximately equal proportion of the world's people. Nor is this situation changing appreciably; the growth rate over the period 1960-70 was three times greater for the rich countries than for the poorest. Narrowing the gap is as far away as ever.

Only the expectations have changed. Not of the goal, of course—if anything, the poor are less resigned to their fate. But there is a lot more realism now about the likelihood of a voluntary fundamental shift of resources, and of the role of aid in this process. The first development decade expired on the new cry, "trade, not aid." The spotlight turned from the Pearson Report and official development assistance targets to UNCTAD commodity conferences, the General Agreement on Tariffs and Trade, and negotiations for a new international economic order.

As aid performance has deteriorated—most industrialized countries are closer to .35 per cent than the target of .7 per cent of GNP set by the UN years ago and Canada has slipped back from .56 per cent in 1975 to .48 per cent in 1976—the focus of attention has shifted from national aid appropriations to bargaining between economic and political power blocs. Voluntary, and therefore arbitrary, decisions about the allocation of national resources to meet international objectives have given way to international negotiations for a structural transformation of the world economic system.

The limitations of aid, presented as a kind of state philanthropy, have been underlined during the present economic crisis in the West. Adverse economic conditions produce popular pressures to restrict aid spending, whether in an absolutely rich country like West Germany, or in a relatively rich country like Britain, where in a recent survey 64 per cent of the respondents said Britain was too poor to give aid. This might be compared to a decision, on the national level, to cut back unemployment insurance because there are too many without work.

If voluntary measures are not enough, can we foresee alternatives? Over the last century in North America the credo of individual free enterprise has been tamed and circumscribed in order to meet a range of social objectives. Can voluntary action on the national level be replaced by a set of international obligations to reach the overriding goal of meeting the basic needs of the majority of mankind? Glimmerings of this may already be discerned in the negotiations for a new international economic order and discussions about sharing the benefits to be derived from exploiting new areas of the globe such as the seabed and Antarctica.

Recently, too, Dame Barbara Ward dusted off an idea first mooted 30 years ago by Trygve Lie, first UN Secretary General, for a more automatic system of financial transfers in the form of a world tax. And, as in most modern societies, one of the aims of such a tax would be to redress gross inequalities of wealth, shifting resources from the rich North to the poor South.

There are problems in such an idea, of course, notably that of control and use. There would be little enthusiasm for turning over revenues to the United Nations as it presently functions, or for creating another swollen bureaucracy. However, regional bodies, such as the European Economic Commission in Brussels might offer relevant models.

It would be essential that the aim of any form of global tax should be not to substitute for structural reform of the world economic system, but to act as an immediate step toward meeting the basic needs of people in the poorest countries. As such, there would have to be ways of ensuring that it was the people who benefited—not, as has been the case with much aid under present systems, a narrow local elite. Merely reinforcing governmental structures, particularly in repressive societies, is no recipe for development.

However, channels for wider popular involvement in development issues exist in most industrialized countries (voluntary agencies, education and pressure groups, the overseas linkages of trade unions and professional bodies), and mechanisms for government support of these have evolved.

A widening of our sense of social responsibility beyond national boundaries, like the introduction of the graduated income tax, would be resisted by the privileged but could eventually be seen as necessary for the greater good of society. Problems in instituting it could be overcome; what is needed is the political will to achieve the goal for which men and women have struggled. In the words of William Shakespeare more than 350 years ago: "So distribution should undo excess and each man have enough."

Reprinted from *Development Directions*, CIDA, Ottawa, May, 1978, p. 32.

debt load of the LDCs is highly concentrated, with about ten nations accounting for well over half the debt. Among the principal debtor nations are India, Pakistan, Zaire, Brazil and Mexico. Brazil and Mexico together in 1977 had a debt load of $60 billion. Such concentration of debt is hazardous for lenders as well as borrowers, for a major default could conceivably set off a chain reaction within the international banking and financial system, with catastrophic effects.

In the face of such rising dependence on international agreements and sources of credit, the LDCs have been demanding a greater voice in organizations such as the World Bank and the International Monetary Fund. The alternative, in their eyes, is to run the risk of having a new form of colonial status imposed through some form of financial controls. Such circumstances brought Egypt under British control a century ago. The LDCs today wish to avoid either the reality or even the appearance of the loss of full independence which, in many cases, has been achieved only recently.

Within the LDCs, a range of special stresses and strains are increasing. In some countries such as Mexico, rapid shifts of population to urban areas create special problems. At its present level of 12 million, Mexico City is one of the largest urban centers in the world. Fueled by urbanization and a Mexican net rate of population growth of 3.5%, Mexico City could reach 30 million by the end of the century.

Political and social pressures are rising. The push for evolution or revolution seems to be intensifying, promoted by mixes of urban and rural forces. In many cases, major internal social adjustments and power shifts seem likely. External relationships face increased pressure as well. Despite (or, to some degree, because of) their dependence on the developed nations, there seem to be signs of growing hostility toward developed nations within the LDCs. This may take the form of rhetoric; it may be directed at foreign-owned firms or property within the LDCs; it may take the form of playing major powers against each other; or it could ultimately combine with other forces and lead to direct conflicts.

Two significant recent studies have dealt with the potential political effects if we fail to come to grips with economic inequalities. *Mankind At the Turning Point,* a 1974 study for the Club of Rome, was somewhat more optimistic about our economic prospects than its predecessor volume, *The Limits to Growth.* The need for effective action was highlighted as the point of concern. The basic view was that, if we act, the world can avoid economic and social disaster. But if we do not move in time, the economic and social pressures may well trigger political forces which could undermine world peace and whatever stability does exist. In his introduction to a sequel report, *RIO-Reshaping the International Order,* (coordinated by Nobel prizewinner, Jan Tinbergen), U.N. Secretary-General Kurt Waldheim states clearly his view that "the existing gap between these groups of nations (the rich and the poor) will increasingly represent a potential threat to international peace and security."

RIO, published in 1976, outlines a sweeping set of proposals for changes in world priorities. Modifications of existing international agreements and institutions are suggested to promote development in priority sectors, such as agriculture, and to increase the flows of trade and technology in ways most helpful to the LDCs. A recurring theme is the need for people to realize how crucial it is to solve this range of international economic problems. Failure to do so invites disaster for poor and rich nations alike.

A slightly newer, massive, UN-sponsored study entitled *The Future of the World Economy* has failed to add much optimism. The research team, headed by Wassily Leontief, has not, in its initial releases, touched on political issues to the same degree as the Club of Rome reports. But Leontief's economic projections are fairly compatible with the others: his outlook is gloomy as well. Based on projections of growth rates even higher than those actually reached in the 1970s, his model did not project any significant narrowing of the gap between rich and poor nations before the end of this century. In order to achieve a major narrowing of the gaps, the model required rates of investment and growth which seem far beyond our realistic capacities. In other words, *The Future of the World Economy* also projects that humankind will have to "run even harder" to simply maintain our place on the treadmill. In the short run, immediate survival seems the best we can expect, globally.

To attain even this minimum short-run goal, major efforts and sacrifices are called for. To go beyond these minimum goals, the costs will be even greater for both the LDCs and the developed nations. The costs of meeting these requirements will impose a heavy burden in future decades, but the failure to achieve the goals poses an even greater threat to mankind.

A New International Economic Order?—Related Reading

Mesarovic, M. and Pestel, E., *Mankind at the Turning Point,* Toronto: Clarke, Irwin, 1974.

Tinbergen, Jan, *RIO: Reshaping the International Order,* Toronto: Clarke, Irwin, 1976.

Laszlo, Ervin, *et. al., Goals for Mankind,* Toronto: Clarke, Irwin, 1977.

Leontief, Wassily, *The Future of the World Economy,* New York: United Nations/Oxford University Press, 1977.

For much more concise comments, see:

"Can Canada Help Achieve a New World Order?" Douglas Roche, M.P. in *Saturday Night,* May, 1975, pp. 11-13.

"The Case for a Global Marshall Plan", *Time,* June 12, 1978, pp. 58-59.

SUMMARY

The low-income countries of the world, which include about two-thirds of the world's population, are struggling to achieve economic development and a higher standard of living for their people. It is in the interests (humanitarian, political, and economic) of the developed countries to see the low-income countries succeed in their effort.

However, the poor countries are facing formidable obstacles to their advancement. Many are short of adequate—or adequately diversified—natural resources. Many, with only one or a few resources in surplus for export, are dependent upon fluctuations in world trade. A fall in the demand for and price of their limited export resources may mean the choking off of their development program. Human resources are short in the low-income countries, not in the quantitative but rather in the qualitative sense. While commonly suffering from overpopulation, low-income countries have severe shortages of the skilled manpower, competent managers, and enterprising businessmen essential to economic growth in the modern industrial world. The low-income countries are also very short of real capital resources; their low income itself makes it difficult for them to save enough to form sufficient capital. Their political and economic instability frequently aggravates this problem of insufficient saving and investment. Their common suspicion and hostility toward foreign private investment further complicate the problem.

The developing nations have acute need of wise economic management by their governments, but this is often lacking. Many new and inexperienced governments try to do too much too soon to raise the people's living standards by increasing expenditures without raising enough funds through taxation. This often breeds inflation, which is compounded by incompetent handling of monetary policy. When inflation breaks out, it tends to check economic growth by discouraging saving and investment in productive enterprises; it, rather, encourages hoarding, speculation, or capital flight. Inflation also damages the country's balance of payments position, often leading it to adopt protectionist economic policies. These may, in turn, lead to further inflation, further inefficiency, and further payments difficulties.

The above generalizations apply in widely differing degrees among the low-income countries. These countries differ markedly in size, density of population, income, growth rates, and rates of inflation. Very generally, however, they face problems of overpopulation and inadequate food supplies, both because of inadequate emphasis on improving agricultural production and because of their inability to restrain the rate of population increase.

There is a growing sense of crisis about the plight of the less developed nations. Needs for more assistance in more appropriate forms are increasing but not being met. As a result, some observers feel that the options are narrowing and may reach the point of forcing us to experience global economic and social adjustments in the distribution of wealth. Whether, or how, such global evolution or revolution takes place is one of the most critical issues facing mankind.

KEY CONCEPTS

overpopulation

social overhead capital

QUESTIONS FOR REVIEW AND DISCUSSION

1. Why should people in Canada be concerned with economic development in the less developed nations of the world?
2. What are some of the general characteristics that seem to impede economic growth in the less developed countries of the world? Classify these characteristics under the general categories of scarce resources used in Chapter 3, i.e. natural resources, human resources (including entrepreneurship), real capital goods, technology, and environment for enterprise (social and cultural values). Can you think of other sets of non-economic categories into which the general characteristics of low-income countries might be classified? Explain your answer.
3. Are all low-income countries identical? What are some of the ways in which they differ?
4. What is meant by the term *social overhead capital*? How was such capital acquired in the Canadian economy? Do you think most low-income countries today should use the same or different techniques? Why?
5. Does inflation present any special problems to low-income countries that it does not present to high-income countries? Do you think that a low-income country might have more or less difficulty in using monetary and fiscal policies to fight inflation? Why?
6. Do you agree with the statement that "low-income countries are caught in a series of vicious cycles?" What might some of these cycles be? How might they be broken?

PROBLEMS AND EXERCISES TO SHARPEN YOUR UNDERSTANDING

Suggest some policies to promote economic growth and improve the standard of living in the world's less developed countries. What are the main obstacles to having each of these policies successfully implemented? Can these obstacles be overcome?

Compare your policies with those of other members of your class, and after a thorough discussion, try to reach an agreement on the policy or policies most likely to achieve success.

To obtain more detailed, up-to-date information on governmental development aid from Canada, obtain a copy of the latest CIDA Report from the Canadian International Development Agency, Ottawa. What information can you find about current efforts of private agencies such as CUSO or OXFAM?

CHAPTER 35

THE WORLD POPULATION PROBLEM

■ CONFLICTING PREDICTIONS ■ PREDICTION TECHNIQUES ■ CONFLICTING ATTITUDES ■ THE PESSIMISM OF MALTHUS ■ ANTI-MALTHUSIAN POPULATION THEORIES ■ NEO-MALTHUSIAN POPULATION THEORIES ■ POPULATION GROWTH IN ECONOMICALLY DEVELOPED COUNTRIES ■ POPULATION PRESSURE IN LESS DEVELOPED COUNTRIES ■ SUMMARY

The world's population, according to United Nations data in the mid-1970s, was increasing by 75 million a year. This annual increase equals the present total of the populations of Canada and Britain. And forecasts generally agree that by the end of this century the world's 1975 population of 4 billion will have increased to about 6.5 billion.

CONFLICTING PREDICTIONS

But are these forecasts any good? Population experts differ by billions when they look only a couple of generations ahead. In the 1950s two leading demographers, W. S. and E. S. Woytinsky, did a monumental study in which they forecast the world's population at 3.2 billion in 2000. In 2050, said the Woytinskys, world population would reach 3.6 billion; thereafter, it would grow very slowly and level off at about 4 billion. However, three California Institute of Technology scientists, Professors Harrison Brown, James Bonner, and John Weir soon afterward "conservatively" forecast a world population of 7 billion in the year 2050.

But when we look at these older forecasts, compared to current actual population figures and trends, we can see world population reaching the Brown-Bonner-Weir projection almost fifty years sooner than originally predicted, and running at double the figure projected by the Woytinskys. Obviously population prediction is not an easy task.

PREDICTION TECHNIQUES

Different conclusions on how long present rapid population growth will continue stem essentially from different techniques of prediction. There are three chief techniques.

1. Historical—This treats population growth as an aspect of cultural development. Nations with similar cultures—industrial or agrarian—will have similar birth and death patterns, according to this theory. When the economies of poor countries come more nearly to resemble those of the more developed Western nations, their birth and death rates will drop, and their fast rates of population growth will decline.

2. Statistical—This is based on an application of recent birth and death rates to existing population groups. High and low assumptions are made as to how much existing rates may vary over the forecast period.

3. Mathematical—This assumes that total population grows over time according to some definite mathematical formula. The demographer fits a curve to past population data, then lets the curve extend into the future.

All these techniques are full of possible flaws which may lead to bigger and bigger errors as they stretch further out into time.

For instance, the link between culture and population growth, assumed by the historical technique, is extremely unsteady. Four decades or so ago, most demographers assumed that the industrial North American population had settled down to a very stable, scarcely growing trend. But after World War II, the North American population became one of the fastest growing in the world. In the late 1940s and 1950s, North America's population was growing as fast as southeast Asia, faster than the Soviet Union or south central Asia. As the birth rate began to decline in the early 1960s, there was again reason to wonder whether North America's population growth rate would not again slow down.

Even quite short-run statistical forecasts can go haywire fast. Slight underestimates of both birth and death rates can result in errors running into the tens of millions in only a decade.

CONFLICTING ATTITUDES

The difficulty in assessing the accuracy of population predictions is certainly compounded if you ask whether a rapid increase in numbers is a good thing or not. To most businessmen, a fast-growing population has usually seemed highly desirable—a stimulus to investment, profits, consumer demand, technological development, and economic growth.

But to many an economist, geochemist, and biologist, rapid population growth is the bane of economic progress. In the 1960s, Mao Tse-tung said in an ideological lecture to the Chinese people, "This figure [30 million Chinese births a year] must be of great concern to us all. . . . The increase in the grain harvest for the last two years has been barely sufficient to cover the needs of our growing population. . . . Steps must therefore be taken to keep our population for a long time at a stable level, say of 600 million."

Is rapid population growth, then, bad for China but good for Canada? Some economists hold that—though years ago North America was underpopulated—nowadays rapid population growth is a drag, not a stimulus, to the individual's economic wel-

Table 35-1. COMPARATIVE POPULATION GROWTH RATES, 1970-76

	Average Annual Rates, 1970-76, Per Hundred People		
Country	Births	Deaths	Net Growth*
Bolivia	4.37	1.80	2.57
Burma	3.95	1.58	2.37
Egypt	3.77	1.23	2.54
Ethiopia	4.94	2.56	2.38
Haiti	3.58	1.63	1.95
India	3.45	1.44	2.01
Nigeria	4.93	2.27	2.66
Sri Lanka	2.99	.78	2.21
Turkey	3.96	1.46	2.50
Australia	1.67	.83	.84
Austria	1.16	1.26	−.10
Canada	1.58	.72	.86
Denmark	1.29	1.07	.22
Iceland	1.94	.69	1.32
Kuwait	4.71	.53	3.43
Sweden	1.19	1.10	.09
Switzerland	1.17	.90	.27
United States	1.47	.89	.58

Note: *The data exclude the factor of migration of people.
Source: Data from *United Nations Statistical Yearbook, 1977,* New York: United Nations, 1978.

Expression of the rates in terms of a quantity per hundred people permits easy expression as a percentage. Note the selection of the two groups is that of the first and last groups of nations from Table 1-1. What generalizations can you make? What exceptions do you find to these generalizations?

fare, just as it is in China. Any country, advanced or less developed, they maintain, can have the gains of economic growth gobbled up by increasing numbers of people.

The debate over population can at least be neatly organized—into four opposing positions.

1. Population will go on growing rapidly, and this is bad.
2. Population will not go on growing rapidiy, and this is bad.
3. Population will go on growing rapidly, and this is good.
4. Population will not go on growing rapidly, and this is good.

Without resolving the issue, which includes moral and religious as well as political, social, and economic factors, we can at least clarify the problem.

THE PESSIMISM OF MALTHUS

The founding father of the pessimistic school of thought on population growth was Thomas R. Malthus, the English clergyman-economist, who held that population (like money in a savings account) tended to grow by a geometrical progression—while resources showed no such tendency. In fact, as limited resources were more intensively used, diminishing output per capita would set in—and per capita income would keep slipping below the starvation level, thereby restoring the balance between resources and people (just about at the starvation level). In short, improved standards of living are unattainable.

Obviously, Malthus was too gloomy. Since his *Essay in Population* was published in 1800, world population has trebled, and certainly in the West, living standards have risen enormously. The Malthusian devil retreated before the onrush of modern technology, including fertilizers and other agricultural improvements that greatly increased the crop yields of land. Malthus' fundamental error was in regarding resources as fixed and not as a function of changing technology. In the short term, at least, Malthus seemed to be proved wrong.

ANTI-MALTHUSIAN POPULATION THEORIES

In fact, only four decades ago, most economists were more worried that population decline, not growth, would breed economic misery. For, in the 1930s, in Western nations, the falling birth rate and falling national incomes seemed causally related—and the cause-effect chain was taken to run from population decline to income decline.

An outstanding proponent of this theory at that time was a leading Swedish economist, Gunnar Myrdal[1] who was later to be the co-recipient of the Nobel Prize in Economics in 1974. The worst effect of a shrinking population, said Myrdal in the 1930s, is that it dries up investment opportunities and creates wasteful imbalances in an economy's capital structure. For instance, Myrdal asked, what happens if you make a mistake and build too many of the wrong kind of apartments in a growing city? Nothing serious—because, as the city grows, people will at length occupy your apartments. But, if the city's population were shrinking, nobody would ever occupy them—capital would be tied up in useless property. The same holds for much of the economy, said Myrdal. A shrinking population multiplies investment risks. On the contrary, he held, a growing market—growing in population—is the basic condition of a free, unregulated capitalist system. Moreover, Myrdal argued, a declining population is an aging population—and such a society becomes dominated by old people and suffers a loss of vigor and opportunity.

Myrdal's case was powerfully impressive to a world worrying in the 1930s about social decay, economic stagnation, and the threat of world war, for which large numbers might mean national survival. His argument, and

[1] A widely-acclaimed work by Myrdal, *Asian Drama*, provides one of the best detailed examinations of the entire range of the problems of LDCs. (Myrdal altered his judgment about the need for population growth in Europe and this earlier opinion does not form any part of his analysis of LDCs in *Asian Drama* or other recent works.)

Radio Times Hulton Picture Library

Prints Division of the New York Public Library

The Rev. Thomas R. Malthus was the economist who first developed a theory to show why population growth might be a serious barrier to economic progress. The second picture shows the living conditions of the working class in London in the nineteenth century—the social setting in which Malthus' ideas became popular.

others like it, helped lead governments to adopt population policies aimed at stimulating the birth rate by devices such as housing subsidies and family allowances.

To many the postwar boom in both population and income appeared further to confirm the Myrdal position. Since the war, many companies have based their expansion plans significantly on population forecasts—taking for granted the positive correlation between rising population and rising national income. These plans were and are, however, based on the assumption that growth rates can be achieved that will more than support increases in population.

NEO-MALTHUSIAN POPULATION THEORIES

But a growing number of economists think this is a false assumption. Some, such as Professor Joseph J. Spengler of Duke University, argue that population growth actually depresses income. Here are the main points in the anti-population growth argument.

1. Population growth does create a need for more investment (if you are going to maintain living standards), but it does not necessarily create an effective demand. For instance, increasing numbers of people in less developed nations may need more housing, but the capacity to acquire it indi-

A Demographic Time Bomb

Professor Joseph J. Spengler, one of the world's leading demographers (population experts), warns his fellow economists that excessive population growth poses a serious danger to the future of mankind.

Unless man halts population growth, population growth will halt man. . . . Between 1960 and 2000, according to United Nations estimates, world population will grow nearly twice as fast as in 1920-60—around 113 per cent to between 6 and 7 billion. The proportion in the developed world will fall to around 22 per cent, since its numbers will grow only 61 per cent, or but two-fifths as fast as the population of the underdeveloped world, which is expected to increase about 151 per cent. Should world population continue to grow about 2 per cent per year* it would number 16-18 billion by 2050 and 43-50 billion by 2100. Even if it should proceed only 1.5 per cent per year, it would number 13-15 billion by 2050 and 43-50 billion by 2100. Acres of all sorts per capita, still about 4.7 to 5.5 in 2000, will then have fallen to 0.6-1.25 by 2100, and close to one-half of this amount will be unfit for habitation except by Lower Slobbovians. Man will have become essentially spaceless in a space age, unless competition for living space should accidentally transform the "ultimate deterrent" into the "ultimate detergent" and, as D. M. Heer estimates (in his *After Nuclear Attack*), destroy perhaps 30 per cent of the population, mostly in heavily urbanized areas.

Given growth of the order suggested as likely in the absence of concerted efforts to limit numbers, food shortages would eventually develop despite schemes for deriving protein from coal and petroleum as well as subsistence from algae and other crude organic matter, or for supporting a man on 20 well-cultivated square metres of soil. . . .

As matters stand, the longer-run prospect is definitely Malthusian, with man sitting on a demographic time bomb into which legislators and others, here and abroad, continue to shovel combustibles.

* It might be noted that as of 1976, the world rate was holding very close to this—at 1.9%.

From J. J. Spengler, "The Economist and the Population Question," Presidential address delivered at the Seventy-eighth Annual Meeting of the American Economic Association, New York, December 29, 1965.

vidually or provide it collectively is not necessarily there. Even in advanced countries, more people may effectively demand more housing—but at the expense of other kinds of investment that would raise per capita output and income.

2. A growing population reduces the relative size of the age group (say, 20 to 65) that actually produces income and increases the part of the population that must be supported. The population, thanks to a rise in the birth rate and a drop in the death rate, is, in fact, growing fastest at both ends—thus providing double burdens on the working people in the middle.

3. Population growth is already pressing hard against certain resources, depressing income in hard-to-measure ways. It is causing serious problems of congestion, which require fantastically expensive capital expenditures (on highways, bridges, tunnels, and so on). It is causing air pollution and is eating up clean and pleasant country and beach land. As time goes on, growing population will press still harder against domestic and world supplies of minerals and fossil

fuels and push raw material costs higher.

4. A rising population is no guarantee against economic depression. The depressions of the nineteenth century, for instance, certainly occurred in the midst of rapidly rising population movements.

5. A rising birth rate is not essential for the maintenance of full employment. That depends more on factors such as monetary and fiscal policies, technological change, trade patterns and other non-demographic factors. Rising population does stimulate certain kinds of investment, as in housing or schools, but there is no reason why the society could not just as well devote more of its income either to other kinds of investment or to raising consumption levels without the pressure of population increase.

The key to both riddles about population—how much and how fast it will go on growing and whether continued growth is economically good or bad—lies in the answer to this question: Can technological progress keep usable resources growing faster than numbers of people? Conceivably, even the living-space problem might be solved technologically—by emigration to the moon and other planets.

POPULATION GROWTH IN ECONOMICALLY DEVELOPED COUNTRIES

There is no doubt that a rate of population growth in excess of the rate of economic growth actually depresses living standards. If the real income of a nation grows by 3 percent per year and its population grows at the same rate, per capita real income obviously does not rise at all.

But as we have seen, some economists would argue that the rapid rate of population growth would, in fact, have an even more adverse effect on the rise in living standards. This would happen because the heavy investment needed to provide housing, schools, sewage systems, roads, hospitals, and other necessary facilities for the larger population would divert the use of resources away from investment in productivity-increasing plant and equipment that would otherwise stimulate a more rapid rate of growth.

They would further argue that, although per capita real income remained the same statistically if both population and national income grew at the same rate, the actual wellbeing of the average person would decline. This would result because greater numbers of people would mean more crowding in cities, longer trips to work, more air pollution (and more spending to cure it), and faster deterioration of existing roads, highways, and other facilities.

Professor Spengler has, in fact, estimated that it takes an increase of 4 percent to 5 percent of national income to support an annual rate of population growth of 1 percent. Although it is difficult to put the cost of population increase in precise dollar figures, it is clear enough that there are additional costs to providing for more people in an already populous society that go beyond the provision of additional food, clothing, and similar goods for greater numbers. For instance, if increasing population causes land values to increase, the existing population must spend more money for land (and housing), but in return it receives no increased real value. If anything, because of greater crowding and less convenient location, it receives less value for higher priced acreage.

Even in technologically advanced countries, there is apparently a growing realization on the part of economists, businessmen, and the general public that a slower rate of population growth may be more conducive to increased material welfare than rapid population growth. Many young couples who want smaller families clearly hope to be able to spend more on each child at critical points in their lives. It is this desire for a higher standard of living and all it implies that ap-

FIG. 35-1.

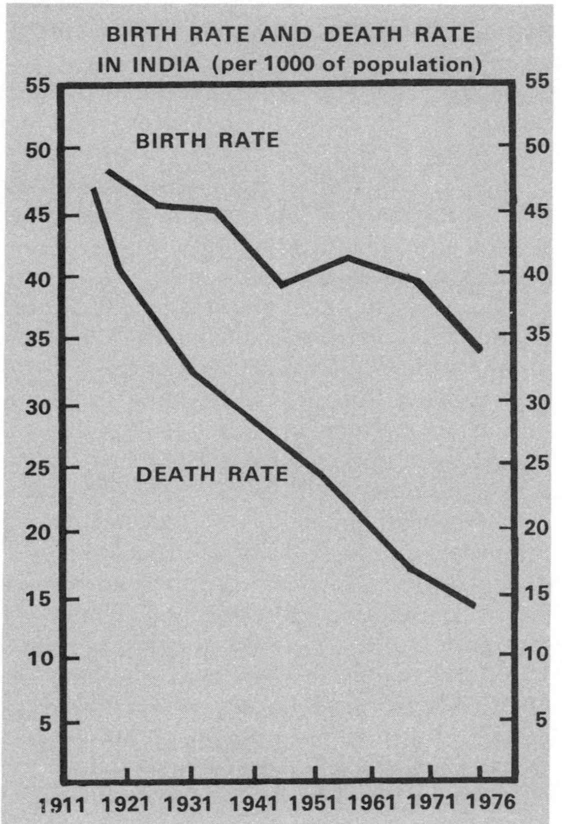

This graph clearly illustrates the population crunch facing many of the less developed nations. Birth rates are falling but death rates have fallen more rapidly. The result is a higher net rate of population growth, immigration factors being excluded. India's net rate of increase during the period 1970-1976 was 2.1% per year.
Based on data from United Nations and the International Bank for Reconstruction and Development.

pears to be behind the lower birth rates of highly developed countries.

POPULATION PRESSURE IN LESS DEVELOPED COUNTRIES

In the less developed countries of the world, the adverse affect upon individual well-being of rapid population growth is a matter of far more serious concern because masses of people in those poor countries live close to the margin of starvation. Any decline in their real income can lead to wide-spread famine and death.

The so-called population explosion in the poor countries is a result primarily of the widespread medical programs that have led to falling death rates, while the birth rates have remained high. For instance, in Sri Lanka (formerly known as Ceylon), an intensive health program in the 1950s achieved a drastic decline in the incidence of malaria. The death rate dropped by almost half in the six years from 1946 to 1952. As a result, for nearly two decades, the population grew at a rate which was one of the highest in the world. Another country suffering from rapid population growth is India. During the first 20 years of this century, the Indian population was static; from 1920 until 1950, it grew by 1 percent per year, compounded. But then, following more vigorous national health programs, the length of life of the typical Indian began to increase. With falling death rates and persistently high birth rates, the Indian population now appears to have increased by over 100 million in the decade between 1966 and 1976.

What to do about population growth is obviously a moral as well as an economic problem, since it involves human life and death and religious beliefs. Clearly, there are tremendous humane, emotional, and moral forces behind the efforts to reduce the death rate. Hence, there is enormous popular pressure to extend international health programs through the World Health Organization and through national medical programs.

If, however, as a result of the programs, the death rate falls and the birth rate stays high, the inevitable consequence is a great increase in population, which, ironically, may reduce the already low living standards of populations in backward countries and keep

The paradox of improving public health: At this village well in the Punjab, India, villagers get a drink, bring cattle to water, and even bathe. Due to faulty well construction, surface water goes right back into the well (behind the child), carrying pollution with it. New improved wells were built in this village to overcome the problem. But these measures to improve public health obviously lengthen the life span of the people, increase the population, and help create the population problem that can lead to famine.

Photo Courtesy A.I.D.

them in a permanent state of poverty. If present rates of population growth should continue, hundreds of millions of people in Asia, Africa, the Middle East, and Latin America might wind up *worse* off than they were before the medical progress was made.

This population pressure might lead to an outbreak of the old natural checks on population growth of famine and pestilence, or of such horrible social checks as warfare or internal violence and mass murders.

It was for fear of the possible horrors of overpopulation that Malthus favored late marriages as a curb on population growth and that many economists and government officials today favor birth control. But whether nations and the individuals who compose them will limit their numbers will depend on their moral and religious beliefs, their social and cultural attitudes, their desire for higher living standards, and upon the kind of population policies supported by national governmental and spiritual leaders.

By and large, it is apparent from examining the birth rates in economically advanced nations that the achievement of higher living standards and families' aspirations for still further opportunities for their children tend, typically, to lead to lower birth rates.

It would appear, therefore, that economic progress itself may provide the cultural conditions that will cause nations to bring population explosions under control. The danger of the immediate present is that economic progress will be too slow to avoid the famines, pestilences, or wars that might come if there is too great a delay in controlling the rate of the world population increase.

SUMMARY

World population is growing by over 75 million people a year; at present rates of growth, the projections are that the global population of 4 billion in 1975 may increase by 65% by the end of the twentieth century. This population explosion creates serious concerns that excessive population growth may depress world living standards, frustrate economic growth, and result in famines or wars.

Forecasting future population growth is hazardous, as past failures of population forecasts demonstrate. Analogies with historical experiences of countries that have achieved higher living standards do not always prove correct; statistical projections are uncertain, since apparently small changes in either birth rates or death rates compound rather quickly to throw off forecasts; and efforts to fit mathematical curves to past growth trends have been relatively poor at prediction.

The first economist who sought to describe the limits on population growth was Thomas Malthus. He contended that while population could grow at a geometric rate, the resources of the earth were limited. Thus he felt that diminishing returns on the fixed supply of land would depress per capita income, and, if population growth continued, it would eventually lead to famines that would wipe out surplus population. Malthus did not foresee the extent to which technological progress could increase the ability of a relatively fixed amount of land and other resources to support much greater populations than in his day.

During the Great Depression of the 1930s, anti-Malthusian economic theories of population growth became popular because the stagnation (and apparently imminent decline) of population appeared to be a threat to economic prosperity and growth. Population growth seemed to some economists—and businessmen—like a strong stimulus to investment.

However, the postwar decades of rapid population increase—facilitated by the spread of modern health programs to the people of less developed countries and by prosperity in the advanced countries—have seen the revival of Malthus' ideas. Many economists and government leaders are now concerned that rapid population increase may eat up the fruits of economic growth—and, if unchecked by human controls, population pressure might eventually bring on serious famines, social conflict, and war.

Even in advanced countries, a decline in the rate of population increase no longer appears to threaten continuing prosperity, since modern methods of economic management, especially through fiscal and monetary policy, helps to keep levels of demand high enough to sustain high levels of employment. Genuine economic growth in human well-being appears to depend far more upon scientific and technological progress and upon improving the knowledge and skills of the population than upon increasing sheer numbers of people.

QUESTIONS FOR REVIEW AND DISCUSSION

1. What are the three main techniques of predicting future population growth? What are the main weaknesses of each of these techniques?
2. What were the population views of Thomas R. Malthus? Have his views been borne out when applied to the Canadian economy? Have his views been borne

out when applied to economies in other parts of the world? What key variable has determined whether Malthus' views have been borne out or not?

3. Why do some people think a rapid increase in population is a bad thing? Why do others think that a rapid increase in population is a good thing? Which view do you think is the more accurate? Why?
4. In what ways are the problems presented by a rapidly increasing population the same for a developed economy as they are for a lesser developed economy? In what ways do the problems differ?
5. What has been the main cause of the population explosion in many of the world's less developed countries? What, if anything, do you think should be done about the population problem in these countries?

PROBLEMS AND EXERCISES TO SHARPEN YOUR UNDERSTANDING

1. If a country's birth rate is 35 per thousand, and its death rate is 30 per thousand, what would be its current annual rate of population growth?
2. Which of the following would you predict as the most likely course of this country's future population growth? Why?
   a. Both the birth rate and the death rate will probably stay about the same, and the annual rate of population increase will probably stay about the same as at present.
   b. There will probably be a sharp drop in both the birth rate and the death rate, and the annual rate of population increase will probably stay about the same as at present.
   c. There will probably be a sharp drop in the birth rate, but the death rate will probably remain about the same, causing the annual rate of population increase to drop.
   d. There will probably be a sharp drop in the death rate, but the birth rate will probably remain about the same, causing the annual rate of population increase to rise.

UNIT 5 REVIEW

1. Explain the difference between absolute advantage and comparative advantage in international trade. Are there significant differences between the benefits to be derived from domestic as opposed to international division of labor and exchange? Can tariffs and other protectionist measures ever be justified? How?
2. What are the advantages and disadvantages of floating exchange rates, fixed exchange rates under the gold standard, and pegged (but movable) exchange rates under the International Monetary Fund?
3. What causes a nation to incur a persistent deficit in its balance of payments? How can this be cured?
4. What are the main obstacles to the economic growth of less developed countries? Which of these do you regard as most crucial to overcome?
5. What has caused the rapid increase in world population? If this rate of population expansion continues, will it stimulate or retard economic development?

CONCLUSION

Using What You Have Learned of Economics is a short concluding chapter in which the authors stress the importance of the concept of interdependence.

USING WHAT YOU HAVE LEARNED OF ECONOMICS

■ RECOGNIZING INTERDEPENDENCE ■ UNDERSTANDING OUR ECONOMIC SYSTEM ■ USING YOUR ECONOMICS

And so you have come to the end of your introduction to economics.

We hope it will not be the end of your interest in the subject. We do not really see how it *can* be—since you will spend the rest of your life living economics, as a buyer and seller of goods and services, as a citizen of your country, and as an inhabitant of a small planet with limited resources and a growing population.

We hope you will find that a knowledge of economics will help you to solve many of the problems you will face and to make your life a better one. We have sought to stress that economics is a science. But it is more than a science because it seeks not just to explain or predict economic events but also to increase human welfare, including your own. Once you try to solve an economic problem, especially an important one, you inevitably get involved in social, political, and moral issues.

Nevertheless, economics *is* a science in the sense that it seeks objectively to observe and measure economic events, to clarify those events by concepts and analytical models, and to explain those events. As an objective discipline, economic analysis provides policy makers with a sound basis for making *intelligent* subjective choices and decisions.

■ RECOGNIZING INTERDEPENDENCE

What is an intelligent subjective choice? It is one that enables you to accomplish what you intend—to solve a problem in a way that you yourself regard as satisfactory. Conversely, an unintelligent choice or decision is one that prevents you from achieving what you intend—or one that produces side-effects that you yourself find so undesirable that you regret your decision.

For instance, if you want to get out of a crowded, burning theater as fast as possible, it is unintelligent for you to race for an exit, but intelligent for you and everyone else in the theater to walk calmly toward the exits. The proof would be found in terms of whether your life and the lives of others were saved.

Similarly, if you want to advance your standard of living, it is unintelligent for you to set so high a price for your services that you cannot even get a job; you cannot alone control the situation—you must adjust your wants and needs to the wants and needs of others. But it *is* intelligent for you to increase your skills and ability to perform useful work so that you can earn a higher salary.

The same principle applies to national and international problems. The Canadian government may ardently desire to give the nation stable prices and a balanced budget. But the government would be acting unintelligently if, at a time when the national economy was already weak and declining, it voted to increase taxes and to reduce government expenditures. These actions would be likely to aggravate the recession, cause prices to decline, cause tax receipts to fall,

Canadian Forces Photo

Economic disaster can play a role in leading to even wider social misery. Economic problems in post-World War I Europe were significant factors in the rise of fascism in Italy and Germany. This in turn led to World War II with its catastrophic results. This Canadian Forces photo shows the impact of air raid damage to the rail yards at Munster, Germany, at the end of the war.

and thus achieve neither price stability nor a balanced budget. At the same time, such actions would also produce undesirable side-effects in the form of higher unemployment, more business failures, lower living standards, and a retardation of national economic growth.

In all such cases intelligence implies the recognition of **interdependence.** This means that the policy maker (you, the head of a business, or the head of a nation) cannot act intelligently without taking account of the consequences for others of your action—and the effect of their actions upon you.

It may be that the single most important idea that you ought to carry away from this course in economics is this concept of interdependence. You have seen a great many instances of it in this book—in our discussion of the market, of the national economy as a whole, of the role of economic institutions in our country and other countries, and of international relations.

The concept of interdependence is, in fact, basic to the very notion of an economic system. In both market and command economic systems, what happens to prices will affect wages; what happens to wages will affect prices; what happens in some industries will affect other industries; what happens to total demand will affect unemployment; what happens to employment will affect prices;

Ridding the World of Economic Misery

John Maynard Keynes, the economist who, more than any other, developed the ideas that made it possible for modern industrial economies to cure mass unemployment, here takes an optimistic look ahead to a future when the burdens of economic hardship and necessity are lifted from mankind.

For at least another hundred years we must pretend to ourselves and to every one that fair is foul and foul is fair; for foul is useful and fair is not. Avarice and usury and precaution must be our gods for a little longer still. For only they can lead us out of the tunnel of economic necessity into daylight.

I look forward, therefore, in days not so very remote, to the greatest change which has ever occurred in the material environment of life for human beings in the aggregate. But, of course, it will all happen gradually, not as a catastrophe. Indeed, it has already begun. The course of affairs will simply be that there will be ever larger and larger classes and groups of people from whom problems of economic necessity have been practically removed. The critical difference will be realized when this condition has become so general that the nature of one's duty to one's neighbour is changed. For it will remain reasonable to be economically purposive for others after it has ceased to be reasonable for oneself.

The *pace* at which we can reach our destination of economic bliss will be governed by four things—our power to control population, our determination to avoid wars and civil dissensions, our willingness to entrust to science the direction of those matters which are properly the concern of science, and the rate of accumulation as fixed by the margin between our production and our consumption; of which the last will easily look after itself, given the first three.

From J. M. Keynes, *Essays in Persuasion*, Harcourt, Brace & World, Inc., New York, 1932, pp. 372-373.

and so on. To the untrained eye, an economic system is a "great buzzing, blooming confusion," to use the phrase of William James; the aim of economic analysis is to reduce the confusion.

UNDERSTANDING OUR ECONOMIC SYSTEM

We hope this book has given you a clearer picture of our economic system in particular. Ours is far from a perfect system in any sense; indeed, it is hard to imagine what a perfect economic system would be, given the continuously emerging problems created by technological, social, and political forces in the world. Our system must constantly adapt itself to cope with the new problems and conditions. It is never fixed; indeed, its strength is that it is constantly changing and evolving.

The major weakness of market economic systems historically has been their tendency to undergo wide swings from boom to bust. There are many in Canada who recall both the events and the impact of the Great Depression of the 1930s. The Depression was a terrible tragedy for many millions of people in this country and other countries and had much to do with the coming of the Second World War. Thanks to the progress of economics since then, we now can be more confident that we have the knowledge that will enable us to avoid repeating the catastrophe of deep depression. We also know enough economics to cope with catastrophic inflation. In fact, there is good reason to think that we now know enough about managing the economy to ensure that its performance will assure a reasonable standard of security for most of our people. However, not all problems for all people will be avoided. Of that, unfortunately, we can be certain.

Another serious question that remains is whether or not we will use intelligently what economic knowledge we do have. There is still considerable economic illiteracy among politicians, businessmen, and the general public. Political opportunism and narrow, unintelligent self-interest may frustrate the sensible application of economic policy for preserving high employment and balanced growth and for dealing with our many other problems.

A free society requires a well-informed citizenry, competent to reason for itself and to act sensibly on important private and public economic matters. You should be able to help there—certainly as a voter but perhaps also as a teacher, businessman, labor leader, public official, or possibly even (who knows?) as an economist. It takes all kinds—with different political views and judgments—to make this a better world.

I was an economic expert—what did you do?

Courtesy of the *Vancouver Sun*

USING YOUR ECONOMICS

The aim of this book has been to help you see more clearly your choices. The book has tried to do this by increasing your awareness of economic *interdependence* and your understanding of the causes of economic *change*—for instance: What causes sales of a product to rise or decline? What makes prices rise or decline? What causes a shortage of hospital beds or a surplus of wheat? What causes unemployment to increase or decrease? What causes a nation to grow or stagnate?

Having a better sense of the answers to such questions will not necessarily make you favor higher sales for either automobiles or pogo sticks, favor price stability rather than inflation or deflation, favor an equilibrium in the market for hospital beds or wheat, or favor full employment or economic growth or anything else. However, if you happen to favor or oppose any of those things, what you have learned of economics should help you to achieve or prevent them.

Economics—a way of reasoning, of weighing alternatives, of gathering information, and analyzing a problem—should help you to get where you want to go and possibly to make it a good place for others as well as yourself when you get there. Interdependence appears again.

A final word: Economics is not everything. Let us end our introduction to economics with a quotation from the most famous economist of the twentieth century, John Maynard Keynes: ". . . Do not let us overestimate the importance of the economic problem or sacrifice to its supposed necessities other matters of greater and more permanent significance."

What are those other matters of greater significance? The answer to that obviously will draw you beyond the realm of economics deep into the area of human values. Consideration of the question should prompt you to turn to other ideas and other books—many other books. It is also an appropriate final question to pose as a completion to this text.

KEY CONCEPT

interdependence

UNIT 6 REVIEW

1. What do you consider to be the principal problems facing Canada and the world today? Which of these are *primarily* economic problems? In what ways can economics contribute to a solution of all these major problems, economic or noneconomic?
2. Heraclitus, the ancient Greek philosopher, said, "You never swim in the same river twice." Is the economy similarly undergoing constant change? How can the knowledge of economics help you to anticipate change? How can economic knowledge help an individual, a business, or a nation to control change?
3. What do we mean by interdependence? In what sense could it be said that the central problem of modern man is to achieve both interdependence and dependence?
4. How did Adam Smith see the problem of interdependence being solved by "the invisible hand?" Can you give some examples where the market does not provide satisfactory solutions to the problem of interdependence? What should be done about such problems?
5. What things do you value most in life? How can a knowledge of economics help you to achieve your aims? What else will it take?

"WOULD YOU MIND GIVING THIS TO JOE?"

Reprinted with permission—*The Toronto Star*

This Macpherson cartoon appeared following the defeat of the Trudeau government in 1979. In its depiction of the problems to be assumed by the new Clark administration, it provides a good indication of the mix of economic issues that faced the country at the beginning of the 1980s.

TIME LINE OF ECONOMICS

SEVENTEENTH CENTURY

1626 Death of Sir Francis Bacon, "the Father of Experimental Philosophy"
1670 Founding of the Hudson's Bay Company
1690 Publication of Sir William Petty's *Political Arithmetick*, first important work on economic statistics
1694 Foundation of the Bank of England
1698 Foundation of the London Stock Exchange

EIGHTEENTH CENTURY

1712 Invention of steam engine by Thomas Newcomen
1720 The South Sea Bubble; major decline in English share values
1758 Publication of Francois Quesnay's *Tableau Economique*, first diagram to show the flow of output and income
1767 Invention of the spinning jenny by James Hargreaves
1776 Publication of Adam Smith's *Wealth of Nations*, the first major treatise on the functioning of market economies
1798 Publication of T. R. Malthus' *Essay on Population*—which warned of coming overpopulation

NINETEENTH CENTURY

1800

1817 Foundation of Bank of Montreal
1825 Publication of David Ricardo's *Principles of Political Economy*, a work that did much to give economics its basic analytical method
1825 First use of George Stephenson's steam locomotive
1835 Charles Babbage develops basic ideas of modern electronic computer
1848 Publication of *The Communist Manifesto* by Karl Marx and Friedrich Engels—the work that heralded coming Communist revolutions
1848 Publication of John Stuart Mills' *Principles of Political Economy*, the book that summed up classical economics

1850

1867 B.N.A. Act
1867 Publication of Karl Marx's *Das Kapital (Capital)*, the major intellectual attack on the market economic system
1874 Publication of Leon Walras' *Elements d'economie politique pure (Elements of pure economics)*, the first presentation of an abstract model of a complete economic system; foundation of Montreal Stock Exchange
1876 Invention of the first successful internal combustion engine by Nikolaus Otto
1876 Alexander Graham Bell invents the telephone
1885 Canadian Pacific Transcontinental Rail Line completed
1886 Trades and Labor Congress established
1890 Publication of Alfred Marshall's *Principles of Economics*, a major refinement and clarification of economic theory
1899 Publication of Thorstein Veblen's *Theory of the Leisure Class*, a work that helped instill concern with social institutions into the thinking of economists

TWENTIETH CENTURY

1900

1903 The Wright Brothers build the first successful motor-driven airplane
1908 Henry Ford uses an assembly line in manufacturing his Model T automobile
1911 Free trade with United States rejected in Canadian federal election
1917 The Russian Revolution. Personal income tax introduced in Canada
1919 The Versailles Peace Conference; publication of John Maynard Keynes' *The Economic Consequence of the Peace*—which warned of another European breakdown; the Winnipeg General Strike
1927 Invention of television by J. L. Baird
1929 The Great Crash in the New York Stock Exchange; start of the Great Depression
1931 Devaluation of the British pound, and collapse of the international monetary system
1933 The coming to power of the Nazis in Germany; Regina Manifesto, founding of C.C.F.
1935 Bank of Canada established
1936 Publication of John Maynard Keynes' *General Theory of Employment, Interest, and Money,* the key work in developing modern economic policy to cure depressions
1939 War in Europe; end of the Great Depression
1941 Publication of Simon Kuznets' *National Income and Its Composition*—a pioneer work on gross national product
1944 The Bretton Woods international monetary conference; formation of the International Monetary Fund and International Bank for Reconstruction and Development
1945 Foundation of the United Nations
1947 Alberta oil discoveries
1948 Publication of Paul Samuelson's *Foundations of Economic Analysis,* the basics of economics set forth mathematically

1950

1958 Publication of J. Kenneth Galbraith's *The Affluent Society*—a sharp critique of the market economy of the U.S. for its neglect of social problems. Formation of the European Economic Community; St. Lawrence Seaway opened
1961 The Coyne Affair
1963 Establishment of Economic Council of Canada
1967 International Monetary Fund approves the plan to create a new international currency
1968 Report of (Watkins) Royal Commission on Foreign ownership in Canadian Industry
1969 First Nobel Prize in economics; Prices and Incomes Commission established
1970 Canada floats the dollar again
1971 Wage and price controls in the U.S.A.; U.S. suspends guarantee to redeem dollars from foreign central banks with gold
1972 Publication of *The Limits to Growth*
1973 Britain, Denmark and Eire join the E.E.C.; FIRA established; Mid-East war starts recurring series of energy crises
1975 The A.I.B.—wage and price controls in Canada
1976 IMF recognizes floating rates to replace Bretton Woods system
1977 Canada's dollar starts to slide down on world money markets
1978 AIB controls end
1979 Tokyo round of tariff agreements; crises in Iran trigger new energy problems

BIBLIOGRAPHY

FOR FURTHER READING AND STUDENT RESEARCH

NEWSPAPERS AND MAGAZINES

You should, at minimum, try to keep up with economic issues as covered in your local daily newspaper. Frequently, such daily newspaper coverage lacks the detail and depth of coverage which might be desired. Consequently, you should try to supplement your current news reading through more detailed sources. On a daily basis, the "Report on Business" section of the Toronto *Globe and Mail* is the most comprehensive source in Canada. Weekly newsmagazines and papers are also very valuable. The *Financial Post* and the *Financial Times* are excellent for the observer of the economy.

STATISTICAL DATA

If you have access to a library depository, Statistics Canada's publications will provide almost anything you want to know—and then some. For most up-to-date material, see their monthly *Canadian Statistical Review*. For a comprehensive package, though a time-lag problem exists, see the annual *Canada Yearbook*. An excellent small publication is a chart booklet, *Canada's Business Climate*, published quarterly by the Toronto-Dominion Bank and readily available through any branch of the bank. More detailed readily available sources are the *Annual Reports* of the Bank of Canada and the Economic Council of Canada. The *Bank of Canada Review*, published monthly, is a good source of current data as is the annual *Economic Review* of the Federal Department of Finance. On an historical basis, *Historical Statistics of Canada*, ed. Buckley and Urquhart, Toronto, Macmillan, 1965 is still the definitive work.

GENERAL TEXTS

Armstrong, Muriel: *The Canadian Economy and Its Problems*, 2nd Edition, Toronto, Prentice-Hall, 1977

McConnell and Pope: *Economics*, 1st Edition, Toronto, McGraw-Hill Ryerson, 1978

Samuelson and Scott: *Economics*, 5th Canadian Edition, Toronto, McGraw-Hill Ryerson, 1980

ANTHOLOGIES OF READINGS

Keirstead, Earl, Brander and Waddell: *Economics Canada: Selected Readings*, Toronto, Macmillan, 1974

Kennedy and Dorosh: *Dateline Canada*, Toronto, Prentice-Hall, 1978

MacDonald, A. H.: *Readings in the World of Economics*, Toronto, McGraw-Hill Ryerson, 1973

Officer and Smith: *Issues in Canadian Economics*, Toronto, McGraw-Hill Ryerson, 1974

MICROECONOMIC TOPICS

Adams, Ian: *The Poverty Wall*, Toronto, McClelland and Stewart, 1970

__________: *The Real Poverty Report*, Edmonton, Hurtig, 1971

Arbella, Irving: *On Strike*, Toronto, James Lorimer, 1974

Armitage, Andrew: *Social Welfare in Canada*, Toronto, McClelland and Stewart, 1975

Bassett, John M.: *Timothy Eaton*, Toronto, Fitzhenry and Whiteside, 1975

Canadian Foundation for Economic Education: "Government and the Economy" Series;
- —*Government and the Economy—How Much? 1977*
- —*Government and the Economy—Stabilization Policies*, 1977
- —*Government and the Economy—Taxation*, 1978
- —*Government and the Economy—Federal-Provincial Relations*, 1979

Clement, Wallace: *The Canadian Corporate Elite*, Toronto, McClelland and Stewart, (Carlton Library #89), 1975

Clements, Muriel: *By Their Bootstraps: The Credit Union Movement in Saskatchewan*, Toronto, Clarke Irwin, 1965

Galbraith, John Kenneth: *The Affluent Society*, Boston, Houghton Mifflin, 1958

__________: *The New Industrial State*. Boston, Houghton Mifflin, 1967

Gouin, S., Portis, B. and Campbell, B: *The Teenage Market in Canada*, London, Ontario, School of Business Administration, University of Western Ontario, 1967

Harker, Douglas: *The Woodwards*, Vancouver, Mitchell Press, 1976

Hunt, Russell, and Campbell, Robert: *K. C. Irving*, Toronto, McClelland and Stewart, 1973

Laxer, Robert: *Canada's Unions*, Toronto, James Lorimer, 1976

__________: *Unions and the Collective Bargaining Process*, Toronto, O.I.S.E., 1978

Loyns, R. M. A.: *Understanding Canadian Agriculture*, Toronto, Canadian Foundation for Economic Education, 1978

MacEwan, Paul: *Miners and Steelworkers; Labour in Cape Breton*, Toronto, Hakkert, 1976

MacPherson, Ian: *Each for All: A History of the Co-operative Movement in Canada*, Toronto, McClelland and Stewart, (Carlton Library #116), 1979

Neufeld, E. P.: *The Financial System of Canada*, Toronto, Macmillan, 1972

Newman, Peter: *Bronfman Dynasty*, Toronto, McClelland and Stewart, 1978

__________: *The Canadian Establishment*, (vol. 1), Toronto, McClelland and Stewart, 1975

__________: *Flame of Power*, Toronto, McClelland and Stewart, 1959

Penner, Norman (ed.): *Winnipeg, 1919*, Toronto, James, Lewis and Samuel, 1973

Peterson, Rein: *Small Business: Building a Balanced Economy*, Erin, Ontario, Press Porcepic, 1977

Ross, Alexander: *The Risk-Takers*, Toronto, Financial Post-Macmillan, 1975

Royal Commission on Corporate Concentration: Ottawa,
Background Reports:
Argus Corporation Ltd. (RCCC Study #1)
Power Corporation Ltd. (RCCC Study #10)
George Weston Ltd. (RCCC Study #12)
Final Report, 1978

Senate of Canada: *Poverty in Canada*, (Cat. YC2-283/2-01), 1971

Stewart, Walter, *Strike*, Toronto, McClelland and Stewart, 1977

* * * *

Note also the bibliographic information on page 224.

MACROECONOMIC TOPICS

Beigie, Carl E.: *Inflation Is A Social Malady*, Montreal, C. D. Howe Research Institute, (British-North American Committee), 1979

Brewis, T. N. (ed.): *Growth and the Canadian Economy*, Toronto, McClelland and Stewart, (Carlton Library #39), 1968

Brewis, T. N.: *Regional Economic Policies in Canada*, Toronto, Macmillan, 1969

Economic Council of Canada: *Living Together: A Study of Regional Disparity*, Ottawa, 1977

__________: *People and Jobs: A Study of the Canadian Labor Market*, Ottawa, 1976

Galbraith, John Kenneth: *The Age of Uncertainty*, Boston, Houghton Mifflin, 1977

__________: *Money: Whence It Came, Where It Went*, Boston, Houghton Mifflin, 1975

__________: *Economics and the Public Purpose*, Boston, Houghton Mifflin, 1973

Gonick, Cy: *Out of Work*, Toronto, James Lorimer, 1978

Gordon, Walter: *Storm Signals*, Toronto, McClelland and Stewart, 1975

Holt, Geoffrey: *Understanding Unemployment*, Toronto, Canadian Foundation for Economic Education, 1976

Joyce, Libby: *Understanding Productivity*, Toronto, Canadian Foundation for Economic Education, 1977

Krueger, Ralph, and Koegler, John: *Regional Development in Northeast New Brunswick*, Toronto, McClelland and Stewart (Canada Studies Foundation), 1975

Krueger, Irving and Vincent: *Regional Patterns: Disparities and Development*, Toronto, McClelland and Stewart (Canada Studies Foundation), 1975

Langman, R. C.: *Poverty Pockets—The Limestone Plains of Southern Ontario*, Toronto, McClelland and Stewart (Canada Studies Foundation), 1975

Mathias, Phillip: *Forced Growth*, Toronto, James, Lewis and Samuel, 1971

Phillips, Paul: *Regional Disparities*, Toronto, James Lorimer, 1978

Robinson, H. L.: *Rising Prices*, Toronto, James Lorimer, 1978

Sheehan, Patricia: *Social Change in the Alberta Foothills*, Toronto, McClelland and Stewart (Canada Studies Foundation), 1975

Starks, Richard: *Industry In Decline*, Toronto, James Lorimer, 1978

Westell, Anthony: *The New Society*, Toronto, McClelland and Stewart, 1977

* * * *

Note also the bibliographic information on pages 371 and 399.

INTERNATIONAL ECONOMICS

Brown, Lester R: *In the Human Interest*, New York, W. W. Norton, 1974. (An analysis of population problems)

Cornell, Peter: *Understanding Canada's International Trade Policy*, Toronto, Canadian Foundation for Economic Education, 1977

Donaldson, P.: *Worlds Apart*, Harmondsworth, Penguin, 1975. (The worlds of the rich and poor nations)

Economic Council of Canada: *Looking Outward: A New Trade Strategy for Canada*, Ottawa, 1975

__________: *For A Common Future: A Study of Canada's Relations With Developing Countries*, Ottawa, 1978

Gordon, J. King: *The New International Economic Order*, Toronto, Canadian Institute for International Affairs (Behind the Headlines Series, XXXIV, 5), 1976

Grubel, H. G.: *The International Monetary System*, Harmondsworth, Penguin, 1977

International Bank for Reconstruction and Development: *Partners in Development*, New York, Praeger, 1969

Jackson, Eric: *The Great Canadian Debate: Foreign Ownership*, Toronto, McClelland and Stewart, 1975

Marchak, Patricia: *In Whose Interests: Multinationals in a Canadian Context*, Toronto, McClelland and Stewart, 1979

Plumptre, A. W. F: *Three Decades of Decision; Canada and the International Monetary System, 1944-75*, Toronto, McClelland and Stewart, 1977

* * * *

Note also the bibliographic information on pages 439-40, 481, and 501.

ECONOMIC HISTORY/HISTORICAL APPROACHES

Carrigan, D. O.: *Canadian Party Platforms, 1867-1968*, Toronto, Copp, Clark, 1968

Easterbrook and Watkins (eds.): *Approaches To Canadian Economic History*, Toronto, McClelland and Stewart (Carlton Library #31), 1967

Galbraith, John Kenneth: *The Age of Uncertainty*, Boston, Houghton Mifflin, 1977

________: *The Great Crash*, Boston, Houghton Mifflin, 1961

Heilbroner, Robert L.: *The Making of Economic Society*, Englewood Cliffs, N.J., Prentice-Hall, 1975

Hodgetts, B. and Burns, J. D.: *Decisive Decades*, Toronto, Thomas Nelson, 1973

Horn, Michael (ed), *The Dirty Thirties*, Toronto, Copp Clark, 1972

Safarian, A. E.: *The Canadian Economy in The Great Depression*, Toronto, McClelland and Stewart (Carlton Library #54), 1970

ECONOMISTS AND ECONOMIC THOUGHT

Breit, W. and Ransom, R. L.: *The Academic Scribblers*, New York, Holt, Rinehart and Winston, 1971

Heilbroner, Robert, *The Worldly Philosophers*, New York, Simon and Schuster, 1969

Hession, C. H.: *John Kenneth Galbraith and His Critics*, Toronto, McLeod, 1972

Neill, R. F.: *A New Theory of Value: The Canadian Economics of H. A. Innes*, Toronto, University of Toronto Press, 1972

Robinson, Joan: *Economic Philosophy*, Harmondsworth, Penguin Books, 1964

Silk, Leonard, *The Economists*, New York, Basic Books, 1976

Soule, George: *Ideas of the Great Economists*, New York, Mentor, 1962.

DICTIONARIES AND BIBLIOGRAPHIES

Bannock, Baxter and Rees: *A Dictionary of Economics*, Harmondsworth, Penguin, 1972

Greenwald, Douglas and Associates: *The McGraw-Hill Dictionary of Modern Economics*, New York, McGraw-Hill, 1973

* * * *

Clement, Wallace and Drache, Daniel: *A Practical Guide to Canadian Political Economy*, Toronto, James Lorimer, 1978. (A wide-ranging annotated guide to sources in Canadian economics

* * * *

Also: See bibliographies compiled by Canadian Foundation for Economic Education and in the *Teachers' Manual for The World of Economics*.

INDEX OF KEY CONCEPTS

Location is designated on a chapter basis. The letter "A" following a number indicates the chapter appendix is the location.

INDEX